Twelve Major Plays

Twelve Major Plays

August Strindberg

Translated from the Swedish by
Elizabeth Sprigge

AldineTransaction
A Division of Transaction Publishers
New Brunswick (U.S.A.) and London (U.K.)

First paperback printing 2008

This book is printed on acid-free paper that meets the American National Standard for Permanence of Paper for Printed Library Materials.

Library of Congress Catalog Number: 2008015397
ISBN: 978-0-202-36191-8
Printed in the United States of America

Library of Congress Cataloging-in-Publication Data

Strindberg, August, 1849-1912
[Plays. English. Selections]
Twelve major plays / August Strindberg ; translated from the Swedish by Elizabeth Sprigge. —1st Transaction printing
p. cm.
Originally published under title Plays: Chicago : Aldine Pub. Co., [c1962]
ISBN 978-0-202-36191-8
1. Strindberg, August, 1849-1912—Translations into English. I. Sprigge, Elizabeth, 1900- II. Title.

PT9811.A3S59 2008
839.72'6—dc22

2008015397

CONTENTS

INTRODUCTION

Johan August Strindberg was born in Stockholm on January 22, 1849. He was the fourth child, and the first born in wedlock, of Carl Oscar Strindberg, a shipping agent of good education, and Ulrica Eleanora Norling, who had been a servant girl. At the time of his birth—he was a seven months' child—his father was bankrupt and his mother worn down by poverty. After their twelfth child, when August Strindberg was thirteen, she died at the age of thirty-nine and his father married the housekeeper.

The conflicts bred of the bourgeois-proletarian union of his parents and the miseries of an over-sensitive childhood made a lasting impression on Strindberg and are described in his first autobiographical novel. While he despised the hypocrisy of bourgeois respectability and espoused the cause of the oppressed, he also deplored the ignorance and gullibility of the working classes and felt that he never properly belonged to any class himself. It is hardly surprising that these obsessions, coupled with a frustrated mother-love, coloured so much of his work.

He went to a number of schools of different social status and was an ambitious if erratic pupil. His favourite subjects were languages and science, and he developed a love of nature which remained throughout his life. With difficulty he got to Uppsala University and lived there in dire poverty, leaving without taking a degree. He was by turn tutor, journalist, art critic, actor and telegraph clerk, and he taught himself enough Chinese to catalogue the Chinese manuscripts in the Royal Library at Stockholm, which last position improved his social standing.

In 1875, when Strindberg was twenty-six, the actress Siri von Essen divorced her husband, Baron Wrangel, to marry him. They had three children, and the first years of this marriage, spent mainly in Switzerland, France and Denmark, were the happiest of his life.

In his university days Strindberg had begun to write plays, chiefly in verse, one of which, *The Outlaw,* earned him a temporary stipend from the King. His first masterpiece, begun soon after this, was *Master Olof,* an historical drama with the Swedish reformer, Olaus Petri, as its central figure and its theme the relativity of truth. Public recognition, however, was slow in coming. It was nine years after he wrote the first prose version of *Master Olof* that this was at last staged. Then Strindberg, with the added incentive of providing parts for his young actress wife, returned to writing for the theatre and produced *Herr Bengt's Wife,* an historical play with a mediæval setting, the first of his works to treat of marriage. This was Strindberg's reaction to Ibsen's recently-produced *A Doll's House,* a play which he considered "sick like its author." In *Herr Bengt's Wife* the sanctity of marriage and parenthood is finally saved, and Strindberg followed it by one of his happiest fantasies, *Lucky Peter's Journey.*

Fame, however, eluded him until his dark side was uppermost again. In 1879 his novel, *The Red Room,* a satire of Stockholm society, earned him the name of "the Swedish Zola," although he had not then read the French master. At the same time it roused fury against him, soon to be exacerbated by *Married,* two volumes of ironic short stories in which, most daringly for the day, he analysed marital relations and for the first time reviled women.

Having read Darwin, Kirkegaard and Brandes, Strindberg was ripe for the agnosticism and new radicalism of the day; but the question of the emancipation of women, now sweeping Scandinavia largely as a result of *A Doll's House,* confounded him. Although he believed in individual rights, he feared and distrusted feminine nature. All the same, he never acknowledged the term "mysogonist," which has stuck to him so persistently that it blinds many people to anything else in his life or his work. It was Strindberg's deep love of women, not hatred, he declared, which made him rail against them—

and indeed it was his love of life itself which made him rage against the mess mankind had made of it.

For *Married* Strindberg was prosecuted, not for his attack on women or society but for blasphemy, on account of his denunciation of the Communion Service as humbug. He was finally acquitted, but the opprobrium remained.

Strindberg's religious life was as eccentric as his domestic one. He had been brought up in the narrow path of Pietism and in his adolescence had gone through a variety of hysterical, religious and erotic experiences. Now he swung from atheism to faith, vainly seeking a creed in eastern and western religions, until in the nineties he discovered the teaching of Swedenborg which spoke to his condition, although even then he was not entirely converted.

In 1887, while his first marriage was breaking up, he produced *The People of Hemsö.* This novel about life in the Swedish skerries, in which he gave rein to his love of nature, was written at the same period as the autobiographical novels, *The Son of a Maidservant* and *A Fool's Defence,* and the so-called "naturalist" dramas which established his European reputation. Here he acknowledged the brothers de Goncourt, besides Zola and Nietzsche, as influences. The most widely known of these plays are *The Father, Miss Julie, Creditors* and the one-act monologue, *The Stronger. The Father* was at once published in Sweden and translated into French (with an introduction by Zola), German and Danish. Sponsored by Georg Brandes, it was first produced and acclaimed in Copenhagen and then even more successfully presented in Paris by Antoine at his *Théâtre Libre,* for whom Strindberg thereupon wrote *Miss Julie* and *Creditors.* In Berlin, too, these plays were soon to be famous, but in Stockholm *The Father* was viewed with unmitigated horror and only ran for a few nights. Strindberg made little money from these early productions, but he had now, at the age of forty, made his name as an avant-garde dramatist. He might be loathed, but he would never again be ignored. He was no longer overshadowed by Ibsen.

In 1891, Strindberg and Siri von Essen were divorced on

grounds of incompatibility. How impossible marriage was for him! He expected each young woman he fell in love with to be not only his wife, his mistress and the mother of his children, but his own mother too. To his grief, for his paternal affection was deep, Siri von Essen was given the custody of the children, and Strindberg satirized the proceedings in the excellent short play, *The Bond*. The following year he married Frida Uhl, an ambitious young Austrian journalist. He lived for long periods now in Germany, Austria and Moravia and made his only visit to England, finding a champion of his plays in the theatrical manager, J. T. Grein.

The marriage to Frida Uhl, by whom he had one daughter, only lasted a year and passed in a kind of materialised nightmare. Scientific studies had always fascinated Strindberg —he was a considerable botanist—and he now began to make chemical experiments and wrote *Antibarbarus*, a treatise concerned with the nature of sulphur and the belief that "all is in all." Living alone in Paris in small hotels on the left bank, almost penniless, Strindberg now proceeded from chemistry to alchemy (always, one way or another, he was trying to make gold) and consorted with the celebrated Parisian occultists of the day. This brought about the crisis that marked the climax of his psychosis, which he minutely describes in his novel, *Inferno*, "the diary of a soul in hell." This is a strange indeed but remarkably lucid account of the psychic phenomena he experienced during the crisis and for which he could find no explanation except that he was being pursued by what he called "The Powers." And only, he came to believe, by admitting his guilt and doing penance could he escape from his torments.

Thus he emerged with a belief in God, and in 1898 expressed the rebirth of faith in his impressive pilgrimage drama, *To Damascus*. Far from his creative powers being impaired, after this crisis Strindberg produced much of his finest work, including his boulevard play, *Crime and Crime* (a psychological thriller produced by the young Reinhardt), and the great historical cycle begun with *Master Olof*—

Gustavus Vasa, Erik XLV, etc.—besides his little play of redemption, *Easter*.

In 1901 Strindberg married the young Norwegian actress, Harriet Bosse, who created the parts of the Lady in *To Damascus* and Eleanora in *Easter*. Harriet Bosse, too, gave him a daughter, but the marriage soon ended, although this time in an amicable separation.

In spite of the new religious note in his work, Strindberg now returned to the old theme of married misery and wrote the powerful drama, *The Dance of Death*. Two fairy plays, strongly influenced by Reinhardt, followed, and then came the wonderful symbolic *Dream Play*, one of Reinhardt's most famous productions.

In his last years Strindberg lived as a recluse in Stockholm and his enormous output of plays continued, besides such works of philosophic reflection as *The Blue Books* and *Alone*. In 1907 he realised his life-long wish for an Intimate Theatre of his own and wrote for it a series of very effective Chamber Plays, of which the best is the macabre *Ghost Sonata*. His last work for the theatre was another pilgrimage play, *The Great Highway*, written chiefly in unrhymed verse, in which he sums up his strange life's journey. It ends with a prayer:

> Bless me, whose deepest suffering,
> deepest of human suffering, was this—
> I could not be the one I longed to be.

What he longed to be was a whole and happy traveller on life's highway, but introvert and schizophrenic (his first biographers speak of "paranoia simplex chronica" and "melancholia dæmomaniaca"), he was split from reality, split in himself, and divided against himself. His attacks on women are, for example, attacks on himself, on the femininity of his own nature with which he was unable to come to terms.

His work is the key to his complexities, since all of it is in some measure autobiographical. This is true not only of his writings but of his paintings—mostly turbulent seascapes, executed with a knife—and it is impossible to consider his work apart from his life, for his schizophrenia prevented him from knowing himself where reality began or imagination ended. "I don't know if *The Father* is an invention or if my life has been like this. . . ." All his writing was intensely subjective:

> Could I but sit among the audience
> and watch the play!
> But I must mount the stage, take
> part and act,
> And once I play a part, I'm lost,
> forgetting who I am.*

He was impelled to write, his mind and his emotions were in a state of seething ferment until he had expressed his vision. He worked against time, with a shadow over his shoulder, and completion left him in a state of physical collapse. But if he had not been able to write, surely he would have quite succumbed to his illness; his work was his outlet, his therapy. He wrote on the ascent and descent of his attacks, and between the giddy slopes lay the unforbidding plateau of reality, where he was never at home. He let his plays develop of their own accord, in later days scarcely correcting a word, but in life he could never let any relationship alone. Whether with his wife, friend or foe, he was forever digging the plant up to examine its growth. "The personality of the author is just as much a stranger to me as to the reader," he declared shortly before he died, "and just as unsympathetic." He invites us to dislike him, but at the same time provokes us into trying to understand his complicated and tortured nature.

Strindberg was ahead of his time, but at last we have begun to catch him up. Or, rather, it is truer to say that we have now begun to accept him, for as Gertrude Stein points out, "no one is ahead of his time, it is only that the particular variety of creating time is the one his contemporaries who are also creating their own time refuse to accept."

Without any doubt Strindberg has exerted a strong influ-

* *The Great Highway.*

ence on twentieth-century writers. The productions of his plays in Munich in 1915 "almost, yes almost, reconciled" Rilke with the theatre; Thomas Mann described his "aggressive worth" as "an indisputable asset" to the youth of his generation, and Eugene O'Neill hailed him in the twenties as "the precursor of all modernity in our present theatre, just as Ibsen, a lesser man as he himself surmised, was the father of the modernity of twenty years or so ago." J. B. Priestley agrees with this view and declares that "no sound critic of the drama doubts his genius," while Sean O'Casey is lyrical in his appreciation. One can trace Strindberg's mark on many American dramatists, including O'Neill, Tennessee Williams and Arthur Miller, while the French playwright Arthur Adamov has always acknowledged him as his first great influence—*A Dream Play* particularly being a source of inspiration. To Jean Cocteau, Strindberg's enchantment lies in the fact that he cannot be "coined": *"Il tombe de la lune. Ne le ramasse pas qui veut."* And yet, different as are the styles of these two writers, it is not difficult to see, for instance, *Les Parents Terribles* as a Strindbergian tragicomedy or *A Dream Play* as a fantasy by Cocteau. Nor can Anouilh's *Waltz of the Toreadors* fail to remind one of *The Dance of Death,* and when I see a production of one of Strindberg's domestic satires, such as *Playing with Fire,* I am haunted by Ionesco. This is partly because the fashion now is to burlesque these Strindberg plays.

Strindberg does not seem to have directly influenced English dramatists, which is not surprising as so few of his works have been produced in England. Although he wrote more than fifty plays, to most English theatre-goers he is known only for *The Father* and *Miss Julie.* But indirectly, as a pioneer of Expressionism and through his outspoken insight before Freud, Jung and D. H. Lawrence led the next generation into sexual and psychological exploration, he is a source in England as elsewhere of twentieth-century literature and drama.

Strindberg's works present many difficulties to his translators. His style varies from the terse to the lyrical—he was a poet, which should never be forgotten—and it is not always easy even for his compatriots. Also, he sometimes slips quotations—from the Bible or Shakespeare, for instance—into his text without comment. One has to know what he was doing and reading at the time of writing in order to follow his thought. At times, too, Strindberg is slapdash in his stage directions, and I have therefore occasionally edited these to help production of the plays.

ELIZABETH SPRIGGE.

THE FATHER

A Tragedy in Three Acts

INTRODUCTION

In the last half-century Strindberg has enjoyed a growing reputation both on the continent and, latterly, in England, for the simple reason that of all nineteenth-century dramatists, he is the least dated. He developed at a time when theatre had begun to be a contemporary affair, a platform for moral debate, an organ of modern thought which influenced public opinion, thus changing customs and even laws, and so the playwright had become an important international figure.

Until Zola, in the 'seventies, made his dramatic assault on the theatre, demanding the whole of life, by which he meant the most crude and violent aspects of life upon the stage, drama had, as usual, lagged behind the times. Now, stripped of romanticism, refinement and rhetoric, led by that pioneer of little theatre clubs, Antoine's Théâtre Libre, it exploded into so-called Naturalism. In came Ibsen with GHOSTS and the stage was set for THE FATHER.

Yet to call THE FATHER a naturalist play is absurd. As the Swedish authority Martin Lamm points out, Strindberg intended it to be the modern equivalent of AGAMEMNON, the Swedish captain like the Greek king victim of woman's sex hatred and lust for power. OTHELLO, MACBETH and KING LEAR were also in Strindberg's mind as he conceived THE FATHER, and he deliberately drew his hero larger than life. The strength of the play can thus be said to be due partly to the influence of Aeschylus; the plot is stark, the construction economic, the pace swift and the movement towards fatality inevitable. The Captain is a giant who, like Strindberg himself, impresses us with his size and shocks us with his clumsy weakness. In fact, in this play Strindberg gives a penetrating diagnosis of his state of mind at its most unhappy and it is his own hysteria which prevents THE FATHER from being wholly great.

While the play grips us with its dramatic force, shatters us with its brutality and leaves us admiring its craftsmanship, there is no aftermath of imagination, no echo of beauty. In spite of the Captain's good points, the play is consistently black, particularly when played, for it is usually produced with unrelieved violence. This, to do the author justice, was not his intention. In a letter to Lundegård, the Swedish critic, at the time of the first production in Copenhagen in 1887, Strindberg stated that the Captain should be presented "as a normally robust man with a taste for irony and self-mockery, and the lightly sceptical tone of a man of the world." He also directed that the part should be played "subtly, calmly, resignedly," and described the Captain—here we see the Greek influence—as "going to meet his fate almost light-heartedly, wrapping himself in his winding-sheet of spiders' webs, which the laws of nature will not permit him to destroy." True, Strindberg declares elsewhere that the protagonists in THE FATHER should be acted with complete abandon—consistency was not his bugbear—but certainly one cannot afford to miss one spark of the Captain's humour. "By and large," Strindberg said, "he symbolises a masculinity which society is trying to invalidate and hand over to the third sex."

Laura is a more difficult character to analyse. Certainly she symbolises a terrible femininity, and is Strindberg's answer to Ibsen and women's emancipation. But she is neither a blue-stocking nor a virago. It is her lack of common-sense, not her lack of morals, that the Captain criticises when he upbraids her for ruining his life. It is only her brother who sees her as clever because of her stubbornness in getting her own way. Her husband's attitude so riles her that her parting shot, before he throws the lamp at her, is: ". . . now you have seen my wits are as strong as my will."

The play falls to pieces if we cannot see Laura as an ordinary, rather stupid, middle-class girl, brought up in ignorance, and the Captain as an intelligent, ambitious young man, walking in the springtime woods and falling in love. Later, through sex difficulties and the sex conflict, both of them are caught in a trap of domesticity and debt and doubt—all of which were Strindberg's own unending problems.

A further problem for the producer is the child Bertha. We are told that she is seventeen, but she behaves as if she is seven—about the age of Strindberg's eldest daughter when he wrote the play after the frenzied break-up of his own marriage. Laura is a silly featureless little girl and the other minor characters, too, are merely sketches. "Ordinary people," Strindberg calls them in his preface to MISS JULIE, "as country pastors and provincial doctors usually are," but to us they seem extraordinary, and he mocks both church and medicine. Indeed, with his characteristic economy of words and the lack of stage directions—it is a matter of chance whether he even remembers to bring a character on or take him off again—Strindberg sets his readers and translators, producers and players, a hard task. Much is asked of an audience too, but the dramatic reward is unique and justifies the toil.

E. S.

Characters

THE CAPTAIN

LAURA, *his wife*

BERTHA, *their daughter*

DOCTOR ÖSTERMARK

THE PASTOR

THE NURSE

NÖJD

THE ORDERLY

The whole play takes place in the central living-room of the Captain's home. He is a cavalry officer in a remote country district of Sweden.

It is about 1886, shortly before Christmas.

At the back of the room, towards the right, a door leads to the hall. In the left wall there is a door to other rooms, and in the right-hand corner another, smaller door, covered in the same wall-paper as the walls, opens on to a staircase leading to the Captain's room above.

In the centre of the room stands a large round table on which are newspapers, magazines, a big photograph album and a lamp. On the right are a leather-covered sofa, arm chairs and a smaller table. On the left is a writing-bureau with a pendulum clock upon it. Arms, guns and gun-bags hang on the walls, and military coats on pegs by the door to the hall.

ACT ONE

Early evening. The lamp on the table is lighted. The Captain and the Pastor are sitting on the sofa talking. The Captain is in undress uniform with riding-boots and spurs; the Pastor wears black, with a white cravat in place of his clerical collar, and is smoking a pipe.

The Captain rises and rings a bell. The Orderly enters from the hall.

ORDERLY. Yes, sir?

CAPTAIN. Is Nöjd there?

ORDERLY. Nöjd's in the kitchen, sir, waiting for orders.

CAPTAIN. In the kitchen again, is he? Send him here at once.

ORDERLY. Yes, sir.

Exit.

PASTOR. Why, what's the trouble?

CAPTAIN. Oh, the ruffian's been at his tricks again with one of the servant girls! He's a damn nuisance, that fellow!

PASTOR. Was it Nöjd you said? Didn't he give some trouble back in the spring?

CAPTAIN. Ah, you remember that, do you? Look here, you give him a bit of a talking to, there's a good chap. That might have some effect. I've sworn at him and thrashed him, without making the least impression.

PASTOR. So now you want me to preach to him. How much impression do you think God's word is likely to make on a trooper?

CAPTAIN. Well, my dear brother-in-law, it makes none at all on me, as you know, but . . .

PASTOR. As I know only too well.

CAPTAIN. But on him? Worth trying anyhow.

Enter NÖJD.

What have you been up to now, Nöjd?

NÖJD. God bless you, sir, I can't talk about that—not with Pastor here.

PASTOR. Don't mind me, my lad.

NÖJD. Well you see, sir, it was like this. We was at a dance at Gabriel's, and then, well then Ludwig said as . . .

CAPTAIN. What's Ludwig got to do with it? Stick to the point.

NÖJD. Well then Emma said as we should go in the barn.

CAPTAIN. I see. I suppose it was Emma who led you astray.

NÖJD. Well, not far from it. What I mean is if the girl's not game, nothing don't happen.

CAPTAIN. Once and for all—are you the child's father or are you not?

NÖJD. How's one to know?

CAPTAIN. What on earth do you mean? Don't you know?

NÖJD. No, you see, sir, that's what you never can know.

CAPTAIN. You mean you weren't the only man?

NÖJD. That time I was. But you can't tell if you've always been the only one.

CAPTAIN. Are you trying to put the blame on Ludwig? Is that the idea?

NÖJD. It's not easy to know who to put the blame on.

CAPTAIN. But, look here, you told Emma you would marry her.

NÖJD. Oh well, you always have to say that, you know.

CAPTAIN, *to the* PASTOR. This is atrocious.

PASTOR. It's the old story. Come now, Nöjd, surely you are man enough to know if you are the father.

NÖJD. Well, sir, it's true, I did go with her, but you know yourself, Pastor, that don't always lead to nothing.

PASTOR. Look here, my lad, it's you we are talking about. And you are not going to leave that girl destitute with a child.

You can't be forced to marry her, but you must make provision for the child. That you must do.

NÖJD. So must Ludwig then.

CAPTAIN. If that's how it is, the case will have to go before the Magistrate. I can't settle it, and it's really nothing to do with me. Dismiss!

PASTOR. One moment, Nöjd. Ahem. Don't you think it's rather a dirty trick to leave a girl destitute with a child like that? Don't you think so—eh?

NÖJD. Yes, if I knew I was the father, it would be, but I tell you, Pastor, you never can know that. And it wouldn't be much fun slaving all your life for another chap's brat. You and the Captain must see that for yourselves.

CAPTAIN. That will do, Nöjd.

NÖJD. Yes, sir, thank you, sir.

CAPTAIN. And keep out of the kitchen, you scoundrel!

Exit NÖJD.

Why didn't you haul him over the coals?

PASTOR. What do you mean? Didn't I?

CAPTAIN. No, you just sat there muttering to yourself.

PASTOR. As a matter of fact, I scarcely knew what to say to him. It's hard on the girl, of course, but it's hard on the boy too. Supposing he's not the father? The girl can nurse the baby for four months at the orphanage, and after that it will be taken care of for good. But the boy can't nurse the child, can he? Later on, the girl will get a good place in some respectable family, but if the boy is cashiered, his future may be ruined.

CAPTAIN. Upon my soul, I'd like to be the magistrate and judge this case! Maybe the boy is responsible—that's what you can't know. But one thing you *can* know—if anybody's guilty, the girl is.

PASTOR. Well, I never sit in judgment. Now what was it we were talking about when this blessed business interrupted us? Yes, Bertha and her confirmation, wasn't it?

CAPTAIN. It's not just a question of confirmation, but of her whole future. The house is full of women, all trying to mould this child of mine. My mother-in-law wants to turn her into a spiritualist; Laura wants her to be an artist; the governess would have her a Methodist, old Margaret a Baptist, and the servant girls a Salvation Army lass. You can't make a character out of patchwork. Meanwhile I . . . I, who have more right than all the rest to guide her, am opposed at every turn. So I must send her away.

PASTOR. You have too many women running your house.

CAPTAIN. You're right there. It's like going into a cage of tigers. They'd soon tear me to pieces, if I didn't hold a red-hot poker under their noses. It's all very well for you to laugh, you blackguard. It wasn't enough that I married your sister; you had to palm off your old stepmother on me too.

PASTOR. Well, good Lord, one can't have stepmothers in one's house!

CAPTAIN. No, you prefer mothers-in-law—in someone else's house, of course.

PASTOR. Well, well, we all have our burdens to bear.

CAPTAIN. I daresay, but I have more than my share. There's my old nurse too, who treats me as if I still wore a bib. She's a good old soul, to be sure, but she shouldn't be here.

PASTOR. You should keep your women-folk in order, Adolf. You give them too much rope.

CAPTAIN. My dear fellow, can you tell me how to keep women in order?

PASTOR. To tell the truth, although she's my sister, Laura was always a bit of a handful.

CAPTAIN. Laura has her faults, of course, but they are not very serious ones.

PASTOR. Oh come now, I know her!

CAPTAIN. She was brought up with romantic ideas and has always found it a little difficult to come to terms with life. But she is my wife and . . .

PASTOR. And because she is your wife she must be the best of women. No, brother-in-law, it's she not you who wears the trousers.

CAPTAIN. In any case, the whole household has gone mad. Laura's determined Bertha shan't leave her, and I won't let her stay in this lunatic asylum.

PASTOR. So Laura's determined, is she? Then there's bound to be trouble, I'm afraid. As a child she used to lie down and sham dead until they gave in to her. Then she would calmly hand back whatever she'd set her mind on, explaining it wasn't the thing she wanted, but simply to get her own way.

CAPTAIN. So she was like that even then, was she? Hm. As a matter of fact, she does sometimes get so overwrought I'm frightened for her and think she must be ill.

PASTOR. What is it you want Bertha to do that's such a bone of contention? Can't you come to some agreement?

CAPTAIN. Don't think I want to turn her into a prodigy—or into some image of myself. But I will not play pander and have my daughter fitted for nothing but the marriage market. For then, if she didn't marry after all, she'd have a wretched time of it. On the other hand, I don't want to start her off in some man's career with a long training that would be entirely wasted if she did marry.

PASTOR. Well, what do you want then?

CAPTAIN. I want her to be a teacher. Then, if she doesn't marry she'll be able to support herself, and at least be no worse off than those unfortunate schoolmasters who have to support families on their earnings. And if she does marry, she can educate her own children. Isn't that reasonable?

PASTOR. Reasonable, yes—but what about her artistic talent? Wouldn't it be against the grain to repress that?

CAPTAIN. No. I showed her attempts to a well-known painter who told me they were nothing but the usual sort of thing learnt at school. Then, during the summer, some young jackanapes came along who knew better and said she was a genius—whereupon the matter was settled in Laura's favour.

PASTOR. Was he in love with Bertha?

CAPTAIN. I take that for granted.

PASTOR. Well, God help you, old boy, I don't see any solution. But it's a tiresome business, and I suppose Laura has supporters . . . *indicates other rooms* in there.

CAPTAIN. You may be sure of that. The whole household is in an uproar, and between ourselves the method of attack from that quarter is not exactly chivalrous.

PASTOR, *rising*. Do you think I haven't been through it?

CAPTAIN. You too?

PASTOR. Yes, indeed.

CAPTAIN. But to me the worst thing about it is that Bertha's future should be decided in there from motives of sheer hate. They do nothing but talk about men being made to see that women can do this and do that. It's man versus woman the whole day long . . . Must you go? Won't you stay to supper? I don't know what there is, but do stay. I'm expecting the new doctor, you know. Have you seen him yet?

PASTOR. I caught a glimpse of him on my way here. He looks a decent, reliable sort of man.

CAPTAIN. That's good. Do you think he may be my ally?

PASTOR. Maybe. It depends how well he knows women.

CAPTAIN. But won't you stay?

PASTOR. Thank you, my dear fellow, but I promised to be home this evening, and my wife gets anxious if I'm late.

CAPTAIN. Anxious! Furious, you mean. Well, as you please. Let me help you on with your coat.

PASTOR. It's certainly very cold to-night. Thank you. You must look after yourself, Adolf. You seem a bit on edge.

CAPTAIN. On edge? Do I?

PASTOR. Yes. You aren't very well, are you?

CAPTAIN. Did Laura put this into your head? For the last twenty years she's been treating me as if I had one foot in the grave.

PASTOR. Laura? No, it's just that I'm . . . I'm worried about you. Take my advice and look after yourself. Goodbye, old man. By the way, didn't you want to talk about the confirmation?

CAPTAIN. By no means. But I give you my word this shall take its own course—and be chalked up to the official conscience. I am neither a witness to the truth, nor a martyr. We have got past that sort of thing. Goodbye. Remember me to your wife.

PASTOR. Goodbye, Adolf. Give my love to Laura.

Exit PASTOR. *The* CAPTAIN *opens the bureau and settles down to his accounts.*

CAPTAIN. Thirty-four—nine, forty-three—seven, eight, fifty-six.

LAURA, *entering from the next room.* Will you please . . .

CAPTAIN. One moment!—Sixty-six, seventy-one, eighty-four, eighty-nine, ninety-two, a hundred. What is it?

LAURA. Am I disturbing you?

CAPTAIN. Not in the least. Housekeeping money, I suppose?

LAURA. Yes, housekeeping money.

CAPTAIN. If you put the accounts down there, I will go through them.

LAURA. Accounts?

CAPTAIN. Yes.

LAURA. Do you expect me to keep accounts now?

CAPTAIN. Of course you must keep accounts. Our position's most precarious, and if we go bankrupt, we must have accounts to show. Otherwise we could be accused of negligence.

LAURA. It's not my fault if we're in debt.

CAPTAIN. That's what the accounts will show.

LAURA. It's not my fault the tenant farmer doesn't pay.

CAPTAIN. Who was it recommended him so strongly? You. Why did you recommend such a—shall we call him a scatterbrain?

LAURA. Why did you take on such a scatterbrain?

CAPTAIN. Because I wasn't allowed to eat in peace, sleep in

peace or work in peace till you got him here. You wanted him because your brother wanted to get rid of him; my mother-in-law wanted him because I didn't; the governess wanted him because he was a Methodist, and old Margaret because she had known his grandmother as a child. That's why, and if I hadn't taken him I should be in a lunatic asylum by now, or else in the family vault. However, here's the housekeeping allowance and your pin money. You can give me the accounts later.

LAURA, *with an ironic bob.* Thank you so much.—By the way, do you keep accounts yourself—of what you spend outside the household?

CAPTAIN. That's none of your business.

LAURA. True. As little my business as the future of my own child. Did you gentlemen come to any decision at this evening's conference?

CAPTAIN. I had already made my decision, so I merely had to communicate it to the only friend I have in the family. Bertha is going to live in town. She will leave in a fortnight's time.

LAURA. Where, if I may ask, is she going to stay?

CAPTAIN. At Sävberg's—the solicitor's.

LAURA. That Freethinker!

CAPTAIN. According to the law as it now stands, children are brought up in their father's faith.

LAURA. And the mother has no say in the matter?

CAPTAIN. None whatever. She sells her birthright by legal contract and surrenders all her rights. In return the husband supports her and her children.

LAURA. So she has no rights over her own child?

CAPTAIN. None at all. When you have sold something, you don't expect to get it back and keep the money too.

LAURA. But supposing the father and mother were to decide things together . . . ?

CAPTAIN. How would that work out? I want her to live in town; you want her to live at home. The mathematical mean would be for her to stop at the railway station, midway between home and town. You see? It's a deadlock.

LAURA. Then the lock must be forced. . . . What was Nöjd doing here?

CAPTAIN. That's a professional secret.

LAURA. Which the whole kitchen knows.

CAPTAIN. Then doubtless you know it too.

LAURA. I do.

CAPTAIN. And are ready to sit in judgment?

LAURA. The law does that.

CAPTAIN. The law doesn't say who the child's father is.

LAURA. Well, people know that for themselves.

CAPTAIN. Discerning people say that's what one never can know.

LAURA. How extraordinary! Can't one tell who a child's father is?

CAPTAIN. Apparently not.

LAURA. How perfectly extraordinary! Then how can the father have those rights over the mother's child?

CAPTAIN. He only has them when he takes on the responsibility—or has it forced on him. But of course in marriage there is no doubt about the paternity.

LAURA. No doubt?

CAPTAIN. I should hope not.

LAURA. But supposing the wife has been unfaithful?

CAPTAIN. Well, such a supposition has no bearing on our problem. Is there anything else you want to ask me about?

LAURA. No, nothing.

CAPTAIN. Then I shall go up to my room. Please let me know when the doctor comes. *Closes the bureau and rises.*

LAURA. I will.

CAPTAIN, *going out by the wall-papered door.* As soon as he comes, mind. I don't want to be discourteous, you understand.

Exit.

LAURA. I understand. *She looks at the bank-notes she is holding.*

MOTHER-IN-LAW, *off.* Laura!

LAURA. Yes, Mother?

MOTHER-IN-LAW. Is my tea ready?

LAURA, *at the door to the next room.* It's coming in a moment.

The ORDERLY *opens the hall door.*

ORDERLY. Dr. Östermark.

Enter DOCTOR. *Exit* ORDERLY, *closing the door.*

LAURA, *shaking hands.* How do you do, Dr. Östermark. Let me welcome you to our home. The Captain is out, but he will be back directly.

DOCTOR. I must apologize for calling so late, but I have already had to pay some professional visits.

LAURA. Won't you sit down?

DOCTOR. Thank you.

LAURA. Yes, there is a lot of illness about just now, but I hope all the same that you will find this place suits you. It is so important for people in a lonely country district like this to have a doctor who takes a real interest in his patients. I have heard you so warmly spoken of, Dr. Östermark, I hope we shall be on the best of terms.

DOCTOR. You are too kind, dear lady. I hope, however, for your sake that my visits here will not often be of a professional nature. I take it that the health of your family is, on the whole, good, and that . . .

LAURA. Yes, we have been fortunate enough not to have any serious illnesses, but all the same things are not quite as they should be.

DOCTOR. Indeed?

LAURA. No, I'm afraid not really at all as one would wish.

DOCTOR. Dear, dear, you quite alarm me!

LAURA. In a family there are sometimes things which honour and duty compel one to keep hidden from the world.

DOCTOR. But not from one's doctor.

LAURA. No. That is why it is my painful duty to tell you the whole truth from the start.

DOCTOR. May we not postpone this conversation until I have had the honour of meeting the Captain?

LAURA. No. You must hear what I have to say before you see him.

DOCTOR. Does it concern him then?

LAURA. Yes, him. My poor, dear husband.

DOCTOR. You are making me most uneasy. Whatever your trouble, Madam, you can confide in me.

LAURA, *taking out her handkerchief.* My husband's mind is affected. Now you know, and later on you will be able to judge for yourself.

DOCTOR. You astound me. The Captain's learned treatise on mineralogy, for which I have the greatest admiration, shows a clear and powerful intellect.

LAURA. Does it? I shall be overjoyed if we—his relatives—are mistaken.

DOCTOR. It is possible, of course, that his mind is disturbed in other ways. Tell me . . .

LAURA. That is exactly what we fear. You see, at times he has the most peculiar ideas, which wouldn't matter much for a scientist, if they weren't such a burden on his family. For instance, he has an absolute mania for buying things.

DOCTOR. That is significant. What kind of things?

LAURA. Books. Whole cases of them, which he never reads.

DOCTOR. Well, that a scholar should buy books isn't so alarming.

LAURA. You don't believe what I am telling you?

DOCTOR. I am convinced, Madam, that you believe what you are telling me.

LAURA. Well, then, is it possible for anyone to see in a microscope what's happening on another planet?

DOCTOR. Does he say he can do that?

LAURA. Yes, that's what he says.

DOCTOR. In a microscope?

LAURA. In a microscope. Yes.

DOCTOR. That is significant, if it is so.

LAURA. If it is so! You don't believe me, Doctor. And here have I let you in to the family secret.

DOCTOR. My dear lady, I am honoured by your confidence, but as a physician I must observe and examine before giving an opinion. Has the Captain shown any symptoms of instability, any lack of will power?

LAURA. Has he, indeed! We have been married twenty years, and he has never yet made a decision without going back on it.

DOCTOR. Is he dogmatic?

LAURA. He certainly lays down the law, but as soon as he gets his own way, he loses interest and leaves everything to me.

DOCTOR. That is significant and requires careful consideration. The will, you see, Madam, is the backbone of the mind. If it is injured, the mind falls to pieces.

LAURA. God knows how I have schooled myself to meet his every wish during these long hard years. Oh, if you knew what I have been through with him, if you only knew!

DOCTOR. I am profoundly distressed to learn of your trouble, Madam, and I promise I will do what I can. You have my deepest sympathy and I beg you to rely on me implicitly. But now you have told me this, I am going to ask one thing of you. Don't allow anything to prey on the patient's mind. In a case of instability, ideas can sometimes take hold and grow into an obsession—or even monomania. Do you follow me?

LAURA. . . . You mean don't let him get ideas into his head.

DOCTOR. Precisely. For a sick man can be made to believe anything. He is highly susceptible to suggestion.

LAURA. I see . . . I understand. Yes, indeed. *A bell rings within.* Excuse me. That's my mother ringing. I won't be a moment . . . Oh, here's Adolf!

As LAURA *goes out, the* CAPTAIN *enters by the wall-papered door.*

CAPTAIN. Ah, so you have arrived, Doctor! You are very welcome.

DOCTOR. How do you do, Captain. It's a great honour to meet such a distinguished scientist.

CAPTAIN. Oh please! Unfortunately, my military duties don't give me much time for research . . . All the same, I do believe I am now on the brink of a rather exciting discovery.

DOCTOR. Really?

CAPTAIN. You see, I have been subjecting meteoric stones to spectrum analysis, and I have found carbon—an indication of organic life. What do you say to that?

DOCTOR. Can you see that in a microscope?

CAPTAIN. No, in a spectroscope, for heaven's sake!

DOCTOR. Spectroscope! I beg your pardon. Then you will soon be telling us what is happening on Jupiter.

CAPTAIN. Not what is happening, what *has* happened. If only that blasted Paris bookseller would send my books. I really think the whole book-trade must be in league against me. Think of it, for two months I've not had one single answer to my orders, my letters or my abusive telegrams! It's driving me mad. I can't make out what's happened.

DOCTOR. Well, what could it be but ordinary carelessness? You shouldn't let it upset you.

CAPTAIN. Yes, but the devil of it is I shan't be able to get my article finished in time.—I know they're working on the same lines in Berlin . . . However, that's not what we should be talking about now, but about you. If you would care to live here, we can give you a small suite of rooms in that wing. Or would you prefer your predecessor's house?

DOCTOR. Whichever you please.

CAPTAIN. No, whichever *you* please. You have only to say.

DOCTOR. It's for you to decide, Captain.

CAPTAIN. Nothing of the kind. It's for you to say which you prefer. I don't care one way or the other.

DOCTOR. But I really can't . . .

CAPTAIN. For Christ's sake, man, say what you want! I haven't any opinion, any inclination, any choice, any preference at all. Are you such a milksop that you don't know what you want? Make up your mind, or I shall lose my temper.

DOCTOR. If I am to choose, I should like to live here.

CAPTAIN. Good!—Thank you. *Rings.* Oh dear me!—I apologise, Doctor, but nothing irritates me so much as to hear people say they don't care one way or the other.

The NURSE *enters.*

Ah, it's you, Margaret. Look here, my dear, do you know if the rooms in the wing are ready for the doctor?

NURSE. Yes, Captain, they're ready.

CAPTAIN. Good. Then I won't detain you, Doctor, for you must be tired. Goodnight, and once again—welcome. I look forward to seeing you in the morning.

DOCTOR. Thank you. Goodnight.

CAPTAIN. By the way, I wonder if my wife told you anything about us—if you know at all how the land lies?

DOCTOR. Your good lady did suggest one or two things it might be as well for a newcomer to know. Goodnight, Captain.

The NURSE *shows the* DOCTOR *out and returns.*

CAPTAIN. What is it, old girl? Anything the matter?

NURSE. Now listen, Mr. Adolf, dear.

CAPTAIN. Yes, go on, Margaret, talk. You're the only one whose talk doesn't get on my nerves.

NURSE. Then listen, Mr. Adolf. Couldn't you go halfway to meet the mistress in all this bother over the child? Think of a mother . . .

CAPTAIN. Think of a father, Margaret.

NURSE. Now, now, now! A father has many things besides his child, but a mother has nothing but her child.

CAPTAIN. Quite so, my friend. She has only one burden, while I have three and bear hers too. Do you think I'd have been stuck in the army all my life if I hadn't had her and her child to support?

NURSE. I know, but that wasn't what I wanted to talk about.

CAPTAIN. Quite. What you want is to make out I'm in the wrong.

NURSE. Don't you believe I want what's best for you, Mr. Adolf?

CAPTAIN. I'm sure you do, my dear, but you don't know what is best for me. You see, it's not enough to have given the child life. I want to give her my very soul.

NURSE. Oh, that's beyond me, but I do think you two ought to come to terms.

CAPTAIN. Margaret, you are not my friend.

NURSE. Not your friend! Ah God, what are you saying, Mr. Adolf? Do you think I ever forget you were my baby when you were little?

CAPTAIN. Well, my dear, am I likely to forget it? You have been like a mother to me, and stood by me against all the others. But now that things have come to a head, you're deserting—going over to the enemy.

NURSE. Enemy?

CAPTAIN. Yes, enemy. You know perfectly well how things are here. You've seen it all from beginning to end.

NURSE. Aye, I've seen plenty. But, dear God, why must two people torment the lives out of each other? Two people who are so good and kind to everyone else. The mistress never treats me wrong or . . .

CAPTAIN. Only me. I know. And I tell you, Margaret, if you desert me now, you'll be doing a wicked thing. For a net is closing round me, and that doctor is no friend of mine.

NURSE. Oh, goodness, Mr. Adolf, you believe the worst of everyone! But that's what comes of not having the true faith. That's your trouble.

CAPTAIN. While you and the Baptists have found the one true faith, eh? You're lucky.

NURSE. Aye, luckier than you, Mr. Adolf. Humble your heart

and you will see how happy God will make you in your love for your neighbour.

CAPTAIN. Isn't it strange—as soon as you mention God and love, your voice grows hard and your eyes fill with hate. No, Margaret, I'm sure you haven't found the true faith.

MARGARET. However proud you are and stuffed with book-learning, that won't get you anywhere when the pinch comes.

CAPTAIN. How arrogantly thou speakest, O humble heart! I'm well aware that learning means nothing to creatures like you.

NURSE. Shame on you! Still, old Margaret loves her great big boy best of all. And when the storm breaks, he'll come back to her, sure enough, like the good child he is.

CAPTAIN. Forgive me, Margaret. You see, you really are the only friend I have here. Help me, for something is going to happen. I don't know what, but I know it's evil, this thing that's on its way. *A scream from within.* What's that? Who's screaming?

BERTHA *runs in.*

BERTHA. Father, Father! Help me! Save me!

CAPTAIN. What is it? My darling, tell me.

BERTHA. Please protect me. I know she'll do something terrible to me.

CAPTAIN. Who? What do you mean? Tell me at once.

BERTHA. Grandmother. But it was my fault. I played a trick on her.

CAPTAIN. Go on.

BERTHA. Yes, but you mustn't tell anyone. Promise you won't.

CAPTAIN. Very well, but what happened?

Exit NURSE.

BERTHA. You see, sometimes in the evening she turns the lamp down and makes me sit at the table holding a pen over a piece of paper. And then she says the spirits write.

CAPTAIN. Well, I'll be damned! And you never told me.

BERTHA. I'm sorry, I didn't dare. Grandmother says spirits

revenge themselves on people who talk about them. And then the pen writes, but I don't know if it's me doing it or not. Sometimes it goes well, but sometimes it doesn't work at all. And when I get tired nothing happens, but I have to make something happen all the same. This evening I thought I was doing rather well, but then Grandmother said it was all out of Stagnelius* and I had been playing a trick on her. And she was simply furious.

CAPTAIN. Do you believe there are spirits?

BERTHA. I don't know.

CAPTAIN. But I know there are not.

BERTHA. Grandmother says you don't understand, and that you have worse things that can see into other planets.

CAPTAIN. She says that, does she? And what else does she say?

BERTHA. That you can't work miracles.

CAPTAIN. I never said I could. You know what meteorites are, don't you?—stones that fall from other heavenly bodies. Well, I examine these and see if they contain the same elements as the earth. That's all I do.

BERTHA. Grandmother says there are things she can see and you can't.

CAPTAIN. My dear, she is lying.

BERTHA. Grandmother doesn't lie.

CAPTAIN. How do you know?

BERTHA. Then Mother does too.

CAPTAIN. Hm!

BERTHA. If you say Mother is a liar, I'll never believe a word you say again.

CAPTAIN. I didn't say that, so now you must believe me. Listen. Your happiness, your whole future depends on your leaving home. Will you do this? Will you go and live in town and learn something useful?

BERTHA. Oh yes, I'd love to live in town—anywhere away from here! It's always so miserable in there, as gloomy

*Erik Johan Stagnelius, Swedish poet and dramatist. (1793–1823.)

as a winter night. But when you come home, Father, it's like a spring morning when they take the double windows down.

CAPTAIN. My darling, my beloved child!

BERTHA. But, Father, listen, you must be kind to Mother. She often cries.

CAPTAIN. Hm! . . . So you would like to live in town?

BERTHA. Oh yes!

CAPTAIN. But supposing your mother doesn't agree?

BERTHA. She must.

CAPTAIN. But supposing she doesn't?

BERTHA. Then I don't know what will happen. But she must, she must!

CAPTAIN. Will you ask her?

BERTHA. No, you must ask her—very nicely. She wouldn't pay any attention to me.

CAPTAIN. Hm! . . . Well now, if you want this and I want it and she doesn't want it, what are we to do then?

BERTHA. Oh, then the fuss will begin all over again! Why can't you both . . .

Enter LAURA.

LAURA. Ah, so you're here, Bertha! Well now, Adolf, as the question of her future is still to be decided, let's hear what she has to say herself.

CAPTAIN. The child can hardly have anything constructive to say about the development of young girls, but you and I ought to be able to sum up the pros and cons. We've watched a good number grow up.

LAURA. But as we don't agree, Bertha can give the casting vote.

CAPTAIN. No. I won't allow anyone to interfere with my rights —neither woman nor child. Bertha, you had better leave us.

Exit BERTHA.

LAURA. You were afraid to hear her opinion because you knew she would agree with me.

CAPTAIN. I know she wants to leave home, but I also know you have the power to make her change her mind.

LAURA. Oh, have I much power?

CAPTAIN. Yes, you have a fiendish power of getting your own way, like all people who are unscrupulous about the means they employ. How, for instance, did you get rid of Dr. Norling? And how did you get hold of the new doctor?

LAURA. Yes, how did I?

CAPTAIN. You ran the old doctor down until he had to leave, and then you got your brother to canvass for this one.

LAURA. Well, that was quite simple and perfectly legal. Then is Bertha to leave home?

CAPTAIN. Yes, in a fortnight's time.

LAURA. I warn you I shall do my best to prevent it.

CAPTAIN. You can't.

LAURA. Can't I? Do you expect me to give up my child to be taught by wicked people that all she has learnt from her mother is nonsense? So that I would be despised by my own daughter for the rest of my life.

CAPTAIN. Do you expect me to allow ignorant and bumptious women to teach my daughter that her father is a charlatan?

LAURA. That shouldn't matter so much to you—now.

CAPTAIN. What on earth do you mean?

LAURA. Well, the mother's closer to the child, since the discovery that no one can tell who the father is.

CAPTAIN. What's that got to do with us?

LAURA. You don't know if you are Bertha's father.

CAPTAIN. Don't know?

LAURA. How can you know what nobody knows?

CAPTAIN. Are you joking?

LAURA. No, I'm simply applying your own theory. How do you know I haven't been unfaithful to you?

CAPTAIN. I can believe a good deal of you, but not that. And if it were so, you wouldn't talk about it.

LAURA. Supposing I were prepared for anything, for being turned out and ostracised, anything to keep my child under my own control. Supposing I am telling the truth now when I say: Bertha is my child but not yours. Supposing . . .

CAPTAIN. Stop it!

LAURA. Just supposing . . . then your power would be over.

CAPTAIN. Not till you had proved I wasn't the father.

LAURA. That wouldn't be difficult. Do you want me to?

CAPTAIN. Stop.

LAURA. I should only have to give the name of the real father —with particulars of place and time, of course. For that matter—when was Bertha born? In the third year of our marriage . . .

CAPTAIN. Will you stop it now, or . . .

LAURA. Or what? Very well, let's stop. All the same, I should think twice before you decide anything. And, above all, don't make yourself ridiculous.

CAPTAIN. I find the whole thing tragic.

LAURA. Which makes you still more ridiculous.

CAPTAIN. But not you?

LAURA. No, we're in such a strong position.

CAPTAIN. That's why we can't fight you.

LAURA. Why try to fight a superior enemy?

CAPTAIN. Superior?

LAURA. Yes. It's odd, but I have never been able to look at a man without feeling myself his superior.

CAPTAIN. One day you may meet your master—and you'll never forget it.

LAURA. That will be fascinating.

Enter NURSE.

NURSE. Supper's ready. Come along now, please.

LAURA. Yes, of course. *The* CAPTAIN *lingers and sits down in an armchair near the sofa.* Aren't you coming?

CAPTAIN. No, thank you, I don't want any supper.

LAURA. Why not? Has anything upset you?

CAPTAIN. No, but I'm not hungry.

LAURA. Do come, or they'll start asking questions, and that's not necessary. Do be sensible. You won't? Well, stay where you are then!

Exit.

NURSE. Mr. Adolf, whatever is it now?

CAPTAIN. I don't know yet. Tell me—why do you women treat a grown man as if he were a child?

NURSE. Well, goodness me, you're all some woman's child, aren't you?—All you men, big or small . . .

CAPTAIN. While no woman is born of man, you mean. True. But I must be Bertha's father. You believe that, Margaret, don't you? Don't you?

NURSE. Lord, what a silly boy you are! Of course you're your own child's father. Come along and eat now. Don't sit here sulking. There now, come along, do.

CAPTAIN, *rising.* Get out, woman! To hell with the hags! *At the hall door.* Svärd! Svärd!

ORDERLY, *entering.* Yes, sir?

CAPTAIN. Have the small sleigh got ready at once.

Exit ORDERLY.

NURSE. Now listen, Captain . . .

CAPTAIN. Get out, woman! Get out, I say!

NURSE. God preserve us, whatever's going to happen now?

CAPTAIN, *putting on his cap.* Don't expect me home before midnight.

Exit.

NURSE. Lord Jesus! What *is* going to happen?

ACT TWO

The same as before, late that night. The DOCTOR *and* LAURA *are sitting talking.*

DOCTOR. My conversation with him has led me to the conclusion that your suspicions are by no means proved. To begin with, you were mistaken in saying that he had made these important astronomical discoveries by using a microscope. Now I have learnt that it was a spectroscope. Not only is there no sign in this of mental derangement—on the contrary, he has rendered a great service to science.

LAURA. But I never said that.

DOCTOR. I made a memorandum of our conversation, Madam, and I remember questioning you on this vital point, because I thought I must have misheard. One must be scrupulously accurate when bringing charges which might lead to a man being certified.

LAURA. Certified?

DOCTOR. I presume you are aware that if a person is certified insane, he loses both his civil and his family rights.

LAURA. No, I didn't know that.

DOCTOR. There is one other point I should like to be clear about. He spoke of not getting any replies from his booksellers. May I ask whether—from the best of intentions, of course—you have been intercepting his correspondence?

LAURA. Yes, I have. It is my duty to protect the family. I couldn't let him ruin us all and do nothing about it.

DOCTOR. Excuse me, I do not think you understand the possible consequences of your action. If he realises you have been interfering with his affairs behind his back, his suspicions will be aroused and might even develop into a persecution mania. Particularly, as by thwarting his will, you have already driven him to the end of his tether.

Surely you know how enraging it is to have your will opposed and your dearest wishes frustrated.

LAURA. Do I not!

DOCTOR. Then think what this means to him.

LAURA, *rising*. It's midnight and he's not back yet. Now we can expect the worst.

DOCTOR. Tell me what happened this evening after I saw him. I must know everything.

LAURA. He talked in the wildest way and said the most fantastic things. Can you believe it—he even suggested he wasn't the father of his own child!

DOCTOR. How extraordinary! What can have put that into his head?

LAURA. Goodness knows, unless it was an interview he had with one of his men about maintenance for a child. When I took the girl's part, he got very excited and said no one could ever tell who a child's father was. God knows I did everything I could to calm him, but I don't believe anything can help him now. *Weeps.*

DOCTOR. This can't go on. Something must be done—without rousing his suspicions. Tell me, has he had any such delusions before?

LAURA. As a matter of fact, he was much the same six years ago, and then he actually admitted—in a letter to his doctor—that he feared for his reason.

DOCTOR. I see, I see. A deep-seated trouble. But . . . er . . . the sanctity of family life . . . and so forth . . . I mustn't probe too far . . . must keep to the surface. Unfortunately what is done cannot be undone, yet the remedy should have been applied to what is done . . . Where do you think he is now?

LAURA. I can't imagine. He has such wild notions these days . . .

DOCTOR. Would you like me to stay until he comes in? I could explain my presence by saying—well, that your mother is ill and I came to see her.

LAURA. That's a very good idea. Please stand by us, Doctor.

If you only knew how worried I am! . . . But wouldn't it be better to tell him straight out what you think of his condition?

DOCTOR. We never do that with mental patients, unless they bring the subject up themselves, and rarely even then. Everything depends on how the case develops. But we had better not stay here. May I go into some other room, to make it more convincing?

LAURA. Yes, that will be best, and Margaret can come in here. She always waits up for him. *At the door.* Margaret! Margaret! She is the only one who can manage him.

NURSE, *entering.* Did you call, Madam? Is Master back?

LAURA. No, but you are to wait here for him. And when he comes, tell him that my mother is unwell and the doctor is with her.

NURSE. Aye, aye. Leave all that to me.

LAURA, *opening the door.* If you will be so good as to come in here, Doctor . . .

DOCTOR. Thank you.

They go out. The NURSE *sits at the table, puts on her glasses and picks up her hymn-book.*

NURSE. Ah me! Ah me! *Reads softly:*

A sorrowful and grievous thing
Is life, so swiftly passing by,
Death shadows with his angel's wing
The whole earth, and this his cry:
'Tis Vanity, all Vanity!

Ah me! Ah me!

All that on earth has life and breath,
Falls low before his awful might,
Sorrow alone is spared by Death,
Upon the yawning grave to write:
'Tis Vanity, all Vanity!

Ah me! Ah me!

During the last lines, BERTHA *enters, carrying a tray with a coffee-pot and a piece of embroidery.*

BERTHA, *softly.* Margaret, may I sit in here with you? It's so dismal up there.

NURSE. Saints alive! Bertha, are you still up?

BERTHA. Well, you see, I simply must get on with Father's Christmas present. And here's something nice for you.

NURSE. But, sweetheart, this won't do. You have to be up bright and early, and it's past twelve now.

BERTHA. Oh, that doesn't matter! I daren't stay up there all alone. I'm sure there are ghosts.

NURSE. There now! What did I tell you? Mark my words, there's no good fairy in this house. What was it? Did you hear something, Bertha?

BERTHA. Oh Margaret, someone was singing in the attic!

NURSE. In the attic? At this time of night?

BERTHA. Yes. It was such a sad song; the saddest I ever heard. And it seemed to come from the attic—you know, the one on the left where the cradle is.

NURSE. Oh dear, dear, dear! And such a fearful night too. I'm sure the chimneys will blow down. "Alas, what is this earthly life? Sorrow, trouble, grief and strife. Even when it seems most fair, Nought but tribulation there."—Ah, dear child, God grant us a happy Christmas!

BERTHA. Margaret, is it true Father's ill?

NURSE. Aye, that's true enough.

BERTHA. Then I don't expect we shall have a Christmas party. But why isn't he in bed if he's ill?

NURSE. Well, dearie, staying in bed doesn't help his kind of illness. Hush! I hear someone in the porch. Go to bed now —take the tray with you, or the Master will be cross.

BERTHA, *going out with the tray.* Goodnight, Margaret.

NURSE. Goodnight, love. God bless you.

Enter the CAPTAIN.

CAPTAIN, *taking off his overcoat.* Are you still up? Go to bed.

NURSE. Oh, I was only biding till . . .

The CAPTAIN *lights a candle, opens the bureau, sits down at it and takes letters and newspapers from his pocket.*

Mr. Adolf . . .

CAPTAIN. What is it?

NURSE. The old mistress is ill. Doctor's here.

CAPTAIN. Anything serious?

NURSE. No, I don't think so. Just a chill.

CAPTAIN, *rising*. Who was the father of your child, Margaret?

NURSE. I've told you often enough, it was that heedless fellow Johansson.

CAPTAIN. Are you sure it was he?

NURSE. Don't talk so silly. Of course I'm sure, seeing he was the only one.

CAPTAIN. Yes, but was he sure he was the only one? No, he couldn't be sure, only you could be. See? That's the difference.

NURSE. I don't see any difference.

CAPTAIN. No, you don't see it, but it's there all the same.

Turns the pages of the photograph album on the table.

Do you think Bertha's like me?

NURSE. You're as like as two peas in a pod.

CAPTAIN. Did Johansson admit he was the father?

NURSE. Well, he was forced to.

CAPTAIN. How dreadful!—Here's the doctor.

Enter DOCTOR.

Good evening, Doctor. How is my mother-in-law?

DOCTOR. Oh, it's nothing much. Just a slight sprain of the left ankle.

CAPTAIN. I thought Margaret said it was a chill. There appear to be different diagnoses of the case. Margaret, go to bed.

Exit NURSE. *Pause.*

Won't you sit down, Dr. Östermark?

DOCTOR, *sitting*. Thank you.

CAPTAIN. Is it true that if you cross a mare with a zebra you get striped foals?

DOCTOR, *astonished.* Perfectly true.

CAPTAIN. And that if breeding is then continued with a stallion, the foals may still be striped?

DOCTOR. That is also true.

CAPTAIN. So, in certain circumstances, a stallion can sire striped foals, and vice versa.

DOCTOR. That would appear to be the case.

CAPTAIN. So the offspring's resemblance to the father proves nothing.

DOCTOR. Oh . . .

CAPTAIN. You're a widower, aren't you? Any children?

DOCTOR. Ye-es.

CAPTAIN. Didn't you sometimes feel rather ridiculous as a father? I myself don't know anything more ludicrous than the sight of a man holding his child's hand in the street, or hearing a father say: "My child." "My wife's child," he ought to say. Didn't you ever see what a false position you were in? Weren't you ever haunted by doubts—I won't say suspicions, as a gentleman I assume your wife was above suspicion?

DOCTOR. No, I certainly wasn't. There it is, Captain, a man—as I think Goethe says—must take his children on trust.

CAPTAIN. Trust, where a woman's concerned? A bit of a risk.

DOCTOR. Ah, but there are many kinds of women!

CAPTAIN. The latest research shows there is only one kind . . . when I was a young fellow and not, if I may say so, a bad specimen, I had two little experiences which afterwards gave me to think. The first was on a steamer. I was in the saloon with some friends, and the young stewardess told us—with tears running down her cheeks—how her sweetheart had been drowned at sea. We condoled with her and I ordered champagne. After the second glass I touched her foot, after the fourth her knee, and before morning I had consoled her.

DOCTOR. One swallow doesn't make a summer.

CAPTAIN. My second experience was a summer swallow. I was staying at Lysekil and got to know a young married woman who was there with her children—her husband was in town. She was religious and high-minded, kept preaching at me and was—or so I thought—the soul of virtue. I lent her a book or two which, strange to relate, she returned. Three months later, I found her card in one of those books with a pretty outspoken declaration of love. It was innocent—as innocent, that's to say, as such a declaration from a married woman could be—to a stranger who had never made her any advances. Moral: don't believe in anyone too much.

DOCTOR. Don't believe too little either.

CAPTAIN. The happy mean, eh? But you see, Doctor, that woman was so unaware of her motives she actually told her husband of her infatuation for me. That's where the danger lies, in the fact that women are unconscious of their instinctive wickedness. An extenuating circumstance, perhaps, but that can only mitigate the judgment, not revoke it.

DOCTOR. You have a morbid turn of mind, Captain. You should be on your guard against this.

CAPTAIN. There's nothing morbid about it. Look here. All steam-boilers explode when the pressure-gauge reaches the limit, but the limit isn't the same for all boilers. Got that? After all, you're here to observe me. Now if I were not a man I could sniff and snivel and explain the case to you, with all its past history. But as unfortunately I am a man, like the ancient Roman I must cross my arms upon my breast and hold my breath until I die. Goodnight.

DOCTOR. If you are ill, Captain, there's no reflection on your manhood in telling me about it. Indeed, it is essential for me to hear both sides of the case.

CAPTAIN. I thought you were quite satisfied with one side.

DOCTOR. You're wrong. And I should like you to know, Captain, that when I heard that Mrs. Alving* blackening her late husband's memory, I thought what a damned shame it was that the fellow should be dead.

CAPTAIN. Do you think if he'd been alive he'd have said any-

*Reference to Mrs. Alving in Ibsen's GHOSTS.

thing? Do you think if any husband rose from the dead he'd be believed? Goodnight, Doctor. Look how calm I am. It's quite safe for you to go to bed.

DOCTOR. Then I will bid you goodnight. I wash my hands of the whole business.

CAPTAIN. So we're enemies?

DOCTOR. By no means. It's just a pity we can't be friends. Goodnight.

The CAPTAIN *shows the* DOCTOR *out by the hall door, then crosses to the other and slightly opens it.*

CAPTAIN. Come in and let's talk. I knew you were eavesdropping.

Enter LAURA, *embarrassed. The* CAPTAIN *sits at the bureau.*

It's very late, but we'd better have things out now. Sit down. *She sits. Pause.* This evening it was I who went to the post office and fetched the mail, and from my letters it is clear to me that you have been intercepting my correspondence—both in and out. The result of this has been a loss of time which has pretty well shattered the expectations I had for my work.

LAURA. I acted from the best of intentions. You were neglecting your military duties for this other work.

CAPTAIN. Scarcely the best of intentions. You knew very well that one day I should win more distinction in this field than in the Army, but what you wanted was to stop me winning laurels of any kind, because this would stress your own inferiority. Now, for a change, I have intercepted letters addressed to you.

LAURA. How chivalrous!

CAPTAIN. In keeping with the high opinion you have of me. From these letters it appears that for a long time now you've been setting my old friends against me, by spreading rumours about my mental condition. So successful have your efforts been that now scarcely one person from Colonel to kitchen-maid believes I am sane. The actual facts about my condition are these. My reason is, as you know, unaffected, and I am able to discharge my duties both as soldier and father. My emotions are still pretty well under control, but only so long as my will-power remains intact. And you have so gnawed and gnawed at my will that at any moment it may slip its cogs, and then the whole bag of tricks will go to pieces. I won't appeal to your feelings, because you haven't any—that is your strength. I appeal to your own interests.

LAURA. Go on.

CAPTAIN. By behaving in this way you have made me so full of suspicion that my judgment is fogged and my mind is beginning to stray. This means that the insanity you have been waiting for is on its way and may come at any moment. The question you now have to decide is whether it is more to your advantage for me to be well or ill. Consider. If I go to pieces, I shall have to leave the Service, and where will you be then? If I die, you get my life-insurance. But if I take my own life, you get nothing. It is therefore to your advantage that I should live my life out.

LAURA. Is this a trap?

CAPTAIN. Certainly. You can avoid it or stick your head in it.

LAURA. You say you'd kill yourself, but you never would.

CAPTAIN. Are you so sure? Do you think a man can go on living when he has nothing and nobody to live for?

LAURA. Then you give in?

CAPTAIN. No, I offer peace.

LAURA. On what terms?

CAPTAIN. That I may keep my reason. Free me from doubt and I will give up the fight.

LAURA. Doubt about what?

CAPTAIN. Bertha's parentage.

LAURA. Are there doubts about that?

CAPTAIN. Yes, for me there are, and it was you who roused them.

LAURA. I?

CAPTAIN. Yes. You dropped them like henbane in my ear, and

circumstances encouraged them to grow. Free me from uncertainty. Tell me straight out it is so, and I will forgive you in advance.

LAURA. I can scarcely admit to guilt that isn't mine.

CAPTAIN. What can it matter to you, when you know I won't reveal it? Do you think any man would proclaim his shame from the housetops?

LAURA. If I say it isn't so, you still won't be certain, but if I say it is, you will believe me. You must want it to be true.

CAPTAIN. Strangely enough I do. Perhaps because the first supposition can't be proved, while the second can.

LAURA. Have you any grounds for suspicion?

CAPTAIN. Yes and no.

LAURA. I believe you want to make out I'm guilty, so you can get rid of me and have absolute control of the child. But you won't catch me in any such trap.

CAPTAIN. Do you think, if I were convinced of your guilt, I should want to take on another man's child?

LAURA. No, I'm sure you wouldn't. So evidently you were lying when you said you'd forgive me in advance.

CAPTAIN, *rising*. Laura, save me and my reason! You can't have understood what I was saying. If the child's not mine, I have no rights over her, nor do I want any. And that's how you'd like it, isn't it? But that's not all. You want complete power over the child, don't you, with me still there to support you both?

LAURA. Power, that's it. What's this whole life and death struggle for if not power?

CAPTAIN. For me, as I don't believe in a life to come, this child was my life after death, my conception of immortality—the only one, perhaps, that's valid. If you take her away, you cut my life short.

LAURA. Why didn't we separate sooner?

CAPTAIN. Because the child bound us together, but the bond became a chain. How was that? I never thought of this before, but now memories return, accusing, perhaps condemning. After two years of marriage we were still childless—you know best why. Then I was ill and almost died. One day, between bouts of fever, I heard voices in the next room. You and the lawyer were discussing the property I still owned then. He was explaining that as there were no children, you could not inherit, and he asked if by any chance you were pregnant. I did not hear your reply. I recovered and we had a child. Who is the father?

LAURA. You are.

CAPTAIN. No, I am not. There's a crime buried here that's beginning to stink. And what a fiendish crime! You women, who were so tender-hearted about freeing black slaves, kept the white ones. I have slaved for you, your child, your mother, your servants. I have sacrificed career and promotion. Tortured, beaten, sleepless—my hair has gone grey through the agony of mind you have inflicted on me. All this I have suffered in order that you might enjoy a care-free life and, when you were old, relive it in your child. This is the lowest form of theft, the cruellest slavery. I have had seventeen years of penal servitude—and I was innocent. How can you make up to me for this?

LAURA. Now you really are mad.

CAPTAIN, *sitting*. So you hope. I have watched you trying to conceal your crime, but because I didn't understand I pitied you. I've soothed your conscience, thinking I was chasing away some nightmare. I've heard you crying out in your sleep without giving your words a second thought. But now . . . now! The other night—Bertha's birthday—comes back to me. I was still up in the early hours, reading, and you suddenly screamed as if someone were trying to strangle you. "Don't! Don't!" you cried. I knocked on the wall—I didn't want to hear any more. For a long time I have had vague suspicions. I did not want them confirmed. This is what I have suffered for you. What will you do for me?

LAURA. What can I do? Swear before God and all that I hold sacred that you are Bertha's father?

CAPTAIN. What good would that do? You have already said

that a mother can and ought to commit any crime for her child. I implore you by the memory of the past, I implore you as a wounded man begs to be put out of his misery, tell me the truth. Can't you see I'm helpless as a child? Can't you hear me crying to my mother that I'm hurt? Forget I'm a man, a soldier whose word men—and even beasts—obey. I am nothing but a sick creature in need of pity. I renounce every vestige of power and only beg for mercy on my life.

LAURA, *laying her hand on his forehead.* What? You, a man, in tears?

CAPTAIN. Yes, a man in tears. Has not a man eyes? Has not a man hands, limbs, senses, opinions, passions? Is he not nourished by the same food as a woman, wounded by the same weapons, warmed and chilled by the same winter and summer? If you prick us, do we not bleed? If you tickle us, do we not laugh? If you poison us, do we not die? Why should a man suffer in silence or a soldier hide his tears? Because it's not manly? Why isn't it manly?

LAURA. Weep, then, my child, and you shall have your mother again. Remember, it was as your second mother that I came into your life. You were big and strong, yet not fully a man. You were a giant child who had come into the world too soon, or perhaps an unwanted child.

CAPTAIN. That's true. My father and mother had me against their will, and therefore I was born without a will. That is why, when you and I became one, I felt I was completing myself—and that is why you dominated. I—in the army the one to command—became at home the one to obey. I grew up at your side, looked up to you as a superior being and listened to you as if I were your foolish little boy.

LAURA. Yes, that's how it was, and I loved you as if you were my little boy. But didn't you see how, when your feelings changed and you came to me as a lover, I was ashamed? The joy I felt in your embraces was followed by such a sense of guilt my very blood seemed tainted. The mother became the mistress—horrible!

CAPTAIN. I saw, but I didn't understand. I thought you despised my lack of virility, so I tried to win you as a woman by proving myself as a man.

LAURA. That was your mistake. The mother was your friend, you see, but the woman was your enemy. Sexual love is conflict. And don't imagine I gave myself. I didn't give. I only took what I meant to take. Yet you did dominate me . . . I felt it and wanted you to feel it.

CAPTAIN. You always dominated me. You could hypnotise me when I was wide awake, so that I neither saw nor heard, but simply obeyed. You could give me a raw potato and make me think it was a peach; you could make me take your ridiculous ideas for flashes of genius. You could corrupt me—yes, make me do the shabbiest things. You never had any real intelligence, yet, instead of being guided by me, you would take the reins into your own hands. And when at last I woke to the realisation that I had lost my integrity, I wanted to blot out my humiliation by some heroic action—some feat, some discovery—even by committing *hara-kiri.* I wanted to go to war, but I couldn't. It was then that I gave all my energies to science. And now—now when I should be stretching out my hand to gather the fruit, you chop off my arm. I'm robbed of my laurels; I'm finished. A man cannot live without repute.

LAURA. Can a woman?

CAPTAIN. Yes—she has her children, but he has not . . . Yet you and I and everyone else went on living, unconscious as children, full of fancies and ideals and illusions, until we woke up. Right—but we woke topsy-turvy, and what's more, we'd been woken by someone who was talking in his own sleep. When women are old and stop being women, they grow beards on their chins. What do men grow, I wonder, when they are old and stop being men? In this false dawn, the birds that crowed weren't cocks, they were capons, and the hens that answered their call were sexless, too. So when the sun should have risen for us, we found ourselves back among the ruins in the full moonlight, just as in the good old times. Our light morning sleep had only been troubled by fantastic dreams—there had been no awakening.

LAURA. You should have been a writer, you know.

CAPTAIN. Perhaps.

LAURA. But I'm sleepy now, so if you have any more fantasies, keep them till to-morrow.

CAPTAIN. Just one thing more—a fact. Do you hate me?

LAURA. Sometimes—as a man.

CAPTAIN. It's like race-hatred. If it's true we are descended from the ape, it must have been from two different species. There's no likeness between us, is there?

LAURA. What are you getting at?

CAPTAIN. In this fight, one of us must go under.

LAURA. Which?

CAPTAIN. The weaker naturally.

LAURA. Then is the stronger in the right?

CAPTAIN. Bound to be as he has the power.

LAURA. Then I am in the right.

CAPTAIN. Why, what power have you?

LAURA. All I need. And it will be legal power to-morrow when I've put you under restraint.

CAPTAIN. Under restraint?

LAURA. Yes. Then I shall decide my child's future myself out of reach of your fantasies.

CAPTAIN. Who will pay for her if I'm not there?

LAURA. Your pension.

CAPTAIN, *moving towards her menacingly*. How can you have me put under restraint?

LAURA, *producing a letter*. By means of this letter, an attested copy of which is already in the hands of the authorities.

CAPTAIN. What letter?

LAURA, *retreating*. Your own. The one in which you told the doctor you were mad. *He stares at her in silence.* Now you have fulfilled the unfortunately necessary functions of father and bread-winner. You are no longer needed, and you must go. You must go, now that you realise my wits are as strong as my will—you won't want to stay and acknowledge my superiority.

The CAPTAIN *goes to the table, picks up the lighted lamp and throws it at* LAURA, *who escapes backward through the door.*

ACT THREE

The same. The following evening. A new lamp, lighted, is on the table. The wall-papered door is barricaded with a chair. From the room above comes the sound of pacing footsteps. The NURSE *stands listening, troubled. Enter* LAURA *from within.*

LAURA. Did he give you the keys?

NURSE. Give? No, God help us, I took them from the coat Nöjd had out to brush.

LAURA. Then it's Nöjd who's on duty?

NURSE. Aye, it's Nöjd.

LAURA. Give me the keys.

NURSE. Here you are, but it's no better than stealing. Hark at him up there! To and fro, to and fro.

LAURA. Are you sure the door's safely bolted?

NURSE. It's bolted safe enough. *Weeps.*

LAURA, *opening the bureau and sitting down at it.* Pull yourself together, Margaret. The only way we can protect ourselves is by keeping calm. *A knock at the hall door.* See who that is.

NURSE, *opening door.* It's Nöjd.

LAURA. Tell him to come in.

NÖJD, *entering.* Despatch from the Colonel.

LAURA. Give it to me. *Reads.* I see . . . Nöjd, have you removed the cartridges from all the guns and pouches?

NÖJD. Yes, Ma'am, just as you said.

LAURA. Wait outside while I write to the Colonel.

Exit NÖJD. LAURA *writes. Sound of sawing above.*

NURSE. Listen, Madam. Whatever is he doing now?

LAURA. Do be quiet. I'm writing.

NURSE, *muttering.* Lord have mercy on us! What will be the end of all this?

LAURA, *holding out the note.* Here you are. Give it to Nöjd. And, remember, my mother's to know nothing of all this.

Exit NURSE *with note.* LAURA *opens the bureau drawers and takes out papers. Enter* PASTOR.

PASTOR. My dear Laura! As you probably gathered, I have been out all day and only just got back. I hear you've been having a terrible time.

LAURA. Yes, brother, I've never been through such a night and day in all my life!

PASTOR. Well, I see you're looking none the worse for it.

LAURA. No, thank heaven, I wasn't hurt. But just think what might have happened!

PASTOR. Tell me all about it. I've only heard rumours. How did it begin?

LAURA. It began by him raving about not being Bertha's father, and ended by him throwing the lighted lamp in my face.

PASTOR. But this is appalling. He must be quite out of his mind. What in heaven's name are we to do?

LAURA. We must try to prevent further violence. The doctor has sent to the hospital for a strait-jacket. I have just written a note to the Colonel, and now I'm trying to get some idea of the state of our affairs, which Adolf has so shockingly mismanaged. *Opens another drawer.*

PASTOR. It's a miserable business altogether, but I always feared something of the kind might happen. When fire and water meet, there's bound to be an explosion. *Looks in drawer.* Whatever's all this?

LAURA. Look! This is where he's kept everything hidden.

PASTOR. Good heavens! Here's your old doll! And there's your christening cap . . . and Bertha's rattle . . . and your letters . . . and that locket . . . *Wipes his eyes.* He must have loved you very dearly, Laura. I never kept this kind of thing.

LAURA. I believe he did love me once, but time changes everything.

PASTOR. What's this imposing document? *Examines it.* The purchase of a grave! Well, better a grave than the asylum! Laura, be frank with me. Aren't you at all to blame?

LAURA. How can I be to blame because someone goes out of his mind?

PASTOR. We—ell! I will say no more. After all, blood's thicker than water.

LAURA. Meaning what, if I may ask?

PASTOR, *gazing at her.* Oh come now!

LAURA. What?

PASTOR. Come, come! You can scarcely deny that it would suit you down to the ground to have complete control of your daughter.

LAURA. I don't understand.

PASTOR. I can't help admiring you.

LAURA. Really?

PASTOR. And as for me—I shall be appointed guardian to that Freethinker whom, as you know, I always regarded as a tare among our wheat.

LAURA *gives a quick laugh which she suppresses.*

LAURA. You dare say that to me, his wife?

PASTOR. How strong-willed you are, Laura, how amazingly strong-willed! Like a fox in a trap that would gnaw off its own leg rather than be caught. Like a master-thief working alone, without even a conscience for accomplice. Look in the mirror! You daren't.

LAURA. I never use a mirror.

PASTOR. No. You daren't look at yourself. Let me see your hand. Not one tell-tale spot of blood, not a trace of that subtle poison. A little innocent murder that the law cannot touch. An unconscious crime. Unconscious? A stroke of genius that. Listen to him up there! Take care, Laura! If that man gets loose, he will saw you in pieces too.

LAURA. You must have a bad conscience to talk like that. Pin the guilt on me if you can.

PASTOR. I can't.

LAURA. You see? You can't, and so—I am innocent. And now, you look after your charge and I'll take care of mine. *Enter* DOCTOR.

Ah, here is the Doctor! *Rises.* I'm so glad to see you, Doctor. I know I can count on you to help me, although I'm afraid not much can be done now. You hear him up there. Are you convinced at last?

DOCTOR. I am convinced there has been an act of violence. But the question is—should that act of violence be regarded as an outbreak of temper or insanity?

PASTOR. But apart from this actual outbreak, you must admit that he suffers from fixed ideas.

DOCTOR. I have a notion, Pastor, that *your* ideas are even more fixed.

PASTOR. My firmly rooted convictions of spiritual . . .

DOCTOR. Convictions apart, it rests with you, Madam, to decide if your husband is to be fined or imprisoned or sent to the asylum. How do you regard his conduct?

LAURA. I can't answer that now.

DOCTOR. Oh? Have you no—er—firmly rooted convictions of what would be best for the family? And you, Pastor?

PASTOR. There's bound to be a scandal either way. It's not easy to give an opinion.

LAURA. But if he were only fined for violence he could be violent again.

DOCTOR. And if he were sent to prison he would soon be out again. So it seems best for all parties that he should be treated as insane. Where is the nurse?

LAURA. Why?

DOCTOR. She must put the strait-jacket on the patient. Not at once, but after I have had a talk with him—and not then until I give the order. I have the—er—garment outside. *Goes out to hall and returns with a large parcel.* Kindly call the nurse.

LAURA *rings. The* DOCTOR *begins to unpack the strait-jacket.*

PASTOR. Dreadful! Dreadful!

Enter NURSE.

DOCTOR. Ah, Nurse! Now please pay attention. You see this jacket. When I give you the word I want you to slip it on the Captain from behind. So as to prevent any further violence, you understand. Now it has, you see, unusually long sleeves. That is to restrict his movements. These sleeves must be tied together behind his back. And now here are two straps with buckles, which afterwards you must fasten to the arm of a chair—or to whatever's easiest. Can you do this, do you think?

NURSE. No, Doctor, I can't. No, not that.

LAURA. Why not do it yourself, Doctor?

DOCTOR. Because the patient distrusts me. You, Madam, are the proper person, but I'm afraid he doesn't trust you either. LAURA *grimaces.* Perhaps you, Pastor . . .

PASTOR. I must beg to decline.

Enter NÖJD.

LAURA. Did you deliver my note?

NÖJD. Yes, Madam.

DOCTOR. Oh, it's you, Nöjd! You know the state of things here, don't you? You know the Captain has had a mental breakdown. You must help us look after the patient.

NÖJD. If there's aught I can do for Captain, he knows I'll do it.

DOCTOR. You are to put this jacket on him.

NURSE. He's not to touch him. Nöjd shan't hurt him. I'd rather do it myself, gently, gently. But Nöjd can wait outside and help me if need be—yes, that's what he'd best do.

A pounding on the paper-covered door.

DOCTOR. Here he is! *To* NURSE. Put the jacket on that chair under your shawl. And now go away, all of you, while the Pastor and I talk to him. That door won't hold long. Hurry!

NURSE, *going out.* Lord Jesus, help us!

LAURA *shuts the bureau and follows the* NURSE. NÖJD *goes out to the hall. The paper-covered door bursts open, the lock broken and the chair hurled to the floor. The* CAPTAIN *comes out, carrying a pile of books.*

CAPTAIN, *putting the books on the table.* Here it all is. You can read it in every one of these volumes. So I wasn't mad after all. *Picks one up.* Here it is in the Odyssey, Book I, page 6, line 215 in the Uppsala translation. Telemachus speaking to Athene: "My mother says I am Odysseus' son; but for myself I cannot tell. It's a wise child that knows its own father."* And that's the suspicion Telemachus has about Penelope, the most virtuous of women. Fine state of affairs, eh? *Takes up another book.* And here we have the Prophet Ezekiel: "The fool saith, Lo, here is my father; but who can tell whose loins have engendered him?" That's clear enough. *Picks up another.* And what's this? A history of Russian literature by Merzlyakov. Alexander Pushkin, Russia's greatest poet, was mortally wounded—but more by the rumours of his wife's unfaithfulness than by the bullet he received in his breast at the duel. On his deathbed he swore she was innocent. Jackass! How could he swear any such thing? I *do* read my books, you see! Hullo, Jonas, are you here? And the Doctor, of course. Did I ever tell you what I said to the English lady who was deploring the habit Irishmen have of throwing lighted lamps in their wives' faces? "God, what women!" I said. "Women?" she stammered. "Of course," I replied. "When things get to such a pass that a man who has loved, has worshipped a woman, picks up a lighted lamp and flings it in her face, then you may be sure . . ."

PASTOR. Sure of what?

*English translation E. V. Rieu. Penguin Classics.

CAPTAIN. Nothing. You can never be sure of anything—you can only believe. That's right, isn't it, Jonas? One believes and so one is saved. Saved, indeed! No. One can be damned through believing. That's what I've learnt.

DOCTOR. But, Captain . . .

CAPTAIN. Hold your tongue! I don't want any chat from you. I don't want to hear you relaying all the gossip from in there like a telephone. In there—you know what I mean. Listen to me, Jonas. Do you imagine you're the father of your children? I seem to remember you had a tutor in the house, a pretty boy about whom there was quite a bit of gossip.

PASTOR. Take care, Adolf!

CAPTAIN. Feel under your wig and see if you don't find two little nobs. Upon my soul, he's turning pale! Well, well! It was only talk, of course, but my God, how they talked! But we married men are all figures of fun, every man Jack of us. Isn't that right, Doctor? What about your own marriage bed? Didn't you have a certain lieutenant in your house, eh? Wait now, let me guess. He was called . . . *Whispers in the* DOCTOR'S *ear.* By Jove, he's turned pale too! But don't worry. She's dead and buried, so what was done can't be done again. As a matter of fact, I knew him, and he's now—look at me, Doctor—no, straight in the eyes! He is now a major of Dragoons. Good Lord, I believe *he* has horns too!

DOCTOR, *angrily.* Be so good as to change the subject, Captain.

CAPTAIN. See! As soon as I mention horns he wants to change the subject.

PASTOR. I suppose you know, brother-in-law, that you're not in your right mind?

CAPTAIN. Yes, I do know. But if I had the handling of your decorated heads, I should soon have you shut up too. I am mad. But how did I become mad? Doesn't that interest you? No, it doesn't interest anyone. *Takes the photograph album from the table.* Christ Jesus, there is my daughter! Mine? That's what we can never know.

Shall I tell you what we should have to do so as to know? First marry, in order to be accepted by society, then immediately divorce; after that become lovers and finally adopt the children. That way one could at least be sure they were one's own adopted children. Eh? But what good's that to me? What good's anything now you have robbed me of my immortality? What can science or philosophy do for me when I have nothing left to live for? How can I live without honour? I grafted my right arm and half my brain and spinal cord on to another stem. I believed they would unite and grow into a single, more perfect tree. Then someone brought a knife and cut below the graft, so now I'm only half a tree. The other part, with my arm and half my brain, goes on growing. But I wither—I am dying, for it was the best part of myself I gave away. Let me die. Do what you like with me. I'm finished.

The DOCTOR *and* PASTOR *whisper, then go out. The* CAPTAIN *sinks into a chair by the table.* BERTHA *enters.*

BERTHA, *going to him.* Are you ill, Father?

CAPTAIN, *looking up stupidly at word "Father."* Me?

BERTHA. Do you know what you did? You threw a lamp at Mother.

CAPTAIN. Did I?

BERTHA. Yes. Supposing she'd been hurt!

CAPTAIN. Would that have mattered?

BERTHA. You're not my father if you talk like that.

CAPTAIN. What d'you say? Not your father? How d'you know? Who told you? Who is your father, then? Who?

BERTHA. Not you, anyway.

CAPTAIN. Anyone but me! Who then? Who? You seem well informed. Who told you? That I should live to hear my own child tell me to my face I am not her father! Do you realise you're insulting your mother by saying this? Don't you understand that, if it's true, *she* is disgraced?

BERTHA. You're not to say anything against Mother, I tell you!

CAPTAIN. Yes, all in league against me, just as you've always been.

BERTHA. Father!

CAPTAIN. Don't call me that again!

BERTHA. Father, Father!

CAPTAIN, *drawing her to him.* Bertha, my beloved child, yes, you *are* my child. Yes, yes, it must be so—it *is* so. All that was only a sick fancy—it came on the wind like an infection or a fever. Look at me! Let me see my soul in your eyes . . . But I see *her* soul as well. You have two souls. You love me with one and hate me with the other. You must love me and only me. You must have only one soul or you'll have no peace—neither shall I. You must have only one mind, fruit of my mind. You must have only one will—mine!

BERTHA. No, no! I want to be myself.

CAPTAIN. Never! I am a cannibal, you see, and I'm going to eat you. Your mother wanted to eat me, but she didn't succeed. I am Saturn who devoured his children because it was foretold that otherwise they would devour him. To eat or to be eaten—that is the question. If I don't eat you, you will eat me—you've shown your teeth already. *Goes to the rack.* Don't be afraid, my darling child. I shan't hurt you. *Takes down a revolver.*

BERTHA, *dodging away from him.* Help! Mother, help! He wants to kill me!

NURSE, *hurrying in.* What in heaven's name are you doing, Mr. Adolf?

CAPTAIN, *examining the revolver.* Did you remove the cartridges?

NURSE. Well, I did just tidy them away, but sit down here and take it easy and I'll soon fetch them back.

She takes the CAPTAIN *by the arm and leads him to a chair. He slumps down. She picks up the strait-jacket and goes behind the chair.* BERTHA *creeps out.*

Mr. Adolf, do you remember when you were my dear little boy, and I used to tuck you up at night and say your prayers with you? And do you remember how I used to get up in the night to get you a drink when you were thirsty? And how, when you had bad dreams and couldn't go to sleep again, I'd light the candle and tell you pretty stories. Do you remember?

CAPTAIN. Go on talking, Margaret. It soothes my mind. Go on talking.

NURSE. Aye, that I will, but you listen carefully. D'you remember how once you took a great big kitchen knife to carve a boat with, and I came in and had to trick the knife away from you? You were such a silly little lad, one had to trick you, you never would believe what anyone did was for your own good . . . "Give me that snake," I said, "or else he'll bite you." And then, see, you let go of the knife. *Takes the revolver from his hand.* And then, too, when it was time for you to dress yourself, and you wouldn't. I had to coax you, and say you should have a golden coat and be dressed just like a prince. Then I took your little tunic, that was just made of green wool, and held it up in front of you and said: "In with your arms, now, both together." *Gets the jacket on.* And then I said: "Sit nice and still now, while I button it up behind." *Ties the sleeves behind him.* And then I said: "Up with you, and walk across the floor like a good boy, so Nurse can see how it fits." *Leads him to the sofa.* And then I said: "Now you must go to bed."

CAPTAIN. What's that? Go to bed, when I'd just been dressed? My God! What have you done to me? *Tries to get free.* Oh you fiendish woman, what devilish cunning! Who would have thought you had the brains for it? *Lies down on the sofa.* Bound, fleeced, outwitted and unable to die!

NURSE. Forgive me, Mr. Adolf, forgive me! I had to stop you killing the child.

CAPTAIN. Why didn't you let me kill her? If life's hell and death's heaven, and children belong to heaven?

NURSE. What do you know of the hereafter?

CAPTAIN. It's the only thing one does know. Of life one knows nothing. Oh, if one had known from the beginning!

NURSE. Humble your stubborn heart, Mr. Adolf, and cry to God for mercy! Even now it's not too late. It wasn't too late for the thief on the Cross, for Our Saviour said: "To-day shalt thou be with me in paradise."

CAPTAIN. Croaking for a corpse already, old crow? *She takes her hymn-book from her pocket. He calls.* Nöjd! Are you there, Nöjd?

Enter NÖJD.

Throw this woman out of the house or she'll choke me to death with her hymn-book. Throw her out of the window, stuff her up the chimney, do what you like only get rid of her!

NÖJD, *staring at the* NURSE. God save you, Captain—and that's from the bottom of my heart—but I can't do that, I just can't. If it were six men now, but a woman!

CAPTAIN. What? You can't manage one woman?

NÖJD. I could manage her all right, but there's something stops a man laying hands on a woman.

CAPTAIN. What is this something? Haven't they laid hands on me?

NÖJD. Yes, but I just can't do it, Sir. Same as if you was to tell me to hit Pastor. It's like religion, it's in your bones. I can't do it.

Enter LAURA. *She signs to* NÖJD, *who goes out.*

CAPTAIN. Omphale! Omphale! Playing with the club while Hercules spins your wool.

LAURA, *approaching the sofa.* Adolf, look at me! Do you believe I'm your enemy?

CAPTAIN. Yes, I do. I believe all you women are my enemies. My mother did not want me to come into the world because my birth would give her pain. She was my enemy. She robbed my embryo of nourishment, so I was born incomplete. My sister was my enemy when she made me knuckle under to her. The first woman I took in my arms was my enemy. She gave me ten years of sickness in return for the love I gave her. When my daughter had to choose between you and me, she became my enemy. And you, you, my wife, have been my mortal enemy, for you have not let go your hold until there is no life left in me.

LAURA. But I didn't mean this to happen. I never really thought it out. I may have had some vague desire to get rid of you—you were in my way—and perhaps, if you see some plan in my actions, there was one, but I was unconscious of it. I have never given a thought to my actions—they simply ran along the rails you laid down. My conscience is clear, and before God I feel innocent, even if I'm not. You weighed me down like a stone, pressing and pressing till my heart tried to shake off its intolerable burden. That's how it's been, and if without meaning to I have brought you to this, I ask your forgiveness.

CAPTAIN. Very plausible, but how does that help me? And whose fault is it? Perhaps our cerebral marriage is to blame. In the old days one married a wife. Now one goes into partnership with a business woman or sets up house with a friend. Then one rapes the partner or violates the friend. What becomes of love, the healthy love of the senses? It dies of neglect. And what happens to the dividends from those love shares, payable to holder, when there's no joint account? Who is the holder when the crash comes? Who is the bodily father of the cerebral child?

LAURA. Your suspicions about our daughter are entirely unfounded.

CAPTAIN. That's the horror of it. If they had some foundation, there would at least be something to catch hold of, to cling to. Now there are only shadows, lurking in the undergrowth, peering out with grinning faces. It's like fighting with air, a mock battle with blank cartridges. Reality, however deadly, puts one on one's mettle, nerves body and soul for action, but as it is . . . my thoughts dissolve in fog, my brain grinds a void till it catches fire . . . Put a pillow under my head. Lay something over me. I'm cold. I'm terribly cold.

LAURA *takes off her shawl and spreads it over him. Exit* NURSE.

LAURA. Give me your hand, my dear.

CAPTAIN. My hand! Which you have bound behind my back. Omphale, Omphale! But I can feel your shawl soft against my mouth. It's warm and gentle like your arms and smells of vanilla like your hair when you were young. When you were young, Laura, and we used to walk in the birch woods. There were primroses and thrushes—lovely, lovely! Think how beautiful life was then—and what it has become! You did not want it to become like this, neither did I. Yet it has. Who then rules our lives?

LAURA. God.

CAPTAIN. The God of strife then—or nowadays the Goddess!

Enter NURSE *with a pillow.*

Take away this cat that's lying on me. Take it away! NURSE *removes the shawl and puts the pillow under his head.* Bring my uniform. Put my tunic over me. *The* NURSE *takes the tunic from a peg and spreads it over him. To* LAURA. Ah, my tough lion's-skin that you would take from me! Omphale! Omphale! You cunning woman, lover of peace and contriver of disarmament. Wake, Hercules, before they take away your club! You would trick us out of our armour, calling it tinsel. It was iron, I tell you, before it became tinsel. In the old days the smith forged the soldier's coat, now it is made by the needlewoman. Omphale! Omphale! Rude strength has fallen before treacherous weakness. Shame on you, woman of Satan, and a curse on all your sex! *He raises himself to spit at her, but sinks back again.* What sort of a pillow have you given me, Margaret? How hard and cold it is! So cold! Come and sit beside me on this chair. *She does so.* Yes, like that. Let me put my head on your lap. Ah, that's warmer! Lean over me so I can feel your breast. Oh how sweet it is to sleep upon a woman's breast, be she mother or mistress! But sweetest of all a mother's.

LAURA. Adolf, tell me, do you want to see your child?

CAPTAIN. My child? A man has no children. Only women have children. So the future is theirs, while we die childless. O God, who holds all children dear!

NURSE. Listen! He's praying to God.

CAPTAIN. No, to you, to put me to sleep. I'm tired, so tired. Goodnight, Margaret. "Blessed art thou among women."

He raises himself, then with a cry falls back on the NURSES's *knees.*

LAURA, *at the door, calling.* Doctor!

Enter DOCTOR *and* PASTOR.

Help him, Doctor—if it's not too late! Look, he has stopped breathing!

DOCTOR, *feeling his pulse.* It is a stroke.

PASTOR. Is he dead?

DOCTOR. No, he might still wake—but to what, who can say?

PASTOR. ". . . once to die, but after this the judgment."*

DOCTOR. No judgment—and no recriminations. You who believe that a God rules over human destiny must lay this to his charge.

NURSE. Ah Pastor, with his last breath he prayed to God!

PASTOR, *to* LAURA. Is this true?

LAURA. It is true.

DOCTOR. If this be so, of which I am as poor a judge as of the cause of his illness, in any case my skill is at an end. Try yours now, Pastor.

LAURA. Is that all you have to say at this deathbed, Doctor?

DOCTOR. That is all. I know no more. Let him who knows more, speak.

BERTHA *comes in and runs to* LAURA.

BERTHA. Mother! Mother!

LAURA. My child! My own child!

PASTOR. Amen.

*HEBREWS: ix, 27.

END

MISS JULIE

A Tragedy in One Act

AUTHOR'S FOREWORD

Theatre has long seemed to me—in common with much other art—a *Biblia Pauperum*, a Bible in pictures for those who cannot read what is written or printed; and I see the playwright as a lay preacher peddling the ideas of his time in popular form, popular enough for the middle-classes, mainstay of theatre audiences, to grasp the gist of the matter without troubling their brains too much. For this reason theatre has always been an elementary school for the young, the semi-educated and for women who still have a primitive capacity for deceiving themselves and letting themselves be deceived—who, that is to say, are susceptible to illusion and to suggestion from the author. I have therefore thought it not unlikely that in these days, when that rudimentary and immature thought-process operating through fantasy appears to be developing into reflection, research and analysis, that theatre, like religion, might be discarded as an outworn form for whose appreciation we lack the necessary conditions. This opinion is confirmed by the major crisis still prevailing in the theatres of Europe, and still more by the fact that in those countries of culture, producing the greatest thinkers of the age, namely England and Germany, drama—like other fine arts—is dead.

Some countries, it is true, have attempted to create a new drama by using the old forms with up-to-date contents, but not only has there been insufficient time for these new ideas to be popularized, so that the audience can grasp them, but also people have been so wrought up by the taking of sides that pure, disinterested appreciation has become impossible. One's deepest impressions are upset when an applauding or a hissing majority dominates as forcefully and openly as it can in the theatre. Moreover, as no new form has been devised for these new contents, the new wine has burst the old bottles.

In this play I have not tried to do anything new, for this cannot be done, but only to modernize the form to meet the demands which may, I think, be made on this art today. To this end I chose—or surrendered myself to—a theme which claims to be outside the controversial issues of today, since questions of social climbing or falling, of higher or lower, better or worse, of man and woman, are, have been and will be of lasting interest. When I took this theme from a true story told me some years ago, which made a deep impression, I saw it as a subject for tragedy, for as yet it is tragic to see one favoured by fortune go under, and still more to see a family heritage die out, although a time may come when we have grown so developed and enlightened that we shall view with indifference life's spectacle, now seeming so brutal, cynical and heartless. Then we shall have dispensed with those inferior, unreliable instruments of thought called feelings, which become harmful and superfluous as reasoning develops.

The fact that my heroine rouses pity is solely due to weakness; we cannot resist fear of the same fate overtaking us. The hyper-sensitive spectator may, it is true, go beyond this kind of pity, while the man with belief in the future may actually demand some suggestion for remedying the evil—in other words some kind of policy. But, to begin with, there is no such thing as absolute evil; the downfall of one family is the good fortune of another, which thereby gets a chance to rise, and, fortune being only comparative, the alternation of rising and falling is one of life's principal charms. Also, to the man of policy, who wants to remedy the painful fact that the bird of prey devours the dove, and lice the bird of prey, I should like to put the question: why should it be remedied? Life is not so mathematically idiotic as only to permit the big to eat the small; it happens just as often that the bee kills the lion or at least drives it mad.

That my tragedy depresses many people is their own fault. When we have grown strong as the pioneers of the French revolution, we shall be happy and relieved to see the national parks cleared of ancient rotting trees which have stood too long in the way of others equally entitled to a period of growth—as relieved as we are when an incurable invalid dies.

My tragedy "The Father" was recently criticised for being too sad—as if one wants cheerful tragedies! Everybody is clamouring for this supposed "joy of life," and theatre managers demand farces, as if the joy of life consisted in being ridiculous and portraying all human beings as suffering from St. Vitus's dance or total idiocy. I myself find the joy of life in its strong and cruel struggles, and my pleasure in learning, in adding to my knowledge. For this reason I have chosen for this play an unusual situation, but an instructive one—an exception, that is to say, but a great exception, one proving the rule, which will no doubt annoy all lovers of the commonplace. What will offend simple minds is that my plot is not simple, nor its point of view single. In real life an action—this, by the way, is a somewhat new discovery—is generally caused by a whole series of motives, more or less fundamental, but as a rule the spectator chooses just one of these—the one which his mind can most easily grasp or that does most credit to his intelligence. A suicide is committed. Business troubles, says the man of affairs. Unrequited love, say the women. Sickness, says the invalid. Despair, says the down-and-out. But it is possible that the motive lay in all or none of these directions, or that the dead man concealed his actual motive by revealing quite another, likely to reflect more to his glory.

I see Miss Julie's tragic fate to be the result of many circumstances: the mother's character, the father's mistaken upbringing of the girl, her own nature, and the influence of her fiancé on a weak, degenerate mind. Also, more directly, the festive mood of Midsummer Eve, her father's absence, her monthly indisposition, her pre-occupation with animals, the excitement of dancing, the magic of dusk, the strongly aphrodisiac influence of flowers, and finally the chance that drives the couple into a room alone —to which must be added the urgency of the excited man.

My treatment of the theme, moreover, is neither exclusively physiological nor psychological. I have not put the blame wholly on the inheritance from her mother, nor on her physical condition at the time, nor on immorality. I have not even preached a moral sermon; in the absence of a priest I leave this to the cook.

I congratulate myself on this multiplicity of motives as being up-to-date, and if others have done the same thing before me, then I congratulate myself on not being alone in my "paradoxes," as all innovations are called.

In regard to the drawing of the characters, I have made my people somewhat "characterless" for the following reasons. In the course of time the word character has assumed manifold meanings. It must have originally signified the dominating trait of the soul-complex, and this was confused with temperament. Later it became the middle-class term for the automaton, one whose nature had become fixed or who had adapted himself to a particular rôle in life. In fact a person who had ceased to grow was called a character, while one continuing to develop—the skilful navigator of life's river, sailing not with sheets set fast, but veering before the wind to luff again—was called characterless, in a derogatory sense, of course, because he was so hard to catch, classify and keep track of. This middle-class conception of the immobility of the soul was transferred to the stage where the middle-class has always ruled. A character came to signify a man fixed and finished: one who invariably appeared either drunk or jocular or melancholy, and characterization required nothing more than a physical defect such as a club-foot, a wooden leg, a red nose; or the fellow might be made to repeat some such phrase as: "That's capital!" or: "Barkis is willin'!" This simple way of regarding human beings still survives in the great Molière. Harpagon is nothing but a miser, although Harpagon might have been not only a miser, but also a first-rate financier, an excellent father and a good citizen. Worse still, his "failing" is a distinct advantage to his son-in-law and his daughter, who are his heirs, and who therefore cannot criticise him, even if they have to wait a while to get to bed. I do not believe, therefore, in simple stage characters; and the summary judgments of authors—this man is stupid, that one brutal, this jealous, that stingy, and so forth—should be challenged by the Naturalists who know the richness of the soul-complex and realise that vice has a reverse side very much like virtue.

Because they are modern characters, living in a period of transition more feverishly hysterical than its predecessor at least, I have drawn my figures vacillating, disintegrated, a blend of old and new. Nor does it seem to me unlikely that, through newspapers and conversations, modern ideas may have filtered down to the level of the domestic servant.

My souls (characters) are conglomerations of past and present stages of civilization, bits from books and newspapers, scraps of humanity, rags and tatters of fine clothing, patched together as is the human soul. And I have added a little evolutionary history by making the weaker steal and repeat the words of the stronger, and by making the characters borrow ideas or "suggestions" from one another.

Miss Julie is a modern character, not that the half-woman, the man-hater, has not existed always, but because now that she has been discovered she has stepped to the front and begun to make a noise. The half-woman is a type who thrusts herself forward, selling herself nowadays for power, decorations, distinctions, diplomas, as formerly for money. The type implies degeneration; it is not a good type and it does not endure; but it can unfortunately transmit its misery, and degenerate men seem instinctively to choose their mates from among such women, and so they breed, producing offspring of indeterminate sex to whom life is torture. But fortunately they perish, either because they cannot come to terms with reality, or because their repressed instincts break out uncontrollably, or again because their hopes of catching up with men are shattered. The type is tragic, revealing a desperate fight against nature, tragic too in its Romantic inheritance now dissipated by Naturalism, which wants nothing but happiness—and for happiness strong and sound species are required.

But Miss Julie is also a relic of the old warrior nobility now giving way to the new nobility of nerve and brain. She is a victim of the discord which a mother's "crime" has produced in a family, a victim too of the day's complaisance, of circumstances, of her own defective constitution, all of which are equivalent to the Fate or Universal Law of former days. The Naturalist has abolished guilt with God, but the consequences of the action—punishment, imprisonment or the fear of it—he cannot abolish, for the simple reason that they remain whether he is acquitted or not. An injured fellow-being is not so complacent as outsiders, who have not been injured, can afford to be. Even if the father had felt impelled to take no vengeance, the daughter would have taken vengeance on herself, as she does here, from that innate or acquired sense of honour which the upper-classes inherit—whether from Barbarism or Aryan forebears, or from the chivalry of the Middle Ages, who knows? It is a very beautiful thing, but it has become a danger nowadays to the preservation of the race. It is the nobleman's *hara-kiri,* the Japanese law of inner conscience which compels him to cut his own stomach open at the insult of another, and which survives in modified form in the duel, a privilege of the nobility. And so the valet Jean lives on, but Miss Julie cannot live without honour. This is the thrall's advantage over the nobleman, that he lacks this fatal preoccupation with honour. And in all of us Aryans there is something of the nobleman, or the Don Quixote, which makes us sympathize with the man who commits suicide because he has done something ignoble and lost his honour. And we are noblemen enough to suffer at the sight of fallen greatness littering the earth like a corpse—yes, even if the fallen rise again and make restitution by honourable deeds. Jean, the valet, is a race-builder, a man of marked characteristics. He was a labourer's son who has educated himself towards becoming a gentleman.

He has learnt easily, through his well-developed senses (smell, taste, vision)—and he also has a sense of beauty. He has already bettered himself, and is thick-skinned enough to have no scruples about using other people's services. He is already foreign to his associates, despising them as part of the life he has turned his back on, yet also fearing and fleeing from them because they know his secrets, pry into his plans, watch his rise with envy, and look forward with pleasure to his fall. Hence his dual, indeterminate character, vacillating between love of the heights and hatred of those who have already achieved them. He is, he says himself, an aristocrat; he has learned the secrets of good society. He is polished, but vulgar within; he already wears his tails with taste, but there is no guarantee of his personal cleanliness.

He has some respect for his young lady, but he is frightened of Kristin, who knows his dangerous secrets, and he is sufficiently callous not to allow the night's events to wreck his plans for the future. Having both the slave's brutality and the master's lack of squeamishness, he can see blood without fainting and take disaster by the horns. Consequently he emerges from the battle unscathed, and probably ends his days as a hotel-keeper. And even if *he* does not become a Roumanian Count, his son will doubtless go to the university and perhaps become a county attorney.

The light which Jean sheds on a lower-class conception of life, life seen from below, is on the whole illuminating—when he speaks the truth, which is not often, for he says what is favourable to himself rather than what is true. When Miss Julie suggests that the lower-classes must be oppressed by the attitude of their superiors, Jean naturally agrees, as his object is to gain her sympathy; but when he perceives the advantage of separating himself from the common herd, he at once takes back his words.

It is not because Jean is now rising that he has the upper hand of Miss Julie, but because he is a man. Sexually he is the aristocrat because of his virility, his keener senses and his capacity for taking the initiative. His inferiority is mainly due to the social environment in which he lives, and he can probably shed it with his valet's livery.

The slave mentality expresses itself in his worship of the Count (the boots), and his religious superstition; but he worships the Count chiefly because he holds that higher position for which Jean himself is striving. And this worship remains even when he has won the daughter of the house and seen how empty is that lovely shell.

I do not believe that a love relationship in the "higher" sense could exist between two individuals of such different quality, but I have made Miss Julie imagine that she is in love, so as to lessen her sense of guilt, and I let Jean suppose that if his social position were altered he would truly love her. I think love is like the hyacinth which has to strike roots in darkness *before* it can produce a vigorous flower. In this case it shoots up quickly, blossoms and goes to seed all at the same time, which is why the plant dies so soon.

As for Kristin, she is a female slave, full of servility and sluggishness acquired in front of the kitchen fire, and stuffed full of morality and religion, which are her cloak and scape-goat. She goes to church as a quick and easy way of unloading her household thefts on to Jesus and taking on a fresh cargo of guiltlessness. For the rest she is a minor character, and I have therefore sketched her in the same manner as the Pastor and the Doctor in "The Father," where I wanted ordinary human beings, as are most country pastors and provincial doctors. If these minor characters seem abstract to some people this is due to the fact that ordinary people are to a certain extent abstract in pursuit of their work; that is to say, they are without individuality, showing, while working, only one side of themselves. And as long as the spectator does not feel a need to see them from other sides, there is nothing wrong with my abstract presentation.

In regard to the dialogue, I have departed somewhat from tradition by not making my characters catechists who ask stupid questions in order to elicit a smart reply.

I have avoided the symmetrical, mathematical construction of French dialogue, and let people's minds work irregularly, as they do in real life where, during a conversation, no topic is drained to the dregs, and one mind finds in another a chance cog to engage in. So too the dialogue wanders, gathering in the opening scenes material which is later picked up, worked over, repeated, expounded and developed like the theme in a musical composition.

The plot speaks for itself, and as it really only concerns two people, I have concentrated on these, introducing only one minor character, the cook, and keeping the unhappy spirit of the father above and behind the action. I have done this because it seems to me that the psychological process is what interests people most today. Our inquisitive souls are no longer satisfied with seeing a thing happen; we must also know how it happens. We want to see the wires themselves, to watch the machinery, to examine the box with the false bottom, to take hold of the magic ring in order to find the join, and look at the cards to see how they are marked.

In this connection I have had in view the documentary novels of the brothers de Goncourt, which appeal to me more than any other modern literature.

As far as the technical side of the work is concerned I have made the experiment of abolishing the division into acts. This is because I have come to the conclusion that our capacity for illusion is disturbed by the intervals, during which the audience has time to reflect and escape from the suggestive influence of the author-hypnotist. My play will probably take an hour and a half, and as one can listen to a lecture, a sermon or a parliamentary debate for as long as that or longer, I do not think a theatrical performance will be fatiguing in the same length of time. As early as 1872, in one of my first dramatic attempts, "The Outlaw," I tried this concentrated form, although with scant success. The play was written in five acts, and only when finished did I become aware of the restless, disjointed effect that it produced. The script was burnt and from the ashes rose a single well-knit act—fifty pages of print, playable in one hour. The form of the present play is, therefore, not new, but it appears to be my own, and changing tastes may make it timely. My hope is one day to have an audience educated enough to sit through a whole evening's entertainment in one act, but one would have to try this out to see. Meanwhile, in order to provide respite for the audience and the players, without allowing the audience to escape from the illusion, I have introduced three art forms: monologue, mime and ballet. These are all part of drama, having their origins in classic tragedy, monody having become monologue and the chorus, ballet.

Monologue is now condemned by our realists as unnatural, but if one provides motives for it one makes it natural, and then can use it to advantage. It is, surely, natural for a public speaker to walk up and down the room practicing his speech, natural for an actor to read his part aloud, for a servant girl to talk to her cat, a mother to prattle to her child, an old maid to chatter to her parrot, and a sleeper to talk in his sleep. And in order that the actor may have a chance, for once, of working independently, free from the author's direction, it is better that the monologue should not be written, but only indicated. For since it is of small importance what is said in one's sleep or to the parrot or to the cat—none of it influences the action—a talented actor, identifying himself with the atmosphere and the situation, may improvise better than the author, who cannot calculate ahead how much may be said or how long taken without waking the audience from the illusion.

Some Italian theatres have, as we know, returned to improvisation, thereby producing actors who are creative, although within the bounds set by the author. This may well be a step forward, or even the beginning of a new art-form worthy to be called *productive*.

In places where monologue would be unnatural I have used mime, leaving here an even wider scope for the actor's imagination, and more chance for him to win independent laurels. But so as not to try the audience beyond endurance, I have introduced music—fully justified by the Midsummer Eve dance—to exercise its powers of persuasion during the dumb show. But I beg the musical director to consider carefully his choice of compositions, so that conflicting moods are not induced by selections from the current operetta or dance show, or by folk-tunes of too local a character.

The ballet I have introduced cannot be replaced by the usual kind of "crowd-scene," for such scenes are too badly played—a lot of grinning idiots seizing the opportunity to show off and thus destroying the illusion. And as peasants cannot improvise their taunts, but use ready-made phrases with a double meaning, I have not composed their lampoon, but taken a little-known song and dance which I myself noted down in the Stockholm district. The words are not quite to the point, but this too is intentional, for the cunning, i.e. weakness, of the slave prevents him from direct attack. Nor can there be clowning in a serious action, or coarse joking in a situation which nails the lid on a family coffin.

As regards the scenery, I have borrowed from impressionist painting its asymmetry and its economy; thus, I think, strengthening the illusion. For the fact that one does not see the whole room and all the furniture leaves scope for conjecture—that is to say imagination is roused and complements what is seen. I have succeeded too in getting rid of those tiresome exits through doors, since scenery doors are made of canvas, and rock at the slightest touch. They cannot even express the wrath of an irate head of the family who, after a bad dinner, goes out slamming the door behind him, "so that the whole house shakes." On the stage it rocks. I have also kept to a single set, both in order to let the characters develop in their métier and to break away from over-decoration. When one has only one set, one may expect it to be realistic; but as a matter of fact nothing is harder than to get a stage room that looks something like a room, however easily the scene painter can produce flaming volcanoes and water-falls. Presumably the walls must be of canvas; but it seems about time to dispense with painted shelves and cooking utensils. We are asked to accept so many stage conventions that we might as least be spared the pain of painted pots and pans.

I have set the back wall and the table diagonally so that the actors may play full-face and in half-profile when they are sitting opposite one another at the table. In the opera AÏDA I saw a diagonal background, which led the eye to unfamiliar perspectives and did not look like mere reaction against boring straight lines.

Another much needed innovation is the abolition of foot-lights. This lighting from below is said to have the purpose of making the actors' faces fatter. But why, I ask, should all actors have fat faces? Does not this under-lighting flatten out all the subtlety of the lower part of the face, specially the jaw, falsify the shape of the nose and throw shadows up over the eyes? Even if this were not so, one thing is certain: that the lights hurt the performers' eyes, so that the full play of their expression is lost. The foot-lights strike part of the retina usually protected—except in sailors who have to watch sunlight on water—and therefore one seldom sees anything other than a crude rolling of the eyes, either sideways or up towards the gallery, showing their whites. Perhaps this too causes that tiresome blinking of the eyelashes, especially by actresses. And when anyone on the stage wants to speak with his eyes, the only thing he can do is to look straight at the audience, with whom he or she then gets into direct communication, outside the framework of the set—a habit called, rightly or wrongly, "greeting one's friends."

Would not sufficiently strong side-lighting, with some kind of reflectors, add to the actor's powers of expression by allowing him to use the face's greatest asset:—the play of the eyes?

I have few illusions about getting the actors to play *to* the audience instead of *with* it, although this is what I want. That I shall see an actor's back throughout a critical scene is beyond my dreams, but I do wish crucial scenes could be played, not in front of the prompter's box, like duets expecting applause, but in the place required by the action. So, no revolutions, but just some small modifications, for to make the stage into a real room with the fourth wall missing would be too upsetting altogether.

I dare not hope that the actresses will listen to what I have to say about make-up, for they would rather be beautiful than life-like, but the actor might consider whether it is to his advantage to create an abstract character with grease-paints, and cover his face with it like a mask. Take the case of a man who draws a choleric charcoal line between his eyes and then, in this fixed state of wrath, has to smile at some repartee. What a frightful grimace the result is! And equally, how is that false forehead, smooth as a billiard ball, to wrinkle when the old man loses his temper?

In a modern psychological drama, where the subtlest reactions of a character need to be mirrored in the face rather than expressed by sound and gesture, it would be worth while experimenting with powerful side-lighting on a small stage and a cast without make-up, or at least with the minimum.

If, in addition, we could abolish the visible orchestra, with its distracting lamps and its faces turned toward the audience; if we could have the stalls raised so that the spectators' eyes were higher than the players' knees; if we could get rid of the boxes (the centre of my target), with their tittering diners and supper-parties, and have total darkness in the auditorium during the performance; and if, first and foremost, we could have a *small* stage and a *small* house, then perhaps a new dramatic art might arise, and theatre once more become a place of entertainment for educated people. While waiting for such a theatre it is as well for us to go on writing so as to stock that repertory of the future.

I have made an attempt. If it has failed, there is time enough to try again.

Characters

MISS JULIE, *aged 25*
JEAN, *the valet, aged 30*
KRISTIN, *the cook, aged 35*

Scene: The large kitchen of a Swedish manor house in a country district in the eighties.
Midsummer eve.
The kitchen has three doors, two small ones into Jean's and Kristin's bedrooms, and a large, glass-fronted double one, opening on to a courtyard. This is the only way to the rest of the house.
Through these glass doors can be seen part of a fountain with a cupid, lilac bushes in flower and the tops of some Lombardy poplars. On one wall are shelves edged with scalloped paper on which are kitchen utensils of copper, iron and tin.
To the left is the corner of a large tiled range and part of its chimney-hood, to the right the end of the servants' dinner table with chairs beside it.
The stove is decorated with birch boughs, the floor strewn with twigs of juniper. On the end of the table is a large Japanese spice jar full of lilac.
There are also an ice-box, a scullery table and a sink. Above the double door hangs a big old-fashioned bell; near it is a speaking-tube.
A fiddle can be heard from the dance in the barn near-by. Kristin is standing at the stove, frying something in a pan. She wears a light-coloured cotton dress and a big apron.
Jean enters, wearing livery and carrying a pair of large riding-boots with spurs, which he puts in a conspicuous place.

JEAN. Miss Julie's crazy again to-night, absolutely crazy.

KRISTIN. Oh, so you're back, are you?

JEAN. When I'd taken the Count to the station, I came back and dropped in at the Barn for a dance. And who did I see there but our young lady leading off with the gamekeeper. But the moment she sets eyes on me, up she rushes and invites me to waltz with her. And how she waltzed—I've never seen anything like it! She's crazy.

KRISTIN. Always has been, but never so bad as this last fortnight since the engagement was broken off.

JEAN. Yes, that was a pretty business, to be sure. He's a decent enough chap, too, even if he isn't rich. Oh, but they're choosy! *Sits down at the end of the table.* In any case, it's a bit odd that our young—er—lady would rather stay at home with the yokels than go with her father to visit her relations.

KRISTIN. Perhaps she feels a bit awkward, after that bust-up with her fiancé.

JEAN. Maybe. That chap had some guts, though. Do you know the sort of thing that was going on, Kristin? I saw it with my own eyes, though I didn't let on I had.

KRISTIN. You saw them . . . ?

JEAN. Didn't I just! Came across the pair of them one evening in the stable-yard. Miss Julie was doing what she called "training" him. Know what that was? Making him jump over her riding-whip—the way you teach a dog. He did it twice and got a cut each time for his pains, but when it came to the third go, he snatched the whip out of her hand and broke it into smithereens. And then he cleared off.

KRISTIN. What goings on! I never did!

JEAN. Well, that's how it was with that little affair . . . Now, what have you got for me, Kristin? Something tasty?

KRISTIN, *serving from the pan to his plate.* Well, it's just a little bit of kidney I cut off their joint.

JEAN, *smelling it.* Fine! That's my special delice. *Feels the plate.* But you might have warmed the plate.

KRISTIN. When you choose to be finicky you're worse than the Count himself. *Pulls his hair affectionately.*

JEAN, *crossly.* Stop pulling my hair. You know how sensitive I am.

KRISTIN. There, there! It's only love, you know.

JEAN *eats.* KRISTIN *brings a bottle of beer.*

JEAN. Beer on Midsummer Eve? No thanks! I've got something better than that. *From a drawer in the table brings out a bottle of red wine with a yellow seal.* Yellow seal, see! Now get me a glass. You use a glass with a stem of course when you're drinking it straight.

KRISTIN, *giving him a wine-glass.* Lord help the woman who gets you for a husband, you old fusser! *She puts the beer in the ice-box and sets a small saucepan on the stove.*

JEAN. Nonsense! You'll be glad enough to get a fellow as smart as me. And I don't think it's done you any harm people calling me your fiancé. *Tastes the wine.* Good. Very good indeed. But not quite warmed enough. *Warms the glass in his hand.* We bought this in Dijon. Four francs the litre without the bottle, and duty on top of that. What are you cooking now? It stinks.

KRISTIN. Some bloody muck Miss Julie wants for Diana.

JEAN. You should be more refined in your speech, Kristin. But why should you spend a holiday cooking for that bitch? Is she sick or what?

KRISTIN. Yes, she's sick. She sneaked out with the pug at the lodge and got in the usual mess. And that, you know, Miss Julie won't have.

JEAN. Miss Julie's too high-and-mighty in some respects, and not enough in others, just like her mother before her. The Countess was more at home in the kitchen and cowsheds than anywhere else, but would she ever go driving with only one horse? She went round with her cuffs filthy, but she had to have the coronet on the cuff-links. Our young lady—to come back to her—hasn't any proper respect for herself or her position. I mean she isn't refined. In the Barn just now she dragged the gamekeeper away from Anna and made him dance with her—no waiting to be asked. We wouldn't do a thing like that. But that's what happens when the gentry try to behave like the common people—they become common . . . Still she's a fine girl. Smashing! What shoulders! And what—er—etcetera!

KRISTIN. Oh come off it! I know what Clara says, and she dresses her.

JEAN. Clara? Pooh, you're all jealous! But I've been out riding with her . . . and as for her dancing!

KRISTIN. Listen, Jean. You will dance with me, won't you, as soon as I'm through.

JEAN. Of course I will.

KRISTIN. Promise?

JEAN. Promise? When I say I'll do a thing I do it. Well, thanks for the supper. It was a real treat. *Corks the bottle.*

JULIE *appears in the doorway, speaking to someone outside.*

JULIE. I'll be back in a moment. Don't wait.

JEAN *slips the bottle into the drawer and rises respectfully.* JULIE *enters and joins* KRISTIN *at the stove.*

Well, have you made it? KRISTIN *signs that* JEAN *is near them.*

JEAN, *gallantly.* Have you ladies got some secret?

JULIE, *flipping his face with her handkerchief.* You're very inquisitive.

JEAN. What a delicious smell! Violets.

JULIE, *coquettishly.* Impertinence! Are you an expert of scent too? I must say you know how to dance. Now don't look. Go away. *The music of a schottische begins.*

JEAN, *with impudent politeness.* Is it some witches' brew you're cooking on Midsummer Eve? Something to tell your stars by, so you can see your future?

JULIE, *sharply.* If you could see that you'd have good eyes. *To* KRISTIN. Put it in a bottle and cork it tight. Come and dance this schottische with me, Jean.

JEAN, *hesitating.* I don't want to be rude, but I've promised to dance this one with Kristin.

JULIE. Well, she can have another, can't you, Kristin? You'll lend me Jean, won't you?

KRISTIN, *bottling.* It's nothing to do with me. When you're so condescending, Miss, it's not his place to say no. Go on, Jean, and thank Miss Julie for the honour.

JEAN. Frankly speaking, Miss, and no offence meant, I wonder if it's wise for you to dance twice running with the same partner, specially as those people are so ready to jump to conclusions.

JULIE, *flaring up.* What did you say? What sort of conclusions? What do you mean?

JEAN, *meekly.* As you choose not to understand, Miss Julie, I'll have to speak more plainly. It looks bad to show a preference for one of your retainers when they're all hoping for the same unusual favour.

JULIE. Show a preference! The very idea! I'm surprised at you. I'm doing the people an honour by attending their ball when I'm mistress of the house, but if I'm really going to dance, I mean to have a partner who can lead and doesn't make me look ridiculous.

JEAN. If those are your orders, Miss, I'm at your service.

JULIE, *gently.* Don't take it as an order. To-night we're all just people enjoying a party. There's no question of class. So now give me your arm. Don't worry, Kristin. I shan't steal your sweetheart.

JEAN *gives* JULIE *his arm and leads her out.*

Left alone, KRISTIN *plays her scene in an unhurried, natural way, humming to the tune of the schottische, played on a distant violin. She clears* JEAN'S *place, washes up and puts things away, then takes off her apron, brings out a small mirror from a drawer, props it against the jar of lilac, lights a candle, warms a small pair of tongs and curls her fringe. She goes to the door and listens, then turning back to the table finds* MISS JULIE'S *forgotten handkerchief. She smells it, then meditatively smooths it out and folds it.*

Enter JEAN.

JEAN. She really *is* crazy. What a way to dance! With people standing grinning at her too from behind the doors. What's got into her, Kristin?

KRISTIN. Oh, it's just her time coming on. She's always queer then. Are you going to dance with me now?

JEAN. Then you're not wild with me for cutting that one.

KRISTIN. You know I'm not—for a little thing like that. Besides, I know my place.

JEAN, *putting his arm round her waist.* You're a sensible girl, Kristin, and you'll make a very good wife . . .

Enter JULIE, *unpleasantly surprised.*

JULIE, *with forced gaiety.* You're a fine beau—running away from your partner.

JEAN. Not away, Miss Julie, but as you see back to the one I deserted.

JULIE, *changing her tone.* You really can dance, you know. But why are you wearing your livery on a holiday. Take it off at once.

JEAN. Then I must ask you to go away for a moment, Miss. My black coat's here. *Indicates it hanging on the door to his room.*

JULIE. Are you so shy of me—just over changing a coat? Go into your room then—or stay here and I'll turn my back.

JEAN. Excuse me then, Miss. *He goes to his room and is partly visible as he changes his coat.*

JULIE. Tell me, Kristin, is Jean your fiancé? You seem very intimate.

KRISTIN. My fiancé? Yes, if you like. We call it that.

JULIE. Call it?

KRISTIN. Well, you've had a fiancé yourself, Miss, and . . .

JULIE. But we really were engaged.

KRISTIN. All the same it didn't come to anything.

JEAN *returns in his black coat.*

JULIE. Très gentil, Monsieur Jean. Très gentil.

JEAN. Vous voulez plaisanter, Madame.

JULIE. Et vous voulez parler français. Where did you learn it?

JEAN. In Switzerland, when I was sommelier at one of the biggest hotels in Lucerne.

JULIE. You look quite the gentleman in that get-up. Charming. *Sits at the table.*

JEAN. Oh, you're just flattering me!

JULIE, *annoyed.* Flattering you?

JEAN. I'm too modest to believe you would pay real compliments to a man like me, so I must take it you are exaggerating—that this is what's known as flattery.

JULIE. Where on earth did you learn to make speeches like that? Perhaps you've been to the theatre a lot.

JEAN. That's right. And travelled a lot too.

JULIE. But you come from this neighbourhood, don't you?

JEAN. Yes, my father was a labourer on the next estate—the District Attorney's place. I often used to see you, Miss Julie, when you were little, though you never noticed me.

JULIE. Did you really?

JEAN. Yes. One time specially I remember . . . but I can't tell you about that.

JULIE. Oh do! Why not? This is just the time.

JEAN. No, I really can't now. Another time perhaps.

JULIE. Another time means never. What harm in now?

JEAN. No harm, but I'd rather not. *Points to* KRISTIN, *now fast asleep.* Look at her.

JULIE. She'll make a charming wife, won't she? I wonder if she snores.

JEAN. No, she doesn't, but she talks in her sleep.

JULIE, *cynically.* How do you know she talks in her sleep?

JEAN, *brazenly.* I've heard her. *Pause. They look at one another.*

JULIE. Why don't you sit down?

JEAN. I can't take such a liberty in your presence.

JULIE. Supposing I order you to.

JEAN. I'll obey.

JULIE. Then sit down. No, wait a minute. Will you get me a drink first?

JEAN. I don't know what's in the ice-box. Only beer, I expect.

JULIE. There's no only about it. My taste is so simple I prefer it to wine.

JEAN *takes a bottle from the ice-box, fetches a glass and plate and serves the beer.*

JEAN. At your service.

JULIE. Thank you. Won't you have some yourself?

JEAN. I'm not really a beer-drinker, but if it's an order . . .

JULIE. Order? I should have thought it was ordinary manners to keep your partner company.

JEAN. That's a good way of putting it. *He opens another bottle and fetches a glass.*

JULIE. Now drink my health. *He hesitates.* I believe the man really is shy.

JEAN *kneels and raises his glass with mock ceremony.*

JEAN. To the health of my lady!

JULIE. Bravo! Now kiss my shoe and everything will be perfect. *He hesitates, then boldly takes hold of her foot and lightly kisses it.* Splendid. You ought to have been an actor.

JEAN, *rising.* We can't go on like this, Miss Julie. Someone might come in and see us.

JULIE. Why would that matter?

JEAN. For the simple reason that they'd talk. And if you knew the way their tongues were wagging out there just now, you . . .

JULIE. What were they saying? Tell me. Sit down.

JEAN, *sitting.* No offence meant, Miss, but . . . well, their language wasn't nice, and they were hinting . . . oh, you know quite well what. You're not a child, and if a lady's seen drinking alone at night with a man—and a servant at that—then . . .

JULIE. Then what? Besides, we're not alone. Kristin's here.

JEAN. Yes, asleep.

JULIE. I'll wake her up. *Rises.* Kristin, are you asleep? KRISTIN *mumbles in her sleep.* Kristin! Goodness, how she sleeps!

KRISTIN, *in her sleep.* The Count's boots are cleaned—put the coffee on—yes, yes, at once . . . *Mumbles incoherently.*

JULIE, *tweaking her nose.* Wake up, can't you!

JEAN, *sharply.* Let her sleep.

JULIE. What?

JEAN. When you've been standing at the stove all day you're likely to be tired at night. And sleep should be respected.

JULIE, *changing her tone.* What a nice idea. It does you credit. Thank you for it. *Holds out her hand to him.* Now come out and pick some lilac for me.

During the following KRISTIN *goes sleepily in to her bedroom.*

JEAN. Out with you, Miss Julie?

JULIE. Yes.

JEAN. It wouldn't do. It really wouldn't.

JULIE. I don't know what you mean. You can't possibly imagine that . . .

JEAN. I don't, but others do.

JULIE. What? That I'm in love with the valet?

JEAN. I'm not a conceited man, but such a thing's been known to happen, and to these rustics nothing's sacred.

JULIE. You, I take it, are an aristocrat.

JEAN. Yes, I am.

JULIE. And I am coming down in the world.

JEAN. Don't come down, Miss Julie. Take my advice. No one will believe you came down of your own accord. They'll all say you fell.

JULIE. I have a higher opinion of our people than you. Come and put it to the test. Come on. *Gazes into his eyes.*

JEAN. You're very strange, you know.

JULIE. Perhaps I am, but so are you. For that matter everything is strange. Life, human beings, everything, just scum drifting about on the water until it sinks—down and down. That reminds me of a dream I sometimes have, in which I'm on top of a pillar and can't see any way of getting down. When I look down I'm dizzy; I have to get down but I haven't the courage to jump. I can't stay there and I long to fall, but I don't fall. There's no respite. There can't be any peace at all for me until I'm down, right down on the ground. And if I did get to the ground I'd want to be under the ground . . . Have you ever felt like that?

JEAN. No. In my dream I'm lying under a great tree in a dark wood. I want to get up, up to the top of it, and look out over the bright landscape where the sun is shining and rob that high nest of its golden eggs. And I climb and climb, but the trunk is so thick and smooth and it's so far to the first branch. But I know if I can once reach that first branch I'll go to the top just as if I'm on a ladder. I haven't reached it yet, but I shall get there, even if only in my dreams.

JULIE. Here I am chattering about dreams with you. Come on. Only into the park. *She takes his arm and they go towards the door.*

JEAN. We must sleep on nine midsummer flowers tonight; then our dreams will come true, Miss Julie. *They turn at the door. He has a hand to his eye.*

JULIE. Have you got something in your eye? Let me see.

JEAN. Oh, it's nothing. Just a speck of dust. It'll be gone in a minute.

JULIE. My sleeve must have rubbed against you. Sit down and let me see to it. *Takes him by the arm and makes him sit down, bends his head back and tries to get the speck out with the corner of her handkerchief.* Keep still now, quite still. *Slaps his hand.* Do as I tell you. Why, I believe you're trembling, big, strong man though you are! *Feels his biceps.* What muscles!

JEAN, *warning.* Miss Julie!

JULIE. Yes, Monsieur Jean?

JEAN. Attention. Je ne suis qu'un homme.

JULIE. Will you stay still! There now. It's out. Kiss my hand and say thank you.

JEAN, *rising.* Miss Julie, listen. Kristin's gone to bed now. Will you listen?

JULIE. Kiss my hand first.

JEAN. Very well, but you'll have only yourself to blame.

JULIE. For what?

JEAN. For what! Are you still a child at twenty-five? Don't you know it's dangerous to play with fire?

JULIE. Not for me. I'm insured.

JEAN, *bluntly.* No, you're not. And even if you are, there's still stuff here to kindle a flame.

JULIE. Meaning yourself?

JEAN. Yes. Not because I'm me, but because I'm a man and young and . . .

JULIE. And good-looking? What incredible conceit! A Don Juan perhaps? Or a Joseph? Good Lord, I do believe you are a Joseph!

JEAN. Do you?

JULIE. I'm rather afraid so.

JEAN *goes boldly up and tries to put his arms round her and kiss her. She boxes his ears.*

How dare you!

JEAN. Was that in earnest or a joke?

JULIE. In earnest.

JEAN. Then what went before was in earnest too. You take your games too seriously and that's dangerous. Anyhow I'm tired of playing now and beg leave to return to my work. The Count will want his boots first thing and it's past midnight now.

JULIE. Put those boots down.

JEAN. No. This is my work, which it's my duty to do. But I never undertook to be your playfellow and I never will be. I consider myself too good for that.

JULIE. You're proud.

JEAN. In some ways—not all.

JULIE. Have you even been in love?

JEAN. We don't put it that way, but I've been gone on quite a few girls. And once I went sick because I couldn't have the one I wanted. Sick, I mean, like those princes in the Arabian Nights who couldn't eat or drink for love.

JULIE. Who was she? *No answer.* Who was she?

JEAN. You can't force me to tell you that.

JULIE. If I ask as an equal, ask as a—friend? Who was she?

JEAN. You.

JULIE, *sitting.* How absurd!

JEAN. Yes, ludicrous if you like. That's the story I wouldn't tell you before, see, but now I will . . . Do you know what the world looks like from below? No, you don't. No more than the hawks and falcons do whose backs one hardly ever sees because they're always soaring up aloft. I lived in a labourer's hovel with seven other children and a pig, out in the grey fields where there isn't a single tree. But from the window I could see the wall round the Count's park with apple-trees above it. That was the Garden of Eden, guarded by many terrible angels with flaming swords. All the same I and the other boys managed to get to the tree of life. Does all this make you despise me?

JULIE. Goodness, all boys steal apples!

JEAN. You say that now, but all the same you do despise me. However, one time I went into the Garden of Eden with my mother to weed the onion beds. Close to the kitchen garden there was a Turkish pavilion hung all over with jasmine and honeysuckle. I hadn't any idea what it was used for, but I'd never seen such a beautiful building. People used to go in and then come out again, and one day the door was left open. I crept up and saw the walls covered with pictures of kings and emperors, and the windows had red curtains with fringes—you know now what the place was, don't you? I . . . *Breaks off a piece of lilac and holds it for* JULIE *to smell. As he talks, she takes it from him.* I had never been inside the manor, never seen anything but the church, and this was more beautiful. No matter where my thoughts went, they always came back—to that place. The longing went on growing in me to enjoy it fully, just once. Enfin, I sneaked in, gazed and admired. Then I heard someone coming. There was only one way out for the gentry, but for me there was another and I had no choice but to take it. JULIE *drops the lilac on the table.* Then I took to my heels, plunged through the raspberry canes, dashed across the strawberry beds and found myself on the rose terrace. There I saw a pink dress and a pair of white stockings—it was you. I crawled into a weed pile and lay there right under it among prickly thistles and damp rank earth. I watched you walking among the roses and said to myself: "If it's true that a thief can get to heaven and be with the angels, it's pretty strange that a labourer's child here on God's earth mayn't come in the park and play with the Count's daughter."

JULIE, *sentimentally.* Do you think all poor children feel the way you did?

JEAN, *taken aback, then rallying. All* poor children? . . . Yes, of course they do. Of course.

JULIE. It must be terrible to be poor.

JEAN, *with exaggerated distress.* Oh yes, Miss Julie, yes. A dog may lie on the Countess's sofa, a horse may have his nose stroked by a young lady, but a servant . . . *change of tone* well, yes, now and then you meet one with guts enough to rise in the world, but how often? Anyhow, do you know what I did? Jumped in the millstream with my clothes on, was pulled out and got a hiding. But the next Sunday, when Father and all the rest went to Granny's, I managed to get left behind. Then I washed with soap and hot water, put my best clothes on and went to church so as to see you. I did see you and went home determined to die. But I wanted to die beautifully and peacefully, without any pain. Then I remembered it was dangerous to sleep under an elder bush. We had a big one in full bloom, so I stripped it and climbed into the oats-bin with the flowers. Have you ever noticed how smooth oats are? Soft to touch as human skin . . . Well, I closed the lid and shut my eyes, fell asleep, and when they woke me I was very ill. But I didn't die, as you see. What I meant by all that I don't know. There was no hope of winning you —you were simply a symbol of the hopelessness of ever getting out of the class I was born in.

JULIE. You put things very well, you know. Did you go to school?

JEAN. For a while. But I've read a lot of novels and been to the theatre. Besides, I've heard educated folk talking—that's what's taught me most.

JULIE. Do you stand round listening to what we're saying?

JEAN. Yes, of course. And I've heard quite a bit too! On the carriage box or rowing the boat. Once I heard you, Miss Julie, and one of your young lady friends . . .

JULIE. Oh! Whatever did you hear?

JEAN. Well, it wouldn't be nice to repeat it. And I must say I was pretty startled. I couldn't think where you had learnt such words. Perhaps, at bottom, there isn't as much difference between people as one's led to believe.

JULIE. How dare you! We don't behave as you do when we're engaged.

JEAN, *looking hard at her*. Are you sure? It's no use making out so innocent to me.

JULIE. The man I gave my love to was a rotter.

JEAN. That's what you always say—afterwards.

JULIE. Always?

JEAN. I think it must be always. I've heard the expression several times in similar circumstances.

JULIE. What circumstances?

JEAN. Like those in question. The last time . . .

JULIE, *rising*. Stop. I don't want to hear any more.

JEAN. Nor did *she*—curiously enough. May I go to bed now please?

JULIE, *gently*. Go to bed on Midsummer Eve?

JEAN. Yes. Dancing with that crowd doesn't really amuse me.

JULIE. Get the key of the boathouse and row me out on the lake. I want to see the sun rise.

JEAN. Would that be wise?

JULIE. You sound as though you're frightened for your reputation.

JEAN. Why not? I don't want to be made a fool of, nor to be sent packing without a character when I'm trying to better myself. Besides, I have Kristin to consider.

JULIE. So now it's Kristin.

JEAN. Yes, but it's you I'm thinking about too. Take my advice and go to bed.

JULIE. Am I to take orders from you?

JEAN. Just this once, for your own sake. Please. It's very late and sleepiness goes to one's head and makes one rash. Go to bed. What's more, if my ears don't deceive me, I hear people coming this way. They'll be looking for me, and if they find us here, you're done for.

The CHORUS *approaches, singing. During the following dialogue the song is heard in snatches, and in full when the peasants enter.*

Out of the wood two women came,
Tridiri-ralla, tridiri-ra.
The feet of one were bare and cold,
Tridiri-ralla-la.

The other talked of bags of gold,
Tridiri-ralla, tridiri-ra.
But neither had a sou to her name,
Tridiri-ralla-la.

The bridal wreath I give to you,
Tridiri-ralla, tridiri-ra.
But to another I'll be true,
Tridiri-ralla-la.

JULIE. I know our people and I love them, just as they do me. Let them come. You'll see.

JEAN. No, Miss Julie, they don't love you. They take your food, then spit at it. You must believe me. Listen to them, just listen to what they're singing . . . No, don't listen.

JULIE, *listening.* What are they singing?

JEAN. They're mocking—you and me.

JULIE. Oh no! How horrible! What cowards!

JEAN. A pack like that's always cowardly. But against such odds there's nothing we can do but run away.

JULIE. Run away? Where to? We can't get out and we can't go into Kristin's room.

JEAN. Into mine then. Necessity knows no rules. And you can trust me. I really am your true and devoted friend.

JULIE. But supposing . . . supposing they were to look for you in there?

JEAN. I'll bolt the door, and if they try to break in I'll shoot. Come on. *Pleading.* Please come.

JULIE, *tensely.* Do you promise . . . ?

JEAN. I swear!

JULIE *goes quickly into his room and he excitedly follows her.*

Led by the fiddler, the peasants enter in festive attire with flowers in their hats. They put a barrel of beer and a keg of spirits, garlanded with leaves, on the table, fetch glasses and begin to carouse. The scene becomes a ballet. They form a ring and dance and sing and mime: "Out of the wood two women came." *Finally they go out, still singing.*

JULIE *comes in alone. She looks at the havoc in the kitchen, wrings her hands, then takes out her powder puff and powders her face.*

JEAN *enters in high spirits.*

JEAN. Now you see! And you heard, didn't you? Do you still think it's possible for us to stay here?

JULIE. No, I don't. But what can we do?

JEAN. Run away. Far away. Take a journey.

JULIE. Journey? But where to?

JEAN. Switzerland. The Italian lakes. Ever been there?

JULIE. No. Is it nice?

JEAN. Ah! Eternal summer, oranges, evergreens . . . ah!

JULIE. But what would we do there?

JEAN. I'll start a hotel. First-class accommodation and first-class customers.

JULIE. Hotel?

JEAN. There's life for you. New faces all the time, new languages—no time for nerves or worries, no need to look for something to do—work rolling up of its own accord. Bells ringing night and day, trains whistling, buses coming and going, and all the time gold pieces rolling on to the counter. There's life for you!

JULIE. For *you*. And I?

JEAN. Mistress of the house, ornament of the firm. With your looks, and your style . . . oh, it's bound to be a success! Terrific! You'll sit like a queen in the office and set your slaves in motion by pressing an electric button. The guests will file past your throne and nervously lay their treasure on your table. You've no idea the way people tremble when they get their bills. I'll salt the bills and you'll sugar them with your sweetest smiles. Ah, let's get away from here! *Produces a time-table.* At once, by the next train. We shall be at Malmö at six-thirty, Hamburg eight-forty next morning, Frankfurt-Basle the following day, and Como by the St. Gothard pass in—let's see—three days. Three days!

JULIE. That's all very well. But Jean, you must give me courage. Tell me you love me. Come and take me in your arms.

JEAN, *reluctantly.* I'd like to, but I daren't. Not again in this house. I love you—that goes without saying. You can't doubt that, Miss Julie, can you?

JULIE, *shyly, very feminine.* Miss? Call me Julie. There aren't any barriers between us now. Call me Julie.

JEAN, *uneasily.* I can't. As long as we're in this house, there *are* barriers between us. There's the past and there's the Count. I've never been so servile to anyone as I am to him. I've only got to see his gloves on a chair to feel small. I've only to hear his bell and I shy like a horse. Even now, when I look at his boots, standing there so proud and stiff,

I feel my back beginning to bend. *Kicks the boots.* It's those old, narrow-minded notions drummed into us as children . . . but they can soon be forgotten. You've only got to get to another country, a republic, and people will bend themselves double before my porter's livery. Yes, double they'll bend themselves, but I shan't. I wasn't born to bend. I've got guts, I've got character, and once I reach that first branch, you'll watch me climb. Today I'm valet, next year I'll be proprietor, in ten years I'll have made a fortune, and then I'll go to Roumania, get myself decorated and I may, I only say *may*, mind you, end up as a Count.

JULIE, *sadly.* That would be very nice.

JEAN. You see in Roumania one can buy a title, and then you'll be a Countess after all. My Countess.

JULIE. What do I care about all that? I'm putting those things behind me. Tell me you love me, because if you don't . . . if you don't, what am I?

JEAN. I'll tell you a thousand times over—later. But not here. No sentimentality now or everything will be lost. We must consider this thing calmly like reasonable people. *Takes a cigar, cuts and lights it.* You sit down there and I'll sit here and we'll talk as if nothing has happened.

JULIE. My God, have you no feelings at all?

JEAN. Nobody has more. But I know how to control them.

JULIE. A short time ago you were kissing my shoe. And now . . .

JEAN, *harshly.* Yes, that was then. Now we have something else to think about.

JULIE. Don't speak to me so brutally.

JEAN. I'm not. Just sensibly. One folly's been committed, don't let's have more. The Count will be back at any moment and we've got to settle our future before that. Now, what do you think of my plans? Do you approve?

JULIE. It seems a very good idea—but just one thing. Such a big undertaking would need a lot of capital. Have you got any?

JEAN, *chewing his cigar.* I certainly have. I've got my professional skill, my wide experience and my knowledge of foreign languages. That's capital worth having, it seems to me.

JULIE. But it won't buy even one railway ticket.

JEAN. Quite true. That's why I need a backer to advance some ready cash.

JULIE. How could you get that at a moment's notice?

JEAN. You must get it, if you want to be my partner.

JULIE. I can't. I haven't any money of my own. *Pause.*

JEAN. Then the whole thing's off.

JULIE. And . . . ?

JEAN. We go on as we are.

JULIE. Do you think I'm going to stay under this roof as your mistress? With everyone pointing at me. Do you think I can face my father after this? No. Take me away from here, away from this shame, this humiliation. Oh my God, what have I done? My God, my God! *Weeps.*

JEAN. So that's the tune now, is it? What have you done? Same as many before you.

JULIE, *hysterically.* And now you despise me. I'm falling, I'm falling.

JEAN. Fall as far as me and I'll lift you up again.

JULIE. Why was I so terribly attracted to you? The weak to the strong, the falling to the rising? Or was it love? Is that love? Do you know what love is?

JEAN. Do I? You bet I do. Do you think I never had a girl before?

JULIE. The things you say, the things you think!

JEAN. That's what life's taught me, and that's what I am. It's no good getting hysterical or giving yourself airs. We're both in the same boat now. Here, my dear girl, let me give you a glass of something special. *Opens the drawer, takes out the bottle of wine and fills two used glasses.*

JULIE. Where did you get that wine?

JEAN. From the cellar.

JULIE. My father's burgundy.

JEAN. Why not, for his son-in-law?

JULIE. And I drink beer.

JEAN. That only shows your taste's not so good as mine.

JULIE. Thief!

JEAN. Are you going to tell on me?

JULIE. Oh God! The accomplice of a petty thief! Was I blind drunk? Have I dreamt this whole night? Midsummer Eve, the night for innocent merrymaking.

JEAN. Innocent, eh?

JULIE. Is anyone on earth as wretched as I am now?

JEAN. Why should *you* be? After such a conquest. What about Kristin in there? Don't you think she has any feelings?

JULIE. I did think so, but I don't any longer. No. A menial is a menial . . .

JEAN. And a whore is a whore.

JULIE, *falling to her knees, her hands clasped.* O God in heaven, put an end to my miserable life! Lift me out of this filth in which I'm sinking. Save me! Save me!

JEAN. I must admit I'm sorry for you. When I was in the onion bed and saw you up there among the roses, I . . . yes, I'll tell you now . . . I had the same dirty thoughts as all boys.

JULIE. You, who wanted to die because of me?

JEAN. In the oats-bin? That was just talk.

JULIE. Lies, you mean.

JEAN, *getting sleepy.* More or less. I think I read a story in some paper about a chimney-sweep who shut himself up in a chest full of lilac because he'd been summonsed for not supporting some brat . . .

JULIE. So this is what you're like.

JEAN. I had to think up something. It's always the fancy stuff that catches the women.

JULIE. Beast!

JEAN. Merde!

JULIE. Now you have seen the falcon's back.

JEAN. Not exactly its *back*.

JULIE. I was to be the first branch.

JEAN. But the branch was rotten.

JULIE. I was to be a hotel sign.

JEAN. And I the hotel.

JULIE. Sit at your counter, attract your clients and cook their accounts.

JEAN. I'd have done that myself.

JULIE. That any human being can be so steeped in filth!

JEAN. Clean it up then.

JULIE. Menial! Lackey! Stand up when I speak to you.

JEAN. Menial's whore, lackey's harlot, shut your mouth and get out of here! Are you the one to lecture me for being coarse? Nobody of my kind would ever be as coarse as you were tonight. Do you think any servant girl would throw herself at a man that way? Have you ever seen a girl of my class asking for it like that? I haven't. Only animals and prostitutes.

JULIE, *broken*. Go on. Hit me, trample on me—it's all I deserve. I'm rotten. But help me! If there's any way out at all, help me.

JEAN, *more gently*. I'm not denying myself a share in the honour of seducing you, but do you think anybody in my place would have dared look in your direction if you yourself hadn't asked for it? I'm still amazed . . .

JULIE. And proud.

JEAN. Why not? Though I must admit the victory was too easy to make me lose my head.

JULIE. Go on hitting me.

JEAN, *rising*. No. On the contrary I apologise for what I've said. I don't hit a person who's down—least of all a woman. I can't deny there's a certain satisfaction in finding that what dazzled one below was just moonshine, that that falcon's back is grey after all, that there's powder on the lovely cheek, that polished nails can have black tips, that the handkerchief is dirty although it smells of scent. On the other hand it hurts to find that what I was struggling to reach wasn't high and isn't real. It hurts to see you fallen so low you're far lower than your own cook. Hurts like when you see the last flowers of summer lashed to pieces by rain and turned to mud.

JULIE. You're talking as if you're already my superior.

JEAN. I am. I might make you a Countess, but you could never make me a Count, you know.

JULIE. But I am the child of a Count, and you could never be that.

JEAN. True, but I might be the father of Counts if . . .

JULIE. You're a thief. I'm not.

JEAN. There are worse things than being a thief—much lower. Besides, when I'm in a place I regard myself as a member of the family to some extent, as one of the children. You don't call it stealing when children pinch a berry from overladen bushes. *His passion is roused again.* Miss Julie, you're a glorious woman, far too good for a man like me. You were carried away by some kind of madness, and now you're trying to cover up your mistake by persuading yourself you're in love with me. You're not, although you may find me physically attractive, which means your love's no better than mine. But I wouldn't be satisfied with being nothing but an animal for you, and I could never make you love me.

JULIE. Are you sure?

JEAN. You think there's a chance? Of my loving you, yes, of course. You're beautiful, refined—*takes her hand*—educated, and you can be nice when you want to be. The fire you kindle in a man isn't likely to go out. *Puts his arm round her.* You're like mulled wine, full of spices, and your kisses . . . *He tries to pull her to him, but she breaks away.*

JULIE. Let go of me! You won't win me that way.

JEAN. Not that way, how then? Not by kisses and fine speeches, not by planning the future and saving you from shame? How then?

JULIE. How? How? I don't know. There isn't any way. I loathe you—loathe you as I loathe rats, but I can't escape from you.

JEAN. Escape with me.

JULIE, *pulling herself together.* Escape? Yes, we must escape. But I'm so tired. Give me a glass of wine. *He pours it out. She looks at her watch.* First we must talk. We still have a little time. *Empties the glass and holds it out for more.*

JEAN. Don't drink like that. You'll get tipsy.

JULIE. What's that matter?

JEAN. What's it matter? It's vulgar to get drunk. Well, what have you got to say?

JULIE. We've got to run away, but we must talk first—or rather, I must, for so far you've done all the talking. You've told me about your life, now I want to tell you about mine, so that we really know each other before we begin this journey together.

JEAN. Wait. Excuse my saying so, but don't you think you may be sorry afterwards if you give away your secrets to me?

JULIE. Aren't you my friend?

JEAN. On the whole. But don't rely on me.

JULIE. You can't mean that. But anyway everyone knows my secrets. Listen. My mother wasn't well-born; she came of quite humble people, and was brought up with all those new ideas of sex-equality and women's rights and so on. She thought marriage was quite wrong. So when my father proposed to her, she said she would never become his *wife* . . . but in the end she did. I came into the world, as far as I can make out, against my mother's will, and I was left to run wild, but I had to do all the things a boy does—to prove women are as good as men. I had to wear boys' clothes; I was taught to handle horses—and I wasn't allowed in the dairy. She made me groom and harness and go out hunting; I even had to try to plough. All the men on the estate were given the women's jobs, and the women the men's, until the whole place went to rack and ruin and we were the laughing-stock of the neighbourhood. At last my father seems to have come to his senses and rebelled. He changed everything and ran the place his own way. My mother got ill—I don't know what was the matter with her, but she used to have strange attacks and hide herself in the attic or the garden. Sometimes she stayed out all night. Then came the great fire which you have heard people talking about. The house and the stables and the barns—the whole place burnt to the ground. In very suspicious circumstances. Because the accident happened the very day the insurance had to be renewed, and my father had sent the new premium, but through some carelessness of the messenger it arrived too late. *Refills her glass and drinks.*

JEAN. Don't drink any more.

JULIE. Oh, what does it matter? We were destitute and had to sleep in the carriages. My father didn't know how to get money to rebuild, and then my mother suggested he should borrow from an old friend of hers, a local brick manufacturer. My father got the loan and, to his surprise, without having to pay interest. So the place was rebuilt. *Drinks.* Do you know who set fire to it?

JEAN. Your lady mother.

JULIE. Do you know who the brick manufacturer was?

JEAN. Your mother's lover?

JULIE. Do you know whose the money was?

JEAN. Wait . . . no, I don't know that.

JULIE. It was my mother's.

JEAN. In other words the Count's, unless there was a settlement.

JULIE. There wasn't any settlement. My mother had a little money of her own which she didn't want my father to control, so she invested it with her—friend.

JEAN. Who grabbed it.

JULIE. Exactly. He appropriated it. My father came to know all this. He couldn't bring an action, couldn't pay his wife's lover, nor prove it was his wife's money. That was my mother's revenge because he made himself master in his own house. He nearly shot himself then—at least there's a rumour he tried and didn't bring it off. So he went on living, and my mother had to pay dearly for what she'd done. Imagine what those five years were like for me. My natural sympathies were with my father, yet I took my mother's side, because I didn't know the facts. I'd learnt from her to hate and distrust men—you know how she loathed the whole male sex. And I swore to her I'd never become the slave of any man.

JEAN. And so you got engaged to that attorney.

JULIE. So that he should be my slave.

JEAN. But he wouldn't be.

JULIE. Oh yes, he wanted to be, but he didn't have the chance. I got bored with him.

JEAN. Is that what I saw—in the stable-yard?

JULIE. What did you see?

JEAN. What I saw was him breaking off the engagement.

JULIE. That's a lie. It was I who broke it off. Did he say it was him? The cad.

JEAN. He's not a cad. Do you hate men, Miss Julie?

JULIE. Yes . . . most of the time. But when that weakness comes, oh . . . the shame!

JEAN. Then do you hate me?

JULIE. Beyond words. I'd gladly have you killed like an animal.

JEAN. Quick as you'd shoot a mad dog, eh?

JULIE. Yes.

JEAN. But there's nothing here to shoot with—and there isn't a dog. So what do we do now?

JULIE. Go abroad.

JEAN. To make each other miserable for the rest of our lives?

JULIE. No, to enjoy ourselves for a day or two, for a week, for as long as enjoyment lasts, and then—to die . . .

JEAN. Die? How silly! I think it would be far better to start a hotel.

JULIE, *without listening* . . . die on the shores of Lake

Como, where the sun always shines and at Christmas time there are green trees and glowing oranges.

JEAN. Lake Como's a rainy hole and I didn't see any oranges outside the shops. But it's a good place for tourists. Plenty of villas to be rented by—er—honeymoon couples. Profitable business that. Know why? Because they all sign a lease for six months and all leave after three weeks.

JULIE, *naïvely*. After three weeks? Why?

JEAN. They quarrel, of course. But the rent has to be paid just the same. And then it's let again. So it goes on and on, for there's plenty of love although it doesn't last long.

JULIE. You don't want to die with me?

JEAN. I don't want to die at all. For one thing I like living and for another I consider suicide's a sin against the Creator who gave us life.

JULIE. You believe in God—*you*?

JEAN. Yes, of course. And I go to church every Sunday. Look here, I'm tired of all this. I'm going to bed.

JULIE. Indeed! And do you think I'm going to leave things like this? Don't you know what you owe the woman you've ruined?

JEAN, *taking out his purse and throwing a silver coin on the table*. There you are. I don't want to be in anybody's debt.

JULIE, *pretending not to notice the insult*. Don't you know what the law is?

JEAN. There's no law unfortunately that punishes a woman for seducing a man.

JULIE. But can you see anything for it but to go abroad, get married and then divorce?

JEAN. What if I refuse this mésalliance?

JULIE. Mésalliance?

JEAN. Yes, for me. I'm better bred than you, see! Nobody in my family committed arson.

JULIE. How do you know?

JEAN. Well, you can't prove otherwise, because we haven't any family records outside the Registrar's office. But I've seen your family tree in that book on the drawing-room table. Do you know who the founder of your family was? A miller who let his wife sleep with the King one night during the Danish war. I haven't any ancestors like that. I haven't any ancestors at all, but I might become one.

JULIE. This is what I get for confiding in someone so low, for sacrificing my family honour . . .

JEAN. Dishonour! Well, I told you so. One shouldn't drink, because then one talks. And one shouldn't talk.

JULIE. Oh, how ashamed I am, how bitterly ashamed! If at least you loved me!

JEAN. Look here—for the last time—what do you want? Am I to burst into tears? Am I to jump over your riding whip? Shall I kiss you and carry you off to Lake Como for three weeks, after which . . . What am I to do? What do you want? This is getting unbearable, but that's what comes of playing around with women. Miss Julie, I can see how miserable you are; I know you're going through hell, but I don't understand you. We don't have scenes like this; we don't go in for hating each other. We make love for fun in our spare time, but we haven't all day and all night for it like you. I think you must be ill. I'm sure you're ill.

JULIE. Then you must be kind to me. You sound almost human now.

JEAN. Well, be human yourself. You spit at me, then won't let me wipe it off—on you.

JULIE. Help me, help me! Tell me what to do, where to go.

JEAN. Jesus, as if I knew!

JULIE. I've been mad, raving mad, but there must be a way out.

JEAN. Stay here and keep quiet. Nobody knows anything.

JULIE. I can't. People do know. Kristin knows.

JEAN. They don't know and they wouldn't believe such a thing.

JULIE, *hesitating.* But—it might happen again.

JEAN. That's true.

JULIE. And there might be—consequences.

JEAN, *in panic*. Consequences! Fool that I am I never thought of that. Yes, there's nothing for it but to go. At once. I can't come with you. That would be a complete give-away. You must go alone—abroad—anywhere.

JULIE. Alone? Where to? I can't.

JEAN. You must. And before the Count gets back. If you stay, we know what will happen. Once you've sinned you feel you might as well go on, as the harm's done. Then you get more and more reckless and in the end you're found out. No. You must go abroad. Then write to the Count and tell him everything, except that it was me. He'll never guess that—and I don't think he'll want to.

JULIE. I'll go if you come with me.

JEAN. Are you crazy, woman? "Miss Julie elopes with valet." Next day it would be in the headlines, and the Count would never live it down.

JULIE. I can't go. I can't stay. I'm so tired, so completely worn out. Give me orders. Set me going. I can't think any more, can't act . . .

JEAN. You see what weaklings you are. Why do you give yourselves airs and turn up your noses as if you're the lords of creation? Very well, I'll give you your orders. Go upstairs and dress. Get money for the journey and come down here again.

JULIE, *softly*. Come up with me.

JEAN. To your room? Now you've gone crazy again. *Hesitates a moment*. No! Go along at once. *Takes her hand and pulls her to the door.*

JULIE, *as she goes*. Speak kindly to me, Jean.

JEAN. Orders always sound unkind. Now you know. Now you know.

Left alone, JEAN *sighs with relief, sits down at the table, takes out a note-book and pencil and adds up figures, now and then aloud. Dawn begins to break.* KRISTIN *enters dressed for church, carrying his white dickey and tie.*

KRISTIN. Lord Jesus, look at the state the place is in! What have you been up to? *Turns out the lamp.*

JEAN. Oh, Miss Julie invited the crowd in. Did you sleep through it? Didn't you hear anything?

KRISTIN. I slept like a log.

JEAN. And dressed for church already.

KRISTIN. Yes, you promised to come to Communion with me today.

JEAN. Why, so I did. And you've got my bib and tucker, I see. Come on then. *Sits.* KRISTIN *begins to put his things on. Pause. Sleepily.* What's the lesson today?

KRISTIN. It's about the beheading of John the Baptist, I think.

JEAN. That's sure to be horribly long. Hi, you're choking me! Oh Lord, I'm so sleepy, so sleepy!

KRISTIN. Yes, what have you been doing up all night? You look absolutely green.

JEAN. Just sitting here talking with Miss Julie.

KRISTIN. She doesn't know what's proper, that one. *Pause.*

JEAN. I say, Kristin.

KRISTIN. What?

JEAN. It's queer really, isn't it, when you come to think of it? Her.

KRISTIN. What's queer?

JEAN. The whole thing. *Pause.*

KRISTIN, *looking at the half-filled glasses on the table.* Have you been drinking together too?

JEAN. Yes.

KRISTIN. More shame you. Look me straight in the face.

JEAN. Yes.

KRISTIN. Is it possible? Is it possible?

JEAN, *after a moment.* Yes, it is.

KRISTIN. Oh! This I would never have believed. How low!

JEAN. You're not jealous of her, surely?

KRISTIN. No, I'm not. If it had been Clara or Sophie I'd have scratched your eyes out. But not of her. I don't know why; that's how it is though. But it's disgusting.

JEAN. You're angry with her then.

KRISTIN. No. With you. It was wicked of you, very very wicked. Poor girl. And, mark my words, I won't stay here any longer now—in a place where one can't respect one's employers.

JEAN. Why should one respect them?

KRISTIN. You should know since you're so smart. But you don't want to stay in the service of people who aren't respectable, do you? I wouldn't demean myself.

JEAN. But it's rather a comfort to find out they're no better than us.

KRISTIN. I don't think so. If they're no better there's nothing for us to live up to. Oh and think of the Count! Think of him. He's been through so much already. No, I won't stay in the place any longer. A fellow like you too! If it had been that attorney now or somebody of her own class . . .

JEAN. Why, what's wrong with . . .

KRISTIN. Oh, you're all right in your own way, but when all's said and done there is a difference between one class and another. No, this is something I'll never be able to stomach. That our young lady who was so proud and so down on men you'd never believe she'd let one come near her should go and give herself to one like you. She who wanted to have poor Diana shot for running after the lodge-keeper's pug. No, I must say. . . ! Well, I won't stay here any longer. On the twenty-fourth of October I quit.

JEAN. And then?

KRISTIN. Well, since you mention it, it's about time you began to look around, if we're ever going to get married.

JEAN. But what am I to look for? I shan't get a place like this when I'm married.

KRISTIN. I know you won't. But you might get a job as porter or caretaker in some public institution. Government rations are small but sure, and there's a pension for the widow and children.

JEAN. That's all very fine, but it's not in my line to start thinking at once about dying for my wife and children. I must say I had rather bigger ideas.

KRISTIN. You and your ideas! You've got obligations too, and you'd better start thinking about them.

JEAN. Don't *you* start pestering me about obligations. I've had enough of that. *Listens to a sound upstairs.* Anyway we've plenty of time to work things out. Go and get ready now and we'll be off to church.

KRISTIN. Who's that walking about upstairs?

JEAN. Don't know—unless it's Clara.

KRISTIN, *going.* You don't think the Count could have come back without our hearing him?

JEAN, *scared.* The Count? No, he can't have. He'd have rung for me.

KRISTIN. God help us! I've never known such goings on. *Exit.*

The sun has now risen and is shining on the treetops. The light gradually changes until it slants in through the windows. JEAN *goes to the door and beckons.* JULIE *enters in travelling clothes, carrying a small bird-cage covered with a cloth which she puts on a chair.*

JULIE. I'm ready.

JEAN. Hush! Kristin's up.

JULIE, *in a very nervous state.* Does she suspect anything?

JEAN. Not a thing. But, my God, what a sight you are!

JULIE. Sight? What do you mean?

JEAN. You're white as a corpse and—pardon me—your face is dirty.

JULIE. Let me wash then. *Goes to the sink and washes her face and hands.* There. Give me a towel. Oh! The sun is rising!

JEAN. And that breaks the spell.

JULIE. Yes. The spell of Midsummer Eve . . . But listen, Jean. Come with me. I've got the money.

JEAN, *sceptically*. Enough?

JULIE. Enough to start with. Come with me. I can't travel alone today. It's Midsummer Day, remember. I'd be packed into a suffocating train among crowds of people who'd all stare at me. And it would stop at every station while I yearned for wings. No, I can't do that, I simply can't. There will be memories too; memories of Midsummer Days when I was little. The leafy church—birch and lilac—the gaily spread dinner table, relatives, friends—evening in the park—dancing and music and flowers and fun. Oh, however far you run away—there'll always be memories in the baggage car—and remorse and guilt.

JEAN. I will come with you, but quickly now then, before it's too late. At once.

JULIE. Put on your things. *Picks up the cage.*

JEAN. No luggage mind. That would give us away.

JULIE. No, only what we can take with us in the carriage.

JEAN, *fetching his hat*. What on earth have you got there? What is it?

JULIE. Only my greenfinch. I don't want to leave it behind.

JEAN. Well, I'll be damned! We're to take a bird-cage along, are we? You're crazy. Put that cage down.

JULIE. It's the only thing I'm taking from my home. The only living creature who cares for me since Diana went off like that. Don't be cruel. Let me take it.

JEAN. Put that cage down, I tell you—and don't talk so loud. Kristin will hear.

JULIE. No, I won't leave it in strange hands. I'd rather you killed it.

JEAN. Give the little beast here then and I'll wring its neck.

JULIE. But don't hurt it, don't . . . no, I can't.

JEAN. Give it here. I *can*.

JULIE, *taking the bird out of the cage and kissing it*. Dear little Serena, must you die and leave your mistress?

JEAN. Please don't make a scene. It's *your* life and future we're worrying about. Come on, quick now!

He snatches the bird from her, puts it on a board and picks up a chopper. JULIE *turns away.*

You should have learnt how to kill chickens instead of target-shooting. Then you wouldn't faint at a drop of blood.

JULIE, *screaming.* Kill me too! Kill me! You who can butcher an innocent creature without a quiver. Oh, how I hate you, how I loathe you! There is blood between us now. I curse the hour I first saw you. I curse the hour I was conceived in my mother's womb.

JEAN. What's the use of cursing. Let's go.

JULIE, *going to the chopping-block as if drawn against her will.* No, I won't go yet. I can't . . . I must look. Listen! There's a carriage. *Listens without taking her eyes off the board and chopper.* You don't think I can bear the sight of blood. You think I'm so weak. Oh, how I should like to see your blood and your brains on a chopping-block! I'd like to see the whole of your sex swimming like that in a sea of blood. I think I could drink out of your skull, bathe my feet in your broken breast and eat your heart roasted whole. You think I'm weak. You think I love you, that my womb yearned for your seed and I want to carry your offspring under my heart and nourish it with my blood. You think I want to bear your child and take your name. By the way, what is your name? I've never heard your surname. I don't suppose you've got one. I should be "Mrs. Hovel" or "Madam Dunghill." You dog wearing my collar, you lackey with my crest on your buttons! I share you with my cook; I'm my own servant's rival! Oh! Oh! Oh! . . . You think I'm a coward and will run away. No, now I'm going to stay—and let the storm break. My father will come back . . . find his desk broken open . . . his money gone. Then he'll ring that bell—twice for the valet —and then he'll send for the police . . . and I shall tell everything. Everything. Oh how wonderful to make an end of it all—a real end! He has a stroke and dies and that's the end of all of us. Just peace and quietness . . . eternal rest. The coat of arms broken on the coffin and the Count's line extinct . . . But the valet's line goes on in an orphanage, wins laurels in the gutter and ends in jail.

JEAN. There speaks the noble blood! Bravo, Miss Julie. But now, don't let the cat out of the bag.

KRISTIN *enters dressed for church, carrying a prayer-book.* JULIE *rushes to her and flings herself into her arms for protection.*

JULIE. Help me, Kristin! Protect me from this man!

KRISTIN, *unmoved and cold.* What goings-on for a feast day morning! *Sees the board.* And what a filthy mess. What's it all about? Why are you screaming and carrying on so?

JULIE. Kristin, you're a woman and my friend. Beware of that scoundrel!

JEAN, *embarrassed.* While you ladies are talking things over, I'll go and shave. *Slips into his room.*

JULIE. You must understand. You must listen to me.

KRISTIN. I certainly don't understand such loose ways. Where are you off to in those travelling clothes? And he had his hat on, didn't he, eh?

JULIE. Listen, Kristin. Listen, I'll tell you everything.

KRISTIN. I don't want to know anything.

JULIE. You must listen.

KRISTIN. What to? Your nonsense with Jean? I don't care a rap about that; it's nothing to do with me. But if you're thinking of getting him to run off with you, we'll soon put a stop to that.

JULIE, *very nervously.* Please try to be calm, Kristin, and listen. I can't stay here, nor can Jean—so we must go abroad.

KRISTIN. Hm, hm!

JULIE, *brightening.* But you see, I've had an idea. Supposing we all three go—abroad—to Switzerland and start a hotel together . . . I've got some money, you see . . . and

Jean and I could run the whole thing—and I thought you would take charge of the kitchen. Wouldn't that be splendid? Say yes, do. If you come with us everything will be fine. Oh do say yes! *Puts her arms round* KRISTIN.

KRISTIN, *coolly thinking*. Hm, hm.

JULIE, *presto tempo*. You've never travelled, Kristin. You should go abroad and see the world. You've no idea how nice it is travelling by train—new faces all the time and new countries. On our way through Hamburg we'll go to the zoo—you'll love that—and we'll go to the theatre and the opera too . . . and when we get to Munich there'll be the museums, dear, and pictures by Rubens and Raphael—the great painters, you know . . . You've heard of Munich, haven't you? Where King Ludwig lived—you know, the king who went mad. . . . We'll see his castles—some of his castles are still just like in fairy-tales . . . and from there it's not far to Switzerland—and the Alps. Think of the Alps, Kristin dear, covered with snow in the middle of summer . . . and there are oranges there and trees that are green the whole year round . . .

JEAN *is seen in the door of his room, sharpening his razor on a strop which he holds with his teeth and his left hand. He listens to the talk with satisfaction and now and then nods approval.* JULIE *continues, tempo prestissimo.*

And then we'll get a hotel . . . and I'll sit at the desk, while Jean receives the guests and goes out marketing and writes letters . . . There's life for you! Trains whistling, buses driving up, bells ringing upstairs and downstairs . . . and I shall make out the bills—and I shall cook them too . . . you've no idea how nervous travellers are when it comes to paying their bills. And you—you'll sit like a queen in the kitchen . . . of course there won't be any standing at the stove for you. You'll always have to be nicely dressed and ready to be seen, and with your looks—no, I'm not flattering you—one fine day you'll catch yourself a husband . . . some rich Englishman, I shouldn't wonder—they're the ones who are easy—*slowing down*—to catch . . . and then we'll get rich and build ourselves a villa on Lake Como . . . of course it rains there a little now and then—but—*dully*—the sun must shine there too sometimes—even though it seems gloomy—and if not—then we can come home again—come back—*pause*—here—or somewhere else . . .

KRISTIN. Look here, Miss Julie, do you believe all that yourself?

JULIE, *exhausted.* Do I believe it?

KRISTIN. Yes.

JULIE, *wearily.* I don't know. I don't believe anything any more. *Sinks down on the bench; her head in her arms on the table.* Nothing. Nothing at all.

KRISTIN, *turning to* JEAN. So you meant to beat it, did you?

JEAN, *disconcerted, putting the razor on the table.* Beat it? What are you talking about? You've heard Miss Julie's plan, and though she's tired now with being up all night, it's a perfectly sound plan.

KRISTIN. Oh, is it? If you thought I'd work for that . . .

JEAN, *interrupting.* Kindly use decent language in front of your mistress. Do you hear?

KRISTIN. Mistress?

JEAN. Yes.

KRISTIN. Well, well, just listen to that!

JEAN. Yes, it would be a good thing if you did listen and talked less. Miss Julie is your mistress and what's made you lose your respect for her now ought to make you feel the same about yourself.

KRISTIN. I've always had enough self-respect—

JEAN. To despise other people.

KRISTIN. —not to go below my own station. Has the Count's cook ever gone with the groom or the swineherd? Tell me that.

JEAN. No, you were lucky enough to have a high-class chap for your beau.

KRISTIN. High-class all right—selling the oats out of the Count's stable.

JEAN. You're a fine one to talk–taking a commission on the groceries and bribes from the butcher.

KRISTIN. What the devil . . . ?

JEAN. And now you can't feel any respect for your employers. You, you!

KRISTIN. Are you coming to church with me? I should think you need a good sermon after your fine deeds.

JEAN. No, I'm not going to church today. You can go alone and confess your own sins.

KRISTIN. Yes, I'll do that and bring back enough forgiveness to cover yours too. The Saviour suffered and died on the cross for all our sins, and if we go to Him with faith and a penitent heart, He takes all our sins upon Himself.

JEAN. Even grocery thefts?

JULIE. Do you believe that, Kristin?

KRISTIN. That is my living faith, as sure as I stand here. The faith I learnt as a child and have kept ever since, Miss Julie. "But where sin abounded, grace did much more abound."

JULIE. Oh, if I had your faith! Oh, if . . .

KRISTIN. But you see you can't have it without God's special grace, and it's not given to all to have that.

JULIE. Who is it given to then?

KRISTIN. That's the great secret of the workings of grace, Miss Julie. God is no respecter of persons, and with Him the last shall be first . . .

JULIE. Then I suppose He does respect the last.

KRISTIN, *continuing* . . . and it is easier for a camel to go through the eye of a needle than for a rich man to enter into the kingdom of God. That's how it is, Miss Julie. Now I'm going–alone, and on my way I shall tell the groom not to let any of the horses out, in case anyone should want to leave before the Count gets back. Goodbye.

Exit.

JEAN. What a devil! And all on account of a greenfinch.

JULIE, *wearily*. Never mind the greenfinch. Do you see any way out of this, any end to it?

JEAN, *pondering*. No.

JULIE. If you were in my place, what would you do?

JEAN. In your place? Wait a bit. If I was a woman—a lady of rank who had—fallen. I don't know. Yes, I do know now.

JULIE, *picking up the razor and making a gesture*. This?

JEAN. Yes. But *I* wouldn't do it, you know. There's a difference between us.

JULIE. Because you're a man and I'm a woman? What is the difference?

JEAN. The usual difference—between man and woman.

JULIE, *holding the razor*. I'd like to. But I can't. My father couldn't either, that time he wanted to.

JEAN. No, he didn't want to. He had to be revenged first.

JULIE. And now my mother is revenged again, through me.

JEAN. Didn't you ever love your father, Miss Julie?

JULIE. Deeply, but I must have hated him too—unconsciously. And he let me be brought up to despise my own sex, to be half woman, half man. Whose fault is what's happened? My father's, my mother's or my own? My own? I haven't anything that's my own. I haven't one single thought that I didn't get from my father, one emotion that didn't come from my mother, and as for this last idea—about all people being equal—I got that from him, my fiancé—that's why I call him a cad. How can it be my fault? Push the responsibility on to Jesus, like Kristin does? No, I'm too proud and —thanks to my father's teaching—too intelligent. As for all that about a rich person not being able to get into heaven, it's just a lie, but Kristin, who has money in the savings-bank, will certainly not get in. Whose fault is it? What does it matter whose fault it is? In any case I must take the blame and bear the consequences.

JEAN. Yes, but . . . *There are two sharp rings on the bell.* JULIE *jumps to her feet.* JEAN *changes into his livery.* The Count is back. Supposing Kristin . . . *Goes to the speaking-tube, presses it and listens.*

JULIE. Has he been to his desk yet?

JEAN. This is Jean, sir. *Listens.* Yes, sir. *Listens.* Yes, sir, very good, sir. *Listens.* At once, sir? *Listens.* Very good, sir. In half an hour.

JULIE, *in panic.* What did he say? My God, what did he say?

JEAN. He ordered his boots and his coffee in half an hour.

JULIE. Then there's half an hour . . . Oh, I'm so tired! I can't do anything. Can't be sorry, can't run away, can't stay, can't live—can't die. Help me. Order me, and I'll obey like a dog. Do me this last service—save my honour, save his name. You know what I ought to do, but haven't the strength to do. Use your strength and order me to do it.

JEAN. I don't know why—I can't now—I don't understand . . . It's just as if this coat made me—I can't give you orders—and now that the Count has spoken to me—I can't quite explain, but . . . well, that devil of a lackey is bending my back again. I believe if the Count came down now and ordered me to cut my throat, I'd do it on the spot.

JULIE. Then pretend you're him and I'm you. You did some fine acting before, when you knelt to me and played the aristocrat. Or . . . Have you ever seen a hypnotist at the theatre? *He nods.* He says to the person "Take the broom," and he takes it. He says "Sweep," and he sweeps . . .

JEAN. But the person has to be asleep.

JULIE, *as if in a trance.* I am asleep already . . . the whole room has turned to smoke—and you look like a stove—a stove like a man in black with a tall hat—your eyes are glowing like coals when the fire is low—and your face is a white patch like ashes. *The sunlight has now reached the floor and lights up* JEAN. How nice and warm it is! *She holds out her hands as though warming them at a fire.* And so light—and so peaceful.

JEAN, *putting the razor in her hand.* Here is the broom. Go now while it's light—out to the barn—and . . . *Whispers in her ear.*

JULIE, *waking.* Thank you. I am going now—to rest. But just tell me that even the first can receive the gift of grace.

JEAN. The first? No, I can't tell you that. But wait . . . Miss Julie, I've got it! You aren't one of the first any longer. You're one of the last.

JULIE. That's true. I'm one of the very last. I *am* the last. Oh! . . . But now I can't go. Tell me again to go.

JEAN. No, I can't now either. I can't.

JULIE. And the first shall be last.

JEAN. Don't think, don't think. You're taking my strength away too and making me a coward. What's that? I thought I saw the bell move . . . To be so frightened of a bell! Yes, but it's not just a bell. There's somebody behind it—a hand moving it—and something else moving the hand—and if you stop your ears—if you stop your ears—yes, then it rings louder than ever. Rings and rings until you answer—and then it's too late. Then the police come and . . . and . . . *The bell rings twice loudly.* JEAN *flinches, then straightens himself up.* It's horrible. But there's no other way to end it . . . Go!

JULIE *walks firmly out through the door.*

CURTAIN

CREDITORS

A Tragi-Comedy

FOREWORD

Creditors is one of the most brilliant of Strindberg's short plays. It was written in 1888, the same year as *Miss Julie,* the year following *The Father,* the first of his so-called Naturalist plays.

At the time of writing it Strindberg was thirty-nine. His first marriage—to Siri von Essen, whom he had once adored and who had borne him children—had finally crashed. True, they were still living under the same roof in Copenhagen, but Strindberg no longer considered her his wife. He thought of her as his housekeeper and former mistress, and if he referred to his marriage at all, it was as an affair too ludicrous to be taken seriously. Hypersensitive and deeply wounded by his failure as a husband, Strindberg dreaded ridicule and judged it better to do the laughing himself.

Before writing *Creditors* he finished his autobiographical novel, *A Fool's Defence,* based on his relations with Siri and her former husband, Baron Carl Gustav Wrangel, and describing the wife's anxiety to be rid of her present husband, "the troublesome creditor." Both in the novel and in *Creditors* he called the former husband Gustav, Baron Wrangel's second name, and referred to him as "an idiot," and it is evident that the play grew directly out of this book. *Creditors* also contains other biographical details, such as the reference to the death of Tekla's child by Gustav.

Another influence on this play was Strindberg's current interest in hypnosis, which also appears in *Miss Julie.*

The Father had been accepted by Antoine for his Théâtre Libre in Paris, and *Creditors* was intended for this *avant-garde* theatre and for the Scandinavian Experimental Theatre Strindberg was now hoping to have himself. He felt that in *Creditors* he had taken "the new form" even further than in his earlier plays. *The Father* and *Miss Julie* are described by him as tragedies; *Creditors* is called a tragi-comedy, and Strindberg wrote to his publisher that the play was "humane, good-humoured, with all three characters sympathetic." This is characteristic and revealing, for although on occasion Strindberg recognised his own virulence, he more often saw the softer, even sentimental side there was to his nature. And this side should never be forgotten in the production of any of his plays. Strindberg's heroines were conceived as good, feminine women and his heroes as fine, intellectual men, who have only grown evil through the demoralising influence of sex warfare. When, for instance, Laura in *The Father* is played from the first line to the last as a vixen, so that one cannot believe that she and the Captain were once a happily married couple, the point of the plot is lost. And it is relevant that he intended Siri to play the part of Tekla when *Creditors* was performed in Scandinavia, although this she did not in fact do.

This, however, is not to say that one can regard *Creditors* as "humane" or "good-humoured." The content is serious, but the tone is ironical and the whole work reflects the cynicism of Strindberg's outlook at this time. The dialogue has sharpened since the earlier plays, possibly owing to Strindberg's growing admiration for the Paris theatre, and there is ample opportunity for satirical production, so long as it is remembered that he pillories people not from cruelty, but from his misery at mankind's wickedness and folly. He caricatures life's tragedy.

Many of Strindberg's recurrent themes appear in *Creditors,* such as Adolf's statement that he had birth-pangs while his wife was in labour, and Gustav's assertion that a child resembling a former husband is no proof that the child is his.

Strindberg's scheme for a Scandinavian Experimental Theatre petered out from excess of strain (his wife, in spite of their estrangement, was in charge of the management) and lack of funds, after single performances of *Miss Julie* and *Creditors,* and Strindberg did not achieve a real theatre of his own until 1907, five years before his death.

In 1893, however, by which time Strindberg was coming

to the end of his second marriage, following the great success in Paris of *The Father* and *Miss Julie*, Lugné Poë, founder of the Théâtre Nouveau, put on *Creditors* with himself in the part of Adolf. The play was enthusiastically received and in the same year was produced at the Residentz Theatre in Berlin, where it gained more laurels. Since then it has often been performed on the Continent and several times in London, the latest production being that of the 59 Theatre Company in 1959.

E. S.

CHARACTERS

TEKLA

ADOLF, *her husband, a painter*

GUSTAV, *her divorced husband, a schoolmaster, travelling under an assumed name*

Non-speaking parts, appearing once briefly: TWO LADIES *and a* WAITER

SCENE: *A sitting-room in a hotel at a Swedish watering-place in the eighties*

At the back a door to a verandah, with a view of the landscape. On the right a door leading to another room.

Centre right a table with newspapers on it, and beyond that a sofa. To the left a chair beside a small modelling stand.

GUSTAV *is sitting on the sofa, smoking a cigar.*

ADOLF *is at the modelling stand, working on a wax figure. His crutches stand beside him.*

ADOLF. . . . and for all this I have you to thank.

GUSTAV, *puffing at his cigar.* Oh nonsense!

ADOLF. But certainly. For the first days after my wife went off on this trip, I just lay on a sofa, unable to do anything but long for her. It was as if she had taken my crutches with her, so I couldn't move at all. Then when I'd slept for a couple of days, I came to and began to pull myself together. My mind, which had been working deliriously, began to calm down. Old thoughts that I had had in the past rose up again; the desire to work, to create, came back, and my eyes regained their old power of looking at things truthfully and boldly. And then you turned up.

GUSTAV. You were wretched enough when I first met you, I admit, and you had to use your crutches; but that doesn't make me responsible for your recovery. You needed a rest and you needed male company.

ADOLF. Yes, that's true enough, like everything you say. I used to have men as friends in the old days, but after I was married they seemed superfluous. I was content with the one person I had chosen. Then I found myself in new circles, where I made many acquaintances, but my wife was jealous of them—she wanted to have me to herself. But what was worse, she also wanted to have my friends to herself. And so I was left alone with my jealousy.

GUSTAV. You're given to that disease, aren't you?

ADOLF. I was afraid of losing her and tried to prevent it. Was that unreasonable? But I was never afraid of her being unfaithful.

GUSTAV. A married man never is afraid of that.

ADOLF. No, isn't it extraordinary? What I was afraid of was that these friends would get an influence over her and so indirectly have power over me. And that I couldn't stand.

GUSTAV. So your opinions differed, your wife's and yours.

ADOLF. Having heard so much, you'd better hear it all. My wife has an independent nature—what are you smiling at?

GUSTAV. Go on. She has an independent nature. . . .

ADOLF. So she won't accept my ideas. . . .

GUSTAV. Only everybody else's.

ADOLF, *after a pause*. Yes. It really has seemed as if she hated my ideas just because they were mine, and not because she found them preposterous. You see, quite often she has brought out some former opinion of mine and forced it on everyone as her own. Yes, and then on other occasions, when some friend of mine passed on views he had got directly from me, she'd think them fine. Everything was fine as long as it didn't come from me.

GUSTAV. In other words, you are not very happy.

ADOLF. Yes, I am happy. I have the person I chose and I have never wanted anyone else.

GUSTAV. And never wanted to be free?

ADOLF. No, I can't say that. At times it has seemed to me that it would be—well, a rest to be free. But the moment she leaves me, I am consumed with need for her—as I need my own arms and legs. It's really extraordinary. I sometimes feel she isn't a separate being at all, but an actual part of me . . . an intestine that carries away my will, my will to live. It's as if I'd given into her keeping my very solar plexus that the anatomists talk of.

GUSTAV. Perhaps, by and large, that is what has happened.

ADOLF. And where would we be then? After all, she's an independent being with a mind of her own. And when I first met her I was just a boy artist whose education she took in hand.

GUSTAV. But before long you were shaping her thoughts and educating her, weren't you?

ADOLF. No. She stopped growing and I went on.

GUSTAV. Yes, it's curious how her writing deteriorated after that first book, or anyhow did not improve. But that time she had an easy subject—it's supposed to be a portrait of her husband, you know. Did you ever meet him? He seems to have been a bit of an idiot.

ADOLF. I never met him because he'd gone away for six months, but he must have been a prize idiot, to judge from her description. *Pause.* And her description was accurate. You can be sure of that.

GUSTAV. I am. But why did she take him?

ADOLF. Because she didn't know him. People never do seem to know one another until afterwards.

GUSTAV. Then people shouldn't marry until—afterwards! But he was a tyrant, of course.

ADOLF. Of course?

GUSTAV. Well, all married men are that. *Feeling his way.* And you not least.

ADOLF. I? Who allow my wife to come and go as she pleases?

GUSTAV. Oh, then you certainly are the least! Perhaps you ought to lock her up. Do you like her spending whole nights away?

ADOLF. No, I certainly do not.

GUSTAV. You see! *Turning.* Actually you'd be ridiculous if you did.

ADOLF. Ridiculous? Can a man be ridiculous because he trusts his wife?

GUSTAV. Certainly he can. And you already are. Utterly ridiculous.

ADOLF, *vehemently*. What? That's the last thing I mean to be. . . . And things will have to be changed.

GUSTAV. Don't get so excited. You'll have another attack.

ADOLF. And why isn't *she* ridiculous when I spend nights away?

GUSTAV. Why? That's no concern of yours—that's how it is—and while you're wondering why, there's your disaster.

ADOLF. What disaster?

GUSTAV. Well, her husband was a tyrant and she took him so as to get her freedom. A girl can only get that by providing herself with a chaperon—in other words, a husband.

ADOLF. Of course.

GUSTAV. And now you are the chaperon.

ADOLF. I?

GUSTAV. Well, you're her husband, aren't you?

ADOLF *looks bewildered.*

Isn't that right?

ADOLF, *uneasily*. I don't know. You live with a woman for years and you never think about her or your relationship with her—and then—suddenly you begin to wonder and the whole thing starts. . . . Gustav, you are my friend, the only friend I have of my own sex. During this week you've given me back my will to live. It's as if I'd been charged by your magnetism. You've been like a watchmaker, mending the works in my head and winding up the spring again. Can't you hear for yourself how much clearer my thoughts are and how lucidly I'm talking? And it seems to me that my voice has got back its old ring.

GUSTAV. Yes, I think it has. I wonder why.

ADOLF. Perhaps one gets used to lowering one's voice when talking to a woman. Certainly Tekla always used to accuse me of shouting.

GUSTAV. So you lowered your voice and bowed to the apron strings.

ADOLF. Don't put it like that. *Reflects*. As a matter of fact, it's worse than that. But don't let's talk about it now . . . Where was I? Yes, you came here and opened my eyes to the truth of my art. As a matter of fact, I had felt my interest in painting waning for some time, as paint didn't seem the right medium for what I wanted to express. But it was only when you gave me the reason for this, and explained that painting could not be the proper form for creative art today, that I saw the light and realised it would be impossible for me ever to work in colour again.

GUSTAV. Are you really convinced that you won't paint any more? That you won't have a relapse?

ADOLF. Absolutely convinced. I've proved it. When I went to bed that night after we had that conversation, I went through all your arguments, point by point, and I knew you were right. But when I woke after a sound night's sleep with a clear head, it came to me in a flash that you might be mistaken. I jumped out of bed, grabbed my brushes, and began to paint. But it was all over. I no longer had any illusions. It was only daubs of paint, and I was amazed to think that I had believed and made others believe that a painted canvas was anything more than a painted canvas. The veil had fallen from my eyes and it was just as impossible for me to go on painting as it was for me to become a child again.

GUSTAV. And then you realised that the naturalistic trend of today with its demand for realism and tangibility could only find its proper form in sculpture, which gives you body, projection in three dimensions.

ADOLF, *hesitating*. The three dimensions . . . yes, that's to say, body.

GUSTAV. And so you became a sculptor. Or rather you were one already, but you had gone astray, and it only needed a guide to put you on the right road. . . . Tell me, are you getting great satisfaction now from your work?

ADOLF. Now I'm living.

GUSTAV. May I see what you are doing?

ADOLF. A female figure.

GUSTAV, *looking at it*. Without a model? And so lifelike.

ADOLF, *flatly*. Yes, but all the same it's like someone. It's extraordinary how that woman is in my body, just as I'm in hers.

GUSTAV. Not really so extraordinary. You know what transfusion is?

ADOLF. Blood transfusion? Yes.

GUSTAV. Well, you seem to have bled yourself. But looking at this figure I understand several things I only suspected before. You have made love to her passionately.

ADOLF. Yes, so passionately that I couldn't tell if she were I, or I, she. When she smiles, I smile; when she weeps, I weep. And when she—can you imagine it?—when she was giving birth to our child, I felt the pains in my own body.

GUSTAV. You know, my dear friend—it gives me great pain to say this—but you have the first symptoms of epilepsy.

ADOLF, *agitated*. What? How can you say such a thing?

GUSTAV. Well, I've seen the symptoms before—in a younger brother I had, who indulged in amorous excesses.

ADOLF. How . . . how did it show itself, this thing?

GUSTAV. It was terrible to witness. If you're feeling at all weak, I won't upset you by describing it.

ADOLF, *urgently*. No, go on, go on!

GUSTAV. Well, the boy had got himself married to an innocent young girl with curls and dove's eyes—the face of a child and the soul of an angel. But none the less, she managed to usurp the prerogative of the male . . .

ADOLF. What's that?

GUSTAV. Initiative, of course. With the result that the angel nearly carried him off to heaven. But first he had to be crucified and feel the nails in his flesh. It was horrible.

ADOLF, *breathlessly*. But what happened?

During the following passage GUSTAV *graphically illustrates his words and* ADOLF *listens so intently that he unconsciously imitates* GUSTAV'S *gestures.*

GUSTAV, *slowly*. We would be sitting talking, he and I, and when I'd been speaking for a while, his face would turn as white as chalk, his arms and legs would grow stiff, and his thumbs would be twisted into the palms of his hands, like this! *Gesture, imitated by* ADOLF. Then his eyes would grow bloodshot and he would begin to masticate, like this! *Gesture, imitated by* ADOLF. The saliva rattled in his throat; his chest was constricted as if in a vice; the pupils of his eyes flickered like gas jets; his tongue worked till he foamed at the mouth, and then . . . he sank . . . slowly . . . down . . . backwards . . . into his chair, as if he were drowning. And then . . .

ADOLF, *in a whisper.* Stop!

GUSTAV. And then . . . Are you ill?

ADOLF. Yes.

GUSTAV *fetches a glass of water.*

GUSTAV. There. Drink this, and we'll talk about something else.

ADOLF, *feebly.* Thank you. . . . Go on now.

GUSTAV. Then, when he came to, he didn't remember anything at all. He had been completely unconscious. Has this ever happened to you?

ADOLF. Well, I do have attacks of giddiness sometimes, but the doctor says it's anaemia.

GUSTAV. Yes, but that's the beginning, you know. You must believe what I say. It will turn into epilepsy if you don't take care of yourself.

ADOLF. What ought I to do then?

GUSTAV. To begin with, you should practise complete sexual abstinence.

ADOLF. How long for?

GUSTAV. Six months at least.

ADOLF. I can't do that. It would destroy our married life.

GUSTAV. Goodbye to you then.

ADOLF, *covering the wax figure.* I couldn't do that.

GUSTAV. Not to save your life? But tell me—as you have taken me so far into your confidence—isn't there anything else, any secret wound that's troubling you? It's rare to find only one reason for discord when life is so varied and so rich in opportunities for destruction. Isn't there some skeleton in your cupboard that you're hiding from yourself? . . . You said just now, for example, that you had a child which was sent away. Why doesn't it live with you?

ADOLF. My wife didn't want it to.

GUSTAV. And her reason? Out with it.

ADOLF. When the child was about three years old it began to look like him, her former husband.

GUSTAV. Ah! Have you ever seen her former husband?

ADOLF. No, never. I just had a brief glance at a bad portrait, but I couldn't see any likeness.

GUSTAV. Portraits never are like the person anyway, and he may have changed since it was done. But I hope this didn't arouse your suspicions?

ADOLF. Certainly not. The child was born a year after our marriage, and her husband was abroad when I first met Tekla here—it was at this very place—actually in this house. That's why we come here every summer.

GUSTAV. Then you couldn't possibly have any suspicions. And you wouldn't need to in any case, for the children of a widow who remarries are often like her dead husband. It's vexing, of course—that's why they used to burn the widows in India, you know . . . But tell me, have you never felt jealous of him, of his memory? Wouldn't it sicken you to meet him out somewhere and hear him—with his eyes on your Tekla—saying "we" instead of "I"? *We!*

ADOLF. I can't deny that thought has haunted me.

GUSTAV. There you are. And you'll never get rid of it. There are discords in life, you see, that never can be resolved. So you had better just put wax in your ears and work. Work, grow older, and pile up new impressions against the cupboard door, so that the skeleton can't get out.

ADOLF. Excuse me interrupting you, but it's amazing how like Tekla you are sometimes when you are talking. You have a way of blinking your right eye as if you were taking aim, and when you look at me your eyes have the same effect on me as hers do sometimes.

GUSTAV. No, really?

ADOLF. And then you said that "No, really?" in just the indifferent tone she uses. She says "No, really?" very often too.

GUSTAV. Perhaps we are distantly related, as all human beings come from the same stock. But it's strange anyhow, and it will be interesting to meet your wife and see this likeness.

ADOLF. But you know she never picks up an expression from me. She seems rather to avoid my vocabulary and I have never seen her use any of my mannerisms. Although married couples are supposed to become rather alike.

GUSTAV. Yes, and do you know why not? That woman has never loved you.

ADOLF. What the devil do you mean?

GUSTAV. I . . . I beg your pardon, but, you see, a woman loves by taking, by receiving, and if she doesn't take anything from a man, she doesn't love him. She has never loved you.

ADOLF. Do you think she's unable to love more than once?

GUSTAV. Yes, one only lets oneself be taken in once. After that one keeps one's eyes open. You have never been taken in, but you had better beware of those that have. They are dangerous, those.

ADOLF. Your words cut into me like knives, and I feel something pierced inside me without my being able to prevent it. Yet the piercing is something of a relief, like the lancing of boils which would not come to a head. . . . She has never loved me. . . . Then why did she take me?

GUSTAV. Tell me first how she came to take you, and if it was you who took her, or her, you.

ADOLF. God knows if I can answer that. . . . Or say how it came about. It didn't happen all in one day.

GUSTAV. Shall I try to guess how it came about?

ADOLF. You couldn't do that.

GUSTAV. Oh, with the help of all you have told me about yourself and your wife, I think I can reconstruct the course of events. Listen now and you'll see. *Lightly, almost jokingly.* The husband had gone abroad to study, and she was alone. At first she found her freedom rather pleasant, then she had a sense of emptiness. Yes, I think she felt pretty empty when she had been living by herself for a fortnight. Then *he* turned up and gradually the emptiness was filled. By comparison the absent one began to fade, for the simple reason that he was at a distance—you know, the law of quadratics. But when they felt passion stirring they were troubled—for themselves and their consciences and for him. To protect themselves, they sheltered behind their fig leaves, played brother and sister, and the more physical their emotions became, the more spiritual they declared their relationship to be.

ADOLF. Brother and sister? How do you know that?

GUSTAV. I guessed it. Children play at being papa and mamma, but when they are older they play at being brother and sister, in order to hide what must be hidden . . . And then they took a vow of chastity, and then they played hide-and-seek, till they found one another in a dark corner where they were sure of not being seen. *With mock severity.* But they felt that there was *one* who could see them in the darkness . . . and they grew frightened, and in their terror the figure of this absent one began to haunt them—to assume gigantic proportions, to be changed, to become a nightmare which disturbed their amorous slumbers, a creditor who knocked at the doors. They saw his dark hand between theirs as they sat at table; they heard his harsh voice in the stillness of the night, which should only have been broken by the beating of their hearts. He did not stop them from possessing one another, but he spoiled their happiness. And when they discovered his invisible power to spoil their happiness, and at last fled—but fled in vain—from the memories that pursued them and the debts they left behind them, and the public opinion they dared not face, they hadn't the strength to carry their own guilt, and so a scapegoat had to be brought in from outside to be sacrificed. They were freethinkers, but they hadn't the courage to go and speak openly to him and say: "We love one another." No, they were cowards, and therefore the tyrant had to be slaughtered. Is that right?

ADOLF. Yes. But you have forgotten how she improved me, how she inspired me with new thoughts. . . .

GUSTAV. I haven't forgotten that. But can you tell me why

she didn't improve the other one too—into a freethinker?

ADOLF. Oh, he was just an idiot!

GUSTAV. Yes, of course. He was an idiot. But that's a somewhat ambiguous term, and in her novel his idiocy seemed to consist mainly of his not understanding her. Excuse the question, but is your wife really so profound? I haven't seen anything profound in her writing.

ADOLF. Nor have I. But I must confess that I too have some difficulty in understanding her. It's as if the mechanism of our brains didn't interlock, as if something goes to pieces in my head when I try to understand her.

GUSTAV. Perhaps you are an idiot too.

ADOLF. No, I don't think I'm that, and I nearly always think she's wrong. . . . Will you read this letter, for instance, that I got today?

Takes a letter from his pocket-book and hands it to GUSTAV.

GUSTAV, *glancing through it.* Hm! The handwriting seems familiar.

ADOLF. Rather masculine, do you think?

GUSTAV. Well, I have seen *one* man at least who writes something like that. . . . She calls you "brother," I see. Do you still play that comedy for each other? With the fig leaves still in place, though withered. Aren't you less formal when you address her?[1]

ADOLF. No, I think respect is lost if one does that.

GUSTAV. I see. Is it to make you respect her then that she calls herself your sister?

ADOLF. I want to respect her more than I respect myself. I want her to be my better part.

GUSTAV. Why not be the better part yourself? Surely that would be less tiresome than someone else being it. You don't want to be inferior to your wife.

ADOLF. Yes, I do. I enjoy always being a little beneath her. For instance, I taught her to swim, and now I like to hear her boasting that she's better at it and braver than I am. At first I pretended to be weak and timid just to give her

[1] NOTE. Literally: "Don't you '*tutoyer*' her?" E.S.

courage, but one fine day I found that I really was weaker and less brave than she. It was as if she had actually taken my courage.

GUSTAV. Have you taught her anything else?

ADOLF. Yes—but this is between ourselves. I taught her to spell, which she couldn't do before. And do you know what happened then? When she took on our correspondence, I stopped writing and—would you believe it?—over the years, with lack of practice, I've even forgotten bits of my grammar. But do you imagine that she remembers it was I who taught her at the start? No, it's I, of course, who am the idiot now.

GUSTAV. Ah, so you are the idiot after all!

ADOLF. That's just a joke, of course.

GUSTAV. Yes, naturally. But all this is pure cannibalism. Do you know what I mean? Well, savages eat their enemies so that they'll get their strength for themselves. She has eaten your soul, this woman, your courage, your knowledge . . .

ADOLF. And my faith. It was I who urged her to write her first book. . . .

GUSTAV, *grimacing*. Is that so?

ADOLF. It was I who boosted her even when I found her writing cheap. It was I who took her into literary circles, where she could sip honey from the ornamental plants. It was I who, through personal influence, kept the critics at bay and blew up her self-confidence, blew so hard that I lost my own breath. I gave, I gave, I gave—until I had nothing left for myself. You know—I'm telling you everything now—it really seems to me that one's soul is pretty extraordinary. When my artistic success threatened to put her in the shade and ruin her reputation, I tried to bolster up her courage by belittling myself and making my work seem inferior to hers. I talked so much about the insignificant part played on the whole by painters, talked so much and invented so many reasons for this, that one fine day I found I had convinced myself of the futility of painting. So all you had to do was to blow down a house of cards.

GUSTAV. Excuse me for reminding you, but at the beginning

of our talk you declared that she never took anything from you.

ADOLF. She doesn't now. There's nothing left to take.

GUSTAV. Now the snake, being full, vomits.

ADOLF. Perhaps she took more from me than I realised.

GUSTAV. You can be sure of that. She took when you weren't looking, and that's known as stealing.

ADOLF. Perhaps she didn't educate me after all.

GUSTAV. But you, her. Very likely. And she tricked you into believing the opposite. May I ask how she set about your education?

ADOLF. Well, first of all . . . hm!

GUSTAV. Yes?

ADOLF. Well, I . . .

GUSTAV. No, surely it was *she*.

ADOLF. Really, I don't know now.

GUSTAV. You see!

ADOLF. Anyhow, she ate up my faith and that sank me, until you came and gave me a new faith.

GUSTAV, *smiling*. In sculpture?

ADOLF, *uncertainly*. Yes.

GUSTAV. You really believe in it? In this abstract, antiquated art from the childhood of the human race. You believe you can work in pure form, in three dimensions—eh? In the realistic vein of today and produce the necessary illusion without colour—without colour, mind you. Do you really believe you can do that?

ADOLF, *crushed*. No.

GUSTAV. And nor do I.

ADOLF. Then why did you say so?

GUSTAV. Because I pitied you.

ADOLF. Yes, I am to be pitied. For now I am bankrupt. Finished. And the worst thing of all is that I haven't got her.

GUSTAV. What use would she be if you had?

ADOLF. She would be what God was for me before I became an atheist. Something I could reverence.

GUSTAV. Reverence be blowed! Cultivate something else instead. A little wholesome contempt, for example.

ADOLF. I can't live without something to look up to. . . .

GUSTAV. Slave!

ADOLF. Without a woman to respect and worship.

GUSTAV. Oh hell! You'd better take God back if you need something to genuflect to. What an atheist! All fuddled up in this superstition about woman. Do you know what that mysterious, sphinx-like profundity in your wife really is? It is pure stupidity. Look here, she doesn't even speak correctly! You see, something's wrong with the mechanism. The watch-case looks expensive, but the works inside are cheap. It's the skirts that do it, nothing else at all. Put a pair of trousers on her and draw a moustache under her nose with a bit of charcoal. Then sober yourself up and listen to her again and you'll see how different it sounds. Nothing but a phonograph, repeating your own words and other people's, a bit thinned down. . . . Have you ever looked at a naked woman? Yes, of course you have. A youth with breasts on his chest, an immature man, a child that's shot up but not developed, a chronic anaemic, who has haemorrhages regularly thirteen times a year! What can you expect of such a creature?

ADOLF. If all you say is true, then how is it that I think of her as my equal?

GUSTAV. Hallucination. The hypnotising power of skirts. Or —because you actually have become equal. The levelling process is complete. Her capillary capacity has equalised the water level. . . . Look here . . . *Takes out his watch* . . . we have been talking for six hours and your wife ought to be here soon. Hadn't we better stop, so that you can have a rest?

ADOLF. No, don't leave me! I daren't be alone.

GUSTAV. It's only for a little while. Then your wife will be here.

ADOLF. Yes, she will be here. . . . It's quite extraordinary. I am longing for her to come; yet I am afraid of her. She caresses me; she is tender, but there is something suffocating about her kisses, something weakening and numbing.

It's as if I were a circus child being pinched behind the scenes by the clown, so as to look rosy to the audience.

GUSTAV. My dear friend, it gives me great pain to see the state you are in. Without being a physician I can tell that you are a dying man. One only has to look at your last pictures to perceive this quite clearly.

ADOLF. What did you say? How do you mean?

GUSTAV. The colour is a washy blue, pallid, thin, with the canvas showing through, yellow as a corpse. It's as if I saw your sunken, putty-coloured cheeks sticking out . . .

ADOLF. Stop it! Stop it!

GUSTAV. Well, that's not just my personal opinion. Haven't you seen today's paper?

ADOLF, *shuddering.* No.

GUSTAV. It's there on the table.

ADOLF, *stretching out his hand, but not daring to take the paper.* Does it say that?

GUSTAV. Read it. Or shall I?

ADOLF. No.

GUSTAV. I'll go if you like.

ADOLF. No! No! No! . . . I don't know. . . . I think I'm beginning to hate you and yet I can't let you go. . . . You pull me out of the hole where I've fallen through the ice, but as soon as I'm out, you hit me on the head and push me under again. As long as I kept my secrets to myself I still had my vitals, but now I am empty. There's a picture by some Italian master—of a torture—a saint whose intestines are being wound out on a winch. The martyr is lying there watching himself growing thinner and thinner, as the roll on the winch gets thicker. . . . Well, it seems to me as if you had swelled since you emptied me out, and when you go you'll take my vitals with you and leave an empty shell.

GUSTAV. Oh, the things you imagine! But anyway isn't your wife coming home and bringing your heart with her?

ADOLF. No, not now. Not since you have burnt her to ashes for me. You have left everything in ashes—my art, my love, my hope, my faith.

GUSTAV. They were pretty well done for already.

ADOLF. But they might have been saved. Now it's too late. Incendiary!

GUSTAV. We have cleared the ground a bit, that's all. Now we will sow in the ashes.

ADOLF. I hate you! I curse you!

GUSTAV. That's a good sign. You still have some strength left. Now I'll pull you out of the ice again. Listen! Will you listen to me and obey me?

ADOLF. Do what you will with me. I'll obey.

GUSTAV, *rising*. Look at me!

ADOLF, *gazing at* GUSTAV. Now you are looking at me again with those other eyes that draw me to you.

GUSTAV. And now listen to me.

ADOLF. Yes, but talk about yourself. Don't talk about me any more. I am like an open wound and cannot bear to be touched.

GUSTAV. But there's nothing to say about me. I am a teacher of dead languages and a widower, and that's all there is to it. Now take my hand.

ADOLF, *doing so*. What terrific power you must have! It's like taking hold of an electric generator.

GUSTAV. And remember, I have been as weak as you are now. . . . Stand up!

ADOLF *rises and falls on* GUSTAV's *neck*.

ADOLF. My bones are as weak as a baby's. And my mind is all at sea.

GUSTAV. Walk about a bit.

ADOLF. I can't.

GUSTAV. You must, or I'll hit you.

ADOLF, *straightening himself up*. You'll *what?*

GUSTAV. I said I'll hit you.

ADOLF *starts back from him, furious.*

ADOLF. You . . . !

GUSTAV. That's better. You've got some blood to your brain

and your self-confidence has come back. Now for some electric current. . . . Where is your wife?

ADOLF. Where is she?

GUSTAV. Yes.

ADOLF. She is . . . at . . . a meeting.

GUSTAV. Are you quite certain?

ADOLF. Quite.

GUSTAV. What sort of meeting?

ADOLF. An orphanage committee.

GUSTAV. Did you part friends?

ADOLF, *hesitating*. No, not friends.

GUSTAV. Enemies, eh? What did you say that made her so furious?

ADOLF. You're uncanny. You terrify me. How do you know?

GUSTAV. It's quite simple. There are three known factors and from them I can deduce the unknown . . . What did you say to her?

ADOLF. I said . . . only two words, but they were terrible, and I regret them, regret them very much.

GUSTAV. You shouldn't regret. What were these words?

ADOLF. I said: "You old flirt."

GUSTAV. What else?

ADOLF. I didn't say anything else.

GUSTAV. That's what you tell me, but you're forgetting the rest—perhaps because you daren't remember it. You've put it in a secret drawer, but now you've got to bring it out.

ADOLF. I don't remember what . . .

GUSTAV. But I know what you said. This. "You ought to be ashamed of flirting, considering you are so old that you can't get any more lovers."

ADOLF. Did I say that? I suppose I did. But how on earth can you know about it?

GUSTAV. I heard her telling the story on the boat on my way here.

ADOLF. Who to?

GUSTAV. To the four youths she was with. Of course, she always did have a fancy for innocent youths, so as to . . .

ADOLF. There's no harm in that.

GUSTAV. . . . so as to play brother and sister instead of papa and mamma.

ADOLF. You have seen her then.

GUSTAV. Yes, I have. But *you* have never seen her when you weren't seeing her—seen her, I mean, when you weren't there. And that's why—you follow me?—a husband can *never* know his wife . . . Have you got a picture of her?

Mystified, ADOLF *takes a photograph from his pocket-book.*

You weren't there when this was taken?

ADOLF. No.

GUSTAV. Look at it. . . . Is it like the portrait you painted of her? . . . No! The features are the same, but the expression is different. But you can't see that because you force your own image of her in between. Look at this as a painter now, without considering the original. . . . What does it represent? I can't see anything but a study of a coquette, out to attract. Do you see that cynical expression of the mouth, which you are never allowed to see? Do you see those glances aimed at a man who is not you? Do you see how low the dress is cut, how cunningly the hair is combed up, and how the sleeve has managed to slip back?

ADOLF. Yes, I do see it—now.

GUSTAV. Beware, my boy!

ADOLF. What of?

GUSTAV. Her revenge. Don't forget that when you said she couldn't attract a man, you wounded her in the most vital and sacred spot. If you had said that what she wrote was trash, she would have laughed at your bad taste—but as it is, believe you me, it will not be her fault if she hasn't taken her revenge already.

ADOLF. I must know.

GUSTAV. Find out.

ADOLF. Find out?

GUSTAV. Use your eyes. I'll help you if you like.

ADOLF. Well, as I'm going to die anyway, let it come. Now's as good a time as another. What are we to do?

GUSTAV. First for a piece of information. Hasn't your wife any point that's specially vulnerable?

ADOLF. Scarcely. She's like a cat with nine lives.

The hoot of a steamer is heard.

GUSTAV. Ah! That was the steamer hooting in the Sound. She will be here at any moment.

ADOLF. I must go down and meet her.

GUSTAV. No. You must stay here. You've got to be rude. If she has a clear conscience you'll get a hailstorm about your ears. If she's guilty she'll cover you with caresses.

ADOLF. Are you quite sure of that?

GUSTAV. Not quite, for the hare sometimes doubles back—but I'll look out for that. *Points to the door on the right.* I'll take up my position in my room there and watch while you play your scene in here. And when you've finished yours, we'll change roles. I'll go into the cage and engage the serpent, while you take your place at the key-hole. Afterwards we'll meet in the park and compare notes. But stand up for yourself! If you begin to weaken I shall knock twice on the floor with a chair.

ADOLF. Very well. . . . But don't go away. I must know you're in that room there.

GUSTAV. You can take my word for it that I shall be. . . . But don't be alarmed later on, when you watch me dissecting a human soul and exposing its entrails on the table. They say it's rather hard for a novice to take, but when you've seen it once it doesn't worry you. . . . But one thing you must remember. Not a single word about meeting me or having made any new acquaintance during her absence. Not one word. I'll seek out her vulnerable point for myself. Hush! She is already here—she's in her room. . . . She's humming. . . . That means she's in a rage. Now, pull yourself together and sit down there in your chair. Then she'll have to sit on the sofa, and I shall be able to watch you both at the same time.

ADOLF. It's only an hour till dinner time, and no new guests have arrived or the bell would have rung. That means we shall be alone, I'm sorry to say.

GUSTAV. Are you such a coward?

ADOLF. I am nothing. . . . Yes, I am afraid of what is going to happen now. But I can't stop it happening. The stone is rolling, but it wasn't the last drop of water that set it rolling, nor the first one either—it was all the drops together.

GUSTAV. Let it roll then. . . . There will be no peace until it has. Goodbye for now.

ADOLF *nods.*

Exit GUSTAV.

ADOLF *stands still holding the photograph. Then he tears it up and throws the pieces under the table. He sits down on his chair, pulls nervously at his tie, runs his fingers through his hair, fidgets with his lapels, and so on.*

TEKLA *enters, goes straight up to him, and kisses him. She is friendly, frank, gay, and attractive.*

TEKLA. Hullo, little brother! How are you?

ADOLF *is almost won over by her manner and speaks reluctantly and as if joking.*

ADOLF. What mischief have you been up to that makes you come and kiss me like that?

TEKLA. I'll tell you. I've spent a frightful lot of money.

ADOLF. Did you have a good time then?

TEKLA. Yes, very. But not at that old crèche meeting. That was just shit—as the Danes would say. But how has my little brother amused himself while Squirrel was away?

TEKLA'S *eyes roam round the room as if she is looking for someone or suspecting something.*

ADOLF. I've been bored stiff.

TEKLA. Didn't anyone come to keep you company?

ADOLF. No, I've been quite alone.

TEKLA, *watching him as she sits down on the sofa.* Who has been sitting here?

ADOLF. There? Nobody.

TEKLA. That's odd. The sofa's still warm and here's a hollow that seems to have been made by an elbow. Have you had some lady friends?

ADOLF. You know I haven't.

TEKLA. But you're blushing. Little brother, I believe you're telling fibs. Come over here and tell Squirrel what's on your conscience.

She draws him to her. He sinks down with his head on her knees.

ADOLF, *smiling*. You're a devil. Did you know that?

TEKLA. No, I don't know anything about myself.

ADOLF. I see. You never give a thought to your own reactions.

TEKLA, *warily*. On the contrary, I never think about anything but myself—I'm a terrible egoist. You're very philosophical all of a sudden!

ADOLF. Put your hand on my forehead.

TEKLA, *soothingly*. Have you been having another brain-storm? Poor head! Let me see what I can do. *Kisses his forehead.* There, is it better now?

ADOLF. Yes, it's better now.

Pause.

TEKLA. Well, tell me how you have been amusing yourself? Have you painted anything?

ADOLF. No, I've done with painting.

TEKLA. What? Done with painting?

ADOLF. Yes. But don't nag me about it. It's not my fault I can't paint any more.

TEKLA. But what will you do then?

ADOLF. I'm going to be a sculptor.

TEKLA. O Lord, another whole lot of new ideas!

ADOLF. Yes, but don't be cross. . . . Take a look at that figure over there.

TEKLA *uncovers the wax figure.*

TEKLA. Well I never! Who is it supposed to be?

ADOLF. Guess!

TEKLA, *gently*. Is it meant to be Squirrel? Aren't you ashamed of yourself?

ADOLF. Isn't it a good likeness?

TEKLA. How can I tell when it hasn't got a face?

ADOLF. Yes, but there's so much else—beautiful!

TEKLA, *caressing his cheek.* Hold your tongue or I'll kiss you.

ADOLF, *backing.* Now, now! Somebody might come in.

TEKLA. What do I care? Mayn't I kiss my own husband then? Surely that's my legal right.

ADOLF. Yes, but do you know what? Here in the hotel they don't believe we're married, because we kiss so often. And the fact that we quarrel sometimes makes no difference—lovers are known to do that too.

TEKLA. Yes, but why should we quarrel? Why can't you always be as nice as you are now? Tell me. Don't you want to be? Don't you want us to be happy?

ADOLF. Oh, I do! But . . .

TEKLA. What is all this business anyhow? Who has put it into your head that you're not going to paint any more?

ADOLF. Who? You're always suspecting there's someone behind me and my thoughts. You're jealous.

TEKLA. Yes, I am. I'm afraid someone may come and take you away from me.

ADOLF. You're afraid of that? When you know no woman can cut you out, and that I can't live without you.

TEKLA. It's not a woman I'm afraid of, but your friends who put ideas into your head.

ADOLF, *looking at her searchingly.* You really are frightened. What frightens you?

TEKLA, *rising.* Someone has been here. Who has been here?

ADOLF. Don't you like me to look at you?

TEKLA. Not like that. That's not how you usually look at me.

ADOLF. How was I looking at you then?

TEKLA. Under your lids.

ADOLF. And under *yours!* Yes, I want to see what's behind them.

TEKLA. Look as much as you like. There's nothing to hide. But —you're talking in a different way too—you're using strange expressions—— *Searchingly.* You're philosophising. Why? *Going up to him threateningly.* Who has been here?

ADOLF. Only my doctor.

TEKLA. Your doctor? Who's that?

ADOLF. The doctor from Strömstad.

TEKLA. What's his name?

ADOLF. Sjöberg.

TEKLA. What did he say?

ADOLF. He said—well, among other things, he said I was on the brink of epilepsy.

TEKLA. Among other things? What else did he say?

ADOLF. Well, something very upsetting.

TEKLA. Tell me.

ADOLF. He said we were not to live together as man and wife for a time.

TEKLA. Did he then! I can well believe it. They want to separate us. I have noticed that for a long time.

ADOLF. You can't have noticed what's never happened.

TEKLA. Haven't I though!

ADOLF. How can you see what doesn't exist? Or is your imagination so distraught by fear that you see what has never existed? What is it you are so afraid of? That I shall borrow somebody else's eyes so as to see you as you are, instead of as you appear to be?

TEKLA. Keep your fancies in check, Adolf! They come from the beast in the human soul.

ADOLF. Wherever did you learn that? From those innocent youths on the boat? Eh?

TEKLA, *without losing her composure.* Well, as a matter of fact, there is a lot to be learned from youth.

ADOLF. I think you're beginning to be infatuated by youth.

TEKLA. I always have been. That's why I fell in love with you. Do you mind?

ADOLF. No, but I'd rather be the only one.

TEKLA, *lightly.* My heart is so big, you see, little brother, that there's room in it for many more than you.

ADOLF. Little brother doesn't want any other brothers.

TEKLA. Come to Squirrel then, and get your hair pulled for being so jealous—no, envious is the word.

Two knocks are heard from GUSTAV's *room.*

ADOLF. No, I don't want to fool now. I want to talk seriously.

TEKLA, *as if talking to a baby.* O Jesus, does he want to talk seriously then? It's frightful how serious he's grown.

She takes his face in her hands and kisses him.

Now just a little smile.

ADOLF *unwillingly smiles.*

There!

ADOLF. You devilish woman! I really believe you can cast spells.

TEKLA. You see! So don't start any trouble or I'll spirit you away.

ADOLF, *rising.* Tekla! Will you pose a moment for me—in profile? So I can put the face on your figure.

TEKLA. Of course I will.

She turns her head so that he can see her profile. He gazes at her and pretends to model.

ADOLF. Don't think about me now. Think about somebody else.

TEKLA. I'll think about my latest conquest.

ADOLF. The chaste youth?

TEKLA. Exactly. He had such a sweet little moustache and cheeks like a peach. They were so smooth and rosy one wanted to bite them.

ADOLF, *grimly.* Keep that expression on your face!

TEKLA. What expression?

ADOLF. A cynical, brazen one I have never seen before.

TEKLA, *making a face.* Like this?

ADOLF. Yes, like that. *Rises.* Do you know how Bret Harte describes an adultress?

TEKLA, *smiling.* No, I have never read Bret whatever-you-call-him.

ADOLF. As a pallid creature who never blushes.

TEKLA. Never? But when she meets her lover she's bound to

blush, though her husband and Mr. Bret aren't there to see it.

ADOLF. Are you sure?

TEKLA, *as before.* Of course. As the husband is incapable of bringing the blood to her head, he can't ever see that charming spectacle.

ADOLF, *furiously.* Tekla!

TEKLA. You little ninny!

ADOLF. Tekla!

TEKLA. You should call me your squirrel, then I'd blush beautifully for you. Don't you want me to?

ADOLF, *disarmed.* I'm so furious with you, you little monster, I could bite you.

TEKLA, *playfully.* Come and bite me then. Come on!

She stretches out her arms to him. ADOLF *takes her in his arms and kisses her.*

ADOLF. Yes, I will bite you to death!

TEKLA, *teasing him.* Now, now! Somebody might come in.

ADOLF. What do I care? What do I care about anything in the world, so long as I've got you?

TEKLA. And if you hadn't got me any more?

ADOLF. Then I should die.

TEKLA. But you're not afraid of that happening because I'm so old no one else would have me.

ADOLF. Oh Tekla, you have not forgotten those words of mine! But I take them all back.

TEKLA. Can you explain why you're so jealous and yet at the same time so confident?

ADOLF. No, I can't explain anything. But it's possible the thought that another man once possessed you still rankles in me. Sometimes it seems to me that our love is nothing but a fiction, a self-defence, a passion held to as a matter of honour. But there's nothing I would hate more than for *him* to know I'm not happy. Oh! Though I've never seen him, the mere thought of somebody waiting for my downfall obsesses me. Somebody who's raining curses on my head every day of the year, and would laugh his head off at my ruin. The mere idea of that haunts me, drives me to you, fascinates me, cripples me.

TEKLA. Do you think I'd allow him that satisfaction? Do you think I want to make his prophecy come true?

ADOLF. I don't want to think so.

TEKLA. Then why don't you keep calm?

ADOLF. You go on upsetting me with your coquettishness. Why do you play these tricks?

TEKLA. They're not tricks. I want to be liked, that's all.

ADOLF. But only by men?

TEKLA. Of course. A woman's never really liked by other women, you know.

ADOLF. Tell me—have you heard from him—recently?

TEKLA. Not for the last six months.

ADOLF. Do you ever think about him?

TEKLA. No. When our child died there was no further link between us.

ADOLF. And you haven't seen him anywhere?

TEKLA. No, he's said to be living somewhere on the west coast. But why are you worrying about all that now?

ADOLF. I don't know. But these last days, while I've been alone, I've found myself thinking how he must have felt, when he was left alone that time.

TEKLA. I believe you have a bad conscience.

ADOLF. I have.

TEKLA. I suppose you feel like a thief.

ADOLF. Pretty nearly.

TEKLA. That's beautiful! Men can steal women just as children and chickens are stolen. So you only think of me as one of his goods and chattels. Thank you very much.

ADOLF. No, I think of you as his wife. And that's more than property. It's something that can't be replaced.

TEKLA. Of course it can! If you were to hear he had married again, all those silly ideas would go out of your head. After all, haven't you replaced him in my life?

ADOLF. Have I? And did you love him once?

TEKLA. I most certainly did.

ADOLF. And then . . . ?

TEKLA. I got tired of him.

ADOLF. Supposing you were to get tired of me too.

TEKLA. I shan't do that.

ADOLF. Supposing somebody else came along who had the qualities you want in a man *now*. Then you'd give me up.

TEKLA. No.

ADOLF. Supposing he captivated you. So you couldn't give him up. Then you'd leave me, of course.

TEKLA. No, that's not true.

ADOLF. Surely you couldn't love two men at the same time.

TEKLA. Yes. Why not?

ADOLF. I don't understand.

TEKLA. Things can be, even though you don't understand them. All people are not made alike, you know.

ADOLF. Now I begin to see.

TEKLA. No, really?

ADOLF. No, really?

Pause. ADOLF *seems to be struggling with some memory he cannot grasp.*

Tekla, you know your frankness is beginning to trouble me.

TEKLA. But that used to be the virtue you put highest—and you taught it to me.

ADOLF. Yes, but it seems to me you're hiding something now behind your frankness.

TEKLA. That's the new tactics, you see.

ADOLF. I don't know why, but I'm beginning to dislike this place. If you don't mind, we'll go home—this evening.

TEKLA. What sort of whim is this? I've only just arrived. I don't want to start on another journey.

ADOLF. But I do.

TEKLA. What's it got to do with me what you want? You can go.

ADOLF. I command you to come with me by the next boat.

TEKLA. Command me! What sort of talk's that?

ADOLF. Do you realise that you are my wife?

TEKLA. Do you realise that you are my husband?

ADOLF. Yes, there's a difference between the one and the other.

TEKLA. So that's the line you're taking. You have never loved me.

ADOLF. Haven't I?

TEKLA. No, for to love is to give.

ADOLF. To love as a man is to give, but to love as a woman is to take. And I have given, given, given!

TEKLA. Oh? What have you given?

ADOLF. Everything.

TEKLA. That's a lot. And if it's so, then I've taken it. Are you giving me the bills for your gifts now? And if I have taken them, that's a proof that I loved you. A woman only takes gifts from her lover.

ADOLF. Her lover, yes. You used the right word. I have been your lover, but never your husband.

TEKLA. Well, isn't that much pleasanter—to escape being the chaperon? But if you're not satisfied with that position, you can take yourself off. I don't want a husband.

ADOLF. No, I've noticed that. And lately, when I've watched you sneaking away from me like a thief and making friends of your own, among whom you could flaunt my feathers and glitter with my jewels, I've tried to remind you of your debt. Then at once I became the unwelcome creditor whom one only wants to get rid of. You wanted to repudiate your notes of hand, and so as not to increase your debt to me, you stopped pillaging my treasure chest and started on other people's. I became your husband without wanting to be, and then you began to hate me. But now, as I mayn't be your lover, I am going to be your husband, whether you want it or not.

TEKLA, *playfully*. My sweet idiot, don't talk such nonsense!

ADOLF. You know it's risky to go round thinking everyone's an idiot but yourself.

TEKLA. Well, everyone does.

ADOLF. And I'm beginning to suspect that he—your former husband—possibly wasn't such an idiot after all.

TEKLA. O God, I believe you're beginning to sympathise with him!

ADOLF. A little bit, yes.

TEKLA. Well I never! Perhaps you would like to make his acquaintance and have a heart to heart. What a beautiful picture! But I'm beginning to be rather drawn to him too, as I'm tired of playing nursemaid. He was at least a man, although he had the disadvantage of being my husband.

ADOLF. Look here, don't talk so loud! People will hear us.

TEKLA. What does it matter if they take us for a married couple?

ADOLF. So now you're beginning to be infatuated by virile men and chaste youths all at the same time.

TEKLA. As you see, my infatuations haven't got any limits. My heart is open to everybody and everything, big and small, beautiful and ugly, young and old. I love the whole world.

ADOLF. Do you know what that means?

TEKLA. No, I don't know anything. I only feel.

ADOLF. It means that you are getting old.

TEKLA. There you go again! Take care!

ADOLF. Take care yourself!

TEKLA. What of?

ADOLF, *picking up one of his tools.* This knife.

TEKLA, *lightly.* You shouldn't play with such dangerous things, little brother.

ADOLF. I'm not playing now.

TEKLA. Oh, this is serious, is it? Dead serious. Then I'll show you—that you're under a delusion. That's to say, you'll never be able to see it, you'll never know it, but the whole rest of the world will know it, everyone but you. But you will suspect it; you will have a sense of it, and you will never have another moment's peace. You will feel that you're ridiculous, that you're deceived, but you'll never have proof of it—a married man never does have that. That's what you'll find out.

ADOLF. You hate me then?

TEKLA. No, I don't. And I don't believe I ever shall. But that of course is because you are a child.

ADOLF. Now, yes. But do you remember how it was when the storm broke over us? Then you would lie crying like a small baby; then you would have to sit on my lap while I kissed your eyes to sleep. It was I who was the nurse then. I had to see that you didn't go out without doing your hair, had to send your shoes to the cobbler and see that there was food to cook. I had to sit by your side and hold your hand for hours at a time. You were frightened, frightened of the whole world, because you hadn't a single friend left and you were crushed by public opinion. I had to talk courage into you until my mouth was dry and my head ached. I had to imagine I was strong and force myself to believe in the future. And at last I managed to bring you back to life, although you seemed half dead. Then you admired me. Then I was the man—not the athlete you had left, but the man of will-power. The mesmerist who instilled new energy into your flabby muscles and charged your empty brain with new electricity. And then I gave you back your reputation, provided you with new friends, surrounded you with a little court of people whom I tricked, out of their friendliness to me, into admiring you. I set you over me and my house, and then I painted my most beautiful pictures—rose-red and azure blue against golden backgrounds, and there wasn't one exhibition then where you did not hold the place of honour. Sometimes you were St. Cecilia, sometimes Mary Stuart, Karin Månsdotter,[2] or Ebba Brahe.[3] I made everyone interested in you and compelled the booing mob to see you with my own infatuated vision. I plagued people with your personality and forced you on them, till you had won their all-important good opinion—and could stand on your own feet. But by the time you could do that, my strength was finished and I collapsed from exhaustion. In lifting you up, I had overstrained myself. I was taken ill, and my illness infuriated you, coming now when at last life had begun

[2] Mistress, later wife, of Erik XIV of Sweden.
[3] Loved by King Gustavus Adolfus.

to smile on you. Sometimes, it seemed to me, you had a secret longing to be rid of your creditor and witness. . . . Your love begins to take on the character of an overbearing sister's, and for want of a better I have to learn the new part of little brother. Your tenderness remains; it even increases, but it has in it a suggestion of pity that's not far from contempt—and which changes into open scorn when my talent wanes and your sun rises. But somehow your fountain of inspiration seems to dry up when mine can no longer replenish it, or rather when you want to show that you don't draw on mine. And so both of us sink. And then you have to have somebody to blame. Somebody new. For you are weak and can never shoulder your own guilt. . . . So I became the scapegoat to be sacrificed alive. But when you cut my sinews, you didn't realise you were also crippling yourself, for the years had joined us as twins. You were an offshoot of my tree, but you tried to make your shoot grow before it had any roots. That's why you couldn't develop on your own. And my tree couldn't spare its vital branch—so both of them died.

TEKLA. What you mean to say by all this is that you wrote my books.

ADOLF. No, that's what *you* mean to say, so as to prove me a liar. I don't express myself as crudely as you do, and I have talked for these five minutes so as to get in all the half-tones and nuances and variations. But your barrel-organ has only one note.

TEKLA. Yes, yes, but the gist of it all is that you wrote my books.

ADOLF. There isn't any gist. You can't reduce a chord to a single note. You can't express a varied life in a single number. I didn't say anything so crude as that I wrote your books.

TEKLA. But that's what you meant.

ADOLF, *furiously*. That's not what I meant.

TEKLA. But the sum of it . . .

ADOLF, *distraught*. There can't be a sum if you don't add things up. If you divide and the figure doesn't go into the other one evenly, you get a quotient which is a long, unending, decimal fraction. I haven't added it up.

TEKLA. No, but I can add it up.

ADOLF. No doubt you can, but I haven't.

TEKLA. But you wanted to.

ADOLF, *exhausted, closing his eyes.* No, no, no! Don't talk to me any more! I shall have an attack. Be quiet! Go away! You destroy my brain with your clumsy pincers—you claw my thoughts and tear them to pieces.

ADOLF *seems almost to lose consciousness and sits staring in front of him, rolling his thumbs.*

TEKLA, *tenderly.* What is it? Adolf, are you ill?

He motions her away.

Adolf!

He shakes his head.

Adolf!

ADOLF. Yes?

TEKLA. Don't you think you were unfair just now?

ADOLF. Yes, yes, yes, yes, I admit it.

TEKLA. And do you apologise?

ADOLF. Yes, yes, yes, I apologise. If only you won't talk to me.

TEKLA. Then kiss my hand.

ADOLF, *kissing her hand.* I'll kiss your hand. If only you won't talk to me.

TEKLA. And now go out and get some fresh air before dinner.

ADOLF. I certainly need it. *Rises.* And then we'll pack and go.

TEKLA. No.

ADOLF. Why not? There must be some reason.

TEKLA. I've promised to go to the concert tonight. That's the reason.

ADOLF. Oh, so that's it!

TEKLA. That's it. I've promised to be there and . . .

ADOLF. Promised? I expect you only said you might go. That doesn't stop you from saying now that you can't.

TEKLA. No, unlike you, I keep my word.

ADOLF. One can keep one's promise without having to stand by every casual word one says. Perhaps someone made you promise to go.

TEKLA. Yes.

ADOLF. Even so, you can be released from your promise, as your husband is ill.

TEKLA. No, I don't want to be. And you aren't so ill that you can't come with me.

ADOLF. Why do you always want to have me with you? Do you feel more at ease then?

TEKLA. I don't know what you mean.

ADOLF. That's what you always say when you know I mean something you don't like.

TEKLA. Really? What is it I don't like now?

ADOLF. Stop it, will you! Don't start that again! Goodbye for the moment. And think what you are doing.

Exit ADOLF *by the door to the verandah, turning to the right.*

TEKLA *is left alone.*

After a moment GUSTAV *enters and goes straight to the table, as if looking for a newspaper. He pretends not to see* TEKLA. *She is agitated but controls herself.*

TEKLA. Is it you?

GUSTAV. It is I. Please excuse me.

TEKLA. How did you get here?

GUSTAV. By land. But I'm not going to stay. I . . .

TEKLA. Do stay. . . . Well, it's been a long time.

GUSTAV. Yes, a long time.

TEKLA. You have changed a lot.

GUSTAV. And you are as charming as ever. And even younger. But you must excuse me. I am not going to spoil your happiness by my presence. If I had known you would be here, I should never . . .

TEKLA. If you don't think it's improper, I should like you to stay.

GUSTAV. There's nothing against it from my point of view, but I'm afraid whatever I say is bound to offend you.

TEKLA. Sit down for a moment. You won't offend me. You have that rare quality—you always had it—of tact and courtesy. . . .

GUSTAV. You flatter me. But one can't expect your husband to regard my qualities so leniently.

TEKLA. As a matter of fact, he was expressing his sympathy for you just now.

GUSTAV. Oh? Well, of course everything vanishes in time—like one's name cut in a tree. Even hatred can't stay in one's mind for ever.

TEKLA. He has never disliked you. How could he when he's never seen you? And as for me, I've always dreamt of seeing you two once as friends, or at least of seeing you meet once in my presence, shake hands, and part.

GUSTAV. And it has been my secret desire to see if she whom I loved better than my life was in truly good hands. I have certainly heard good accounts of him and I know his work well, but even so I should have liked, before I grew old, to take his hand and look into his eyes and beg him to guard the treasure providence has put into his keeping. At the same time I should have liked to put an end to the instinctive hatred there was bound to be between us, and give my soul some peace and humility to live by for the rest of my sorrowful days.

TEKLA. You have spoken my very thoughts. You have understood me. Thank you for that.

GUSTAV. Oh, I am a poor man—I was too insignificant ever to put you in the shade. The monotony of my life, the drudgery of my work, and the narrowness of my horizon were not for your adventurous spirit. I realise that, but you, who have studied the human soul so deeply, must realise what it cost me to confess this to myself.

TEKLA. It is noble, it is great to be able to acknowledge one's own weaknesses, and not everyone is capable of it. *Sighs.* But yours was always an honest, faithful, trustworthy nature—which I respected, although . . .

GUSTAV. I wasn't like that then—not at that time—but suffering purifies one, sorrow ennobles one—and I have suffered.

TEKLA. Poor Gustav! Can you forgive me? Tell me. Can you?

GUSTAV. Forgive you? What are you saying? It is for me to ask your forgiveness.

TEKLA, *fencing.* Why, I believe we're both crying. At our age!

GUSTAV, *parrying.* Our age! Ah yes, I am old! But you get younger and younger.

Unobtrusively he sits down on the chair, left, whereupon TEKLA *seats herself on the sofa.*

TEKLA. Do you think so?

GUSTAV. And you know how to dress.

TEKLA. I learnt that from you. Don't you remember how you found the best colours for me?

GUSTAV. No.

TEKLA. Yes. Don't you remember? Hm, I even remember a time when you were cross with me if I didn't wear some touch of scarlet.

GUSTAV. I wasn't cross. I was never cross with you.

TEKLA. Oh yes, you were! When you tried to teach me how to think. Don't you remember that? I couldn't do it at all.

GUSTAV. Of course you could think. Everyone can do that. And now you are quite intelligent—in your writing at least.

TEKLA *is embarrassed and rushes on with the conversation.*

TEKLA. It's delightful to see you again anyway, dear Gustav. Specially in such a peaceful way.

GUSTAV. Well, I never was exactly rowdy. You always had a peaceful time with me.

TEKLA. Yes, a bit too peaceful.

GUSTAV. Oh! But you see that's how I thought you wanted me to be. That's how it seemed when we were engaged.

TEKLA. One doesn't know what one wants then. Besides, I'd been told by Mamma to make a good impression on you.

GUSTAV. Well, you live in a whirl now. The artistic life is always dazzling, and your husband doesn't seem to be exactly lethargic.

TEKLA. One can have too much of a good thing, you know.

GUSTAV, *once again changing his tactics.* I say! I do believe you are still wearing my earrings.

TEKLA, *embarrassed.* Well, why shouldn't I? We've never quarrelled—so I thought I might wear them as a token . . . as a reminder that we were not enemies. . . . Besides, you know, it's impossible to get earrings like this nowadays. *She takes one off.*

GUSTAV. That's all very well, but what does your husband say about it?

TEKLA. Why should I care what he says?

GUSTAV. Don't you care? But you do him a wrong by that. It could make him ridiculous.

TEKLA, *quickly, as if to herself.* He is that already.

She has difficulty in putting her earring on again.

GUSTAV *rises.*

GUSTAV. Perhaps you'll let me help you . . .

TEKLA. Thank you so much.

Putting the earring on, GUSTAV *pinches her ear.*

GUSTAV. Supposing your husband could see us now!

TEKLA. Yes, what a wail there would be!

GUSTAV. He's very jealous then?

TEKLA. Jealous? I should say he is.

Sounds from the adjacent room.

GUSTAV. Who has that room next door?

TEKLA. I don't know. . . . Well, tell me how you are getting along and what you are doing.

GUSTAV. Tell me how *you* are getting along.

Trying to think how to answer, TEKLA *inadvertently uncovers the wax figure.*

I say! Whoever's that? By Jove, it's you!

TEKLA. I don't think so.

GUSTAV. Well, it's just like you.

TEKLA, *cynically.* In your view.

GUSTAV. That reminds me of the story . . . "How could Your Majesty see that?"

TEKLA *bursts out laughing.*

TEKLA. You're impossible! Do you know any new stories?

GUSTAV. No, but surely you should.

TEKLA. Oh, I never hear anything funny now!

GUSTAV. Is he prudish?

TEKLA. Well—in speech he is.

GUSTAV. But not in—other ways?

TEKLA. He's not well just now.

GUSTAV. Poor dear! But little brother shouldn't go poking his nose into other people's wasps'-nests.

TEKLA, *laughing.* You're quite impossible!

GUSTAV. Do you remember once, when we were newly married, we stayed in this very room? Eh? It was furnished differently then. There was a chest of drawers against that wall, and the bed was over there . . .

TEKLA. Stop it!

GUSTAV. Look at me!

TEKLA. Well, that I can do.

They gaze at one another.

GUSTAV. Do you think one can forget something that has made a very deep impression?

TEKLA. No. Memories have tremendous power. Specially youthful ones.

GUSTAV. Do you remember when I first met you? You were a charming little girl—a small slate on which parents and governesses had made some scrawls, which I had to wipe off. Then I wrote new texts to suit my own ideas, until you felt your slate was full. That's why, you see, I shouldn't like to be in your husband's place—but that's his business. It's also why I have so much pleasure in seeing you again. Our thoughts match so well. Sitting here talking with you is like opening bottles of old wine of my own tapping. Yes, I have my own wine again, but it has matured. And now that I have a fancy to marry again, I have purposely chosen a young girl, whom I can educate to my own way of thinking. For the woman, you see, is the man's child, and if she is not, he becomes hers, and that makes a topsy-turvy world.

TEKLA. You're going to marry again?

GUSTAV. Yes, I mean to tempt fortune once more, but this time I shall harness the mare better, so she won't bolt.

TEKLA. Is she pretty?

GUSTAV. To me she is. But I may be too old. And curiously enough, now that chance has brought you and me together once more, I am beginning to doubt if it is possible to play that game again.

TEKLA. How do you mean?

GUSTAV. I feel that my roots are still in your soil, and the old wounds are opening. You are a dangerous woman, Tekla!

TEKLA. Oh! But my young husband says I shan't be able to make any more conquests.

GUSTAV. In other words, he no longer loves you.

TEKLA. I don't understand what he means by love.

GUSTAV. You have played hide-and-seek so long that now you can't find each other. That's what happens. You have gone on playing the innocent until now he doesn't dare. . . . Yes, you see, change has its disadvantages. It has its disadvantages.

TEKLA. Is that a reproach?

GUSTAV. By no means. To a certain extent, whatever happens has to happen. If it didn't happen, something else would. This did happen and there it is.

TEKLA. What an enlightened man you are! I have never met anyone with whom I so much liked exchanging ideas. You are so free from moralising and preaching, and make so few demands on people, that one feels at ease in your company. You know, I'm jealous of your wife to be.

GUSTAV. You know, I'm jealous of your husband.

TEKLA, *rising*. And now we must part. For ever.

GUSTAV. Yes, we must part. But not without taking leave. Eh?

TEKLA, *uneasily*. No.

GUSTAV, *following her*. Yes! We must take leave of each other. We must drown our memories in an intoxication so deep that when we wake we shall have forgotten those memories. There is such an intoxication, you know. *Puts his arm round her.* You have been dragged down by a sick soul who has infected you with his own disease. I will breathe new life into you. I will make your talent bloom again like an autumn rose. I will . . .

TWO LADIES *in travelling dress come on to the verandah. Seeing the couple, they look surprised, point at them, laugh, and go off.*

TEKLA, *freeing herself.* Who was that?

GUSTAV, *indifferently.* Some visitors.

TEKLA. Go away! I'm frightened of you.

GUSTAV. Why?

TEKLA. You take away my soul.

GUSTAV. And give you mine in exchange. Anyhow, you haven't got a soul. That's just an illusion.

TEKLA. You say the most impertinent things in a way that makes it impossible to be angry with you.

GUSTAV. That's because you know I have the first mortgage. Now tell me. When and where?

TEKLA. No. It wouldn't be fair on him. He really does still love me, and I don't want to do any more harm.

GUSTAV. He doesn't love you. Do you want proof of it?

TEKLA. How could you give me that?

GUSTAV *picks up the pieces of photograph from the floor.*

GUSTAV. Here you are. See for yourself.

TEKLA. Oh, this is scandalous!

GUSTAV. You see for yourself. So . . . when and where?

TEKLA. The deceitful wretch!

GUSTAV. When?

TEKLA. He is going tonight by the eight o'clock boat.

GUSTAV. Then . . .

TEKLA. Nine o'clock.

Noises from the room are heard.

Whoever can have taken that room and be making such a din?

GUSTAV. Let's see. *Peers through the key-hole.* A table has been overturned and a water carafe smashed. That's all. Perhaps they have shut up a dog in there. . . . Nine o'clock then.

TEKLA. Very well. He has only himself to blame. . . . To think of him being so false, when he's always preaching honesty and making me tell the truth. . . . But wait a moment . . . How was it? . . . He received me rather coldly—he didn't come down to the jetty—and then he said something about the youths on the boat, which I pretended not to take in. . . . But how could he have known about them? . . . Wait a minute . . . After that he began philosophising about women—and you seemed to be haunting him. . . . And then he talked about becoming a sculptor, and how sculpture was the art of today—just as you used to say once.

GUSTAV. No, really?

TEKLA. No, really! Ah, now I understand! Now I begin to see what an absolute monster you are. You have been here stabbing him to death. It was you who had been sitting on the sofa. It was you who made him think he had epilepsy and must live as a celibate—and that he must show he was a man by taking a stand against his wife. Yes, it was you! How long have you been here?

GUSTAV. I have been here for a week.

TEKLA. So it *was* you I saw on the boat.

GUSTAV. It was me.

TEKLA. And then you thought you would trap me.

GUSTAV. I have done so.

TEKLA. Not yet.

GUSTAV. Yes.

TEKLA. You stole on my lamb like a wolf. You came here with a fiendish scheme to destroy my happiness, and you were carrying it out when my eyes were opened and I foiled it.

GUSTAV. It wasn't quite as you say. This is what actually happened. I admit I had a secret hope things would go wrong with you, but I was pretty certain no interference on my part would be needed. Besides, I was too much taken up with other things to have time for intriguing. Then, when I happened to be away and at a loose end, I saw you on the boat with those young men, and I decided the time had come to have a look at you. I came here, and your lamb immediately threw himself into the arms of the wolf. I won his sympathy through a kind of reflex action I won't be so discourteous as to try and explain. At first I was sorry for him, as he seemed to be in the same fix as I once was. But then he began to probe old wounds—the book, you know, and the idiot—and I was seized with the desire to pull him to pieces and mix the pieces up so thoroughly that he could never be put together again. And thanks to your conscientious groundwork, I succeeded. But I still had you to deal with. You were the mainspring of the works and had to be twisted to bits. What a buzz! When I came in here, I didn't really know what I was going to say. I had various schemes, but as in chess, my play depended on your moves. One thing led to another, chance helped, and so I had you ditched. Now you're caught.

TEKLA. No.

GUSTAV. Yes, you are. The last thing you wanted has happened. The world—in the guise of two lady travellers, whom I did not send for, being no intriguer—the world has seen you reconciled with your former husband, creeping repentantly back into his faithful arms. Isn't that enough?

TEKLA. It should be enough for your revenge. But tell me, you who are so enlightened and just, how can you, who think whatever happens has to happen and we are not free to act . . .

GUSTAV, *correcting her.* Not entirely free.

TEKLA. It's the same thing.

GUSTAV. No.

TEKLA. . . . how can you, who hold me guiltless since I was driven by my nature and the circumstances to behave as I did, how can you believe you have any cause for revenge?

GUSTAV. For that very reason. Because my nature and the circumstances drove me to seek revenge. Which makes it quits, doesn't it? But do you know why you two were bound to get the worst of it in this fight?

TEKLA *looks scornful.*

And why you let yourselves be tricked? Because I'm stronger than you and wiser too. It's you who have been the idiot—and so has he. And now you can see that one isn't necessarily an idiot because one doesn't write novels or paint pictures. Bear that in mind.

TEKLA. Have you no feelings at all?

GUSTAV. None. That's why I can think, you know, a process of which you have little experience. And act—as you have recently discovered.

TEKLA. All this merely because I wounded your vanity!

GUSTAV. There's no *merely* about that. You'd better stop wounding people's vanity. It's their most vulnerable spot.

TEKLA. You vindictive creature! Shame on you!

GUSTAV. You wanton creature! Shame on you!

TEKLA. It's my nature, isn't it?

GUSTAV. It's *my* nature, isn't it? One should learn something of human nature in general before giving one's own nature free rein. Otherwise one may get hurt, and then what a wailing and gnashing of teeth!

TEKLA. Can't you ever forgive?

GUSTAV. Yes. I have forgiven you.

TEKLA. Have you?

GUSTAV. Certainly. Have I lifted a finger against you in all these years? No. And now I only came here to have a look at you—and then you went to pieces. Have I reproached you or moralised or preached? No. I played a bit of a joke on your spouse and that was enough to burst his bubble. And now here am I, the plaintiff, defending myself. Tekla, have you nothing to reproach yourself with?

TEKLA. Nothing at all. Christians say our actions are ruled by providence, and others call it fate. So we're guiltless, aren't we?

GUSTAV. Up to a point, yes. But there's always a place where the guilt creeps in. And the creditors present themselves sooner or later. Guiltless but responsible. Guiltless before Him, who no longer exists. Responsible to oneself and one's fellow creatures.

TEKLA. So you came here to dun me.

GUSTAV. I came here to recover what you had stolen, not what you had had as a gift. You stole my honour and I could only regain it by taking yours. Wasn't that my right?

TEKLA. Honour! Hm! Well, are you satisfied now?

GUSTAV. Yes, I am satisfied. *Rings the bell.*

TEKLA. And now you are going home to your fiancée.

GUSTAV. I have no fiancée. And I shall never have one. And I am not going home, for I have no home. Nor do I want one.

A WAITER *enters.*

Will you bring my bill, please. I am leaving by the eight o'clock boat.

The WAITER *bows and goes out.*

TEKLA. Without atonement?

GUSTAV. Atonement? You use so many words that have lost their meaning. Atonement? Are we perhaps all three to live together? It's you who should do the atoning, by making good my losses—but you can't. You did nothing but take, and what you took you have devoured, so you can't return it. Will it satisfy you if I say: Forgive me for your having clawed my heart to pieces. Forgive me for your having disgraced me. Forgive me for having been the daily laughing-stock of my pupils for seven years. Forgive me for setting you free from the domination of your parents, for releasing you from the tyranny of ignorance and superstition, for setting you over my house, for giving you friends and a position, for making a woman of the mere child you were. Forgive me, as I forgive you! . . . So, I have cancelled my note of hand. Now go and settle your account with the other one.

TEKLA. What have you done with him? I'm beginning to suspect—something terrible.

GUSTAV. Done with him? Why, do you love him?

TEKLA. Yes.

GUSTAV. Just now it was me. Was that true?

TEKLA. It was true.

GUSTAV. Do you know what you are then?

TEKLA. You despise me?

GUSTAV. I pity you. It's a trait—I don't say a fault but a trait—which has disastrous consequences. Poor Tekla! Do you know I feel almost remorseful, although I am as free from guilt as—as you are. But perhaps you will enjoy knowing just how I felt that time. . . . Do you know where your husband is?

TEKLA. I think now I do know. . . . He is in that room there. And he has heard everything. And seen everything. And he who sees his familiar spirit dies.

ADOLF *appears in the verandah doorway. He is white as a corpse. There is a bleeding scratch on one cheek. His eyes are staring without expression and he is frothing at the mouth.*

GUSTAV, *backing*. Well, there he is! Settle up with him now and see if he is as generous as I have been. . . . Goodbye.

GUSTAV *goes towards the other room and stops.*

TEKLA *runs to* ADOLF *with arms outstretched.*

TEKLA. Adolf!

ADOLF *leans against the verandah door and collapses on the floor.*

TEKLA *throws herself across his body, caressing him.*

TEKLA. Adolf! My darling child! Are you still alive? Oh speak, speak! Forgive your wicked Tekla! Forgive, forgive, forgive! You must answer me, little brother. Can you hear? . . . No, O my God, he doesn't hear! He is dead. O God in heaven! O God, help us, help us!

GUSTAV. She really does love him too. Poor creature!

THE STRONGER

THE STRONGER was written in 1889, when Strindberg was still writing plays for Antoine's Théâtre Libre, and hoping to form an experimental theatre of his own in Stockholm. This project was not realised until 1907, when THE STRONGER had its première with one of Strindberg's new Chamber Plays, THE BURNED SITE. Since then it has been performed often and in many countries, and is acclaimed as a jewel among monologues.

E. S.

Characters

MRS. X., *actress, married*
MISS Y., *actress, unmarried*
A WAITRESS

Scene: A corner of a ladies' café (in Stockholm in the eighteen eighties). Two small wrought-iron tables, a red plush settee and a few chairs.

MISS Y. *is sitting with a half-empty bottle of beer on the table before her, reading an illustrated weekly which from time to time she exchanges for another.*

MRS. X. *enters, wearing a winter hat and coat and carrying a decorative Japanese basket.*

MRS. X. Why, Millie, my dear, how are you? Sitting here all alone on Christmas Eve like some poor bachelor.

MISS Y. *looks up from her magazine, nods, and continues to read.*

MRS. X. You know it makes me feel really sad to see you. Alone. Alone in a café and on Christmas Eve of all times. It makes me feel as sad as when once in Paris I saw a wedding party at a restaurant. The bride was reading a comic paper and the bridegroom playing billiards with the witnesses. Ah me, I said to myself, with such a beginning how will it go, and how will it end? He was playing billiards on his wedding day! And she, you were going to say, was reading a comic paper on hers. But that's not quite the same.

A WAITRESS *brings a cup of chocolate to* MRS. X. *and goes out.*

MRS. X. Do you know, Amelia, I really believe now you would have done better to stick to him. Don't forget I was the first who told you to forgive him. Do you remember? Then you would be married now and have a home. Think how happy you were that Christmas when you stayed with your fiancé's people in the country. How warmly you spoke of domestic happiness! You really quite longed to

Note: Translator's addition to scene bracketed. First mention of Miss Y. and Mrs. X. reversed.

be out of the theatre. Yes, Amelia dear, home is best—next best to the stage, and as for children—but you couldn't know anything about that.

MISS Y.'s *expression is disdainful.* MRS. X. *sips a few spoonfuls of chocolate, then opens her basket and displays some Christmas presents.*

MRS. X. Now you must see what I have bought for my little chicks. *Takes out a doll.* Look at this. That's for Lisa. Do you see how she can roll her eyes and turn her head. Isn't she lovely? And here's a toy pistol for Maja.* *She loads the pistol and shoots it at* MISS Y. *who appears frightened.*

MRS. X. Were you scared? Did you think I was going to shoot you? Really, I didn't think you'd believe that of me. Now if *you* were to shoot *me* it wouldn't be so surprising, for after all I did get in your way, and I know you never forget it—although I was entirely innocent. You still think I intrigued to get you out of the Grand Theatre, but I didn't. I didn't, however much you think I did. Well, it's no good talking, you will believe it was me . . . *Takes out a pair of embroidered slippers.* And these are for my old man, with tulips on them that I embroidered myself. As a matter of fact I hate tulips, but he has to have tulips on everything.

MISS Y. *looks up, irony and curiosity in her face.*

MRS. X., *putting one hand in each slipper.* Look what small feet Bob has, hasn't he? And you ought to see the charming way he walks—you've never seen him in slippers, have you?

MISS Y. *laughs.*

MRS. X. Look, I'll show you. *She makes the slippers walk across the table, and* MISS Y. *laughs again.*

MRS. X. But when he gets angry, look, he stamps his foot like this. "Those damn girls who can never learn how to make coffee! Blast! That silly idiot hasn't trimmed the lamp properly!" Then there's a draught under the door and his

*Pronounced Maya.

feet get cold. "Hell, it's freezing, and the damn fools can't even keep the stove going!" *She rubs the sole of one slipper against the instep of the other.* MISS Y. *roars with laughter.*

MRS. X. And then he comes home and has to hunt for his slippers, which Mary has pushed under the bureau . . . Well, perhaps it's not right to make fun of one's husband like this. He's sweet anyhow, and a good, dear husband. You ought to have had a husband like him, Amelia. What are you laughing at? What is it? Eh? And, you see, I know he is faithful to me. Yes, I know it. He told me himself—what *are* you giggling at?—that while I was on tour in Norway that horrible Frederica came and tried to seduce him. Can you imagine anything more abominable? *Pause.* I'd have scratched her eyes out if she had come around while I was at home. *Pause.* I'm glad Bob told me about it himself, so I didn't just hear it from gossip. *Pause.* And, as a matter of fact, Frederica wasn't the only one. I can't think why, but all the women in the Company* seem to be crazy about my husband. They must think his position gives him some say in who is engaged at the Theatre. Perhaps you have run after him yourself? I don't trust you very far, but I know he has never been attracted by you, and you always seemed to have some sort of grudge against him, or so I felt. *Pause. They look at one another guardedly.*

MRS. X. Do come and spend Christmas Eve with us tonight, Amelia—just to show that you're not offended with us, or anyhow not with me. I don't know why, but it seems specially unpleasant not to be friends with you. Perhaps it's because I did get in your way that time . . . *slowly* or—I don't know—really, I don't know at all why it is. *Pause.* MISS Y. *gazes curiously at* MRS. X.

MRS. X., *thoughtfully.* It was so strange when we were getting to know one another. Do you know, when we first met, I was frightened of you, so frightened I didn't dare let you out of my sight. I arranged all my goings and

*"In the Company" translator's addition.

comings to be near you. I dared not be your enemy, so I became your friend. But when you came to our home, I always had an uneasy feeling, because I saw my husband didn't like you, and that irritated me—like when a dress doesn't fit. I did all I could to make him be nice to you, but it was no good—until you went and got engaged. Then you became such tremendous friends that at first it looked as if you only dared show your real feelings then —when you were safe. And then, let me see, how was it after that? I wasn't jealous—that's queer. And I remember at the christening, when you were the godmother, I told him to kiss you. He did, and you were so upset . . . As a matter of fact I didn't notice that then . . . I didn't think about it afterwards either . . . I've never thought about it—until *now! Rises abruptly.* Why don't you say something? You haven't said a word all this time. You've just let me go on talking. You have sat there with your eyes drawing all these thoughts out of me—they were there in me like silk in a cocoon—thoughts . . . Mistaken thoughts? Let me think. Why did you break off your engagement? Why did you never come to our house after that? Why don't you want to come to us tonight?

MISS Y. *makes a motion, as if about to speak.*

MRS. X. No. You don't need to say anything, for now I see it all. That was why—and why—and why. Yes. Yes, that's why it was. Yes, yes, all the pieces fit together now. That's it. I won't sit at the same table as you. *Moves her things to the other table.* That's why I have to embroider tulips, which I loathe, on his slippers—because you liked tulips. *Throws the slippers on the floor.* That's why we have to spend the summer on the lake—because you couldn't bear the seaside. That's why my son had to be called Eskil—because it was your father's name. That's why I had to wear your colours, read your books, eat the dishes you liked, drink your drinks—your chocolate, for instance. That's why—oh my God, it's terrible to think of, terrible! Everything, everything came to me from you—even your passions. Your soul bored into mine like a worm into an apple, and ate and ate and burrowed and burrowed, till nothing was left but the skin and a little black mould. I wanted to fly from you, but I couldn't. You were there like a snake, your black eyes fascinating me. When I spread my wings, they only dragged me down. I lay in the water with my feet tied together, and the harder I worked my arms, the deeper I sank—down, down, till I reached the bottom, where you lay in waiting like a giant crab to catch me in your claws—and now here I am. Oh how I hate you! I hate you, I hate you! And you just go on sitting there, silent, calm, indifferent, not caring whether the moon is new or full, if it's Christmas or New Year, if other people are happy or unhappy. You don't know how to hate or to love. You just sit there without moving—like a cat* at a mouse-hole. You can't drag your prey out, you can't chase it, but you can out-stay it. Here you sit in your corner—you know they call it the rat-trap after you—reading the papers to see if anyone's ruined or wretched or been thrown out of the Company. Here you sit sizing up your victims and weighing your chances—like a pilot his shipwrecks for the salvage. *Pause.* Poor Amelia! Do you know, I couldn't be more sorry for you. I know you are miserable, miserable like some wounded creature, and vicious because you are wounded. I can't be angry with you. I should like to be, but after all you are the small one—and as for your affair with Bob, that doesn't worry me in the least. Why should it matter to me? And if you, or somebody else taught me to drink chocolate, what's the difference? *Drinks a spoonful. Smugly.* Chocolate is very wholesome anyhow. And if I learnt from you how to dress, *tant mieux!*—that only gave me a stronger hold over my husband, and you have lost what I gained. Yes, to judge from various signs, I think you have now lost him. Of course, you meant me to walk out, as you once did, and which you're now regretting. But I won't do that, you may be sure. One shouldn't be narrow-minded, you know. And why should nobody else want what I have? *Pause.* Perhaps, my dear, taking everything into consideration, at this moment it is I who

*In Swedish, "stork."

am the stronger. You never got anything from me, you just gave away—from yourself. And now, like the thief in the night, when you woke up I had what you had lost. Why was it then that everything you touched became worthless and sterile? You couldn't keep a man's love—for all your tulips and your passions—but I could. You couldn't learn the art of living from your books—but I learnt it. You bore no little Eskil, although that was your father's name. *Pause.* And why is it you are silent—everywhere, always silent? Yes, I used to think this was strength, but perhaps it was because you hadn't anything to say, because you couldn't think of anything. *Rises and picks up the slippers.* Now I am going home, taking the tulips with me—*your* tulips. You couldn't learn from others, you couldn't bend, and so you broke like a dry stick. I did not. Thank you, Amelia, for all your good lessons. Thank you for teaching my husband how to love. Now I am going home—to love him.

Exit.

THE BOND

FOREWORD

The Bond was written in 1892, a year after Strindberg and his first wife were granted the year's judicial separation which preceded their divorce, and cynically portrays the proceedings.

Strindberg was now forty-three. He had returned to Sweden, after living abroad for many years, and having won fame with *The Father* and *Miss Julie* was engaged in writing a number of biting, naturalistic one-act plays for the Intimate Theatre he was eager to establish. All these short plays depict the horror and futility of Strindberg's own life, and *The Bond,* with its caricature of a Court of Justice, is perhaps the best.

E. S.

Characters

THE DISTRICT JUDGE, *aged 27*
THE PASTOR, *aged 60*
THE BARON, *aged 42*
THE BARONESS, *aged 40*
THE TWELVE JURYMEN
THE SHERIFF
THE VILLAGE CONSTABLE
THE ADVOCATE
FARMER ALEXANDERSSON
THE SERVANT GIRL, ALMA JONSSON
THE DAIRYMAID
THE THRESHER
THE NOTARY
THE PUBLIC

Scene: A Court of Justice in a Swedish village in the 1880's.

At the back, a door and window. Through the window are seen the churchyard and belfry.

To the right, a door. To the left, the Bench in the form of a desk on a dais, the desk bearing a gilt emblem of the Sword and Scales. On both sides of the Bench, chairs and tables for the Jury. In the middle of the floor, benches for the public.

The walls are formed by fixed cupboards, on the doors of which appear tables of tariffs and public notices.

The Sheriff and the Village Constable are preparing the Court for a Session.

SHERIFF. Did you ever see so many people at the Summer Assizes before?

CONSTABLE. No, not since we had the great Alsjö murder fifteen years ago.

SHERIFF. Aye, and this is something of an affair, which may be just as good as the murder of both parents. It's bad enough in any case for the Baron and Baroness to be getting a divorce; but when it comes to the relatives starting to wrangle over the property and estates—well one can imagine the fat will be in the fire! It just needed them to quarrel over their only child and King Solomon himself couldn't have given judgment.

CONSTABLE. Yes, what are the rights of the case? Some say one thing and some another; but surely somebody must be to blame.

SHERIFF. That's none so certain. Sometimes it's nobody's fault when two people fall out, and occasionally only one of them is to blame for the quarrel. My old shrew at home, for instance, she goes and has a big quarrel by herself when I'm not there, so they tell me. However, this isn't just a quarrel; it's a proper legal case, and in most of those there's one party prosecuting, that's to say the injured party, and the other party, the guilty, defending. Which is guilty in this case, it is not easy to say, for both parties are prosecuting and both defending.

CONSTABLE. Yes, yes, these are queer times! The women seem to have gone mad. My old woman has a way of saying that if there were any justice in the world I should bear the children—as if the Lord didn't know how to make his own creatures. And then I get long stories about how she, too, is a human being, as if I hadn't known that before or had said anything to the contrary, and about her having no mind to be my servant—when really I am her drudge.

SHERIFF. Ah, so you have that trouble in your home, too! Mine is always reading a newspaper which she gets from the manor, and so one day she tells me as something wonderful that a Dalecarlian girl has started bricklaying, and another time that an old woman has set upon her sick husband and beaten him. I don't know what things are coming to; but she seems to be angry with me just because I am a man.

CONSTABLE. Yes, it's a queer business altogether. *Offers snuff.* Lovely weather. The rye's standing like a pelt, and we got through the frosty nights capitally.

SHERIFF. I haven't any crops myself, and good years are bad years for me: no distraints, no auctions. Do you know the new judge who is holding the Assizes today?

CONSTABLE. No, but he appears to be a young gentleman who has just passed his examination and is now holding his first Assizes.

SHERIFF. And he is said to be rather religious too. Hm!

CONSTABLE. Hm, hm! The Assize sermon is lasting a long time today.

The SHERIFF *lays out a great Bible on the Notary's table and twelve small ones on the Jurymen's.*

SHERIFF. It can't be very long now before it's over. They will soon have been at it a whole hour.

CONSTABLE. He's a beggar for preaching, the parson, when once he gets started. *Pause.* Are the couple appearing in person?

SHERIFF. Both of them. So there'll be no end of a row.

A bell rings in the belfry outside.

Ah, there now, it's over! Just dust the table a bit, and then I suppose we can begin.

CONSTABLE. And is there ink in the inkpots?

Enter, back, the BARON *and the* BARONESS.

BARON, *in an undertone to the* BARONESS. Then before we separate for this year, we are entirely agreed on all points. In the first place: no recriminations in Court?

BARONESS. Do you suppose I should want to stand here and lay bare all the details of our life together, before a pack of curious peasants?

BARON. Good! Further: you keep the child during the year of separation, with the proviso that it visits me whenever I please, and that it is brought up according to the principles I have laid down and you have approved?

BARONESS. Exactly.

BARON. And that I, during the year of separation, allow three thousand crowns from the revenues of the estate for you and the child?

BARONESS. Exactly.

BARON. Then I have nothing more to add except to bid you farewell. Why we are parting, only you and I know, and for our son's sake no one else must know. But I beg you, also for his sake, not to start any dispute, which might provoke us into blacking his parents' name. In any case he will suffer enough out in the cruel world, from the fact that his parents are divorced.

BARONESS. I shall start no dispute so long as I may keep my child.

BARON. Then let us concentrate our attention solely upon

the child's welfare, and forget what has been between us. And consider one more point: if we wrangle about the child and challenge each other's claim to have charge of it, the Judge can order it to be taken from us both, and handed over to pietists to bring up in hatred and contempt of its parents.

BARONESS. That is not possible!

BARON. Well, my dear, it's the law.

BARONESS. It's a stupid law.

BARON. That may be, but it is valid and applies even to you.

BARONESS. It's unnatural. And I should never submit to it.

BARON. Nor need you, since we have done with recriminations. We have never agreed before; but on this point at least we are at one, that we should separate without discord. *To the* SHERIFF. May the Baroness be permitted to wait in that room?

SHERIFF. Walk in, please.

The BARON *accompanies the* BARONESS *to the door, right, then goes out himself through the door, back.*

Enter back, the ADVOCATE, *the* SERVANT GIRL, *the* DAIRYMAID, *the* THRESHER.

ADVOCATE, *to the* SERVANT GIRL. Look here, my girl. I do not for a moment doubt that you did steal; but, inasmuch as your master has no evidence of it, you are innocent. And as your master called you a thief in the presence of two witnesses, he is guilty of slander. So now you are plaintiff and he defendant. Now remember this rule: a guilty party's first duty is to deny.

SERVANT GIRL. Yes, but you said just now I wasn't the guilty party, but the master was.

ADVOCATE. You are the guilty party inasmuch as you have stolen, but inasmuch as you have asked for counsel, it is my clear duty to whitewash you and to have your master convicted. Therefore, and for the last time, deny! *To the Witnesses.* And you witnesses, what evidence are you going to give? Listen to me: a good witness must stick to the facts. Note well, therefore, that the question is not whether Alma stole or not; the question is only whether Alexandersson said that she stole; for, mark this, Alexandersson hasn't the right to substantiate his assertion, and we have. Why, the devil only knows! But that does not concern you. So then: your tongues between your teeth and your fingers on the Bible!

DAIRYMAID. Lord Jesus, I'm that scared I don't know what to say!

THRESHER. Say what I say and you'll tell no lies.

Enter, back, the DISTRICT JUDGE *and the* PASTOR.

JUDGE. Thank you for your sermon, Rector.

PASTOR. Don't mention it, Judge.

JUDGE. Well, as you know, this is my first Assizes. I have really been frightened of this career into which I have been thrown almost against my will. For one thing, law is so imperfect, the course of justice so uncertain, and human nature so full of falsehood and dissimulation, that I have often wondered how a judge can have the courage to pronounce a definite opinion. And today you have reawakened my misgivings.

PASTOR. To be conscientious is indeed a duty; but it does not do to be over-sensitive. And since all else on earth is imperfect, we can hardly expect judges and their judgments to be infallible.

JUDGE. That may be, but it does not prevent me from feeling an immense responsibility when I hold men's fates in my hands, and when a word from me may affect future generations. I am thinking now especially of this divorce suit between the Baron and his wife, and I must ask you, who gave the husband and wife two warnings in the Church Council, what your opinion is of their mutual relations and relative guilt.

PASTOR. That is to say, you will either make me the judge or base your judgment upon my testimony. I can only refer you to the minutes of the Church Council.

JUDGE. Oh, I know the minutes; but it is just what does not appear in them that I need to know.

PASTOR. What accusations the pair brought against each other in private examination is my secret. Besides, how am I to know which of them was speaking the truth and which lying? I can only say to you, as I said to them—that I have no reason to believe the one more than the other.

JUDGE. But surely you have been able to form some opinion during these proceedings?

PASTOR. I came to one conclusion after hearing one side, and I came to another after hearing the other side. In a word, I cannot have any fixed opinion in this matter.

JUDGE. But I have to pronounce a definite opinion, I who know nothing at all.

PASTOR. That is a judge's heavy task, which I should never be able to carry out.

JUDGE. But surely there are witnesses to be called, evidence to be produced?

PASTOR. No, the pair will not accuse one another in public. And besides, two false witnesses are complete evidence and one perjuror equally good. Do you suppose I would base my judgment upon maids' gossip, the chatter of jealous neighbours, or the spite of interested relatives?

JUDGE. You are a terrible sceptic, Pastor!

PASTOR. One becomes so when one has lived sixty years, and has held a cure of souls for forty. Falsehood persists like original sin, and I believe that all men are liars. In childhood one lies from fear; as one grows older from interest, necessity, the instinct of self-preservation; and there are those, too, who lie out of pure human kindness. In the present case, as regards this pair, I fancy you will have great difficulty in making out which of them is speaking the more truthfully, and I only wish to warn you not to let any prejudice come upon you unawares. You yourself are newly married and under the spell of a young woman; you may therefore easily be swayed in favour of a young and charming lady, who is an unhappy wife and, furthermore, a mother. On the other hand, you yourself have recently become a father and, as such, cannot but be moved by the father's impending separation from his only child. Beware of sympathy with either side, for sympathy with one is cruelty towards the other.

JUDGE. There is one thing, however, that lightens my task, and that is that the pair are agreed upon the main point.

PASTOR. Don't rely upon that; they all say so, but when they come before the Court, the thing bursts into a blaze. It only needs a spark to set it alight. Here comes the Jury. Good-bye for the moment. I will remain, although I do not have to appear.

Enter, back, the twelve JURYMEN. *The* SHERIFF *rings a bell in the open doorway, back. The members of the Court take their seats. People pour in.*

JUDGE. In accordance with the provisions of the Penal Code, relating to the Peace of Assize, in its eleventh chapter, fifth, sixth and eighth paragraphs, I hereby declare the proceedings of the Court open. *Whispers to the* NOTARY, *then aloud:* The newly elected jury will please take the oath.

The JURYMEN *rise, holding their Bibles.*

NOTARY, *followed in turn by the* JURYMEN.

I, Alexander Eklund,
I, Emanuel Wickberg,
I, Karl Johan Sjöberg,
I, Erik Otto Boman,
I, Erenfrid Söderberg,
I, Olof Andersson of Vik,
I, Karl Peter Andersson of Berga,
I, Axel Vallin,
I, Anders Erik Ruth,
I, Sven Oskar Erlin,
I, August Alexander Vass,
I, Ludwig Östman

JURYMEN, *together, in time, in a low tone.* promise and swear by God and His Holy Gospel, that I will and shall, to the best of my understanding and conscience, in all verdicts do justice, not less to the poor than to the rich, and will judge according to the law of God and of Sweden, and as the law directs; (*in a higher tone and louder voices*) never to distort law or to favour wrong for kinship's sake, by blood or marriage, friendship's sake, envy, illwill or fear, nor yet for bribes and gifts or any other consideration whatever, and not to declare him guilty who is guiltless, nor him guiltless who is guilty. *Raising their voices still higher.* Neither will I, before judgment nor after, reveal to those in Court, nor yet to others, the deliberations which the Court holds within locked doors. All this I will and shall as an honest and upright judge truly hold without evil craft or contrivance. *Pause.* So help me God in body and soul!

The JURYMEN *sit down.*

JUDGE, *to the* SHERIFF. Call the case of Alma Jonsson versus Farmer Alexandersson.

SHERIFF, *calling.* The servant girl, Alma Jonsson, versus Farmer Alexandersson.

ADVOCATE. I submit the power of attorney of the plaintiff, Alma Jonsson.

JUDGE, *examining the document.* The servant girl, Alma Jonsson, in the summons taken out against her former master, Alexandersson, claims that he is liable, pursuant to the sixteenth chapter of the Penal Code, paragraph eight, to be imprisoned for six months or to pay a fine, on the ground that he, Alexandersson, called her a thief without having substantiated his charge or instituted proceedings. Alexandersson, what have you to say?

ALEXANDERSSON. I called her a thief because I saw her stealing.

JUDGE. Have you witnesses to the fact that she stole?

ALEXANDERSSON. No, as a matter of fact I had no one with me. I mostly go about alone.

JUDGE. Why did you not prosecute the girl?

ALEXANDERSSON. Because I never do go to law. For the matter of that, it's not the way of us masters to make a fuss about house-thefts—partly because they're so common, partly because we don't want to ruin the servants' future.

JUDGE. Alma Jonsson, what have you to say in answer to this?

SERVANT GIRL. We . . e . . ell . . .

ADVOCATE. You be quiet! *To the* JUDGE. Alma Jonsson, who in this case is not defendant but plaintiff, asks that her witnesses be heard in order that Alexandersson's slander may be proved.

JUDGE. Since Alexandersson pleads guilty to the slander, I require no witnesses. On the other hand, it is important for me to know whether Alma Jonsson is guilty of the offence; for if Alexandersson had reasonable grounds for his statement, that will have the effect of mitigating the sentence.

ADVOCATE. I must take exception to that contention of the Judge, in virtue of the sixteenth chapter of the Penal Code, paragraph thirteen, whereby one charged with slander is debarred from bringing evidence of the truth of his defamation.

JUDGE. The parties, the witnesses and the public will retire while the Court deliberates.

All go out, right, except the members of the Court.

Is Alexandersson a trustworthy and honest man?

JURYMEN. Alexandersson is a trustworthy man.

JUDGE. Is Alma Jonsson known as an honest servant?

BOMAN. Alma Jonsson was dismissed for pilfering at my house last year.

JUDGE. None the less, I must now sentence Alexandersson to pay a fine. There is no help for it. Is he poor?

ÖSTMAN. He is in arrears with his taxes and his crops failed last year; so he's in no position to stand a fine.

JUDGE. And yet I can find no reason to adjourn the case, since the facts are clear and Alexandersson is debarred from calling evidence. Has anyone anything to add or objections to raise?

EKLUND. I'd just like to allow myself a general observation. A case like this, in which one who is not only innocent but also the injured party, must bear the punishment, while the thief has her so-called honour restored, may easily result in people growing less lenient with their neighbours and law-suits becoming commoner.

JUDGE. That is very possible, but general observations are out of place in the records, and judgment must be pronounced. I therefore only ask the Jury whether Alexandersson can be held guilty according to the sixteenth chapter of the Penal Code, paragraph thirteen.

JURYMEN. Yes!

JUDGE, *to the* SHERIFF. Call in the parties and the witnesses.

All come in, right.

In the case between Alma Jonsson and Farmer Alexandersson, Alexandersson is sentenced to pay a fine of one hundred crowns for slander.

ALEXANDERSSON. But I actually saw her stealing! That's what one gets for being soft-hearted.

ADVOCATE, *to the* SERVANT GIRL. Now, you see. If only you deny a charge, everything goes right. Alexandersson was foolish and denied nothing. If I had been his Counsel and he had denied the charge, I should at once have challenged your witnesses, and where would you have been then? Now let us go out and settle up this business.

He goes out, right, with the SERVANT GIRL *and the witnesses.*

ALEXANDERSSON, *to the* SHERIFF. And now I suppose I

shall have to make out a testimonial for Alma, and put down that she was honest and well-behaved.

SHERIFF. That is not my affair.

ALEXANDERSSON, *to the* CONSTABLE. And as a consequence, I must sell up. Who would have thought that justice was like this, that the thief should get the honour and the victim get the rod? Devil take it! Come along now and have a coffee with something in it, Oman!

CONSTABLE. Yes, I'll come presently, but don't yell!

ALEXANDERSSON. Yes, I'll be damned if I don't yell, even if it costs me three months.

CONSTABLE. Now don't yell, don't yell!

JUDGE, *to the* SHERIFF. Call the divorce case between Baron Sprengel and his wife, born Malmberg.

SHERIFF. The divorce case between Baron Sprengel and his wife, born Malmberg.

Enter the BARON *and the* BARONESS.

JUDGE. In the charge laid against his wife, Baron Sprengel has made it clear that he does not intend to continue the marriage further and, since the warnings of the Church Council have proved unavailing, petitions for one year's separation in bed and board. What objection, Baroness, have you to make to this?

BARONESS. I make no objection to the separation, if only I may keep my child. That is my condition.

JUDGE. The law recognises no conditions in a case like this, and it is for the Court to determine the question of the custody of the child.

BARONESS. That is most extraordinary.

JUDGE. And it is therefore of great importance for the Judge to ascertain who is the cause of the dissension, upon which the plea for separation is based. From the minutes submitted by the Church Council, it appears that the wife allowed that she had at times a quarrelsome and difficult temper, while the husband admitted no fault. The Baroness thus appears to have acknowledged . . .

BARONESS. It is a lie.

JUDGE. I cannot easily admit that the minutes of the Church Council, attested by the Rector and eight other credible witnesses, are in error.

BARONESS. The document is false.

JUDGE. Such expressions cannot be addressed to the Court with impunity.

BARON. I beg to call attention to the fact that I have voluntarily resigned my child to the Baroness upon certain conditions.

JUDGE. And I repeat once more what I said just now, that it is for the Judge and not the parties to decide the issue. And so, Baroness, you deny that you are the cause of the dissension?

BARONESS. Yes, indeed I do. It takes two to make a quarrel.

JUDGE. Baroness, this is not a quarrel but a legal action. Moreover, you seem now to be displaying a contentious disposition and an uncompromising attitude.

BARONESS. But you don't know my husband.

JUDGE. Please explain yourself, for I cannot pronounce judgment upon insinuations.

BARON. In that case I ask that the suit be dismissed, so that I may seek divorce by other means.

JUDGE. The case is already before the Court and must proceed. You assert then, Baroness, that your husband caused the breach. Can this be proved?

BARONESS. Yes, it can be proved.

JUDGE. Then kindly do so; but bear in mind that this will involve depriving the Baron of his rights both of fatherhood and property.

BARONESS. He has forfeited these many times over. Not least when he denied me sleep and food.

BARON. As to that, I must explain that I have never denied her sleep. I have only begged her not to sleep till midday, since that involved neglecting the house and leaving the child without supervision. As for food I have always left the management of that to the mistress of the house, and I only objected to a number of extravagant entertainments, at a time when the ill-run household could not stand such expense.

BARONESS. And he has left me lying ill and refused to send for the doctor.

BARON. The Baroness had a habit of falling ill whenever she did not get her own way, but that kind of illness was soon over. After having, on one occasion, called in a specialist from the town, who made it clear that her illness was nothing but a sham, I summoned no doctor for her next attack—due to the new pier-glass being cheaper by fifty crowns than the one she wanted.

JUDGE. None of this is of a nature which can be taken into consideration in determining so grave a case. There must be more serious grounds.

BARONESS. Surely it ought to be counted a serious ground that a father will not allow a mother to bring up her own child.

BARON. In the first place, the Baroness has left the care of the child to a maid, and when she herself has taken a hand in its supervision, things have always gone wrong. In the second place, she has wanted to bring the boy up to become a woman instead of a man; thus, she let him go about in girls' clothes until he was four years old and, to this day, at eight, he wears his hair long like a girl, is made to sew and crochet and even to play with dolls, all of which I consider harmful to the child's normal development into a man. At the same time, she has amused herself by dressing the daughters of people on the estate as boys, has cut off their hair and set them to work such as is usually done by boys. In a word, I took my son's upbringing in hand when I noticed these insane symptoms, which before now have been seen to lead to conflict with the eighteenth chapter of the Penal Code.

JUDGE.* And yet now you are willing to leave the child in the mother's care?

BARON. Yes, for I never entertained the cruel idea of separating mother and child; besides, the mother has promised improvement. However, I only promised conditionally and on the assumption that the law did not concern itself with the question; but since we have started recriminations, I have changed my mind, especially as from being plaintiff I have come to be defendant.

BARONESS. That's the way this man always keeps his promises.

BARON. My promises, like other people's, were always conditional, and so long as the conditions were observed, I kept them.

BARONESS. For instance, he promised me personal freedom in marriage . . .

BARON. On the assumption, naturally, that the rules of propriety would not be violated; but when all bounds were overstepped, and license crept in under the name of freedom, I considered my promise void.

BARONESS. And consequently he plagued me with the most preposterous jealousy, which is in itself enough to make married life intolerable. He was even ridiculous enough to be jealous of the doctor.

BARON. This jealousy amounted to my protesting against the employment of a notorious and gossiping masseur for an ailment usually treated by a woman, unless the Baroness is referring to the occasion when I turned out the bailiff, who was smoking in the drawing-room and offering her cigars.

BARONESS. Since we seem to be abandoning all decency, it is as well for the whole truth to come out. The Baron has committed adultery. Isn't that enough to make him unfit for the sole charge of my child?

JUDGE. Can you prove this?

* In the Swedish text this speech is given to the Baroness, which is surely an error. E.S.

BARONESS. Yes, indeed I can. Here are the letters.

JUDGE, *taking the letters.* How long ago was this?

BARONESS. It was a year ago.

JUDGE. Then the time for instituting proceedings has expired; but the fact itself weighs heavily against the husband, and could result in him losing the child and his share in the settlement. Do you admit the adultery, Baron?

BARON. Yes, with remorse and shame; but there are mitigating circumstances. I was forced into a humiliating celibacy by the calculating coldness of the Baroness, although I only asked courteously, as a favour, that which the law allows me as a right. I grew weary of buying her love, when she introduced prostitution into my marriage and sold her favours, first for power, then for gifts and money, and I found myself finally, and with the Baroness's express approval, compelled to enter into an irregular union.

JUDGE. Did you give your consent, Baroness?

BARONESS. It is not true. I demand proof.

BARON. It is true, but I cannot prove it; since the only witness, my wife, denies it.

JUDGE. Unproven is not necessarily untrue; but an agreement of this kind, contrary to the law of the land, is *pactum turpe* and invalid. Baron, you still have everything against you.

BARONESS. And, as the Baron has confessed the offence with remorse and shame, I, who am now plaintiff instead of defendant, ask that the Court proceed to judgment, since further details are unnecessary.

JUDGE. In my capacity of President of the Court, I require to hear what the Baron can allege in his defence or at least in extenuation.

BARON. I have just admitted my adultery and have alleged as mitigating circumstances, both that it occurred by reason of imperative need since, after ten years of marriage, I suddenly found myself unmarried, and that it was with the Baroness's own sanction. As I have now reason to believe that all this was a trap to make a case against me, it is my duty, for my son's sake, to go further . . .

BARONESS, *crying out involuntarily.* Axel!

BARON. What caused my adultery was the infidelity of the Baroness.

JUDGE. Can you prove that the Baroness was unfaithful?

BARON. No. For I was zealous for the honour of the family and destroyed all the evidence which came into my hands; but I venture, nevertheless, to assume that the Baroness will confirm here the confession which she once made to me.

JUDGE. Baroness, do you confess your adultery prior to and therefore probably conducive to the Baron's misconduct?

BARONESS. No.

JUDGE. Will you swear that you are innocent of this charge?

BARONESS. Yes.

BARON. Good God! No! She mustn't do that. No perjury, I beg.

JUDGE. I ask yet once more: Baroness, will you take the oath?

BARONESS. Yes.

BARON. Permit me to observe that the Baroness is at the moment plaintiff and one does not plead on oath.

JUDGE. Since you have brought a charge against her, she is defendant. What is the opinion of the Jury?

WICKBERG. As the Baroness is a party to the suit, it appears to me that she can hardly give evidence on her own behalf.

ERLIN. It seems to me, that, if the Baroness is to give evidence on oath, the Baron should be allowed to do the same; but if oath does not tally with oath, the whole affair will remain obscure.

VASS. This is, in fact, not a question of the oath of a witness, but of an oath establishing innocence.

RUTH. That, surely, is the first question to decide.

VALLIN. But not in the presence of the parties; the deliberations of the Court are not public.

SJÖBERG. The Jury's right to speak is not limited by any conditions of secrecy.

JUDGE. I can obtain no guidance from so many dissimilar opinions. But, since the Baron's offence can be proved, and that of the Baroness is yet unproven, I must require the Baroness to take the oath of innocence.

BARONESS. I am ready.

JUDGE. No. One moment! Baron, if you are given time, can you produce evidence or witnesses in support of your charge?

BARON. I neither can nor will, for I am not anxious to have my dishonour made public.

JUDGE. The proceedings of the Court are adjourned, while I confer with the President of the Church Council.

He steps down from the Bench and goes out, right. The Jurymen confer among themselves in low tones. Members of the public talk in groups. The BARON *and the* BARONESS *move away from the rest.*

BARON, *to the* BARONESS. You do not shrink from perjury?

BARONESS. I shrink from nothing where my child is concerned.

BARON. Supposing I have evidence?

BARONESS. But you haven't.

BARON. The letters were burned, but certified copies are in existence.

BARONESS. You are lying to frighten me.

BARON. To show you how deeply I love my child and to save the mother, at least, since I am lost, here, take the proofs—but do not be ungrateful! *Hands her a packet of letters.*

BARONESS. That you were a liar, I knew before, but even so I didn't believe you were scoundrel enough to have the letters copied.

BARON. What gratitude! But now we are both lost.

BARONESS. Yes, let us both go under—then there will be an end to the strife.

BARON. Is it better for the child to lose both parents and be left alone in the world?

BARONESS. That can never happen.

BARON. Your preposterous conceit, which leads you to believe yourself above the law and your fellow creatures, has deluded you into starting this quarrel, in which there can be only one loser—our son! What were you thinking of when you began this attack which could not fail to provoke a defence? It was not of the child. Was it of revenge? Revenge for what? For my discovery of your misconduct?

BARONESS. The child? Were you thinking of the child, when you stood there and besmirched me before this rabble?

BARON. Hélène! We have torn one another as bloodily as wild beasts; we have laid bare our shame before all these people who rejoice at our ruin, for we have not one friend in this room. Henceforward our child will not be able to speak with pride of his parents; he will go out into life without the recommendation of a father and a mother; he will see his home shunned and us, in our old age, alone and scorned, and the day will come when he will flee from us.

BARONESS. What do you want to do then?

BARON. We will go abroad as soon as the place is sold.

BARONESS. And begin the quarrel over again. I know how it will be. You will be mild enough for a week, and then you will abuse me.

BARON. Think, our fate is even now being settled in there! You cannot count on one good word from the Pastor, whom you have just called a liar; I, who am known to be an unbeliever, can expect no mercy. Oh, that I could lie beneath a vault of roots out in the forest and thrust my head under a stone—I am so ashamed!

BARONESS. It is true; the Pastor hates us both, and it may turn out as you say. You had better speak to him.

BARON. What about? A reconciliation?

BARONESS. Anything you please, if only it is not too late! Think if it were too late! What does that Alexandersson want, slinking round us all the time? I am afraid of that man.

BARON. Alexandersson is a decent fellow.

BARONESS. To you, yes, but not to me. I have seen those looks before. Go to the Pastor now, but first take my hand—I am so frightened.

BARON. Of what, my dear, of what?

BARONESS. I don't know—everything, everyone!

BARON. But not of me?

BARONESS. Not any longer. It is as if we have been dragged into a mill and got our clothes caught in the wheels. And all these malicious people stand looking on, laughing. What have we done? What have we done in our anger? Think how they will enjoy it, all these people, seeing the Baron and Baroness stripped and scourging one another. Oh, I feel as if I were standing here naked!

She fastens her cloak again.

BARON. Calm yourself, my dear! This is hardly the place to say to you what I have said before: one has only one friend and one home, but we could begin over again. God knows! No, we can't do that. It has gone too far. It is finished. And this last, yes, let it be the last! And it had to follow after all the rest . . . No, we are enemies for life. And if I let you go now with the child, you may marry again—I see that now—and then my child will have a step-father, and I shall see another man going about with my wife and my child. Or else I myself may be going about with another man's harlot on my arm. No! Either you or I! One of us must go under. You or I!

BARONESS. You! For if I let you go with the child, then you

will be able to marry again, and I may come to see another woman mother of my child. Oh, the thought is enough to make me a murderess! A step-mother for *my* child!

BARON. You might have thought of that before; but when you saw how I gnawed at the chain of love that bound me to you, you supposed that I could not love another.

BARONESS. Do you suppose I ever loved you?

BARON. Yes, at one time at least. When I was unfaithful to you. Then your love was sublime. And your pretended scorn made you irresistible. But you even came to respect me after my misconduct—whether it was the male or the culprit you most admired, I don't know, but I think it was both—it must have been both, for you are the most feminine woman I have known. And you are already jealous of the wife of whom I have not even thought. What a pity you became my wife! As my mistress you would have had an undisputed triumph, and your infidelities would have been merely a bouquet added to the wine of my youth.

BARONESS. Yes, your love was always sensual.

BARON. Sensual like all things spiritual; spiritual like all things sensual. My weakness towards you, which was the strength of my feeling, gave you the notion that you were the stronger, whereas you were only more malicious, more brutal, more unscrupulous than I.

BARONESS. You the stronger? You who never want the same thing for two minutes together and, when all is said, don't know what you want!

BARON. Yes, I know very well what I want; but there is room in me for both hatred and love, and I love you at one moment and hate you the next. And now I hate you.

BARONESS. And are you thinking of the child now?

BARON. Yes, now and always. And do you know why? Because he is our love which took flesh. He is the memory of our most beautiful moments, the bond which unites our souls, the meeting-place where we come together always, whether we will or no. And that is why we can never be parted, even if we are divorced. Oh, if only I could hate you as I would!

Enter the JUDGE *and the* PASTOR *in conversation.*

JUDGE. Thus I recognise the utter hopelessness of seeking justice or discovering the truth. And it seems to me that the laws are a couple of centuries behind our notions of right. Did I not have to punish Alexandersson who was innocent, and to exonerate that thieving servant girl? And as to this divorce case, so far I know nothing, and cannot take it on my conscience to give judgment.

PASTOR. Yet judgment must be given.

JUDGE. Not by me. I shall resign my office and choose another career.

PASTOR. Oh, a scandal like that would only make you a byword and close all careers to you! Go on for a few years as a judge, and you will find that it becomes quite easy to crush human destinies like egg-shells. For the rest, if you want to get out of this affair, just let the Jury outvote you, and the responsibility will be theirs.

JUDGE. That is one way, and I believe they will be practically unanimous against me; for I have an opinion in this matter, although I reached it intuitively and dare not therefore rely upon it . . . Thank you for the advice.

The SHERIFF, *who has been talking to* ALEXANDERSSON, *comes up to the* JUDGE.

SHERIFF. In my capacity of Public Prosecutor, I have to announce Farmer Alexandersson as a witness against the Baroness Sprengel.

JUDGE. Touching the adultery?

SHERIFF. Yes.

JUDGE, *to the* PASTOR. This gives a new turn to the investigation.

PASTOR. There are plenty of clues, if one can only follow them.

JUDGE. But in any case it is horrible to see two people who

have loved one another destroying each other in this way. It is like looking on at a slaughter.

PASTOR. That you see, Judge, is love.

JUDGE. What then is hate?

PASTOR. It is the lining of the garment.

The JUDGE *goes over and speaks with the* JURYMEN. *The* BARONESS *turns towards the* PASTOR.

BARONESS. Help us, Pastor! Help us!

PASTOR. I cannot and, as a minister, I must not. Besides, did I not warn you against playing with such serious matters? You thought it so simple to separate. Well, separate then! The law is not hindering you, so do not put the blame on that.

JUDGE. The Court will now resume its deliberations. According to the report of the Public Prosecutor, Sheriff Viberg, a witness has come forward against the Baroness and corroborates her adultery. Farmer Alexandersson!

ALEXANDERSSON. Present!

JUDGE. Alexandersson, how can you prove your statement?

ALEXANDERSSON. I saw the offence committed.

BARONESS. He is lying. He'll have to prove it.

ALEXANDERSSON. Prove it? I'm here to give evidence.

BARONESS. Your evidence is no proof, even if you are called a witness for the occasion.

ALEXANDERSSON. Maybe the witness ought to bring two witnesses, and the two witnesses more witnesses?

BARONESS. Yes, that may be necessary when one doesn't know whether they are all lying.

BARON. Alexandersson's testimony is superfluous. I beg leave to hand to the Judge the whole correspondence, which gives full proof of the Baroness's adultery . . . Here are the originals; copies of them will be found on the person of the defendant.

The BARONESS *gives a cry, but recovers herself.*

JUDGE. Yet a moment ago, Baroness, you were prepared to take the oath?

BARONESS. But I did not do so. Anyway, now I suppose we are quits, the Baron and I.

JUDGE. We do not set off one offence against another. Each one's claim must be settled separately.

BARONESS. Then I demand to put in a claim now against the Baron for my dowry which he has dissipated.

JUDGE. If the Baron has dissipated the Baroness's dowry, it would be best to settle the matter now.

BARON. The Baroness brought to the marriage six thousand crowns in shares which were unsaleable and became worthless. As at the time of the marriage she was employed as a telegraph operator, and made it clear that she had no wish to be supported by her husband, we entered into an agreement on the understanding that each would be self-supporting. However, after the marriage she lost her position, and I have been supporting her ever since. To this I have made no objection; but since she now raises the question of accounts, I shall take the liberty of presenting my counter-claim. It amounts to thirty-five thousand crowns, this being one-third of the expenses of the household during our marriage, for I take two-thirds upon myself.

JUDGE. Have you this agreement in writing?

BARON. No, I have not.

JUDGE. Have you, Baroness, any documents showing the disposal of your dowry?

BARONESS. I didn't think it necessary at the time to have anything in writing, since I supposed myself to be dealing with honourable people.

JUDGE. Then I cannot take the question into consideration. The Jury will kindly retire to the small Court to deliberate and prepare their verdict.

The JURYMEN *and the* JUDGE *go out, right.*

ALEXANDERSSON, *to the* SHERIFF. I can't make head or tail of this justice.

SHERIFF. I think it would be wisest for you to go home now, otherwise the same thing might happen to you that happened to the peasant from Mariestad. Did you hear about that?

ALEXANDERSSON. No.

SHERIFF. Well, he went to the Court as an onlooker, was drawn into the case as a witness, became a party to it and ended by getting twenty lashes.

ALEXANDERSSON. The devil he did! But I can believe it of them. I believe there's nothing they wouldn't do.

Exit ALEXANDERSSON, *back. The* BARON *joins the* BARONESS *in the foreground.*

BARONESS. You find it hard to keep away from me?

BARON. Hélène, in stabbing you, I bleed myself, for your blood is mine . . .

BARONESS. And how good you are at making claims.

BARON. No, only counter-claims. Your courage is that of despair—of the doomed. And when you leave here, you will go to pieces. Then you will no longer have me to load your sorrow and guilt on to, and then you will suffer agonies of conscience. Do you know why I have not killed myself?

BARONESS. You dare not.

BARON. No, it is not from fear of everlasting torments—I do not believe in them—but because I reflected that even if you got the child, you would be gone in five years—so the doctor says. And then the child would be without both father and mother. Think of it—alone in the world.

BARONESS. Five years! It is a lie.

BARON. In five years. Then I shall be left with the child, whether you wish it or not.

BARONESS. Oh no, my dear! Then my family would take proceedings to remove the child from you. I shall not die when I die.

BARON. Evil never dies—that is true . . . But can you explain why you grudge the child to me, and me to the child when it needs me? Is it just out of malice and vindictiveness that you punish the child?

The BARONESS *is silent.*

Do you know, I told the Rector that I thought you possibly had some doubt as to the child's paternity, and this was the reason why you did not wish me to have the child—lest I should build my happiness upon false grounds. To that he answered: "No, I do not credit her with so fine a motive." I don't believe you know yourself why you are so fanatical upon this point; but it is the struggle for survival which presses us on and will not allow us to let go. Our son has your body, but my soul, and that you cannot uproot. You will find me again in him when you least expect it; you will find my thoughts, my tastes, my passions in him, and for these one day you will hate him as you hate me. It is this I fear.

BARONESS. You still seem a little afraid that he will be mine.

BARON. In your character of mother and woman you have an advantage over me with these gentlemen who are our judges, and although no doubt Justice throws the dice blindfold, they are always loaded.

BARONESS. You can still make pretty speeches at the moment of separation. Perhaps you don't hate me as much as you pretend to?

BARON. Frankly speaking, I suppose it is my dishonour rather than you that I hate—although I do that too. And why this terrible hatred? Perhaps I had forgotten that you were nearly forty, and that a certain masculinity had begun to grow in you. Perhaps it is just this masculinity which I have perceived in your kisses and your embraces, and which is so repulsive to me.

BARONESS. Perhaps that is it. For the great sorrow of my life, unknown to you, has been that I was not born a man.

BARON. Perhaps that has come to be the sorrow of *my* life. And now you are revenging yourself for nature's trick by trying to bring up your son as a woman. Will you promise me one thing?

BARONESS. Will *you* promise me one thing?

BARON. What's the use of promising? We never keep our promises.

BARONESS. No, let us make no more promises.

BARON. Will you give me a true answer to one question?

BARONESS. Even if I told you the truth, you would think I was lying.

BARON. Yes, so I should.

BARONESS. You see now that it is the end—for ever.

BARON. For ever! For ever, as once we swore to love one another.

BARONESS. It is wrong to have to swear such things.

BARON. Why so? At least it's some kind of bond.

BARONESS. I never could endure a bond.

BARON. Do you think it would have been better if we had not bound ourselves?

BARONESS. Yes, for me.

BARON. I wonder. Then you would have had no hold on me.

BARONESS. Nor you on me.

BARON. Then it would have come to exactly the same thing —like a reduced fraction. So, not the law's fault, not our fault, no one else's fault. And yet we must bear the blame.

The SHERIFF *approaches.*

Ah! Now our fate is decided. Farewell, Hélène!

BARONESS. Farewell—Axel!

BARON. It is hard to part. And impossible to live together. But at least the strife is over.

BARONESS. If only it were! I fear it is only beginning.

SHERIFF. The parties are to withdraw while the Court deliberates.

BARONESS. Axel, a word before it is too late! It is quite possible that they will remove the child from both of us. So drive home and take the boy to your mother; then later we will flee—far away!

BARON. I believe you mean to trick me again.

BARONESS. No, I don't. I am not thinking of you any longer, nor of myself, nor of revenge. Only save the child! Do you hear? Do it!

BARON. I will. But if you are deceiving me . . . However, I will do it.

The BARON *goes quickly out, back. The* BARONESS *goes out, right. The* JURYMEN *and the* JUDGE *enter, right, and resume their seats.*

JUDGE. The case being now complete, I will ask the Jury to state their views before judgment is given. For my own part, I can see no reasonable course other than to assign the child to the mother, since both parties are equally to blame for the separation, and the mother surely must be considered better qualified than the father to be the guardian of the child.

Silence.

EKLUND. According to the law as it stands, the wife takes the husband's status and condition, not the husband the wife's.

WICKBERG. And the husband is the wife's legal guardian.

SJÖBERG. The marriage ceremony, which seals the union, requires the wife to obey her husband, whence it seems to me that the man comes before the woman.

BOMAN. And the children are to be brought up in the father's faith.

SÖDERBERG. From which it follows that the child should go with the father and not with the mother.

ANDERSSON OF VIK. But, as in the case before us, both are equally to blame and, in view of all that has come to light, equally unfit to bring up a child, I consider that the child ought to be removed from both.

ANDERSSON OF BERGA. Concurring with Olof Andersson, I call to mind that in such cases the Judge nominates two trustees as guardians of the children and the property, maintenance being allowed from this for husband, wife and children.

VALLIN. In that case, I would like to propose as trustees, Alexander Eklund and Erenfrid Söderberg, who are both known for their upright life and Christian character.

RUTH. I agree with Olof Andersson of Vik as to the separation of the child from both father and mother, and with Axel Vallin concerning the trustees, whose Christian character renders them peculiarly fitted for the upbringing of the child.

ERLIN. I agree with the aforesaid.

VASS. Agreed!

ÖSTMAN. Agreed!

JUDGE. As the majority opinion of the Jury now seems to be directly opposed to mine, I will ask the Jury to proceed to a vote. I ought perhaps to put as a motion Olof Andersson's proposal to remove the child from both father and mother and to appoint trustees. Is this the unanimous opinion of the Jury?

JURYMEN. Yes.

JUDGE. If anyone dissents from the motion, let him hold up his hand. *No one moves.* The opinion of the Jury has consequently prevailed over mine, and I shall enter upon the record a protest against what seems to me a needlessly cruel verdict. The husband and wife are sentenced to one year's separation in bed and board, on pain of imprisonment if during that time they approach one another. *To the* SHERIFF. Call in the parties!

The BARONESS *and the Public enter.*

JUDGE. Is Baron Sprengel not present?

BARONESS. The Baron will be here directly.

JUDGE. He who is not in time has only himself to blame.

The judgment of the Court is that the spouses Sprengel be sentenced to one year's separation in bed and board, and that the child be removed from the parents and assigned to two trustees to bring up, whereunto the Court has accordingly nominated and appointed the Jurors, Alexander Eklund and Erenfrid Söderberg.

The BARONESS *screams and sinks to the floor. The* SHERIFF *and the* CONSTABLE *lift her up and place her on a chair. Some of the public leave. The* BARON *enters.*

BARON, *to the* JUDGE. My Lord, having heard outside the judgment of the Court, I wish to protest both against the Jury, who are my personal enemies, and against the trustees, Alexander Eklund and Erenfrid Söderberg, neither of whom possesses the financial status required of trustees; moreover, I shall take proceedings against the Judge for incompetence in the discharge of his office, in that he failed to discern that the party who first broke the marriage tie was the cause of the other's breach, and that therefore both are not equally responsible.

JUDGE. Whoever is not satisfied with the judgment is at liberty to appeal to the High Court within the prescribed period. The Jury will please proceed to the inspection of dilapidations at the Rectory in and for the case against the surveyors to the Local Council.

The JUDGE *and* JURYMEN *go out, back. As the* BARON *and* BARONESS *begin speaking, the rest of the public stroll out.*

BARONESS, *rising*. Where is Emile?

BARON. He had gone.

BARONESS. You are lying.

BARON, *after a pause*. Yes. I did not take him to my mother because I do not trust her, but to the Rectory.

BARONESS. To the Rector!

BARON. Your one trustworthy enemy. Yes. Whom else dared I trust? And I did it because just now I saw a look in your eyes which said that you might possibly kill both yourself and the child.

BARONESS. You saw that! Oh, why did I let myself be fooled into trusting you?

BARON. And what have you to say about all this now?

BARONESS. I don't know. But I am so tired that I no longer feel the blows. It comes almost as a relief to have had the finishing stroke.

BARON. You don't realise what will happen now: how your son will be brought up by two peasants, whose want of breeding and coarse ways will gradually torture the child to death; how he will be forced down into their narrow sphere; how his intelligence will be choked by religious superstition; how he will be taught contempt for his father and mother . . .

BARONESS. Stop! Don't say any more or I shall lose my reason. My Emile among peasant wives, who do not know how to wash themselves, who have bugs in the beds and can't tell if a comb is clean! My Emile! No, it's impossible.

BARON. That is exactly the position, and you have no one but yourself to blame.

BARONESS. Myself? Yes, but did I make myself? Put the evil tendencies, the hatred and wild passions into myself? No! Who denied me the power and the will to fight them? When I look at myself at this moment I feel I should be pitied. Shouldn't I?

BARON. Indeed you should. We should both be pitied. We tried to avoid the rocks of marriage by living as man and wife without being married; but even so we quarrelled, and we missed one of life's greatest boons—the respect of our fellows—and so we married. But we thought to outwit society and its laws; we would have no wedding ceremony, so we entangled ourselves in a civil contract. We would not be dependent upon one another . . . not have a common purse, claim no rights of possession over one another's person—and then it all went back into the old rut again. Marriage, without the ceremony and with the contract. And then that broke down. I forgave your infidelity, and for the child's sake we lived together in voluntary separation—how voluntary! But I grew tired of presenting my friend's mistress as my wife—and so we had to part. Do you know with what, do you know with whom we strove? You call him God, but I call him Nature. And that power incited us to hatred, just as he incites mankind to love. And now we are doomed to lacerate each other so long as one spark of life remains in us. New proceedings in the Court of Appeal, revision of the case, Church Council's hearing, Chapter's pronouncement, Supreme Court's decision. And then come my notice to the Solicitor General, my application for the custody, your protest and counter proceedings—from pillar to post! And without finding one merciful executioner. Mismanagement of the estate, financial ruin, the child's neglected upbringing. And why do we not put an end to these two miserable lives? Because the child holds us back. You weep, but I cannot. Not even when I think of the night about to fall on that deserted home. And you, poor Hélène, who are to go back to your mother! Your mother, whom you once left with a glad heart to come to a home of your own. To become her daughter again . . . perhaps that will prove worse than being a wife . . . One year . . . two years . . . countless years . . . How many more do you think we can still endure?

BARONESS. I will never go back to my mother. Never. I shall wander about the roads and in the woods, so as to hide myself and be able to scream—scream myself tired against God who has put this devilish love into the world to torment mankind. And when it grows dark, I shall lay myself down in the Rectory barn, so that I may sleep near my child.

BARON. You think you will sleep tonight, do you?

THE END

CRIME AND CRIME

A Comedy

FOREWORD

Crime and Crime was written early in 1899. Although the play is set in Paris, it was now four years since Strindberg, after the terrible ordeals there, described in *Inferno,* had returned to live in Sweden. He refers to *Advent,* the play preceding *Crime and Crime,* as a Swedenborgian drama, and this treats mystically of sin and retribution. In *Crime and Crime* Strindberg further develops the Swedenborgian view that crime is its own punishment; but this time the treatment is realistic, and the play is something of a psychological thriller at one level and a spiritual adventure at a deeper one. It is extremely autobiographical: the scenes set in places Strindberg himself frequented, and the hero a playwright, with much of his own strange temperament, at the moment of his first brilliant success in the Paris theatre. Although Maurice's play is spoken of as redeeming slandered human nature, which could not be said of *The Father,* even if true of some of the later plays, Strindberg was certainly thinking of the fame which came to him overnight with the first performance of *The Father* in Antoine's Théâtre Libre. And the sense of guilt and mutual torture dominating *Crime and Crime* were among Strindberg's deepest obsessions, as was too belief in the destructive power of evil thought. During the *Inferno* period he had practised black magic and believed that he had once caused the illness of one of his children, although he had not actually, like Maurice, "wished the life out of" the child.

Madame Cathérine, Henriette, and the Abbé all have their origins in people who played a part in Strindberg's Paris life. He called *Crime and Crime* his "boulevard" play, and surely its swift action and dialogue were influenced by the French theatre. Although Strindberg never again lived there, his attachment to France remained, and he continued to correspond with Antoine, Lugné Poë, and other Frenchmen connected with literature and the theatre. E. S.

CHARACTERS

MAURICE, *a playwright*

JEANNE, *his mistress*

MARION, *their daughter, aged five*

EMILE, *Jeanne's brother, a workman*

ADOLPHE, *an artist*

HENRIETTE, *his mistress*

MADAME CATHÉRINE, *proprietress of the Crémerie*

THE ABBÉ

A KEEPER, *in the Cemetery*

THE WOMAN, *in the Cemetery (non-speaking)*

THE COMMISSAIRE

FIRST DETECTIVE

SECOND DETECTIVE

THE HEAD WAITER *(non-speaking)*

A WAITER

A KEEPER, *in the Luxembourg Gardens*

A SERVING GIRL

ACT I, SCENE 1, *The Cemetery at Montparnasse*
SCENE 2, *The Crémerie*

ACT II, SCENE 1, *The Auberge des Adrets*
SCENE 2, *A Restaurant in the Bois de Boulogne*

ACT III, SCENE 1, *The Crémerie*
SCENE 2, *The Auberge des Adrets*

ACT IV, SCENE 1, *The Luxembourg Gardens*
SCENE 2, *The Crémerie*

The whole action of the play takes place in Paris in the nineties

ACT I

SCENE 1

SCENE: *The upper end of the cypress avenue in the cemetery at Montparnasse. Seen in the background are burial chapels and stone crosses bearing the inscription:* O Crux! Ave spes unica! *Also the ivy-clad ruin of a windmill.*

A well-dressed WOMAN *in mourning is kneeling beside a flower-decked grave, murmuring prayers.*

JEANNE *is walking to and fro, as if expecting somebody.*

MARION *is playing with some withered flowers she has picked up from a rubbish heap on the path.*

The ABBÉ *is walking at the far end of the avenue, reading his breviary.*

The KEEPER *enters.*

KEEPER, *to* JEANNE. Look here, this isn't a playground.

JEANNE, *meekly.* I'm only waiting for someone who's bound to be here soon. . . .

KEEPER. That's as it may be, but no one's allowed to take any flowers. . . .

JEANNE, *to* MARION. Put the flowers down, dear.

The ABBÉ *approaches and is saluted by the* KEEPER.

ABBÉ. But, Keeper, surely the child may play with those flowers which have been thrown away?

KEEPER. The regulations forbid anyone to touch any flowers, even those that have been thrown away. They are supposed to be contagious—whether it's true or not.

ABBÉ, *to* MARION. In that case, there is nothing for us to do but obey. What is your name, my little friend?

MARION. I'm called Marion.

ABBÉ. And what is your papa's name?

MARION *bites her fingers and does not answer.*

The KEEPER *goes out.*

To JEANNE. Pardon my question, Madame. I did not mean to intrude. I was simply talking to calm the little girl.

JEANNE. I realised that at once, Reverend Father, and I was wishing you would say something to calm me too, for I am very troubled after waiting here for two whole hours.

ABBÉ. Two hours—for him? How human beings can torture one another! *O Crux! Ave spes unica!*

JEANNE. Yes, what do they mean—those words which are written all over this place?

ABBÉ. They mean: O Cross! Our only hope!

JEANNE. Is it our only one?

ABBÉ. Our only sure one.

JEANNE. I shall soon believe that you are right, Father.

ABBÉ. May I ask why?

JEANNE. You have already guessed. When a man keeps a woman and child waiting for two hours in a cemetery, the end is not far off.

ABBÉ. And when he does abandon you, what then?

JEANNE. The river.

ABBÉ. Ah, no, no!

JEANNE. Yes, yes!

MARION. I want to go home, Mamma. I'm hungry.

JEANNE. Be patient just a little longer, my darling, and then we will go.

ABBÉ. Woe, woe upon them who call evil good and good evil!

JEANNE. What is that woman doing at that grave?

ABBÉ. She appears to be talking to the dead.

JEANNE. But can you do that?

ABBÉ. She seems to be able to.

JEANNE. Then won't there be an end to the misery even when this is over?

ABBÉ. Do you not know that?

JEANNE. Where can you find out?

ABBÉ. Hm! Next time you feel you need some enlightenment on this well-known question, come and find me in the Chapel of Our Lady in the Church of Saint-Germain. *Looking off.* Here comes, surely, the one you are expecting.

JEANNE, *embarrassed.* It's not him, but I know this one too.

ABBÉ, *to* MARION. Goodbye, little Marion. May God keep you! *Kisses the child. To* JEANNE. In Saint Germain-des-Prés.

Exit the ABBÉ.

Enter EMILE.

EMILE. Why, Sister, what are you doing here?

JEANNE. Waiting for Maurice.

EMILE. Then you'll have to wait a long time, for I saw him lunching on the boulevard with some friends an hour ago. And how's dear little Marion? *Kisses the child.*

JEANNE. Were there women with him?

EMILE. Yes, of course, but that doesn't mean anything. He writes plays and his new one's opening tonight. They were probably some of his actresses.

JEANNE. Did he recognise you?

EMILE. No. He doesn't know who I am and there's no reason why he should. I know my place as a workman and I don't want any favours from those above me.

JEANNE. But suppose he leaves us high and dry?

EMILE. Now, look, when that happens it will be time enough for me to introduce myself. But surely you don't expect anything of the kind, because he really thinks the world of you, and above all he's set on the child.

JEANNE. I don't know—I just feel something frightful is going to happen to me.

EMILE. Has he promised to marry you?

JEANNE. No, he hasn't promised, but he's led me to hope.

EMILE. Hope, eh? Don't you remember what I said at the start? Don't hope, for those on top don't marry beneath them.

JEANNE. But it does happen.

EMILE. Of course it does. But would you be happy in his set? I bet you wouldn't—you wouldn't even understand what they were talking about. I eat there sometimes—in the kitchen—at the place he has his meals, and I can't make out a word they say.

JEANNE. Really, you eat there?

EMILE. Yes, in the kitchen.

JEANNE. To think he's never invited me there.

EMILE. You can give him credit for that. It shows he has some respect for Marion's mother, for the ladies who go there are a queer lot.

JEANNE. Oh . . . !

EMILE. But Maurice doesn't bother with the ladies. No, there's something *straight* about that chap.

JEANNE. I think so too, but when a woman comes along, men lose their heads.

EMILE, *smiling*. You're telling me. But listen. Are you short of money?

JEANNE. No, not that.

EMILE. Then all's well so far. Look! Over there, down the avenue. There he comes! And I'll be on my way. Goodbye, little girl.

JEANNE. Is he coming? Yes, it is him.

EMILE, *going*. Now don't drive him crazy with your jealousy, Jeanne.

JEANNE. Of course I won't.

Exit EMILE.

Enter MAURICE.

MARION *runs to him and he catches her up in his arms.*

MARION. Papa, Papa!

MAURICE. My pet, my darling! *Turning to* JEANNE. Jeanne, can you forgive me for keeping you waiting so long? Can you?

JEANNE. Of course I can.

MAURICE. But say it so I can hear that you forgive me.

JEANNE. Come here and I'll whisper it to you.

MAURICE *comes close to her.*

JEANNE *kisses him on the cheek.*

MAURICE. I didn't hear.

JEANNE *kisses him on the mouth.*

I heard then. . . . Well . . . I suppose you know this is the day on which my fate will be decided. My play is to be presented and has every chance of success—or failure.

JEANNE. I'll pray for you; then you'll have a success.

MAURICE. Thank you. Even if that doesn't help, it can't do any harm. . . . Look down there in the valley, in the sun haze. There lies Paris. Today Paris does not know who Maurice is, but within twenty-four hours it will know. The cloud of smoke which has hidden me for thirty years will disperse as I blow upon it, and I shall be seen. I shall take shape and begin to be somebody. My enemies, that's to say all those who wish they could do what I have done, will writhe with pain, and that will give me pleasure—to see them suffering what I have suffered.

JEANNE. Don't talk like that, don't!

MAURICE. But that's how it is.

JEANNE. Yes, but don't talk about it. . . . And then?

MAURICE. Then we'll be in clover, and you and Marion will bear the name I have made famous.

JEANNE. You do love me then?

MAURICE. I love you both, one as much as the other, or Marion even a little more.

JEANNE. I'm glad of that, for you may tire of me, but not of her.

MAURICE. You don't trust my feeling for you?

JEANNE. I don't know, but I'm afraid of something, something terrible. . . .

MAURICE. You're tired and depressed by this long wait. Once more, please forgive me. What have you to be afraid of?

JEANNE. The unknown—that you can have a presentiment about without a real reason.

MAURICE. Well, the only presentiment I have is—success, and

with real reasons: the sure instincts of theatre folk and their experience of the public, not to mention their personal acquaintance with the critics. So now you must be calm and . . .

JEANNE. I can't, I can't! Do you know, there was an Abbé here just now who talked so kindly to us. You haven't wiped out my faith, but you have smeared it over like when you whiten windows, so I couldn't get at it. But this old man passed his hand over the chalk and the light came through, and you could see again that the family was at home inside. I shall pray for you this evening in Saint-Germain.

MAURICE. Now it's I who am frightened.

JEANNE. Fear of God is the beginning of wisdom.

MAURICE. God? What is that? Who is He?

JEANNE. He who gave joy to your youth and strength to your manhood. And it is He who will support us in the terrors that lie ahead.

MAURICE. What lies ahead? What do you know? Where have you learnt this? This that I don't know.

JEANNE. I can't tell. I haven't dreamt anything, seen anything, heard anything. But during these two dreadful hours, I have lived through such an eternity of pain that I am ready for the very worst.

MARION. I want to go home now, Mamma. I'm hungry.

MAURICE. You shall go home, my darling. *Hugs her.*

MARION, *whimpering.* Oh, you hurt me, Papa!

JEANNE. We must go home to dinner. So goodbye, Maurice. And good luck!

MAURICE, *to* MARION. How could I hurt you? You know I only want to be kind to my little girl.

MARION. Come home with us then, if you're kind.

MAURICE, *to* JEANNE. You know, when I hear the child talk like that, I feel I ought to do as she says. But then reason and duty step in. . . . Goodbye, little daughter.

He kisses the child, who puts her arms round his neck.

JEANNE. When do we meet again?

MAURICE. Tomorrow, my dear, we shall meet. And never more to part.

JEANNE *embraces him.*

JEANNE. Never, never more to part.

She makes the sign of the cross on his forehead.

May God keep you!

MAURICE, *moved in spite of himself.* My own beloved Jeanne!

JEANNE *and* MARION *move right.*

MAURICE *moves left.*

Both turn at the same moment and kiss hands to one another.

Turning back. Jeanne, I'm ashamed of myself. I'm always forgetting you, and you are the last to remind me. Here is your ticket for tonight.

JEANNE. Thank you, my dear, but–you must be at your post alone, and I shall be at mine–with Marion.

MAURICE. Your wisdom is as great as your goodness of heart. Yes, I swear no other woman would sacrifice a pleasure in order to do her man a service. I need to be quite free tonight, and a man doesn't take his wife and children to the battlefield with him. This you understood.

JEANNE. Maurice, don't think too highly of a simple woman like me, then you won't have to lose your illusions. . . . And now you will see I am as forgetful as you were. Here is a tie and a pair of gloves I've bought you. I thought you might do me the honour of wearing them on your great day.

MAURICE, *kissing her hand.* Thank you, my love.

JEANNE. And then, Maurice, don't forget, as you so often do, to go to the barber. I want you to look handsome, so that others will like you too.

MAURICE. You aren't jealous at all, are you?

JEANNE. Don't use that word. It rouses bad thoughts.

MAURICE. Do you know, at this moment I could forego tonight's victory–yes, it will be a victory. . . .

JEANNE. Hush, hush, hush!

MAURICE. And come home with you.

JEANNE. But you mustn't. Go! Your fate is waiting for you.

MAURICE. Goodbye then. And let come what may.

Exit MAURICE.

JEANNE, *alone with* MARION. *O Crux! Ave spes unica!*

SCENE 2

SCENE: *The Crémerie. The same afternoon.*

Right, a buffet, on which stands an aquarium containing goldfish, a palm, vegetables, fruits, preserves, etc.

Back, a door to the kitchen, where workmen are gathered, with a further door to the garden.

Left, a raised counter and shelves holding many kinds of bottles.

Down right, one long marble-topped table against the wall, and another parallel with it, nearer in. Wicker chairs stand beside the tables. The walls are covered with paintings.

MADAME CATHÉRINE *is sitting at the counter.*

MAURICE *is leaning against the counter with his hat on, smoking a cigarette.*

MME CATHÉRINE. So tonight the balloon goes up for you, eh, Monsieur Maurice?

MAURICE. Yes, tonight.

MME CATHÉRINE. Are you nervous?

MAURICE. Cool as a cucumber.

MME CATHÉRINE. Well, I wish you luck, you deserve it, Monsieur Maurice, after fighting difficulties such as yours.

MAURICE. Thank you, Madame Cathérine. You have been very kind to me. Without your help, by now I'd be down and out.

MME CATHÉRINE. We won't talk about that now. Where I see hard work and the will to get on, I help, though, mind you, I don't like to be exploited. . . . Can we trust you to come back here when the play's over and let us drink a glass of wine with you?

MAURICE. Of course you can trust me. I've already given you my promise.

Enter HENRIETTE, *right.*

MAURICE *turns, raises his hat, and gazes at* HENRIETTE, *who regards him appraisingly.*

HENRIETTE, *to* MME CATHÉRINE. Isn't Monsieur Adolphe here?

MME CATHÉRINE. No, Madame. But he will be here soon. Please take a seat.

HENRIETTE. Thank you. But I would prefer to wait for him outside.

Exit HENRIETTE.

MAURICE. Who . . . was . . . that?

MME CATHÉRINE. That was Monsieur Adolphe's lady friend.

MAURICE. Was . . . that . . . she?

MME CATHÉRINE. Haven't you ever seen her before?

MAURICE. No, he has been hiding her from me, just as if he were afraid I would take her from him.

MME CATHÉRINE. Aha! Well, what do you think of her looks?

MAURICE. Her looks? Let me see. I don't know . . . I didn't see her, for it was as if she had flown straight into my arms. She came so close that I had no view. And she left her impression on the air. I can still see her standing there.

He goes towards the door and mimes putting his arm round someone's waist.

Ow! *Mimes having pricked his finger.* She has pins in her waistband. She is one of the kind that stings.

MME CATHÉRINE, *smiling.* You and your ladies—you're crazy!

MAURICE. Yes, I'm crazy, crazy! But I tell you what, Madame Cathérine—I'm going to leave before she comes back, for if I don't, if I don't . . . Oh, she is a terrible woman!

MME CATHÉRINE. Are you scared?

MAURICE. Yes, I'm scared for myself and scared for some others . . .

MME CATHÉRINE. Well then, go.

MAURICE. Listen. When she drifted out of that door, it made a little whirlwind which sucked me in too. . . . You may laugh, but look how that palm on the buffet is still trembling! She is a devil of a woman.

MME CATHÉRINE. Well then, go, my dear man, before you're stark staring mad.

MAURICE. I want to go, but I can't. . . . Do you believe in destiny, Madame Cathérine?

MME CATHÉRINE. No, I believe in the good God, who protects us from evil powers, if we ask Him nicely.

MAURICE. So, anyway there are evil powers. . . . Isn't it *them* I hear in the entrance now?

MME CATHÉRINE. It certainly is. She rustles so much it's like the draper tearing off a length of material. Go on! Get out! Through the kitchen.

MAURICE *dashes to the kitchen door and collides with* EMILE *coming out.*

EMILE. A thousand pardons! *Backs into the kitchen, shutting the door.*

Enter ADOLPHE, *followed by* HENRIETTE.

ADOLPHE. Why, there's Maurice! Good day to you! Let me introduce you! My dear friend, Mademoiselle Henriette, and my oldest and best friend, Monsieur Maurice.

MAURICE, *bowing stiffly.* Enchanted.

HENRIETTE. We have seen one another before.

ADOLPHE. Really? But when, if I may ask?

MAURICE. Just now. In here.

ADOLPHE. Oh, I see! Well, now you mustn't go until we've had a talk.

MME CATHÉRINE *signals to* MAURICE.

MAURICE. I only wish I had time.

ADOLPHE. Make time. We are not staying long.

HENRIETTE. I won't disturb you, if you gentlemen want to talk business.

MAURICE. Any business we have is too bad to talk about.

HENRIETTE. Then we'll talk about something else.

She takes MAURICE'*s hat and hangs it up.*

Be kind now and let me make the acquaintance of the great author.

MME CATHÉRINE *signs to* MAURICE, *but he pays no attention.*

ADOLPHE. That's right, Henriette, you take him prisoner.

They seat themselves at a table.

HENRIETTE, *to* MAURICE. You certainly have a good friend in Adolphe, Monsieur Maurice. He never talks about anything but you, so much so that I often feel quite put in the shade.

ADOLPHE. I like that! I may tell you, Maurice, that Henriette doesn't give me a moment's peace about you. She has read everything you have written and is always wanting to know where you got *this* from and where that. She has asked me what you look like, how old you are, what you care about most. In a word, I've had you morning, noon, and night. We've been as good as living together, the three of us.

MAURICE, *to* HENRIETTE. Good gracious! Why didn't you come here and take a look at this prodigy? Then your curiosity would have been satisfied at once.

HENRIETTE. Adolphe didn't want me to.

ADOLPHE *looks embarrassed.*

Not that he was jealous . . .

MAURICE. Why should he be, when he knew my affections were otherwise engaged?

HENRIETTE. He may not have trusted the constancy of your affections.

MAURICE. I don't see why not. I'm famous for my fidelity.

ADOLPHE. It wasn't that. It . . .

HENRIETTE, *interrupting, to* MAURICE. Perhaps because it's never been put to the test. . . .

ADOLPHE. Oh really, you know . . . !

HENRIETTE, *interrupting.* Well, the world has never yet seen a faithful man.

MAURICE. Then it's going to see one.

HENRIETTE. Where?

MAURICE. Here.

HENRIETTE *laughs.*

ADOLPHE. Well, that sounds . . .

HENRIETTE, *interrupting and continuing to address herself to* MAURICE. Do you think I'd trust my dear Adolphe for more than a month or so?

MAURICE. It's not my business to challenge your lack of confidence, but I'd go bail for Adolphe's fidelity.

HENRIETTE. You needn't do that. . . . My tongue just ran away with me, and I take it back. Not only so I don't feel less high-minded than you, but because it really is so. . . . It's a bad habit of mine only to see the worst, and I go on doing it, even when I know better. But if I could be with you two for a while longer, I would grow good again in your company. Forgive me, Adolphe.

She lays her hand against his cheek.

ADOLPHE. You always talk so ill and behave so well. What you really think, I don't know.

HENRIETTE. Who does know that?

MAURICE. If we had to answer for our thoughts, who would stand a chance?

HENRIETTE. Do you have evil thoughts too?

MAURICE. Yes, of course. Just as I do the cruellest things—in dreams.

HENRIETTE. In dreams, ah! Just think I . . . no, I'm ashamed to talk about it. . . .

MAURICE. Go on, go on!

HENRIETTE. Last night I dreamt I was coolly dissecting the muscles of Adolphe's chest. I'm a sculptor, you know—and he, who is always so sweet, made no resistance, but actually helped me over the difficulties, as he knows more anatomy than I do.

MAURICE. Did he seem to be dead?

HENRIETTE. No, he was alive.

MAURICE. How horrible! How could you bear to do it?

HENRIETTE. I didn't mind at all. That's what surprised me, because I'm pretty sensitive about other people's sufferings. That's true, isn't it, Adolphe?

ADOLPHE. Absolutely true. Specially where animals are concerned.

MAURICE. I, on the other hand, am rather indifferent to my own sufferings and those of others.

ADOLPHE. Now he's telling lies about himself. Isn't he, Madame Cathérine?

MME CATHÉRINE. Monsieur Maurice is kind to the point of folly. Just think, he nearly called in the police because I hadn't changed the goldfishes' water—those on the buffet there. Look at them! You'd think they could hear what I'm saying.

MAURICE. And here we sit, you see, white-washing ourselves into angels, when by and large any one of us is capable of committing some polite atrocity where glory, gold, or women are concerned. . . . So you are a sculptor, Mademoiselle Henriette?

HENRIETTE. Bit of a one. Good enough anyhow to do a bust. And to do one of you. That's been my dream for a long time, and I'm sure I could.

MAURICE. At your service. That dream at least can be realised at once.

HENRIETTE. But I don't want to visualise you until after tonight's success, when you first become what you really should be.

MAURICE. How certain you are of victory!

HENRIETTE. Yes. It's written in your face that you're going to win this battle, and you must be feeling that yourself.

MAURICE. Why so?

HENRIETTE. Because I feel it. You know, I wasn't well this morning, but now I'm fine again.

ADOLPHE *begins to look depressed.*

MAURICE, *embarrassed.* Listen, I have one theatre ticket left —but only one. It's at your disposal, Adolphe.

ADOLPHE. Thank you, old man, but I surrender it to Henriette.

HENRIETTE. Oh, but would that do?

ADOLPHE. Why not? And I never go to the theatre anyhow. I can't stand the heat.

HENRIETTE. But you will at least come and fetch me when the play's over?

ADOLPHE. If you insist. Or why not come back here with Maurice, where we shall all be waiting for him?

MAURICE. Surely you can take the trouble to come and meet us. I want you to. I beg you to do so. Look here, if you don't want to wait outside the theatre, there's the Auberge des Adrets. You can meet us there. Is that settled?

ADOLPHE. Wait a bit. You have a way of settling things to suit yourself, before one has time to consider.

MAURICE. What is there to consider? It's just a matter of escorting your lady or not.

ADOLPHE. You never know what may come out of such a simple matter. I have a sense of foreboding.

HENRIETTE. Tut, tut! You can't be spooky in broad daylight. *To* MAURICE. Whether he turns up or not, we can always come back here.

ADOLPHE *rises.*

ADOLPHE. Well, anyway, I must leave you now. I have a model coming. Goodbye. Good luck, Maurice! Tomorrow you will have got there. Goodbye, Henriette.

HENRIETTE. Do you really have to go?

ADOLPHE. Must.

MAURICE. Goodbye, then. See you later.

ADOLPHE *salutes* MME CATHÉRINE *and goes out.*

HENRIETTE. To think that we should meet at last!

MAURICE. Do you find that so remarkable?

HENRIETTE. It's as if it were meant to happen, though Adolphe has done his best to prevent it.

MAURICE. Has he?

HENRIETTE. Surely you noticed that.

MAURICE. I did notice it. So why should you mention it?

HENRIETTE. I had to.

MAURICE. Well, I don't have to tell you that I meant to escape through the kitchen just now so as to avoid meeting you, but was stopped by someone shutting the door in my face.

HENRIETTE. Why talk about that now?

MAURICE. Don't know.

MME CATHÉRINE *upsets a number of glasses and bottles.* Don't upset yourself, Madame Cathérine, there's no danger.

HENRIETTE. Was that meant as a signal or a warning?

MAURICE. Probably both.

HENRIETTE. Am I a locomotive that I need signalmen?

MAURICE. And switchmen. The most dangerous part is the switch-over.

HENRIETTE. How wicked you can be!

MME CATHÉRINE. Monsieur Maurice is not wicked at all. Up to now, nobody could have been kinder or more loyal to those who belong to him or those he's under an obligation to.

MAURICE. Hush, hush, hush!

HENRIETTE, *to* MAURICE. How that old woman pokes her nose in!

MAURICE. We can go over to the boulevard if you like.

HENRIETTE. By all means. This is no place for me. I feel hatred clawing at me.

HENRIETTE *goes out.*

MAURICE *begins to follow her.*

MAURICE. Goodbye, Madame Cathérine.

MME CATHÉRINE. One moment. May I say a word, Monsieur Maurice?

MAURICE, *stopping unwillingly.* What is it?

MME CATHÉRINE. Don't do it! Don't do it!

MAURICE. What?

MME CATHÉRINE. Don't do it!

MAURICE. Have no fear. This lady is not my kind. She just interests me. Scarcely even that.

MME CATHÉRINE. Don't trust yourself!

MAURICE. Yes, I do trust myself. Goodbye.

MAURICE *goes out.*

ACT II

SCENE 1

SCENE: *The Auberge des Adrets the same night.*

A café in theatrical seventeenth-century style, with alcoves containing tables and chairs.

The walls hung with armour and weapons, the shelves along the panelling holding glasses, pitchers, etc.

On one side a fireplace.

MAURICE *and* HENRIETTE, *in evening dress, sit facing one another at a table, on which stand a bottle of champagne and three filled glasses. The third glass is on the far side of the table and a third chair is placed for the expected third person.*

MAURICE *puts his watch on the table.*

MAURICE. If he doesn't come in five minutes, he won't come at all. . . . Shall we drink meanwhile with his ghost?

He touches the third glass with his own.

HENRIETTE *does likewise.*

HENRIETTE. Your health, Adolphe!

MAURICE. He won't come.

HENRIETTE. He will.

MAURICE. He won't.

HENRIETTE. He will.

MAURICE. What an evening! What a wonderful day! I can't grasp it yet—that a new life has begun. Just imagine, the manager believes I can count on at least a hundred thousand francs. I shall buy a villa for twenty thousand—outside the city—and I shall still have eighty thousand left. I shan't be able to take it all in until tomorrow. I'm so tired, tired, tired. *Sinks back in his chair.* Have you ever had a real stroke of luck?

HENRIETTE. Never. What does it feel like?

MAURICE. Well, how shall I put it? I can't really express it. But what I'm chiefly thinking about is the chagrin of my enemies. It's unpleasant of me, but that's how it is.

HENRIETTE. What's the point of thinking about one's enemies?

MAURICE. The conqueror always counts the enemy's dead and wounded in order to gauge his victory.

HENRIETTE. Are you as bloodthirsty as that?

MAURICE. Not really. But when you have felt other people's heels trampling on your chest for years, it's very pleasant to shake the enemy off and breathe.

HENRIETTE. Don't you find it strange to be sitting here alone with me, an insignificant girl and a stranger to you? On a night like this, when by rights you should be showing yourself as the triumphant hero to all the people on the boulevards and in the big restaurants.

MAURICE. Well, it is a little odd, but I like it here, and your company is all I want.

HENRIETTE. You're not very gay, are you?

MAURICE. No, I'm feeling rather sad. I should like to shed a few tears.

HENRIETTE. But why?

MAURICE. Success recognising its own emptiness and anticipating disaster.

HENRIETTE. How sad, how truly sad! What more can you want?

MAURICE. The one thing that makes life worth living. . . .

HENRIETTE. Then . . . you no longer love her?

MAURICE. No, not in the way I understand love. Do you imagine she has read my play or wants to see it? Oh, she is so good, so self-sacrificing and considerate, but she would think it wrong to go out and celebrate like this tonight. You know, I did once treat her to champagne and, instead of being pleased, she picked up the wine list to see what it cost. And when she saw the price, she cried. Cried because Marion needed new stockings. . . . Beautiful if you like, very moving. But what pleasure can one have when that's the way things are? And I want some pleasure before I get any older. So far I have lived in privation, but now, now . . . life is beginning for me.

A clock strikes twelve.

Now a new day is beginning. A new era.

HENRIETTE. Adolphe's not coming.

MAURICE. No, he's not coming. And now it's too late to go to the Crémerie.

HENRIETTE. But they are expecting you.

MAURICE. Then they must expect. They made me promise to come and I take my promise back. . . . Do you want to go there?

HENRIETTE. Far from it.

MAURICE. Then will you give me the pleasure of your company?

HENRIETTE. Willingly. If you can put up with it.

MAURICE. Well, considering I've begged you for it! Strange that the victor's crown should be worthless if you can't lay it at some woman's feet. That everything is worthless if you haven't a woman. . . .

HENRIETTE. Surely you have no need to be without a woman? You!

MAURICE. A question.

HENRIETTE. Don't you know that at the moment of success and fame a man is irresistible?

MAURICE. No, I don't. I haven't had that experience.

HENRIETTE. You are an extraordinary person. At this moment, when you're the most envied man in Paris, you just sit here brooding. Perhaps you have a bad conscience because you've neglected the invitation to drink chicory coffee with the old woman in the milk shop.

During the following dialogue somebody in the adjacent room begins to play the finale of Beethoven's Piano Sonata in D major (Op. 31, No. 3). The final Allegretto is played softly at first, but growing louder and more passionate until it ends in complete abandon.

MAURICE. Yes, my conscience does prick me on that score, and even here I can sense their resentment, their wounded feelings, their justifiable indignation. My comrades in distress had the right to demand my presence tonight. The good Madame Cathérine had a special stake in my success, which was to have given a glimmer of hope to the poor fellows who haven't had any luck as yet. . . . And I have cheated them of their good faith in me. I can hear them swearing: "Maurice will come. He's a good chap. He doesn't look down on us and he won't break his word." Now I have broken my word and theirs. . . . Who can be playing here at this time of night?

HENRIETTE. Some nightbird like us, I suppose. . . . But look, you're not putting the case as it is. Don't forget Adolphe promised to meet us. We have waited and he has broken his promise. So you are not to blame.

MAURICE. Is that what you think? I believe you while you're talking, but when you stop, my conscience starts up again. . . . What have you got there?

HENRIETTE. Oh, it's only a laurel wreath. I meant to send it up on to the stage, but I didn't get the chance. Let me give it to you now. It's supposed to cool the heated brow.

She rises, places the wreath on his head, and kisses his forehead.

Hail, victor!

MAURICE. No, don't!

HENRIETTE, *kneeling*. Hail, King!

MAURICE, *rising and taking off the wreath*. Don't! It frightens me.

HENRIETTE. How timid you are! So timid you're even scared of good fortune. Who took away your self-esteem and turned you into a dwarf?

MAURICE. Dwarf? Yes, you're right. I don't work up in the clouds like a giant, crashing and booming, but forge my sword down in the silent heart of the mountain. You think my modesty shrinks from the victor's wreath. No, I despise it because it's too slight for me. You think I fear the ghost sitting there with the green eyes of jealousy, keeping a watch on my feelings—of whose strength you have no notion. Away with you, ghost!

He sweeps the third, untasted, glass of champagne off the table.

Away, you unwanted third! You absent one, who have lost your rights if you ever had any. You shunned the field of battle because you knew yourself already beaten. So, as I crush this glass beneath my foot, I will crush to pieces the image you set up for yourself in a little temple which shall never again be yours.

HENRIETTE. Bravo! That's how it will be. Bravo, my hero!

MAURICE. Now I have sacrificed my best friend, my most faithful supporter, on your altar, Astarte. Are you satisfied?

HENRIETTE. Astarte. That's a beautiful name and I shall keep it. You must be in love with me, Maurice.

MAURICE. Naturally . . . *Femme fatale,* who scents the victim and rouses man's passion, where have you come from and where will you lead me? When they spoke of you, I trembled. And when I saw you—in the doorway—your spirit flew to mine. When you went away, you were still there in my arms. I wanted to flee from you, but something stopped me, and tonight we are driven together like quarry in the hunter's net. Who is to blame? Your friend, who played pander for us.

HENRIETTE. Blame or no blame, what's that got to do with it? What does it mean? Adolphe is to blame because he didn't bring us together before. He is guilty of the crime of robbing us of two weeks' life of bliss, to which he had no right. I am jealous of him on your behalf; I hate him for cheating you of your true love; I should like to blot him out of the numbers of the living and his memory too, to obliterate him from the past and make him unmade, unborn.

MAURICE. Then we will bury him under our own memories. We will peg him down in the depths of the forest and pile stones over him so that he can never raise his head again. *Raising his glass.* Our fate is sealed. Woe betide us! What is to happen now?

HENRIETTE. Now a new era will begin. . . . What's in that packet?

MAURICE. I don't remember.

HENRIETTE *opens the packet and brings out a tie and a pair of gloves.*

HENRIETTE. What a frightful tie! It must have cost quite fifty centimes.

MAURICE *snatches the things from her.*

MAURICE. Don't touch those!

HENRIETTE. Are they from her?

MAURICE. Yes, they are.

HENRIETTE. Give them to me.

MAURICE. No! She's better than us, better than us all.

HENRIETTE. I don't believe it. She's just simpler and stingier. A woman who cries because there's champagne . . .

MAURICE. When there aren't any stockings for her child. Yes, she's good.

HENRIETTE. You bourgeois! You'll never be an artist. But I am an artist, and I shall make a bust of you with a shopkeeper's cap instead of a laurel wreath. . . . Is she called Jeanne?

MAURICE. Yes. How do you know?

HENRIETTE. That's what all housekeepers are called.

MAURICE. Henriette!

HENRIETTE *picks up the gloves and the tie and throws them into the fireplace.*

Weakly. Astarte! Now you're demanding the sacrifice of women. That you shall have. But if it's to be innocent children, then you must go.

HENRIETTE. Do you know what it is that binds you to me?

MAURICE. If I knew, I would tear myself away. But I believe it is your evil qualities which I need. I believe it is the vice in you which attracts me with the irresistible pleasure of the new. . . .

HENRIETTE. Haven't you ever committed a crime?

MAURICE. No, not a real one. Have you?

HENRIETTE. Yes.

MAURICE. Well? What was that like?

HENRIETTE. It outweighed doing any good deed, for that only puts you on a level with others. It outweighed performing any feat, because that puts you above others and is rewarded. This crime put me outside, on the other side of life and society and my fellow-beings. Since that time, I have only been living a half life, a dream life, so reality no longer has any meaning for me.

MAURICE. What did you do?

HENRIETTE. I won't tell you. You'd be afraid again.

MAURICE. Can you never be found out?

HENRIETTE. Never. But that doesn't stop me from often seeing the five stones in the Place de Roquette, where the scaffold used to stand. And that's why I never touch cards, for the five of diamonds always comes up. . . .

MAURICE. Was it that kind of crime?

HENRIETTE. Yes, that kind.

MAURICE. That's pretty horrible, but it's interesting. Have you never had a conscience?

HENRIETTE. Never. But if we might talk about something else, I should be grateful.

MAURICE. What shall we talk about—love?

HENRIETTE. You don't talk about that until it's over.

MAURICE. Were you in love with Adolphe?

HENRIETTE. I don't know. The purity of his nature attracted me like some beautiful forgotten memory of childhood, but there was a great deal about his person that offended my eye. It took me a long time to erase, change, and add to and take from, so as to make a passable figure of him. When he talked, I could tell he had learnt his views from you, and they were often half understood and clumsily applied. So you can imagine how poor the copy appears now that I can see the original. That's why he was scared of letting us two meet, and when it did happen, he knew at once his time was up.

MAURICE. Poor Adolphe!

HENRIETTE. I'm sorry for him too. He must be suffering torments.

MAURICE. Hush! Someone's coming.

HENRIETTE. Suppose it is he?

MAURICE. That would be intolerable.

HENRIETTE. It isn't he, but if it had been, what do you think would have happened?

During the following dialogue the pianist in the adjacent room practises the D major Sonata, sometimes pianissimo, sometimes wildly fortissimo. At times there is silence: at others only bars 96–107 of the Finale are heard.

MAURICE. At first he would have been rather cross with you, because he had made a mistake about the café—looked for us in vain in the wrong place—but his arrogance would soon have given way to pleasure at seeing us—at seeing that we hadn't deceived him. And in his joy at finding he had wronged us by his suspicions, he would have loved us both, and so been delighted to find that we were such good friends. It had always been his dream—hm, this is him speaking now—his dream, that the three of us would make a trio and show the world a fine example of a friendship making no demands. "Yes, I trust you, Maurice, partly because you are my friend, partly because your affections are engaged elsewhere."

HENRIETTE. Bravo! Have you been in such a situation before that you are able to reproduce it so exactly? You know, Adolphe is just the kind that has to be a third, who can't enjoy his girl unless he has a friend along.

MAURICE. That is why I was called upon to entertain you. . . . Hush, there's someone outside! . . . It is he.

HENRIETTE. No, these are the hours when ghosts walk, you know, and when one hears so many things and sees them sometimes too. To be awake at night, when one should be sleeping, has the same charm for me as crime. One has set oneself above and beyond the laws of nature.

MAURICE. But the penalty is heavy. I am shivering or trembling, whichever it is.

HENRIETTE *takes her opera cloak and puts it round him.*

HENRIETTE. Have this round you. That will warm you.

MAURICE. It's beautiful. It's as if I were inside your skin, as if my vigil-worn body were recast in your form. I can feel it being moulded. But I am getting a new soul too, new thoughts, and here, my own breast is filling the curve which yours has left.

The music interrupts his thought.

What a monster to sit there all night practising the piano! I'm sick of it. I tell you what. We will drive out to the Bois de Boulogne and have breakfast in the Pavilion and watch the sun rise over the lake.

HENRIETTE. Good!

MAURICE. But first I must send a note home, so that my mail and the morning papers and the rest are sent out by messenger to the breakfast place. Listen, Henriette. Shall we invite Adolphe?

HENRIETTE. Yes, it's too crazy, but why not? The ass can surely be harnessed to the triumphal chariot. Let him come.

They rise.

MAURICE *removes the cloak.*

MAURICE. Then I'll ring.

HENRIETTE. Wait a moment!

She throws herself into his arms.

SCENE 2

SCENE: *The Bois de Boulogne. Dawn.*

A large, magnificently furnished room of a restaurant, with rugs and mirrors, chaise-longues and divans.

Back, French windows overlooking the water.

Centre, a table spread with flowers, bowls of fruit, decanters of wine, oyster platters, many kinds of wine glasses, and two lighted candelabra.

Right, a low table with newspapers and telegrams.

MAURICE *and* HENRIETTE *are sitting opposite one another at this table.*

The sun is rising.

MAURICE. There is no longer any doubt. The press says it is so, and these telegrams congratulate me on my success. This is a new life beginning, and my life is wedded to yours through this night, in which you alone have shared my hopes and my triumphs. It was from your hand I received my laurels and I feel everything has come to me from you.

HENRIETTE. What a wonderful night! Have we dreamt it or have we really lived it?

MAURICE, *rising*. And what a dawn for such a night! I feel as if it were the world's first day now being lighted by the rising sun. The earth has just been created and spun itself free of those white membranes now floating away. There lies the Garden of Eden in the rosy light of dawn, and here is the first pair of human beings. . . . Do you know, I am so happy I could weep to think that the whole of mankind is not as happy as I am. . . . Listen to that distant murmur, like waves on a pebbly beach, like the wind in the woods. Do you know what that is? It is Paris whispering my name. Do you see the smoke spiralling up to the sky in thousands and tens of thousands? That is Paris whispering my name. Those are my altar fires—or if they aren't, they shall be, for I will it to be so. At this very moment every telegraph in Europe is tapping out my name; the Oriental express is carrying the news to the Far East, into the rising sun, and the ocean liners to the furthest West . . . the earth is mine, and so it is beautiful. Now I wish for wings for both of us, so we could take flight far, far away, before anyone can spoil my happiness, before envy wakes me from my dream—because this probably is a dream.

HENRIETTE, *giving him her hand*. Feel! You are not dreaming.

MAURICE. It is not a dream, yet it has been one. You know, when as a penniless young man I used to walk down there in the woods and look up at this Pavilion, I saw it as an enchanted castle, and I always imagined myself up in this room with its balcony and its rich curtains—a place of pure bliss. To be here with a beloved woman, watching the sunrise with the candles still alight, was the most audacious dream of my youth. Now it has come true, and now I have no more to ask of life. . . . Would you like to die—now, with me?

HENRIETTE. No, you idiot! Now I want to begin to live.

MAURICE. To live is to suffer. Now comes reality. I hear his footsteps on the stairs. He is panting with anxiety; his heart is pounding with the dread of having lost the most precious thing of all. Believe me, Adolphe is under this roof. In one moment he will be standing here in the room.

HENRIETTE, *uneasily*. It was a stupid idea to invite him here, and I already regret it. . . . Well, at least we shall see if your forecast was right.

MAURICE. Of course, one can easily be mistaken about a person's feelings.

The HEAD WAITER *enters and hands him a card.*

Ask the gentleman to come in.

Exit the HEAD WAITER.

I am afraid we *shall* regret it.

HENRIETTE. Too late to think of that. Hush!

Enter ADOLPHE, *white and hollow-eyed.*

MAURICE, *trying to speak naturally*. So here you are! Wherever did you get to last night?

ADOLPHE. I went to join you at the Hôtel des Arrêts and waited a whole hour. . . .

MAURICE. But you went to the wrong place. We waited a couple of hours for you at the Auberge des Adrets and are still waiting, as you see.

ADOLPHE, *relieved*. Thank God!

HENRIETTE. Good morning, my dear. You are a gloomy bird, always expecting the worst. I suppose you imagined we were trying to avoid your company, and although you know we sent for you, you still think yourself *de trop*.

ADOLPHE. Accept my apologies. I was wrong, but the night was frightful.

They sit down. Embarrassed silence.

HENRIETTE, *to* ADOLPHE. Well, aren't you going to congratulate Maurice on his great success?

ADOLPHE. Oh, yes! You have had a real success—that envy itself can't deny. Everybody is at your feet. You make me feel quite small.

MAURICE. What nonsense! Henriette, pour Adolphe out a glass of wine.

ADOLPHE. Thank you, not for me. Nothing.

HENRIETTE, *to* ADOLPHE. What's the matter? Are you ill?

ADOLPHE. No, but I feel I may be.

HENRIETTE. Your eyes . . .

ADOLPHE. What about them?

MAURICE. How was it at the Crémerie last night? I suppose they're offended with me.

ADOLPHE. No one's offended with you, but your absence cast a gloom that was painful to see. But no one was offended, I assure you. Your understanding friends regarded you and your absence with sympathy and tolerance. Madame Cathérine herself took on your defence and proposed your health. We all rejoiced in your success as if it had been our own.

HENRIETTE. But what nice people! What good friends you have, Maurice!

MAURICE. Yes, better than I deserve.

HENRIETTE. No one has better friends than he deserves, and you are blessed in your friends. . . . Can't you feel how the very air is softened for you today by the stream of pure good wishes reaching you from a thousand hearts?

MAURICE *rises to conceal his emotion.*

ADOLPHE. From a thousand hearts which you have set free from the nightmare which had oppressed them all their lives. Human nature had been slandered and you have redeemed it, so people are grateful to you. Today they lift their heads again, saying: "See, we are better than our reputations!" And the thought makes them better.

HENRIETTE *tries to hide her emotion.*

Am I bothering you? Let me just warm myself for a moment in your sunshine, Maurice. Then I will go.

MAURICE. Why should you go when you have only just come?

ADOLPHE. Why? Because I have seen what I need never have seen, because I know now that my time is over. *Silence.* That you sent for me I take as a sign of consideration, an acknowledgement of what has happened, a candour less wounding than deceit. You know, Maurice, how well I think of human nature, and it's you who taught me to, Maurice. *Silence.* But, my friend, just now I went into the Church of Saint-Germain, and there I saw a woman and a child. I'm not sorry that you weren't there to see them, because what has happened cannot be changed; but if you had given them a thought or a word before you set them adrift on the open seas of the great city, then you might enjoy your good fortune in peace. And now I bid you goodbye.

HENRIETTE. Why are you going?

ADOLPHE. You ask that! Do you want me to tell you?

HENRIETTE. No, I don't.

ADOLPHE. Then goodbye.

Exit ADOLPHE.

MAURICE. The Fall. "And lo, they knew that they were naked."

HENRIETTE. How different this scene was from the one we imagined. He is better than we are.

MAURICE. I feel now everyone is better than we are.

HENRIETTE. Do you see? The sun has gone behind the clouds and the wood has lost its rosy tint.

MAURICE. I do see. And the blue water is black. Let us flee to where the sky is always clear and the trees are always green.

HENRIETTE. Yes, let us do that. But without farewells.

MAURICE. No, with farewells.

HENRIETTE. We should fly. You offered me wings, but your feet are of lead. I am not jealous; but if you go to say goodbye and find two pairs of arms about your neck, you will not be able to break away.

MAURICE. You are perfectly right, except that only one small pair of arms is needed to hold me.

HENRIETTE. It is the child that holds you then, not the woman.

MAURICE. It is the child.

HENRIETTE. The child! Another's child! And for that I am to suffer. Why should that child block the path, the path I must now take?

MAURICE. Why, indeed? Better if it had never existed.

HENRIETTE. Yes, but it does exist. Like a stone on the road, an immovable boulder which cannot fail to upset the carriage.

MAURICE. The triumphal chariot! The ass is driven to its death, but the boulder remains. Confound it!

Silence.

HENRIETTE. There's nothing to be done.

MAURICE. Yes. We must get married; then *our* child will make us forget the other one.

HENRIETTE. The other one would kill ours.

MAURICE. Kill? What a thing to say!

HENRIETTE, *changing her tone.* Your child will kill our love.

MAURICE. No, my dear. Our love will kill everything that stands in its way, but it will not be killed.

HENRIETTE *picks up a pack of cards from the mantelpiece.*

HENRIETTE. Look! The five of diamonds. The scaffold. Is it possible that our fates are predestined? That our thoughts are led as if through pipes, the way they must go, without our being able to stop them? No, I don't want to go that way! I don't want to! Do you realise I should go to the scaffold if my crime were discovered?

MAURICE. Tell me about your crime. This is the moment.

HENRIETTE. No, I should regret it afterwards, and you would loathe me. . . . No, no, no! *Pause.* Have you ever heard that one can hate a person to death? Well, my father came to be hated by my mother and his children, and he melted away like wax before a fire. Horrible! Let's talk about something else. . . . Above all, let's leave Paris. Here the air is poisoned; tomorrow your laurels will be withered, the triumph forgotten, and in a week all eyes will be on another victor. Away from here, to work for new victories! But first of all, Maurice, you must go and embrace your child and provide for its immediate future. The mother, you need not see.

MAURICE. Thank you. Your heart does you honour, and you are all the more dear to me when you show the kindness you sometimes hide.

HENRIETTE. And then go to the Crémerie and say goodbye to the old woman and your friends. Leave nothing behind you undone that might weigh on your mind on our journey.

MAURICE. I will do everything that should be done, and to-night we will meet at the railway station.

HENRIETTE. Agreed! And so, away from here, en route for the sunshine and the sea!

ACT III

SCENE 1

SCENE: *The Crémerie. Evening of the same day.*

The gas is lighted.

MADAME CATHÉRINE *is sitting beside the buffet.*

ADOLPHE, *at a table.*

MME CATHÉRINE. Such is life, my dear Monsieur Adolphe. But you young people are always demanding too much and then coming here and moaning about it.

ADOLPHE. No, it's not like that. I don't reproach anyone and I am still as fond as ever of them both. But there is something that makes me rather sick. You see, I was so much attached to Maurice, yes, so much that I wanted him to have everything that would make him happy. But now I have lost him; that hurts me more than the loss of her. I have lost them both, and so my loneliness is doubly painful. But there is something else too which I'm not quite clear about.

MME CATHÉRINE. Don't brood so much. Work and find things to do. Do you ever go to church, for example?

ADOLPHE. What should I do there?

MME CATHÉRINE. Oh, there's so much to see! And then there's the music. That at least is not banal.

ADOLPHE. Possibly not. But I don't belong to the fold, because I'm not devout. You see, Madame Cathérine, faith is undoubtedly a gift, and one that so far I have not got.

MME CATHÉRINE. Wait then, till you do get it. . . . But what is this tale I heard today? Is it true you have sold a picture in London at a very high price and won the top award?

ADOLPHE. Yes, it's true.

MME CATHÉRINE. But good heavens! And you haven't said a word about it?

ADOLPHE. I'm afraid of good fortune, and anyway it's almost worthless to me at this moment. I'm afraid, in the way one is of ghosts. It's bad luck to speak of having seen one.

MME CATHÉRINE. Well, you always were a strange fellow.

ADOLPHE. No, Madame, but I have seen so much bad luck follow on good, and I have seen how in misfortune one always has true friends, and in success only false ones . . . You asked me if I ever went to church and I didn't give you a straight answer. I did go into Saint-Germain this very morning, without quite knowing why. It was as if I went to look for someone to whom I could offer silent thanks—but I didn't find anyone. Then I put a gold coin in the poor box—that's all I got out of my churchgoing—and it was pretty banal.

MME CATHÉRINE. It was something at least. It was good to think about the poor when you were in luck.

ADOLPHE. It was neither good nor bad; it was just something I did because I couldn't help myself. But something else happened to me in the church too. I saw Maurice's friend Jeanne and his child. Struck down, crushed by his triumphal chariot; it was as if they bore the whole weight of his past misfortunes.

MME CATHÉRINE. Well, my child, how you come to terms with your consciences, I don't know. But that a decent person, a kindly, conscientious man like Monsieur Maurice, can throw over a woman and child in the twinkling of an eye—explain that to me.

ADOLPHE. I can't explain it, and he doesn't seem to understand it himself. I saw them this morning and it all seemed to them so natural, so right, that they couldn't imagine things otherwise. It was as if they were enjoying the satisfaction of having done some good deed or performed some sacred duty. There are things we can't explain, Madame Cathérine, and therefore it is not for us to judge. Besides, surely you saw how it came about. Maurice felt the danger in the air. I had a premonition; I tried to prevent their meeting. It's really as if an intrigue had been woven by some invisible power, as if they had been driven by a trick into one another's arms. I'm certainly disqualified in this case, but I don't hesitate to pronounce the verdict: not guilty.

MME CATHÉRINE. Well now, look, to be able to forgive as you do, that's religion.

ADOLPHE. Good heavens! Am I religious without knowing it?

MME CATHÉRINE. But, you see, to *let* oneself be driven or tempted into evil like Monsieur Maurice, that's either weakness or wickedness. And if you feel your strength failing, then you pray for help, and you get it. But he didn't do that—he was too stuck-up. . . . Who's this coming? Oh, I think it's the Abbé.

ADOLPHE. What does he want here?

Enter the ABBÉ.

ABBÉ. Good evening, Madame. Good evening, Monsieur.

MME CATHÉRINE. What can I do for you, Monsieur l'Abbé?

ABBÉ. Has Monsieur Maurice, the author, been here today?

MME CATHÉRINE. No, not today. There's this play of his on at the theatre, and that is probably keeping him busy.

ABBÉ. I have . . . bad news to give him. Bad in many respects.

MME CATHÉRINE. Dare I ask what kind of . . . ?

ABBÉ. Yes, there is no secret about it. His daughter, by Jeanne, born out of wedlock, is dead.

MME CATHÉRINE. Dead!

ADOLPHE. Marion dead!

ABBÉ. Yes. She died suddenly this morning, without any previous illness.

MME CATHÉRINE. O God! Who can tell Thy ways?

ABBÉ. The mother's despair calls for Monsieur Maurice's presence, and we must try to find him. . . . And now a question—in confidence. Was Monsieur Maurice known to be fond of the child, or was he indifferent to her?

MME CATHÉRINE. Did he love his little Marion? Monsieur l'Abbé, we all know how he doted upon her.

ADOLPHE. There is no doubt of that, Monsieur l'Abbé.

ABBÉ. I am glad to hear it. As far as I am concerned, that doubt is dispelled.

MME CATHÉRINE. Has there been a doubt?

ABBÉ. Unfortunately, yes. An evil rumour has been running round the *Quartier* that he had abandoned the child and its mother in order to go off with a strange woman. In a few hours this rumour has developed into definite accusations, and the feeling against him has now reached such a pitch that his life is threatened, and he is being called a murderer.

MME CATHÉRINE. O God, what is all this? What is it?

ABBÉ. I will tell you my own view. I am convinced that the man is innocent of this charge, and the mother is as sure of this as I am. But Monsieur Maurice has appearances against him, and he will not find it easy to clear himself, when the police come to interrogate him.

MME CATHÉRINE. Have the police got hold of the matter?

ABBÉ. Yes, the police have to be prepared to protect him from these evil rumours and the people's anger. I believe the Commissaire is on his way here now.

MME CATHÉRINE, *to* ADOLPHE. You see what happens when a man can't tell the difference between good and evil and flirts with vice. The Lord punishes.

ADOLPHE. Then He is more merciless than man.

ABBÉ. What do you know about this matter?

ADOLPHE. Nothing much more, but I can see how it happened. . . .

ABBÉ. And understand it too?

ADOLPHE. Not yet perhaps.

ABBÉ. Let us look more closely at the matter. . . . Here is the Commissaire.

Enter the COMMISSAIRE.

COMMISSAIRE. Messieurs, Madame, I must trouble you for a moment with some enquiries about Monsieur Maurice Gérard, who, as you have probably heard, is the object of a hideous rumour, which, by the way, I don't myself believe.

MME CATHÉRINE. None of us believe it either.

COMMISSAIRE. That strengthens my own opinion; but for his own sake I must give him a chance to defend himself.

ABBÉ. That is good. And he will surely find justice, hard though it may be.

COMMISSAIRE. Appearances are terribly against him, and I have seen innocent people mount the scaffold before their innocence was discovered. Listen to what they say against him. The child, Marion, left alone by her mother, was secretly visited by the father, who seems to have chosen the hour when the child would be alone. A quarter of an hour after the visit the mother returned and found the child dead. This is a serious situation for the accused. . . . The post-mortem shows no sign of violence nor any trace of poison, but the doctors affirm that there are newly discovered poisons which leave no trace. . . . To me this visit seems a coincidence, and I am well used to those. But worse was to come. Last night Monsieur Maurice was seen at the Auberge des Adrets with a strange lady. The conversation, according to the waiter, turned to crime. The Place de Roquette and the scaffold were mentioned. An unusual topic of conversation between lovers of good breeding and position. However this could have been, and we know from experience that people, who are short of sleep and have been drinking a good deal, tend to dig up the worst from the depths of their souls. More serious still is the evidence of the head waiter from the champagne breakfast in the Bois de Boulogne this morning. He states that he heard them wishing the life out of a child. The man appears to have said: "Better if it had never existed," to which the woman replied: "Yes, but it does exist." And later in the conversation came these words: "The other one would kill ours," to which the answer was: "Kill! What a thing to say!" and: "Our love will kill everything that stands in its way." And then: "The five of diamonds," "the scaffold," "the Place de Roquette." . . . All this, you see, is hard to explain away, and so finally is this foreign journey planned for tonight. These are serious matters.

ADOLPHE. He is lost.

MME CATHÉRINE. It is a horrifying story. What is one to believe?

ABBÉ. This is not the work of man. God have mercy on him!

ADOLPHE. He is caught in the net and will never get out.

MME CATHÉRINE. Why did he let himself get into it?

ADOLPHE. Are you beginning to suspect him, Madame Cathérine?

MME CATHÉRINE. Yes and no. I can no longer have any opinion in the matter. . . . Hasn't one seen angels turn into devils in the twinkling of an eye and then become angels again?

COMMISSAIRE. It's an extraordinary business. However, we must just wait and hear what he has to say. Nobody is condemned unheard. Good evening, Messieurs, good evening, Madame.

Exit the COMMISSAIRE.

ABBÉ. This is not the work of man.

ADOLPHE. It certainly looks like the work of demons for man's undoing.

ABBÉ. It is either retribution for hidden sins, or else a fearful test.

Enter JEANNE, *wearing mourning.*

JEANNE. Good evening. Excuse my asking, but has Monsieur Maurice been here?

MME CATHÉRINE. No, Madame. But he might come in at any moment. . . . Then you haven't seen him since . . .

JEANNE. Not since this morning.[1]

MME CATHÉRINE. Please accept my sympathy in your great sorrow.

JEANNE. Thank you, Madame. *To the* ABBÉ. Ah, you are here, Father!

ABBÉ. Yes, my child. I thought I might be of some help to you here. And it was fortunate, as I was able to have a few words with the Commissaire just now.

[1] NOTE. In the Swedish: "*yesterday* morning," which does not fit with Maurice's line in Act IV, Scene 1.

JEANNE. The Commissaire! He doesn't suspect Maurice too, does he?

ABBÉ. No, he does not, and nor do any of us here. But appearances are terribly against him.

JEANNE. You mean because of that conversation the waiter overheard . . . That means nothing to me. I've heard the same sort of things before when Maurice has had a few drinks. It's his habit then to speculate on crime and punishment. Besides, it seems to have been the woman he had with him who made the most dangerous remarks. I should like to look that woman in the eyes.

ADOLPHE. My dear Jeanne, however much wrong that woman may have unintentionally done you, she had no evil purpose, no evil purpose at all. She just followed the dictates of her heart. I know she is good and could look anyone straight in the eyes.

JEANNE. Your judgement in this matter is of great value to me, Adolphe, and I believe you. So there is no one I can blame for what has happened but myself. Yes, it is my heedlessness that is now being punished. *She weeps.*

ABBÉ. Do not reproach yourself unjustly. I know you, and how seriously you took your motherhood. That this responsibility was not sanctioned by the Church and Civil Law is not your fault. No, here we are facing something different.

ADOLPHE. What?

ABBÉ. Who can say?

Enter HENRIETTE *in travelling dress.*

ADOLPHE *rises resolutely and goes to meet her.*

ADOLPHE. You here?

HENRIETTE. Yes, where is Maurice?

ADOLPHE. Do you know . . . or don't you?

HENRIETTE. I know everything. Excuse me, Madame Cathérine, but I was all ready for the journey and had to come in here for a moment. *To* ADOLPHE. Who is that woman? . . . Ah!

HENRIETTE *and* JEANNE *stare at one another.*

EMILE *is seen in the doorway of the kitchen.*

To JEANNE. I ought to say something, but I don't know what, because whatever I say will sound crude or mocking. . . . But, Madame, if I ask you quite simply to believe that I share in your deep sorrow, as much as anyone closer to you does, then you must not repulse me. . . . You must not, for I deserve your pity, if not your forbearance.

HENRIETTE *holds out her hand to* JEANNE. JEANNE *gazes at her.*

JEANNE. I believe you now, but in another moment I shall not believe you.

JEANNE *takes* HENRIETTE'S *hand.*

HENRIETTE, *kissing her hand.* Thank you.

JEANNE *draws back her hand.*

JEANNE. No, don't. I don't deserve that. I don't deserve it.

ABBÉ. Forgive me, but while we are all gathered here, in harmony, so it seems, for the moment, won't you shed some light, Mademoiselle Henriette, on the uncertainty and darkness surrounding the main point of this accusation? I ask you, as among friends, to tell us what you meant by what you said about death and crime and the Place de Roquette. We are all convinced that these words had no connection with the death of the child, but it would relieve us to hear what that conversation meant. Will you tell us?
Pause.

HENRIETTE. I can't tell you. I can't.

ADOLPHE. Tell us, Henriette. Say the words that will bring peace to us all.

HENRIETTE. I can't. Don't ask me to do that.

ABBÉ. This is not the work of man.

HENRIETTE. To think that this moment had to come! And like this, like this! *To* JEANNE. Madame, I swear that I am not guilty of your child's death. Is that not enough?

JEANNE. It is enough for us, but not for justice.

HENRIETTE. Justice! If you knew how true your words were!

ABBÉ, *to* HENRIETTE. And if you understood what you said just now.

HENRIETTE. Do you understand it better than I?

ABBÉ. Yes.

HENRIETTE *gazes at the* ABBÉ.

Have no fear. For even if I guess your secret, I will not betray it. For that matter, human justice is not my concern. But divine grace is.

MAURICE *enters hastily, in travelling clothes. He does not look at the rest of the company in the foreground, but goes straight to the counter, where* MADAME CATHÉRINE *is sitting.*

MAURICE. Madame Cathérine, you are not angry with me for staying away? Anyway, I have come now to ask you to forgive me, before I start South at eight o'clock tonight.

MADAME CATHÉRINE *is too much taken aback to speak.*

Then you are angry with me. *Looks round.* What is all this? Is it a dream, or isn't it? . . . Yes, I see it is real, but it looks like a wax tableau. . . . There is Jeanne like a statue—all in black . . . And Henriette like a corpse . . . What does this mean?

Silence.

No one answers. . . . Then it means something terrible.

Silence.

But please *speak!* Adolphe, you are my friend, what is it? *Indicates* EMILE. And—there is a detective.

ADOLPHE, *coming forward.* You know nothing then?

MAURICE. Nothing. But I must know.

ADOLPHE. Well then . . . Marion is dead.

MAURICE. Marion—dead?

ADOLPHE. Yes, she died this morning.

MAURICE, *to* JEANNE. And that is why you are in mourning. Jeanne, Jeanne, who has done this to us?

JEANNE. He who holds life and death in His hand.

MAURICE. But I saw her well and rosy this very morning. How did it happen? Who did it? Somebody did this to us.

His eyes seek HENRIETTE.

ADOLPHE. Don't look for the guilty one here, for it is no one here. Unfortunately the police have turned their suspicions in a direction where there should be none.

MAURICE. Where is that?

ADOLPHE. Well . . . You must know that your reckless conversation last night and this morning has placed you in a light that is anything but favourable.

MAURICE. Were they listening to us? Let me think what it was that was said? . . . It's true . . . Yes, then I am lost.

ADOLPHE. But explain your thoughtless words. And we will believe you.

MAURICE. I can't. I will not. I shall be sent to prison, but that's nothing. Marion is dead! Dead! And I have killed her.

General consternation.

ADOLPHE. Think what you are saying! Weigh your words! Do you realise what you said?

MAURICE. What did I say?

ADOLPHE. You said that you had killed Marion.

MAURICE. Could anyone believe that I am a murderer and could kill my own child? Madame Cathérine, you who know me, tell me, do you believe it, do you believe it?

MME CATHÉRINE. I don't any longer know what to believe. What's in the heart the tongue will speak, and you have spoken evil words.

MAURICE. She does not believe me.

ADOLPHE. Well, but explain yourself. Explain what you meant by your love would kill everything that stood in its way.

MAURICE. I see. They know that too. Henriette, will you explain that?

HENRIETTE. I can't do that.

ABBÉ. Yes. There is something wrong behind all this, and you have lost our sympathy, my friends. Just now I would have sworn that you were innocent, but I cannot do that now.

MAURICE, *to* JEANNE. What you say means more to me than anything else.

JEANNE, *coldly*. First answer this question: who was it you cursed during that orgy out in the Bois?

MAURICE. Did I do that? Perhaps. Yes, yes, I am guilty, and at the same time guiltless. Let me go away from here, for I am ashamed, and my misdeeds are greater than I can forgive myself.

HENRIETTE, *to* ADOLPHE. Go with him or he will do himself some harm.

ADOLPHE. I?

HENRIETTE. Who else?

ADOLPHE, *without bitterness.* You were nearest. Hush! There's a carriage.

MME CATHÉRINE. It's the Commissaire. I have seen a great deal of life. But never would I have believed that success and fame were such brittle things.

MAURICE, *to* HENRIETTE. From the triumphal chariot to the police van.

JEANNE, *simply.* And the ass drawing it—who was that?

ADOLPHE. That was certainly me.

Enter the COMMISSAIRE, *with papers in his hand.*

COMMISSAIRE. A summons to appear at the Préfecture immediately, this evening, for Monsieur Maurice Gérard . . . and Mademoiselle Henriette Mauclerc. Present?

MAURICE *and* HENRIETTE. Yes.

MAURICE. Is this an arrest?

COMMISSAIRE. No, not yet. This is only a summons to attend in person.

MAURICE. And after that?

COMMISSAIRE. One does not know.

MAURICE *and* HENRIETTE *move towards the door.*

MAURICE. Goodbye to you all!

Everyone shows emotion.

The COMMISSAIRE, MAURICE, *and* HENRIETTE *go out.*

EMILE *enters and goes up to* JEANNE.

EMILE. Now, my dear sister, I will see you home.

JEANNE. And what do you think about all this?

EMILE. The man is innocent.

ABBÉ. Yes, but in my view it is and always will be despicable to break one's promise, and unpardonable where a woman and a child are concerned.

EMILE. I should certainly be inclined to feel the same as you now, as this concerns my sister, but I am unfortunately prevented from casting the first stone, because I have committed the same offence myself.

ABBÉ. Although I am innocent in this respect, I still cast no stones; but the act condemns itself and is punished by its consequences.

JEANNE. Pray for him! For them!

ABBÉ. No, that I shall not do, for it is presumptuous to wish to change the counsels of the Lord. And what has happened is surely not the work of man.

SCENE 2

SCENE: *The Auberge des Adrets. Evening of the following day.*

ADOLPHE *and* HENRIETTE *are sitting at the table where* MAURICE *and* HENRIETTE *sat in Act II, Scene 1.*

ADOLPHE *has a cup of coffee in front of him.* HENRIETTE, *nothing.*

ADOLPHE. You really believe he will come here?

HENRIETTE. Without any doubt. He was released this morning for lack of evidence, but he did not want to show himself outside until dusk.

ADOLPHE. Poor fellow. You know, life has seemed quite horrible to me since yesterday.

HENRIETTE. And what about me? I am afraid to live, scarcely dare breathe, scarcely dare think even, as I know someone is spying not only on my words but on my thoughts.

ADOLPHE. So you were here that night when I couldn't find you.

HENRIETTE. Yes, but don't speak of it. I could die of shame when I think of it. Adolphe, you are made of other and better stuff than he and I. . . .

ADOLPHE. No, no, no!

HENRIETTE. Yes, yes. And what persuaded me to stay? I was lazy; I was tired. His success bewitched me. I can't explain it. But if you had come, it would never have happened. . . . And today you are the great one and he the little, least of the least. Yesterday he had a hundred thousand francs, and today he is penniless, as his play has been withdrawn. He will never be cleared in public opinion, for it will condemn him for his infidelity as severely as if he were the murderer. Anyhow, the most considered opinion is that the child died from sorrow, so he *was* the cause of its death.

ADOLPHE. Henriette, you know my opinion, but I should like to be sure you are both completely innocent. Won't you tell me what your terrible words meant? It can't have been just idle chatter on such a festive occasion to talk so much of killing and the scaffold.

HENRIETTE. It wasn't idle chatter. It was something that had to be said and something I can't talk about. But I have no right to appear innocent in your eyes, for I am not innocent.

ADOLPHE. I don't understand.

HENRIETTE. Then let's talk about something else. . . . Has it ever occurred to you that there are many unpunished criminals at large, even among our intimate friends?

ADOLPHE, *uneasily*. How so? What do you mean?

HENRIETTE. Don't you think everyone at some time in his life does something that would be against the law if it were found out?

ADOLPHE. Yes, I think that is so, but no misdeed remains unpunished, at least by conscience.

He rises and unbuttons his coat.

And . . . nobody is a really good human being who has not erred. *Breathing heavily.* For to know how to forgive, one must have needed forgiveness oneself. . . . I once had a friend whom we called the Saint; he never spoke an ill word about anyone, forgave everything and everybody, and received insults with an extraordinary kind of satisfaction which we couldn't explain. At last, late in life, he told me his secret in a word: "I am a penitent."

He sits down. HENRIETTE *regards him silently, in surprise.* ADOLPHE *continues as if to himself.*

There are crimes not mentioned in the Criminal Code, and

they are the worst ones, for we have to punish them ourselves, and no judge is so severe as oneself.

Pause.

HENRIETTE. Well, this friend of yours, did he find peace?

ADOLPHE. After years of self-torture, he attained a certain degree of peace, but life never held any pleasure for him. He dared not accept any mark of distinction and never felt he deserved a kind word or well-earned praise. In a word, he could never forgive himself.

HENRIETTE. Never? What had he done?

ADOLPHE. He wished the life out of his father, and when the father suddenly died, the son imagined he had killed him. These imaginings were taken as symptoms of sickness, and he was put into a Home, from which after a while he emerged cured—so they said. But he still had his sense of guilt, and so he continued to punish himself for his evil thoughts.

HENRIETTE. Are you sure an evil will cannot kill?

ADOLPHE. In a mystic way, you mean?

HENRIETTE. If you like. Let's call it mystic. In my family I am sure that my mother, and we brothers and sisters, killed my father with our hatred. You see, he had a terrible way of systematically opposing all our likes and desires, and where he found any real vocation he tried to uproot it. And so he roused an opposition that became charged with hatred, and in the end it grew so powerful that he pined away, was neutralised, lost his will-power, and finally wished himself dead.

ADOLPHE. And your conscience never reproached you?

HENRIETTE. No. For that matter, I don't know what conscience is.

ADOLPHE. Don't you? Well, you will know soon. *Silence.* How do you think Maurice will look when he walks in here? What do you think he will say?

HENRIETTE. Do you know, yesterday, while we were waiting for you, he and I tried to make the same sort of guesses about you.

ADOLPHE. And?

HENRIETTE. We guessed completely wrong.

ADOLPHE. Can you tell me why you sent me that message?

HENRIETTE. Malice, recklessness, sheer cruelty.

ADOLPHE. Strange, the way you recognise your misdeeds but don't repent of them.

HENRIETTE. It's surely because I don't feel fully responsible for them. They are like the dirt left by all the things one handles during the day that one washes off at night. . . . But tell me something. Do you really think as highly of human nature as you profess to?

ADOLPHE. Well, we are a little better than our reputation—and a little worse.

HENRIETTE. That's not a direct answer.

ADOLPHE. No, it's not. But will you give me a direct answer when I ask you: do you still love Maurice?

HENRIETTE. I don't know until I see him. But at this moment I feel no longing for him, and I think I could live very well without him.

ADOLPHE. I think that's quite likely. But you are chained now to his fate. . . . Hush! Here he comes.

HENRIETTE. How everything repeats itself! Just the same situation and the same words as yesterday, when it was *you* who were expected.

MAURICE *enters, white as death, hollow-eyed, unshaven.*

MAURICE. Here I am, dear friends, if this be me. For last night in the cell has changed me into another person. *Gazes at* HENRIETTE *and* ADOLPHE.

ADOLPHE. Sit down and pull yourself together. Then we can talk things over.

MAURICE, *to* HENRIETTE. Perhaps I am *de trop.*

ADOLPHE. Don't be bitter towards us.

MAURICE. I have grown evil in these twenty-four hours, and so suspicious that I shall soon have to go my way alone. Anyhow, who wants to keep a murderer company?

HENRIETTE. Surely you have been cleared.

MAURICE, *picking up a newspaper.* By the police, yes, but not by the public. Here you see the murderer, Maurice Gérard, once the playwright, and his mistress, Henriette Mauclerc . . .

HENRIETTE. Oh my mother! My brothers and sisters! Lord Jesus, help us!

MAURICE. Do you see? I really do look like a murderer too. And it's also hinted that I stole my play. So not a trace is left of yesterday's conqueror. And in his place my rival, Octave, appears on the playbill. And it is he who will collect my hundred thousand francs. O Solon, Solon! Such is fortune, such is fame! You are lucky, Adolphe, not to have had any success so far.

HENRIETTE. Oh, but don't you know Adolphe has had a great success in London and won the top award?

MAURICE, *darkly.* No, I didn't know. Is that true, Adolphe?

ADOLPHE. Perfectly true, but I have refused the award.

HENRIETTE, *pointedly.* That I didn't know. Are you debarred from accepting distinctions—like your friend?

ADOLPHE. My friend? *Embarrassed.* Oh yes, yes!

MAURICE. I'm glad of your success, but it makes a gulf between us.

ADOLPHE. I expected that. I'm bound to be as lonely with my success as you with your adversity. To think that one's good fortune should hurt others. Life is appalling.

During the following speech two men in civilian clothes enter unnoticed and sit at a table in the background.

MAURICE. You say that. And what am I to say? It's as if a black veil had been pulled over my eyes and changed the whole shape and colour of life. This room is like yesterday's room, but it is quite different. I recognise you both, it is true, but you have new faces. I'm searching for words, because I don't know what to say to you. I ought to defend myself, but I can't. And I almost miss my cell, which at least protected me from those curious glances which pierce right through me. The murderer Maurice and his mistress. You don't love me any more than I care for you. Today you are ugly, clumsy, empty, repellent.

ADOLPHE. Come, come, pull yourself together! That you have been discharged, cleared of all suspicion, is bound to appear in some evening paper. And that will put an end to all the accusations. Your play is certain to be put on again, and at worst you can write a new one. Leave Paris for a year and let the whole thing be forgotten. You, who exonerated human nature, will be reinstated yourself.

MAURICE. Ha ha! Human nature! Ha ha!

ADOLPHE. Have you lost your faith in its goodness?

MAURICE. Yes. If I ever believed in it. Perhaps that was just a mood, a way of looking at things, a courtesy to wild beasts. If I, who was held to be among the better ones, can be so utterly base, how vile the others must be!

ADOLPHE. Now I'm going out to buy all the evening papers. Then we shall certainly have a basis for new points of view.

MAURICE, *turning*. Two detectives . . . That means I am released under surveillance, so as to give myself away by careless talk.

ADOLPHE. They aren't detectives. That's just your imagination. I recognise them both. *Begins to go.*

MAURICE. Don't leave me alone, Adolphe. I fear Henriette and I may come to open explanations.

ADOLPHE. Be reasonable, Maurice, and think of your future. Try to calm him, Henriette. I shall be back in a moment. *Exit* ADOLPHE.

HENRIETTE. Maurice, what do you think now about our guilt or guiltlessness?

MAURICE. I have not murdered. I only talked a lot of hot air when I was drunk. But it is your crime which walks again—and you have grafted it on to me.

HENRIETTE. Is that the tone you're taking? Was it not you who cursed your own child, who wished that it did not exist, and wanted to go away without farewells? And was it not I who begged you to go and see Marion and pay a visit to Madame Cathérine's place?

MAURICE. Yes, you are right. Forgive me. You were more humane than I, and the guilt is all mine. Forgive me. But at the same time I am guiltless. Who has tied this net out of which I can never escape? Guilty and guiltless, guiltless and guilty. This is driving me mad. Look! They are sitting over there, listening. . . . And no waiter cares to serve us. I shall go and order a cup of tea. Do you want anything?

HENRIETTE. Nothing.

Exit MAURICE.

The FIRST DETECTIVE *approaches* HENRIETTE.

DETECTIVE. Let me look at your papers, young woman.[2]

HENRIETTE. Young woman! How dare you!

DETECTIVE. Dare? I'll teach you, you tart!

HENRIETTE. Whatever do you mean?

DETECTIVE. Prostitutes are under my supervision. Well, yesterday you were here with one man, today with another. That amounts to prostitution. And unescorted ladies are not served here. So come along. Follow me!

HENRIETTE. My escort will be back in a minute.

DETECTIVE. Nice kind of escort. Hardly a protection for a lady.

HENRIETTE. O God! My mother! My brothers and sisters! . . . Don't you realise that I'm of good family?

DETECTIVE. A fine one, I'm sure. But anyway, the evening papers have made you famous. Come along!

HENRIETTE. Where to? Where am I to go?

DETECTIVE. To the Bureau, of course. To get a little card; a license which obliges you to have free medical attention.

HENRIETTE. Lord Jesus Christ, this can't be true!

DETECTIVE, *taking her arm*. Not true, eh?

HENRIETTE, *falling on her knees*. Save me! Maurice, help!

DETECTIVE. Hold your tongue! Don't struggle, damn you!

Enter MAURICE, *followed by the* WAITER.

WAITER. Gentlemen of your kind are not served here. Pay and get out! And take your tart with you.

MAURICE *desperately searches his pocket-book.*

MAURICE. Henriette, pay for me and let's get away. I haven't a sou on me.

HENRIETTE *looks in her purse.*

[2] NOTE. In the original, the Detective uses the familiar second person to Henriette, which enrages her. "Young woman" is used as an equivalent insult.

WAITER. So it's the lady who pays for her "Alphonse." "Alphonse!" Do you know what that means?

HENRIETTE. My God! I haven't any money either. Why doesn't Adolphe come back?

DETECTIVE. What a damned pack of people! Get going! Leave something as security. Women like her usually have their fingers covered with rings.

MAURICE. Is it possible that we have sunk so low?

HENRIETTE *pulls off a ring and hands it to the* WAITER.

HENRIETTE. The Abbé was right. This is not the work of man.

MAURICE. No, it's the work of the devil. . . . But if we leave before Adolphe comes back, he will think that we have deceived him and slipped away.

HENRIETTE. That would be in keeping with the rest. Anyhow, it's the river for us now, isn't it?

MAURICE *takes* HENRIETTE'S *hand as they go out.*

MAURICE. The river, yes!

ACT IV

SCENE 1

SCENE: *Beside the statue of Adam and Eve in the Luxembourg Gardens, late afternoon the following day.*

The wind is blowing in the trees and stirring leaves, straws, and bits of paper on the ground.

MAURICE *and* HENRIETTE *are seated on a bench.*

HENRIETTE. You don't want to die?

MAURICE. No, I daren't. I imagine myself freezing in the grave, with only a sheet over me and a few shavings underneath. Besides, it seems to me that I still have something left undone, although I don't know what it is.

HENRIETTE. I can guess what it is.

MAURICE. Tell me.

HENRIETTE. It is revenge. . . . You, like me, suspect Jeanne and Emile of having set those detectives on me yesterday. Only a woman could think up such a revenge on a rival.

MAURICE. Those were my thoughts. But you know my suspicions go even further. It's as if these last days of suffering have sharpened my wits. For instance, can you explain why the waiter at the Auberge des Adrets and the head waiter at the Pavilion were not called to give evidence at the hearing?

HENRIETTE. I hadn't thought of it before, but yes, I do know why. They had no evidence to give, because they had not listened to our conversation at all.

MAURICE. Then how did the Commissaire know what we had said?

HENRIETTE. He didn't know, but he figured it out. He guessed and guessed right. Perhaps he has had a similar case before.

MAURICE. Or else he knew from our looks what we had said. There certainly are people who can read the thoughts of others. He found it quite natural that we should call Adolphe, as he was the dupe, the ass. That appears to be the rule, with the slight exception that he is generally called the idiot. But as there was talk of a chariot, a triumphal chariot, ass came more readily to mind. It's simple to find the fourth factor when you know three.

HENRIETTE. To think that we let ourselves be so completely taken in!

MAURICE. That's due to thinking well of people. That's what one gets for it. But I may tell you that, behind this Commissaire, who, by the way, must be an unmitigated scoundrel, I suspect there is another.

HENRIETTE. You mean the Abbé, who was playing the part of private detective.

MAURICE. That's who I mean. That man has to hear so many confessions. And don't forget this—Adolphe told me himself he had been in Saint-Germain that morning. What did he do there? Told the tale, of course, and bewailed his fate. And then the Abbé added two and two together for the Commissaire.

HENRIETTE. Tell me something. Do you trust Adolphe?

MAURICE. I don't trust any human being any longer.

HENRIETTE. Not even Adolphe?

MAURICE. Him least of all. How can I trust an enemy, a man whose mistress I stole?

HENRIETTE. Well, as you said it first, I will give you a few details about our friend. You know he refused that award from London. Can you think of any reason?

MAURICE. No.

HENRIETTE. Well, he considers himself unworthy of it, and he has taken a penitential vow not to receive any distinctions.

MAURICE. Is that possible? Why, what has he done?

HENRIETTE. He has committed a crime which is not punishable by law. That's what he told me, in an indirect way.

MAURICE. He too! He, the best, the most perfect of men, who never speaks ill of anyone, and forgives everything.

HENRIETTE. Yes. So you see, we are no worse than others. Although we are hunted as if by devils night and day.

MAURICE. He too! Then human nature has not been slandered. . . . But if he was capable of *one* crime, then one may expect anything of him. Perhaps it was he who set the police on you yesterday. Now that I come to think of it, it was he who sneaked away from us, when he saw us in the newspaper, and he was lying when he insisted those fellows weren't police. One may expect anything of a lover who has been deceived.

HENRIETTE, Would he be so low? No, it's impossible. Impossible.

MAURICE. Why? As he is a scoundrel . . . What did you talk about yesterday before I came?

HENRIETTE. He spoke nothing but good of you.

MAURICE. You're lying.

HENRIETTE, *collecting herself and changing her tone.* Listen, there's still one person you haven't suspected at all—I don't know why. Have you considered Madame Cathérine's changing attitude about all this? In the end, didn't she say right out that she believed you capable of anything?

MAURICE. Yes, she certainly did say that—and that shows what kind of a person she is. Because to think so ill of another without good reason, you must be a complete scoundrel yourself.

HENRIETTE *stares at him. Silence.*

HENRIETTE. To think so ill of another, you must be a complete scoundrel yourself.

MAURICE. What do you mean?

HENRIETTE. What I said.

MAURICE. Do you mean that I . . . ?

HENRIETTE. Yes, that's what I do mean now. Listen. Did you meet anyone but Marion on your visit that morning?

MAURICE. Why do you ask?

HENRIETTE. Why do you think?

MAURICE. Well, as you appear to know it, yes, I met Jeanne too.

HENRIETTE. Then why did you lie to me?

MAURICE. I wanted to spare you.

HENRIETTE. And now you want me to believe someone who has lied to me. No, my dear, now I believe that you committed that murder.

MAURICE. Wait a minute! Now we have reached the point where my thoughts have been heading, but which I resisted for as long as possible. . . . It is remarkable how the thing that lies nearest is the last thing one sees, and what one does not want to believe, one does not believe. . . . Tell me something. Where did you go yesterday morning, after we parted in the Bois?

HENRIETTE. Why?

MAURICE. You were either at Adolphe's, which you couldn't have been, because he was giving a lesson, or you went—to—Marion.

HENRIETTE. Now I am convinced that you are the murderer.

MAURICE. And I that you are the murderess. Because you alone had an interest in the child being out of the way—the stone upsetting the carriage, as you so aptly put it.

HENRIETTE. That was your expression.

MAURICE. And the one who had the interest committed the crime.

HENRIETTE. Maurice, we have been running round and round this treadmill, scourging one another. Let us stop now or else we shall go quite mad.

MAURICE. You are that already.

HENRIETTE. Don't you think it is time for us to part, before we drive one another insane?

MAURICE. Yes, I do think so.

HENRIETTE, *rising*. Then, goodbye.

Two men in civilian clothes appear in the background.

HENRIETTE *turns back to* MAURICE.

There they are again.

MAURICE. The dark angels who will drive us from the garden.

HENRIETTE. And force us upon each other, as if we were welded together.

MAURICE. Or as if we were condemned to life-long marriage. Should we in fact marry? Share the same home, and be able to shut the door on the world and perhaps in the end find peace?

HENRIETTE. Shut ourselves in to torture one another to death; lock ourselves in, each with his ghost as marriage portion, you tormenting me with Adolphe's memory and I torturing you with Jeanne's—and Marion's.

MAURICE. Never mention Marion's name again! You know that she is being buried today—perhaps at this very moment.

HENRIETTE. And you are not there. What does that mean?

MAURICE. It means that both Jeanne and the police have warned me of the crowd's fury.

HENRIETTE. Coward too?

MAURICE. All the vices. How could you care for me?

HENRIETTE. Because two days ago you were a different person, worthy of being loved.

MAURICE. And now sunk to such depths.

HENRIETTE. Not that. But you are beginning to flaunt bad qualities which are not your own.

MAURICE. But yours.

HENRIETTE. Perhaps. For when you appear worse, I at once feel rather better.

MAURICE. It's like going about, passing on a certain kind of disease.

HENRIETTE. And you have become coarse too!

MAURICE. I notice that myself. I don't recognise myself since that night in gaol. They put in one person and let out another, through that gate that separates us from society. You know, now I feel I am the enemy of mankind. I should like to set fire to the earth and dry up the sea, for nothing less than a world conflagration can wipe out my dishonour.

HENRIETTE. I had a letter from my mother today. My mother is the widow of a major and has high-minded, old-fashioned ideas about honour and all that. Would you care to read the letter? No, you wouldn't! Do you realise I am an outcast? My respectable acquaintances won't have anything to do with me, and if I go about alone, the police will take me up. Do you understand now that we must marry?

MAURICE. We hate one another and yet we must marry. That is hell itself. But, Henriette, before we join our destinies, you must tell me your secret, so that we are more evenly matched.

HENRIETTE. Very well, I will tell you. I had a friend who got into trouble . . . you understand me? I wanted to help her, for her future was at stake. And as I was unskilled, she died.

MAURICE. That was a rash thing to do, but it was rather noble.

HENRIETTE. So you say now, but next time you are angry, you will reproach me with it.

MAURICE. No, I won't do that . . . but I cannot deny that this shakes my confidence. I'm afraid to be with you. Tell me —is her lover still alive and does he know you were responsible?

HENRIETTE. He was just as guilty.

MAURICE. Then suppose his conscience were to awake—that often does happen—and he felt obliged to denounce you. Then you would be lost.

HENRIETTE. I know that very well, and it is this constant dread which drives me to live so fast and furiously, so as not to have time to wake to full consciousness.

MAURICE. And now you want me to take my marriage portion of your dread. That is asking too much.

HENRIETTE. But since I have shared the dishonour of Maurice, the murderer . . .

MAURICE. Let's put an end to . . .

HENRIETTE. No, this is not the end yet, and I shall not loose my hold until I have seen right through you. For you shan't go round thinking yourself better than I am.

MAURICE. You want to fight me, do you? Very well, you shall.

HENRIETTE. For life and death.

A roll of drums in the distance.

MAURICE. The garden is to be closed. "Cursed is the ground for thy sake . . . thorns also and thistles shall it bring forth to thee."

HENRIETTE. "And the Lord said unto the woman . . ."

The park KEEPER, *in uniform, approaches.*

KEEPER, *courteously.* Monsieur, Madame, the garden must be closed.

SCENE 2

SCENE: *The Crémerie. The same evening.*

MADAME CATHÉRINE *at the counter, making entries in a book.*

ADOLPHE *and* HENRIETTE *at a table.*

ADOLPHE, *calmly, kindly.* But if for the hundredth time I swear that I did not sneak away, but on the contrary thought you had given me the slip, that ought to convince you.

HENRIETTE. But why did you fool me by saying they weren't police?

ADOLPHE. I didn't think they were myself, and I also said it to reassure you.

HENRIETTE. When you put it that way, I do believe you. And

now you must believe me too, when I reveal my innermost thoughts to you.

ADOLPHE. Go on.

HENRIETTE. But you mustn't make your usual retort about fancy and imagination.

ADOLPHE. You seem to have reason to fear I may.

HENRIETTE. I don't fear anything, but I know you and your scepticism. . . . Well then . . . but you mustn't tell anyone this. Promise me that.

ADOLPHE. I promise.

HENRIETTE. Well, you've got to take in, terrible though it is, that I have some proof that Maurice is guilty—or at least reasonable grounds for suspicion. . . .

ADOLPHE. What are you saying?

HENRIETTE. Listen. Then you can judge. When Maurice left me in the Bois, he said he was going to see Marion alone, while the mother was out. But now, afterwards, it has come out that he did meet the mother. So he was lying to me.

ADOLPHE. That's possible, and probably from the best of motives, but how can anyone conclude from that that he committed murder?

HENRIETTE. Can't you see? Don't you understand?

ADOLPHE. Not in the least.

HENRIETTE. Because you don't want to. Well, then I have no choice but to inform on him, and then we will see if he can establish an alibi.

ADOLPHE. Henriette, let me tell you the whole grim truth. You and he are both on the brink—of madness. You are in the grip of the demons of suspicion, and each of you is tearing the other to pieces with your sense of partial guilt. Let me see if my guess is right. Doesn't he also suspect you of murdering his child?

HENRIETTE. Yes, he's as insane as that.

ADOLPHE. You call his suspicions insane, but not your own.

HENRIETTE. Prove the contrary—or that I suspect him unjustly.

ADOLPHE. Yes, that is easily done. A further autopsy has proved that Marion died of a recognised disease—with a strange name I can't now remember.

HENRIETTE. Is that true?

ADOLPHE. The official report is in today's paper.

HENRIETTE. You can't go by that. It may have been falsified.

ADOLPHE. Henriette! Take care, or you may go over the edge without realising it. Above all, beware of making accusations which might land you in prison. Beware! *He puts his hand on her head.* Do you hate Maurice?

HENRIETTE. Beyond all bounds.

ADOLPHE. Where love turns to hatred, the love was already tainted.

HENRIETTE, *more calmly.* What shall I do? Tell me, you who alone understand me.

ADOLPHE. But you don't want any sermons.

HENRIETTE. Have you nothing else to offer me?

ADOLPHE. Nothing. But they have helped me.

HENRIETTE. Preach away then.

ADOLPHE. Try to turn your hatred against yourself. Lance your own boil, because that is the seat of *your* evil.

HENRIETTE. Explain yourself!

ADOLPHE. First, break with Maurice, so you haven't a chance to cultivate your consciences together. Put an end to your artistic career, for which your only vocation was a desire for the gay Bohemian life, as they call it. You see now how gay it is! Go home to your mother.

HENRIETTE. Never.

ADOLPHE. Somewhere else then.

HENRIETTE. Adolphe, I presume you know I have guessed your secret and realise why you wouldn't accept that award.

ADOLPHE. I suppose you understood that half-hinted story?

HENRIETTE. Well, yes. But what did you do to gain peace?

ADOLPHE. As I intimated. I grew conscious of my guilt, repented, resolved to atone, and lived the life of a penitent.

HENRIETTE. How can you repent when, like me, you haven't any conscience? Is repentance a grace one gets like faith?

ADOLPHE. Everything is grace, but one doesn't get it, you know, unless one seeks for it. . . . Seek!

HENRIETTE *is silent.*

And don't let the time go by. If you do, you may harden and go to pieces among those past helping.

HENRIETTE, *after a further silence.* Is conscience fear of punishment?

ADOLPHE. No, it is the hatred of our better natures for the misdeeds of our lower natures.

HENRIETTE. In that case, I have a conscience too.

ADOLPHE. Of course you have, but . . .

HENRIETTE. Tell me, Adolphe, are you what one means by religious?

ADOLPHE. Not in the least.

HENRIETTE. It's all so extraordinary. Whatever is religion?

ADOLPHE. I just don't know, and I don't believe anyone can tell you. It seems to me sometimes that it's a punishment, because no one gets religion who hasn't a bad conscience.

HENRIETTE. Yes, it is a punishment. . . . Now I know what I must do. . . . Goodbye, Adolphe.

ADOLPHE. Are you going away?

HENRIETTE. Yes, I am going away . . . To where you said. Goodbye, my friend. Goodbye, Madame Cathérine.

MME CATHÉRINE. Are you off in such a hurry?

HENRIETTE. Yes.

ADOLPHE. Would you like me to come with you?

HENRIETTE. That wouldn't do. I must go alone, as alone as I came in here one spring day, here where I didn't belong, believing that there was something called freedom, which doesn't exist. Goodbye.

Exit HENRIETTE.

MME CATHÉRINE. I hope that lady never comes back and I wish she had never come here at all.

ADOLPHE. Who knows if she had not some mission to fulfil here? And in any case, she deserves pity, boundless pity.

MME CATHÉRINE. I don't deny that, for we all deserve it. . . .

ADOLPHE. She has actually done less wrong than the rest of us. . . .

MME CATHÉRINE. Possible, but not probable.

ADOLPHE. You are always hard, Madame Cathérine. Tell me something. Haven't you ever done anything wrong?

MME CATHÉRINE, *startled.* Certainly, for I am a sinful human being. But anyone who has fallen through thin ice has the right and the duty to tell others not to go that way. And without being considered hard or uncharitable. Didn't I say to Monsieur Maurice, when that same lady came in here: "Take care! Don't go there!" But he went and so he fell in. Like a naughty, self-willed child. And whoever behaves in that way gets a thrashing like a disobedient boy.

ADOLPHE. Well, hasn't he had his thrashing?

MME CATHÉRINE. Yes, but it doesn't seem to have been enough, for he's still going round pitying himself.

ADOLPHE. That is a very popular interpretation of this complicated matter.

MME CATHÉRINE. Bosh! You do nothing but philosophise about your vices, and while you're at it, the police come and solve the riddle. Now leave me in peace to do my accounts.

ADOLPHE. Here is Maurice.

MME CATHÉRINE. Yes, God bless him!

MAURICE *enters, very flushed, and sits down beside* ADOLPHE.

MAURICE. Good evening.

MADAME CATHÉRINE *nods and goes on adding.*

ADOLPHE. How are things with you?

MAURICE. Well, beginning to straighten out now.

ADOLPHE *hands him a newspaper, which he does not take.*

ADOLPHE. So you have seen the paper?

MAURICE. No, I don't read the papers any more. There's nothing in them but infamy.

ADOLPHE. Well, but you had better read this before . . .

MAURICE. No, I won't. It's only lies. But now you shall hear a new view. . . . Have you guessed who committed the murder?

ADOLPHE. No one! No one!

MAURICE. Do you know where Henriette was during that quarter of an hour when the child was alone? Well, she was *there*. And it is she who did it.

ADOLPHE. You are crazy, man!

MAURICE. Not I, but Henriette is crazy, for she suspects me and has threatened to inform on me.

ADOLPHE. Henriette was here just now and used the same words as you. You are both crazy, for it has now been established by a second autopsy that the child died from a recognised disease, the name of which escapes me.

MAURICE. That's not true.

ADOLPHE. That's what she said too. But the official report is there in the paper.

MAURICE. Official report? Then it's been falsified.

ADOLPHE. She said that too. You have the same mental sickness, the two of you. But I managed to make her see her lunacy.

MAURICE. Where has she gone?

ADOLPHE. She has gone far away—to begin a new life.

MAURICE. Mm, mm! . . . Did you go to the funeral?

ADOLPHE. Yes, I was there.

MAURICE. Well?

ADOLPHE. Well, Jeanne was calm and had no hard word to say about you.

MAURICE. She is a good woman.

ADOLPHE. Then why did you throw her over?

MAURICE. I was crazy, quite beyond myself, and then we drank champagne . . .

ADOLPHE. Do you understand now why she cried when you drank champagne?

MAURICE. Yes, I understand now. . . . And because I do, I have already written and asked her to forgive me. . . . Do you think she will forgive me?

ADOLPHE. I am sure she will, for she hasn't it in her to hate anyone.

MAURICE. Do you think she will really forgive, so that she will want to come back to me?

ADOLPHE. I don't know about that. You have given such proof of your infidelity that she can hardly trust her fate to you any longer.

MAURICE. Yes, but I can feel that her affection for me has not gone. I know she will come back.

ADOLPHE. How do you know that? What makes you believe it? Didn't you suspect her and that decent brother of hers of revenging themselves by setting the police on Henriette as a prostitute?

MAURICE. I don't think that any longer. Although Emile is a queer customer.

MME CATHÉRINE. Now look here, what are you saying about Monsieur Emile? Of course, he is only a workman, but if only everyone was as correct as he is! There's no flaw in him, and he has understanding and tact . . .

Enter EMILE.

EMILE. Monsieur Gérard?

MAURICE. Here I am.

EMILE. Excuse me, but I have something private to say to you.

MAURICE. Please say it. We are all friends here.

The ABBÉ *enters and seats himself.*

EMILE *glances at him.*

EMILE. Perhaps after all . . .

MAURICE. It makes no difference. The Abbé is a friend too, although he and I hold different opinions.

EMILE. You know who I am, Monsieur Gérard? My sister has only asked me to give you this package as an answer to your letter.

MAURICE *takes the package and opens it.*

Now I only have to add, as I am, as it were, my sister's guardian, that on her behalf and on my own, I acknowledge you, Monsieur Gérard, free of all obligations, now that the natural bond between you no longer exists.

MAURICE. But you must have a grudge against me.

EMILE. Must I? No, I don't see why. On the other hand, I should like to have a declaration from you, Monsieur Gérard, here in the presence of your friends, that you don't think me or my sister so low that we could have put the police on Mademoiselle Henriette.

MAURICE. I wish to take back what I said and offer you my apologies, if you will accept them.

EMILE. They are accepted. I wish you all a good evening.

ALL. Good evening.

Exit EMILE.

MAURICE. The tie and the gloves which Jeanne gave me for the opening night of my play, and which I let Henriette throw into the fireplace. Who snatched them back? Everything is dug up; everything repeats itself. . . . And when she gave them to me in the cemetery, she said I was to look fine and handsome, so that others would like me too. . . . She stayed at home herself. . . . This hurt her too deeply, and well it might. I should not be in the company of decent people. Oh, have I done this? Scoffed at a gift from a kind heart, scorned a sacrifice to my own good. This I threw away for—a laurel wreath, which is lying on the rubbish heap, and a bust which should stand in the pillory. . . . Monsieur l'Abbé, now I put myself in your hands.

ABBÉ. Welcome!

MAURICE. Say the word I need.

ABBÉ. Do you mean me to contradict your self-accusations and inform you that you have done nothing wrong?

MAURICE. Say the right word!

ABBÉ. With your permission then, I must say that I have found your behaviour as abominable as you have found it yourself.

MAURICE. What shall I do? What shall I do to get free of all this?

ABBÉ. You know as well as I do.

MAURICE. No, I only know that I am lost, that my life is ruined, my career closed, my reputation in this world lost for ever.

ABBÉ. And so you are looking for a new existence in another, better world, in which you are beginning to believe?

MAURICE. That is so.

ABBÉ. You have been living for the flesh and now you wish to live for the spirit. Are you sure then that this world no longer holds any attractions for you?

MAURICE. None. Honour—an illusion; gold—dry leaves; women—intoxicants . . . Let me hide behind your consecrated walls and forget this appalling dream, which has taken two days and lasted two eternities.

ABBÉ. Very well. But this is not the place to go into the matter more closely. Let us arrange to meet in Saint-Germain this evening at nine o'clock. I am going, as it happens, to preach to the penitentiaries of Saint-Lazare, and that can be your first step on the hard road of penance.

MAURICE. Penance?

ABBÉ. Yes, did you not wish . . . ?

MAURICE. Yes, yes!

ABBÉ. After that we have a vigil from midnight until two o'clock.

MAURICE. That will be good.

ABBÉ. Give me your hand, so that you will not look back.

MAURICE, *rising and giving him his hand.* Here is my hand with all my heart.

The SERVING GIRL *enters from the kitchen.*

GIRL. There is a telephone call for Monsieur Maurice.

MAURICE. Who from?

GIRL. From the theatre.

MAURICE *tries to break away from the* ABBÉ, *but he holds him fast.*

ABBÉ, *to the* GIRL. Ask what it is about.

GIRL. Well, they want to know if Monsieur Maurice will be at the performance tonight.

ABBÉ, *to* MAURICE, *who is still trying to get free.* No, I will not let go.

MAURICE, *to the* GIRL. What performance is it?

ADOLPHE. Why don't you read the paper?

MME CATHÉRINE *and* ABBÉ. He hasn't read the paper!

MAURICE. It's all lies and slander. *To the* GIRL. Tell them at the theatre that I am engaged tonight. I am going to church. *The* GIRL *goes out to the kitchen.*

ADOLPHE. As you won't read the paper, I had better tell you that the theatre is putting on your play again, now that you are exonerated. And your literary friends have arranged to pay a tribute to you tonight—on the stage with the curtain up—a tribute to your uncontested talent.

MAURICE. It's not true.

ALL. It is true.

MAURICE, *after a silence.* I don't deserve this.

ABBÉ. Good!

ADOLPHE. And there's more still, Maurice.

MAURICE, *hiding his face in his hands.* More!

MME CATHÉRINE. A hundred thousand francs. You see how they have come back to you. And the villa outside the city. Everything is coming back, except Mademoiselle Henriette.

ABBÉ, *smiling.* You should take it all a little more seriously, Madame Cathérine.

MME CATHÉRINE. No, but you see I can't, I can't keep serious any longer.

She puts her handkerchief to her face and bursts out laughing.

ADOLPHE. Well, Maurice, it's eight o'clock at the theatre.

ABBÉ. But it's nine o'clock at the church.

ADOLPHE. Maurice!

MME CATHÉRINE. Monsieur Maurice, we must hear the end now.

MAURICE *puts his head on his arms on the table.*

ADOLPHE. Free him, Monsieur l'Abbé!

ABBÉ. It is not for me to set free or to bind. He must do that himself.

MAURICE, *rising.* Very well, I shall go with the Abbé.

ABBÉ. No, my young friend. I have nothing to give you but

a scolding, which you can give yourself. And you have a responsibility to yourself and your good reputation. That you have come through this so quickly is to me a sign that you suffered your punishment as intensely as if it had lasted an eternity. And when Providence has granted you absolution, there is nothing for me to add.

MAURICE. Why was I punished so severely when I was guiltless?

ABBÉ. Severely? Only two days. And guiltless you were not, for we are responsible for our thoughts, our words, and our desires. You murdered in your mind when you wished the life out of your child.

MAURICE. You are right. . . . But my decision is made. Tonight I will meet you at the church to have a reckoning with myself about all this—but tomorrow I shall go to the theatre.

MME CATHÉRINE. A good solution, Monsieur Maurice.

ADOLPHE. Yes, that's the solution. Phew!

ABBÉ. Yes, that is it.

EASTER
A Play in Three Acts

INTRODUCTION

EASTER has long been a favourite among Strindberg's plays, both in Sweden and in England. The small cast of six characters and the single set of a verandah furnished as a living-room, put it within the scope of the smallest theatre, while the opportunities for fine acting and imaginative production are large. Nor in this modern Mystery or Morality Play is there any of the grim tragedy found in many of Strindberg's dramas. It is tender, sensitive and has a haunting quality of goodness.

Strindberg tells us that the mood of Easter was suggested by Haydn's *Sieben Worte des Erlösers* ("The Seven Words of the Redeemer"), and its form by the three poignant days of the Christian calendar—Maundy Thursday, Good Friday and Easter Eve. The Christian message is woven into that of Nature herself, as spring comes to the frozen north, and man's pride cracks with the melting ice.

The Heyst family is seen in a provincial university town, where the father is serving a term of imprisonment for embezzling trust funds. His wife displays a fanatical belief in his innocence, and Elis, the schoolmaster son, is weighed down with shame, for in addition to his father's dishonour and debts, Eleanora, the young daughter, has been sent away to a mental hospital. Kristina, Elis's fiancée, and Benjamin, one of his pupils whose inheritance was purloined by the father, make up the household.

Maundy Thursday brings further difficulties and disappointments, and Lindkvist, the Heysts' heaviest creditor, comes to live across the road and remind them by his presence that he can sell up their home whenever he pleases. But it also brings Eleanora, half child, half angel, to breathe peace among them in spite of her own trouble.

Good Friday is dark indeed. Elis is forced to go vainly through all the reports of his father's case again, and he believes he has lost Kristina to a friend who has already played him false. Eleanora fears that she may be arrested for taking a daffodil from a closed shop, and over the whole family looms the shadow of the Creditor.

On Easter Eve the clouds gradually lift, until at the end the Creditor comes not as ogre, but as guardian angel, and the future promises fair for the little family which has gone through "the school of suffering."

The theme is slight, but the play is rich in imagery, of which the producer could make far better use than is usually made. Some of the characters, such as Mrs. Heyst and Kristina the fiancée, are shadowily sketched and need plenty of invention to bring them into the round. Elis, on the other hand, is fully drawn—a portrait of young, frustrated manhood, blinded by self pity; and so is Eleanora, the "Easter Girl"—one of the strangest and most poetic of Strindberg's creations. Simple, child-like, clairvoyant, she can hear the language of flowers and read the hearts of human beings, and the words of the Scriptures pour unpremeditated from her lips, because God is her friend.

All Strindberg's work is, in some degree, autobiographical, and it is a help to the interpretation of this play to notice some of the threads woven into it. EASTER was written in Stockholm in the autumn of 1900, when the dramatist, at the age of fifty-one, had returned to his own country and to the theatre after a long absence. While recovering from a prolonged nervous breakdown he lived at Lund, the University town in the South of Sweden which, as a Stockholmer with an adoration for the skerries and the Mälar Lake, he did not like. He therefore chose this town as the purgatory of the Heyst family. While he was there his sister Elisabeth was sent into a mental hospital. Strindberg believed that she had taken the sins of their whole family on her shoulders and she was never out of his mind as he modelled his "Easter Girl." Eleanora was also influenced by Balzac's Séraphita, and Strindberg endowed her with all his own hypersensitiveness and clairvoyance, and gave her into the bargain the flower-like patience in suffering he could never achieve himself. To Elis he gave much of his own pride, his moodiness, jealousy and timidity, and his own detested days both as schoolmaster and pupil are reflected in the play. Here too we find the garden of the Deaf and Dumb which one of his lodgings in Paris overlooked, and some of the phenomena of birds and flowers he had gathered up on his travels for a Book of Miracles. EASTER also contains some of Strindberg's favourite themes, to be found in many of his works, such as the law of recurrence—"everything happens again," and the doctrine of crime as punishment.

Here and there a little knowledge of Swedish life helps to explain the action. The examination, for instance, in which, in the first act, Benjamin knows himself to have failed, is the annual Student Examination, which bestows the right to enter a university. The students usually make a rough copy of their papers, and this is what Benjamin shows Elis. The disappointment of failing to pass at the right age (16–17) would be heavy in any case, but for Benjamin his failure involves a further year of living in the home of the man who stole his inheritance. Then, again, when a Swedish graduate presents his thesis for a Doctor's degree in any subject, the thesis is printed and distributed, and its author is called upon to defend his work in a public debate. In Act One Peter Holmblad has just done this, and is giving a dinner to celebrate his success. The Lenten Birch, ancient symbol of penance, decorates many Swedish homes at this season, its original grimness disguised with bright ribbons and tassels.

The Swedish Church is, of course, Lutheran, and Strindberg was brought up as a Pietist, a strict sect of this denomination. Although he broke away, a puritanical influence remained; but it is essential that the religious message of EASTER should not obscure the Northerner's passion for spring itself. The taking down of double windows and the laying aside of heavy winter clothing are poignant expressions of release from the long imprisonment of winter, and although the whole play takes place within a verandah, Nature plays an important part in the action.

Strindberg's stage directions are always capricious. He brings characters on and omits to take them off again; he instructs them to stand up when it seems unlikely that they would have been sitting, and often gives no indication at all when one is most anxious to see the action through his eyes. The same with properties. Some object is suddenly presented as important, when we have never heard of it before. Take, for instance, the pendulum clock in Act Two. This was the family possession that Eleanora loved best of all. Would she then not have looked for it in Act One, when she came back from the asylum, "bare and white as a bathroom", to the dear familiarity of her home? And the piano that is mentioned just once, when Eleanora describes the bad clock that always began to strike when Elis played, should this not be used too? Might not Elis in one of his moods—perhaps when he thinks Kristina has deserted him—be heard playing that piano?—another precious possession, by the way, that the Creditor has the power to seize. Then there is the birch, symbol of "the school of suffering" through which the family is passing. It comes as a present to Elis, to warn him of his pride—just as his own voice on the telephone tries to warn him to stand the test to which Kristina is compelled to put him. The Lenten Birch and the Lenten Lily, symbol of healing, dominate the play. Elis hears the galoshes of the Creditor swishing like the birch in use and works himself up into a frenzy of flagellation. Yet he has simply stuck the birch behind the mirror, where Strindberg leaves it to speak for itself. There are many more such instances of the dramatist's reliance on the imagination of his producer, and in return we should remember two things. First that Strindberg often criticised a producer's lack of boldness, and second that he was a pioneer of Expressionism. He is essentially a twentieth century, not a nineteenth century writer. He was bent on breaking the bourgeois tradition of the theatre of his age, and should never be limited by the dates of his life. His plays, whether historical or contemporary, are not period pieces; they all have a quality of timelessness.

This translation was made while two different amateur companies were putting the play on, and I had the benefit of constantly hearing the lines spoken. I have taken a few liberties with the original text, but only, of course, in the matter of stage directions, based on the experience of these productions. I have, for example, left the placing of the furniture to the discretion of the producer, and omitted the indications "Left" or "Right" in entrances or exits. Apropos, it is interesting to note that when Lindkvist makes his only entrance in Act Three, Strindberg has him coming from the side. Much emphasis is laid in Act One on the open front door in the centre of the back wall, and in Act Two on the gigantic shadow of the Creditor thrown right across the back, a device actually suggested to Strindberg by a Shadow Play of *The Giant of the Skinflint Mountains.* But when at last Lindkvist enters in the flesh, his creator slips him in at the side. The only reason for this would seem to be that Mrs. Heyst should see Lindkvist first in the kitchen, as she describes his appearance to Elis; but this reason is refuted as Lindkvist himself shortly afterwards wonders if Mrs. Heyst is at home. When the Uppsala students performed the play in England, they followed Strindberg's direction, but it was certainly an anti-climax, robbing Lindkvist of a most dramatic entry and Elis of scope for reaction. And so, occasionally, I have left out Strindberg's stage directions, and where I felt it was quite necessary to make his meaning clear, I have added to them.

The world première of EASTER was at Frankfurt in March 1901, and the first Swedish performance followed at the Dramatic Theatre in Stockholm on Maundy Thursday of the same year, with Harriet Bosse, the talented young Norwegian actress who was shortly to become Strindberg's third wife, creating the part of Eleanora. It was revived next in 1908 for Strindberg's own Intimate Theatre when it had an outstanding success, and since then has been very often played in Sweden. The first English performance appears to have been by a small experimental theatre group in 1924, and it is interesting to remember that in 1928 it was produced at the Arts Theatre Club with John Gielgud and Peggy Ashcroft in the principal parts.

E. S.

Characters

MRS. HEYST
ELIS, *her son (a Schoolmaster)*
ELEANORA, *her daughter*
KRISTINA, *Elis's fiancée*
BENJAMIN, *a Pupil at the grammar school*
LINDKVIST

SET FOR ALL THREE ACTS

The whole play takes place inside the glass verandah of a house in a small university town in the south of Sweden, furnished as the living-room of a middle-class family.

In the centre of the back wall is the front door leading into a garden, with a fence and a gate to the street. Across the street which, like the house, is on a height, can be seen another low fence round a garden sloping down to the town. The trees in this garden are breaking into leaf, and beyond them are a church tower and the imposing gable of a house. In the street is a lamp post with an incandescent lamp.

The glass windows of the verandah, stretching across the back and two sides of the stage, are hung with curtains of a pale yellow flowery material which can be drawn. On one side of the front door hangs a mirror with a calendar below it.

There are two other doors, one leading to the kitchen, the other to the rest of the house.

The furniture consists of a big porcelain stove with mica panes, a dining-table, a sideboard, a large writing table on which stand books, writing materials and a telephone, and a sewing table, arm chairs, lamps, etc.

ACT ONE

MAUNDY THURSDAY

Musical Prelude: Haydn: The Seven Words of the Redeemer. Introduction: Maestoso Adagio.

A shaft of sunlight falls across the room, reaching one of the arm chairs by the sewing-table. In the other chair, out of the sun, sits KRISTINA, *threading a tape through a pair of freshly ironed white curtains.*

ELIS *enters, leaving the front door open. He is wearing his winter overcoat, unbuttoned, and carries a bundle of papers. He and* KRISTINA *greet one another affectionately.*

ELIS. My dear!

KRISTINA. Ah Elis, here you are!

ELIS *flings down the papers and they embrace. Then, as he takes off his coat, he gazes round the room in delight.*

ELIS. The double windows have been taken down—oh, and the floor has been scrubbed and fresh curtains put up! Yes, it's spring again. They have hacked up the ice in the street, and down by the river the willows are in leaf. Yes, it's spring again—and I can put away my winter overcoat. *He weighs the coat in his hands, and his mood quickly changes to bitterness.* Look how heavy it is. As if it had soaked up all the hardships of winter—the sweat of anguish, and the dust of school. *He throws the coat down on a chair.*

KRISTINA, *soothing him.* But now you have a holiday.

ELIS. Yes, the Easter Holiday. Five glorious days to make the most of—to breathe and forget. *He takes her hands and they sit down together.* Look, the sun has come back. It went away in November. I remember the very day when it disappeared over there behind the brewery. Oh, what a winter, what an endless winter!

KRISTINA, *anxiously, indicating the kitchen door.* Hush!

ELIS. Don't worry my dear. I'm going to be quite calm. It's just that I'm so glad it's over. Ah, this good sun! *He springs up.* I want to wash myself in sunshine. I want to bathe myself in light after all this filth and darkness.

KRISTINA, *again glancing anxiously towards the kitchen.* Hush, Elis, hush.

ELIS, *recovering.* But you know I really believe peace is on the way—that our misfortunes are wearing themselves out at last.

KRISTINA. What makes you think that?

ELIS. Well . . . partly because just now as I was passing the cathedral, a white dove came flying by. It swooped down to the pavement and dropped the twig it was carrying in its beak right at my feet.

KRISTINA. Did you see what kind of twig it was?

ELIS. I suppose it couldn't really have been an olive branch, but I feel sure it was a sign of peace. And now at this moment, I feel such a saving, sunlit calm . . . *With sudden anxiety.* Where is Mother?

KRISTINA. In the kitchen.

ELIS, *reassured, closes his eyes, smiles and speaks softly and happily.* I *hear* that it is spring. I hear that the double windows have been taken out. Do you know what tells me? *Pause.* First, the creaking of the cart-wheels . . . And now what's that? The chatter of the chaffinch. And they're hammering in the shipyard . . . and there's a smell of paint . . . the red-lead paint they are using for the steamers.

KRISTINA. Can you get all that here?

ELIS. Here? *He opens his eyes and his smile fades.* Yes, true enough, we are—*here. With growing misery.* But I was *there,* far away up north where our home is. Why did we ever come to this odious town where people all hate each other, and one is always lonely? Yes, it was to get our daily bread, but the bread was spread with calamities—with Father's crime and my little sister's sickness. *Pause.*

Do you know if Mother got permission to see Father in prison?

KRISTINA. As a matter of fact I believe she was there today.

ELIS. What did she say about it?

KRISTINA. Not a word. She talked about other things.

ELIS. All the same something has been achieved. After the verdict, there was an end of suspense. There was even a kind of strange calm once the papers had dropped the subject. And now one year is over. In another year he will be out, and then we can make a new start.

KRISTINA. I admire your patience in suffering.

ELIS. Don't. Don't admire anything about me, for I am nothing but faults. Now you know—and you'll have to believe me.

KRISTINA. It's not as if it were your own faults you're suffering for. It's other people's.

ELIS, *to change the subject.* What's that you're making?

KRISTINA. Curtains for the kitchen, dear.

ELIS. They look like a bridal veil . . . In the autumn, Kristina, you will be my bride.

KRISTINA. Yes . . . But we have the summer to look forward to first.

ELIS, *excited.* Yes, the summer. *He fetches his bank book from the writing table and shows it to her.* Look how much money I have saved already. As soon as term is over we will set out for the north, for our own country, for the Mälar Lake. The cottage stands there waiting, just as it was when we were children. The lime trees are there —and the boat moored under the willows. Ah, that it were summer now and I could bathe in the lake! This family disgrace has smeared me all over—body and soul, so that I pine for a lake to wash myself in.

KRISTINA. Have you heard at all from your sister?

ELIS. Yes. Poor little Eleanora. She's miserable and she writes letters that make my heart bleed. Naturally she begs to be let out and allowed to come home. But you see, the Principal of the Institution dare not let her go, because she does things which might land her in prison. All the same I sometimes feel conscience-stricken for having given my consent to her being shut up there.

KRISTINA. You blame yourself for everything, dearest, but surely—as things were—it was a mercy to have her properly taken care of, poor little thing.

ELIS. You are perfectly right, and I know very well how much better things are this way. Yes, she is as well off there as she could possibly be anywhere. And when I think of the shadow she threw over any glimmer of happiness when she was here, of how her condition weighed on us like a nightmare, tormenting us past bearing, I am selfish enough to feel such relief that it is almost happiness. The worst misfortune I can imagine at this moment would be to see her come through that door. What a wretch I am!

KRISTINA. How human you are.

ELIS. But all the same I'm tormented. Tormented by the thought of her misery and my father's.

KRISTINA. It's as if some people were born to suffering.

ELIS. Poor you—to come into a family doomed from the beginning . . . and damned.

KRISTINA. Elis, you can't tell whether all this is a punishment or just a kind of test.

ELIS. I don't know what it can be for you. You, of all people, are free from guilt.

KRISTINA. Well, there's the saying "tears in the morning, laughter at eve." Dearest, perhaps I can help you to get through . . .

ELIS. Do you think Mother has a clean white tie for me?

KRISTINA, *uneasily*. Are you going out?

ELIS. Yes. You know, Peter presented his thesis yesterday, and tonight he's giving a dinner to celebrate getting his doctor's degree.

KRISTINA. Do you want to go to it?

ELIS. You mean I ought to stay away, considering what an ungrateful pupil he has turned out.

KRISTINA. I admit I'm shocked by his disloyalty—promising to quote your work, and then lifting whole passages from it without acknowledgment.

ELIS. Oh, that's always the way. And I get a certain satisfaction from knowing it's really my own work.

KRISTINA. Has he invited you?

ELIS, *surprised.* Come to think of it, he hasn't. That's really most extraordinary, for he's been talking about this dinner for years, as if I were certain to be there—and I've talked about it too, to other people. If now I'm not invited it's a public insult. No matter, it's not the first I've had, nor will it be the last. *Pause.*

KRISTINA. Benjamin's late. Do you think he'll have passed?

ELIS. I certainly hope so—with a credit in Latin.

KRISTINA. He's a nice boy, Benjamin.

ELIS. Uncommonly nice, although he does rather brood over things . . . Kristina, I suppose you know why he is living here with us?

KRISTINA, *hesitating.* Is it because . . . ?

ELIS, *harshly.* Because, as in the case of so many others, my father embezzled the money that was in trust for the boy. That's what's so horrible, Kristina. In school I have to see all these fatherless children whom my father robbed and who now have the humiliation of being charity pupils. And you can imagine how they look at me. I have to go on reminding myself of the miserable plight they are in so as to forgive their cruelty.

KRISTINA. I believe your father is really better off than you are.

ELIS. Undoubtedly.

KRISTINA. Elis, we must think of the summer, and not of the past.

ELIS. Yes, of the summer. Do you know, last night I was woken up by students singing the song that goes "Yes, I am coming. Happy winds, go tell the earth, tell the birds I love them. Tell the birches and limes, the mountains and lakes, I long to see them once again—to see them as when I was a child."* Shall I "see them once again?" Shall I ever escape from this dreadful town—from Ebal, the mount of curses, and behold Gerizim once more?

KRISTINA. —Yes, yes, you will.

ELIS. But even then, shall I see my birches and limes as I saw them when I was a child? Won't the same black veil cling to them that clings to all nature—*He moves as if trying to free his body from this terrible clinging gloom* —that has clung to life itself ever since that day . . . *He breaks off and points to the arm chair which is now in shadow.* Look, the sun has gone?

KRISTINA. It will come again, and next time it will stay longer.

ELIS. That's true. The days are lengthening, and the shadows growing shorter.

KRISTINA. We are moving towards the light, Elis—believe me.

ELIS. Sometimes I do believe it. When I think of past days and compare them with these now, I am happy. Last year you were not sitting there. You had left me—you had broken off our engagement. You know, for me that was the darkest time of all. I literally died, bit by bit—but when you came back, I came to life again. Why did you go away? KRISTINA *shakes her head.* Can't you remember?

KRISTINA. No, I don't remember. It seems now as if there was no real reason. I just felt I was being told to go, and so I went—as if I were walking in my sleep. When I saw you again, I woke up and was happy.

ELIS. And now we will never part again. If you left me now, I really should die . . . Here's Mother. Don't say anything. Let her go on living in her world of illusion, believing that Father is a martyr and all his victims are swindlers. MRS. HEYST *comes in from the kitchen, wearing an apron and peeling an apple. She speaks in a kindly, absent-minded way.*

MRS. HEYST. Good evening, children. Would you like your apple sauce† cold or hot?

*Lines from a well-known student song.

†Soup in the original.

ELIS. Cold, Mother dear.

MRS. HEYST. That's right, my son. You always know what you want and say so. You can't do that, Kristina. Elis learnt it from his father. He always knew what he wanted and what he was about. People can't stand that, and so things went badly for him. But his day will come, when he will be proved right and the others wrong. Now, wait a minute, what was it I wanted to tell you? . . . Oh yes. Have you heard that Lindkvist has come to town? Lindkvist, the greatest swindler of them all.

ELIS, *agitated.* He has come here?

MRS. HEYST. Yes, he's living just across the street.

ELIS. Then we're bound to see him passing every day. That too!

MRS. HEYST. Just let me have a word with him, and he'll never show his face again, for I know a thing or two about him . . . Well, Elis, how did Peter get on with his thesis?

ELIS. Very well.

MRS. HEYST. I can quite believe it. And when are you going to present your thesis?

ELIS. When I can afford to, Mother.

MRS. HEYST. When I can afford to—that's no answer. And Benjamin? Has he got through his exam?

ELIS. We don't know yet, but he'll be in soon.

MRS. HEYST. I see. You know, I'm not sure I quite like Benjamin. He goes round giving himself airs, as if he had some claim on us, but we'll cure him of that, he's a nice boy really. Oh yes, there's a parcel for you, Elis. *She goes out to the kitchen.*

ELIS. You know, Mother doesn't miss much. I sometimes think she's not so simple as she makes out.

MRS. HEYST, *coming in and handing* ELIS *a parcel.* Here it is. Lina took it in.

ELIS. A present? I'm afraid of presents, since that day I was sent a box of stones. *He puts it down.*

MRS. HEYST. I'm going back to the kitchen. *She looks anx-*

iously at the front door, as if fearing an intruder. Isn't it too cold with that door open?

ELIS. No no, not at all, Mother.

MRS. HEYST. Elis, you shouldn't leave your overcoat there—it looks so untidy. Well, Kristina, are my curtains nearly ready?

KRISTINA. Yes, Mother, in just a few minutes. *She begins to work again.*

MRS. HEYST. You know I like that Peter—he's rather a favourite of mine . . . Aren't you going to his dinner, Elis?

ELIS. Yes, yes—why, certainly—of course.

MRS. HEYST. Then why did you say you wanted your apple sauce cold, if you're going out? You're so vague, Elis. But Peter isn't. Shut the door if there's a draught, so you don't catch cold. *She goes out to the kitchen.*

ELIS. Poor dear Mother. And it's always Peter. What's her idea? Is she trying to tease you about Peter?

KRISTINA. Me?

ELIS. Well, you know the queer notions old women get.

KRISTINA. What is your present?

ELIS *opens the parcel and slowly draws out a bundle of birch twigs tied together.*

ELIS. A Lenten birch.

KRISTINA. Who's it from?

ELIS. It doesn't say. Well, it's harmless enough. I shall put it in water and it will blossom like Aaron's rod. *Then suddenly he cuts the air with it and speaks cynically.* "Birch . . . as when I was a child" . . . And as for limes—Lindkvist—the twig of lime*—has come here.

KRISTINA. Why does it matter so much?

ELIS, *laying down the birch.* We owe him more money than all the rest.

KRISTINA. But surely *you* don't owe him anything?

*Lindkvist means in Swedish "Twig of Lime." I have added these words after his name to give point to "birches and limes," etc., otherwise lost in English.

ELIS. *We* do. We are all in this together. The family name is dishonoured so long as one debt remains.

KRISTINA. Change your name.

ELIS. Kristina!

KRISTINA. Thank you, Elis. I only wanted to test you.

ELIS. But you mustn't tempt me. Lindkvist is a poor man. He needs what belongs to him. Wherever my father went, the place became like a battlefield strewn with dead and wounded. Yet my mother believes he is the victim. *Pause.* Would you like to come for a walk?

KRISTINA. And find the sun? With all my heart.

ELIS, *thinking it out.* Do you understand this, Kristina? The Redeemer suffered for our sins, yet we have to go on paying. No one is paying for me.

KRISTINA. But if someone were paying for you, would you understand then?

ELIS. Yes, of course, then I should understand. . . . *Listening.* Here comes Benjamin. Can you see if he is looking cheerful?

KRISTINA, *looking out.* He's walking very slowly . . . and now he's stopping at the fountain, and bathing his eyes.

ELIS. That too.

KRISTINA. Wait a little. . . .

ELIS. Tears, tears!

KRISTINA. Be patient.

BENJAMIN *comes in, polite but sad. . . . He is carrying some books and a satchel.*

ELIS. Well, how did the Latin go?

BENJAMIN. Badly.

ELIS. May I see your notes? What went wrong?

BENJAMIN. I used "ut" with the indicative where I knew it should be the subjunctive.

ELIS. Then you're done for. But what on earth made you do such a thing?

BENJAMIN, *humbly.* I can't make it out. I knew how it ought to go, and I wanted to write it that way—but I wrote it wrong.

A long pause, while ELIS *looks through the papers.* BENJAMIN *slumps down at the table.*

ELIS. Yes, here it is, the indicative. O Lord!

KRISTINA, *to* BENJAMIN. Well, better luck next time. Life is long, terribly long.

BENJAMIN, *bitterly*. Yes, it certainly is.

ELIS, *sadly, but without bitterness.* That everything should happen at once like this. You were my best pupil, so what can I expect of the others? My reputation as a teacher will be ruined. I shall get no more tutoring and so—well, everything's gone to pieces. *Seeing* BENJAMIN'S *distress* . . . Don't take it so hard, it's not your fault.

KRISTINA, *urgently*. Elis, for heaven's sake, have courage.

ELIS. Where am I to find it?

KRISTINA. Where you found it before.

ELIS. This isn't the same as before. I seem to have fallen from grace.

KRISTINA. It is a sign of grace to suffer when you are innocent. Don't be tempted to impatience. Stand the test—for this is only a test. I feel sure of that.

ELIS. Can the year Benjamin must go through now be less than 365 days?

KRISTINA. Yes, a cheerful heart makes time go quickly.

ELIS, *ironically*. Blow on the sore and make it better—that's what they tell children.

KRISTINA, *to* ELIS *gently*. Be a child then, and I'll comfort you like one. Think of your mother, how she bears it all.

ELIS. Give me your hand, I am sinking. KRISTINA *gives him her hand.* Your hand is trembling.

KRISTINA. I don't feel it.

ELIS. You're not so strong as you make out.

KRISTINA. I don't feel any weakness.

ELIS. Then why can't you give me strength?

KRISTINA. I have none to spare.

ELIS, *turns to the window. Pause.* Look who's coming—the Creditor!

KRISTINA, *looking out of the window too.* This is too much.

ELIS, *hysterically.* The Creditor. The man who can take all our furniture, everything we own, whenever he pleases. Lindkvist, who has come here to sit like a spider in the centre of his web and watch the flies.

KRISTINA, *catching hold of him and pointing to the kitchen.* Go away.

ELIS. No, I won't. Just now when you grew weak, I grew strong. Now he's coming up the street. He has already cast his evil eye on his prey.

KRISTINA. At least keep out of his sight.

ELIS. No, now I find him amusing. He seems to be gloating over his quarry caught in the trap. Come on, my friend! He's measuring the distance to the gate. He sees by the open door that we are at home . . . But now he has met someone. He's stopping to talk. They're talking about us—he's glancing this way.

KRISTINA. So long as he doesn't meet Mother. If she gives him the sharp edge of her tongue, there'll be no hope at all. Don't let that happen, Elis.

ELIS. Now he's shaking his stick, as if to declare that in this case mercy shall not take the place of justice. He's unbuttoning his overcoat to show that at least we've left him the clothes he stands up in. I can see by his lips what he's saying. What shall I answer? Sir, you are right. Take everything, it belongs to you?

KRISTINA. That's all you can say.

ELIS. Now he's laughing. *Pause. Surprised.* But it's a kind laugh, not a cruel one. Perhaps he's not so cruel after all, even if he does want his money. I wish he'd come on in and stop that blessed chatter. *Watches.* Now he's waving his stick again—they always have sticks—those creditors that come to dun you—and galoshes that go "swish, swish";—like a cane through the air. *He holds Kristina's* *hand against his heart.* Feel how my heart is pounding. There's a throbbing in my right ear like an ocean liner. Ah, now he's saying goodbye. And here come the galoshes "swish, swish" like the Lenten birch. But he has a watch chain, with trinkets dangling from it—so he's not quite destitute. They always wear trinkets made of cornelian—like chunks of flesh cut off their neighbour's backs. Listen to the galoshes. *Working himself up into a flagellating frenzy.* Swish, swish, beast, beasts, hard, harder, harder! Swish, swish!* Look out! He's seen me, he's seen me! *Bows towards the street.* He bowed to me first. He's smiling. He's waving his hand—and . . . he has gone the other way. *He collapses at the writing table.*

KRISTINA. Thank God.

ELIS. He has gone away, but he will come again. *Long pause.* Let us go out into the sun.

KRISTINA. But what about Peter's dinner?

ELIS. As I haven't been invited, I'm not going. Anyhow, what have I to do with people celebrating? Why go to meet a disloyal friend? I should suffer just the same, but blame it all on him.

KRISTINA. So you're going to stay at home with us. Oh thank you!

ELIS. You know very well that's what I want to do. Shall we go?

KRISTINA. Yes—this way. *She goes out to the kitchen.*

ELIS *begins to follow her, but stops to pick up the birch. As he passes* BENJAMIN, *he puts a hand on his head.*

ELIS. Courage, boy! BENJAMIN *hides his face.* ELIS *puts the birch behind the mirror. Sadly.* It was no olive branch the dove brought, but a birch.

He goes out.

Pause. The Haydn is heard from the Church.

*In the original this is "vargar, vargar, argar, argare" . . . meaning "wolves, angry, angrier," etc. As it is impossible to reproduce the rhyme, I have simply chosen words to produce a plausible sound and meaning.

Eleanora comes in from the street. She looks about sixteen, has her hair in plaits, and wears the plain dress of an institution. She carries a yellow daffodil in a pot. Without seeming to see BENJAMIN, *she puts the daffodil on the side-board and waters it, then looks lovingly round her familiar home. Then she moves the flower to the dining-table, sits down opposite* BENJAMIN, *watches him and mimics his movements. He looks up at her in amazement.*

ELEANORA, *pointing to the daffodil.* Do you know what that is?

BENJAMIN, *boyishly.* Of course I do, it's a daffodil. But who are you?

ELEANORA, *echoes, sadly and gently.* Yes, who are you?

BENJAMIN. I am called Benjamin, and I'm boarding here at Mrs. Heyst's.

ELEANORA. I see. I am called Eleanora and I'm the daughter of the house.

BENJAMIN. How queer! They've never talked about you.

ELEANORA. One doesn't talk about the dead.

BENJAMIN. The dead?

ELEANORA. In the eyes of the world I am dead, for I have done something very wicked.

BENJAMIN. You?

ELEANORA. Yes, I embezzled trust funds– Of course that doesn't matter very much–for ill-gotten gains never prosper. But my old father was blamed for it and put in prison, and that, you see, can never be forgiven.

BENJAMIN. How strangely and beautifully you speak. It never occurred to me that my inheritance might have been ill-gotten.

ELEANORA. We should not bind people but set them free.

BENJAMIN. Yes, you have set me free–from the shame of feeling myself cheated.

ELEANORA. So you're being brought up by guardians, too.

BENJAMIN. Yes, it's my miserable fate to be kept here by these unhappy people–serving a sentence for their crime.

ELEANORA, *shrinking.* You mustn't use hard words, or I shall go away. I am so soft I can't bear anything hard. *Pause.* But you—are you bearing all this because of me?

BENJAMIN. Because of your father.

ELEANORA. It's all one, for he and I are one and the same person. *Pause.* I have been very ill . . . Why are you so sad?

BENJAMIN. Oh, I've had rather a blow.

ELEANORA. Why be sad about that? "The rod and reproof give wisdom, and he that hateth correction shall die." What was the blow?

BENJAMIN. I failed in my Latin exam—when I was absolutely sure I'd get through.

ELEANORA. I see. So sure, so cocksure, that you'd have even bet your pocket money on it.

BENJAMIN. Yes—I did.

ELEANORA. I thought so. Don't you see it happened like that just because you were so sure?

BENJAMIN. Do you think that was the reason?

ELEANORA. Of course it was. Pride goes before a fall.

BENJAMIN, *smiling.* Well, I'll remember that next time.

ELEANORA. Good. And a sacrifice acceptable to God is a broken spirit.

BENJAMIN, *boyishly.* Are you religious?

ELEANORA. Yes, I am religious.

BENJAMIN. Really? A believer, I mean?

ELEANORA. Yes, that's what I mean. So if you say anything bad about God, who is my friend, I won't sit at the same table with you.

BENJAMIN. How old are you?

ELEANORA. For me there is neither time nor space. I am everywhere and of all times. I am in my father's prison and in my brother's schoolroom, I am in my mother's kitchen, and in my sister's shop, far away in America. When sales are good I share her joy, when they aren't I'm sorry, but not so sorry as when she does something bad.

Benjamin—you are called Benjamin because you are the youngest of my friends—yes, all human beings are my friends—Benjamin, if you trust yourself to me, I will suffer for you too.

BENJAMIN. I don't really understand your words, but I seem to know what you mean all the same—and so I'll do whatever you want me to.

ELEANORA. Then, to begin with, stop judging people—even those who are convicted of sin.

BENJAMIN. Yes, but I must have a reason for that. You see, I've studied philosophy.

ELEANORA. Oh, have you? Then you can help me to understand these words of a great philosopher. He says "He who hateth the righteous shall himself become a sinner."

BENJAMIN. By all the laws of logic that means that man can be foredoomed to sin.

ELEANORA. And the sin itself is punishment.

BENJAMIN. That's really deep. One could take it for Kant or Schopenhauer.

ELEANORA. I don't know them.

BENJAMIN. Where did you read that?

ELEANORA. In the Holy Scriptures.

BENJAMIN. Really? Are there things like that in them?

ELEANORA. How ignorant you are! You've been neglected. If only I could bring you up.

BENJAMIN, *laughing*. You're very sweet.

ELEANORA. But it's clear there's nothing bad in you. In fact you look very good to me. What's the name of your Latin Master?

BENJAMIN. Dr. Algren.*

*According to Swedish authorities Strindberg originally meant to give Dr. Algren the part of Lindkvist. As it is, he is twice mentioned in the text, but this leads to nothing. He can well be cut in production, specially as the mentioning of him is inconsistent with Elis's vexation that *his* best pupil should fail in the examination.

ELEANORA. I shall remember that. *Pause. . . . Then she gets up and cries out in agony.* Oh, now my father is in great trouble! They're being cruel to him. *She stands still, listening.* Do you hear how the telephone wires are wailing? That's because of the hard words the beautiful soft red copper can't bear. When people speak ill of one another on the telephone the copper wails and wails. *Sternly.* And every word is written in the Book, and at the end of time will come the reckoning.

BENJAMIN. How stern you are!

ELEANORA. I? Oh, no, no! How would I dare be? I, I! *Her mood changes. She becomes quiet and crafty, looks round, tiptoes to the stove, opens the door and takes out several torn-up pieces of white note-paper.* BENJAMIN *goes over to watch as she pieces the letter together on the sewing table.* How careless people are—leaving their secrets in stoves! Wherever I am I go straight to the stove. But I never misuse anything I find. I wouldn't dare. If I did, something awful would happen to me . . . Now what's this? *Reads.*

BENJAMIN. It's Mr. Peter writing to Kristina to ask her to meet him . . . I've been expecting this for some time.

ELEANORA, *putting her hand over the papers.* Oh you, what have you been expecting? You wicked creature, always thinking the worst of people. This letter has nothing but good in it. I know Kristina—she is going to be my sister-in-law. This meeting will prevent a misfortune to my brother Elis. Benjamin, will you promise not to say a word about this?

BENJAMIN. I wouldn't dare talk about it.

ELEANORA. It's wrong of people to have secrets. They think themselves wise and are fools. *She gathers up the pieces and puts them back in the stove.* Now what made me do that?

BENJAMIN. Yes, why are you so inquisitive?

ELEANORA. You see, that's my sickness. I must know everything. I can't rest until I do.

BENJAMIN. Know everything?

ELEANORA, *sadly*. Yes, it's a fault I can't overcome. *Gaily*. Anyhow, I know what the starlings say.

BENJAMIN. Can they talk?

ELEANORA. Haven't you heard of starlings being taught to speak?

BENJAMIN. Yes, taught.

ELEANORA. Well then, they can learn. And there are some that teach themselves. They sit and listen—without our knowing, of course—and then they mimic us. Just now as I came along, I heard a couple chatting in the walnut tree.

BENJAMIN. What fun you are! What did they say?

ELEANORA. Well, one said "Peter!" and the other said "Judas!" "Much of a muchness," said the first, "Fie, fie, fie!" said the second. And have you noticed the only place the nightingales sing is over there in the garden of the Deaf and Dumb.

BENJAMIN. Yes, everybody knows that. Why is it?

ELEANORA. Because those who have hearing don't hear what the nightingales say, but the deaf and dumb people do hear it. *Pause*.

BENJAMIN. Tell me some more fairy tales.

ELEANORA. I will if you're kind to me.

BENJAMIN. How do you mean—kind?

ELEANORA. Well you must never hold me to my words—never say "then you said that, and now you say this." See? . . . Now I'll tell you some more about birds. There is a bad one called the rat-buzzard because he feeds on rats. Because he's bad it's made hard for him to catch them. He can only say one word and that sounds like a cat's "miaow." So when the buzzard says "miaow," the rats run away and hide. But the buzzard doesn't understand what he's saying—so he goes without food very often. Do you want to hear any more? Or shall I tell you about flowers? You see, when I was ill I had to take some medicine with henbane in it. That turns your eye into a magnifying glass —just the opposite of belladonna, which makes you see everything small. So now I can see further than other people. I can see the stars in daylight.

BENJAMIN. The stars aren't up then.

ELEANORA. Silly! The stars are always up. Why at this moment I'm sitting facing north and looking at Cassiopea like a W in the middle of the Milky Way. Can you see it?

BENJAMIN. No, I can't.

ELEANORA. There you are—one person can see what another can't. So don't be so cocksure. Now I'll tell you about this flower on the table. It's a Lenten Lily, and its home is in Switzerland. It has a chalice, full of sunlight—that's why it's yellow—and it has the power of soothing pain. *Pause.* I passed a flower shop on my way, and saw it. *Tenderly.* I wanted it—to give my brother Elis. I went up to the door, but the shop was shut—of course because it's Confirmation Day. So as I had to have the flower, I took out my keys and tried them. And what do you think? My latchkey fitted—and I went in. *Pause.* Oh, if only you understood the silent language of flowers! Every scent says so many things. I was quite overwhelmed. And with my magnifying eye I looked right into their works which no one else sees, and they told me how they suffered at the hands of the careless gardener—I don't say cruel, for he is only thoughtless. Then I put a coin on the counter with my card, took the flower and came away.

BENJAMIN. But how rash of you. Suppose they miss the flower and don't find the money.

ELEANORA. That's true. You're right.

BENJAMIN. A coin gets lost so easily, and if they only find your card, you're done for.

ELEANORA. But surely no one would believe I'd just take something?

BENJAMIN, *looking hard at her.* Wouldn't they?

ELEANORA, *hurt.* Oh, I know what you mean! Like father, like child. How thoughtless of me! *For a moment she is silent, then depression changes to resignation.* Oh, well, what must be, must be . . . That's all there is to it.

BENJAMIN. Can't we do something to put it right?

ELEANORA. Hush . . . Let's talk about something else. Dr. Algren. Poor Elis . . . poor all of us. But this is Easter, and we must suffer. There'll be the Easter Concert tomorrow, won't there? They'll play Haydn's "Seven Words of the Redeemer"—"Mother, behold thy son!" *She weeps.*

BENJAMIN, *after a long pause.* What sort of illness was it you had?

ELEANORA. My illness is not sickness unto death, but unto the honour of God. I expected good and evil came; I expected light and darkness came . . . What was *your* childhood like, Benjamin?

BENJAMIN. Oh, I don't know—pretty miserable. And yours?

ELEANORA. I never had one. I was born old . . . I knew everything when I was born, and when I learnt anything, it was just like remembering. I knew all about people—their blindness and folly—when I was four years old. That's why they were unkind to me.

BENJAMIN. Everything you say I seem to have thought myself.

ELEANORA. I expect you have. What made you think the coin I left in the flower shop would get lost?

BENJAMIN. Because that annoying sort of thing always does happen.

ELEANORA. So you've found that too . . . Hush, someone's coming! *She listens.* I can hear . . . that it's Elis. Oh, how lovely! My one and only friend on earth. *Her happiness vanishes.* But he's not expecting me. And he won't be glad to see me. Of course he won't . . . Benjamin, Benjamin, be friendly and look happy when my poor brother comes in. I'll go, and you must break it to him that I'm here. But no hard words, remember, they hurt me so. Give me your hand. *He does so and she kisses him on the head.* Now you're my dear brother too. God bless you and keep you. *As she passes* ELIS's *overcoat she pats the sleeve affectionately. . . .* BENJAMIN *watches her.* Poor Elis. ELEANORA *goes into the house. . . .* ELIS *comes in from the street, looking troubled and goes to the writ-*

ing table. Before BENJAMIN *can tell him of the arrival,* MRS. HEYST *enters from the kitchen.*

ELIS. Ah, there you are, Mother!

MRS. HEYST. Was that you? I thought I heard a strange voice.

ELIS, *brusquely.* I've got some news. I met our lawyer in the street.

MRS. HEYST. Yes?

ELIS. The case is going to the Court of Appeal, and to save time I've got to read through the whole report of the proceedings. *He pulls some documents from a drawer.*

MRS. HEYST. Well, that won't take you long.

ELIS. Oh, I thought all that was over, and now I have to go through it all again—that long tale of suffering—with all the accusations, all the witnesses, all the evidence . . . the whole thing over again.

MRS. HEYST. Yes. But then he'll be acquitted by the Court of Appeal.

ELIS. No, he won't, Mother. You know he confessed.

MRS. HEYST. But there may be some legal error. That was the last thing the lawyer said to me.

ELIS. He only said it to comfort you.

MRS. HEYST. Oughtn't you to be off to that dinner?

ELIS. No.

MRS. HEYST. Now you've changed your mind again.

ELIS. I know.

MRS. HEYST. You shouldn't do that.

ELIS. I can't help it. I'm tossed about like drift-wood in a storm.

MRS. HEYST. I was quite sure I heard a strange voice that I recognized—but I must have been wrong. *Points to the overcoat.* That coat shouldn't be left there, as I said before. *She goes out to the kitchen.*

ELIS, *catching sight of the daffodil, to* BENJAMIN. Where did that flower come from?

BENJAMIN. A young lady brought it.

ELIS. Young lady? What's happened now? Who was it?

BENJAMIN. It was . . .

ELIS. Was it . . . my sister?

BENJAMIN. Yes. ELIS *sits down at the table. Pause.*

ELIS. Did you speak to her?

BENJAMIN. Oh yes!

ELIS. My God, is there no end to it? Did she . . . behave badly?

BENJAMIN. Oh no! She was very, very nice.

ELIS. How extraordinary! Did she mention me? Is she very angry with me?

BENJAMIN. On the contrary. She said you were her one and only friend on earth.

ELIS. What an amazing change!

BENJAMIN. And when she left she patted that coat of yours on the sleeve.

ELIS. Left? Where did she go?

BENJAMIN, *pointing.* In there.

ELIS. You mean she's there now?

BENJAMIN. Yes.

ELIS. You look so happy and friendly, Benjamin.

BENJAMIN. She talked so beautifully.

ELIS. What did she talk about?

BENJAMIN. She told me fairy tales—and then there was a lot about religion.

ELIS, *rising.* And that made you happy? BENJAMIN *nods.* Poor Eleanora she's so unhappy herself, and yet she can make others happy. *Reluctantly he goes towards the door to face the ordeal of meeting* ELEANORA. God help me!

ACT TWO

GOOD FRIDAY

Musical Prelude: Haydn: The Seven Words of the Redeemer. Largo No. 1 Pater dimitte illis.

The scene is the same, but the curtains are drawn and light comes through them from the lamp in the street. The hanging lamp is lighted and also a small lamp on the table. A fire is burning in the stove.

ELIS *and* KRISTINA *are sitting by the sewing-table, talking.* ELEANORA *and* BENJAMIN *are sitting opposite one another at the dining-table, with the lamp between them.* ELEANORA *is reading the Bible and* BENJAMIN *has some books. The weather is cold.* ELEANORA *has a wrap over her shoulders. All are dressed in black.* ELIS *and* BENJAMIN *are wearing white ties. The writing table is strewn with legal documents. The daffodil stands on the sewing-table. On the dining-table is an old pendulum clock.*

From time to time the shadow of someone passing in the street falls on the curtains. The organ can be heard in the distance, playing the Haydn Largo.

ELIS, *to* KRISTINA, *low.* Good Friday . . . yes, Long Friday,* as they call it—and how terribly long! The snow lies in the streets like the straw they spread outside the houses of the dying. Every sound is blotted out—except for the deep notes of the organ, which one can catch even in here.

KRISTINA. I suppose Mother went to evening service.

ELIS. Yes. She couldn't bear to go in the morning. She's so hurt by the way people look at her.

KRISTINA. They are extraordinary, those people. They seem to expect us all to keep out of sight, as if that was the correct way for us to behave.

*The Swedish for Good Friday.

ELIS. Perhaps they're right.

KRISTINA. One person makes a false step, and the whole family is ostracized.

ELIS. Yes, that's how it is.

ELEANORA *pushes the lamp towards* BENJAMIN *so that he shall see better.*

ELIS, *indicating* ELEANORA *and* BENJAMIN. Look at those two.

KRISTINA, *low.* Isn't it a charming sight? They get on so well together.

ELIS. It is such a mercy Eleanora's so calm. If only it would last.

KRISTINA. Why shouldn't it?

ELIS. Because . . . well, good times don't usually last long. And today I'm afraid of everything.

BENJAMIN, *smiling, pushes the lamp back to* ELEANORA.

KRISTINA. Look at them.

ELIS. Have you noticed how changed Benjamin is? That sulky defiance has quite gone. He's so gentle and willing.

KRISTINA. There is something exquisite about her whole nature. Even the word "beautiful" isn't quite right.

ELEANORA *begins to cry silently as she reads.*

ELIS. Yes, she has brought an angel of peace with her, who walks unseen and breathes repose. Even Mother was curiously calm when she saw Eleanora, and that I didn't expect.

KRISTINA. Do you think she's cured?

ELIS. I would think so, if it were not for that oversensitiveness. Look, she can't help weeping as she reads the story of Christ's passion.

KRISTINA. Well I remember doing the same thing—at school on Ash Wednesdays.

ELIS. Don't talk so loud; she'll hear.

KRISTINA. No. At the moment she's too far away.

ELIS. Have you noticed that something dignified—almost noble —has come into Benjamin's face?

KRISTINA. Suffering has done that. Pleasure makes things commonplace.

ELIS. Or perhaps it's rather love. Do you think those two young creatures . . . ?

KRISTINA. Ssh, ssh! Don't touch the butterfly's wings or it will fly away.

ELIS. They are looking at each other now, and only pretending to read. I can't hear any pages being turned.

KRISTINA. Hush!

ELEANORA *gets up and puts her wrap round* BENJAMIN'S *shoulders . . . He demurs mildly, then gives in. She sits down, and pushes the lamp towards him again.*

ELIS, *during this action.* She can't help doing these things.

KRISTINA. Poor Eleanora, she has no idea how good she is.

ELIS, *rising.* I must get back to my documents.

KRISTINA. Do you see any point in reading all that?

ELIS. Only one—to keep hope alive for Mother. But though I too only pretend to read, the words prick my eyes like thorns. *Picks up documents.* The evidence of the witnesses, the rows of figures, Father's admissions—as, for example, "the accused confessed with tears" . . . So many tears, so many tears. *Displays documents.* And the documents themselves, stamped like counterfeit money, or prison bars. And the strings . . . and the red seals like the five wounds of Jesus . . . and the sentences that run on for ever . . . endless torture. This is Good Friday Penance. Yesterday the sun shone, yesterday our imagination carried us out into the countryside. Kristina, suppose we had to stay here all the summer.

KRISTINA. Well, we should save a lot of money, but it would be sad.

ELIS. I couldn't bear it. I've spent three summers here and it's like a tomb. Mid-day—and one sees the long grey street winding like an unending trench. Not a man, not a horse, not a dog. Only the rats coming out of the sewers because the cats are on holiday. And the few people left sit at their window mirrors,* spying on their neighbours' clothes, prying on their down-at-heel boots and shabby ways. "Look, that fellow's wearing his winter suit!" And cripples, who had hidden, creep out from the slums, and people without noses and ears—miserable, evil people. There they sit on the promenade, sunning themselves, just as if they had taken the town by storm. There, where a little while before, pretty, well-dressed children played—encouraged with tender words by their lovely mothers—now a crowd of ragged hooligans swarm, cursing and tormenting each other. I remember one midsummer day two years ago . . .

KRISTINA. Elis, Elis, you must look to the future.

ELIS. Is it brighter there?

KRISTINA. Let us believe it is.

ELIS. If only it were not snowing. Then we could go out and walk.

KRISTINA. Oh, my dear, only yesterday evening you wanted the darkness to return so as to hide us from people's glances. "The darkness is so good, so blessed," you said, "it's like drawing the blankets up over one's head."

ELIS. Well, there you are—the misery's as great either way. *Picks up documents.* The worst part of these proceedings is the impertinent questions about my father's way of living. It says here that we gave grand parties. One witness declares that Father drank. It's too much. I can't go on. And yet I must—to the bitter end. *He shivers.* Aren't you cold?

KRISTINA. No, but it's not exactly warm. Isn't Lina in?

ELIS. You know very well she went to Church.†

KRISTINA. Surely Mother will be back soon.

ELIS. I'm always terrified when she comes back from the town. She hears so much, and sees so much—and all of it's wrong.

*Mirrors set at an angle inside windows so that one can see who is approaching in the street. They appear in several of Strindberg's plays.

†Literally Communion.

KRISTINA. There's a queer, melancholy strain in your family.

ELIS. That's why only melancholy people have anything to do with us. The happy ones avoid us.

KRISTINA. There's Mother coming in now—by the kitchen door.

ELIS. Don't be impatient with her, Kristina.

KRISTINA. Of course not. It's harder for her than for any of us. But I don't understand her.

ELIS. She hides her shame as best she can—and that makes her difficult. Poor Mother.

MRS. HEYST *comes in. . . . She is dressed in black and carries a prayer book and a handkerchief.*

MRS. HEYST. Good evening, my dears. *All greet her affectionately, except* BENJAMIN *who only bows.* You're all in black—as if you were in mourning. *Silence.*

ELIS. Is it still snowing?

MRS. HEYST. Yes, great wet flakes. It's cold in here. *Goes over to* ELEANORA *and caresses her.* Well, my chick, at your studies I see. *To* BENJAMIN. But you're not studying much, are you?

ELEANORA *holds her mother's hand against her face and kisses it.* MRS. HEYST *tries to hide her emotion.*

MRS. HEYST. There, my pet, there, there.

ELIS. So you've been to evening service, Mother.

MRS. HEYST. Yes, the Vicar took it, and I don't like him.

ELIS. Did you meet anyone you know?

MRS. HEYST, *sitting down by the sewing table.* It would have been better if I hadn't.

ELIS. Then I have no doubt who . . .

MRS. HEYST, *nodding.* Lindkvist—and he came straight up to me . . .

ELIS. How cruel, how very cruel!

MRS. HEYST. And asked me how we were. And then . . . you can imagine what a shock it was to me—he asked if he might call on us this evening.

ELIS. Good Friday evening!

MRS. HEYST. I couldn't speak. And he took my silence for consent. *Pause.* He'll be here any moment.

ELIS. Here? Now?

MRS. HEYST, *vaguely.* He said he wanted to leave a paper, and it was urgent.

ELIS. He's going to take the furniture.

MRS. HEYST. His manner was so odd, I didn't know what to make of it.

ELIS. Let him come then. He has the law on his side and we must submit. *To them all.* We must receive him correctly when he comes.

MRS. HEYST. If only I needn't see him.

ELIS. Well, you can stay in your room.

MRS. HEYST. But he mustn't take the furniture. How shall we manage if he takes everything away? We can't live in empty rooms, can we?

ELIS. The foxes have holes and the birds have nests. Some homeless people live in the woods.

MRS. HEYST. That's the right place for swindlers, not honest people.

ELIS, *sits down at the writing table.* I must get on with this reading, Mother.

MRS. HEYST. Have you found an error yet?

ELIS. No, I don't believe there is one.

MRS. HEYST. But I met the Notary just now. He says we ought to be able to find something—an unqualified witness or an unproved statement—or some contradiction. You can't be reading carefully enough.

ELIS. Of course I am, Mother—but it's very painful.

MRS. HEYST. Listen, I did meet the Notary just now—it was quite true what I said. And he also told me about a case of shop-breaking. In the town, yesterday, in broad daylight.

ELEANORA *and* BENJAMIN *prick up their ears.*

ELIS. Shop-breaking? Here, in the town? Where?

MRS. HEYST. It was at the flower shop in Convent Street. The whole thing was very odd. This is what seems to have happened. The shopkeeper locked up the shop so as to go to the church where his son—or perhaps it was his daughter—was being confirmed. When he came back at three o'clock—or perhaps it was four—but that doesn't make any difference—what do you think? The shop door was open and his flowers had vanished—masses of them, and in particular—and this was the first thing he missed—a yellow tulip.

ELIS. A tulip! If it had been a daffodil I should have been worried.

MRS. HEYST. No, it was a tulip. That's quite definite. However, the police are investigating. ELEANORA *rises as if to speak, but* BENJAMIN *pulls her back and whispers to her.* Just think, shop-breaking on Maundy Thursday while the children were being confirmed. Nothing but swindlers, the whole town. And then they have to put innocent people in prison.

ELIS. Have they any notion who did it?

MRS. HEYST. No. But it was a peculiar kind of thief, because he didn't take any money from the till.

KRISTINA. Oh, that this day were over!

MRS. HEYST. I wish Lina would come in . . . By the way, everyone was talking about Peter's dinner last night. The Governor was there.

ELIS. Was he? That surprises me. Peter's always been opposed to the Governor's policy.

MRS. HEYST. Then he must have changed.

ELIS. He isn't called Peter for nothing it seems.

MRS. HEYST. What have you got against the Governor?

ELIS. He's an obstructionist. He obstructs everything. He fought against the workers' colleges and military training for the boys. He even wanted to prohibit perfectly harmless bicycles—not to speak of those splendid summer camps. And he has always been against me.

MRS. HEYST. I don't know anything about that, but it doesn't matter. The point is that the Governor made a speech, and Peter thanked him.

ELIS. With emotion, I suppose. And denied his teacher and said "I know not the man." And the cock crew a second time. Isn't the Governor called Pontius, with the surname Pilate?

ELEANORA *rises again as if to speak, but controls herself.*

MRS. HEYST. You shouldn't be so bitter, Elis. Men are human, and one must take them as they are.

ELIS. Ssh. I can hear Lindkvist coming.

MRS. HEYST. Can you hear him in the snow?

ELIS. I hear his stick tapping the pavement . . . and his galoshes . . . You had better go away, Mother.

MRS. HEYST. No, I've decided to stay and give him a piece of my mind.

ELIS. Mother dear, please go. This is intolerable.

MRS. HEYST, *rising in great agitation.* May the day I was born be blotted out!

KRISTINA. Oh don't blaspheme!

MRS. HEYST, *passionately.* Were it not more just that the unrighteous should suffer this anguish and the evil doer this tribulation?

ELEANORA, *with a cry of agony.* Mother!

MRS. HEYST. My God, why hast Thou forsaken me—and my children? *She goes out.*

ELIS, *listening.* He has stopped. Perhaps he realises it's not correct to call on Good Friday. Or perhaps he thinks it's too cruel. But of course he wouldn't think that, or he couldn't write such terrible letters. They were always on blue note-paper. I've never been able to see a blue letter since without trembling.

KRISTINA. What are you going to say? What will you suggest to him?

ELIS. I don't know. I can't think clearly any more. Shall I fall on my knees and beg for mercy? Can you hear him? All I can hear now is the blood singing in my ears.

KRISTINA. Let's be prepared for the worst. Suppose he does take everything?

ELIS. Then the landlord will come and ask for a guarantee, which I shall be unable to give him. He'll want a guarantee because the furniture will no longer be a security for the rent.

KRISTINA, *looking through the curtains.* He's not there. He must have gone.

ELIS *gives a long sigh of relief. Pause.*

ELIS. You know Mother's apathy troubles me far more than these outbursts.

KRISTINA. That apathy's not real. It's put on to deceive us or herself. There was something of the roaring of the lioness in her last words. Did you see how she grew—how big she became?

ELIS. Do you know, just then, as I was thinking about Lindkvist, I saw him as a good-natured giant who does nothing worse than frighten children. I wonder what made me think of that just then.

KRISTINA. Thoughts come and go.

ELIS. It was a good thing I wasn't at that dinner yesterday. I should have made a speech against the Governor, and that would have ruined everything, for myself and for us all. Yes, it really was a good thing.

KRISTINA. You see?

ELIS. Thanks for the advice. So you knew your Peter.

KRISTINA. *My* Peter?

ELIS. I meant—mine. Look, here he is again. Mercy upon us!

*Against the curtains appears the shadow of a man drawing nearer and nearer. It grows steadily until it is gigantic.**

The giant! Look at the giant who is coming to devour us.

*This is where the shadow appears in the Swedish text, but surely it should be seen by the audience when Elis says the earlier lines about the giant.

KRISTINA. This is something to smile at—a kind of fairy tale.

ELIS. I don't know how to smile any more. *The shadow crosses the back until it disappears.*

KRISTINA. Look at his stick and you'll have to laugh.

ELIS. He's gone. Now I can breathe again. He won't come again now—until tomorrow. *He sighs with relief.*

KRISTINA. And tomorrow the sun will shine, for it is the eve of the Resurrection. The snow will have melted and the birds will sing.

ELIS, *closing his eyes.* Go on talking like that. I can see all that you're saying.

KRISTINA. Oh, if only you could see into my heart, could see my thoughts, my real purpose, my fervent prayer, when now I . . . *Breaks off.* Elis, Elis . . .

ELIS. When what?

KRISTINA. When now I ask something of you.

ELIS. Go on.

KRISTINA. It's a test. Remember that, Elis, please—it's a test.

ELIS. Test? Well, what is it?

KRISTINA. Let me . . . no, I daren't . . . it might not work.

ELEANORA *grows alert.*

ELIS. Why do you torment me?

KRISTINA. I shall regret it I know . . . but it must be said. Elis, let me go to that concert this evening.

ELIS. What concert?

KRISTINA. In the cathedral—Haydn's "Seven Words."

ELIS. Who with?

KRISTINA. With Alice . . .

ELIS. And?

KRISTINA. Peter.

ELIS. With Peter?

KRISTINA: There—you are angry. I regret it already—but it's too late.

ELIS. Yes, it is rather late. But you had better explain.

KRISTINA. I've been trying to warn you that I can't explain. That's why I want you to trust me completely.

ELIS, *softly*. Go then. I do trust you, but all the same it is an agony to me that you should choose the company of that traitor.

KRISTINA. I know it is—but it's only a test.

ELIS. One which I can't stand.

KRISTINA. You will.

ELIS. I want to, but I can't. But anyhow you shall go.

KRISTINA. Give me your hand.

ELIS, *giving it to her*. There.

The telephone rings.

ELIS, *at telephone*. Hullo! . . . No answer . . . Hullo . . . My own voice is answering . . . Who is it? . . . How extraordinary! . . . I hear my own words like an echo.

KRISTINA. That does sometimes happen.

ELIS. Hullo! How uncanny! *Rings off*. Go now, Kristina, without explanations, without fuss. I shall stand the test.

KRISTINA. If you do, then all will be well with us.

ELIS. I will. KRISTINA *moves towards the kitchen*. Why are you going that way?

KRISTINA. My coat is out there. Well then, goodbye for the moment. *She goes out.*

ELIS. Goodbye, my dear. *Pause*. For ever! *He rushes out the other way.*

ELEANORA. Oh heavens! And what have I done? The police are looking for the thief, and if I am discovered, poor Mother, poor Elis!

BENJAMIN, *boyishly*. Eleanora, you must say I did it.

ELEANORA. You're only a child. How could you bear another's guilt?

BENJAMIN. That's easy when one knows one's innocent.

ELEANORA. But we mustn't deceive people.

BENJAMIN. Then let me telephone the flower shop and explain what happened.

ELEANORA. No. I did wrong, and I must be punished with this anxiety. I've woken their fear of burglars, so I have to be frightened too.

BENJAMIN. But if the police come?

ELEANORA. It will be terrible. But if they do, that's how it's to be. Oh, that this day were over! *Draws the pendulum clock on the table towards her and moves the hands.* Dear clock, please go a little faster. Tick, tock, ping, ping, ping. Now it's eight. Ping, ping, ping. Now it's nine. Ten. Eleven . . . Twelve! Now it's Easter eve. Soon the sun will be rising, and we shall write on the Easter eggs. I shall write this: "The Adversary hath desired to have you that he may sift you as wheat, but I have prayed for thee."

BENJAMIN. Why do you give yourself such a bad time, Eleanora?

ELEANORA. A *bad* time? Me? *She shakes her head.* Benjamin, think of all the flowers that have come out—the anemones and snowdrops that have to stand in the snow the whole day long—and all through the night, too, freezing in the darkness. Think how they suffer. The night's the worst, because then it's dark, and they are afraid of the dark and can't run away. They just stand and wait for the day to come.* Everything, everything suffers, but the flowers most of all. And the birds who have already come back from the South—where will they sleep tonight?

BENJAMIN. In hollow trees, of course.

ELEANORA. There aren't enough hollow trees for them all. I've only seen two in the gardens here, and owls live in those. They kill little birds. *Pause.* Poor Elis. He thinks Kristina has left him, but I know she'll come back.

BENJAMIN. If you knew, why didn't you say so?

ELEANORA. Because Elis must suffer. Everyone has to suffer today, Good Friday, so as to remember Christ's suffering on the cross. *A whistle is heard outside.* ELEANORA *starts.* What was that?

BENJAMIN, *rising.* Don't you know?

*Unconsciously thinking of herself in the asylum.

ELEANORA. No.

BENJAMIN. It's the police.

ELEANORA. The police! Oh! Yes, that was the sound when they came to take Father away. And then I was ill. And now they're coming to take me. BENJAMIN *takes his stand between* ELEANORA *and the door.*

BENJAMIN. No, they shan't take you. I will defend you, Eleanora.

ELEANORA. That's fine of you, Benjamin, but you mustn't.

BENJAMIN, *peeping through the curtains.* There are two of them. ELEANORA *tries to take his place. He resists.* Not you, Eleanora. I wouldn't want to go on living if anything happened to you.

ELEANORA, *firmly.* Benjamin, go and sit down—in that chair. Go on. BENJAMIN *obeys as if hypnotised.* ELEANORA *draws back the curtains and looks boldly out of the window.* It's just a couple of boys. Oh, we of little faith! How could we believe God would be so cruel, when I've done nothing wicked, only acted thoughtlessly? It serves me right. Why did I doubt?

BENJAMIN. All the same, there's still that man coming tomorrow to take away the furniture.

ELEANORA. Yes. He must come—and we must go. And leave everything behind—all the old furniture Father collected for our home, and which I've known ever since I was little. *She goes round touching the furniture.* We should have nothing to bind us to earth. We must climb the stony paths that wound our feet and weary us so.

BENJAMIN. Now you're tormenting yourself again, Eleanora.

ELEANORA. Let me. But do you know what I shall find it hardest to part from? It's this clock. It was there when I was born. It measured all my hours and all my days. *She lifts the clock up.* Do you hear it beating like a heart? Exactly like a heart. It stopped just at the hour my grandfather died—we had it even then. Goodbye, little clock. Please stop again soon . . . Do you know, Benjamin, this clock had a way of going faster when there was bad luck in the house, as if it wanted to hurry over the trouble—for our sakes, of course. But when things were going well it slowed down to let us enjoy them longer. This was the good clock—but we had a bad one too. It's hanging in the kitchen still. It couldn't bear music. As soon as Elis began to play the piano it started to strike. We all noticed it, not only I. That's why it was put in the kitchen, because it was so naughty. But Lina doesn't like it either. It won't keep quiet at night, and one can't cook eggs by it. They're always hard-boiled, Lina says . . . Now you're laughing.

BENJAMIN. How can I help it?

ELEANORA. You're a nice boy, Benjamin, but you must be serious. Think of the birch there behind the mirror.

BENJAMIN. But they're such fun, the things you say. I can't help smiling. And why should we cry all the time?

ELEANORA. If we don't weep here in this vale of tears, where shall we weep?

BENJAMIN. Hm!

ELEANORA. You'd like to smile all day, that's why you got into trouble. But I only really like you when you're serious. Don't forget that.

BENJAMIN. Eleanora, do you think we'll ever get out of all this?

ELEANORA. Yes. Most of it will clear up once Good Friday is over—although not everything. Today the birch, tomorrow Easter eggs. Today snow, tomorrow thaw. Today death, tomorrow resurrection.

BENJAMIN. You're very wise.

ELEANORA. I can feel already that it's clearing up into lovely weather. The snow is melting—there's the smell of melting snow in here already . . . Tomorrow the violets will be out against the south wall. The clouds have lifted—I can feel it as I breathe. Oh, I know so well when the heavens are open! Benjamin pull back the curtains. I want God to see us. BENJAMIN *obeys. The room is flooded, with moonlight.* Look at the full moon. The Easter moon. And, you know, the sun is there—although the moon is giving us the light.

ACT THREE

EASTER EVE

Musical Prelude: Haydn: Seven Words of The Redeemer. No. 5 Adagio.

The curtains are drawn back, disclosing grey misty weather. The door to the street is closed. The stove is alight, and ELEANORA *sits beside it holding a bunch of hepatica.* BENJAMIN *comes in from the kitchen.*

ELEANORA. Where have you been all this time, Benjamin?

BENJAMIN. It wasn't long.

ELEANORA. I missed you.

BENJAMIN. Well, where have *you* been, Eleanora?

ELEANORA. I went to the market and bought these flowers. Now I'm warming them—they were frozen, poor things.

BENJAMIN. And where's your sun now?

ELEANORA. Behind the mist. There are no clouds today—only mist from the sea. It smells of salt.

BENJAMIN. Did you see if the birds were still alive?

ELEANORA. Yes. Not a single one can fall to the ground unless God wills it. But in the market there were dead birds.

ELIS *comes in.*

ELIS. Has the paper come?

ELEANORA. No, Elis.

ELIS *crosses the verandah. When he's half way,* KRISTINA *comes in from the other side and ignores him.*

KRISTINA, *to* ELEANORA. Has the paper come?

ELEANORA. No, not yet.

ELIS *and* KRISTINA, *paying no attention to one another, cross and go out.*

ELEANORA. Oh, how cold it has grown! Hate has come into the house. While there was love one could bear it all. But now, oh dear, it's so cold!

BENJAMIN. Why do they want the paper?

ELEANORA. Don't you realize? It will be in it.

BENJAMIN. What will?

ELEANORA. Everything. The shop-breaking, the police—and more too.

MRS. HEYST, *entering from the kitchen.* Has the paper come?

ELEANORA. No, Mother dear.

MRS. HEYST, *going back to the kitchen.* When it comes, let me know first.

ELEANORA. The paper, the paper. Oh, that the printing press had broken down, or the editor gone sick! No, one mustn't wish such things. Do you know, I was with Father last night.

BENJAMIN. Last night?

ELEANORA. Yes, in my sleep. And I was in America, too, with my sister. On Thursday she sold something for thirty dollars and made five dollars profit.

BENJAMIN. Is that a lot or a little?

ELEANORA. Quite a lot.

BENJAMIN, *artfully.* Did you meet anyone you knew in the market?

ELEANORA. Why do you ask me that? You mustn't pry, Benjamin. You want to know my secrets, but you can't.

BENJAMIN. But you expect to find out mine.

ELEANORA. Listen to the telephone wires humming. So now the paper has come out, and people are ringing each other up. "Have you read about it?" "Yes I've read it." "Isn't it frightful?"

BENJAMIN. What's frightful?

ELEANORA. Everything. The whole of life is frightful—but we have to accept it all the same. Look at Elis and Kristina. They're so fond of one another, yet they hate each other—so much that the thermometer drops when they walk through the room. Yesterday Kristina went to the concert, and today they aren't speaking. Why? Why?

BENJAMIN. Because your brother's jealous.

ELEANORA. Don't say that word. What do we know about it, anyway, except that it's an illness and therefore a punishment? One mustn't touch evil, or one may catch it. Look at Elis. Have you noticed how changed he is since he began reading those documents?

BENJAMIN. About the trial?

ELEANORA, *going over to the writing table.* Yes. It's as if the evil in them had got right into his soul, and flamed out in his face and eyes. Kristina feels it—and so as not to catch his evil, she's put on an armour of ice. Oh, these documents! If only I could burn them. Cruelty and lies and revenge pour out of them. That's why you must keep evil and dirty things away from you, Benjamin—away from your lips and your heart too.

BENJAMIN. What a lot you see in everything.

ELEANORA, *after a pause.* Do you know what's in store for me, if Elis and the others find out it was I who bought the daffodil in such an odd way?

BENJAMIN. What will they do to you?

ELEANORA. I shall be sent back . . . back to that place I came from. Where the sun doesn't shine, where the walls are white and bare like a bathroom. Where you hear only weeping and wailing. Where I have lost a whole year of my life.

BENJAMIN. Where do you mean?

ELEANORA. Where you are tortured worse than in prison, where the damned dwell, where unrest has its home, where despair keeps watch day and night. A place from which no one ever returns.

BENJAMIN. Did you say worse than prison?

ELEANORA. In prison you are condemned, but there you are doomed. In prison you are examined and heard, there you are unheard. Poor daffodil, the cause of it all. I meant so well and did so badly.

BENJAMIN. But why don't you go to the flower shop and explain how it happened. You're just like a lamb going to the slaughter.

ELEANORA. When it knows it has to be slaughtered it doesn't complain or try to run away. There's nothing it can do.

ELIS *enters, a letter in his hand.*

ELIS. Hasn't the paper come yet?

ELEANORA. No, brother.

ELIS, *calling into the kitchen.* Lina, go and get a paper!

MRS. HEYST *comes in from the kitchen. At the look of her* ELEANORA *and* BENJAMIN *are frightened.*

MRS. HEYST. Children, will you go away for a few minutes please. *They go out.* You've had a letter?

ELIS. Yes.

MRS. HEYST. From the asylum?

ELIS. Yes.

MRS. HEYST. What do they say?

ELIS. They want Eleanora back.

MRS. HEYST. They shan't have her. She's my child.

ELIS. My sister.

MRS. HEYST. What do you mean by that?

ELIS. I don't know. I can't think any more.

MRS. HEYST. But I can. Eleanora, this child of sorrow, has brought us joy. Not of this world, it is true—but her unrest has been changed into a peace she shares with us all. Sane or not, for me she is wise—for she knows how to bear life's burdens better than I do, better than any of us. What's more, Elis, if I am sane now, was I sane when I believed my husband innocent? I knew very well he was convicted on factual tangible evidence—and that he had confessed. *Pause.* And you, Elis, are you in your right mind when you can't see that Kristina loves you—when you go on thinking she hates you?

ELIS. It's a queer way of loving.

MRS. HEYST. No. Your coldness freezes her heart. It is you

who are doing the hating. But you're wrong—and so you're suffering.

ELIS. How can I be wrong? Didn't she go out last night with the friend who played me false?

MRS. HEYST. Yes, she did. And with your knowledge. But why did she go? You ought to be able to see why.

ELIS. Well, I can't.

MRS. HEYST. In that case you deserve what you get.

The kitchen door opens; MRS. HEYST *goes to it and returns with the newspaper which she hands to* ELIS.

ELIS. That was the worst blow of all. With her I could have borne the rest. Now my last support has gone, and I am falling.

MRS. HEYST. Fall then, but fall in the right way—so you can get up again. Well, what is there in the paper?

ELIS. I don't know. I'm afraid of the paper today.

MRS. HEYST. Give it to me. I'll read it.

ELIS. No, give me time!

MRS. HEYST. What are you afraid of? What are you expecting?

ELIS. The worst possible.

MRS. HEYST. That's happened so many times already. Oh my child, if you only knew my life, if you had been there while I was watching your father going step by step to his destruction—without my being able to warn all those people he was ruining. When the crash came, I knew I was guilty too, for I was fully aware of the crime. If the judge had not been a man of understanding, who saw how difficult my position was as wife, I should have been punished too.

ELIS. What really caused Father's downfall? I've never understood.

MRS. HEYST. Pride, as with us all.

ELIS. But why should we who are innocent suffer for his fault?

MRS. HEYST. Oh, be quiet! *She takes the paper and reads.* ELIS *stands in apprehension, then paces up and down.*

What's this? Didn't I say that among the flowers stolen from that shop was a yellow tulip?

ELIS. Yes, I remembered that distinctly.

MRS. HEYST. But here it says a daffodil.

ELIS, *shocked.* Does it say that?

MRS. HEYST. It was Eleanora. Oh my God, my God! *She collapses into a chair.*

ELIS. So the worst was still to come.

MRS. HEYST. Prison or asylum.

ELIS. It's impossible that she did it, impossible.

MRS. HEYST. Now the family name will be dragged in the mud again.

ELIS. Do they suspect her?

MRS. HEYST, *reading.* It says—clues point in a certain direction. It's pretty clear where.

ELIS. I'll talk to her.

MRS. HEYST, *rising.* Be gentle with her. I can't bear any more. She is lost, found and lost again. Yes, talk to her. *She goes out to the kitchen.* ELIS *looks at the paper, groans, then goes to the other door and calls.*

ELIS. Eleanora, my child, will you come in here a minute? I want to speak to you.

ELEANORA, *off.* I'm just doing my hair.

ELIS. Never mind. Leave it as it is. ELEANORA *comes in with her hair loose.* Tell me, dear. Where did you get that flower?

ELEANORA. I took it.

ELIS. Oh my God!

ELEANORA. But I left the money there.

ELIS. You paid for it?

ELEANORA. Yes and no. Oh, it's always so difficult. But I didn't do anything wrong. I meant to do something nice. You do believe me, don't you?

ELIS. I believe you, my dear—but the newspaper doesn't know you're innocent.

ELEANORA. Oh, Elis, so I must go through that too! What will they do to me? *She hangs her head.* Well–so be it. *Her hair falls over her face.* BENJAMIN *rushes in beside himself.*

BENJAMIN. You mustn't touch her. She's done nothing wrong. I know, because I did it. It was I, I, I who did it.

ELEANORA. Don't believe a word he's saying. It was I.

ELIS. What shall I believe? Which of you shall I believe?

BENJAMIN. Me, me! *He is almost in tears at the thought of* ELEANORA's *peril.*

ELEANORA. Me, me!

BENJAMIN. Let me go to the police.

ELIS. Come now, be quiet!

BENJAMIN. I must go. I will go.

ELEANORA. No, no!

ELIS. Be quiet, both of you! Mother's coming.

MRS. HEYST *comes in, much moved, takes* ELEANORA *in her arms and kisses her.*

MRS. HEYST. Child, child–you are my beloved child and you are to stay with me.

ELEANORA. You're kissing me, Mother. You haven't done that for years. Why now?

MRS. HEYST. Because . . . because . . . My dear, the shopkeeper has come to apologise for causing so much trouble. The lost money has been found with your card.

ELEANORA *leaps into* ELIS's *arms and kisses him, then hugs* BENJAMIN.

ELEANORA. Dear Benjamin, wanting to go through all that for me. Why did you?

BENJAMIN, *shyly, boyishly.* Because I like you so much, Eleanora.

MRS. HEYST. You'd better put your things on, children, and go out into the garden. It's clearing up.

ELEANORA, *happily.* Oh, it's clearing up! Come along, Benjamin. *She takes his hand and pulls him out.*

ELIS. Now can we put the birch on the fire?

MRS. HEYST. Not yet. There's still one thing more.

ELIS. You mean Lindkvist?

MRS. HEYST. He's standing outside. He looks very odd—almost gentle in spite of himself. It's a pity he's so garrulous and will talk so much about himself.

ELIS. Now I've seen a ray of light I'm not afraid to meet the giant. Let him come.

MRS. HEYST. But don't provoke him. Providence has put our fate in his hands. Blessed are the meek . . . and you know only too well what happens to the proud.

ELIS, *impatiently*. Yes, I know all that. Listen to the galoshes. Swish, swish, beast, beasts! Does he intend to come in here with them on? Why not? These are his carpets and his furniture.

MRS. HEYST. Elis, think of us all.

ELIS. I do, Mother.

> MRS. HEYST *goes out to the kitchen.*
> ELIS *opens the front door, and* LINDKVIST *is framed in it. He is an elderly man of fierce appearance with grey hair, black bushy eyebrows, black whiskers and round black-rimmed spectacles. Large cornelian trinkets hang from his watch-chain. A cane is in his hand with which he was about to knock on the door. He wears a black overcoat with a fur collar and large pockets stuffed with papers. He carries a top hat. His galoshes squeak. As he enters he looks piercingly at* ELIS. *Both men bow formally.*

LINDKVIST. My name is Lindkvist.

ELIS, *stiffly*. Mine is Heyst . . . Won't you sit down?

> LINDKVIST *sits by the sewing table and stares at* ELIS. *Pause.*

ELIS. What can I do for you?

LINDKVIST, *formally*. Hm! I had the honour to announce my intention to call yesterday evening, but on second thoughts I decided it was not fitting to talk business on Good Friday.

ELIS. We are very grateful.

LINDKVIST, *sharply.* We are not grateful. *Pause.* However . . . On Thursday I happened to pay a visit to the Governor. *Pauses, and watches to see the impression this makes on* ELIS. Do you know the Governor?

ELIS, *casually.* I have not that honour.

LINDKVIST. Then you shall have that honour. We talked about your father.

ELIS. I can well believe it.

LINDKVIST, *putting a white document on the table.* And I got this paper from him.

ELIS. I've been expecting this for a long time. But before we go further, may I take the liberty of asking a question?

LINDKVIST, *curtly.* Certainly.

ELIS. Why don't you deliver this order to the official receiver, so that at least we may be spared this long and painful execution?

LINDKVIST. So that's the line, young man.

ELIS. Young or not, I don't ask for mercy, only for justice.

LINDKVIST, *balancing the paper on the rim of the table.* So that's the line. No mercy . . . no mercy. You see this paper—balancing here on the edge of the table? Now I take it back. Justice, you say, nothing but justice. Now listen, my friend—once upon a time I was robbed—robbed in an unpleasant way of my money. When I wrote politely asking you when it would be convenient for you to settle, you answered me rudely. You treated me as if I were an usurer, bent on robbing the widowed and fatherless—whereas it was I who was robbed, and your people were the robbers. But, since I have some sense, I was content to answer your rude abuse civilly, though sharply. You know my blue note-paper, eh? I can get it officially stamped too when I wish—but I don't always wish. *Looks round the room.*

ELIS. If you please—the furniture is at your disposal.

LINDKVIST. I wasn't looking at the furniture. I was wondering if your mother was in. I presume she loves justice just as much as you do.

ELIS. I hope so.

LINDKVIST. Good. Do you realise that if the justice which you esteem so highly had taken its course, your mother, as an accessory to the crime, would have been convicted under common law?

ELIS. Oh no!

LINDKVIST. Oh yes! And it's not too late even now. *He takes another paper, a blue one, from his pocket and puts it on the table.*

ELIS. My mother!

LINDKVIST. Look. Now I'm balancing *this* paper on the edge—it's certainly blue—but it's not stamped yet.

ELIS. Almighty God, my Mother! It's happening all over again.

LINDKVIST. Yes, my young lover of justice, everything happens all over again. That's how it is. *Pause.* If I were now to ask myself this question: "You, Andrew John Lindkvist, born in poverty and brought up in toil and privation, is it right that you, in your old age, should deprive yourself and your children—mark that, your children—of the means of support which you by your industry, foresight, and self-denial—mark that, self-denial—have saved up, farthing by farthing? What are you to do, Andrew John Lindkvist, if you want to be just? You robbed nobody, yet if you object to having been robbed—you'll have to leave town. Nobody will have anything to do with the hardhearted man who demanded his own back." *Pause.* But you see, there is a charity which runs counter to the law and is above it . . . That is mercy.

ELIS. You're right. Take everything. It belongs to you.

LINDKVIST. I have the right, but I dare not exercise it.

ELIS. I will think of your children and not complain.

LINDKVIST, *putting the paper away in his coat pocket.* Good, then we'll put this blue paper back too. Now, we'll go a step further.

ELIS. Excuse me, do they really mean to prosecute my mother?

LINDKVIST. We will go a step further first. So you don't know the Governor personally?

ELIS. No, and don't want to.

LINDKVIST, *taking the blue paper out again and waving it.* Come, come! You see, in their young days, the Governor and your father were friends, and he would like to make your acquaintance. Everything happens again, everything. Won't you call on him?

ELIS. No!

LINDKVIST. The Governor . . .

ELIS, *rising impatiently.* Can't we talk about something else?

LINDKVIST. You must be polite to me. I'm defenceless—you have public opinion on your side and I have nothing but—justice. What have you got against the Governor? He doesn't like bicycles and working people's colleges—that's one of his little eccentricities. We needn't exactly admire people's eccentricities, but we can get over them, get over them and keep to essentials. We're all human, and in life's crises we must take one another as we are with all our faults and weaknesses—swallow each other neck and crop. Go to the Governor!

ELIS. Never.

LINDKVIST. Is that the kind of man you are?

ELIS. Yes, that's the kind.

LINDKVIST, *rising and walking across the room, his galoshes swishing and waving the blue paper.* Worse and worse! . . . I'll begin again from the other end . . . A revengeful person intends to bring a charge against your mother. This you can prevent.

ELIS. How?

LINDKVIST. By going to the Governor.

ELIS. No!

LINDKVIST, *taking hold of* ELIS *by the shoulders.* Then you are the most contemptible creature I've ever met in my life. Now I shall go to your mother.

ELIS. No, don't do that.

LINDKVIST. Then will you go to the Governor?

ELIS, *murmurs.* Yes.

LINDKVIST. Say that again, louder.

ELIS. Yes.

LINDKVIST. Then that's settled. *Puts down the blue paper beside* ELIS. There's that paper. ELIS *takes the paper without reading it.* Now we come to number two, which *was* number one. Shall we sit down? *They sit as before.* You see, if only we go to meet each other, the road is just half as long. Number two—my claim on your household effects . . . Have no illusions, for I neither can nor will give away what is the property of my family. I shall extort my claim to the last farthing.

ELIS. I understand that.

LINDKVIST, *sharply.* Oh you understand, do you?

ELIS. I didn't mean to be offensive.

LINDKVIST. No. I quite realise that. *He puts on his spectacles and glares at* ELIS. Beast, angry beast, swish, swish! And the cornelian charms the colour of flesh. The giant from the Skinflint Mountain who doesn't eat children, only frightens them. I'll frighten you, I will, I'll frighten you out of your wits. I'll have the value of every stick of furniture. The inventory's here in my pocket, and if a single item is missing, you'll be clapped into gaol where the sun never shines—nor Cassiopaea. Yes, I can eat children and widows too when I'm provoked. Public opinion? Bah! I'll just move to another town, that's all. ELIS *is speechless.* You had a friend called Peter. Peter Holmblad. He was a linguist—and your pupil in languages. But you wanted to set him up as a sort of prophet . . . Very well, Peter denied you. And the cock crew twice. Isn't that so? ELIS *is silent.* You can't rely on human nature, any more than on the nature of matter or of thought. Peter *was* faithless, I don't deny it—and I don't defend him. Not on that point. But the human heart is fathomless—it has layers of gold—and dross. Peter was a faithless friend, but a friend all the same.

ELIS. A faithless one.

LINDKVIST. A faithless one, yes. But a friend none the less. Unknown to you this faithless friend has done you a great service.

ELIS. That too!

LINDKVIST. Everything happens again, everything.

ELIS. Everything evil, yes. And good is rewarded with evil.

LINDKVIST. Not always. The good comes again too, believe me.

ELIS. I suppose I must believe you, or else you'll torture the life out of me.

LINDKVIST. Not the life, but the pride and wickedness I shall squeeze out of you.

ELIS. Go on then.

LINDKVIST. Peter has done you a service, I tell you.

ELIS. I don't want any services from that fellow.

LINDKVIST. So we're back there, are we? Now listen to this. Through the intervention of your friend Peter, the Governor has been induced to intercede for your mother. So you must write a letter to Peter and thank him. Promise you will.

ELIS. No. To anyone else in the world, but not to him.

LINDKVIST, *pouncing on him.* Then I must squeeze you some more. You've got some money in the bank, haven't you?

ELIS. What's that got to do with you? I'm not responsible for my father's debts, am I?

LINDKVIST. Aren't you? Aren't you? Weren't you here eating and drinking while my children's money was being squandered in this house? Answer me that.

ELIS. I can't deny it.

LINDKVIST. And since the furniture does not suffice to pay the debt, you will now make out a cheque for the balance—you know the amount.

ELIS, *devastated.* That too!

LINDKVIST. That too. Be so good as to write it. ELIS *rises, takes out his cheque book, and sits at the writing-table.* Make it payable to self or bearer.

ELIS. It won't be enough anyhow.

LINDKVIST. Then you must borrow the rest . . . every farthing of it.

ELIS, *handing the cheque to* LINDKVIST. There you are. This is all I possess. It is my summer and my bride. I have no more to give.

LINDKVIST. Then, as I say, you must go and borrow it.

ELIS. I can't do that.

LINDKVIST. Then you must find a guarantor.

ELIS. No one will guarantee a Heyst.

LINDKVIST. I shall now, as my ultimatum, present you with two alternatives—thank Peter or pay up.

ELIS. I'll have nothing to do with Peter.

LINDKVIST. Then you're the most contemptible creature I've ever known. By a simple act of courtesy you can save your mother's home and your own marriage, and you won't do it. There must be some reason you won't admit. Why do you hate Peter?

ELIS. Kill me, but don't torture me any more.

LINDKVIST. You're jealous. So that's the situation. *Walks about the room, thinking*. Have you read today's paper?

ELIS. Yes, worse luck.

LINDKVIST. All of it?

ELIS. No, not all.

LINDKVIST. I see . . . Then . . . er . . . perhaps you don't know that Peter has announced his engagement?

ELIS, *startled*. I didn't know that.

LINDKVIST. And who to? Can you guess?

ELIS. I . . .

LINDKVIST. He is engaged to Miss Alice. It was arranged at a certain concert last night—with the aid of your fiancée.

ELIS. Then why all this secrecy?

LINDKVIST. Haven't two young people the right to keep the secrets of their hearts from you?

ELIS. And I had to suffer this agony for their happiness?

LINDKVIST. Yes. And these have suffered to prepare the way for *your* happiness—your mother, your father, your sweetheart, your sister. Sit down. I want to tell you a story. Quite a short one. ELIS *sits reluctantly. Outside the weather is growing steadily brighter.* It was about forty years ago. I came to town to look for a job. Young, alone, unknown. I had next to no money, and it was a dark night. As I knew of no cheap lodging, I asked the passers-by, but no one would tell me. When I was absolutely desperate, a man came up to me and asked why I was weeping—I was actually in tears. I told him my predicament. Then he turned aside from his own way, took me to a lodging and comforted me with kind words. Just as I was going in, a shop door was flung open and a pane of glass broke against my elbow. The furious shopkeeper grabbed hold of me and said I must pay or he'd call the police. Imagine my despair. A night on the street before me. My unknown benefactor, who had seen what happened, took the trouble of calling the police himself—and saved me. That man was your father. So—everything happens again, the good things too. For your father's sake I have renounced my claim. So take this paper—*hands him the first white paper*—and keep your cheque. *Rising as* ELIS *struggles with his emotions.* As you find it difficult to say thank you, I'll take my leave, specially as I find it painful to be thanked. *As he reaches the street door.* Instead, go in now to your mother and set her mind at rest. *Waves* ELIS *back as he tries to approach him.* Go on. ELIS *rushes into the kitchen. Pause. As* LINDKVIST *turns to go, the front door is quietly opened by* ELEANORA *and* BENJAMIN. *Seeing* LINDKVIST *they start back in alarm.* Well, youngsters, come along in. Don't be frightened. *They enter.* Do you know who I am? *Growls.* I'm the giant of the Skinflint Mountain, who frightens children. Yum, yum, yum! *In his natural voice.* But I'm not really so dangerous. Come here, Eleanora. *Takes her head between his hands and looks into her eyes.* You have your father's good eyes, and he was a good man—although weak. *Kisses her on the forehead.* That's how it was.

ELEANORA. Oh, he's speaking well of Father! Can anyone think well of him?

LINDKVIST. I can. Ask your brother Elis.

ELEANORA. Then you can't want to hurt us.

LINDKVIST. No, no, dear child.

ELEANORA. Then help us!

LINDKVIST. Child, I can't help your father to escape his punishment. *Looking kindly at* BENJAMIN. Nor Benjamin to get through his Latin examination. But the other help has already been given. Life won't give us everything—and nothing gratis. So you must help me too. Will you?

ELEANORA. How can I, who have nothing, help you?

LINDKVIST. What's the date today? Look and see.

ELEANORA, *taking down the calendar.* It's the sixteenth.

LINDKVIST. Very well. Before the twentieth you must get your brother to call on the Governor and to write a letter to Peter.

ELEANORA. Is that all?

LINDKVIST. Oh, child! But if he doesn't do those things, the giant will come again with his yum, yum, yum!

ELEANORA. Why does the giant come and frighten children?

LINDKVIST. To make 'em good.

ELEANORA. Yes, of course. And he's quite right. *Rubs her cheek against the sleeve of his coat.* Thank you, kind giant.

BENJAMIN. You ought to call him Mr. Lindkvist, you know.

ELEANORA. Oh no, that's far too ordinary.

LINDKVIST. Well—goodbye, children. Now you can throw the birch on the fire.

ELEANORA *goes towards the birch then stops and smiles.*

ELEANORA. No, it had better stay there—children are so forgetful.

LINDKVIST, *gently.* How well you know children, little one. *The children show him out and wave as he goes down the street.*

ELEANORA. Oh, Benjamin, just think, we shall be able to go

to the country! In two months. Oh, may they pass quickly! *She tears the sheets off the calendar and strews them in the sunlight now streaming into the room.* KRISTINA *enters and stands watching.* Look how the days are passing! April . . . May . . . June . . . And the sun is shining on them all—see? *She pulls him to the window and stands gazing up.* Now you must thank God for helping us to get to the country.

BENJAMIN, *shyly.* Can't I say it silently?

ELIS *and* MRS. HEYST *come quietly in from the kitchen.* ELIS *and* KRISTINA *look tenderly at one another.*

ELEANORA. Yes, you can say it silently, for now the clouds have lifted, and we can be heard up there.

For a moment all are motionless, then KRISTINA *and* ELIS *move towards each other, but the curtain falls before they meet.*

THE DANCE OF DEATH

A Drama in Two Parts

FOREWORD

After *Crime and Crime* Strindberg wrote a number of historical dramas in which Shakespeare's influence is apparent. Then came *Easter,* his tender play of redemption, but even before his marriage to Harriet Bosse, the wheel had turned and Strindberg was once more plunged into icy gloom. Memories racked him and the old poisoned streams of hatred and suspicion demanded further violent expression. He decided to write a *Dance Macabre,* using Saint-Saëns' music; then, finding that the hated Ibsen had forestalled him by introducing this music in *John Gabriel Borkman,* Strindberg took the march, *Entry of the Boyars,* as theme tune for his new play, called by turn *Dance Macabre, Fight with Death, Death in the Dance, The Vampire,* and finally *The Dance of Death.*

Strindberg was uncertain at first whether to make his leading character a pilot captain, a retired professor, or a doctor, but finally chose a superannuated Captain of Artillery, O.C. of an island fortress. In this grim stone tower, which had once been a prison, Strindberg concentrated his sense of life's malevolence. Again, as in *The Father,* the theme of the play is married misery, and Edgar, the larger-than-life Captain, destroys the peace of all who are in contact with him, as he staggers from one death throe to the next.

The immediate model for Edgar was the son of a Swedish Battery Commander who had fought on the Danish side in the Prusso-Danish war of 1864; but the Captain in the *Dance of Death* is a highly composite character. Not only is he a caricature of a friend of Strindberg's who, as a Customs Inspector, became such an insufferable bully that in the end he had no one left to talk to, but also of several other of Strindberg's former associates, whom he now regarded as enemies—and of course the character also contains a great deal of Strindberg himself. The Captain's behaviour is in the highest degree extraordinary and his defence is Strindberg's own:

> Life is so strange. So against me, so
> vindictive that I became vindictive too . . .

In Kurt, the Quarantine Officer, returned after fifteen years abroad, divorced and robbed of his children, Strindberg depicted another of his selves, sensuous, well-meaning, weak. Even the use of the telegraph apparatus in the play derives from Strindberg's own experience, for he was once apprenticed to the telegraph service and learnt to send out weather reports.

Alice, the Captain's wife, is painted with the venom that memories of his love-hatred for Siri von Essen, his first actress wife, always roused in Strindberg, yet in *The Dance of Death* he does not, in his usual way, lay the chief responsibility for the disastrous marriage on the woman. It is interesting to consider what may have been in Strindberg's mind as he depicted this bizarre couple. We know that at some point he had discovered from his horoscope, cast at his request by a friend, that the hour of his birth was dominated by Saturn and Venus, the most incompatible of planets. He may well have had this planetary conflict in mind while he was creating Edgar and his wife, Alice, in whom the saturnine evil and rancour run parallel with an unresolved passion whose traces influence even their most desperate moments. Another influence in the depiction of this marriage "not made in heaven" may well have been Swedenborg's *De coelo et inferno,* for at this period Strindberg was deeply affected by his work.

By and large, with its battering cynical dialogue, its silent nightmare action, and the pounding of the *Entry of the Boyars,* Part One of *The Dance of Death* is a masterpiece of horror, a caricature of tragedy.[1]

In Part Two, Strindberg for the first time created adolescent characters. There are children in *The Father* and in *Easter,* but here in Judith and Allan, the Captain's daughter and the Quarantine Officer's son, are young adults in the turmoil of first love. It is probable that the fact that Strindberg had spent the summer of 1899 out in his beloved Baltic skerries, with several young nephews and nieces and one of his daughters by

[1] How startlingly modern this play is, comparable with today's offbeat theatre, with, for instance, certain of Eugène Ionesco's grotesque and wildly funny tragedies.

his first marriage, had something to do with this. While maintaining the horrific atmosphere of the play, these young characters are amusingly but tenderly drawn. As Judith's mother, Alice, comments: "To think that flowers can grow out of filth!"

Part One of *The Dance of Death,* being in itself a full-length play, is usually presented alone, while Part Two, which is shorter and could not stand by itself, is seldom seen. But undoubtedly the two parts were intended to be played together as one play. Strindberg's compact scenes and terse dialogue are, of course, difficult to cut, but surely a skilled director could make a single play—even if a long one—out of the two parts.[2]

E. S.

I am indebted to Dr. O. Wieselgren for giving me permission to include, in the above Foreword, material from his programme note to the August 1959 production of *The Dance of Death* in Stockholm.

[2] And would not a Ionesco touch aid the production?

CHARACTERS: PART ONE

EDGAR, *Captain in the Garrison Artillery*

ALICE, *his wife, formerly an actress*

KURT, *Quarantine Officer*

JENNY, *a maid*

AN OLD WOMAN

A SENTRY (*non-speaking*)

The whole action takes place inside a fortress on an island off the coast of Sweden in the nineties.

SCENE: *The living-room in the round, grey stone fortress.*

Centre back is the old main entrance to the fortress: a double stone archway inset with glass doors. Beyond is a beach with gun emplacements and the sea.

In the walls on each side are smaller doors leading to other rooms. The one on the left also leads out of doors.

On either side of the big doorway are windows, in one of which are pots of flowers and in the other a cage of birds.

On the right is a cottage piano; below it a sewing-table and two armchairs.

On the left, towards the centre, is a writing-table equipped with telegraphic apparatus; below this family photographs are ranged on a whatnot. Nearby is a couch and against the wall a sideboard and a round porcelain stove.

Further left, beside the door, is a stand hung with accoutrements: swords and so forth. A mercurial barometer hangs on the wall. Near this is a bureau.

A lamp hangs from the ceiling. Over the piano is a portrait of a woman in theatrical costume between two large, beribboned laurel wreaths.

PART ONE

ACT I

SCENE 1

It is a warm autumn evening. The glass doors are open, and an artilleryman on sentry duty is seen down by the shore battery. He is wearing a busby with brush. Now and then his sword glitters in the red light of the setting sun. The sea is dark and still.

THE CAPTAIN *is sitting in the armchair on the left of the sewing-table, fingering a cigar which has gone out. He is in undress uniform, the worse for wear, with riding-boots and spurs. He looks tired and bored.*

ALICE *is sitting in the armchair on the right, doing nothing. She looks tired but expectant.*

THE CAPTAIN. Won't you play something for me?

ALICE, *indifferently but not crossly.* What shall I play?

THE CAPTAIN. What you like.

ALICE. You don't like my repertoire.

THE CAPTAIN. Nor you mine.

ALICE, *ambiguously.* Do you want the doors left open?

THE CAPTAIN. As you wish.

ALICE. Let's leave them then. *Pause.* Why aren't you smoking?

THE CAPTAIN. I can't stand strong tobacco any longer.

ALICE, *more kindly.* Smoke something milder then. As you say, it's your only joy.

THE CAPTAIN. Joy? Whatever's that?

ALICE. Don't ask me. I know no more of it than you. . . . Won't you have your whisky now?

THE CAPTAIN. I'll wait a little. . . . What's for supper?

ALICE. How should I know? Ask Kristin.

THE CAPTAIN. Oughtn't mackerel to be in soon? It *is* autumn now.

ALICE. Yes, it *is* autumn.

THE CAPTAIN. Outside and in. But, in spite of the cold that autumn brings, outside and in, a broiled mackerel with a slice of lemon and a glass of white burgundy is not to be despised.

ALICE. How eloquent you've become!

THE CAPTAIN. Have we any burgundy in the wine cellar?

ALICE. I'm unaware that we've had a wine cellar for the past five years.

THE CAPTAIN. You never are aware. However, we must get in a supply for our silver wedding.

ALICE. Do you really mean to celebrate that?

THE CAPTAIN. Naturally.

ALICE. It would be more natural to hide our misery, our twenty-five years of misery . . .

THE CAPTAIN. Misery there has been, my dear Alice, but pleasure too now and then. And one must make use of the short time left, for then comes the end.

ALICE. Is it the end? If only it were!

THE CAPTAIN. It *is* the end. Just enough left to wheel out on a barrow and put on a garden plot.

ALICE. All this fuss for a garden plot.

THE CAPTAIN. Well, that's how it is. It's not my doing.

ALICE. All this fuss! *Pause.* Have you had the mail?

THE CAPTAIN. Yes.

ALICE. Did the butcher's bill come?

THE CAPTAIN. Yes.

ALICE. How much was it?

THE CAPTAIN *takes a paper from his pocket and puts on his glasses, but immediately takes them off again.*

THE CAPTAIN. Look for yourself. I can't make it out.

ALICE. What's wrong with your eyes?

THE CAPTAIN. Don't know.

ALICE. Old age.

THE CAPTAIN. What nonsense! Me?

ALICE. Well, not me!

THE CAPTAIN. Hm.

ALICE, *looking at the bill.* Can you pay it?

THE CAPTAIN. Yes, but not at the moment.

ALICE. Later on, of course. In a year, when you've retired on a small pension, and it's too late. Later on, when you get ill again and . . .

THE CAPTAIN. Ill? I've never been ill. Just a little out of sorts once. I shall live for another twenty years.

ALICE. That's not what the doctor thought.

THE CAPTAIN. Doctor!

ALICE. Well, who else could have a sound opinion about an illness?

THE CAPTAIN. I haven't any illness, never have had, and never shall have. I shall just drop down dead like an old soldier.

ALICE. Talking of the doctor, you know he's having a party this evening.

THE CAPTAIN, *irritated.* Well, what of it? We haven't been invited because we don't mix with the doctor's family, and we don't mix with 'em because we don't want to, because I despise them. They're scum.

ALICE. You say that about everyone.

THE CAPTAIN. Everyone is scum.

ALICE. Except you.

THE CAPTAIN. Yes. I've behaved decently whatever's come about. So I am not scum.

Pause.

ALICE. Do you want to play cards?

THE CAPTAIN. Might as well.

ALICE *takes a pack of cards from the drawer of the sewing-table and begins to shuffle.*

ALICE. Just think of them having the band at the doctor's—for a private party!

THE CAPTAIN, *angrily*. That's because he sucks up to the Colonel in town. Sucks up, see? If you can do that . . . !

ALICE, *dealing*. Gerda and I were friends once, but she cheated me.

THE CAPTAIN. They're all cheats, the whole pack of them! . . . What's that card? What's trumps?

ALICE. Put your glasses on.

THE CAPTAIN. They're no use. . . . Well? Well?

ALICE. Spades are trumps.

THE CAPTAIN, *disappointed*. Spades?

ALICE, *playing*. Yes, that may be. In any case, we're written off by the new officers' wives.

THE CAPTAIN, *playing and taking the trick*. What's that matter? We don't give any parties, so it won't be noticed. I can get on alone—I always have.

ALICE. So can I. But the children—the children are growing up without any companions.

THE CAPTAIN. They'll have to find those for themselves in the town. . . . That was my trick. Any trumps left?

ALICE. Yes, one. That was mine.

THE CAPTAIN. Six and eight, that makes me fifteen.

ALICE. Fourteen! Fourteen!

THE CAPTAIN. Six and eight makes me fourteen . . . I seem to have forgotten how to count. And two makes sixteen . . . *Yawns*. Your deal.

ALICE. You're tired.

THE CAPTAIN, *dealing*. Not a bit.

ALICE, *listening*. One can hear the music even here. *Pause*. Do you think Kurt has been invited?

THE CAPTAIN. He arrived in the morning, so I daresay he's had time to unpack his dress suit, even if not to call on us.

ALICE. Quarantine Officer. Will there be quarantine here?

THE CAPTAIN. Yes.

ALICE. After all, he is my cousin—my name was the same as his once.

THE CAPTAIN. No great honour in that.

ALICE, *sharply.* Look here! You leave my family alone, and I'll leave yours!

THE CAPTAIN. Now, now! Don't let's start that again.

ALICE. Is the Quarantine Officer a doctor?

THE CAPTAIN. No. He's just a kind of clerk in the civil administration. Kurt has never got anywhere.

ALICE. He was a poor creature . . .

THE CAPTAIN. Who cost me money . . . And to leave his wife and children like that was scandalous.

ALICE. Don't be too harsh, Edgar!

THE CAPTAIN. Yes, that's what it was. And what's he been doing since, and in America? Eh? I can't say I'm aching for his company here. Although he was a nice lad and I used to enjoy arguing with him.

ALICE. Because he always gave in.

THE CAPTAIN, *haughtily.* Whether he gave in or not, he was at least somebody one could talk to. Here on the island there isn't one person who understands what I say. It's a community of nitwits.

ALICE. It's odd, isn't it, that Kurt should turn up just in time for our silver wedding? Whether it's celebrated or not.

THE CAPTAIN. Why is it odd? Oh yes, of course, it was he who brought us together and got you married, so they said.

ALICE. Didn't he?

THE CAPTAIN. Of course he did. It was all his idea . . . the merits of which I leave you to judge.

ALICE. A frivolous notion . . .

THE CAPTAIN. For which we've had to pay, not he.

ALICE. Yes. Just think if I were still on the stage. All my friends are stars now.

THE CAPTAIN, *rising.* Yes, yes, yes! Now I'll have my grog.

Goes to the cupboard and mixes a drink, which he takes standing.

There ought to be a rail here to put one's foot on. Then one could imagine oneself in Copenhagen at the American Bar.

ALICE. We must have a rail made, just to remind us of Copenhagen. Those really were the best times we had.

THE CAPTAIN, *taking a long drink*. Yes. Do you remember Nimb's *navarin aux pommes? Smacks his lips.*

ALICE. No, but I remember the Tivoli concerts.

THE CAPTAIN. You have such exclusive tastes.

ALICE. You ought to be glad to have a wife with taste.

THE CAPTAIN. On occasions . . .

ALICE. When you want to boast about her.

THE CAPTAIN, *drinking*. They must be dancing at the doctor's. I can hear the bass tubas' three-four time—boom—boom-boom.

ALICE. I can hear the whole tune of the *Alcazar Waltz*. . . . Though the last time I waltzed wasn't yesterday.

THE CAPTAIN. Could you do it still?

ALICE. Still?

THE CAPTAIN. Ye-es. You're a bit past dancing, same as I am.

ALICE. I'm ten years younger than you.

THE CAPTAIN. Then we're the same age—for the lady always has to be ten years younger.

ALICE. How dare you! You're an old man, and I'm in my prime.

THE CAPTAIN. Oh, I know you can be perfectly charming—to others—when you choose.

ALICE. Shall we have the lamps lighted now?

THE CAPTAIN. If you like.

ALICE. Then ring.

THE CAPTAIN *goes slowly to the writing-table and rings a bell.*

Enter JENNY, *right.*

THE CAPTAIN. Will you please light the lamp, Jenny.

ALICE, *sharply*. Light the hanging lamp!

JENNY, *impudently*. Yes, milady!

JENNY *lights the lamp while* THE CAPTAIN *watches her.*

ALICE, *curtly.* Have you cleaned the chimney properly?

JENNY. It will do.

ALICE. That's not the way to answer.

THE CAPTAIN. Now, now . . .

ALICE, *to* JENNY. Go away! I'll light the lamp myself. That's best.

JENNY, *going.* I think so too.

ALICE, *rising.* Go away!

JENNY, *turning.* I wonder what you'd say if I did go, ma'am.

ALICE *does not reply.*

Exit JENNY.

THE CAPTAIN *comes forward and lights the lamp.*

ALICE, *uneasily.* Do you think she will leave?

THE CAPTAIN. Wouldn't surprise me. Then we'd be ditched.

ALICE. It's your fault. You spoil them.

THE CAPTAIN. Rubbish! Look how polite they always are to me.

ALICE. Because you cringe to them. Just as you cringe to all your inferiors. Although you're a despot, at bottom you're a slave.

THE CAPTAIN. Come, come!

ALICE. Yes, you cringe to your men and your non-commissioned officers, but you can't get on with your equals and superiors.

THE CAPTAIN. Ouf!

ALICE. Just like all tyrants! . . . Do you think she'll leave?

THE CAPTAIN. Yes, unless you go and say something nice to her.

ALICE. Me?

THE CAPTAIN. If I go, you'll say I'm flirting with the maids.

ALICE. To think, if she does leave, I'll have to do all that housework like last time, and ruin my hands.

THE CAPTAIN. And what's worse, if Jenny goes, Kristin will go too, and we'll never get another servant on the island. The mate of the steamboat will scare away anyone who comes to apply for the place, and should he forget, then my bombardiers will do it.

ALICE. Yes, your bombardiers, whom I have to feed in my kitchen because you don't dare show them the door.

THE CAPTAIN. No, or they'd go at the end of their service—and then we'd have to close down the gun-shop.

ALICE. That would ruin us!

THE CAPTAIN. Which is why the Officers' Corps intends to request His Majesty for a maintenance grant . . .

ALICE. Who for?

THE CAPTAIN. The bombardiers.

ALICE, *laughing*. You're quite crazy!

THE CAPTAIN. Yes, let's have a little laughter. We may need it.

ALICE. I shall soon have forgotten how to laugh.

THE CAPTAIN, *lighting a cigar*. One must never forget that. It's boring enough as it is.

ALICE. It's certainly not amusing. . . . Do you want to go on playing?

THE CAPTAIN. No, it exhausts me.

Pause.

ALICE. You know, considering he's my cousin, it does annoy me that the new Quarantine Officer should make his first visit here to people who are not our friends.

THE CAPTAIN. Not worth a thought.

ALICE. Well, but did you see in the paper—in the list of arrivals—it said he was of independent means? He must have come into some money.

THE CAPTAIN. Independent means! Aha! A rich relation! Certainly the first in this family.

ALICE. In your family, yes. There have been many in mine.

THE CAPTAIN. If he has any money, he's sure to be stuck-up. But I'll keep him in check, and he won't get a chance of seeing my cards.

The telegraph apparatus begins to tap out a message.

THE CAPTAIN *rises.*

ALICE. Who is it?

THE CAPTAIN, *not moving*. Quiet a moment, please!

ALICE. Well, go and see!

THE CAPTAIN. I can hear. I can hear what they're saying. . . . It's the children.

He goes to the apparatus and taps out a reply.

The apparatus taps for a while and he replies again.

ALICE. Well?

THE CAPTAIN. Wait a minute! . . . *Gives the ending signal.* It was the children. They were at the guardhouse in the town. Judith is off colour again and staying away from school.

ALICE. *Again?* What else did they say?

THE CAPTAIN. Money, of course.

ALICE. Why should Judith be in such a hurry? If she took her exam next year that would be time enough.

THE CAPTAIN. Tell her so and see what effect it has.

ALICE. You ought to tell her.

THE CAPTAIN. Haven't I done so times without number? You know very well children do as they please.

ALICE. In *this* household at any rate.

THE CAPTAIN *yawns.*

Must you yawn in your wife's face?

THE CAPTAIN. What do you suggest I should do? . . . Don't you realise we go through the same rigmarole every day? When you repeated your old dig just now: "In *this* household at any rate," my cue was to retort: "The household isn't just *my* affair." But as I've already said this five hundred times, now I yawn instead. And my yawn can be taken to mean that I can't be bothered to answer, or: "You're perfectly right, my angel," or: "Let's shut up!"

ALICE. You're in good form this evening.

THE CAPTAIN. Isn't it nearly time for supper?

ALICE. Do you know they have ordered supper from the Grand Hotel for the doctor's party?

THE CAPTAIN. Really? Then they will be having woodcock. *Smacks his lips.* You know, woodcock is the best bird there is, but to roast it in pork fat is barbarous.

ALICE. Oh, must we talk about food?

THE CAPTAIN. About wine then? I wonder what the barbarians are drinking with their woodcock.

ALICE. Shall I play for you?

THE CAPTAIN, *seating himself at the writing-table.* The last resource! Yes, if you keep off your funeral marches and dirges—which sound all too appropriate. I always find myself intoning: "See how unhappy I am, miaow, miaow!" Or: "See what a dreadful husband I have! Pom, pom, pom! Oh, if only he would die! Joyful roll of drums! Fanfares! End the *Alcazar Waltz!* The *Champagne Galop!*" Apropos champagne, surely there are two bottles left. Shall we get them up and pretend we have guests?

ALICE. No, we won't. They're mine. They were sent to me.

THE CAPTAIN. You're always economical.

ALICE. And you're always stingy—anyhow to your wife.

THE CAPTAIN. Then I don't know what to suggest. . . . Shall I dance for you?

ALICE. No, thank you. Your dancing days are over.

THE CAPTAIN. You ought to ask some woman here to stay with you.

ALICE. Thanks. You ought to ask some man to stay with you.

THE CAPTAIN. Thanks. That was tried—to our mutual dissatisfaction. But what was interesting in the experiment was how happy we were as soon as we had a stranger in the house—to begin with.

ALICE. And then!

THE CAPTAIN. Oh, don't talk about it!

There is a knock on the door, left.

ALICE. Who can that be at this hour?

THE CAPTAIN. Jenny doesn't usually knock.

ALICE. Go and open it and don't call "come in"—that sounds like a workshop.

THE CAPTAIN, *going to the door.* You don't like workshops.

The knocking is repeated.

ALICE. Open it, do!

THE CAPTAIN *opens it and takes the visiting card which is handed to him.*

THE CAPTAIN. It's Kristin. . . . *To the unseen* KRISTIN. Has Jenny gone? *Her reply is inaudible. To* ALICE. Jenny has gone.

ALICE. So I'm to be the maid again.

THE CAPTAIN. And I the man.

ALICE. Can't we have one of the garrison to help in the kitchen?

THE CAPTAIN. Not these days.

ALICE. But surely it wasn't Jenny who sent in that card?

THE CAPTAIN *puts on his glasses and looks at the card, then hands it to* ALICE.

THE CAPTAIN. You read it. I can't.

ALICE, *looking at the card.* Kurt! It's Kurt. Go and bring him in.

THE CAPTAIN, *going out, left.* Kurt! Well, that is nice!

ALICE *arranges her hair and seems to come to life.*

THE CAPTAIN *and* KURT *enter, left.*

Here he is, the blackguard! Welcome, old man! *Pats him on the back.*

ALICE. Welcome to my home, Kurt!

KURT. Thank you. . . . It's a long time since we saw one another.

THE CAPTAIN. What is it? Fifteen years. And we've grown old.

ALICE. Oh, Kurt looks just as he was to me!

THE CAPTAIN. Sit down, sit down! Now first of all your programme. Any engagement this evening?

KURT. I've been invited to the doctor's, but I haven't promised to go.

ALICE. Then stay with your relatives.

KURT. That would be the natural thing to do, but on the other hand, the doctor is my chief, and there'd be unpleasantness later.

THE CAPTAIN. Nonsense! I've never been afraid of my chiefs.

KURT. Afraid or not, there'd be unpleasantness just the same.

THE CAPTAIN. Here on the island, I'm master. Stick behind me and no one will dare get at you.

ALICE. Be quiet, Edgar! *Takes* KURT's *hand.* Never mind about masters and chiefs—you stay here with us. It's only right and proper.

KURT. So be it. Specially as I find myself welcome here.

THE CAPTAIN. Why shouldn't you be welcome? We haven't any quarrel with you.

KURT *cannot hide a certain embarrassment.*

Why should we have? You were a bit reckless, but you were young, and I've forgotten it. I don't bear grudges.

ALICE *looks vexed.*

All three sit at the sewing-table.

ALICE. Well, have you been round the world?

KURT. Yes, and now I've landed up with you . . .

THE CAPTAIN. Whom you married off twenty-five years ago.

KURT. Hardly that . . . but let it go. It's nice to see that you've stuck together for twenty-five years.

THE CAPTAIN. Yes, we've rubbed along. Sometimes it's been a bit touch and go, but as you say, we've stuck it out. And Alice has had nothing to complain of. Plenty of everything, oodles of money . . . Perhaps you don't know I'm a famous writer—writer of textbooks.

KURT. Yes, I remember when our ways parted you had just brought out a shooting manual that was doing well. Is it still used in the military schools?

THE CAPTAIN. It is still there and still number one, although they've tried to throw it out for an inferior one . . . which of course is used now, though it's utterly worthless.

Embarrassing silence.

KURT. You've been abroad, I hear.

ALICE. Yes, just imagine. We've been to Copenhagen five times.

THE CAPTAIN. Yes. You see, when I took Alice away from the theatre . . .

ALICE. Took me?

THE CAPTAIN. Yes, I took you, as a wife should be taken . . .

ALICE. You're talking very big.

THE CAPTAIN. But afterwards I was always having it thrown at me that I'd ruined her brilliant career. . . . Hm! So I had to make amends by promising to take my wife to Copenhagen. And I've kept my promise faithfully. Five times we've been there. *Holds up the fingers of his left hand.* Five. Have you been to Copenhagen?

KURT, *smiling.* No, I've been chiefly in America.

THE CAPTAIN. America? Pretty low place, what?

KURT, *taken aback.* It's not Copenhagen.

ALICE. Have you . . . heard at all . . . from your children?

KURT. No.

ALICE. Forgive me, my dear, but it was rather heartless to leave them like that.

KURT. I didn't leave them. The Court gave their mother custody.

THE CAPTAIN. We won't talk about that now. Seems to me you were lucky to get out of that mess.

KURT, *to* ALICE. Are your children well?

ALICE. Yes, thank you. They're at school in the town—they'll be grown up soon.

THE CAPTAIN. Yes, they're bright youngsters. The boy has a brilliant mind. Brilliant. He'll be on the General Staff.

ALICE. If they'll have him.

THE CAPTAIN. Have him? The makings of a Minister of War.

KURT. To change the subject . . . There's to be this Quarantine Station here—for plague, cholera, and so forth—and the doctor, as you know, will be my chief. What sort of man is he?

THE CAPTAIN. Man? He's not a man. He's a brainless scoundrel.

KURT, *to* ALICE. How very unpleasant for me!

ALICE. It's not as bad as Edgar says, but I must admit he doesn't appeal to me.

THE CAPTAIN. He's a scoundrel. And so are the rest of them—the Customs Officer, the Postmaster, the telephone girl, the chemist, the pilot—the what-do-they-call-him, the Alderman—scoundrels, the whole pack of them.

KURT. Are you on bad terms with the whole lot?

THE CAPTAIN. The whole lot.

ALICE. Yes, it's true, you can't have anything to do with those people.

THE CAPTAIN. It's as if all the tyrants in the country had been interned on this island.

ALICE, *ironically*. How true!

THE CAPTAIN, *good-humouredly*. Hm. Is that a dig at me? I'm no tyrant, not in my own home at any rate.

ALICE. You be careful!

THE CAPTAIN, *to* KURT. You mustn't believe a word she says. I'm a very good husband and my old woman's the best wife in the world.

ALICE. Would you like a drink, Kurt?

KURT. No thanks, not at the moment.

THE CAPTAIN. You haven't become a . . . ?

KURT. Rather moderate, that's all.

THE CAPTAIN. American?

KURT. Yes.

THE CAPTAIN. I say be immoderate—or leave it alone. A man should be able to hold his liquor.

KURT. To return to our neighbours on the island—my position will bring me into contact with everyone. And it won't be plain sailing, because, however little one wants to, one's bound to become involved in other people's intrigues.

ALICE. Go on then, but you'll always come back to us, because your true friends are here.

KURT. Isn't it frightful to sit here alone surrounded by enemies?

ALICE. It's not pleasant.

THE CAPTAIN. It's not frightful at all. All my life I've had enemies and they've helped rather than harmed me. And when my time comes to die, I shall be able to say: "I owe nobody anything and I've never had anything as a gift. Everything I've got I've had to fight for."

ALICE. Yes, Edgar's path has not been strewn with roses.

THE CAPTAIN. With thorns and stones—flints. But there's your own strength. Do you know what I mean?

KURT, *simply*. Yes, I learnt the limits of mine ten years ago.

THE CAPTAIN. Then you're a milksop.

ALICE. Edgar!

THE CAPTAIN. Well, he is a milksop if he can't rely on his own strength. True, when the mechanism's done for, nothing's left but a barrowful to tip out on a garden plot. But as long as the mechanism's intact, the thing is to kick and fight for all your worth, with both hands and both feet. That's my philosophy.

KURT, *smiling.* You're amusing to listen to.

THE CAPTAIN. But don't you believe it?

KURT. No, I don't believe it.

THE CAPTAIN. Well, anyhow it's true.

During the above scene the wind has risen, and now one of the glass doors slams.

THE CAPTAIN, *rising.* A gale's getting up. I felt it coming.

He shuts the doors and taps the barometer.

ALICE, *to* KURT. You'll stay to supper, won't you?

KURT. Thank you.

ALICE. It will be very simple. Our maid's just left.

KURT. I'm sure it will be fine.

ALICE. You're so easy to please, my dear Kurt.

THE CAPTAIN, *at the barometer.* You should just see how the barometer's falling. I felt it in my bones.

ALICE, *aside to* KURT. He's all on edge.

THE CAPTAIN. It's time we had supper.

ALICE, *rising.* I'm just going to see to it. You two stay here and talk philosophy. *To* KURT, *aside.* But don't contradict him or he'll lose his temper. And don't ask him why he isn't a Major.

KURT *nods assent.* ALICE *goes towards the door, right.*

THE CAPTAIN *sits down at the sewing-table with* KURT.

THE CAPTAIN. See we have something good, old girl!

ALICE. You would have if you gave me some money.

THE CAPTAIN. Always money!

Exit ALICE.

To KURT. Money, money, money! All day long I run round with a purse, till I begin to think I am a purse. Do you know what I mean?

KURT. Surely. With this difference . . . I thought I was a pocket-book.

THE CAPTAIN. Ha! So you know the type—those ladies! Ha! And you picked a proper one.

KURT, *evenly.* All that can be forgotten now.

THE CAPTAIN, *ironically.* A perfect jewel that one. Whereas I —in spite of everything—at least got myself a good woman. For she is honest, in spite of everything.

KURT, *smiling amiably.* In spite of everything!

THE CAPTAIN. Don't laugh.

KURT, *as before.* In spite of everything!

THE CAPTAIN. Yes, she's been a faithful wife . . . a good mother, exceptionally good, but . . . *Glances at the door, right* . . . she has the devil of a temper. There have been times, you know, when I've cursed you for saddling me with her.

KURT, *affably.* But I never did. Listen, my dear fellow . . .

THE CAPTAIN. Damn it, man! You talk a lot of rubbish and forget anything that's unpleasant to remember. . . . Don't get me wrong. You see, I'm used to commanding and blustering, but you know me and won't take offence.

KURT. Of course not. But I didn't saddle you with a wife. On the contrary . . .

THE CAPTAIN, *not allowing his flow to be interrupted.* Don't you think life's an extraordinary business anyway?

KURT. It surely is.

THE CAPTAIN. As for growing old, it's not nice but it's interesting. Of course, I'm not old, but age is beginning to make itself felt. Your acquaintances die off and you grow lonely.

KURT. The man who has a wife to grow old with is fortunate.

THE CAPTAIN. Fortunate? Yes, that is fortunate, for one's children leave one too. You should never have left yours.

KURT. But I didn't. They were taken from me.

THE CAPTAIN. Now you mustn't take offence when I say that.

KURT. But it wasn't so.

THE CAPTAIN. Well, how it happened has been forgotten. But you *are* alone.

KURT. My dear fellow, one gets used to anything.

THE CAPTAIN. Could one . . . could one really get used to being entirely alone?

KURT. Just look at me.

THE CAPTAIN. What have you achieved these fifteen years?

KURT. What a question! These fifteen years.

THE CAPTAIN. They say you've come into some money and are rich.

KURT. I'm not rich . . .

THE CAPTAIN. I wasn't thinking of borrowing.

KURT. If you were, I'm ready . . .

THE CAPTAIN. Thank you so much, but I have my own debit and credit account. You see . . . *Glances at the door, right* . . . in this household there must be no shortage of anything. The day I hadn't any money, off she'd go.

KURT. Oh no!

THE CAPTAIN. Oh yes! I know it. Believe it or not, she's always on the look-out for the times when I do happen to be out of funds, just for the pleasure of proving to me that I don't support my family.

KURT. But I thought you said you had a big income.

THE CAPTAIN. Certainly I have a big income . . . but it isn't enough.

KURT. Then it's not big in the ordinary sense.

THE CAPTAIN. Life is extraordinary, and so are we.

The telegraph begins tapping.

KURT. What's that?

THE CAPTAIN. Only the time signal.

KURT. Haven't you got a telephone?

THE CAPTAIN. Yes, in the kitchen. But we use the telegraph, because the telephone girls repeat everything we say.

KURT. Social life out here must be grim.

THE CAPTAIN. Yes, it's perfectly abominable. The whole of life is abominable. And you, who believe in a sequel, do you think there'll be peace afterwards?

KURT. There's bound to be storm and stress there too.

THE CAPTAIN. There too—if there is a there. Then rather annihilation.

KURT. How do you know annihilation would come without pain?

THE CAPTAIN. I shall drop down dead, without pain.

KURT. I see. You know that, do you?

THE CAPTAIN. Yes, I know it.

KURT. You aren't satisfied with your existence, are you?

THE CAPTAIN, *sighing*. Satisfied? The day I die I shall be satisfied.

KURT. You can't know that. . . . Now, tell me, what are you two up to in this house? What's going on here? The very walls smell of poison—one feels sick the moment one comes in. I'd rather be off, if I hadn't promised Alice to stay. There's a corpse under the floor . . . and such hatred that one can scarcely breathe.

THE CAPTAIN *collapses in his chair and stares vacantly.*

What's wrong with you? Edgar!

THE CAPTAIN *does not move.* KURT *slaps him on the back.*

Edgar!

THE CAPTAIN, *coming to.* Did you say something? *Looking round.* Oh, it's you! I thought it was Alice. . . . Now . . . *Relapses into apathy again.*

KURT. This is terrible. *Goes over and opens the door, right.* Alice!

ALICE *enters, wearing an apron.*

ALICE. What's the matter?

KURT. I don't know. Look at him!

ALICE, *calmly.* He does sometimes lose his senses like this. I'll play—that will bring him round. *Goes towards the piano.*

KURT. No, don't, don't! Let me try. Can he hear? Can he see?

ALICE. At this moment he can neither hear nor see.

KURT. Yet you can speak so calmly. Alice, what are you two up to in this house?

ALICE. Ask that man there.

KURT. That man! Why he's your husband!

ALICE. To me he's a stranger, as much of a stranger as twenty-five years ago. I know nothing about this man except that he . . .

KURT. Stop! He may hear you.

ALICE. He can hear nothing now.

A bugle call is heard.

THE CAPTAIN *springs to his feet and seizes his sword and cap.*

THE CAPTAIN. Excuse me. I must just inspect the posts.

Exit THE CAPTAIN *through the centre doorway.*

KURT. What's the matter with him?

ALICE. I don't know.

KURT. Is he out of his mind?

ALICE. I don't know.

KURT. Does he drink?

ALICE. There's more boasting about it than drinking.

KURT. Sit down and talk. Calmly and truthfully now.

ALICE, *sitting*. What am I to say? That I've been in this tower a lifetime, imprisoned, guarded by a man I've always hated, and now hate so utterly that the day he died, I'd laugh aloud.

KURT. Why haven't you separated?

ALICE. Question! Twice we broke off our engagement, and since then not a day has passed in which we haven't tried to separate. But we are welded together—we can't escape. Once we *did* separate—in our own home—for five years. Now only death can separate us. We know it, so we wait for him as the deliverer.

KURT. Why are you so alone?

ALICE. Because he has isolated me. First he uprooted my brothers and sisters from the house—"uprooted" is his own word for it—and after that my girlhood's friends . . . and the rest.

KURT. But what about *his* relatives? Did you uproot them?

ALICE. Yes. For they were sapping my very life by robbing me of my honour and good name. In the end, my only contact with the world and other human beings was through this telegraph—for the telephone is spied on by the girls. I taught myself how to telegraph, but this he doesn't know. You mustn't tell him or he would kill me.

KURT. Horrible! Horrible! But why does he blame me for your marriage? Let me tell you what really happened. When we were young, Edgar was my friend. He fell in love with you at first sight and came and asked me to act as go-between. I at once refused and, my dear Alice, as I knew you had a cruel and domineering streak in your nature, I warned him. Then, when he insisted, I sent him to ask your brother to plead for him.

ALICE. I believe what you say, but having deceived himself all these years, you'll never get the idea out of his head.

KURT. Very well, let him blame me if that makes him feel better.

ALICE. That's asking too much.

KURT. I'm used to it. . . . But what does hurt is his unjust accusation that I deserted my children.

ALICE. That's how he is. He says what he chooses and believes it. But he seems to like you—chiefly, I suppose, because you don't contradict him. . . . Please try not to get tired of us. . . . I think you've come at a fortunate moment for us, that your coming is an act of providence. . . . Kurt, you mustn't get tired of us! Because we really are the most unhappy people in the whole world. *Weeps.*

KURT. *One* marriage I have seen at close quarters, and that was horrible. But this is almost worse.

ALICE. Do you think so?

KURT. Yes.

ALICE. Whose fault is it?

KURT. Alice, the moment you stop asking whose fault it is, you'll have a sense of relief. Try just to accept it as a fact, as a trial that must be borne.

ALICE. I can't. It's too much. *Rises.* It's hopeless.

KURT. You poor things! Do you know why you hate one another?

ALICE. No, it's a quite unreasoning hatred. It has no cause, no object, but also no end. And why do you think he fears death most? He's afraid I shall marry again.

KURT. Then he loves you.

ALICE. Maybe. But that doesn't stop him from hating me.

KURT, *as if to himself*. That's known as *love-hatred,* and comes from the lowest depths. . . . Does he like you to play to him?

ALICE. Yes, but only hideous tunes—like that revolting *Entry of the Boyars*. When he hears that, he goes quite crazy and has to dance.

KURT. Dance?

ALICE. Yes. He's really very funny sometimes.

KURT. Another thing—forgive my asking. Where are the children?

ALICE. Perhaps you don't know that two of them are dead?

KURT. You've been through that too?

ALICE. What haven't I been through?

KURT. But the two others?

ALICE. In the town. They couldn't stay at home. He set them against me. . . .

KURT. And you against him.

ALICE. Yes, naturally. Then it came to taking sides, canvassing, bribery . . . So, in order not to destroy the children, we parted from them. What should have been a bond drove us apart; the blessing of a home became its curse. . . . Yes, sometimes I think our stock is cursed.

KURT. Since the Fall, yes, that's so.

ALICE, *with a venomous glance, sharply*. What fall?

KURT. Adam and Eve's.

ALICE. Oh, I thought you meant something else!

Embarrassed silence.

ALICE *wrings her hands.*

Kurt! My cousin, my girlhood's friend, I have not always treated you as I should. But now I am punished and you have your revenge.

KURT. Not revenge. There's no revenge about it. Hush!

ALICE. Do you remember one Sunday, when you were engaged? I had invited you to dinner . . .

KURT. Hush!

ALICE. I must speak. Have pity on me. . . . When you came, we were out—you had to go away again.

KURT. You had been asked out yourselves. It's not worth talking about.

ALICE. Kurt, when I asked you to supper just now, I thought there was something in the larder. *Hides her face in her hands.* But there's nothing, not even a bit of bread. . . . *Cries.*

KURT. Poor, poor Alice!

ALICE. And when *he* comes in and wants something to eat and there isn't anything, he'll fly into a rage. You've never seen him in a rage. . . . O God, I'm so humiliated!

KURT. Let me go out and put that right.

ALICE. There's nothing to be got on the island.

KURT. Not for my sake, but for his and yours, I must think of something, something . . . When he comes in, we must make a joke of it. I'll suggest we have a drink, and meanwhile I'll think of something. . . . Get him into a good humour, play to him—play any rubbish he likes. . . . Sit at the piano and be ready.

ALICE. Look at my hands! Are they fit to play? I have to polish the brass and wipe the glasses, do the fires and the rooms . . .

KURT. But you have two servants.

ALICE. We have to say so, because he's an officer . . . but the servants keep on leaving, so sometimes we have none, more times than not. . . . How shall I get out of this—this supper business? Oh, if only the house would catch fire!

KURT. Hush, Alice, hush!

ALICE. Or the sea rise and sweep us away!

KURT. No, no, no, I won't listen to you!

ALICE. What will he say? What will he say? Don't go, Kurt, don't leave me!

KURT. No, my poor friend, I won't go.

ALICE. But when you do go . . .

KURT. Has he ever struck you?

ALICE. Struck me? Oh no, he knows that then I would leave him. One must have some pride.

Outside is heard: Halt! Who goes there? Pass, friend!

KURT, *rising.* Is that him?

ALICE, *nervously.* Yes, it's him.

Pause.

KURT. What on earth shall we do?

ALICE. I don't know, I don't know.

Enter THE CAPTAIN, *back.*

THE CAPTAIN, *gaily.* There we are! Now I'm free. . . . Well, has she got in all her complaints? Wretched life hers, what?

KURT. How's the weather out there?

THE CAPTAIN. Half a gale. *Sets one of the doors ajar. Facetiously.* Sir Bluebeard and the maiden in the tower, and outside the sentry marching with sword drawn, keeping watch over the beautiful maiden . . . And then come the brothers, but the sentry's on guard. Look at him! One, two! He's a fine sentry. Look at him! Meli-tam-tam-ta, meli-ta-lia-lay! Shall we do the sword dance? Kurt ought to see that.

KURT. No, have the *Entry of the Boyars.*

THE CAPTAIN. You know that, do you? Alice, in the kitchen apron, come and play! Come on, I say!

ALICE *goes unwillingly to the piano.*

He pinches her arm.

Been slandering me, haven't you?

ALICE. I?

KURT *turns away.* ALICE *strikes up the* Entry of the Boyars.

THE CAPTAIN *does a kind of Hungarian dance behind the writing-table, knocking with his spurs. Then he sinks to the floor, unobserved by* KURT, *or* ALICE, *who plays the piece to the end.*

Without turning round. Shall we have it again?

Silence.

ALICE *turns and sees* THE CAPTAIN *lying unconscious on the floor behind the writing-table.*

Lord Jesus!

ALICE *stands with her arms crossed over her breast and gives a sigh as of thankfulness and relief.*

KURT *turns and hurries to* THE CAPTAIN.

KURT. What is it? What is it?

ALICE, *in a state of great tension.* Is he dead?

KURT. I don't know. Help me!

ALICE, *without moving.* I can't touch him. . . . Is he dead?

KURT. No. He's alive.

ALICE *sighs.*

KURT *helps* THE CAPTAIN *up into a chair.*

THE CAPTAIN. What happened?

Silence.

What happened?

KURT. You just fell down.

THE CAPTAIN. Was there any . . . ?

KURT. You fell on to the floor. How do you feel now?

THE CAPTAIN. Feel? Nothing at all. I don't know anything about it. Why do you stand there gaping?

KURT. You are ill.

THE CAPTAIN. Fiddlesticks! Go on playing, Alice. . . . Ah! Now it's coming on again. *Clasps his head.*

ALICE. You see, you are ill.

THE CAPTAIN. Don't scream! It's only giddiness.

KURT. We must have the doctor. I'll go and telephone.

THE CAPTAIN. I won't have the doctor.

KURT. You must. We must call him for our own sakes, or we'll be held responsible.

THE CAPTAIN. I'll throw him out if he comes. I'll shoot him . . . Ah, here it is again! *Clasps his head.*

KURT, *going to the door, right.* I'll go and telephone right away.

Exit KURT.

ALICE *takes off her apron.*

THE CAPTAIN. Will you give me a glass of water?

ALICE. I suppose I must.

She gives him a glass of water.

THE CAPTAIN. How amiable!

ALICE. Are you ill?

THE CAPTAIN. Excuse me for not being well.

ALICE. Are you going to look after yourself then?

THE CAPTAIN. You don't seem to want to do it.

ALICE. You can be sure of that.

THE CAPTAIN. The time has come that you have waited for so long.

ALICE. Yes, and which you believed would never come.

THE CAPTAIN. Don't be angry with me.

Enter KURT, *right.*

KURT. That's the limit!

ALICE. What did he say?

KURT. He rang off, without a word.

ALICE, *to* THE CAPTAIN. This is what comes of your monstrous arrogance.

THE CAPTAIN. I think I'm getting worse. . . . Try and get a doctor from the town.

ALICE, *going to the writing-table.* I shall have to telegraph then.

THE CAPTAIN, *half rising, amazed.* Can—you—telegraph?

ALICE, *telegraphing.* Yes, I can.

THE CAPTAIN. Well! Go on then. What deceit! *To* KURT. Come and sit by me.

KURT *does so.*

Take my hand. I seem to be slipping down. Can you understand? Down somehow. It's queer.

KURT. Have you had attacks like this before?

THE CAPTAIN. Never.

KURT. While you're waiting for the answer from the town, I'm going over to have a talk with the doctor. Has he attended you before?

THE CAPTAIN. That he has.

KURT. Then he knows your constitution. *Goes to the door, left.*

ALICE. There'll be an answer here in a moment. It's kind of you, Kurt. But come back quickly.

KURT. As quickly as I can.

Exit KURT.

THE CAPTAIN. He is kind, Kurt. And so changed.

ALICE. Yes, for the better. But it's bad luck on him to be mixed up in our misery just now.

THE CAPTAIN. Good luck for us, though. I wonder how things really are with him. Did you notice he wouldn't talk about his personal affairs?

ALICE. I noticed it, but then I don't think anyone asked him to.

THE CAPTAIN. Think of his life. And ours. I wonder if everyone's life is like this.

ALICE. Perhaps, though they don't talk about it, as we do.

THE CAPTAIN. I've sometimes thought misery attracts misery, and the happy shun unhappiness. That's why we see nothing but misery.

ALICE. Have you ever known any happy people?

THE CAPTAIN. Let me think . . . No. Yes, the Ekmarks.

ALICE. What did you say? She had that operation last year.

THE CAPTAIN. That's true. Well, then I don't know . . . Yes, the von Kraffts.

ALICE. Yes, that whole family lived idyllically for half a century. Well-off, respected, good children, suitable marriages. Then that cousin went and committed a crime—prison and all the rest of it—and that was the end of their peace. The family name was disgraced in all the newspapers. . . . The Krafft murder made it impossible for that highly esteemed family to show their faces. The children had to be taken away from school. Good God!

THE CAPTAIN. I wonder what's the matter with me.

ALICE. What do you think?

THE CAPTAIN. Heart, or head. It's as if my soul is trying to escape and dissolve in smoke.

ALICE. Have you any appetite?

THE CAPTAIN. Yes. What about supper?

ALICE, *walking about, uneasily.* I'll ask Jenny.

THE CAPTAIN. But she's gone.

ALICE. Yes, yes, of course.

THE CAPTAIN. Ring for Kristin, so I can have some fresh water.

ALICE *rings.*

ALICE. Supposing . . . *Rings again.* She doesn't hear.

THE CAPTAIN. Go and see. Supposing she has gone too.

ALICE *opens the door, left.*

ALICE. What's this? Her trunk in the passage, packed.

THE CAPTAIN. Then she has gone.

ALICE. This is hell!

Bursts into tears, falls on her knees, and puts her head on a chair, sobbing.

THE CAPTAIN. And everything at once! Of course Kurt would come and find us in this mess. If there's one humiliation left, let it come now, at once.

ALICE. Oh, do you know what I think? Kurt's gone and won't come back.

THE CAPTAIN. I can quite believe it of him.

ALICE. Yes, we are under a curse.

THE CAPTAIN. What on earth do you mean?

ALICE. Don't you see how everyone avoids us?

THE CAPTAIN. I snap my fingers at them.

The telegraph begins tapping.

Here's the answer. Quiet! Let me listen . . . No one has time . . . Excuses . . .

The tapping ceases.

ALICE. That's what you get for snapping your fingers at your doctors . . . and not paying their fees.

THE CAPTAIN. It's not that.

ALICE. Even when you could, you wouldn't pay them, because you despised their work, just as you despised mine and everybody else's work. . . . They won't come. And the telephone's cut off, because you didn't consider that worth anything either. Nothing's worth anything except your guns and cannons.

THE CAPTAIN. Don't stand there chattering!

ALICE. The wheel is come full circle . . .

THE CAPTAIN. Old wives' tales!

ALICE. You'll see. . . . Do you know we owe Kristin six months' wages?

THE CAPTAIN. Well, she has stolen that much.

ALICE. But I've had to borrow from her too.

THE CAPTAIN. I can believe it of you.

ALICE. How ungrateful you are! You know I lent the money for the children's journey.

THE CAPTAIN. Kurt's made a pretty comeback. Rotter like the rest of them. And coward. Didn't dare say he'd had enough and it was more amusing at the doctor's ball. Suppose he expected a poor supper here. . . . Just like the wretch.

KURT *enters hastily, left.*

KURT. Well, my dear Edgar, this is how it is. The doctor has a thorough knowledge of your heart. . . .

THE CAPTAIN. Heart?

KURT. Yes, for a long time you have had a calcified heart . . .

THE CAPTAIN. Stony heart?

KURT. And . . .

THE CAPTAIN. Is it dangerous?

KURT. Yes, that's to say . . .

THE CAPTAIN. It is dangerous.

KURT. Yes.

THE CAPTAIN. Fatal?

KURT. You must take great care. First of all, cigars—away with them!

THE CAPTAIN *throws away his cigar.*

Then whisky—away with it! . . . And then to bed.

THE CAPTAIN, *alarmed.* No, *that* I won't do. Not bed. That means the end. That means never getting up again. I'll spend the night on the couch. What else did he say?

KURT. He was very friendly and will come at once if you call him.

THE CAPTAIN. Friendly, was he, the hypocrite? I won't see him. Am I allowed to eat?

KURT. Not tonight. And the next few days only milk.

THE CAPTAIN. Milk? I can't stand it.

KURT. You'll have to learn to.

THE CAPTAIN. No, I'm too old to learn. *Clasps his head.* Ah, here it is again!

He remains sitting, staring into space.

ALICE, *to* KURT. What did the doctor say?

KURT. That he *might* die.

ALICE. God be praised!

KURT. Take care, Alice! Take care! . . . And now go and get a pillow and a blanket. I'm going to put him to bed on the couch and spend the night in that chair.

ALICE. And I?

KURT. You go to bed. The sight of you seems to make him worse.

ALICE. Command! I'll obey, for you mean well by us both.

KURT. Both, mark that! I don't take sides.

Exit ALICE, *left.*

KURT *picks up the water carafe. Exit, right.*

The gale outside is heard. Then the glass doors blow open and an OLD WOMAN *of poor and unpleasing appearance peers in.* THE CAPTAIN *comes to, sits up, and looks about him.*

THE CAPTAIN. So they've deserted me, the rotters! *Catches sight of the* OLD WOMAN *and is startled.* Who is it? What do you want?

OLD WOMAN. I just wanted to shut the door, kind sir.

THE CAPTAIN. Why did you? Why?

OLD WOMAN. Because it blew open just as I was passing.

THE CAPTAIN. You meant to steal.

OLD WOMAN. There's not much to take, according to Kristin.

THE CAPTAIN. Kristin!

OLD WOMAN. Good night, sir. Sleep well.

She goes out, shutting the door.

ALICE *enters, left, with pillows and a blanket.*

THE CAPTAIN. Who was that at the door? Was there anybody?

ALICE. Yes, it was old Maja from the poorhouse going by.

THE CAPTAIN. Are you sure?

ALICE. Are you scared?

THE CAPTAIN. Scared? I? No, no!

ALICE. As you don't want to go to bed, lie down here now.

THE CAPTAIN *lies down on the couch.*

THE CAPTAIN. Yes, I'll lie down here.

As ALICE *puts the blanket over him he tries to take her hand, but she draws it away.*

KURT *enters with the water carafe.*

Don't leave me, Kurt!

KURT. I'm staying with you all night. Alice is going to bed.

THE CAPTAIN. Good night then, Alice.

ALICE. Good night, Kurt.

Exit ALICE, *left.*

KURT *draws up a chair and sits down beside the couch.*

KURT. Don't you want to take your boots off?

THE CAPTAIN. No! A soldier must always be equipped.

KURT. Are you expecting a battle then?

THE CAPTAIN. Perhaps. *Sits up.* Kurt, you're the only person I can confide in. Listen to me. If I die tonight . . . look after my children.

KURT. I'll do that.

THE CAPTAIN. Thank you. I trust you.

KURT. Tell me why you trust me?

THE CAPTAIN. We haven't been friends—I don't believe in friendship—and our two families were born enemies and have always been at war. . . .

KURT. And yet you trust me?

THE CAPTAIN. Yes—I don't know why. *Silence.* Do you think I'm going to die?

KURT. You, like everyone else. No exception is made for you.

THE CAPTAIN. You're bitter, aren't you?

KURT. Yes. . . . Are you afraid of dying? The wheelbarrow and the garden plot.

THE CAPTAIN. Think if that were not the end!

KURT. Many people do think it's not.

THE CAPTAIN. And then?

KURT. Utter astonishment, I imagine.

THE CAPTAIN. But one knows nothing for certain.

KURT. No, that's just it. So one has to be ready for anything.

THE CAPTAIN. You're not so childish as to believe in hell, are you?

KURT. Don't you believe in it—you who are right in it?

THE CAPTAIN. Only metaphorically.

KURT. You've described your hell so realistically that metaphors, however poetic, are out of the picture.

Silence.

THE CAPTAIN. If you knew what agonies I'm suffering.

KURT. Physical?

THE CAPTAIN. No, not physical.

KURT. Then they must be spiritual. There's no third alternative.

Pause.

THE CAPTAIN, *raising himself up*. I don't want to die!

KURT. A little while ago you wanted annihilation.

THE CAPTAIN. Yes, if it's painless.

KURT. But we know it's not.

THE CAPTAIN. Is this annihilation?

KURT. The beginning of it.

THE CAPTAIN. Good night.

KURT. Good night.

SCENE 2

SCENE: *The same.*

The lamp is going out. Through the windows and the glass panes of the doors a cloudy morning is seen. The sea is rough.

The SENTRY *is at his post as before.*

THE CAPTAIN *is lying on the couch asleep.*

KURT *is in the chair beside him, pale and vigil-worn.*

ALICE *enters, left.*

ALICE. Is he asleep?

KURT. Yes, since what should have been sunrise.

ALICE. How was the night?

KURT. He slept from time to time, but he would talk so much.

ALICE. What about?

KURT. He kept on arguing about religion like a schoolboy, yet claimed to have solved the riddle of the universe. Finally, towards dawn, he discovered the immortality of the soul.

ALICE. To his own honour.

KURT. Exactly. He really is the most arrogant person I have ever met. "*I* am; therefore God exists."

ALICE. Now you see. . . . Look at those boots! He'd have trampled the earth flat with them if he could. He's trampled other people's fields and gardens with them and other people's toes—and my skull. . . . Killer bear, you've got your bullet now!

KURT. He would be comic if he were not tragic, and there's a touch of greatness in his pettiness. Can't you say one good word for him?

ALICE, *sitting down.* Yes, so long as he doesn't hear it. One word of encouragement sends him mad with pride.

KURT. He can't hear anything. He has had morphia.

ALICE. He was brought up in a poor home with many brothers and sisters, and early on had to support his family by giving lessons, as his father was a waster—or worse. It's pretty hard for a young man to have to forego all the pleasures of youth and slave for a pack of ungrateful children whom he hasn't brought into the world. When I was a little girl I used to see Edgar as a young man; he had no overcoat in winter—in freezing weather—but his little sisters had duffel-coats. That was fine and I admired him, though his ugliness made me shudder. He is extraordinarily ugly, isn't he?

KURT. Yes, and his ugliness can be pretty sinister. I noticed that, specially when we weren't on good terms. And when he wasn't actually present, his image swelled and took on frightful shapes and sizes, so that he literally haunted me.

ALICE. Then think of me! . . . But his years as a young officer were certainly a martyrdom, although now and then he got help from somebody rich. He never will admit that—he's taken everything he could get as a tribute that was his due —without a word of thanks.

KURT. We were to speak well of him.

ALICE. After he's dead. Ah well, I don't remember any more!

KURT. Do you think he's vindictive?

ALICE. Yes—and yet he can be so kind and sentimental. As an enemy, he's simply terrible.

KURT. Why hasn't he been promoted?

ALICE. You ought to know that for yourself. They don't want a man over them who was a tyrant when he was under them. But you mustn't let on you know about that. He says himself he didn't want to be a Major. . . . Did he mention the children at all?

KURT. Yes, he misses Judith.

ALICE. I can well believe it. Oh! Do you know what Judith is? His own image, whom he has trained to bait me. Just think, she, my own daughter, raised her hand against me!

KURT. No, that's going too far!

ALICE. Hush! He's moving. . . . Supposing he heard! . . . He's cunning too.

KURT. He's just waking up.

ALICE. Doesn't he look like an ogre? I'm frightened of him.

Silence.

THE CAPTAIN *stirs, wakes, sits up, and looks about.*

THE CAPTAIN. It's morning. At last!

KURT. How do you feel now?

THE CAPTAIN. Bad.

KURT. Do you want the doctor?

THE CAPTAIN. No. I want to see Judith. My child.

KURT. Wouldn't it be wise to get your affairs in order before —I mean, in case—anything should happen?

THE CAPTAIN. What do you mean? What should happen?

KURT. What happens to us all.

THE CAPTAIN. Oh rot! I shan't die as easily as that, you may be sure. Don't rejoice prematurely, Alice!

KURT. Think of your children. Make your Will, so that at least your wife can keep the furniture.

THE CAPTAIN. Is she to inherit it while I'm still alive?

KURT. No, but if anything does happen, she oughtn't to be thrown out into the street. The person who has looked after these things for twenty-five years and polished and dusted them ought to have the right to keep them. Shall I send for the lawyer?

THE CAPTAIN. No.

KURT. You're a hard man, harder than I thought.

THE CAPTAIN. Here it comes again!

He falls back, unconscious, on the couch.

ALICE, *moving, right.* There's someone in the kitchen. I must go.

KURT. Yes, go. There's nothing much to do here.

Exit ALICE, *right.*

THE CAPTAIN, *regaining consciousness.* Well, Kurt, how do you mean to run this Quarantine Station?

KURT. It will work out.

THE CAPTAIN. But I'm Commandant on the island, so you'll have to deal with me. Don't forget that.

KURT. Have you ever seen a Quarantine Station?

THE CAPTAIN. Have I? Yes, before you were born. And I'll give you a piece of advice. Don't put the disinfecting chambers too near the shore.

KURT. I thought they ought to be near the water.

THE CAPTAIN. That shows how much you know about your business. Why, water's the element of the bacilli, their life element.

KURT. But salt water's essential for washing away impurities.

THE CAPTAIN. Idiot! . . . Now, as soon as you've settled in, you must bring your children here.

KURT. Do you think they'll let themselves be brought?

THE CAPTAIN. Of course, if you're anything of a man. It would make a good impression on the neighbourhood to see you doing your duty in that respect too.

KURT. I've always done my duty in that respect.

THE CAPTAIN, *raising his voice.* It's in that respect you've failed most.

KURT. Haven't I told you that . . . ?

THE CAPTAIN, *going straight on.* Because one doesn't desert one's children in that way.

KURT. How you do go on!

THE CAPTAIN. As a relative of yours, an elder relative, I feel it's my place to tell you the truth, even if it's bitter. . . . And you mustn't take it amiss.

KURT. Are you hungry?

THE CAPTAIN. Yes, I am.

KURT. Would you like something light?

THE CAPTAIN. No, something substantial.

KURT. That would be the end of you.

THE CAPTAIN. Isn't it enough to be ill without starving too?

KURT. That's how it is.

THE CAPTAIN. And not to drink and not to smoke. Such a life's scarcely worth living.

KURT. Death requires sacrifices—or else he comes at once.

ALICE *enters with some flowers, telegrams, and letters.*

ALICE. These are for you.

She throws the flowers on the writing-table.

THE CAPTAIN, *flattered.* For me! Let me see them.

ALICE, *giving him the telegrams and letters.* Oh, they're only from the band and the bombardiers!

THE CAPTAIN. You're jealous.

ALICE. Oh no! If they were laurel wreaths it would be a different matter, but you could never get those.

THE CAPTAIN. Hm! Here's a wire from the Colonel. Read it, Kurt. The Colonel's a gentleman anyhow, though he's a bit of an ass. . . . This one's from—what does it say? It's from Judith. Please wire her to come by the next boat. . . . And this . . . So, one's not without friends after all, and it's good of them to think of a sick man, a deserving man, better than his rank, without fear and without reproach.

ALICE. I don't understand. Are they congratulating you for being ill?

THE CAPTAIN. Hyena!

ALICE, *to* KURT. Yes, we had a doctor here who was so much hated that when he left the island they gave a banquet not *for* him, but *after* him.

THE CAPTAIN. Put the flowers in vases. . . . I'm certainly not credulous, and people are scum, but this simple homage—by God, it's genuine! It can't be anything but genuine.

ALICE. Fool!

KURT, *reading the telegram.* Judith says she can't come because the boat's held up by the storm.

THE CAPTAIN. Is that all?

KURT. No—there's a bit more.

THE CAPTAIN. Out with it!

KURT. Well, she begs Papa not to drink so much.

THE CAPTAIN. What impertinence! There's children for you! There's my own beloved daughter—my Judith, my idol!

ALICE. And image.

THE CAPTAIN. There's life for you and its greatest blessings! Devil take it!

ALICE. Now you're reaping what you sowed. You set her against her mother; now she's turning against her father. Tell me there isn't a God!

THE CAPTAIN, *to* KURT. What does the Colonel say?

KURT. He grants you leave of absence—nothing more.

THE CAPTAIN. Leave of absence? I haven't asked for it.

ALICE. No, but I have.

THE CAPTAIN. I don't accept it.

ALICE. Arrangements have already been made.

THE CAPTAIN. I don't accept that.

ALICE. You see, Kurt, for this man no laws exist; he doesn't recognise any rules or regulations. He's above everything—everybody; the universe is created for his private use; the sun and the moon revolve to carry his praises to the stars. Such is my husband! The insignificant Captain who could never become a Major, whose pompousness makes him a laughing-stock to everyone, while he imagines he is feared! This poor creature who's afraid of the dark and puts his faith in barometers, and all this adds up to what a curtain —a barrowful of manure, and that not of the best quality!

THE CAPTAIN *has been fanning himself complacently with a bunch of flowers and not listening to* ALICE.

THE CAPTAIN. Have you asked Kurt to breakfast?

ALICE. No.

THE CAPTAIN. Then go at once and prepare two steaks, two really good Châteaubriands!

ALICE. Two?

THE CAPTAIN. I'm going to have one.

ALICE. But there are three of us.

THE CAPTAIN. Are you going to have some? Well, get three then.

ALICE. Where am I to get them? Last night you asked Kurt to supper and there wasn't a crust of bread in the house. Kurt has had to keep watch all night on an empty stomach, and he's had no coffee because there isn't any, and our credit's finished.

THE CAPTAIN. She's angry with me for not dying yesterday.

ALICE. No, for not dying twenty-five years ago—for not dying before I was born.

THE CAPTAIN, *to* KURT. Listen to her! This is the result of your match-making, my dear Kurt. Our marriage wasn't made in heaven, that's certain.

ALICE *and* KURT *look at each other meaningly.*

THE CAPTAIN *rises and goes towards the door, left.*

However, say what you will, I'm going on duty now.

He puts on an old-fashioned Artillery helmet, fastens on his sword, and puts on his cape.

ALICE *and* KURT *try to stop him, but in vain.*

Out of my way! *Exit.*

ALICE. Yes, go! You always do go; you always turn your back when the battle gets too hot for you and leave your wife to cover up your retreat. Boozer, boaster, liar! Curses on you!

KURT. This is a bottomless pit.

ALICE. And you don't know it all yet.

KURT. Is there more to come?

ALICE. But I'm ashamed . . .

KURT. Where has he gone now? And how has he got the strength?

ALICE. You may well ask. Well, he has gone down to the bombardiers to thank them for the flowers—and then he'll eat and drink with them and slander his fellow-officers. If you knew how many times he's been threatened with dismissal! Only consideration for his family has kept him his post. And he imagines it's fear of his superiority. And those poor officers' wives who have taken pains on our behalf, he hates and abuses.

KURT. I must confess that I applied for this post in order to get some peace out here by the sea. . . . I knew nothing of your circumstances.

ALICE. Poor Kurt! . . . How will you get something to eat?

KURT. Oh, I'll go to the doctor's. But what about you? Please let me arrange something for you.

ALICE. So long as he doesn't get to know of it—if he did he'd kill me.

KURT, *looking out of the window.* Look, there he is out in the storm on the rampart!

ALICE. He is to be pitied—for being like this.

KURT. You are both to be pitied. What can be done?

ALICE. I don't know. . . . A batch of bills came too, which he didn't see.

KURT. It can be an advantage sometimes not to see.

ALICE, *at the window.* He has opened his cape and is letting the wind blow on to his breast. So he wants to die!

KURT. I don't think he wants to, for, just now, when he felt his own life ebbing away, he held on fast to mine and began to busy himself with my affairs, as if he wanted to get inside me and live my life.

ALICE. That *is* his vampire nature—to seize hold of other people's fates, to suck interest from the lives of others, to order and arrange for others, because his own life is absolutely without interest. So remember, Kurt, never let him into your family life, never allow him to know your friends, for he'll take them from you and make them his own. . . . He's a real wizard at that. If he met your children, you'd soon find they were *his* nearest and dearest, and he'd tell them what to do and bring them up to suit his own ideas, and above all *against* yours.

KURT. Alice, it wasn't he who took my children away from me —at the time I was divorced?

ALICE. Since it's all over now—yes, it was he.

KURT. I suspected it, but never knew. It was he.

ALICE. When, putting your entire trust in my husband, you sent him as a mediator to your wife, he started an affair with her, and put her up to how she could get the children.

KURT. O God! O God in heaven!

ALICE. There you have another side of him.

Silence.

KURT. Do you know, last night, when he thought he was dying . . . he made me promise to look after his children.

ALICE. But surely you won't revenge yourself on my children?

KURT. By keeping my promise? Yes, I shall look after your children.

ALICE. That is really the greatest revenge you could take, for there's nothing he loathes so much as magnanimity.

KURT. So I can consider myself revenged—without taking any revenge.

ALICE. I love the justice of revenge. It delights me to see how evil gets punished.

KURT. You still feel like that?

ALICE. Yes, and always shall. The day I forgave or loved an enemy I should be a hypocrite.

KURT. Alice, it can be a duty not to say everything, not to see everything. That's known as tolerance—a thing we all need.

ALICE. I don't. My life is open and clear, and I have always been above board.

KURT. That's saying a lot.

ALICE. But it's not saying enough. What haven't I gone through for no fault of my own, for this man whom I have never loved?

KURT. Why did you marry?

ALICE. Ask yourself! . . . Because he took me, seduced me. I don't know. And then I wanted to better myself.

KURT. So you abandoned your art.

ALICE. Which was despised. But, you see, he cheated me. He promised me a good life—a beautiful home—and there was nothing but debts. . . . The only gold was on his uniform, and that wasn't gold either. He cheated me.

KURT. Wait a bit. When a young man falls in love, he sees ahead the fulfilment of all his hopes. He must be forgiven if these hopes aren't always realised. I have the same deceit on my own conscience, without considering myself a cheat. . . . What are you looking at out there?

ALICE. I was looking to see if he had fallen.

KURT. Has he fallen?

ALICE. Unfortunately not. He always cheats me.

KURT. Well, I shall go and see the doctor and the District Attorney.

ALICE, *seating herself by a window.* Go, my dear Kurt. I shall sit here and wait. I have learnt how to wait.

ACT II

SCENE 1

Two days later.

SCENE: *The same, by daylight. The sentry is marching by the battery as before.*

ALICE *is sitting in the armchair, right. Her hair is now grey. There is a knock on the door, left, and* KURT *enters.*

KURT. Good morning, Alice.

ALICE. Good morning, my dear. Sit down.

KURT, *sitting in the armchair, left.* The steamer's just coming in.

ALICE. Then I know what we're in for—if he's on it.

KURT. He is. I saw the glitter of his helmet. . . . I wonder what he's been doing in town.

ALICE. I can tell you. As he was in parade dress, he was seeing the Colonel, and as he took his best gloves, he was paying calls.

KURT. Did you notice how quiet he was yesterday? Since he's stopped drinking he's been a different person—calm, reserved, considerate . . .

ALICE. I know. If that man had always kept sober he would have been a power to reckon with. Perhaps it's lucky for people that he has made himself ridiculous and impotent with his whisky.

KURT. The spirit of the bottle has chastened him. . . . But have you noticed that since death has set his mark on him, he has a kind of lofty dignity? It's possible that these new thoughts of immortality have given him a new view of life.

ALICE. You're deceiving yourself. He's up to no good. And don't believe a word he says, because he lies deliberately and knows the art of intrigue better than anybody.

KURT, *gazing at* ALICE. Alice, what's this? In these two nights your hair has turned grey.

ALICE. No, my dear, it has been like that for a long time. I have simply stopped darkening it, as my husband is as good as dead. Twenty-five years in a fortress—did you know this was a prison in olden times?

KURT. Prison! The walls look like it.

ALICE. So does my complexion. Even the children had the pallor of prison here.

KURT. I find it hard to imagine small children prattling within these walls.

ALICE. Nor did they prattle much. And the two who died perished from lack of light.

KURT. What do you think's going to happen now?

ALICE. A determined attack on *us*. I saw a familiar gleam in his eye when you read out that telegram from Judith. It should, of course, have been for her, but she, as you know, always gets off scot free, so his hatred descended on you.

KURT. What does he mean to do to me, do you think?

ALICE. Hard to say, but he's very clever—or lucky—in nosing out other people's secrets. You must have noticed yesterday how he seemed to be living in your Quarantine Station; how he was sucking an interest in life from your existence and eating your children alive? Man-eater, you see—I know him. His own life is ebbing or has already ebbed.

KURT. I have that impression too—that he is already on the other side. His face seems phosphorescent, as if he's begun to decompose—and his eyes flicker like will-o'-the-wisps over graves and swamps. . . . Here he comes! Tell me, have you thought of the possibility of him being jealous?

ALICE. No, he's too conceited for that. "Show me the man I would need to be jealous of!" That's what he says.

KURT. So much the better. Even his faults have their merits. Well, in any case, shall I go and meet him?

ALICE. No. Be ungracious or else he'll think you're insincere. And when he starts lying, pretend to believe him. I'm so good at translating his lies and can always get at the truth with my dictionary. . . . I feel something terrible is going to happen—but, Kurt, don't lose your self-control! My one advantage in the long struggle has been that I was always sober and therefore had my wits about me. He always resorted to his whisky. . . . Now we shall see!

Enter THE CAPTAIN, *left, in parade dress, helmet, cape, and white gloves. Calm, dignified, but pale and hollow-eyed.*

He stumbles forward and sits down, right, still in his helmet and cape, at a distance from KURT *and* ALICE.

During the following dialogue THE CAPTAIN *holds his sword between his knees.*

THE CAPTAIN. Good morning. I apologise for sitting down like this, but I'm rather tired.

ALICE *and* KURT. Good morning.

ALICE. How are you?

THE CAPTAIN. Fine. Just a little tired.

ALICE. What news from town?

THE CAPTAIN. This and that. Among other things, I went to the doctor, and he said it was nothing and I could live another twenty years, if I looked after myself.

ALICE, *to* KURT, *aside.* Now he's lying. *To* THE CAPTAIN. That was very good news, my dear.

THE CAPTAIN. That it was.

Silence, during which THE CAPTAIN *looks at* ALICE *and* KURT *expectantly.*

ALICE, *to* KURT. Don't say anything. Let him talk first, then he'll show his hand.

THE CAPTAIN, *to* ALICE. Did you speak?

ALICE. No, I didn't.

THE CAPTAIN, *slowly.* Listen, Kurt . . .

ALICE, *to* KURT. You see, now it's coming.

THE CAPTAIN. I . . . I was in town, as you know.

KURT *nods assent.*

W-well, I made the acquaintance—among others—of a young cadet . . . *Hesitates* . . . in the Artillery.

Pause, during which KURT *appears uneasy.*

As . . . we are short of cadets here, I arranged with the Colonel that he should come over. . . . That ought to please you, particularly when I tell you that this cadet . . . was . . . your own son.

ALICE, *to* KURT. The vampire! You see!

KURT. In the ordinary way that would please a father, but in my circumstances it is merely painful.

THE CAPTAIN. I don't understand.

KURT. You don't need to. It's enough that I don't want this.

THE CAPTAIN. Really. Is that how you feel? Then you had better know that the young man has been ordered to report here, and from that moment he takes his orders from me.

KURT. Then I shall make him apply to be transferred to another regiment.

THE CAPTAIN. You can't do that, as you have no rights over your son.

KURT. No rights?

THE CAPTAIN. No, the Court assigned those to the mother.

KURT. Then I will get in touch with his mother.

THE CAPTAIN. There's no need to do that.

KURT. No need?

THE CAPTAIN. No, because I've already done it. Ha!

KURT *rises, but subsides again.*

ALICE, *to* KURT. Now he *must* die!

KURT. He really is a man-eater.

THE CAPTAIN. So much for *that*. . . . Did you two say something?

ALICE. No. Is anything wrong with your hearing?

THE CAPTAIN. Yes, slightly. . . . But if you'll come nearer, I'll tell you something in confidence.

ALICE. That's not necessary. And a witness may be an advantage to both parties.

THE CAPTAIN. You're right there. It's always good to have a witness. But first of all, have you got the Will ready?

ALICE, *handing him a document*. The solicitor drew it up himself.

THE CAPTAIN. In your favour. Good.

He reads the document and tears it carefully into strips, which he throws on the floor.

So much for that. Ha!

ALICE, *to* KURT. Did you ever see such a man?

KURT. He isn't a man.

THE CAPTAIN. Now, Alice, I have this to say to you.

ALICE, *uneasily.* Well, go on.

THE CAPTAIN, *calmly, as before.* On account of your long-expressed desire to put an end to this miserable life in an unfortunate union; on account of the lack of affection with which you have treated your husband and children; and on account of your neglect of your household duties, during my visit to town today, I filed a petition for divorce at the County Court.

ALICE. Indeed? On what grounds?

THE CAPTAIN, *calmly, as before.* Apart from the grounds already mentioned, on purely personal ones. In fact, now that it has been established that I may live for another twenty years, I have it in mind to exchange this unfortunate union for one that suits me better. I intend to unite my destiny with that of a woman who will bring into the home, not only devotion to her husband, but youth and, let it be said, a little beauty.

ALICE *takes off her wedding ring and throws it at* THE CAPTAIN.

ALICE. Here you are!

THE CAPTAIN *picks up the ring and puts it in his waistcoat pocket.*

THE CAPTAIN. She has thrown away her ring. Will the witness kindly mark that!

ALICE, *agitated.* So you mean to throw me out and put another woman in my house?

THE CAPTAIN. Maybe.

ALICE. Then we'll have some plain speaking now. Kurt, my cousin, this man is guilty of attempting to murder his wife.

KURT. To murder?

ALICE. Yes, he pushed me into the water.

THE CAPTAIN. There were no witnesses.

ALICE. That's a lie. Judith saw it.

THE CAPTAIN. What's that matter?

ALICE. She can give evidence.

THE CAPTAIN. No, she can't. She says she saw nothing.

ALICE. You've taught the child to lie.

THE CAPTAIN. I had no need to—you had taught her already.

ALICE. Did you see Judith?

THE CAPTAIN. Yes.

ALICE. O God! O God!

THE CAPTAIN. The fortress has surrendered. The enemy is granted ten minutes for evacuation under safe-conduct. *Puts his watch on the table.* Ten minutes by the watch on the table.

THE CAPTAIN *remains standing with his hand on his heart.* ALICE *goes up to him and seizes his arm.*

ALICE. What is it?

THE CAPTAIN. I don't know.

ALICE. Do you want something? A drink?

THE CAPTAIN. Whisky? No, I don't want to die. See? *Straightens up.* Don't touch me! *Draws his sword.* Ten minutes, or the garrison will be cut down. *Exit, back.*

KURT. What is this man?

ALICE. He's a fiend, not a man.

KURT. What does he want with my son?

ALICE. He wants him as a hostage, so that he can be your master. He wants to isolate you from the island authorities. . . . You know that people call this island "Little Hell."

KURT. No, I didn't know. . . . Alice, you are the first woman who has aroused my pity. All the others seemed to me to deserve what they got.

ALICE. Don't desert me now! Don't leave me! He beats me—he has beaten me for twenty-five years—in front of the children too. . . . He has pushed me into the sea.

KURT. After this revelation, I am utterly against him. I came here without ill-feeling, putting out of my mind his former humiliations and slanders. I forgave him, even when you told me that it was he who had separated me from my children—because he was sick and dying. But now that he wants to rob me of my son, he must die—he or I!

ALICE. Well said! No surrender of the fortress. Rather blow it up and him with it, even if we must perish too. I have the gunpowder ready.

KURT. When I came here I bore no malice, and when I felt myself infected by your hatred, I made up my mind to go away. But now I feel impelled to hate this man—as I have hated evil itself. . . . What is to be done?

ALICE. He has taught me the tactics. Rouse his enemies and seek allies.

KURT. To think of him getting in touch with my wife! Why didn't those two meet a generation ago? Then there would have been battles enough to shake the earth.

ALICE. But now these kindred spirits have met—and they must be separated. I think I know his vulnerable point—I have long suspected it.

KURT. Who is his surest enemy on the island?

ALICE. The Quartermaster.

KURT. Is he an honest fellow?

ALICE. Yes, he is. And he knows what I—I know too. He knows what the Sergeant-Major and the Captain have been up to.

KURT. What they've been up to? Do you mean . . . ?

ALICE. Embezzlement.

KURT. That's really shocking. No, I won't have anything to do with that.

ALICE. Aha! So you can't aim a blow at an enemy.

KURT. I could once, but I can't now.

ALICE. Why not?

KURT. Because I have discovered that retribution comes in any case.

ALICE. While you're waiting for it, your son will be taken from you. Look at my grey hair . . . yes, and feel how thick it still is! . . . He means to get married—so I am free—to do the same. I am free! And in ten minutes' time he will be down below, under arrest. *Stamping on the floor.* Down below! And I shall dance on his head. I shall dance the *Entry of the Boyars. . . .*

She dances a few steps with her hands on her hips.

Ha, ha, ha, ha! And I shall play the piano so he hears. *Bangs on the keys.* Ah! The tower is opening its gates, and the guard with the drawn sword will not be guarding me any more—but him! Meli-tam-ta, meli-ta-lia-lay! Him, him, him will he guard.

KURT *watches her, fascinated.*

KURT. Alice! Are you a devil too?

ALICE *jumps on a chair and pulls down the laurel wreaths.*

ALICE. These I will take with me when I make my exit. The laurels of triumph and waving ribbons. A little bit dusty, but eternally green—like my youth. . . . I'm not old, Kurt!

KURT, *with shining eyes.* You're a devil!

ALICE. In Little Hell. Look, now I must make myself beautiful. *Takes down her hair.* In two minutes I shall dress, and in another two go to the Quartermaster. And then, up goes the fortress, sky-high!

KURT, *as before.* You're a devil.

ALICE. You always said that, even when we were children. Do you remember when we were children and got engaged? Ah! You were shy, of course.

KURT, *seriously.* Alice!

ALICE. Yes, you were, and it suited you. You know, there are bold women who like shy men, and . . . it seems there are shy men who like bold women. . . . You did like me rather in those days, didn't you?

KURT. I don't know where I am!

ALICE. With an actress whose manners are free, but who is all the same a very fine woman. Yes, yes! But now I'm free, free, free! Turn your back while I change my blouse.

She unbuttons her blouse.

KURT *rushes forward, takes her in his arms, and lifts her up. He bites her neck and she screams.*

Then KURT *throws* ALICE *down onto the couch and rushes out, left.*

SCENE 2

SCENE: *The same, in the evening.*

The SENTRY *by the battery continues to be seen through the windows of the centre doorway.*

The laurel wreaths are hanging on the arm of a chair. The centre lamp is lighted. Soft music.

THE CAPTAIN, *pale and hollow-eyed, with grizzled hair, in his shabby undress uniform and riding-boots, is sitting at the writing-table, playing patience. He is wearing spectacles.*

The interval music continues after the curtain rises, until the next character appears.

THE CAPTAIN *lays out his patience, but now and then gives a start or looks up and listens anxiously.*

Apparently he can't get the patience out; he grows impatient and sweeps the cards together. Then he goes to the left window, opens it, and throws the pack out. The window remains open, grinding on its hooks.

He goes to the sideboard, is alarmed by the noise made by the window, and turns to see what it is. He takes out three dark, square whisky bottles, examines them, then throws them out of the window.

Next he takes some cigar boxes, sniffs inside one, and throws them out of the window.

After this he removes his spectacles, wipes them, and tests how well he can see with them. Then he throws these too out of the window.

Now he stumbles about among the furniture, as if he can't see properly, and lights the six-candled candelabra on the bureau. Catching sight of the laurel wreaths, he picks them up and goes towards the window, but turns back. He takes the cover off the piano and carefully wraps the wreaths in it, fastening the corners with pins from the writing-table, then lays the bundle on a chair.

He goes to the piano, bangs the keys with his fists, slams the lid, locks it, and throws the key out of the window. Then he lights the piano candles.

He goes to the whatnot, takes his wife's photograph, looks at it, and tears it up, throwing the pieces on to the floor. The window grinds on its hooks and he is again alarmed. When he has calmed down once more, he takes the portraits of his son and daughter, kisses them, and puts them in his breast pocket. The rest of the portraits he sweeps down with his elbow and kicks into a heap.

Then he sits down wearily at the writing-table and clutches his heart; lights the candle on the table and sighs; then stares in front of him as if seeing dreadful visions.

He rises, goes to the bureau, opens the flap, and takes out a bundle of letters tied up with blue ribbon, which he throws into the stove. He closes the bureau.

The telegraph taps once and then stops.

THE CAPTAIN *shrinks back in mortal terror and remains standing with his hand to his heart, listening. When he hears nothing further from the telegraph, he turns, listening, towards the door, left. Then he goes over and opens it, steps out, and returns carrying a cat and stroking its back.*

THE CAPTAIN *goes out, right, with the cat.*

The music stops.

ALICE *comes in from the back. She is in outdoor clothes, with darkened hair, and wears a hat and gloves. She looks round, surprised to see so many lights.*

KURT *comes in left, obviously nervous.*

ALICE. It looks like Christmas Eve in here!

KURT. Well?

ALICE, *holding out her hand for him to kiss.* Thank me!

KURT *reluctantly kisses her hand.*

Six witnesses, four of them firm as rock. The charge has been laid and the reply is coming here—by telegraph—right into the fortress.

KURT. I see.

ALICE. Say thank you, not "I see."

KURT. Why has he lighted so many candles?

ALICE. Because he's afraid of the dark, of course. . . . Look at that telegraph-key. It looks like the handle of a coffee-grinder, doesn't it? I grind, I grind, and the beans crack—like when teeth are drawn out.

KURT. What has he been doing to the room?

ALICE. It looks as if he means to move. And move he shall—down below!

KURT. Alice, don't talk like that! I find it revolting. He was the friend of my youth and did me many a kindness when I was in difficulties. . . . He is to be pitied.

ALICE. Then what about me, who have done nothing wrong and have had to sacrifice my career to this monster?

KURT. What about that career? Was it so brilliant?

ALICE, *furiously.* What on earth do you mean? Don't you know who I am, what I was?

KURT. Now, now!

ALICE. Are you beginning too—already?

KURT. Already?

ALICE *flings her arms round* KURT'S *neck and kisses him.*

KURT *takes hold of her arms and bites her neck. She screams.*

ALICE. You bit me!

KURT, *beside himself.* Yes, I want to bite your throat and suck your blood like a lynx. You have roused the wild beast in me, which for years I've been trying to kill by self-denial and penance. I came here thinking myself rather better than you two, but now I am the vilest of the three. Now that I have seen you—in the full horror of your nakedness—now that passion has distorted my vision, I know the full force of evil. Ugliness has become beauty and goodness is growing ugly and feeble. . . . Come to me! I will suffocate you—with a kiss.

He embraces her.

ALICE, *showing him her ring finger.* Look at the mark of the fetter you have broken! I was a slave and now am free.

KURT. But I shall bind you.

ALICE. You?

KURT. I!

ALICE. I thought at one moment you were . . .

KURT. Pious?

ALICE. Yes, you talked about the Fall.

KURT. Did I?

ALICE. And I thought you had come here to preach.

KURT. Did you? In an hour we shall be in town. Then you shall see what I am.

ALICE. We'll go to the theatre tonight and let everyone see us. The shame will be his if I run away. You realise that, don't you?

KURT. I'm beginning to realise it. Prison is not enough.

ALICE. No, it's not enough. There must be shame too.

KURT. A queer world! You commit a shameful act, and he has to bear the shame.

ALICE. As the world is so stupid.

KURT. It's as if these prison walls had soaked in all the evil of the criminals, and one only had to breathe here to catch it. You were thinking about the theatre and supper, I suppose. I was thinking about my son.

ALICE *strikes him across the mouth with her glove.*

ALICE. Prig!

KURT *raises his hand to box her ears.*

ALICE *shrinks back.*

Tout beau!

KURT. Forgive me!

ALICE. On your knees then!

KURT *falls on his knees.*

On your face!

KURT *touches the floor with his forehead.*

Kiss my foot!

KURT *kisses her foot.*

And never do that again! Get up!

KURT, *rising.* What have I come to? Where am I?

ALICE. You know where.

KURT, *looking round in horror.* I almost think I'm . . .

THE CAPTAIN *enters, right, leaning on a stick and looking wretched.*

THE CAPTAIN. May I talk to you, Kurt? Alone.

ALICE. About the safe-conduct?

THE CAPTAIN, *sitting at the sewing-table.* Will you be so kind as to stay here with me for a moment, Kurt? And, Alice, will you grant us one moment's . . . peace?

ALICE. What is it now then? New signals. *To* KURT. Do sit down.

KURT *unwillingly sits at the sewing-table.*

And listen to the words of age and wisdom. . . . If a telegram comes, let me know.

Exit ALICE, *left.*

THE CAPTAIN, *after a pause, with dignity.* Do you understand a human destiny like mine—like hers and mine?

KURT. No, as little as I understand my own.

THE CAPTAIN. Then what is the meaning of this mess?

KURT. In my better moments I have thought that the meaning was just that we should not understand, and yet submit.

THE CAPTAIN. Submit! Without some fixed point outside myself, I can't submit.

KURT. Obviously not. But as a mathematician, you should be able to find that unknown point from the data given you.

THE CAPTAIN. I have searched for it—but I haven't found it.

KURT. Then you've made some mistake in your calculations. Begin again.

THE CAPTAIN. I will begin again. Tell me, how did you come to be so resigned?

KURT. I'm not any longer. Don't overrate me.

THE CAPTAIN. You may have observed that my practice of the art of living has been—elimination. That's to say, to cancel out and pass on. Early in life I made myself a sack into which I stuffed my humiliations, and when it was full I chucked it into the sea. I don't believe any human being has suffered so many humiliations as I have. But when I cancelled them out and passed on, they ceased to exist.

KURT. I have noticed how you have created your own life in your imagination, and created your own environment.

THE CAPTAIN. How could I have borne life if I hadn't? How could I have endured?

Presses his hand to his heart.

KURT. How are you feeling?

THE CAPTAIN. Bad.

Pause, after which he speaks in an old man's quavering voice, his lower jaw sagging.

But there comes a moment when the ability to create in imagination, as you call it, fails. And then reality stands out in all its nakedness. . . . That's terrible. You see, my dear friend . . . *Controls himself and speaks in his ordinary voice.* Forgive me. When I was in town just now and saw the doctor . . . *His voice breaks again* . . . he said that I was done for . . . *In his ordinary voice* . . . and that I couldn't live for long.

KURT. He said *that?*

THE CAPTAIN. Yes, he said that.

KURT. Then it wasn't true.

THE CAPTAIN. What wasn't? Oh, I see—no, it wasn't true.

Pause.

KURT. Wasn't the other thing true either?

THE CAPTAIN. What, my dear fellow?

KURT. About my son being sent here as a cadet.

THE CAPTAIN. I haven't heard a word about that.

KURT. You know your ability to cancel out your own misdeeds is unparalleled.

THE CAPTAIN. My dear fellow, I don't know what you're talking about.

KURT. Then you *are* done for.

THE CAPTAIN. Yes, there's not much of me left.

KURT. Look here, perhaps you didn't really file a petition for that divorce which would bring your wife into such disgrace.

THE CAPTAIN. Divorce? No, heard nothing of that.

KURT, *rising.* Then you admit you were lying.

THE CAPTAIN. You use such strong language, my dear man. We all need to have allowances made for us.

KURT. You have found that out, have you?

THE CAPTAIN, *firmly, in a clear voice.* Yes, I have found that out. . . . So, forgive me, Kurt! Forgive the whole business!

KURT. Well said. But I have nothing to forgive you. And I'm not now the man you believe me to be—and am quite unworthy to receive your confidences.

THE CAPTAIN, *in a clear voice.* Life has been so strange. So against me, so vindictive . . . and people were so vindictive that I became vindictive too. . . .

KURT *walks about uneasily and looks at the telegraph apparatus.*

What are you looking at?

KURT. Can one switch off a telegraph receiver?

THE CAPTAIN. Hardly.

KURT, *with increasing anxiety.* Who is this Sergeant-Major Östberg?

THE CAPTAIN. An honest enough fellow. Looks after his own interests, of course.

KURT. And what about the Quartermaster?

THE CAPTAIN. He's got his knife into me all right, but I've nothing against him.

KURT *looks out of the window and sees a moving lantern.*

KURT. Why have they got a lantern out on the battery?

THE CAPTAIN. Is there a lantern there?

KURT. Yes, and people moving around.

THE CAPTAIN. It's probably what we call a fatigue-party.

KURT. What's that?

THE CAPTAIN. A few men and a bombardier. Probably some poor fellow's going to be locked up.

KURT. Oh!

Pause.

THE CAPTAIN. Now that you know Alice, what do you think of her?

KURT. I can't tell you . . . I don't understand people at all.

She is as much an enigma to me as you are—as I am myself. The fact is, I'm getting to the age when wisdom admits: "I know nothing, I understand nothing . . ." But when I see an action, I want to know its motive. . . . Why did you push her into the water?

THE CAPTAIN. I don't know. It just seemed perfectly natural to me when I saw her on the jetty that she should go in.

KURT. Didn't you feel any remorse?

THE CAPTAIN. Never.

KURT. That's extraordinary.

THE CAPTAIN. Yes, it certainly is. So extraordinary that I can't believe it was I who behaved in such a caddish way.

KURT. Didn't it occur to you that she'd take her revenge?

THE CAPTAIN. She certainly has—fully—and I find that equally natural.

KURT. How have you arrived so quickly at this cynical resignation?

THE CAPTAIN. Since looking death in the eyes, life has presented itself from another angle. . . . Listen! If you had to judge between Alice and me, which of us would you say was in the right?

KURT. Neither. But I'm desperately sorry for you both, perhaps a little more for you.

THE CAPTAIN. Give me your hand, Kurt.

KURT *gives* THE CAPTAIN *his hand and puts the other on his shoulder.*

KURT. Old friend!

ALICE *enters left, carrying a parasol.*

ALICE. Dear me, what intimacy! Ah, there's friendship for you! . . . Hasn't the telegram come?

KURT, *coldly.* No.

ALICE. I have no patience with this delay. And when I've no patience I speed things up. . . . Watch now, Kurt, I'm going to fire the last bullet at him—and then he'll fall. . . . First, I load—I know the rifle-manual, you see—that famous rifle-manual which never sold five thousand copies . . . Then I take aim . . . *Aims with her parasol* . . . fire! How is the new wife? The young, the lovely, the unknown? You don't know. But I know how my lover is.

She throws her arms round KURT'S *neck and kisses him. He pushes her away.*

He's quite well, but he's still shy. . . . *To* THE CAPTAIN. You poor wretch, whom I have never loved, you who were too conceited to be jealous, you couldn't see how I've been leading you by the nose.

THE CAPTAIN *draws his sword and rushes at her, but only succeeds in striking the furniture.*

Help! Help!

KURT *does not move.*

THE CAPTAIN *falls with the sword in his hand.*

THE CAPTAIN. Judith! Avenge me!

ALICE. Hurrah! He's dead.

KURT *moves towards the door, back.*

THE CAPTAIN, *rising.* Not yet.

He sheathes his sword and goes to sit in the armchair by the sewing-table.

Judith! Judith!

ALICE, *going to* KURT. I'm coming now—with you.

KURT *pushes her away so that she falls to her knees.*

KURT. Go to the hell from which you came! Goodbye for ever.

Turns towards the door.

THE CAPTAIN. Don't leave me, Kurt, she'll kill me!

ALICE. Kurt! Don't desert me! Don't desert us!

KURT. Goodbye.

Exit KURT.

ALICE, *with a complete change of mood.* What a wretch! There's a friend for you!

THE CAPTAIN, *gently.* Forgive me, Alice, and come over here. Come quickly!

ALICE, *going to him.* I've never met such a wretch and such a hypocrite in all my life. . . . You are a man; I will say that for you.

THE CAPTAIN. Alice, listen . . . I can't live much longer.

ALICE. What?

THE CAPTAIN. The doctor said so.

ALICE. Then all that other talk wasn't true.

THE CAPTAIN. No.

ALICE, *distraught.* Oh, what have I done?

THE CAPTAIN. It can all be put right.

ALICE. This can't be put right.

THE CAPTAIN. There's nothing that can't be put right, so long as one cancels it out and passes on.

ALICE. But the telegram! The telegram!

THE CAPTAIN. What telegram?

ALICE *falls on her knees beside* THE CAPTAIN.

ALICE. Are we doomed? Must this happen? I've destroyed myself, destroyed us both! Oh, why did you pretend to have done all that? And why did that man come and tempt me? . . . We are lost! Everything could have been put right; everything could have been forgiven in the bigness of your heart.

THE CAPTAIN. What is there that can't be forgiven? What haven't I forgiven you?

ALICE. That's true . . . but this can't be put right.

THE CAPTAIN. I can't guess this one, although I know your devilish powers of invention.

ALICE. Oh, if I could only get out of this! If I could only get out of this, I'd take such care of you! Edgar, I would love you.

THE CAPTAIN. Just listen to that! Wherever am I?

ALICE. Do you realise no one can help us? No one on earth.

THE CAPTAIN. Who else then?

ALICE, *looking him in the eyes.* I don't know. . . . Oh, what is to become of the children—with their name dishonoured?

THE CAPTAIN. Have you dishonoured their name?

ALICE. Not I! Not I! . . . Now they'll have to leave school. And when they go out into the world, they'll be as lonely as us, and as spiteful as us. . . . Then you didn't meet Judith either? I realise that now.

THE CAPTAIN. No. But cancel that out.

The telegraph taps.

ALICE *jumps up.*

ALICE, *screaming.* Now we are done for! Don't listen to it!

THE CAPTAIN, *calmly.* I won't listen to it, dear child. Calm yourself.

ALICE *stands by the telegraph and gets on her toes so as to see out of the window.*

ALICE. Don't listen! Don't listen!

THE CAPTAIN, *putting his hands over his ears.* I'm stopping my ears, Lisa, my child.

ALICE *kneels with her arms outstretched.*

ALICE. God help us—the fatigue-party is coming!

She moves her lips as if in silent prayer.

The telegraph taps for a little longer, until a long strip of paper has appeared. Then there is silence again.

ALICE *rises, tears off the strip of paper, and reads it to herself. Then she raises her eyes to heaven, goes over and kisses* THE CAPTAIN *on the forehead.*

It is over. It was nothing.

She sits down in the other chair, takes out her handkerchief, and bursts into tears.

THE CAPTAIN. What are all these secrets?

ALICE. Don't ask me. It's over now.

THE CAPTAIN. Just as you please, my child.

ALICE. You wouldn't have said that three days ago. What's happened to you?

THE CAPTAIN. Well, my dear, when I had that first attack, I passed over for a while to the other side of the grave. What I saw I have forgotten, but the effect has lasted.

ALICE. What effect?

THE CAPTAIN. The hope of something better.

ALICE. Something better?

THE CAPTAIN. Yes. I never really have believed that this could be life itself. This is death—or worse.

ALICE. And we . . . ?

THE CAPTAIN. Were destined to torment one another, so it seems.

ALICE. Haven't we tormented one another enough?

THE CAPTAIN. I should think so. What havoc we have played too! *Looks about.* Shall we put the place in order? And clean up?

ALICE, *rising.* Yes, if it's possible.

THE CAPTAIN, *rising and looking round the room.* It can't be done in one day, that's certain.

ALICE. In two, then. Many days.

THE CAPTAIN. Let's hope so.

Pause.

THE CAPTAIN *sits down again.*

So you didn't get free this time. But you didn't get me locked up either.

ALICE *looks surprised.*

Yes, I knew you wanted to put me in prison, but I cancel that out. . . . You have probably done worse things than that.

ALICE *is speechless.*

And I was not guilty of that embezzlement.

ALICE. And now I am to be your nurse?

THE CAPTAIN. If you will.

ALICE. What else is there for me to do?

THE CAPTAIN. I don't know.

ALICE *slumps down in despair.*

ALICE. These are surely the everlasting fires! Is there no end?

THE CAPTAIN. Yes, but we must have patience. Perhaps when death comes, life begins.

ALICE. Ah, if that were so . . . !

Pause.

THE CAPTAIN. You think Kurt was a hypocrite, do you?

ALICE. Yes, I certainly do.

THE CAPTAIN. I don't. But everyone who comes near us grows evil and goes his way. . . . Kurt was weak and evil is strong.

Pause.

How insipid life is now! One used to fight; now one only shakes one's fists. . . . I feel pretty sure that in three months' time we shall be having our silver wedding—with Kurt as best man, and the doctor and Gerda among the guests. The Quartermaster will propose the toast and the Sergeant-Major lead the cheering. And if I know the Colonel, he will invite himself. . . .

ALICE *giggles.*

Makes you laugh, eh? But do you remember Adolf's silver wedding—that fellow in the Rifles? The bride had to wear the ring on her right hand, because in a moment of tenderness the bridegroom had chopped off her left ring-finger with a bill-hook.

ALICE *holds her handkerchief to her face to stifle her laughter.*

Are you crying? No, you're laughing, surely. Yes, child, that's how it is for us—part laughter and part tears. Which it should be, don't ask me! The other day I read in the paper that a man who had been divorced seven times and had married again seven times, finally eloped in his ninety-ninth year and remarried his first wife. There's love for you! Whether life is serious or just trivial, I haven't a clue. It can be its most painful when it's comic, and its most agreeable and peaceful when it's serious. . . . But if you finally decide to take yourself seriously, someone comes and makes a fool of you. Kurt, for example. . . . Do you want a silver wedding?

ALICE *is silent.*

Do say yes. . . . They'll laugh at us, but what does that matter? We'll laugh with them—or else be serious—just as we choose.

ALICE. Yes—very well.

THE CAPTAIN, *seriously.* So silver wedding it is. . . . *Rises.* Cancel out and pass on! So—let us pass on!

CHARACTERS: PART TWO

EDGAR

ALICE

KURT

ALLAN, *Kurt's son*

JUDITH, *Edgar's daughter*

THE LIEUTENANT

The whole action takes place in a house on the island. The following summer.

SCENE: *An oval drawing-room in white and gold.*

In the back wall French windows, through which are seen a terrace with a stone balustrade and light-blue faïence pots of petunias and scarlet geraniums. This terrace is a public promenade. In the background is seen the shore battery with an artilleryman on sentry duty. Beyond, the open sea.

Inside the drawing-room: on the left a gilded sofa, table, and chairs; on the right a fireplace, a grand piano, and a writing-table.

Downstage an American easy chair.

Beside the writing-table is a small table with a copper standard lamp fixed to it.

On the walls are several old oil paintings.

PART TWO

ACT I

SCENE 1

A warm summer morning. The French windows open.

ALLAN *is sitting at the writing-table, making calculations.*

JUDITH *comes in through the French windows, wearing a short-skirted summer dress, her hair in a plait. In one hand she carries her hat, in the other a tennis-racquet. She stops in the entrance.*

ALLAN *rises, serious and courteous.*

JUDITH, *seriously but amiably.* Why don't you come and play tennis?

ALLAN, *shyly, fighting his emotion.* I'm so busy . . .

JUDITH. Didn't you see I left my bicycle *facing* the oak, not with its *back* to the oak?

ALLAN. Yes, I did.

JUDITH. Well, what does that mean?

ALLAN. It means . . . that you want me to come and play tennis. . . . But my work . . . I have some problems to solve . . . and your father is a pretty strict master.

JUDITH. Do you like him?

ALLAN. Yes, I do. He takes such an interest in all his pupils.

JUDITH. He takes an interest in everyone and everything. . . . Are you coming?

ALLAN. You know very well I want to—but I mustn't.

JUDITH. I'll ask Papa to give you leave.

ALLAN. Don't do that. There'd only be a fuss.

JUDITH. I can manage him, you know. What I want, he wants.

ALLAN. That must be because you're so hard—yes!

JUDITH. You ought to be too.

ALLAN. I'm not of the wolf breed.

JUDITH. Then you must be a sheep.

ALLAN. Rather that.

JUDITH. Tell me why you won't come and play tennis.

ALLAN. You know why.

JUDITH. Tell me all the same. The Lieutenant . . .

ALLAN. Yes, you don't care a pin about me, but you don't enjoy being with the Lieutenant unless I'm there too, so you can watch me being tortured.

JUDITH. Am I so cruel? I didn't know that.

ALLAN. You know it now.

JUDITH. Then I'll have to reform, because I don't want to be cruel. I don't want to be bad—in your eyes.

ALLAN. You're just saying that so as to get the upper hand of me. I'm your slave already, but you're not satisfied with that. The slave has to be tortured and thrown to the wild beasts. . . . You've already got the other one in your clutches, so what do you want with me then? Let me go my way and you go yours.

JUDITH. Are you turning me out?

ALLAN *does not answer.*

All right, I'll go. Being cousins, we're bound to meet now and then, but I won't bother you.

ALLAN *sits at the table and goes on with his calculations.*

JUDITH, *instead of going, gradually approaches him.*

Don't worry—I'm just going. I only wanted to see what the Quarantine Officer's quarters were like. . . . *Looks round.* White and gold! . . . And a grand piano—a Bechstein! Ho! We're still in the fortress tower, although Papa's been pensioned off—the tower where Mamma has lived for twenty-five years. . . . And we're only there as a favour too. But your people are rich. . . .

ALLAN, *calmly.* We aren't rich.

JUDITH. So you say, but you're always very well turned out. Though, as a matter of fact, whatever you wear suits you. . . . Do you hear what I'm saying? *Comes closer.*

ALLAN, *resigned.* I hear.

JUDITH. How can you hear while you're adding up, or whatever it is you're doing?

ALLAN. I don't hear with my eyes.

JUDITH. Your eyes . . . By the way, have you ever looked at them in a mirror?

ALLAN. Get along with you!

JUDITH. You despise me, don't you?

ALLAN. My dear girl, I'm not thinking about you at all.

JUDITH, *coming right up to the table.* Archimedes doing his sums, while the soldier comes and cuts him down.

She stirs his papers with her racquet.

ALLAN. Don't touch my papers!

JUDITH. That's what Archimedes said too. . . . You're imagining things, you know. You think I can't live without you.

ALLAN. Why can't you leave me in peace?

JUDITH. Be polite, and I'll help you with your exam.

ALLAN. You?

JUDITH. Yes. I know the examiners.

ALLAN, *severely.* What of it?

JUDITH. Don't you realise one has to be on good terms with one's instructors?

ALLAN. You mean your father and the Lieutenant.

JUDITH. And the Colonel.

ALLAN. You mean that under your protection I shouldn't have to work.

JUDITH. You are a bad translator.

ALLAN. Of a bad original.

JUDITH. You ought to be ashamed.

ALLAN. I am—of your behaviour and my own. I'm ashamed of having listened to you. Why don't you go away?

JUDITH. Because I know you value my company. . . . Yes, your way always leads under my window. You always have something that takes you to town by the same boat as me. You can't go out sailing without having me to man the foresail.

ALLAN, *bashfully.* That's not the way for a young girl to talk.

JUDITH. Do you think I'm a child?

ALLAN. Sometimes you're a good child and sometimes a wicked woman. You seem to have chosen me as your sheep.

JUDITH. You are a sheep. That's why I'm going to protect you.

ALLAN, *rising.* The wolf makes a jolly bad shepherd. . . . You want to eat me—that's the truth of the matter. You want to pledge your pretty eyes so as to redeem my head for yourself.

JUDITH. Oh, have you looked at my eyes? I didn't think you were as bold as that.

ALLAN *gathers up his papers and starts to go out, right.* JUDITH *stands in front of the door.*

ALLAN. Get out of my way, or . . .

JUDITH. Or?

ALLAN. If only you were a boy, I'd . . . But you're just a girl.

JUDITH. So what?

ALLAN. If you had a spark of pride, you'd have gone—so you can consider yourself thrown out.

JUDITH. I'll pay you out for this.

ALLAN. I'm sure of that.

JUDITH, *as she goes, furiously.* I'll—pay—you—out!

Exit JUDITH, *back.*

Enter KURT, *left.*

KURT. Where are you off to, Allan?

ALLAN. Oh, is that you?

KURT. Who made such a violent exit that it made the bushes shake?

ALLAN. That was Judith.

KURT. She is rather violent, but a nice girl.

ALLAN. When a girl is ill-natured and crude, she's always called a nice girl.

KURT. You shouldn't be so intolerant, Allan. Don't you like your relatives?

ALLAN. I like Uncle Edgar.

KURT. Yes, he has many good points. And your other instructors? The Lieutenant, for example.

ALLAN. He's so moody. Sometimes I think he has a down on me.

KURT. Nonsense! You're always thinking things about people. Don't brood. Just do your own job properly and leave other people to do theirs.

ALLAN. Yes, I do, but . . . I don't get any peace. They drag one in—just like the cuttle-fish down by the jetty. . . . They don't bite, but they stir up an eddy that sucks one in.

KURT, *kindly*. I think you're a bit given to melancholy. Don't you like being here with me? Is there something you miss?

ALLAN. I've never had such a good time but . . . There is something here that chokes me.

KURT. Here, by the sea? Don't you like the sea?

ALLAN. Yes, the open sea. But on this shore there's nothing but goose-grass, cuttle-fish, jellyfish, and stingers, or whatever they're called.

KURT. You shouldn't stay indoors so much. Go out and play tennis.

ALLAN. That doesn't amuse me.

KURT. You're angry with Judith, aren't you?

ALLAN. Judith?

KURT. You're so critical of people. You shouldn't be. It makes one lonely.

ALLAN. I'm not critical, but . . . I feel as if I'm at the bottom of a wood-pile waiting my turn to be put on the fire. I'm weighed down, weighed down by all that's on top of me. . . .

KURT. Wait till your turn comes. The pile's diminishing.

ALLAN. Yes, but so slowly, oh so slowly! While I lie there rotting.

KURT. It's not easy to be young. And yet people envy you.

ALLAN. Do they? Would you like to change places with me?

KURT. No, thank you.

ALLAN. Do you know what's hardest of all? To hold one's tongue when one's elders are talking rot. When I know I know more about a subject than they do, and yet have to keep my mouth shut. . . . Oh, I beg your pardon! I wasn't counting you as one of the elders.

KURT. But why not?

ALLAN. Perhaps because we have really only just got to know one another.

KURT. And in the process you've formed a different opinion of me.

ALLAN. Yes.

KURT. I suppose during the years we were apart you didn't always feel very kindly towards me?

ALLAN. No.

KURT. Did you ever see a picture of me?

ALLAN. Only one—and that was most unflattering.

KURT. And old?

ALLAN. Yes.

KURT. Ten years ago my hair turned grey in a single night. Now it has changed back of its own accord. Let's talk about something else. . . . Ah, here comes your aunt, my cousin! What do you think of her?

ALLAN. I'd rather not say.

KURT. Then I won't ask.

Enter ALICE *in a light summer dress, carrying a parasol.*

ALICE. Good morning, Kurt.

Her look indicates that ALLAN *is to go.*

KURT, *to* ALLAN. You had better go.

ALLAN *goes out, right.*

ALICE *sits on the sofa, left, with* KURT *on a chair beside her.*

ALICE, *confused.* He's coming in a moment, so you needn't feel embarrassed.

KURT. Why should I?

ALICE. With your strict principles . . .

KURT. In regard to myself, yes.

ALICE. Yes . . . well . . . I forgot myself once, when I saw you as the liberator, but you kept your presence of mind . . . and so we have a right to forget—what never was.

KURT. Forget it then.

ALICE. However—I don't think *he* has forgotten.

KURT. Do you mean that night he fell down with a heart attack, and you rejoiced too soon, thinking he was dead?

ALICE. Yes. Since then he's been quite himself again, but when he stopped drinking he learnt to hold his tongue, and now he's terrifying. He's up to something I can't grasp.

KURT. Alice, your husband is a good-natured ass who does me endless favours.

ALICE. Beware of his favours! I know them.

KURT. Oh, really . . . !

ALICE. So he's hoodwinked you too. Don't you see the danger? Aren't you aware of the traps?

KURT. No.

ALICE. Then you're doomed to destruction.

KURT. Heaven preserve us!

ALICE. You see! Here am I, watching ruin creeping up on you like a cat. . . . I point it out, but you can't see it.

KURT. Allan, with his unbiased view, can't see it either. For that matter, he doesn't see anything but Judith, and surely that's a guarantee of good relations.

ALICE. Do you know Judith?

KURT. A coquettish little thing in pigtails and rather too short skirts.

ALICE. Quite. But I saw her in a long skirt the other day—and then she was a young lady—not so young either, with her hair up.

KURT. She is slightly precocious, I admit.

ALICE. And she's playing with Allan.

KURT. No harm in that, so long as it is play.

ALICE. I see—that's permitted. . . . Edgar will be here in a moment. He will sit in the easy chair—he has such a passion for it he could steal it.

KURT. He shall have it.

ALICE. Let him sit over there, and we'll stay here. And while he's talking about trivial matters, I'll interpret for you.

KURT. Oh, you're too cautious, too cautious, dear Alice! What could I have to fear, so long as I run the Quarantine Station efficiently and behave properly otherwise?

ALICE. You pin your faith in justice and honour and all that.

KURT. Yes—experience has taught me to. Once I pinned my faith in just the opposite. . . . That cost me dear.

ALICE. Here he comes!

KURT. I've never seen you frightened before.

ALICE. My courage was only unawareness of the danger.

KURT. The danger? You'll begin to frighten me soon.

ALICE. Oh, if only I could! . . . Here he is!

Enter THE CAPTAIN, *back, wearing a buttoned-up black morning coat and officer's cap, and carrying a silver-crooked cane. He greets them with a nod, crosses the room, and sits in the easy chair.*

To KURT. Let him speak first.

THE CAPTAIN. This is a superb chair you have, my dear Kurt. Really superb.

KURT. You shall have it as a present, if you will accept it.

THE CAPTAIN. I didn't mean that.

KURT. But that's what I mean. Just think of all I've had from you.

THE CAPTAIN, *volubly.* What rot! . . . And sitting here, I get a view of the whole island, of all the walks—I can see all the people on their verandahs, all the ships at sea—coming in and going out . . . You certainly have hit on the best bit of this island, which is by no means one of the Isles of the Blest. Is it, Alice? . . . Yes, it's known as Little Hell, and here Kurt has built himself a Paradise. Without Eve, of course, for when she came that was the end of Paradise.

By the way, did you know this was once a royal hunting lodge?

KURT. So I have heard.

THE CAPTAIN. You live royally, but shame to say, you have me to thank for it.

ALICE, *to* KURT. You see? Now he wants to get you in his clutches.

KURT. I have so much to thank you for.

THE CAPTAIN. Oh nonsense! Listen, did you get those cases of wine?

KURT. Yes.

THE CAPTAIN. And you're satisfied?

KURT. More than satisfied. Please give your wine merchant my compliments and tell him so.

THE CAPTAIN. He always provides first-class stuff.

ALICE, *to* KURT. At second-class prices—and you have to pay the difference.

THE CAPTAIN. What did you say, Alice?

ALICE. I? Nothing.

THE CAPTAIN. Yes. When this Quarantine Station was established, I thought of applying for the post, and to that end made a study of quarantine systems.

ALICE, *to* KURT. That's a lie.

THE CAPTAIN, *boastfully.* The archaic ideas of quarantine held by the authorities were not shared by me. I, in fact, was on the side of the Neptunists—as we called them, because they favoured the water method.

KURT. I beg your pardon! I remember very well that it was I who preached water on one occasion, and you, fire.

THE CAPTAIN. Did I? What rot!

ALICE, *loudly.* Yes, I remember that too.

THE CAPTAIN. You do?

KURT. I remember it all the more clearly because . . .

THE CAPTAIN, *cutting him short.* Well, that may be, but it makes no odds. *Raising his voice.* In any case . . . we have now reached the point when a new state of affairs . . .

KURT *tries to break in.*

don't interrupt! . . . a new state of affairs has arisen, and the quarantine system is about to take a giant step forward.

KURT. Apropos, do you know who it is who writes those silly articles in the newspaper?

THE CAPTAIN, *getting red.* I don't know; but why do you call them silly?

ALICE, *to* KURT. Take care! It was he who wrote them.

KURT, *to* ALICE. He? *To* THE CAPTAIN. Well, shall we say—not very intelligent.

THE CAPTAIN. You're no judge of that.

ALICE. Do you mean to quarrel?

KURT. Oh no!

THE CAPTAIN. It's hard to keep the peace here on the island, but we ought to set a good example.

KURT. Yes. Now can you explain this to me? When I came here I made friends at once with all the officials and was on confidential terms with the lawyer—as confidential, that's to say, as one can be at our time of life. Well, after a time —it was just after you got well again—one and then another began to cold-shoulder me, and yesterday the lawyer cut me on the promenade. I can't tell you how hurt I was.

THE CAPTAIN *is silent.*

Have you noticed any coldness towards yourself?

THE CAPTAIN. No, on the contrary.

ALICE, *to* KURT. Don't you realise he has stolen your friends?

KURT, *to* THE CAPTAIN. I wondered if it could be due to that new issue of shares I refused to have anything to do with.

THE CAPTAIN. No, no. But can you tell me why you wouldn't subscribe?

KURT. Because I'd already put my small savings into your soda factory. And also because a new issue means that the old shares are doing badly.

THE CAPTAIN, *irrelevantly.* That's a superb lamp you have. Where on earth did you get it?

KURT. In the town, of course.

ALICE, *to* KURT. Keep an eye on your lamp, Kurt.

KURT, *to* THE CAPTAIN. You mustn't think I'm ungrateful or haven't confidence in you, Edgar.

THE CAPTAIN. Well, it doesn't show much confidence when you want to back out of a business you helped to start.

KURT. My dear fellow, common prudence requires one to save oneself and what one has, while there's still time.

THE CAPTAIN. Save? Is there danger pending? Do they mean to rob you?

KURT. Why put it so crudely?

THE CAPTAIN. Weren't you pleased when I helped you to invest your capital at six per cent?

KURT. Yes, I was grateful too.

THE CAPTAIN. You are *not* grateful. It's not in your nature to be, but you can't help that.

ALICE, *to* KURT. *Listen* to him!

KURT. There are plenty of shortcomings in my nature and my fight against them is pretty unsuccessful, but I do recognise obligations. . . .

THE CAPTAIN. Show it then! *Puts out his hand and picks up a newspaper.* Look! What's this? . . . An announcement. *Reads.* Death of the Medical Superintendent.

ALICE, *to* KURT. He's already speculating on the corpse.

THE CAPTAIN, *as if to himself.* This will bring about . . . certain changes.

KURT. In what respect?

THE CAPTAIN, *rising.* We shall soon see.

ALICE, *to* THE CAPTAIN. Where are you going?

THE CAPTAIN. I think I'd better go into town.

He catches sight of an envelope on the writing-table, picks it up as if unconsciously, reads the address, and puts it back.

Excuse me for being so absent-minded.

KURT. No harm in that.

THE CAPTAIN. Here's Allan's geometry set. Where is the boy?

KURT. He's out playing with the girls.

THE CAPTAIN. That great boy? I don't like it. And Judith ought not to run about like that. . . . You keep an eye on your young gentleman, and I'll look after my young lady. *Passing the piano, he strikes a few notes.* Superb tone, this instrument. A Steinbech, eh?

KURT. Bechstein.

THE CAPTAIN. Yes, you're well off, Kurt. Thanks to me, who brought you here.

ALICE, *to* KURT. That's a lie. He tried to prevent you coming.

THE CAPTAIN. Goodbye for the moment. I'll take the next boat.

On his way out, he examines the pictures on the walls. Exit.

ALICE. Well?

KURT. Well?

ALICE. I don't understand yet what he's scheming. But—tell me one thing. That envelope he looked at . . . who was the letter from?

KURT. I'm sorry to say, it was my one secret.

ALICE. And he smelt it out. You see, he's a wizard, as I told you before. . . . Is anything printed on the envelope?

KURT. Yes, it says: "Electors' Association."

ALICE. Then he's guessed your secret. I understand—you want to get into Parliament. And now you'll have to watch *him* getting in instead.

KURT. Has he ever thought of that?

ALICE. No, but he's thinking of it now. I read it in his face while he was looking at the envelope.

KURT. Is that why he's going to town?

ALICE. No. He made that decision when he saw the obituary.

KURT. What has he to gain by the death of the Medical Officer?

ALICE. You may well ask. . . . Perhaps he was an enemy who got in the way of his schemes.

KURT. If he's as monstrous as you say, one has good reason to fear him.

ALICE. Didn't you see how he wanted to get you into his clutches and tie your hands, on the grounds of obligations which don't exist? For instance, he did not get you the post; on the contrary, he tried to prevent your getting it. He's a man-eater, an insect, a woodworm who will devour you internally, so that one day you're as hollow as a rotten pine tree. . . . He hates you, though he's bound to you by the memories of your early friendship.

KURT. How sharp-witted you become when you hate!

ALICE. How dull-witted one is when one loves! Blind and dull.

KURT. Oh no, don't say that!

ALICE. Do you know what's meant by a vampire? . . . Well, it's the soul of a dead person looking for a body to live in as a parasite. Edgar has been dead ever since that fall of his. He has no interests of his own, no personality, no initiative. But if only he can get hold of somebody, he clings to him, puts out his suckers, and begins to grow and bloom. Now he's making a set at you.

KURT. If he comes too close, I'll shake him off.

ALICE. Shake off a burr—you'll see! . . . Listen. Do you know why he doesn't want Judith and Allan to play together?

KURT. He's afraid their feelings will run away with them, I suppose.

ALICE. Not at all. He wants to marry Judith off—to the Colonel.

KURT, *shocked.* That old widower?

ALICE. Yes.

KURT. How horrible! And Judith?

ALICE. If she could have the General, who is eighty, she'd take him so as to spite the Colonel, who is sixty. To crush, you see, that's her object in life. Trample and crush, that's the password of *that* family.

KURT. Judith? That glorious proud young beauty.

ALICE. Yes, we know about all that. . . . May I sit here and write a letter?

KURT, *tidying the writing-table.* By all means.

ALICE *takes off her gloves and sits at the writing-table.*

ALICE. Now I'll try the art of war. I failed once when I intended to slay my dragon. But now I've learnt how it's done.

KURT. You know you have to load before you shoot?

ALICE. Yes, and with ball cartridges too.

KURT *goes slowly out, right.*

ALICE *ponders, then writes.*

ALLAN *rushes in without noticing* ALICE *and throws himself full length on the sofa, sobbing into a lace handkerchief.*

ALICE *watches him for a moment, then rises and approaches the sofa.*

Gently. Allan!

ALLAN *sits up, embarrassed, and hides the handkerchief behind his back.*

Gently, motherly, with real emotion. You mustn't be afraid of me, Allan. I'm no danger to you. . . . What's the matter? Are you ill?

ALLAN. Yes.

ALICE. In what way?

ALLAN. I don't know.

ALICE. Have you got a headache?

ALLAN. No-o-o.

ALICE. In your heart? Pain?

ALLAN. Yes!

ALICE. Pain, pain, as if your heart were melting away. And dragging, dragging . . .

ALLAN. How do you know?

ALICE. And then you want to die; you wish you were dead and it's all so grim. And you can only think of one thing . . . one person . . . but when two are thinking of the same person, then sorrow is heavy for one of them.

ALLAN *forgets himself and fingers the handkerchief.*

This is the sickness no one can cure. . . . You cannot eat; you do not want to drink; you only want to weep, and how bitterly one does weep—out in the woods for choice, where no one can see you, for people laugh at this sorrow—cruel people. *Shudders.* What do you want of her? Nothing. You don't want to kiss her lips, for you think if you did you would die. You feel as if death were stealing on you when your thoughts fly to her. And it is death, my child, the death which gives life. But you don't understand that yet. . . .

There's a scent of violets. It is she. *Goes up to* ALLAN *and takes the handkerchief gently away.* It is she. Everywhere she and only she. Ah! Ah! Ah!

ALLAN *cannot do otherwise than hide his face in* ALICE'S *arms.*

Poor boy! Poor boy! Oh, how it hurts, how it hurts!

She dries his tears with the handkerchief.

There, there, there! Cry, cry then! That eases the heart. . . . But now, get up, Allan, and be a man, or she won't look at you. That cruel girl who isn't cruel. Has she been tormenting you? With the Lieutenant? Listen, my boy. You must make friends with the Lieutenant, so that you can talk about her together. That's generally some comfort at least.

ALLAN. I don't want to see the Lieutenant.

ALICE. Listen, little boy. It won't be long before the Lieutenant seeks you out so as to talk about her. Because . . .

ALLAN *looks up with a ray of hope.*

Well, shall I be kind and tell you?

ALLAN *nods.*

He is just as unhappy as you are.

ALLAN, *joyfully.* Is he?

ALICE. Yes, truly, and he needs someone to confide in when Judith hurts him. . . . You seem to be rejoicing rather soon.

ALLAN. Doesn't she want the Lieutenant?

ALICE. She doesn't want you either, my dear boy. What she wants is the Colonel.

ALLAN *grows depressed again.*

Oh, raining again, is it? But you can't have the handkerchief, because Judith is careful of her possessions and likes her dozen complete.

ALLAN *looks crestfallen.*

Yes, you see, that's how Judith is. Now sit there, while I write another letter and then you can do an errand for me.

She goes to the writing-table and writes.

THE LIEUTENANT *enters, back. He is melancholy, but without looking at all comical. He does not notice* ALICE, *but makes straight for* ALLAN.

THE LIEUTENANT. Cadet!

ALLAN *rises and stands to attention.*

Do sit down.

ALICE *watches them.*

THE LIEUTENANT *goes over and sits beside* ALLAN. *He sighs, takes out a handkerchief like the other one, and mops his brow.*

ALLAN *surveys the handkerchief enviously.*

THE LIEUTENANT *surveys* ALLAN *sorrowfully.*

ALICE *coughs.*

THE LIEUTENANT *springs to attention.*

ALICE. Do sit down.

THE LIEUTENANT. I beg your pardon, madam.

ALICE. Don't mention it. . . . Please sit down and keep the Cadet company. He feels rather deserted here on the island. *Writes.*

THE LIEUTENANT, *disconcerted, converses in a low tone with* ALLAN.

THE LIEUTENANT. Frightfully hot, isn't it?

ALLAN. Rather!

THE LIEUTENANT. Have you finished the sixth book yet?

ALLAN. I'm just working at the last proposition.

THE LIEUTENANT. Bit of a teaser, that one.

Silence.

Have you . . . *Seeks for words* . . . been playing tennis today?

ALLAN. No-o. The sun was too hot.

THE LIEUTENANT, *in torment, but still in no way comic.* Yes, it's frightfully hot today.

ALLAN, *whispering.* Yes, it's very hot indeed.

Silence.

THE LIEUTENANT. Have you been out sailing today?

ALLAN. No, I haven't found anyone to act as crew.

THE LIEUTENANT. Would . . . er . . . would you trust me to do it?

ALLAN, *respectfully, as before.* That would be too great an honour for me, Lieutenant.

THE LIEUTENANT. Not at all, not at all . . . Do you think the wind will be good today—round about noon? That's the only time I'm free.

ALLAN, *slyly.* At noon the wind drops . . . and at that time Miss Judith has her lesson.

THE LIEUTENANT, *crestfallen.* I see, I see. . . . Er, do you think . . . ?

ALICE. Would either of you young gentlemen care to take a letter for me . . . ?

ALLAN *and* THE LIEUTENANT *look at one another suspiciously.*

. . . To Miss Judith.

ALLAN *and* THE LIEUTENANT *rise simultaneously and approach* ALICE, *although with a certain dignity to conceal their feelings.*

Both of you? Well, it's all the more certain of being delivered. *Hands the letter to* THE LIEUTENANT. Now, Lieutenant, may I have that handkerchief? My daughter is careful of her linen. She has a touch of meanness in her character. . . . Give me the handkerchief! . . . I don't want to laugh at you, but you shouldn't make yourselves ridiculous without good cause. And the Colonel doesn't want to be Othello. *Takes the handkerchief.* Off with you now, young men, and try to hide your feelings as best you can.

THE LIEUTENANT *bows and goes out, followed by* ALLAN.

Calling. Allan!

ALLAN *reluctantly stops in the doorway.*

ALLAN. Yes, Aunt?

ALICE. Stay here. If you don't want to do yourself more harm than you can stand.

ALLAN. Yes, but he's going!

ALICE. Let him burn his fingers. But you take care!

ALLAN. I don't want to take care.

ALICE. Then it will end in a cry. And I shall have the bother of comforting you.

ALLAN. I want to go.

ALICE. Go then. But if you come back, young madcap, I shall have the right to laugh at you.

ALLAN *hurries after* THE LIEUTENANT.

ALICE *writes once more.*

Enter KURT.

KURT. Alice, I've had an anonymous letter which worries me.

ALICE. Have you noticed that since he's stopped wearing his uniform, Edgar has become another person? I never would have believed a coat could make such a difference.

KURT. You haven't answered my question.

ALICE. It wasn't a question. It was a piece of information. What are you afraid of?

KURT. Everything.

ALICE. He went to town. His journeys to town always bring about something fearful.

KURT. But I can't do anything, because I don't know from which quarter the attack will start.

ALICE *folds up her letter.*

ALICE. We must see if I can't guess.

KURT. Are you going to help me then?

ALICE. Yes. . . . But only as far as my interests allow. Mine —that's to say, my children's.

KURT. I realise that. . . . Alice, listen! How still it is—nature, the sea, everything!

ALICE. But behind the stillness I hear voices . . . murmurs, cries.

KURT. Hush! I hear something too. . . . No, it was only the seagulls.

ALICE. But I—I hear something else. . . . And now I'm going to the post—with this letter.

SCENE 2

SCENE: *The same.*

ALLAN *is sitting at the writing-table, working.*

JUDITH *is standing in the doorway, wearing a tennis hat and holding the handle-bars of a bicycle.*

JUDITH. May I borrow your spanner?

ALLAN, *without looking up.* No, you mayn't.

JUDITH. You're being rude, now that I'm running after you.

ALLAN, *not crossly.* I'm not being anything, but I want to be left in peace.

JUDITH, *advancing.* Allan!

ALLAN. Well, what is it?

JUDITH. You mustn't be angry with me.

ALLAN. I'm not.

JUDITH. Shake hands on it.

ALLAN, *gently.* I don't want to shake hands, but I'm not angry. . . . What do you want with me, really?

JUDITH. You're so stupid.

ALLAN. That may well be.

JUDITH. You think I'm just horrid.

ALLAN. No, I know you're nice too. You *can* be nice.

JUDITH. Well, it's not my fault that . . . that you and the Lieutenant go and cry in the woods. Why do you cry? Tell me.

ALLAN *is embarrassed.*

Tell me. I never cry. And why are you such good friends now? What do you talk about when you're walking arm in arm?

ALLAN *has no answer.*

Allan, soon you will see what I am, and that I can strike a blow for anyone I care about. And one piece of advice I must give you, although I don't want to tell tales. Be prepared!

ALLAN. What for?

JUDITH. For trouble.

ALLAN. From what quarter?

JUDITH. The quarter you least expect.

ALLAN. I'm pretty well used to trouble. I haven't had a very pleasant life. . . . What's brewing now?

JUDITH, *pensively*. You poor boy! Give me your hand!

ALLAN *gives her his hand.*

Look at me. . . . Don't you dare look at me?

ALLAN *hastens out, left, to hide his emotion.*

Enter THE LIEUTENANT, *back.*

THE LIEUTENANT. Excuse me, I thought the Cadet . . .

JUDITH. Listen, Lieutenant. Will you be my friend and confidant?

THE LIEUTENANT. If you will do me that honour.

JUDITH. Well! In a word—don't give Allan up when the disaster comes.

THE LIEUTENANT. What disaster?

JUDITH. You'll soon see—perhaps today. . . . Do you like Allan?

THE LIEUTENANT. That young man is my best pupil, and I value him personally too for his strength of character. . . . Yes, life has moments when that's needed . . . *Emphatically* . . . strength to bear, to endure—in a word, to suffer.

JUDITH. That was more than a word—what you said. However, you approve of Allan.

THE LIEUTENANT. Yes.

JUDITH. Go and find him and keep him company.

THE LIEUTENANT. That's what I came for—*that* and *nothing else*. My visit had no other purpose.

JUDITH. I hadn't imagined anything—in the way you mean. . . . *Pointing left*. Allan went out that way.

THE LIEUTENANT, *going slowly to the door, left*. Yes . . . I'll do that.

JUDITH. Please do.

Exit THE LIEUTENANT, *left.*

Enter ALICE, *back.*

ALICE. What are you doing here?

JUDITH. I wanted to borrow a spanner.

ALICE. Will you listen to me for a moment?

JUDITH. Of course I will.

ALICE *sits on the sofa.*

JUDITH *remains standing.*

But say what you have to quickly. I don't like long lectures.

ALICE. Lectures? . . . Very well. Put your hair up and wear long skirts.

JUDITH. Why?

ALICE. Because you're no longer a child. And you're too young to need to make out you're younger than you are.

JUDITH. What does this mean?

ALICE. That you're old enough to be married. And your way of dressing shocks people.

JUDITH. Then I'll do it.

ALICE. So you have understood?

JUDITH. Yes, of course.

ALICE. And we're agreed.

JUDITH. Absolutely.

ALICE. On all points?

JUDITH. Even on the sorest.

ALICE. And at the same time will you stop playing about—with Allan?

JUDITH. This is to be serious then?

ALICE. Yes.

JUDITH. Then we'd better begin at once.

She puts down the handle-bars, lets down her bicycling skirt, and twists her plait up into a knot, which she fastens with a hairpin taken from her mother's hair.

ALICE. One doesn't do one's toilet in other people's drawing-rooms.

JUDITH. Am I all right like this? . . . Then I'm ready. Now, come who dares!

ALICE. Now at least you look decent. . . . And now—leave Allan in peace!

JUDITH. I don't understand what you mean by that.

ALICE. Don't you see how he's suffering? . . .

JUDITH. Yes, I think I have noticed it, but I don't know why. I'm not suffering.

ALICE. That's your strength. But wait a little—oh, yes, one day you'll know well enough! . . . Go home now, and don't forget you're wearing a long skirt.

JUDITH. Must one walk differently then?

ALICE. Try to.

JUDITH, *trying to walk like a lady.* Oh, I have fetters on my feet! I'm imprisoned. I can no longer run.

ALICE. No, child, now the walking begins—the slow way towards the unknown—which one knows already and yet must pretend not to know. . . . Shorter steps, and slower, much slower. Children's shoes must go and you must have boots, Judith. You don't remember when you gave up wearing babies' socks and had shoes; but I remember.

JUDITH. I shall never be able to stand this.

ALICE. All the same, you must. Must.

JUDITH *goes up to her mother and kisses her lightly on the cheek.*

JUDITH. Goodbye.

She goes out in a dignified manner like a lady, forgetting the handle-bars.

Enter KURT, *right.*

KURT. Are you here already?

ALICE. Yes.

KURT. Has *he* come back?

ALICE. Yes.

KURT. What like?

ALICE. In dress uniform. So he has been at the Colonel's. Two orders on his breast.

KURT. Two? I knew he was to get the Order of the Sword when he retired. What's the other one?

ALICE. I don't know, but it's a white cross inside a red one.

KURT. Portuguese in that case. . . . Let's think. . . . Ah, didn't his newspaper articles describe Quarantine Stations in Portuguese harbours?

ALICE. Yes, so far as I remember.

KURT. And has he ever been to Portugal?

ALICE. Never.

KURT. But I have been there.

ALICE. You shouldn't be so communicative. His hearing is very acute and he has an excellent memory.

KURT. Don't you think it was Judith who got him this decoration?

ALICE. No, really Kurt—there are limits! *Rises.* And you have overstepped them.

KURT. Are we going to bicker now?

ALICE. Depends on you. Don't interfere with my interests.

KURT. If they cross mine, I have to interfere with them, even if with a very cautious hand. . . . Here he comes!

ALICE. It's now that it will happen.

KURT. What will happen?

ALICE. You'll see.

KURT. May it be an attack then, for this state of siege has got on my nerves. I haven't a friend left on the whole island.

ALICE. Quick now! . . . You sit here on this side . . . he'll take the easy chair, of course, and I can prompt you.

Enter THE CAPTAIN, *back, in full dress uniform with the Order of the Sword and the Portuguese Order of Christ.*

THE CAPTAIN. Good morning. So this is the rendezvous.

ALICE. You're tired. Sit down.

THE CAPTAIN, *contrary to expectation, sits on the sofa, left.* Make yourself comfortable.

THE CAPTAIN. It's so nice here. You're very kind.

ALICE, *to* KURT. Take care! He suspects us.

THE CAPTAIN, *testily*. What's that you said?

ALICE, *to* KURT. He's certainly been drinking.

THE CAPTAIN, *bluntly*. No, he hasn't.

Silence.

Well? How have you been amusing yourselves?

ALICE. And you?

THE CAPTAIN. Haven't you noticed my Orders?

ALICE. No . . . o.

THE CAPTAIN. I thought not. You're jealous. It's usual to congratulate people when they're decorated.

ALICE. We have the honour to do so.

THE CAPTAIN. We get these things instead of the laurels actresses get.

ALICE. That refers to the wreaths on the wall at home in the tower . . .

THE CAPTAIN. Which you got from your brother . . .

ALICE. Oh, stop!

THE CAPTAIN. And which I've had to kotow to for twenty-five years . . . and which it has taken me twenty-five years to expose.

ALICE. Have you been seeing my brother?

THE CAPTAIN. From time to time.

ALICE *is taken aback.*

Silence.

Well, Kurt? You're very silent.

KURT. I'm waiting.

THE CAPTAIN. Listen, I suppose you've heard the big news?

KURT. No.

THE CAPTAIN. Well, it's not very pleasant for me to have to be the one to . . .

KURT. Let's have it!

THE CAPTAIN. The soda factory has gone bust.

KURT. That's very bad news. How do you come out of it?

THE CAPTAIN. I'm all right. I sold out in time.

KURT. You did wisely.

THE CAPTAIN. But how do you come out of it?

KURT. Badly.

THE CAPTAIN. You've only yourself to blame. You should have sold out in time or have subscribed to the new shares.

KURT. Then I'd have lost them too.

THE CAPTAIN. Oh no! Because then the Company would have stayed on its feet.

KURT. Not the Company, but the Board. I regarded the new shares as a collection for the directors.

THE CAPTAIN. Can that point of view save you? That's the question now.

KURT. No, I shall have to give up everything.

THE CAPTAIN. Everything?

KURT. Even the house and furniture.

THE CAPTAIN. That's an appalling state of affairs.

KURT. I have been through worse.

Silence.

THE CAPTAIN. That's what happens when amateurs go in for speculation.

KURT. How can you say that? You know if I hadn't subscribed I'd have been boycotted. . . . "Further means of livelihood for coast-dwellers and sea-workers; unlimited capital, unlimited as the sea . . . philanthropy and national gain." That's what you wrote and had printed. And now you call it speculation.

THE CAPTAIN, *unmoved.* What do you mean to do now?

KURT. I may have to have an auction.

THE CAPTAIN. You would do well to.

KURT. What do you mean?

THE CAPTAIN. What I said. *Slowly.* The fact is, there are going to be certain changes here.

KURT. Here on the island?

THE CAPTAIN. Yes. . . . For instance, your official residence will be exchanged for a simpler one.

KURT. Indeed?

THE CAPTAIN. Yes, it's intended to have the Quarantine Station on the far side of the island, by the water.

KURT. My original idea.

THE CAPTAIN, *drily*. I know nothing of that. . . . I don't know your ideas on the subject. However, it's an excellent opportunity for you to get rid of your furniture—like that, it will scarcely be noticed—the scandal.

KURT. What?

THE CAPTAIN. The scandal. *Working himself up*. For it is a scandal to come to a new place and immediately get oneself into financial difficulties. And it's unpleasant for the relatives—most of all for the relatives.

KURT. Unpleasant most of all for me.

THE CAPTAIN. I'll tell you one thing, my dear Kurt. If you hadn't had me on your side in this affair, you would have lost your job.

KURT. That too!

THE CAPTAIN. You find it pretty difficult to be meticulous. There have been criticisms of you in the service.

KURT. Just criticisms?

THE CAPTAIN. Well, yes. For you are—in spite of your other admirable qualities—a slacker. Don't interrupt me! You're a terrible slacker.

KURT. That's marvellous!

THE CAPTAIN. However! The afore-mentioned charge is likely to happen pretty quickly. And I want to advise you to have the auction at once or try to sell privately.

KURT. Privately? Where could I find a buyer here?

THE CAPTAIN. Surely you don't mean I'm to come and settle myself in among your furniture? That would be a fine story. . . . *Jerkily*. Hm! Specially if one . . . considers what happened . . . at one time . . .

KURT. What's that? Do you mean what *didn't* happen?

THE CAPTAIN, *turning*. You're very quiet, Alice. What's the matter, old girl? You're not in your usual form.

ALICE. I'm just thinking.

THE CAPTAIN. O Lord! Thinking, are you? But you have to think quickly, correctly, and clearly if it's to be of any use. . . . Well, think then! One, two, three! . . . Aha, you can't do it! Well, then I'll have a shot. . . . Where's Judith?

ALICE. She's somewhere about.

THE CAPTAIN. Where's Allan?

ALICE *is silent.*

Where's the Lieutenant?

ALICE *is silent.*

Well, Kurt, what do you mean to do with Allan now?

KURT. Do with him?

THE CAPTAIN. Well, you won't have the means to keep him in the Artillery, will you?

KURT. Perhaps not.

THE CAPTAIN. You must try to get him into some cheap Infantry regiment, up in Norrland or somewhere.

KURT. In Norrland?

THE CAPTAIN. Yes. Or else you must make him go in for something practical, right away. If I were in your shoes, I'd put him in an office. . . . Why not?

KURT *is silent.*

In these enlightened times. Well? . . . Alice is so *unusually* silent. . . . Yes, my children, that's the way life's see-saw goes. Now one's on top, looking confidently around; then one's at the bottom, and then up one comes again. And so on. That's how it goes. Yes. . . . *To* ALICE. Did you say something?

ALICE *shakes her head.*

We may expect visitors here in a few days.

ALICE. Were you addressing me?

THE CAPTAIN. We may expect visitors in a few days. Distinguished visitors.

ALICE. Well, who?

THE CAPTAIN. You see! You're interested. . . . Now you can just sit there and guess who's coming. And while you're guessing, you can take this letter and read it once again.

Gives her an opened letter.

ALICE. My letter? Opened? Back from the post?

THE CAPTAIN, *rising.* Yes. In my capacity as head of the family and your guardian, I watch over the family's most sacred interests, and cut with an iron hand every attempt to break family ties through a criminal correspondence. Yes.

ALICE *is beaten.*

I am not dead, Alice, but don't be angry at this moment, when I am trying to lift us all out of an undeserved humiliation—undeserved on my part at least.

ALICE. Judith! Judith!

THE CAPTAIN. And Holofernes? Is that to be me? Pah!

Exit, back.

KURT. Who is this man?

ALICE. I don't know.

KURT. We are beaten.

ALICE. Yes . . . without any doubt.

KURT. He has stripped me to the bone, but so cunningly that I can't accuse him of anything.

ALICE. Accuse? On the contrary, you're under an obligation to him.

KURT. Does he know what he's doing?

ALICE. No, I don't believe he does. He obeys his nature and his instincts, and now he seems to be in favour wherever good and bad luck are meted out.

KURT. It must be the Colonel who is coming here.

ALICE. Probably. And so Allan must go away.

KURT. Do you really think so?

ALICE. Oh yes!

KURT. Then our ways divide.

ALICE, *preparing to go.* For a little while. . . . But we shall meet again.

KURT. Probably.

ALICE. And you know where?

KURT. Here.

ALICE. You realise that?

KURT. It's easy. *He's* going to take over the place and buy the furniture.

ALICE. That's what I believe too. But don't desert me!

KURT. Not for so slight a cause.

ALICE. Goodbye.

KURT, *as* ALICE *goes*. Goodbye.

ACT II

SCENE: *The same. Some weeks later.*

A cloudy day and rain.

Enter ALICE *and* KURT, *back, in raincoats, carrying umbrellas.*

ALICE. So I've got you here! Kurt, I can't be so cruel as to bid you welcome—in your own home.

KURT. Oh! Why not? I've had the bailiffs in three times—and worse. This means nothing to me.

ALICE. Did *he* send for you?

KURT. A formal summons, but I don't understand on what authority.

ALICE. Quite. He's not your chief.

KURT. No, but he has set himself up as king of this island. And if anyone opposes him, he just invokes the Colonel's name, and they all kotow. . . . Tell me, is it today the Colonel's coming?

ALICE. He's expected—but I don't know anything for certain. Do sit down.

KURT, *sitting*. It's all the same as ever here.

ALICE. Don't think about it. Don't open the wound.

KURT. Wound? I only find it a little strange. Strange—like the man himself. You know, when I first met him in my youth, I ran away from him. But he pursued me. Flattered me, offered his help—and bound me. I tried to escape again, but in vain. . . . Now I am his slave.

ALICE. But why? It's he who's indebted to you; yet you who are under an obligation.

KURT. After I was ruined, he offered to help Allan with his examination.

ALICE. That will cost you dear. . . . Does your candidacy for Parliament still hold good?

KURT. Yes, there's no hitch as far as I can see.

Silence.

ALICE. Is Allan leaving today?

KURT. Yes. If I can't prevent it.

ALICE. That was a brief joy.

KURT. Brief, like everything else, except life itself, which is appallingly long.

ALICE. Yes, that it is. . . . Won't you come and wait in the morning-room? Even if these surroundings don't hurt you, they do me.

KURT. As you wish.

ALICE. I'm ashamed. I'm so ashamed that I could die. But I can't alter things.

KURT. Let's go then, if you like.

ALICE. Besides, somebody's coming.

Exeunt ALICE *and* KURT, *left.*

Enter THE CAPTAIN *and* ALLAN, *back, both in uniform with capes.*

THE CAPTAIN. Sit down here, my boy. I want to have a talk with you.

THE CAPTAIN *sits in the easy chair, and* ALLAN *on a chair, left.*

If it wasn't raining today, I should enjoy sitting here, looking out at the sea.

Silence.

Well? You don't want to go, eh?

ALLAN. I don't like leaving my father.

THE CAPTAIN. Your father, yes. He's rather an unfortunate man.

Silence.

And parents seldom know what's best for their children. That's to say—there are exceptions, of course. Hm! Tell me, Allan, are you in touch with your mother?

ALLAN. Yes, she writes to me sometimes.

THE CAPTAIN. You know she's your guardian?

ALLAN. Oh, yes.

THE CAPTAIN. Now, Allan, did you know that your mother had given me full authority to act on her behalf?

ALLAN. No, I didn't know that.

THE CAPTAIN. Anyway, you know it now. And consequently all discussion of your future is at an end. You are going to Norrland. See?

ALLAN. But I haven't the means.

THE CAPTAIN. I've seen to that.

ALLAN. Then I can only thank you, Uncle.

THE CAPTAIN. At least you're grateful—not everybody is. Hm! *Raises his voice.* The Colonel . . . do you know the Colonel?

ALLAN, *puzzled.* No, I don't.

THE CAPTAIN, *emphasizing each syllable.* The Col-onel is a specially good friend of mine . . . *Speeds up* . . . as you probably know. Hm! The Colonel has shown an interest in my family, including my wife's relatives. Through his good offices, the Colonel has been able to arrange for the means needed for the completion of your course. . . . Now you know your indebtedness—and your father's indebtedness to the Colonel. . . . Have I made myself clear?

ALLAN *nods.*

Now go and pack your things. The money will be handed to you at the gangway. And so, goodbye, my boy.

He rises and holds out one finger for ALLAN *to shake.*

Goodbye.

Exit THE CAPTAIN, *right.*

ALLAN *stands alone, looking miserably round the room.*

Enter JUDITH, *back, wearing a hooded cape and carrying an umbrella. Apart from this, she is beautifully turned out, in a long skirt with her hair up.*

JUDITH. Is it you, Allan?

ALLAN *turns and looks* JUDITH *over from head to foot.*

ALLAN. Is it *you,* Judith?

JUDITH. Don't you recognise me? But where have you been all this time? . . . What are you looking at? My long skirt —and my hair? . . . You haven't seen this before.

ALLAN. Well!

JUDITH. Do I look like a woman?

ALLAN *turns away.*

Gravely. What are you doing here?

ALLAN. I have been taking my leave.

JUDITH. What? Are you—going away?

ALLAN. I'm being transferred to Norrland.

JUDITH, *dumbfounded.* To Norrland? When do you go?

ALLAN. Today.

JUDITH. Who arranged this?

ALLAN. Your father.

JUDITH. I might have known. *Walks up and down, stamping her feet.* I wish you could be here today.

ALLAN. So as to meet the Colonel.

JUDITH. What do you know about the Colonel? Must you really go?

ALLAN. I have no choice. And now it's what I want myself.

Silence.

JUDITH. Why do you want to go now?

ALLAN. I want to get away from here. Out into the world.

JUDITH. It's too cramped here. Yes, I understand, Allan. It's unbearable here. People speculate—in soda and in human beings.

Silence.

With real feeling. Allan, I, as you know, am a happy sort of person who doesn't suffer—but now I'm beginning to.

ALLAN. You . . . ?

JUDITH. Yes. Now I'm beginning to.

She presses both hands to her breast.

Oh, how I am suffering! Oh!

ALLAN. What is it?

JUDITH. I don't know. I can't breathe. I think I'm dying.

ALLAN. Judith!

JUDITH, *crying out.* Oh! Is *this* how it feels? Is it like this? Poor boys!

ALLAN. I ought to laugh, if I were as cruel as you.

JUDITH. I'm not cruel, but I didn't know any better. . . . You mustn't go.

ALLAN. I must.

JUDITH. Go then . . . but give me something to remember.

ALLAN. What have I to give you?

JUDITH, *with deep and genuine feeling.* You! . . . No, this I *cannot* live through. *Cries aloud, clasping her breast.* I'm suffering. I'm suffering. . . . What have you done to me? I don't want to live any longer. Allan, don't go—not alone! We'll go together, and we'll take the little cutter—the little white one—and sail out to sea—but with the sheet made fast—there's a splendid wind—and then we'll sail until we founder—out there, right out where there's no goose-grass and no jellyfish. . . . What do you say? Shall we? . . . But we should have washed the sails yesterday—they should be pure white—I want to see whiteness at that moment. . . . And then you will swim with me in your arms until you grow tired—and then we shall sink. . . . *Turns.* We'll do it in style. Far more style that way than staying here, moping, and smuggling letters for Father to open and scoff at. Allan! *She takes hold of his arms and shakes him.* Are you listening?

ALLAN, *who has been watching her with his eyes shining.* Judith! Judith! Why didn't you say this before?

JUDITH. I didn't know it. How could I say what I didn't know?

ALLAN. And now I must leave you. . . . But it surely is the best and only way. I can't compete with a man who . . .

JUDITH. Don't talk about the Colonel!

ALLAN. Isn't it true?

JUDITH. It's true and it's untrue.

ALLAN. Can't it just be untrue?

JUDITH. Yes, it shall be now. In an hour's time.

ALLAN. Will you keep your word? I can wait; I can endure; I can work. . . . Judith!

JUDITH. Don't go yet! How long must I wait?

ALLAN. A year.

JUDITH, *joyfully*. One? I'll wait a thousand years, and if you don't come then, I'll turn the heavens back to front, so the sun comes up in the west. . . . Hush, someone's coming! Allan, we must part. . . . Hush! . . . Take me in your arms. *They embrace.* But you mustn't kiss me. *Turns her head away.* So go now—go now!

ALLAN *puts on his cape. Then they rush into each other's arms, so that* JUDITH *disappears in the cape, and for one moment they kiss.*

ALLAN *rushes out; back.*

JUDITH *throws herself face downwards on the sofa, sobbing.*

ALLAN *comes in again and falls on his knees beside the sofa.*

ALLAN. No, I can't go. I can't leave you now.

JUDITH, *rising*. If you knew how beautiful you are now, if you could see yourself!

ALLAN. No, no, a man can't be beautiful! But you, Judith! That you . . . that you . . . I see so clearly how when you're kind you seem like another Judith . . . who is mine. . . . But if you deceive me, I shall die.

JUDITH. I think I'm dying anyhow! . . . Oh, that I could die now, at this very moment, when I am happy! . . .

ALLAN. Someone's coming.

JUDITH. Let them come. I'm not afraid of anything in the whole world now. But I wish you would take me under your cape. *She plays at hiding under his cape.* And I would fly with you to Norrland. What shall we do in Norrland? Join the Light Infantry . . . the ones with plumes in their hats . . . that's so smart and would suit you beautifully.

She plays with his hair.

He kisses the tips of her fingers, one after the other, and then her boots.

What are you doing, you crazy boy? You will make your mouth black. *Gets up hastily.* And then I shan't be able to kiss you when you go. . . . Come on, I'll go with you!

ALLAN. No, if you did I'd be arrested.

JUDITH. I'll be arrested with you.

ALLAN. They wouldn't let you be. . . . Now we must part.

JUDITH. I shall swim after the steamer . . . and then you'll jump in and rescue me, and then it will be in the newspaper, and then we can get engaged. Shall we do that?

ALLAN. You can still joke, can you?

JUDITH. One can always cry. . . . Now say goodbye.

They fall into one another's arms. Then ALLAN *draws her gently towards the French windows, which are still open, and they embrace outside in the rain.*

ALLAN. It's raining on you, Judith.

JUDITH. What do I care about that?

They tear themselves apart.

ALLAN *goes.*

JUDITH *stays in the rain and the wind, which ruffles her hair and her dress as she stands waving her handkerchief. Then she rushes in again and flings herself on the sofa, with her face in her hands.*

ALICE *comes in, left, and goes up to* JUDITH.

ALICE. What's the matter? . . . Are you ill? Get up and let me look at you.

JUDITH *straightens up.*

ALICE *gazes at her.*

You're not ill. . . . But I'm not going to console you.

Exit ALICE, *right.*

Enter THE LIEUTENANT, *back.*

JUDITH *rises and puts on her hooded cape.*

JUDITH. Lieutenant, will you be so kind as to accompany me to the telegraph office?

THE LIEUTENANT. If I can be of any service to you, Miss Judith . . . but I don't know if it's quite correct.

JUDITH. So much the better. That's just the object—for you to compromise me—but without having any illusions. . . . You go first.

They go out, back.

THE CAPTAIN *and* ALICE *enter, right. He is in undress uniform. He sits in the easy chair.*

THE CAPTAIN. Call him in.

ALICE *goes to the door, left, and opens it. Then she sits on the sofa.*

Enter KURT, *left.*

KURT. You want to see me?

THE CAPTAIN, *amiably, but a trifle patronisingly.* Yes, I have several matters of importance to tell you. Sit down.

KURT *takes the chair on the left.*

KURT. I am all ears.

THE CAPTAIN. Well then . . . *In a haranguing tone.* You are aware that our quarantine system has been in a parlous state for close on a century . . . hm!

ALICE, *to* KURT. That's the parliamentary candidate speaking.

THE CAPTAIN. But in accordance with today's unprecedented development in . . .

ALICE, *to* KURT. Means of communication, naturally.

THE CAPTAIN. . . . in every possible respect, the Government has been considering a policy of expansion. To this end the Ministry of Health has appointed inspectors, and . . .

ALICE, *to* KURT. He's dictating.

THE CAPTAIN. . . . you may as well know it sooner as later—I have been appointed a Quarantine Inspector.

Silence.

KURT. I congratulate you—and at the same time pay my respects.

THE CAPTAIN. Our personal relationship—due to our family connection—will remain unchanged. But now, to speak of another matter—your son Allan has, at my request, been transferred to an Infantry regiment in Norrland.

KURT. But I don't wish him to be.

THE CAPTAIN. Your wishes in this matter are subordinate to those of his mother . . . and since his mother has authorised me to act for her, I have made the afore-mentioned decision.

KURT. I admire you.

THE CAPTAIN. Is that your only reaction in this moment, when you are about to be parted from your son? Have you any really human feelings?

KURT. You mean I ought to be suffering?

THE CAPTAIN. Yes.

KURT. It would please you if I suffered. You want me to have to suffer.

THE CAPTAIN. Can you suffer? Once I was stricken with illness —you were there—and I can only remember an expression of unfeigned pleasure in your face.

ALICE. That's not true. Kurt sat at your bedside all night, and soothed you when your pangs of conscience became too sharp. But when you recovered, you were ungrateful.

THE CAPTAIN, *without appearing to hear* ALICE. Accordingly, Allan is to leave us.

KURT. Who's to provide the means?

THE CAPTAIN. I have already done so. That is to say, we have —a syndicate, which interests itself in the young man's future.

KURT. Syndicate?

THE CAPTAIN. Yes. And so that you may see that it's all in order, you can take a look at these lists.

He hands KURT *some papers.*

KURT. Lists? *Looks at the papers.* Why, these are begging lists!

THE CAPTAIN. Call them that if you like.

KURT. Have you been begging for my son?

THE CAPTAIN. More ingratitude! An ungrateful person is the heaviest burden the earth has to bear.

KURT. Now I'm done for socially, and my candidature will come to nothing.

THE CAPTAIN. What candidature?

KURT. Why, for Parliament.

THE CAPTAIN. Surely you never dreamt of that? Particularly as you must have had a notion that I, as an older resident, intended to propose myself—whom you appear to have underrated.

KURT. Well, so that's finished, that too.

THE CAPTAIN. It doesn't seem to worry you much.

KURT. Now you've taken everything. Do you want anything else?

THE CAPTAIN. Have you anything else? And have you anything to reproach me with? Think hard now if you have anything with which to reproach me.

Silence.

KURT. In actual fact, nothing. Everything has been done correctly and lawfully, as between honest citizens in daily life. . . .

THE CAPTAIN. You say that in a tone of resignation I would call cynical. But your whole nature has a cynical bent, my dear Kurt, and therefore, at moments, I might be tempted to share Alice's opinion of you—that you are a hypocrite, a hypocrite of the first rank.

KURT, *calmly.* Is that Alice's opinion?

ALICE, *to* KURT. It was once. But it isn't any longer, for to bear what you have borne takes sheer heroism, or—something else.

THE CAPTAIN. I think the discussion may now be considered closed. Go and say goodbye to Allan, Kurt. He's taking the next boat.

KURT, *rising.* So soon? . . . Ah well, I've been through worse.

THE CAPTAIN. Yes, you say that so often that I begin to wonder what you were up to in America.

KURT. Up to? I was just dogged by misfortune. And it is the indisputable right of every human being to meet with misfortune.

THE CAPTAIN, *sharply.* There are self-induced misfortunes. Was it that kind?

KURT. Isn't that a question of conscience?

THE CAPTAIN, *shortly.* Have you got a conscience?

KURT. There are wolves and there are sheep. It's no honour to a man to be a sheep; but I'd rather be that than a wolf.

THE CAPTAIN. Don't you know the old truth that everyone shapes his own destiny?

KURT. Is it a truth?

THE CAPTAIN. And don't you know that it's one's own strength . . .

KURT. Yes, I do know that, since the night when your own strength betrayed you, so you were prostrate on the floor.

THE CAPTAIN, *raising his voice.* A deserving man like yours truly—yes, look at me. I have striven for fifty years against a whole world; but I have in the end won the game through perseverance, attention to duty, energy, and—integrity.

ALICE. You should let others say that.

THE CAPTAIN. Others don't, because they're jealous. However! . . . We're expecting visitors here. . . . Today my daughter, Judith, is to meet her fiancé. . . . Where is Judith?

ALICE. She's out.

THE CAPTAIN. In the rain? Send for her!

KURT. Perhaps I might go now?

THE CAPTAIN. No, you stay! . . . Is Judith dressed? Respectably?

ALICE. Yes, she'll do. . . . Has the Colonel said for certain that he's coming?

THE CAPTAIN, *rising.* Yes—that's to say, he's going to arrive and take us by surprise as it were. I'm expecting his telegram at any moment. *Going, right.* Back soon.

Exit THE CAPTAIN.

ALICE. There you have the man. Is he human?

KURT. When you asked me that before, I said he wasn't. Now I believe him to be one of the commonest types that possess the earth. . . . Perhaps we're a bit like that ourselves. Profiting by other people, opportunists.

ALICE. He has eaten you and yours alive. . . . And you defend him?

KURT. I've been through worse. . . . But this man-eater has left my soul untouched—that he could not devour.

ALICE. What is this "worse" you've been through?

KURT. You ask that?

ALICE. Are you being rude?

KURT. No, I don't want to be so—never ask that again.

Enter THE CAPTAIN, *right.*

THE CAPTAIN. The telegram was there already. Read it please, Alice—my sight is so bad. *Sits down heavily in the easy chair.* Read it! You needn't go, Kurt.

ALICE, *having read it quickly to herself, shows consternation.*

Well? Aren't you pleased?

ALICE *stares silently at* THE CAPTAIN.

Ironically. Who's it from?

ALICE. It's from the Colonel.

THE CAPTAIN, *delighted.* You don't say so! . . . Well, what does he say?

ALICE. He says this: "In view of Miss Judith's impertinent telephone message, I regard our relations as broken off—for good."

She stares at THE CAPTAIN.

THE CAPTAIN. Once more, if you please.

ALICE, *reading loudly.* "In view of Miss Judith's impertinent telephone message, I regard our relations as broken off—for good."

THE CAPTAIN, *turning pale.* This is Judith!

ALICE. And here is Holofernes.

THE CAPTAIN. What are you then?

ALICE. You will soon see.

THE CAPTAIN. This is your doing.

ALICE. No.

THE CAPTAIN, *furiously.* This is your doing.

ALICE. No.

THE CAPTAIN *tries to rise and draw his sword, but has a stroke and falls back into his chair.*

Now you've got what you deserve.

THE CAPTAIN, *whimpering senilely.* Don't be angry with me. I'm very ill.

ALICE. Are you? I'm glad to hear it.

KURT. Let's carry him to bed.

ALICE. No, I won't touch him.

She rings the bell.

THE CAPTAIN, *as before.* Don't be angry with me. *To* KURT. Look after my children!

KURT. That's rich. I'm to provide for his children, when he has stolen mine.

ALICE. What self-deception!

THE CAPTAIN. Look after my children!

He continues to babble incoherently.

ALICE. At last that tongue is stayed. It can brag no more, lie no more, wound no more. . . . You, Kurt, who believe in God, thank Him for me. Thank Him for freeing me from the tower, from the wolf, from the vampire.

KURT. Don't, Alice!

ALICE, *in* THE CAPTAIN'S *face.* Where's your own strength now, eh? And your energy?

THE CAPTAIN, *speechless, spits in her face.*

If you can still spit venom, viper, I'll tear the tongue out of your throat.

She gives him a blow on the ear.

The head is off. . . . O Judith, glorious girl, whom I bore like vengeance beneath my heart, you, you have set us free —all of us! If you have any more heads, hydra, we'll take them too!

She pulls his beard.

So there is justice on earth after all! Sometimes I've dreamt of it, but I've never believed it. Kurt, ask God to forgive me for having misjudged Him. Oh, justice does exist! Now I'll become a sheep too. Tell Him that, Kurt. A little good fortune makes us better; it's misfortune that turns us into wolves.

Enter THE LIEUTENANT, *back.*

The Captain has had a stroke. Please help us wheel the chair out.

THE LIEUTENANT. Madam . . .

ALICE. What is it?

THE LIEUTENANT. Well, Miss Judith . . .

ALICE. Help us here first. You can talk about Judith afterwards.

THE LIEUTENANT *wheels the chair out, right.*

Out with the carcass! Out with it and throw everything open! The place must be aired.

She throws open the French windows.

Outside it has cleared.

Ah!

KURT. Are you going to abandom him?

ALICE. A ship that has foundered is abandoned, and the crew saves itself. There's no need for me to lay out a decaying animal. Skinners or scavengers can look after him. A garden plot is too nice a place to receive that barrow-load of filth. . . . Now I'm going to bathe myself—to wash off all this dirt, if I can ever be clean again.

JUDITH *is seen outside by the balustrade, bareheaded, waving her handkerchief towards the sea.*

KURT, *going out, back.* Who's that? Judith! *Calling.* Judith!

Enter JUDITH.

JUDITH, *crying out.* He has gone!

KURT. Who?

JUDITH. Allan has gone.

KURT. Without saying goodbye?

JUDITH. *We* said goodbye, and he sent messages to you, Uncle.

ALICE. Was that how it was?

JUDITH *throws herself into* KURT'S *arms.*

JUDITH. He has gone.

KURT. He'll come back, dear child.

ALICE. Or we'll follow him.

KURT, *pointing to the door, right.* And leave him? What would people . . . ?

ALICE. People? Pah! Judith, come and embrace me!

JUDITH *goes up to* ALICE, *who kisses her on the forehead.*

Do you want to follow him?

JUDITH. Need you ask?

ALICE. But your father is ill.

JUDITH. What do I care about that!

ALICE. That's Judith. Oh how I love you, Judith!

JUDITH. Besides, Papa isn't petty, and he doesn't like being coddled. He has at least got some style, Papa.

ALICE. Yes, in a way.

JUDITH. And I don't think he's anxious to see me after that telephone business. . . . But why should he saddle me with an old man? No! Allan, Allan! *She throws herself into* KURT'S *arms.* I want to go to Allan.

She pulls herself away again and runs out to wave.

KURT *follows her and waves too.*

ALICE. To think that flowers can grow out of filth!

Enter THE LIEUTENANT, *right.*

Well?

THE LIEUTENANT. Well, Miss Judith . . .

ALICE. Is it now so sweet to feel the sound of her name caressing your lips that you forget a dying man?

THE LIEUTENANT. Yes, but she said . . .

ALICE. She? It would be better to call her Judith. . . . But first, what's happening in there?

THE LIEUTENANT. Oh, in there–it's all over!

ALICE. Over? O God, I thank Thee for myself and for all mankind that Thou hast delivered us from this evil! . . . Give me your arm. I want to go out and breathe. To breathe!

THE LIEUTENANT *offers his arm.*

Checking herself. Did he say anything before the end?

THE LIEUTENANT. Miss Judith's father did say a few words.

ALICE. What did he say?

THE LIEUTENANT. He said: "Forgive them, for they know not what they do."

ALICE. Incredible!

THE LIEUTENANT. Yes, Miss Judith's father was a good and noble man.

ALICE. Kurt!

Enter KURT.

It is over.

KURT. Ah! . . .

ALICE. Do you know what his last words were? No, you don't know. "Forgive them, for they know not what they do."

KURT. Can you interpret that?

ALICE. I suppose he meant that *he* had always done right and died as one wronged by life.

KURT. He's sure to get a beautiful funeral oration.

ALICE. And masses of wreaths. From the non-commissioned officers.

KURT. Yes.

ALICE. A year ago he said something like this: "It looks as if life for us were some monstrous joke."

KURT. Do you think he was pulling our legs on his death-bed?

ALICE. No. . . . But now that he's dead I feel a strange inclination to speak well of him.

KURT. Well, let's then.

THE LIEUTENANT. Miss Judith's father was a good and noble man.

ALICE, *to* KURT. You hear!

KURT. "They know not what they do." How many times have I not asked you if he knew what he was doing? And you thought he didn't know. So, forgive him!

ALICE. Riddles! Riddles! . . . But feel the peace in the house now! The wonderful peace of death. Wonderful as that solemn unrest when a child is coming into the world. I can hear the silence . . . and I can see the marks on the floor of the easy chair which bore him away. . . . And I feel that now my own life is over and I am on the way to dissolution. . . . Do you know—it's very strange, but the Lieutenant's simple words—and he is a simple person—still echo in my mind, but now they mean something. My husband, the love of my youth—yes, you may laugh, but he was a good and noble man—in spite of it all.

KURT. In spite of it all. And a brave one too. How he fought for his own existence and what was his!

ALICE. What anxieties! What humiliations! Which he cancelled out—so that he could pass on.

KURT. He was one who was *passed over,* that's the crux of it. Alice, go in to him!

ALICE. No. I can't. For while we have been talking here, I've had a vision of him when he was young. I saw him—I can see him now—as he was when he was twenty. . . . I must have loved that man.

KURT. And hated.

ALICE. *And* hated. . . . Peace be with him!

She moves towards the door, right, where she stands still, her hands clasped.

SWANWHITE

A Fairy Play in Three Acts

FOREWORD

August Strindberg wrote *Swanwhite* in the spring of 1901 as a betrothal gift for his third wife, Harriet Bosse, the young Norwegian actress who had already played the Lady in *To Damascus* and for whom he had created the part of Eleanora in *Easter*.

In spite of his happiness at having won her hand, for he was deeply in love, Strindberg had followed the penitential dramas *To Damascus* and *Easter* with the masterpiece of horror and hatred *The Dance of Death*. Now he was eager to repeople his stage with spirits and prove the power of love.

In his "Open Letters to the Intimate Theatre" he explains how he had long wanted to blend the fairest and ugliest of Swedish folk-lore into a single picture for the stage. So now he took from the old fairy tales the ubiquitous themes of Prince and Princess and Wicked Stepmother, plucked the Maids, the Gardener, and the Young King from their traditional settings, and, in his own words, "threw them all together into the separator . . . so that the cream poured out and was my own creation. More than ever my own because I lived the story in imagination. A springtime in the winter."

Between the conception of *Swanwhite* and its creation he became a disciple of Maeterlinck's. In his Naturalist period Strindberg had distrusted his Belgian contemporary; but now that he had been through his "inferno," Maeterlinck's philosophy spoke to his condition.

Physical love tormented Strindberg all his life, for it seemed always to bring hatred in its wake. He extolled parental love as the purest form of emotion, and now, sending Harriet Bosse this play, he wrote: "It is through the Flower Test in Swanwhite that the Prince wins her, for his desire is purer and therefore stronger. The other is weakness."

Harriet Bosse did not, however, play the part of Swanwhite. The play was first produced in 1908 in Strindberg's own Intimate Theatre, and by this time he and Harriet Bosse were divorced, although they never ceased to be friends. To the actress Anna Flygare, who created the part of Swanwhite, Strindberg wrote:

> Eros is not the main theme; the symbolism relates to Caritas, the great Love, which suffers everything, overcomes everything, forgives, hopes, and believes however much it is betrayed. This is illustrated by the Stepmother's change of character, but most of all by the final scene: love is stronger than death.

Swanwhite was a success in the Intimate Theatre. In the mid-summer of 1909 or 1910 (the dates given in Swedish books vary), the Company gave an open-air performance in a public park, after which it went on tour to various parts of Sweden.

The play was never again performed during Strindberg's lifetime. In 1913, the year after the author's death, Reinhardt produced it in Berlin, and in 1914 it was revived in Stockholm with the *Swanwhite* music which Sibelius had composed in 1907.

Swanwhite has also been played in Finland, Denmark, and Hungary. The Academy of Music in New York produced it in 1920.

It was broadcast by the B.B.C. for the Strindberg centenary in 1949.

This play is a treasure-chest full of the truth that lies in fairy tales and brimful of magic and romance. It is an invitation to imaginative production as a masque, a chamber opera, a children's play, a ballet, or a film in the vein of Jean Cocteau's *La Belle et la Bête*.

E. S.

CHARACTERS

SWANWHITE

THE YOUNG KING

THE DUKE

THE STEPMOTHER

THE PRINCE

SIGNE }
ELSA } MAIDS
TOVA }

THE GARDENER

SWANWHITE'S MOTHER

THE PRINCE'S MOTHER

THE EXECUTIONER

THE EQUERRY

THE STEWARD

THE HERB GARDENER

THE FIRST KNIGHT

THE SECOND KNIGHT

THE FISHERMAN

ETC.

SCENE FOR THE WHOLE PLAY

An Apartment in a mediaeval stone castle. The walls and cross-vaulted ceiling are completely white. At the back, three arches open on to a stone balcony. There are rich curtains with which they can be closed. Below the balcony is a garden, and the tops of rose trees can be seen bearing pink and white blooms. In the distance is a glimpse of a white sandy beach and blue sea.

Right of the triple-arched doorway is a small door which, when open, shows a vista of three Closets, opening one into the other. The first is the Pewter Closet, in which are pewter vessels arranged on shelves. The second is the Clothing Closet, in which can be seen gorgeous raiment, and the third is the Fruit Closet, which reveals a store of apples, pears, pumpkins, and melons.

The whole floor is inlaid with black and red squares. In the centre of the Apartment stands a gilded dining-table covered with a cloth; on it are a clock, a dish of fruit, and a single rose in a vase. Over the table hangs a branch of mistletoe, and beside it stand two ornate gilded stools. On the floor in the foreground a lion-skin is spread. Over the small doorway can be seen two swallows' nests. In the foreground on the left is a white bed with a rose-coloured canopy supported at the head by two posts; at the foot are no posts. The bed coverings are white except for one coverlet of palest blue silk.[1]

Behind the bed is a vast wall cupboard. Beside the bed are a small romanesque gilded table (round on a single column) and a lampstand bearing a Roman lamp of gold. Right is a beautifully carved chimney-piece, on which stands a white lily in a vase. Front right is a gilded treasure-chest.

[1] Strindberg includes a filmy white nightdress lying on the bed. I have omitted this, as it disagrees with the text. The only white garment should be the one brought Swanwhite by her mother. E.S.

In the left arch of the main doorway a peacock is asleep on a perch with its back to the audience. In the right arch is a great golden cage containing two sleeping white doves.

ACT I

As the curtain rises, the three MAIDS *are seen, half-hidden by the doorways of each Closet.* SIGNE, *the false maid, is in the Pewter Closet,* ELSA, *who is tiny and pretty, is in the Clothing Closet,* TOVA, *the ugly faithful maid, is in the Fruit Closet.*

THE DUKE *enters by the main doorway, followed by* THE STEPMOTHER *with a steel whip in her hand.*

The stage is dim as they enter. Outside a horn is blown.

THE STEPMOTHER, *gazing round her.* Is Swanwhite not here?

THE DUKE. You can see. . . .

THE STEPMOTHER. I can see, but I cannot see *her. Calls.* You maids! Signe![2] Elsa! Tova![2]

THE MAIDS *come in, one after the other, and stand in front of* THE STEPMOTHER.

Where is the Lady Swanwhite?

SIGNE *crosses her arms over her breast and is silent.*

You do not know? *Shakes the whip.* Then . . . do you know what I have in my hand? . . . Quick, answer me! *Pause.* Quick! *Swings the whip so that it whistles.* Listen to the whistle of the Falcon. It has claws and a beak of steel. And what is it?

SIGNE. It is the steel whip.

THE STEPMOTHER. Yes, the steel whip. Now—where is the Lady Swanwhite?

SIGNE. I cannot tell what I do not know.

THE STEPMOTHER. Ignorance is a failing, but heedlessness is a

[2] Pronounced Seenya and Toova.

crime. Are you not here to keep watch over your young mistress? Take off your kerchief.

Despairingly, SIGNE *obeys.*

Get down on your knees!

THE DUKE *turns his back in horror at the scene.*

Hold out your neck! Now I shall put such a necklace on it that no young suitor will ever put his lips to it again. . . . Stretch out your neck! Further!

SIGNE. For Christ's sake, have mercy!

THE STEPMOTHER. It is mercy enough that you keep your life.

THE DUKE *draws his sword and tests it first on one of his nails, then on his long beard.*

THE DUKE, *ironically.* Her head should be cut off, put in a sack . . . hung from a tree . . .

THE STEPMOTHER. So it should indeed.

THE DUKE. We are of one mind, you see.

THE STEPMOTHER. We were not so yesterday.

THE DUKE. And perhaps we shall not be tomorrow.

SIGNE, *still on her knees, is stealthily crawling away.*

THE STEPMOTHER. What are you doing? Stay where you are. *She raises the whip and strikes.* SIGNE *turns, so that the lash merely cuts the air.* SWANWHITE *comes from behind the bed and falls on her knees. She is simply dressed and has dirty bare feet.*

SWANWHITE. Here I am, Stepmother. I am the guilty one. Signe is innocent.

THE STEPMOTHER. Say "Mother." Say "Mother."

SWANWHITE. I cannot. No human being has more than one mother.

THE STEPMOTHER. Your father's wife is your mother.

SWANWHITE. My father's second wife is my stepmother.

THE STEPMOTHER. You are a stubborn daughter, but this steel is pliant and makes others pliant. *She lifts the whip to strike* SWANWHITE.

THE DUKE, *raising his sword.* Beware! Your head is in danger.

THE STEPMOTHER. Whose head?

THE DUKE. Your own.

THE STEPMOTHER *recoils in rage, but controls herself and remains silent. Long pause. Then, seeing herself beaten, she changes her tone.*

THE STEPMOTHER. Very well. Now perhaps you will inform your daughter what is in store for her.

THE DUKE, *sheathing his sword.* My beloved child, come and find refuge in my arms.

SWANWHITE, *springing into his arms.* Oh Father, you are like a royal oak tree, and my arms are not long enough to embrace you! But beneath your foliage I can hide from threatening storms . . . *She hides her face in his great beard* . . . and I will swing on your branches like a bird. Lift me up so that I may climb to the very top.

He lifts her on to his shoulder.

Now I have the earth beneath me and the air above. Now I can see out across the rose garden to the white sands and the blue sea, and to all the seven kingdoms. . . .

THE DUKE. Then you can see the Young King, to whom you are betrothed.

SWANWHITE. No, him I cannot see. Him I have never seen. Is he handsome?

THE DUKE. It will depend on your own eyes, dear heart, how he appears to you.

SWANWHITE, *rubbing her eyes.* On my own eyes? . . . All that they see is beautiful.

THE DUKE, *kissing her foot.* Black little foot, foot of my little blackamoor.

During this scene THE STEPMOTHER *has signed to* THE MAIDS *to resume their places in the doorways of the Closets. With the stealthy movement of a panther,* THE STEPMOTHER *goes out through the middle arch.* SWANWHITE *jumps down.* THE DUKE *seats her on the table and sits on a stool beside her.* SWANWHITE *watches* THE STEPMOTHER *disappear and expresses her relief.*

SWANWHITE. Has the sun risen? Has the wind changed to the south? Has spring come back again?

THE DUKE, *putting his hand over her mouth.* Little chatterbox. Joy of my old age—my evening star. Open your rosy ears and shut the little red shell of your mouth. Listen to me. Obey me and all will go well with you.

SWANWHITE, *putting her fingers in her ears.* I hear with my eyes, I see with my ears. Now I cannot see at all. I can only hear.

THE DUKE. Child . . . while you were still in the cradle you were betrothed to the young King of Rigalid.[3] You have never seen him, for such is Court etiquette. Now the day is drawing near when the sacred knot must be tied, but in order to teach you the ways of the Court and the duties of a Queen, the King has sent hither a young Prince, with whom you are to study books, learn to play chess, to dance a measure, and play upon the harp.

SWANWHITE. What is this Prince's name?

THE DUKE. My child, that is something you must never ask, neither of him nor of any other, for it is prophesied that whosoever calls him by his name must love him.

SWANWHITE. Is he handsome?

THE DUKE. Yes—since your eyes see nothing but beauty.

SWANWHITE. But is he not beautiful?

THE DUKE. Yes, he is beautiful. So, set a guard on your young heart, which belongs to the King, and never forget that in the cradle you were made a Queen. . . . And now, my beloved child, I am going to leave you, for I must go to war. Be humble and obedient to your stepmother. She is a hard woman, but your father loved her once, and a sweet nature may melt a heart of stone. *From under his cloak he takes a horn of carved ivory.* If, against her sworn word, her malice should exceed all bounds, then blow upon this horn—and help will come. But do not blow it unless you are in peril, great peril . . . Do you understand?

SWANWHITE. But what am I to do?

THE DUKE. My child, the Prince is below in the Ladies' Chamber. Do you wish to receive him now?

SWANWHITE, *excited.* Do I wish . . . ?

[3] Pronounced Reegaleed.

THE DUKE. Shall I not first bid you farewell?

SWANWHITE. Is the Prince here already?

THE DUKE. He is here already and I am already there—there, far away, where the heron of forgetfulness puts its head under its wing.

SWANWHITE, *throwing herself into* THE DUKE's *arms and burying her face in his beard.* Don't say such things. Don't say them. You cover me with shame.

THE DUKE, *tenderly.* You should be beaten for forgetting your old father so quickly at the thought of a young Prince. . . .

A horn sounds in the distance. He rises hastily, picks SWANWHITE *up in his arms, throws her up, and catches her again.* Fly, little bird, fly! High above the dusty earth with the clear air beneath your wings. . . . *He puts her down.* There. Down once more to earth. . . . I am called by war and glory—you by love and youth. *Girds on his sword.* And now hide your magic horn that no evil eyes may see it.

SWANWHITE. Where shall I hide it? Where?

THE DUKE. Inside your bed.

SWANWHITE, *hiding the horn in the bedclothes.* Sleep there. Sleep well, my little herald. When the time comes, I'll waken you. Do not forget to say your prayers.

THE DUKE. And you, child, do not forget my last behest: obey your stepmother.

SWANWHITE. In everything?

THE DUKE. In everything.

SWANWHITE. Not in what is unclean. My mother gave me two changes of linen every week. *She* gives me only one. My mother gave me water and soap—these my stepmother denies me. You have seen my poor little feet.

THE DUKE. Keep pure within, my daughter, and you shall be pure without. You know that holy men who renounce ablutions for a penance grow white as swans, while the wicked turn black as ravens.

SWANWHITE. Then I will grow so white, so white.

THE DUKE. Come to my arms once more—and then farewell! *They embrace.*

SWANWHITE. Farewell, great warrior—my glorious father. May good fortune follow in your train and make you rich in years and friends and victories.

THE DUKE. Amen. May your gentle prayers protect me.

He closes the visor of his golden helmet.

SWANWHITE, *kissing his visor.* The golden gates are shut, but through the bars I see your kind and watchful eyes. *She knocks at the visor.* Open, open, for Little Red Ridinghood! . . . No one is in. "Come in and see," said the wolf, who was lying in the bed.

THE DUKE. Sweet flower of mine, grow fair and fragrant. If I return—so be it, I return. If not, my eyes will watch over you from the starry vault and never again will you be lost to my sight. For there we mortals shall be all-seeing as our Lord Creator.

He goes out firmly, with a gesture forbidding her to follow. SWANWHITE *falls on her knees and prays.*

A wind sighs. All the rose trees sway. The peacock moves its wings and tail. SWANWHITE *rises, goes to the peacock, and strokes its back and tail.*

SWANWHITE. Pavo, dear Pavo, what do you see? What do you hear? Is someone coming? Who is coming? Is it a young Prince? Is he handsome—and kind? Surely you can see with so many, many blue eyes. *She lifts one of the bird's tail-feathers and gazes intently at its eye, then continues in a changed voice.* Oh, are you going to keep your eye on us, you horrid Argus? Do you mean to watch in case the hearts of two young people beat too fast? You stupid creature! I shall draw the curtain, see! *She draws a curtain so that it hides the peacock, but not the landscape. Then she goes over to the doves.* My white doves—oh so white, white, white! You shall see the whitest thing of all. . . . Hush wind, hush roses, hush doves—my Prince is coming!

For a moment she looks out through the arches, then withdraws to the Pewter Closet. She puts on stockings[4] *while she peeps out at* THE PRINCE, *who does not see her.*

THE PRINCE *enters through the middle arch. He is in black*

[4] Added stage direction, to correspond with the text. E.S.

with steel armour. Having carefully observed everything in the room, he sits down by the table, takes off his helmet, and studies it. His back is turned to the door where SWANWHITE *is hiding.*

THE PRINCE. If anyone is here, let him answer. *Pause.* Someone is here, for I can feel the warmth of a young body wafted to me like a breeze from the south. I can hear breathing—it has the fragrance of roses—and gentle as it is, it stirs the plume on my helmet. *He puts the helmet to his ear.* My helmet murmurs like a great sea-shell. It is the murmuring of the thoughts in my head, swarming like bees in a hive. "Bzz, bzz," they go . . . just like bees. They are buzzing round their Queen—the little queen of my thoughts and my dreams. *He puts the helmet on the table in front of him and gazes at it.* Dark and arched it is, like the night sky—but starless, for ever since my mother died, the black plume has spread darkness everywhere. . . . *He turns the helmet round and stares at it again.* Yet there, deep in the darkness inside it . . . I see beyond, a shaft of light. Is it a rift in the heavens? And there in the rift I see—no, not a star, for that would be a diamond—but a blue sapphire, queen of jewels, blue as the summer sky, set in a milk-white cloud, shaped like the egg of a dove. What is it? Not my ring? Now another feathery cloud, black as velvet, passes by. . . .

SWANWHITE *smiles.*

The sapphire is smiling—so sapphires can smile. Now a flash of lightning, mild and without thunder.

She flashes a startled glance at him.

What are you? Who are you? *He looks at the back of the helmet.* Not there. Not here. Nowhere at all. *He puts his face close to the helmet.* As I draw nearer, you go further away.

SWANWHITE *steals towards him on tiptoe.*

Now there are two . . . two eyes! Young human eyes . . . I kiss you. *He kisses the helmet.*

SWANWHITE *goes to the table and slowly seats herself opposite* THE PRINCE. *He rises, bows with his hand on his heart, and gazes at her.*

SWANWHITE. Are you the Prince?

THE PRINCE. The Young King's faithful servant, and your own.

SWANWHITE. What message has the Young King sent his bride?

THE PRINCE. He sends the Lady Swanwhite a thousand tender greetings. He would have her know that the thought of the sweet joys to come will shorten this long torment of his waiting.

SWANWHITE, *looking searchingly at* THE PRINCE. Will you not be seated, Prince?

THE PRINCE. If I were to sit while you were sitting, when you stood up I should have to kneel.

SWANWHITE. Tell me about the King. What is he like?

THE PRINCE. What is he like? . . . *Puts his hand up to his eyes.* How strange! I can no longer see him.

SWANWHITE. How do you mean?

THE PRINCE. He has gone away. He is invisible.

SWANWHITE. Is he tall?

THE PRINCE, *studying* SWANWHITE. Wait—now I can see him. Taller than you are.

SWANWHITE. And beautiful?

THE PRINCE. He is no match for you.

SWANWHITE. Speak of the King, not of me.

THE PRINCE. I am speaking of the King.

SWANWHITE. Is he fair or dark?

THE PRINCE. If he were dark, seeing you he would at once become fair.

SWANWHITE. There is more flattery than sense in that. Are his eyes blue?

THE PRINCE, *glancing at his helmet.* I had better look.

SWANWHITE, *holding her hand up between them.* Oh you, you!

THE PRINCE. Y-o-u—you. Y-o-u-t-h—youth. .

SWANWHITE. Are you to teach me spelling?

THE PRINCE. The Young King is tall and fair, with blue eyes, broad shoulders, and hair like a young forest. . . .

SWANWHITE. Why do you wear a black plume?

THE PRINCE. His lips are red as berries, his skin is white, and his teeth would not shame a young lion.

SWANWHITE. Why does your forehead glisten?

THE PRINCE. His mind knows no fear, and his heart is free from guilt.

SWANWHITE. Why is your hand trembling?

THE PRINCE. We were to speak of the Young King, not of me.

SWANWHITE. Is it for you to lecture me?

THE PRINCE. That is my duty—to teach you to love the Young King, whose throne you are to share.

SWANWHITE. How did you cross the sea?

THE PRINCE. By bark and sail.

SWANWHITE. With the wind so high?

THE PRINCE. Without wind one cannot sail.

SWANWHITE. How wise you are, boy . . . will you play with me?

THE PRINCE. I shall do whatever is required of me.

SWANWHITE. Now you shall see what I have in my chest. *She kneels beside the chest and takes out a doll, a rattle, and a toy horse. She brings the doll to* THE PRINCE. Here is my doll. It is my child, my child of sorrow who can never keep her face clean. I have carried her down to the laundry myself, and scoured her with silver sand . . . but she only grew dirtier. I have beaten her, but that did not help either. Now I have thought of the worst punishment of all for her.

THE PRINCE. And what is that?

SWANWHITE, *glancing round.* She shall have a stepmother.

THE PRINCE. But how can that be? She must have a mother first.

SWANWHITE. I am her mother, and if I marry again, I shall be her stepmother.

THE PRINCE. Oh no, that is not the way of it!

SWANWHITE. And you will be her stepfather.

THE PRINCE. No, no.

SWANWHITE. But you must be kind to her even if she cannot

wash her face. Take her. Let me see if you know how to hold a child.

THE PRINCE *unwillingly takes the doll.*

You do not know yet, but you will learn. Now take this rattle and rattle it for her. *Gives him the rattle.* I see you do not know how to do that at all. *Takes back the doll and the rattle and throws them into the chest. She brings him the horse.* Here is my steed. It has a saddle of gold and shoes of silver and it can cover forty miles in an hour. On its back I have ridden through the forest, over the great moor, across the King's bridge, along the highway, through the Valley of Fear to the Lake of Tears. Once it dropped a golden shoe.[5] It fell into the lake, but up came a fish and along came a fisherman, and so I got back the golden shoe. That's the end of that story. *She throws the horse back into the chest and brings out a chess-board with red and white squares and chessmen of silver and gold.* If you would like to play with me, come and sit down on the lion-skin. *She seats herself and begins to put up the pieces.* Sit down—the Maids can't see us here.

THE PRINCE *sits shyly down beside her. She runs her hand through the lion's mane.*

It is like sitting on the grass, not the green grass of a meadow, but desert grass which has been burned by the sun. Now you must tell me about myself. Do you like me a little?

THE PRINCE. Shall we play?

SWANWHITE. Play? What do I care about that? *Sighs.* Oh, you should teach me something!

THE PRINCE. Alas, what can I teach you other than how to saddle a horse and carry arms? Such things would be of small service to you.

SWANWHITE. Are you sad?

THE PRINCE. My mother is dead.

SWANWHITE. Poor Prince . . . My mother is in heaven too—

5 Strindberg has this discrepancy—"shoes of silver"—"golden shoe." E.S.

with God. She is an angel now. Sometimes in the night I see her. Do you see your mother?

THE PRINCE, *hesitating*. No.

SWANWHITE. And have you a stepmother?

THE PRINCE. Not yet. It is so short a time since my mother died.

SWANWHITE. You must not be so sad. Everything passes in time. *Pause. She fetches a banner from her chest.* I will give you a banner to gladden your heart. Oh! It is true, I made this one for the Young King—but I will make another one for you. This is the King's, with seven flaming fires—you shall have one with seven red roses. First you must hold this skein of yarn for me. *She takes a skein of rose-coloured yarn from the chest and arranges it over* THE PRINCE'S *hands.* One, two, three. Now I will begin, but you must not let your hands tremble. Perhaps you would like one of my hairs woven into the banner. Pull one out.

THE PRINCE. No, no, I cannot.

SWANWHITE. Then I will do it. *She pulls out one of her hairs and winds it into the ball of yarn.* What is your name?

THE PRINCE. You must not ask that.

SWANWHITE. Why not?

THE PRINCE. Did not the Duke tell you?

SWANWHITE. No. What would happen if I said your name? Something terrible?

THE PRINCE. Surely the Duke told you?

SWANWHITE. I have never heard of such a thing. A person not able to tell his own name!

The curtain behind which the peacock is hidden moves, and a faint sound is heard as of castanets.

THE PRINCE. What was that?

SWANWHITE, *uneasily*. It is Pavo—the peacock. Do you think he understands what we are saying?

THE PRINCE. You never know.

Pause.

SWANWHITE. Tell me your name.

The same sound is repeated.

THE PRINCE. This frightens me. You must not ask me that again.

SWANWHITE. He is snapping his beak, that's all. Keep your hands still. Have you ever heard the story of a Princess who was not allowed to say the Prince's name, for fear something terrible should happen? Do you know what . . . ?

The curtain hiding the peacock is drawn aside. The peacock has turned round and spread his tail. All the "eyes" seem to be gazing at SWANWHITE *and* THE PRINCE.

THE PRINCE. Who drew that curtain? Who told that bird to spy on us with its hundred eyes? You must not ask me that again.

SWANWHITE. Maybe not. Go back and keep quiet, Pavo.

The curtain is drawn again.

There.

THE PRINCE. Is this place haunted?

SWANWHITE. You mean because things like that happen? Yes, many things happen here, but I am used to it. In fact . . . *She lowers her voice* . . . they say that my stepmother is a witch. There, now I have pricked my finger.

THE PRINCE. How did you prick it?

SWANWHITE. There was a splinter in the yarn. When the sheep have been kept in the barns all the winter, that does sometimes happen. Can you take the splinter out?

THE PRINCE. Yes, but we must sit at the table so that I can see.

They seat themselves at the table.

SWANWHITE, *holding out her little finger.* Can you see anything?

THE PRINCE, *rather bolder than hitherto.* What do I see? *He holds her hand up to the light.* The inside of your hand is pink, and through it I see the world and all life in a rosy light.

SWANWHITE. Pull out the splinter. It is hurting me.

THE PRINCE. But I shall have to hurt you. Forgive me first.

SWANWHITE. Yes, yes, but do it now.

THE PRINCE *takes the splinter out of her little finger.*

THE PRINCE. Here is the wretched thing which dared to hurt you.

He throws the splinter on the floor and stamps on it.

SWANWHITE. Now you must suck the blood to keep the wound from festering.

He puts his lips to her finger.

THE PRINCE. Now I have drunk your blood, so I am your foster-brother.

SWANWHITE. My foster-brother. Yes, but you were already that, or how could I have talked to you as I did?

THE PRINCE. Or I to you.

SWANWHITE. Now I have a brother—and that is you. Dear brother, take my hand.

THE PRINCE, *taking her hand.* Dear sister. *He feels the pulse in her finger.* What is it that keeps ticking in there? . . . One, two, three, four . . . *Continues to count soundlessly while looking at the clock.*

SWANWHITE. Yes, what is it that ticks? Tick, tick, tick—so steadily. My heart cannot be in my finger, for it is beneath my breast. . . . Put your hand here and you will feel it.

The doves begin to stir and coo.

What is the matter with my little white creatures?

THE PRINCE, *who has gone on counting.* . . . sixty. Now I know what it is that ticks. It is time. Your little finger is the second-hand. It ticks sixty times for every minute that passes. *Looking at the clock on the table.* Do you think there is a heart inside that clock?

SWANWHITE, *touching the clock.* A clock's works are as secret as a heart's. Feel my heart beating.

SIGNE *enters from the Pewter Closet, carrying the steel whip, which she lays on the table.*

SIGNE. The Duchess commands the Prince and Princess to sit at opposite ends of the table.

They sit as directed. SIGNE *returns to the Pewter Closet.* THE PRINCE *and* SWANWHITE *gaze at each other for a while in silence.*

SWANWHITE. We are far apart, yet nearer even than before.

THE PRINCE. People are never so close as when they are parted.

SWANWHITE. How do you know that?

THE PRINCE. I have just learned it.

SWANWHITE. Now you are beginning to teach me.

THE PRINCE. It is you who are teaching me.

SWANWHITE, *pointing to the dish of fruit.* Will you have some fruit?

THE PRINCE. No, eating is ugly.

SWANWHITE. Yes, it is ugly.

THE PRINCE. Three maids are standing there—one in the Pewter Closet, one in the Clothing Closet, and one in the Fruit Closet. Why are they there?

SWANWHITE. To watch us—lest we do what is forbidden.

THE PRINCE. May we not go into the rose garden?

SWANWHITE. I can only go into the garden in the morning, for my stepmother's bloodhounds are let loose there. And I am never allowed to go down to the sea . . . and so I can never bathe.

THE PRINCE. Have you never seen the sands? Never heard the song of the waves on the beach?

SWANWHITE. No. Only the roaring of the breakers in a storm reaches me here.

THE PRINCE. Have you never heard the murmuring of the winds as they sweep over the water?

SWANWHITE. That cannot reach me here.

THE PRINCE, *pushing his helmet across the table to* SWANWHITE. Hold this to your ear and you will hear it.

SWANWHITE, *holding the helmet to her ear.* What is it I hear?

THE PRINCE. The sea singing and the winds whispering.

SWANWHITE. No, I hear human voices. Hush! It is my stepmother. She is talking to the Steward. She is speaking of me —and of the Young King. She is saying evil things. She is swearing that I shall never be a Queen—and she is vowing . . . that you . . . that you shall marry her daughter . . . that ugly, wicked Lena.

THE PRINCE. Can you hear all that in my helmet?

SWANWHITE. Yes, yes, I can.

THE PRINCE. I did not know it had such power. Yet the helmet was a christening present from my godmother.

SWANWHITE. Will you give me a feather from the plume?

THE PRINCE. With all my heart.

SWANWHITE. Shape it into a quill, so that I may write with it.

THE PRINCE. You know how to write?

SWANWHITE. That my father taught me.

Meanwhile she has pushed the helmet back to THE PRINCE *and he has pulled a black feather from the plume. He takes a silver knife from his belt and shapes the quill.* SWANWHITE *brings out an inkhorn and parchment from the drawer of the table.*

THE PRINCE. Who is this Lady Lena?

He gives SWANWHITE *the quill.*

SWANWHITE, *writing.* Who is she? Do you want her?

THE PRINCE. There is evil brewing in this house.

SWANWHITE. Have no fear. My father left me a gift which will bring help in time of need.

THE PRINCE. What was this gift?

SWANWHITE. The magic horn Standby.

THE PRINCE. Where is it?

SWANWHITE. That you must read in my eyes. I dare not speak, for fear of the Maids.

THE PRINCE, *looking into her eyes.* I have seen.

SWANWHITE, *pushing writing materials across to* THE PRINCE. Write it down.

He writes and hands her the parchment.

Yes, that is the hiding-place. *She writes.*

THE PRINCE. What are you writing?

SWANWHITE. Names. All the beautiful names a Prince may have.

THE PRINCE. All but my own.

SWANWHITE. Yours too.

THE PRINCE. No, no, not that.

SWANWHITE. Now I have twenty names—all that I know—so yours must be among them. *She pushes the parchment across to him.* Read!

He reads.

She claps her hands. Oh, I read it in your eyes!

THE PRINCE. Do not say it. For pity's sake, do not say it.

SWANWHITE. I read it in your eyes.

THE PRINCE. But do not say it. Do not say it.

SWANWHITE. But why? What would happen? . . . Is Lena to say it? Your bride, your love.

THE PRINCE. Hush! Oh hush, hush!

SWANWHITE, *rising and beginning to dance.* I know his name. The most beautiful name in all the land.

THE PRINCE *rises, catches hold of her, and holds his hand over her mouth.*

Now I am biting your hand, now I am drinking your blood, now we are brethren twice over. Do you understand?

THE PRINCE. We are of one blood.

SWANWHITE, *throwing back her head.* O-o-o-h! Look, there is a hole in the roof, and I can see the sky, a tiny piece of heaven, a window pane, and behind the window is a face. Is it an angel's face? . . . Look, look . . . it is your face.

THE PRINCE. The angels are young girls, not boys.

SWANWHITE. But it is you.

THE PRINCE, *gazing up.* It is a mirror.

SWANWHITE. Woe to us then! It is my stepmother's magic mirror. She has seen everything.

THE PRINCE. I can see the hearth in the mirror. There is a pumpkin hanging in it.

SWANWHITE, *taking from the hearth a queerly shaped mottled pumpkin.* What can this be? It has the look of an ear. So the witch has heard us too. Alas, alas! *She throws the pumpkin into the fire and runs towards the bed. Suddenly she stops and raises one foot.* Oh, she has strewn the floor with needles. *She sits down and rubs her foot.*

THE PRINCE *kneels to help her.*

No, you must not touch my foot, you must not.

THE PRINCE. Dear heart, you must take off your stocking if I am to help you.

SWANWHITE, *sobbing*. You must not, you must not see my foot.

THE PRINCE. But why, why?

SWANWHITE, *drawing her foot under her*. I cannot tell you, I cannot. Go away. Leave me. I will tell you tomorrow, but today I cannot.

THE PRINCE. But your poor foot is hurting. I must take out the needle.

SWANWHITE. Go away, oh go away! No, no, you must not touch it. Were my mother alive this would never have happened. Mother, mother, mother!

THE PRINCE. I do not understand. Are you afraid of me?

SWANWHITE. Do not ask. Only go away. Oh!

THE PRINCE, *rising, sadly*. What have I done?

Pause.

SWANWHITE. No, do not leave me. I did not mean to grieve you—but I cannot tell you. Oh, if only I might reach the shore, the white sand of the beach. . . .

THE PRINCE. What then?

SWANWHITE. I cannot say, I cannot tell you.

She hides her face in her hands. Once more the peacock snaps his beak and the doves stir. The three MAIDS *enter one after the other. A gust of wind is heard and the tops of the rose trees sway. The golden clouds that have hung over the sea disappear and the blue sea darkens.* SWANWHITE *watches this transformation and then speaks.*

Is this the judgement of heaven on us? There is ill luck in the house. Oh, that my sorrow could bring back my mother from her dark grave!

THE PRINCE, *with his hand on his sword*. My life for yours.

SWANWHITE. Alas, she can even turn the edge of your sword. . . . Oh, that my sorrow could bring back my mother from her grave!

The swallows in the nest twitter.

What was that?

THE PRINCE, *looking at the nest.* A swallows' nest! I had not noticed it.

SWANWHITE. Neither had I. How did it get there—and when? Surely it is a good omen. . . . Yet the sweat of fear is on my brow . . . and I can scarcely breathe. Look, even the rose is withering as that evil woman draws near—for it is she who is coming.

The rose on the table begins to close and drops a petal.

THE PRINCE. But the swallows, where did they come from?

SWANWHITE. Not from that evil woman—for swallows are good. . . . Here she is!

THE STEPMOTHER *enters through the main arch with her panther-like step. The rose droops.*

THE STEPMOTHER. Signe! Take the horn out of the bed.

SIGNE *obeys.*

THE PRINCE *moves towards the door.*

Where are you going, Prince?

THE PRINCE. The day is almost over, madam. The sun is setting and my bark must set sail for home.

THE STEPMOTHER. The day *is* over. The gates are closed and the hounds let loose. Do you know my bloodhounds?

THE PRINCE. Yes, I know them. But do you know my sword?

THE STEPMOTHER. What is there to know?

THE PRINCE. Sometimes there is blood upon it.

THE STEPMOTHER. Ah, but surely never the blood of women. Will you sleep in the Blue Room, Prince?

THE PRINCE. No, by heaven, I will sleep at home in my own bed.

THE STEPMOTHER. Have you many to aid you?

THE PRINCE. Many?

THE STEPMOTHER. How many? As many as these? One, two, three . . .

As she counts, the members of the household begin to pass across the balcony in single file. All appear grim. Some are armed. None look into the room. Among them are THE STEW-

ARD, THE BAILIFF, THE GUARD, THE CHEF, THE EXECUTIONER, THE EQUERRY, *and* THE GROOM.

THE PRINCE, *crushed.* I will sleep in the Blue Room.

THE STEPMOTHER. I thought you would. And so I bid you a thousand times good night—and so too does Swanwhite.

There is music as of the flight of swans. A swan flies across the garden. A poppy drops from the ceiling on to THE STEPMOTHER. *She and* THE MAIDS *fall asleep on their feet.*

SWANWHITE, *going up to* THE PRINCE. Good night, Prince.

THE PRINCE, *taking her hand and speaking in a low voice.* Good night. I am to sleep under the same roof as my Princess. My dreams shall enfold your dreams, and tomorrow we shall awake to play together and . . .

SWANWHITE, *low.* Now you are the only one I have on earth. You are my father, for she has robbed me of his great strength. Look, she is asleep.

THE PRINCE. Did you see the swan?

SWANWHITE. No, but I heard it. It was my mother.

THE PRINCE. Come, fly with me!

SWANWHITE. That we may not do. Be patient. We shall meet in our dreams, shall we not? But to do this, you must love me more than all the world. Oh, love me, love me! . . .

THE PRINCE. My King, my loyalty.

SWANWHITE. Your Queen, your heart—this is what I am.

THE PRINCE. I am a knight.

SWANWHITE. But I am not. And so, and so, I take you, Prince . . .

She puts her hand to his mouth and whispers his name.

THE PRINCE. Alas, what have you done?

SWANWHITE. I have given myself to you through your own name. With me on your wings you have found yourself again. You . . . *Whispers his name again.*

THE PRINCE, *with a movement of his hand, as if catching the word in the air.* Was that a rose you threw to me? *He throws a kiss to her.* Swanwhite!

SWANWHITE, *catching it and looking in her hand.* You have

given me a violet. It is you. It is your soul. *She puts her hand to her mouth.* Now I drink you in, now I have you in my breast, in my heart.

THE PRINCE. And you are mine. Who then is the owner?

SWANWHITE. We two.

THE PRINCE. We. You and I. My rose.

SWANWHITE. My violet.

THE PRINCE. Rose.

SWANWHITE. Violet.

THE PRINCE. I love you.

SWANWHITE. You love me.

THE PRINCE. You love me.

SWANWHITE. I love you.

The stage grows light again. The rose on the table lifts its head and opens. The faces of THE STEPMOTHER *and* THE MAIDS *are lighted and appear beautiful, kind, and happy.* THE STEPMOTHER *lifts her drowsy head and, with her eyes still closed, appears to be watching the joy of the young people with a sweet smile.*

Look, look! The cruel one is smiling as at a memory of youth. See how false Signe is transformed by truth and hope. How ugly Tova has become beautiful, and little Elsa has grown tall.

THE PRINCE. This is the power of our love.

SWANWHITE. Can love do this? Praise be to God, mighty God the Creator!

She falls on her knees and weeps.

THE PRINCE. Are you weeping?

SWANWHITE. Yes, for I am so full of joy.

THE PRINCE. Come to my arms, and smile.

SWANWHITE. In your arms I shall die.

THE PRINCE. Smile then and die.

SWANWHITE, *rising.* If I might die . . .

THE PRINCE *takes her in his arms.* THE STEPMOTHER *awakens. On seeing the young people embracing, she strikes the table with the whip.*

THE STEPMOTHER. I must have fallen asleep. Ah, so this was your trick! Did I say the Blue Room? It was the Blue Tower I meant. That is where you shall sleep, Prince—with the Iron Maiden. Signe! Elsa!

The three MAIDS *awaken.*

Show the Prince the nearest way to the Blue Tower, and if in spite of your help he should lose his way, call the Guard, the Executioner, the Equerry, and the Groom.

THE PRINCE. There will be no need for them. Wheresoever I go, through fire or water, beneath the earth or above the clouds, there I shall meet my Swanwhite. She will be with me always, and so now I go to meet her—in the Blue Tower. How is that for witchcraft, Witch? Can you surpass it? I think not—for in you there is no love.

He and SWANWHITE *gaze long at one another. Then he goes out, followed by* THE MAIDS. SWANWHITE *approaches* THE STEPMOTHER *with a pleading gesture.*

THE STEPMOTHER. What is it? Do not waste words, but tell me briefly what you wish.

SWANWHITE. Most of all I want pure water in which to bathe my feet.

THE STEPMOTHER. Is the water to be cold or warm?

SWANWHITE. If I may choose, I should like it to be warm.

THE STEPMOTHER. What else do you desire?

SWANWHITE. A comb to take the tangles from my hair.

THE STEPMOTHER. A golden comb or one of silver?

SWANWHITE. Are you—oh, are you being kind to me?

THE STEPMOTHER. Is it to be gold or silver?

SWANWHITE. Wood or horn would do well enough for me.

THE STEPMOTHER. What else do you wish?

SWANWHITE. A clean shift.

THE STEPMOTHER. Of silk or of linen?

SWANWHITE. Of linen.

THE STEPMOTHER. Ha! Now I have heard your wishes, listen to mine. You are to have no water, neither cold nor warm. You are to have no comb, neither of wood nor of horn, still less of gold or of silver. This is my kindness. You are to have no clean shift, but to get you into the closet and cover your body with a coarse black smock. These are my orders. If you were to leave this apartment, which in any case you cannot do, you would be trapped to your death. And if you escaped that, I would mark your pretty face with the steel whip, so that neither Prince nor King would ever look at you again. Now, get yourself to bed!

THE STEPMOTHER *strikes the table with the whip and goes out through the centre archway. She closes the doorway with a golden grille, which squeaks and rattles as she locks it.*

ACT II

SCENE: *As before. The golden grille is still closed. The peacock and the doves are sleeping. Clouds, landscape and sea are dark.*

SWANWHITE *is asleep on the bed in a garment of black homespun.* THE PRINCE'S *helmet still lies on the table.*

In the doorways of the Closets stand the three MAIDS, *their eyes closed and lighted Roman lamps in their hands.*

A swan flies over the garden. Music of swans' flight as in Act I.

THE MOTHER OF SWANWHITE *appears outside the grille, clothed in white. Over one shoulder is the plumage of a swan and she carries a small golden harp. As she touches the grille, it opens of its own accord. She enters and it closes behind her.*

She takes off the plumage and puts the harp on the table. She looks round the room and, as she sees SWANWHITE, *the harp begins to play.* THE MAIDS' *lamps go out one after another, beginning with that furthest away. Then the three Closet doors close one after another, the innermost first.*

Slowly the clouds grow golden.

THE MOTHER *lights the lamp beside the bed and kneels down.*

The harp continues to play during the following scene.

THE MOTHER, *still kneeling, takes off* SWANWHITE'S *stockings. She bends over her daughter's feet as if bathing them with her tears, then wipes them with a white cloth and kisses them. She puts sandals on* SWANWHITE'S *feet, which now appear shining white.*

She takes a comb of gold and smooths SWANWHITE'S *hair, then lays a garment of white linen beside her on the bed. She kisses her daughter on the forehead and prepares to leave. A white swan flies past and the swan music is repeated.* THE PRINCE'S MOTHER *appears. She too is clothed in white and enters the grille in the same way as* SWANWHITE'S MOTHER, *taking off her swan plumage.*

SWANWHITE'S MOTHER. Well met, my sister. How long before cock crow?

THE PRINCE'S MOTHER. Not long, I fear. The dew is rising from the roses, the corn-crake calls, and the breath of dawn is wafted from the sea.

SWANWHITE'S MOTHER. We must make haste with what we have to do.

THE PRINCE'S MOTHER. You called me here for our dear children's sake.

SWANWHITE'S MOTHER. Yes. I remembered how, as I walked in the green fields of the land that knows no sorrow, I met you —whom I had always known, but never seen before. You were lamenting the fate of your poor child, left alone down here in the vale of sorrow. You opened your heart to me and stirred my own thoughts, which shunned the earth they hated. Then my mind turned once more to earth and sought out my poor deserted daughter. I found her destined to marry the Young King, who is a cruel man and evil.

THE PRINCE'S MOTHER. And so I said to you: "Like unto like. May Love, the all-powerful, prevail and join these two lonely hearts so that they may find comfort in each other."

SWANWHITE'S MOTHER. And now their hearts are joined, and the soul of each enfolds the other. May sorrow turn to joy and the earth rejoice at their young happiness!

THE PRINCE'S MOTHER. If this is granted by the Powers on high.

SWANWHITE'S MOTHER. Their love will be tested in the fire of suffering.

THE PRINCE'S MOTHER *takes* THE PRINCE'S *helmet in her hand and changes the black feathers for white and red ones.*

THE PRINCE'S MOTHER. May sorrow turn to joy this very day when he has mourned his mother for a year!

SWANWHITE'S MOTHER. Give me your hand, my sister, and let the test begin.

THE PRINCE'S MOTHER. Here is my hand and with it goes the hand of my son. Now we have pledged them.

SWANWHITE'S MOTHER. In chastity and honour.

THE PRINCE'S MOTHER. I go to open the Blue Tower, that the young lovers may fly to each other's arms.

SWANWHITE'S MOTHER. In chastity and honour.

THE PRINCE'S MOTHER. And you and I shall meet again in the green meadows that know no sorrow.

SWANWHITE'S MOTHER, *with a gesture towards* SWANWHITE. Listen, she is dreaming of him. . . . Oh, foolish cruel woman who believes that lovers can be parted! . . . They are holding one another by the hand as they walk in the Land of Dreams under whispering pines and singing limes. They are laughing and playing . . .

THE PRINCE'S MOTHER. Hush! The dawn is breaking. I hear the robins calling and the stars are fading from the sky. Farewell, my sister.

SWANWHITE'S MOTHER. Farewell.

THE PRINCE'S MOTHER *goes out, drawing her swan's plumage about her.* SWANWHITE'S MOTHER *passes her hand over* SWANWHITE *in blessing, takes her plumage, and leaves. The grille opens and closes as before.*

The clock on the table strikes three. The harp is silent for a moment, then begins to play a new melody, sweeter even than before.

SWANWHITE *awakes, gazes round her, and listens to the harp. She rises, runs her fingers through her hair, and looks with joy at her white feet. She sees the white garment on the bed. She sits at the table where she sat before, and seems to see someone sitting opposite her in* THE PRINCE'S *place. She looks into his eyes and smiles and holds out her hands. Her lips move as if she is speaking, and then she seems to be listening to a reply.*

She points meaningly at the red and white plume on the helmet and bends forward as if whispering. Then she leans her head back and breathes deeply as if inhaling some fragrance. She catches something in the air, kisses her hand, and blows the kiss back. She picks up the quill and caresses it as if it were a bird, then writes and pushes the parchment across the table. She appears to be watching him as he writes an answer; then she takes back the parchment, reads it, and hides it in her dress. She strokes her black dress as if commenting on the sad change in her appearance, then she smiles as if at an answer and finally bursts into ringing laughter. She indicates in mime that her hair has been combed. She rises and goes a little way away from the table, shyly holding out one of her white feet. She stays for a moment like this, awaiting an answer; when she hears it, she is puzzled and hastily hides her foot.

She goes to the chest and takes out the chess-board and men. She places them on the lion-skin with a gesture of invitation, then lies down, puts up the men, and begins to play with an invisible partner.

The harp is silent for a moment, then starts a new melody. The game of chess ends and SWANWHITE *seems again to be talking to her invisible companion. Suddenly she draws away as if he is coming too close. With a warning gesture, she springs lightly to her feet. She gazes long and reproachfully at him, then takes the white garment and hides behind the bed.*

THE PRINCE *appears outside the grille. His hair has grown grey, his cheeks are pale. He tries in vain to open the grille. He raises his eyes to heaven with an expression of despair.*

SWANWHITE, *coming forward.* Who comes with the rising of the sun?

THE PRINCE. Your love, your Prince, your heart's desire.

SWANWHITE. Whence comes my love?

THE PRINCE. From the Land of Dreams, from the flush of

dawn behind the rose-tipped hills, from the whispering pines and singing limes.

SWANWHITE. What did my love in the Land of Dreams behind the rose-tipped hills?

THE PRINCE. He laughed and played. He wrote her name. He sat on the lion-skin at a game of chess.

SWANWHITE. With whom did he laugh? With whom did he play?

THE PRINCE. With Swanwhite.

SWANWHITE. Then you are he. Welcome to my castle, to my table, to my arms.

THE PRINCE. Who will open the golden grille?

SWANWHITE. Give me your hand. . . . It is as cold as your heart is warm.

THE PRINCE. My body slept in the Blue Tower, while my soul escaped to the Land of Dreams. In the Tower it was cold and dark.

SWANWHITE. I will warm your hand against my breast. I will warm you with my gaze and with my kisses.

THE PRINCE. Lighten my darkness with the radiance of your eyes.

SWANWHITE. Are you in darkness?

THE PRINCE. In the Blue Tower there is neither sun nor moon.

SWANWHITE. Rise, sun! Blow warmly, wind! Rock gently, waves! Oh, golden grille, you believe you can hold apart two hearts, two hands, two pairs of lips—but nothing can divide them!

THE PRINCE. Nothing.

Two doors slide in front of the grille and close, so that SWANWHITE *and* THE PRINCE *can no longer see one another.*

SWANWHITE. Alas, what word has fallen? Who heard? Who punishes?

THE PRINCE. I am not parted from you, dear love, for the sound of my voice still reaches you. It goes through copper, steel and stone to touch your ear in sweet caress. In my thoughts you are in my arms; in my dreams I kiss you, and nothing on this earth can part us—nothing.

SWANWHITE. Nothing.

THE PRINCE. I see you, although I cannot see you with my eyes. I taste you, for you fill my mouth with roses.

SWANWHITE. Oh, that I could hold you in my arms!

THE PRINCE. I am in your arms.

SWANWHITE. Alas, I ache to feel the beat of your heart against my own! I yearn to fall asleep within your arms. Oh, grant us each other, dear God, grant us each other!

The swallows chirp. A small white feather falls to the ground. SWANWHITE *picks it up and finds that it is a key. She opens the gates of the grille.* THE PRINCE *enters.* SWANWHITE *springs into his arms and they kiss.*

Why do you not kiss me?

THE PRINCE, *kissing her again.* I kiss you, I kiss you.

SWANWHITE. I cannot feel your kisses.

THE PRINCE. Then you do not love me.

SWANWHITE. Hold me close. I cannot feel your arms.

THE PRINCE. I shall crush the life out of you.

SWANWHITE. I am still breathing.

THE PRINCE. Give me your soul.

SWANWHITE. I have given it to you. So give me yours.

THE PRINCE. Here is my soul. Now I have yours, and you have mine.

SWANWHITE, *breaking away.* I want my soul again.

THE PRINCE, *uneasily.* And I want mine.

SWANWHITE. Search for it.

THE PRINCE. Each of us is lost. You are me and I am you.

SWANWHITE. We are one.

THE PRINCE. God, who is merciful, has heard our prayer. We have each other.

SWANWHITE. We have each other, yet you are no longer mine. I cannot feel the touch of your hand or the caress of your lips. I cannot see your eyes, or hear your voice. You have gone from me.

THE PRINCE. But I am here.

SWANWHITE. You are here on earth. I must meet you in the Land of Dreams.

THE PRINCE. Then let us fly upon the wings of sleep.

SWANWHITE. With my hand in yours.

THE PRINCE. In my embrace.

SWANWHITE. Within your arms.

THE PRINCE. For this is bliss.

SWANWHITE. Eternal bliss without flaw or end.

THE PRINCE. Can any part us now?

THE PRINCE. Are you my bride?

SWANWHITE. Are you my bridegroom?

THE PRINCE. Bridegroom and bride are we in the Land of Dreams—but here we are not.

SWANWHITE. Here? Where are we then?

THE PRINCE. We are below, down below on earth.

SWANWHITE. Where the clouds gather and the ocean rages, where each night the earth sheds its tears upon the grass, waiting for the sun to rise. Where the hawk destroys the dove and the swallow kills the fly, where leaves fall and turn to dust, where hair grows white and cheeks grow hollow, where eyes lose their lustre and hands lose their strength. Down here on earth below.

THE PRINCE. Let us fly.

SWANWHITE. Yes, let us fly.

THE GARDENER *suddenly appears behind the table. He wears cap, apron, and breeches, one side entirely green, the other entirely blue, and has shears and a knife in his belt. He carries a small sack, from which he scatters seed around.*

THE PRINCE. Who are you?

THE GARDENER. I sow, I sow.

THE PRINCE. What do you sow?

THE GARDENER. Seeds, seeds, seeds.

THE PRINCE. What kind of seeds?

THE GARDENER. Onefold and twofold. One pulls this way, the other pulls that way. When the bridal dress is on, unity has gone. In discord I shall sow, and in concord you shall reap. One and one make one, but one and one also make three. One and one make two, but two make three. Do you understand?

THE PRINCE. Earth-worm, mouldwarp. You who live with your nose to the ground and turn your back on heaven—what can you teach me?

THE GARDENER. That you are a mole and an earth-worm. And that since you turn your back on the earth, the earth will turn its back on you. Good day to you.

THE GARDENER *disappears behind the table.*

SWANWHITE. What was that? Who was he?

THE PRINCE. It was the Green Gardener.

SWANWHITE. Green? Surely he was blue.

THE PRINCE. He was green, my love.

SWANWHITE. Why do you say what is not true?

THE PRINCE. Beloved, I said only what is true.

SWANWHITE. Alas, he does not speak the truth!

THE PRINCE. Whose voice is this? Not my Swanwhite's.

SWANWHITE. Who is this my eyes behold? Not my Prince, whose name alone once charmed me like the spell of the water sprite, like the song of a mermaid in green deeps. . . . Who are you, you stranger with evil eyes—and hair grown grey?

THE PRINCE. You see it only now—my hair that turned grey in the Tower, in a single night mourning the loss of Swanwhite, who is no more.

SWANWHITE. But here is Swanwhite.

THE PRINCE. No. I see before me a black-clad maiden whose face too is dark.

SWANWHITE. Did you not see before that I was clad in black? Then you do not love me.

THE PRINCE. Love her who stands there hard and cruel? No.

SWANWHITE. Your vows were false.

THE PRINCE. When I made my vows, another one stood there. Now—now you are filling up my mouth with nettles.

SWANWHITE. Your violets smell of stinkweed—faugh!

THE PRINCE. Now I am punished for betraying my Young King.

SWANWHITE. Would I had awaited the Young King!

THE PRINCE. Wait. He will come.

SWANWHITE. I shall not wait. I shall go and meet him.

THE PRINCE. I will not stop you.

SWANWHITE, *moving towards the doorway.* And this was love.

THE PRINCE, *distraught.* Where is Swanwhite? Where, where is she? The loveliest, the kindest, the most fair.

SWANWHITE. Seek her!

THE PRINCE. Alas, she is not here!

SWANWHITE. Seek her then elsewhere.

She goes sadly out.

Left alone, THE PRINCE *seats himself at the table, covers his face with his hands, and weeps. A gust of wind sets the draperies and curtains fluttering, and a sigh is heard from the strings of the harp.* THE PRINCE *rises and goes over to the bed. He looks at the impression of* SWANWHITE'S *head on a pillow, then picks it up and kisses it. A clamour is heard outside. He hastily seats himself at the table again.*

The doors of the Closets fly open. The three MAIDS *are seen with darkened faces.* THE STEPMOTHER *comes through the arch; her face too is dark.*

THE STEPMOTHER, *sweetly.* Greeting, dear Prince. Did you enjoy a good night's sleep?

THE PRINCE. Where is Swanwhite?

THE STEPMOTHER. She has gone to marry the Young King. *Pause.* Is there no such thought, Prince, in your own mind?

THE PRINCE. In my mind is but one thought.

THE STEPMOTHER. Of young Swanwhite?

THE PRINCE. Is she too young for me?

THE STEPMOTHER. Grey hairs should keep company with good sense. I have a daughter of good sense.

THE PRINCE. And I, grey hairs?

THE STEPMOTHER. He does not know. He does not believe it. Maids! Signe, Elsa, Tova, come look at the young suitor with his grey hairs!

THE MAIDS *laugh and* THE STEPMOTHER *joins in.*

THE PRINCE. Where is Swanwhite?

THE STEPMOTHER. Follow the clues. Here is one.

She hands him a parchment.

THE PRINCE, *reading.* Did she write this?

THE STEPMOTHER. You know the hand—it is hers. What has she written?

THE PRINCE. That she hates me and loves another—that she was only playing with me—that she will spew out my kisses and throw my heart to the swine. My only desire now is to die—for I am dead.

THE STEPMOTHER. A knight does not die because a wench makes a fool of him. He shows his mettle and takes another.

THE PRINCE. Another? When there is only one?

THE STEPMOTHER. There are two at least, and my Magdalena has seven casks of gold.

THE PRINCE. Seven?

THE STEPMOTHER. And more beside.

Pause.

THE PRINCE. Where is Swanwhite?

THE STEPMOTHER. Magdalena is skilled in many crafts.

THE PRINCE. In witchcraft too?

THE STEPMOTHER. She could bewitch a young Prince.

THE PRINCE, *gazing at the parchment.* Did Swanwhite write this?

THE STEPMOTHER. Magdalena would not write in such a way.

THE PRINCE. Is Magdalena kind?

THE STEPMOTHER. Kindness itself. She does not play with sacred feelings, or seek revenge for little slights. She would be true to the one she . . . *Hesitates, cannot say the word "loves"* . . . cares for.

THE PRINCE. Then she is fair.

THE STEPMOTHER. She is not fair.

THE PRINCE. Then she cannot be kind. Tell me more of her.

THE STEPMOTHER. See her for yourself.

THE PRINCE. Where?

THE STEPMOTHER. She shall come here.

THE PRINCE, *looking at the parchment.* But did Swanwhite write this?

THE STEPMOTHER. Magdalena would have written tenderly.

THE PRINCE. What would she have written?

THE STEPMOTHER. That . . . *Hesitates.*

THE PRINCE. Say the word. Say the word "love" if you are able to.

THE STEPMOTHER *stammers and cannot say it.*

You cannot say that word.

She tries again.

No, no, you cannot say it.

THE STEPMOTHER. Magdalena can say it. Shall she come to you?

THE PRINCE. Let her come.

THE STEPMOTHER, *rising and speaking to* THE MAIDS. Blindfold the Prince, then he will find in his embrace a Princess who has no peer within the seven kingdoms.

SIGNE *comes forward and binds* THE PRINCE'S *eyes.*

THE STEPMOTHER *claps her hands. Pause.*

Why does she not come?

The peacock snaps his beak, the doves coo.

Has my art deserted me? What has happened? Where is the bride?

Four YOUNG GIRLS *come through the arches, carrying baskets of pink and white roses. Music is heard from above.* THE GIRLS *strew the bed with roses. Two* KNIGHTS *enter with closed visors. Between them is* THE BRIDE, *deeply veiled.*[6]

With gestures THE STEPMOTHER *bids all depart except the bridal pair. She herself leaves last of all, closing the curtains and locking the grille.*

THE PRINCE. Is my bride here?

THE BRIDE. Who is your bride?

[6] Stage direction slightly altered to agree with Act III. E.S.

THE PRINCE. I have forgotten her name. Who is your bridegroom?

THE BRIDE. He whose name may not be spoken.

THE PRINCE. Speak it if you can.

THE BRIDE. I can, but I will not.

THE PRINCE. Speak it if you can.

THE BRIDE. Speak my name first.

THE PRINCE. Seven casks of gold. Hunchback, Harelip, Hatred. What is my name? Say it if you can.

THE BRIDE. Prince Greyhair.

THE PRINCE. You are right.

THE BRIDE *throws off her veil, and* SWANWHITE *is revealed, dressed in white with a wreath of roses on her hair.*

SWANWHITE. Now who am I?

THE PRINCE. You are a rose.

SWANWHITE. You are a violet.

THE PRINCE, *taking the scarf off his eyes.* You are Swanwhite.

SWANWHITE. And you . . . you are . . .

THE PRINCE. Hush!

SWANWHITE. You are mine.

THE PRINCE. But you went away. You fled from my kisses.

SWANWHITE. I have come back—because I love you.

THE PRINCE. You wrote cruel words.

SWANWHITE, *tearing up the parchment.* I have destroyed them —because I love you.

THE PRINCE. You called me false.

SWANWHITE. What does that matter since you are true?—And I love you.

THE PRINCE. You wished to go to the Young King.

SWANWHITE. But came instead to you—because you are my love.

THE PRINCE. Now tell me how I have offended.

SWANWHITE. I have forgotten—because you are my love.

THE PRINCE. If I am your love, are you my bride?

SWANWHITE. I am your bride.

THE PRINCE. May heaven bless our union.

SWANWHITE. In the Land of Dreams.

THE PRINCE. In my arms.

THE PRINCE *leads* SWANWHITE *to the bed, on which he places his sword. She lies down on one side of the sword and he on the other. The clouds become rose-coloured, the tree-tops murmur, the harp plays softly and sweetly.*

Good night, my Queen.

SWANWHITE. Good morning, oh my soul's beloved! I hear the beating of your heart. I hear it beating like the waves of the sea, like the hoofs of a steed, like the wings of an eagle. Give me your hand.

THE PRINCE. Here is my hand. Now we will take wing.

Pause. Music. THE STEPMOTHER *enters with the three* MAIDS, *carrying torches. All four have become grey-haired.*

THE STEPMOTHER. Now I shall see my work accomplished before the Duke returns. Magdalena, my daughter, is plighted to the Prince, and Swanwhite is shut up in the Tower. *Approaches the bed.* They are asleep in one another's arms. Bear witness to this, Maids!

They approach.

What is this I see? The hair of all three of you is grey.

SIGNE. Your hair too is grey, madam.

THE STEPMOTHER. Mine? Let me see.

ELSA *holds up a mirror.*

This is the work of evil powers—then perhaps the Prince's hair is no longer grey. . . .

THE MAIDS *hold their torches so that they light up the bed.*

Great heaven, that is so! Look! How beautiful they are! But the sword? Who placed the sword between them to sever a plighted troth?

She tries to remove the sword, but, without waking, THE PRINCE *clings to it.*

SIGNE. Here is some devilry, madam.

THE STEPMOTHER. How so?

SIGNE. This is not the Lady Magdalena.

THE STEPMOTHER. Who is it? Give my eyes some help.

SIGNE. See—it is the Lady Swanwhite.

THE STEPMOTHER. Swanwhite? Is this some devilish apparition, or have I done what I least wished?

THE PRINCE, *still sleeping, turns his head so that his lips touch* SWANWHITE'S.

THE STEPMOTHER *is suddenly moved by the beauty of the sight.*

Never have I seen a sight more fair. Two roses blown together by the wind, two stars falling from heaven and joining as they fall. This is beauty itself. Youth, beauty, innocence, love . . . What memories this awakens, what sweet memories of the days when I lived in my father's house and was loved by *him. Breaks off in astonishment.* What did I say?

SIGNE. You said, madam, that you were loved . . .

THE STEPMOTHER. Then I did speak that word of power. Beloved. So he called me once, when he was setting forth for war—Beloved. *She is lost in thought.* He went away . . . and they married me to another, whom I could not love. . . . Now my life is drawing to its close, and I must watch joy and happiness I have never had myself. I must find joy in others' happiness, some kind of joy at least—in others' love . . . some kind of love at least. . . . But my Magdalena, what joy is there for her? O love omnipotent, O eternal God the Creator, how you have softened my heart, my tiger's heart! Where is my power? Where is my hatred, where my vengeance? *She sits on the bed and looks long at the sleeping pair.* I remember a song, a love-song which *he* sang when I was young—which he sang on that last evening. . . . *Suddenly she rises as if waking from a dream and flies into a rage. Shouts:* Here, men of the Castle—Guards, Bailiff, Executioner—all of you, come here! *She tears the sword from the bed and throws it behind her.* Come, all of you, come here!

Clamour. The members of the household enter as before. Behold! The Prince, the Young King's vassal, has defiled his master's bride. Bear witness to the shameful deed. Let the traitor be taken in chains and irons to his lord—and into the spiked cask with the hussy.

THE PRINCE *and* SWANWHITE *awaken.*

Grooms and Executioner, seize the Prince!

They take hold of him.

THE PRINCE, *struggling.* Where is my sword? Not against evil, but for innocence I fight.

THE STEPMOTHER. Whose innocence?

THE PRINCE. My bride's.

THE STEPMOTHER. The hussy's innocence! Prove it.

SWANWHITE. O Mother, Mother!

The white swan flies past.

THE STEPMOTHER. Bring scissors, Maids! I will cut off the harlot's hair.

SIGNE *brings scissors.*

Now I will cut off your beauty and your love.

THE STEPMOTHER *catches hold of a lock of* SWANWHITE'S *hair and tries to cut it, but the blades of the scissors will not close. She is suddenly seized with panic, which spreads to the men and* THE MAIDS.

Is the enemy upon us? Why are you trembling?

SIGNE. Madam, the dogs are barking and the horses neigh. Strangers are approaching.

THE STEPMOTHER. Quick, to the drawbridge, one and all! Man the ramparts! Fire, water, sword, and axe!

Amid great turmoil the curtain falls.

ACT III

The three MAIDS *are standing in the Closets at their work:* SIGNE *in the Pewter Closet,* ELSA *in the Clothing Closet,* TOVA *in the Fruit Closet.*

THE GARDENER *enters and beckons to* SIGNE, *who comes out to meet him.*

THE GARDENER. Signe, my daughter, I need your help.

SIGNE. First tell me who it was that came with so much din and clamour? Was it the Duke, our master, returning from the war?

THE GARDENER. No, it was not the Duke. It was an Envoy from the Young King, Lady Swanwhite's bridegroom, and with him a great armed retinue. Misfortune is upon us. There will be war—and this domain will blaze with fire.

SIGNE. Your seed has grown, your seed of discord. This is the harvest of your sowing.

THE GARDENER. False Signe, it was you who betrayed us, when you obeyed the Duchess and seized the guardian horn Standby.

SIGNE. A faithful servant must be false to her mistress's enemies.

THE GARDENER. But now, if the Duke does not come, the castle will be razed to the ground. How will he get here in time?

SIGNE. Time brings its own solution. However, now there is to be a banquet. I am polishing the pewter, Elsa is arranging the robes, and Tova is preparing the fruit. Are you sure the Young King has not come himself?

THE GARDENER. Only the Envoy and his retinue.

SIGNE. Where then is the Young King?

THE GARDENER. Who knows? Disguised perhaps among the retinue.

SIGNE. And the Prince?

THE GARDENER. In the Tower. Why do you hate him?

SIGNE. Hate him? I do not hate him. Oh no, no!

THE GARDENER. Perhaps you . . . ?

SIGNE. Do not say it.

THE GARDENER. Can one hate the man one loves?

SIGNE. Yes, when one cannot have him.

THE GARDENER. When one cannot have him? But the Lady

Swanwhite cannot have her Prince, yet she loves him unto death and beyond death.

SIGNE. Is the Prince to die?

THE GARDENER. You know that.

SIGNE. No. O God in heaven, he must not die! Save him, save him!

THE GARDENER. How can I?

SIGNE. By the secret passage—you know the way. Here is the entrance to it, here in the floor.

THE GARDENER. The Duchess has already had the secret passage flooded.

SIGNE. You must find a way through. Oh, save him, save him, before it is too late! Get him to a boat and out to sea.

THE GARDENER. I go to mend what I have broken. If I do not come again, you will know I have atoned.

SIGNE. May God protect you on your journey!

SWANWHITE *enters by the archway.*

SWANWHITE. You evil man, why are you here?

THE GARDENER, *falling on his knees.* I am here to right the wrong I did.

He rises and sows seed.

SWANWHITE. How can you do that? You sowed the seed of discord. What are you sowing now?

THE GARDENER. I sow Concord, Heartsease, Peace, Good to all and ill to none. Do not condemn me, Lady, for your dispute was not my fault.

SWANWHITE. Dispute? You mean as to whether you were green or blue?

THE GARDENER. Even so. Look at me now, Lady, with both your lovely eyes.

SWANWHITE. I am looking.

THE GARDENER, *spinning round.* Then see, I am green on one side, and blue upon the other.

SWANWHITE. So you are both colours. Old simpleton, you have taught me wisdom, and I thank you for it.

He goes to the trapdoor.

But where are you going now?

THE GARDENER. To rescue the Prince.

SWANWHITE. You? Can evil turn to good?

THE GARDENER. Not always. . . . Now I shall take the secret passage—and return with him, or not return at all.

SWANWHITE. The blessing of God go with you and protect you on this journey.

THE GARDENER *goes out through the trapdoor in the floor.* THE EXECUTIONER *rolls the spiked cask on to the terrace and stands beside it, half hidden.*[7] SWANWHITE *watches, then turns to* SIGNE.

Have you betrayed your father?

SIGNE. No, not my father.

SWANWHITE. The Prince then?

SIGNE. No, not the Prince.

SWANWHITE. Then me?

SIGNE *is silent.*

Then me?

SIGNE. My young mistress, disaster is upon us all. One alone can save us now—the Duke, your father.

SWANWHITE. Yes, the Duke, my mighty father. But he does not hear us in our need, because you betrayed me and gave the horn into the hands of the Duchess.

SIGNE. Do you know where she has hidden it?

SWANWHITE. Let me think. *She thinks.*

SIGNE. Where?

SWANWHITE. Hush! *Pause.* Now I can see it. . . . It is behind the mirror . . . in . . . in her silver closet.

SIGNE. Then I will fetch it.

SWANWHITE. You will do this—for my sake?

SIGNE. Do not thank me. Disaster is upon us. No, do not thank me.

SWANWHITE. You will not betray us?

SIGNE. Us? Neither all, nor one, nor any if I know it. He whom

[7] Added stage direction. E.S.

one loves, one hates—though not always. But he whom one hates, one does not love—ever. I am quite confused. We shall see Standby. . . . I shall stand by and be perhaps a bystander.

She goes out.

SWANWHITE. She speaks in riddles. Elsa, Tova, come in here!

They obey.

Here, stand close to me, for someone is listening to us. My pretty Elsa, my faithful Tova, stay by my side. I fear something which I cannot explain. Something is coming which I do not know. I hear with the ears of my heart, I see with the eyes of my breast—danger. I feel a breath as cold as ice. A brutal hand clutches at my breast like a bird of prey swooping on a dove. Woe is me, nettles and goatsbeard, foul flesh and all that reeks! . . . He has come, the Young King.

THE YOUNG KING *enters, full of lust and drink.* ELSA *and* TOVA *stand close together, with* SWANWHITE *behind them.* THE KING *comes up to them insolently.*

THE YOUNG KING. Ha, three of you! Do you know who I am?

ELSA. Knight of the wine barrel.

THE YOUNG KING. Impertinent chit. Give me a kiss, for you are little and bad, but pretty. *To* TOVA. You are good, I know, but plain. Tell me where the Princess Swanwhite is.

ELSA. Can you not guess?

THE YOUNG KING. Are you she? . . . Aha! But your hands are red—you are no Princess. Do you know my name?

ELSA. Lord Goat.

THE YOUNG KING. I like impudent girls. You little scamp, come to my arms!

ELSA. Here? Now?

They flirt.

THE YOUNG KING. Think if the Princess were to hear us.

TOVA. She does not hear such things. She has ears only for the song of the nightingales, for the whisper of leaves, for the murmur of the wind and the waves.

THE YOUNG KING. Don't be so long-winded, ugly one. You talk

too much at a time. Remember your manners, chits, and tell me where the Princess is. Or else, by Satan and all his devils, the Stepmother's steel whip shall rain down fire upon your backs. Where is the Princess Swanwhite?

SWANWHITE, *coming forward.* She is here.

THE YOUNG KING, *gazing at her.* She? *Pause.* Impossible. I saw her portrait, and it was beautiful—but that was painted by the wily Prince so as to deceive me. You have no nose, my girl. You are cross-eyed and your lips are too thick. . . . I ask you—is this Swanwhite?

SWANWHITE. I am she.

THE YOUNG KING, *sitting down.* So it is true, well, well . . . Can you dance, play, paint, sing? *Pause.* You can do nothing. And for this nothing, I am about to storm the castle, burn, sack . . . *Pause.* Can't you at least speak? Can you while away a long evening in conversation? *Pause.* Not that either.

SWANWHITE, *whispering.* I can speak, but not to you.

THE YOUNG KING. Your voice is toneless as a feather brush. Perhaps you are deaf?

SWANWHITE. Certain voices do not reach my ears.

THE YOUNG KING. And blind, and lame as well. *Pause.* This is too great a venture for too small a gain. Go in peace—or rather let me go. Prince Faithless may pluck his goose with the plaintiff. And with me.

He strides out. SWANWHITE, ELSA, *and* TOVA *lift their hands in joy. A melody sounds from the harp.*

THE PRINCE *comes up through the trapdoor.* SWANWHITE *springs into his arms. The harp continues to play.* ELSA *and* TOVA *go out through the arch.*

THE PRINCE *and* SWANWHITE *try to speak to each other, but cannot find words.*

THE YOUNG KING *is seen stealing into the Clothing Closet, where he stands hidden, spying and listening.*

SWANWHITE. Is this farewell?

THE PRINCE. Do not say that word.

SWANWHITE. He is here—he has been here, the King, your King.

THE PRINCE. Then it is farewell—for ever.

SWANWHITE. No. He did not see me. He did not hear me. He did not like me.

THE PRINCE. But he seeks my life.

SWANWHITE. All of them seek your life. . . . Where will you go?

THE PRINCE. Down to the shore.

SWANWHITE. Out on the sea in the storm of winds and waves? You who are my love, my heart's delight.

THE PRINCE. In the waves I shall drink our marriage cup.

SWANWHITE. Then I shall die.

THE PRINCE. And we shall meet never to part, never never more to part.

SWANWHITE. Never more. But if I did not die, my sorrow would bring you back from the grave.

The stage begins to darken.

THE PRINCE. For each tear that is shed from your bright eyes, there is a drop of blood in my coffin. Each hour you walk on earth in happiness fills it with petals of roses.

SWANWHITE. It is growing dark.

THE PRINCE. I walk in light, in your light, because I love you.

SWANWHITE. Take my soul, take my life!

THE PRINCE. I have yours. Take mine, take mine! Now my body must depart, but my soul stays here.

SWANWHITE. My body must stay here, but my soul departs—with you.

As before, THE PRINCE *and* SWANWHITE *try to speak, but their lips move soundlessly.* THE PRINCE *goes down through the trapdoor.* THE YOUNG KING *has witnessed the scene with growing emotion. He sees* SWANWHITE *as she really is. He is first ashamed, then enraptured. When* THE PRINCE *has gone,* THE YOUNG KING *hastens out and falls on his knees.*

THE YOUNG KING. Swanwhite, fairest work of God's hand, do not fear me, for now I have seen you in all your perfection, and heard your voice as of silver strings. But it was with *his* eyes that I saw and with *his* ears that I heard. Alone, I had no powers, for I have not your love. . . . Your stony gaze tells me that you do not see me, that you do not hear my words, that you exist for him alone—that if I took you, it would be a corpse that I held in my arms. Forgive what I have destroyed. Forget that I ever was. Believe that I would never dare defile you by one impure thought, though the memory of you will pursue me and be my punishment. One thing alone I ask. Give me your voice in farewell, that I may carry its echo within my heart. One word to remember, one only.

Pause.

SWANWHITE, *harshly.* Go!

THE YOUNG KING, *springing up.* Raven! Now hear my answer: Blood! *He draws his sword.* None shall possess you, save only I. I will have the raven. I love the strong, the fierce, the cruel. The dove is not the bird for me.

SWANWHITE, *retreating behind the table.* Help me, my father! Standby, come to me, come, come!

THE YOUNG KING, *falling back.* There it comes. The silver voice. The sound of the Angelus on some saint's day. My strength is gone from me.

SWANWHITE, *half singing.* Come, come, come!

THE YOUNG KING. Your voice is so lovely that my sword weeps for shame. Go in and hide yourself. No sword then, but fire. Fire to the castle, death to the traitor.

TOVA *steals in with the horn.*

Who is there?

TOVA. Here it is. Take it, take it!

SWANWHITE, *taking it.* You have brought it, not Signe?

TOVA. I took it from Signe. She was faithless still.

SWANWHITE *blows the horn. Another horn answers in the distance.* THE YOUNG KING, *panic-stricken, shouts to his unseen men.*

THE YOUNG KING. To horse! Let loose the reins, press in the spurs, ride for dear life!

He rushes out.

SWANWHITE *blows the horn again, and the other horn answers.*

TOVA. He is coming, the glorious hero. He is coming.

After a pause SWANWHITE *blows again and* THE DUKE *enters.* TOVA *goes out.*

THE DUKE. Sweet treasure of my heart, what is at stake?

SWANWHITE. Your child's life is at stake, Father. Look at the spiked barrel there.

THE DUKE. What has my child done to deserve such a fate?

SWANWHITE. I learned the Prince's name in the way that only those who love can learn. I spoke it and lost my heart to him.

THE DUKE. This does not merit death. What more?

SWANWHITE. I slept beside him—with the sword between.

THE DUKE. Nor does this merit death, although it was not wise. What more?

SWANWHITE. That is all.

THE DUKE, *to* THE EXECUTIONER. Away with the spiked barrel!

He obeys.

And now, my child, where is the Prince?

SWANWHITE. Sailing for home in his coracle.

THE DUKE. Now in this raging storm? Alone?

SWANWHITE. Alone. Oh, what will befall him?

THE DUKE. That is in the hand of God.

SWANWHITE. Is he in danger?

THE DUKE. Fortune sometimes favours the brave.

SWANWHITE. Oh, he deserves it!

THE DUKE. If he is innocent.

SWANWHITE. He is, he is, more innocent than I.

THE STEPMOTHER *enters.*

THE STEPMOTHER, *to* THE DUKE. How did you come here?

THE DUKE. By the shortest way. Would I had been here sooner.

THE STEPMOTHER. Had you come sooner, your daughter would have escaped this injury.

THE DUKE. What injury?

THE STEPMOTHER. The one for which there is no remedy.

THE DUKE. Have you proof?

THE STEPMOTHER. I have eye-witnesses.

THE DUKE. Call the Steward.

THE STEPMOTHER. He knows nothing of this.

THE DUKE, *grasping the hilt of his sword.* Call the Steward!

THE STEPMOTHER *shudders. She claps her hands four times.* THE STEWARD *enters.*

Have a pie prepared without delay—a pie of beasts' entrails, seasoned with fennel, roots, rank herbs, and fungus.

THE STEWARD *glances at* THE STEPMOTHER.

Why this glance? Obey me instantly.

THE STEWARD *goes out.*

To THE STEPMOTHER. Now call the Herb Gardener.

THE STEPMOTHER. He is ignorant.

THE DUKE. And shall remain so. But come he must. Summon him.

THE STEPMOTHER *claps her hands six times.* THE HERB GARDENER *enters.*

Bring me three lilies—one white, one red, one blue.

THE HERB GARDENER *glances at* THE STEPMOTHER. THE DUKE *touches his sword.*

Have a care of your head.

THE HERB GARDENER *goes out.* THE DUKE *turns back to* THE STEPMOTHER.

Now call the witnesses.

THE STEPMOTHER *claps her hands once.* SIGNE *enters.*

What did you see? Give evidence. But choose your words with care.

SIGNE. I saw the Lady Swanwhite and the Prince together in one bed.

THE DUKE. With the sword between?

SIGNE. There was no sword.

SWANWHITE. Signe, Signe, you are bearing false witness against me—I who saved you from the steel whip! You do me such wrong, such wrong. *Pause.* You betrayed me that night—you know it. Why did you do this to me?

SIGNE. I did not know what it was I did. I did what I had no will to do. I did the will of another. Now I no longer wish to live. Forgive me for our Saviour's sake.

SWANWHITE. I forgive you. Do you also forgive yourself, for you are without guilt since an evil will possessed you.

SIGNE. Punish me, punish me!

SWANWHITE. Is not your repentance punishment enough?

THE DUKE. I do not think so. . . . Are there more witnesses?

The two KNIGHTS *enter.*

Were you the Bride's escort? Give your evidence.

THE FIRST KNIGHT. I escorted the Lady Magdalena to her bridal couch.

THE SECOND KNIGHT. I escorted the Lady Magdalena to her bridal couch.

THE DUKE. What is this? A snare that shall entrap the snarer. The next witness.

Enter ELSA.

Give your evidence.

ELSA. I swear, by God the Just, I saw the Lady Swanwhite and the Prince, fully clothed and with the sword between them.

THE DUKE. One for and one against . . . and two not relevant. I leave it to God to judge.

TOVA *enters.*

The flowers shall testify.

TOVA, *coming forward.* My gracious master, noble Lord. . . .

THE DUKE. What have you to tell me?

TOVA. That my sweet Lady is innocent.

THE DUKE. Oh child, child, do you know this? Then let us know it too.

TOVA. I have said what is true.

THE DUKE. And no one believes you. Yet when Signe says what is not true, she is believed. And what does Swanwhite say herself? Does not her pure brow, do not her candid eyes and innocent mouth declare that she is slandered? Do not my own eyes, the eyes of a father, tell me this too? Now Almighty God shall judge, so that all men may believe.

THE HERB GARDENER *enters, carrying the three lilies in narrow vases of glass.* THE DUKE *places them in a semi-circle on the table.* THE STEWARD *enters with a huge platter, on which is a steaming pie.* THE DUKE *places the platter within the semi-circle of flowers.*

For whom does the white lily stand?

ALL, *except* SWANWHITE *and* THE STEPMOTHER. For Swanwhite.

THE DUKE. And the red lily?

ALL, *except* SWANWHITE *and* THE STEPMOTHER. For the Prince.

THE DUKE. And the blue?

ALL, *except* SWANWHITE *and* THE STEPMOTHER. For the Young King.

THE DUKE. So be it. Tova, my child, you who believe in innocence because you are innocent yourself, interpret God's judgement for us. Tell us the subtle secrets of these flowers. What do you see?

TOVA. What is evil I cannot speak.

THE DUKE. I shall do that—you speak the good. In the reek of the burning wild beasts' blood, in the vapours of those sensual herbs, what do you see?

TOVA *gazes at the three lilies, which behave as she describes.*

TOVA. The white lily closes its petals against defilement. This flower is Swanwhite's.

ALL, *as before.* Swanwhite is innocent.

TOVA. The red flower, the Prince's lily, closes too. But the blue, the Young King's flower, opens wide to breathe the sensual fumes.

THE DUKE. Well read. What do you see now?

TOVA. The red lily bows its head in reverent love before the white. But the blue flower writhes with envious rage.

THE DUKE. Well read. Who then shall have Swanwhite?

TOVA. The Prince. His desire is purer and therefore stronger.

ALL, *as before.* The Prince shall have Swanwhite.

SWANWHITE *throws herself into* THE DUKE'S *arms.*

SWANWHITE. Father, Father!

THE DUKE. Call back the Prince! Let every horn and trumpet call him. Let every bark on shore set sail. . . . But one thing more—for whom is the spiked barrel?

All are silent.

Then I will tell you. It is for the Duchess, the arch-liar, the destroyer. Now, evil woman, you have seen that for all the power of your spells, they cannot conquer love. Go, and go quickly!

THE STEPMOTHER *makes a movement with her hands, which for a moment seems to stun* THE DUKE. *Then he lifts* SWANWHITE *on to his shoulder, draws his sword, and points it at* THE STEPMOTHER.

Out upon you, evil one! My sword will pierce your spells.

THE STEPMOTHER *goes slowly out to the balcony backwards, with the dragging step of a panther.*

Now for the Prince.

THE STEPMOTHER *stops on the balcony as if turned to stone, and opens her mouth as if pouring out venom. The peacock and the doves fall down dead. Then* THE STEPMOTHER *begins to swell. Her clothes become inflated until they hide her head and shoulders; then they seem to be on fire, flaming in a pattern of snakes and branches. The sun begins to rise. The ceiling sinks slowly into the room. Smoke and flame pour from the hearth.* THE DUKE *raises the cross-shaped hilt of his sword towards* THE STEPMOTHER.

Pray, people, pray to Christ our Saviour!

ALL. Christ have mercy upon us!

The ceiling returns to its place, the smoke and the fire cease. The sound of many voices is heard outside.

THE DUKE. What is this? What has happened now?

SWANWHITE. I know. . . . I see. I hear the water dripping from his hair, I hear the silence of his heart. I hear that he no longer breathes. . . . I see that he is dead.

THE DUKE. Where do you see this? And who . . . ?

SWANWHITE. Where? . . . I see it.

THE DUKE. I see nothing.

SWANWHITE. Let them come quickly, since they must come.

Four young MAIDS-OF-HONOUR *enter with baskets, from which they strew the floor with branches of yew and white lilies. Next come four* PAGES, *ringing silver bells of different tones. Then a* PRIEST, *bearing a crucifix, and finally the* PALL-BEARERS, *carrying a bier, on which* THE PRINCE *lies under a white shroud strewn with pink and white roses. His hair is dark again and his face youthful, rosy, and radiantly beautiful. His eyes are closed, but he is smiling.*

The harp begins to play. The sun rises fully. The bewitched shape of THE STEPMOTHER *bursts and she resumes her own form. She steps away.*

The bier is set down in the rays of the sun.

SWANWHITE *throws herself on her knees beside it and kisses* THE PRINCE.

All present hide their faces in their hands and weep. THE FISHERMAN, *who has been standing in the doorway, comes in.*

THE DUKE. Tell us the brief tale, Fishernan.

THE FISHERMAN. Does it not tell itself, my noble Lord? The young Prince had scarcely crossed the Sound when he was seized by such longing for his love—that he must return. Since his bark had lost its rudder, he plunged into the water and swam against spring-tide and wave and wind. I saw his young head top the billows, I heard his voice call out her name. . . . Then his dead body dropped gently on the white sand at my feet. His hair had turned grey that night in the Tower, his cheeks had grown hollow with sorrow and care, his lips had lost their power to smile. . . . Now in death he was young again and beautiful. His dark locks framed his rosy cheeks . . . he smiled, and see, he is smiling still. The people gathered on the shore, awed by this sad sweet sight, and one whispered to another: "See, this is Love!"

SWANWHITE. He is dead. His heart no longer sings, his eyes no longer light my life, his breath no longer sheds its dew on me. He smiles, but not at me—it is at heaven that he smiles. I will join him on his journey.

She kisses him and prepares to lie down beside him.

THE DUKE. Do not kiss a dead man's lips, for they bear poison.

SWANWHITE. Sweet poison if it brings me death, that death which for me is life.

THE DUKE. They say, my child, that the dead do not meet again at will, and that what a man has prized in life has little worth beyond it.

SWANWHITE. But love? Can love not reach to the other side of death?

THE DUKE. Our wise men have denied it.

SWANWHITE. Then he must come back to earth again. O God, dear God, send him back from Your heaven!

THE DUKE. A vain prayer, I fear.

SWANWHITE. I cannot pray. Alas, an evil eye still rules this place.

THE DUKE. You mean the witch whom the sunlight pierced. Let her then be taken to the stake and burned alive.

SWANWHITE. Burned alive? No, no. Let her go in peace.

THE DUKE. She shall be burned alive. You men, build the pyre close to the shore, that her ashes may be strewn to the winds.

SWANWHITE *falls on her knees before* THE DUKE.

SWANWHITE. No, no. I pray for her, my executioner. Have mercy on her, mercy!

THE STEPMOTHER *enters, changed. She is freed from the evil powers that have held her under their spell.*

THE STEPMOTHER. Mercy? Who spoke that sacred word? Who prayed a prayer from the heart for me?

SWANWHITE. I prayed for you. . . . I, your daughter . . . Mother.

THE STEPMOTHER. O God in heaven, she calls me Mother! At whose bidding is this?

SWANWHITE. At the bidding of love.

THE STEPMOTHER. Blessed be love that works such miracles. Ah child, it has the power too to call back the dead from death's dark realm! I cannot do this, for love has been denied me. But you, you can do it.

SWANWHITE, *humbly.* I, what can I do?

THE STEPMOTHER. You can love, you can forgive, and so, mighty child, you can do everything. Learn this from me, who may not use my powers. Go to him. Call the name of your beloved and lay your hand upon his heart. Then with the help of Almighty God—but only with His help—your love will hear your voice—if you can believe.

SWANWHITE. I believe. I will. I pray.

She goes to the bier and lays one hand on THE PRINCE'S *heart and raises the other to heaven.*

With my mind.

She bends down and whispers something in his ear.

With my heart.

She whispers again.

With my soul.

She whispers a third time.[8]

THE PRINCE *awakens. He rises and takes* SWANWHITE *in his arms.*

All kneel in praise and thanksgiving.

The music swells to a climax.

[8] Strindberg puts only that Swanwhite whispers three times in the Prince's ear. "With my mind," "with my heart," and "with my soul" have been added to express what is implied: three stages of will. E.S.

A DREAM PLAY

INTRODUCTION

A DREAM PLAY was begun in 1901 shortly after Strindberg's marriage at the age of fifty-two to his third wife, the young Norwegian actress Harriet Bosse.

He had emerged now from the long "Inferno" period in which he had wrestled with his soul and written no plays, only scientific and alchemical treatises. He had been born again into a period of "new productivity, with faith, hope and charity regained—and absolute conviction," and as he had changed, so must his drama, for Strindberg's life and writings are inseparable. In earlier years, although he was "born with a nostalgia for heaven," and had clairvoyant gifts, he chose materialism and forced himself to explain everything by natural phenomena. The last brilliant fruits of that phase were his two Naturalist plays THE FATHER and MISS JULIE, although even then his creation was larger than life. Now, convinced at last of the truth of his poetic vision, he invited spirits to play upon his stage and ignored every restricting convention.

After choosing Harriet Bosse to play The Lady in TO DAMASCUS, the first of his visionary plays, a rôle for which she was really too young, Strindberg, at the time of their betrothal, designed the part of Eleanora in EASTER specially for her. Indra's Daughter, the heavenly visitor in A DREAM PLAY is, Strindberg tells us, Eleanora grown up. The same pity for human suffering and the same horror of ugliness and sin are found in both characters, but whereas Eleanora has vicarious experience of the joys and sorrows of other people, the Daughter of Indra must live through these things herself, in order to achieve a wider comprehension and a deeper compassion.

In spite of his marriage and the fact that Harriet Bosse shortly bore him a child—parenthood was to him the most moving of all human experiences—when Strindberg wrote A DREAM PLAY he was not happy. Although he was no longer persecuted by invisible enemies, his ordeal had left him frail and more sensitive even than before. His wife often went away for weeks at a time; he felt the gulf of age between them, and theatre too, which they both loved so well, conspired to take her from him. A terrible anticipation of new loneliness hung over him, aggravated by fear of losing this child as, in two divorces, he had lost the others. He often felt as if his whole life were a dream, in which everything that had happened was happening again; the idea grew into an obsession, and from it came the seed of this play.

His first title for it was PRISONERS, since it was clear to him that this world which looked so fair was either a prison or a lunatic asylum, then he changed the name to ALLEY DRAMA, after the alley leading to the stage door of the theatre in Stockholm where, night after night, he had waited for Harriet Bosse, and where his fancy had been struck by a mysterious door with an airhole shaped like a four-leafed clover. In this play that door conceals the secret of existence, which turns out to be nothing, since out of nothing God made life. His next title was THE GROWING CASTLE, suggested by the domed roof of the cavalry barracks which he could see from the window of his study, flashing gold above the trees. Everything struggled upwards away from earth's filth, so why not a castle too?

Finally he brought all these ideas together and called the work A DREAM PLAY, explaining in a foreword that it continued the experiment of TO DAMASCUS in reproducing the disconnected yet apparently logical form of a dream. Far ahead of his time, he explored the workings of the subconscious during sleep and saw how the personality of the single dreamer sometimes split into many seemingly different characters.

To the Daughter of Indra (Harriet Bosse's dark beauty influenced the choice this time of a Hindu goddess), Strindberg gave his own agony at being earth-bound, chained within life's limitations. The Officer undergoes Strindberg's own punishment of being endlessly sent back to school to learn the same lessons again; to the Officer too is given his eternal waiting for the perfect love which never came. Then there is the Lawyer, the young idealist, trapped and broken and mirroring in his own ugliness the evil and suffering of the world, and finally the Poet appears, the man who is closest to the heavens, who takes mud-baths to harden his skin, and whose imperfect words, telling of man's plight, the Daughter of Indra promises to interpret to the Gods. All these characters, and that too of the Quarantine Master, wearing a mask so as to appear a shade blacker than he really is, are facets of the dreamer—of Strindberg himself.

There is more poetry both in form and language in A DREAM PLAY than in TO DAMASCUS, and it is filled with imagery. Nor are the images always tormented. Although Kristin pastes man up in his prison and the Lawyer twists the squeaking door handle, which is at the same time the heart of his love, although the rich are tortured on the hell-racks of their gymnasium, Earth itself stretches heavenward, the Castle grows up out of the manure, the giant hollyhocks climb to the light, and man himself ascends by the ladder of suffering. There is much sadness in the play, but no despair. As the Daughter of Indra returns to heaven, the Castle blazes up in an all-purging fire, and although the faces of mankind still mirror agony, the bud on the summit of the Castle, a symbol of faith, bursts at last into a gigantic chrysanthemum. Strindberg believed that if the old pattern were destroyed, a new world would rise, and the golden age of the poet and the dreamer yet be reached.

A DREAM PLAY was first produced in Stockholm in 1907 with Harriet Bosse, now divorced from Strindberg but still his friend, creating the part of Indra's Daughter. Strindberg considered that the Director, Ranft, was not daring enough in his production. In any case the play, called by the critics an interesting experiment, closed after twelve performances.

Since then this play has been little performed except in Germany, until recently Sweden's leading director, Olaf Molander, started a Strindberg renaissance. He has directed several productions of A DREAM PLAY in Scandinavia, each different. To have seen one of these, and to have worked on the London broadcast of my earlier translation, has confirmed my belief that this, in spite of the unevenness which prevents it from being great, is a wonderful piece of work. Had they been written later, A DREAM PLAY, and still more THE GHOST SONATA, might have been called surrealist, but however one classifies these plays, it is clear that Strindberg's dramatic vision was in advance of his own times and is still ahead of ours. He should never be restricted by the convention of any period, and for this reason his work, specially his late poetic drama, invites imaginative and adventurous interpretation.

In Molander's productions and, I feel sure, in earlier ones, no visual resemblance was made between the Officer, the Lawyer, and the Poet; but as these three characters are all facets of one Dreamer I think they should not be quite unlike. The Poet, by Swedish convention, usually resembles Strindberg. The Director of the B.B.C. production, interested in the link between the characters, gave all three parts to one actor, but I myself think this was going too far. Strindberg wrote three characters, not one, although they are seldom on the stage together. Incidentally a number of other characters may be doubled with good effect.

The theme line of the play: "Det är synd om människorna," repeated many times by Indra's Daughter, is exceedingly difficult to translate. "Mankind is pitiable," or "pitiful," "Human beings are to be pitied," are all fair versions of the Swedish, but there is also a suggestion of "it's a shame about human beings." The Daughter, however, is dominated by compassion not contempt, and whenever she says this line one must feel the link between her and her heavenly father Indra, who has sent her down to earth to find out if human complaint is justified. Strindberg never once alters the Daughter's phrase, but after long consideration I have made an occasional slight variation in English, in order that the meaning may be more exact.

Another translation problem is the term: "Alla Rätttänkande," the people who refuse the Lawyer his laurels because he has defended the poor, who fight all reform, and who, the Poet tells the Daughter, crucified the Saviour because He came to liberate. Literally, of course, the term means "right-thinking," but as this does not work easily into the English text, in this version I have used "Righteous," not in the biblical sense, but as having nowadays a flavour "self-righteous" and implying the respectable citizen.

Strindberg's stage directions, even for taking characters on or off the stage, are erratic, and where I have judged necessary I have added a direction, such additions marked by square brackets. I have also occasionally omitted directions such as "Left" or "Right," when they restrict rather than aid visual imagination. Writing in the era of painted backcloths and drops, Strindberg uses these words in his sets. I have substituted "background," and written "the scene changes," rather than "the backdrop rises," as more undated terms. I have also sometimes altered the order of stage directions to make them clearer, but in every other way this text follows the Swedish as closely as possible.

The play needs skilful cutting for production; the Mediterranean scene, for instance, is completely out of date, and no translation can prevent the young lover's song in the Foulstrand scene from tedious sentimentality. Arranging the play for the theatre is not the translator's job but the director's, but I find myself dreaming this fascinating ever-changing dream upon the stage, and I have had both audience and reader in mind while working on the text. A realistic presentation is not only very costly but very cumbersome. What an opportunity for an ingenious use of light and modern methods and materials, and what a film the play would make!

E. S.

AUTHOR'S NOTE

In this dream play, as in his former dream play TO DAMASCUS, the Author has sought to reproduce the disconnected but apparently logical form of a dream. Anything can happen; everything is possible and probable. Time and space do not exist; on a slight groundwork of reality, imagination spins and weaves new patterns made up of memories, experiences, unfettered fancies, absurdities and improvisations.

The characters are split, double and multiply; they evaporate, crystallise, scatter and converge. But a single consciousness holds sway over them all—that of the dreamer. For him there are no secrets, no incongruities, no scruples and no law. He neither condemns nor acquits, but only relates, and since on the whole, there is more pain than pleasure in the dream, a tone of melancholy, and of compassion for all living things, runs through the swaying narrative. Sleep, the liberator, often appears as a torturer, but when the pain is at its worst, the sufferer awakes—and is thus reconciled with reality. For however agonising real life may be, at this moment, compared with the tormenting dream, it is a joy.

*Dramatis Personæ**

(*The voice of*) FATHER INDRA

INDRA'S DAUGHTER

THE GLAZIER

THE OFFICER

THE FATHER

THE MOTHER

LINA

THE DOORKEEPER

THE BILLSTICKER

THE PROMPTER

THE POLICEMAN

THE LAWYER

THE DEAN OF PHILOSOPHY

THE DEAN OF THEOLOGY

THE DEAN OF MEDICINE

THE DEAN OF LAW

THE CHANCELLOR

KRISTIN

THE QUARANTINE MASTER

THE ELDERLY FOP

THE COQUETTE

THE FRIEND

THE POET

HE

SHE (*doubles with Victoria's voice*)

THE PENSIONER

UGLY EDITH

EDITH'S MOTHER

THE NAVAL OFFICER

*There is no list of characters in the original. E. S.

ALICE

THE SCHOOLMASTER

NILS

THE HUSBAND

THE WIFE

THE BLIND MAN

1ST COAL HEAVER

2ND COAL HEAVER

THE GENTLEMAN

THE LADY

SINGERS AND DANCERS (*Members of the Opera Company*)

CLERKS, GRADUATES, MAIDS, SCHOOLBOYS,

CHILDREN, CREW, RIGHTEOUS PEOPLE.

PROLOGUE

An impression of clouds, crumbling cliffs, ruins of castles and fortresses.
The constellations Leo, Virgo and Libra are seen, with the planet Jupiter shining brightly among them.
On the highest cloud-peak stands THE DAUGHTER OF INDRA. INDRA'S VOICE *is heard from above.*

INDRA'S VOICE. *Where art thou, Daughter?*

DAUGHTER. *Here, Father, here!*

INDRA'S VOICE. *Thou hast strayed, my child.*
Take heed, thou sinkest.
How cam'st thou here?

DAUGHTER. *Borne on a cloud, I followed the lightning's*
blazing trail from the ethereal heights.
But the cloud sank, and still is falling.
Tell me, great Father Indra, to what region
am I come? The air's so dense, so hard to breathe.

INDRA'S VOICE. *Leaving the second world thou camest to the third.*
From Cucra, Star of the Morning,
Far art thou come and enterest
Earth's atmosphere. Mark there
The Sun's Seventh House that's called the Scales.
The Morning Star is at the autumn weighing,
When day and night are equal.

DAUGHTER. *Thou speak'st of Earth. Is that the dark*
and heavy world the moon lights up?

INDRA'S VOICE. *It is the darkest and the heaviest*
of all the spheres that swing in space.

DAUGHTER. *Does not the sun shine there?*

INDRA'S VOICE. *It shines, but not unceasingly.*

DAUGHTER. *Now the clouds part, and I can see . . .*

INDRA'S VOICE. *What see'st thou, child?*

DAUGHTER. *I see . . . that Earth is fair . . . It has green woods,*
blue waters, white mountains, yellow fields.

INDRA'S VOICE. *Yes, it is fair, as all that Brahma shaped,*
yet in the dawn of time
was fairer still. Then came a change,
a shifting of the orbit, maybe of more.
Revolt followed by crime which had to be suppressed.

DAUGHTER. *Now I hear sounds arising . . .*
What kind of creatures dwell down there?

INDRA'S VOICE. *Go down and see. The Creator's children I would not decry,*
but it's their language that thou hearest.

DAUGHTER. *It sounds as if . . . it has no cheerful ring.*

INDRA'S VOICE. *So I believe. Their mother-tongue*
is called Complaint. Truly a discontented,
thankless race is this of Earth.

DAUGHTER. *Ah, say not so! Now I hear shouts of joy,*
and blare and boom. I see the lightning flash.
Now bells are pealing and the fires are lit.
A thousand thousand voices rise,
singing their praise and thanks to heaven.
Pause.
Thy judgment is too hard on them, my Father.

INDRA. *Descend and see, and hear, then come again*
and tell me if their lamentations
and complaint are justified.

DAUGHTER. *So be it. I descend. Come with me, Father!*

INDRA. *No. I cannot breathe their air.*

DAUGHTER. *Now the cloud sinks. It's growing dense. I suffocate!*
This is not air, but smoke and water that I breathe,
so heavy that it drags me down and down.
And now I clearly feel its reeling!
This third is surely not the highest world.

INDRA. *Neither the highest, truly, nor the lowest.*
It is called Dust, and whirls with all the rest,

And so at times its people, struck with dizziness,
live on the borderline of folly and insanity . . .
Courage, my child, for this is but a test!

DAUGHTER, *on her knees as the cloud descends.*
I am sinking!

[*The curtain rises on* THE GROWING CASTLE.]

The background shows a forest of giant hollyhocks in bloom: white, pink, crimson, sulphur-yellow and violet. Above this rises the gilded roof of a castle with a flower-bud crowning its summit. Under the walls of the castle lie heaps of straw and stable-muck.

On each side of the stage are stylised representations of interiors, architecture and landscape which remain unchanged throughout the play.

The GLAZIER *and the* DAUGHTER *enter together.*

DAUGHTER. The castle keeps on growing up out of the earth. Do you see how it has grown since last year?

GLAZIER, *to himself.* I've never seen that castle before—and I've never heard of a castle growing . . . but . . . *to the* DAUGHTER *with conviction.* Yes, it's grown six feet, but that's because they've manured it. And if you look carefully, you'll see it's put out a wing on the sunny side.

DAUGHTER. Ought it not to blossom soon? We are already halfway through the summer.

GLAZIER. Don't you see the flower up there?

DAUGHTER, *joyfully.* Yes, I see it. Father, tell me something. Why do flowers grow out of dirt?

GLAZIER. They don't like the dirt, so they shoot up as fast as they can into the light—to blossom and to die.

DAUGHTER. Do you know who lives in the castle?

GLAZIER. I used to know, but I've forgotten.

DAUGHTER. I believe there is a prisoner inside, waiting for me to set him free.

GLAZIER. What will you get if you do?

DAUGHTER. Ones does not bargain about what one has to do. Let us go into the castle.

GLAZIER. Very well, we will.

They go towards the background which slowly vanishes to the sides, disclosing a simple bare room with a table and a few chairs. A screen cuts the stage in two [the other half unlighted]. A YOUNG OFFICER *in an unconventional modern uniform sits rocking his chair and striking the table with his sword.*

[*The* DAUGHTER *and the* GLAZIER *enter.*]

She goes up to the OFFICER *and gently takes the sword from his hands.*

DAUGHTER. No, no, you mustn't do that.

OFFICER. Please, Agnes, let me keep my sword.

DAUGHTER. But you are cutting the table to pieces. *To the* GLAZIER. Father, you go down to the harness room and put in that window pane, and we will meet later.

Exit GLAZIER.

DAUGHTER. You are a prisoner in your own room. I have come to set you free.

OFFICER. I have been waiting for this, but I wasn't sure you would want to.

DAUGHTER. The castle is strong—it has seven walls—but it shall be done. Do you want to be set free—or not?

OFFICER. To tell the truth, I don't know. Either way I'll suffer. Every joy has to be paid for twice over with sorrow. It's wretched here, but I'd have to endure three times the agony for the joys of freedom . . . Agnes, I'll bear it, if only I may see you.

DAUGHTER. What do you see in me?

OFFICER. The beautiful, which is the harmony of the universe. There are lines in your form which I have only found in the movement of the stars, in the melody of strings, in the vibrations of light. You are a child of heaven.

DAUGHTER. So are you.

OFFICER. Then why do I have to groom horses, clean stables and have the muck removed?

DAUGHTER. So that you may long to get away.

OFFICER. I do. But it's so hard to pull oneself out of it all.

DAUGHTER. It is one's duty to seek freedom in the light.

OFFICER. Duty? Life has not done its duty by me.

DAUGHTER. You feel wronged by life?

OFFICER. Yes. It has been unjust. . . .

Voices are now heard from behind the dividing screen, which is drawn aside [as the lights go up on the other set: a homely living-room]. The OFFICER *and the* DAUGHTER *stand watching, gestures and expression held. The* MOTHER, *an invalid, sits at a table. In front of her is a lighted candle, which from time to time she trims with snuffers. On the table are piles of new underclothing, which she is marking with a quill pen. Beyond is a brown cupboard.*

The FATHER *brings her a silk shawl.*

FATHER, *gently*. I have brought you this.

MOTHER. What use is a silk shawl to me, my dear, when I am going to die so soon?

FATHER. You believe what the doctor says?

MOTHER. What he says too, but most of all I believe the voice that speaks within me.

FATHER, *sorrowfully*. Then it really is grave . . . And you are thinking of your children, first and last.

MOTHER. They were my life, my justification, my happiness, and my sorrow.

FATHER. Kristina, forgive me . . . for everything.

MOTHER. For what? Ah, my dear, forgive *me!* We have both hurt each other. Why, we don't know. We could not do otherwise . . . However, here is the children's new linen. See that they change twice a week—on Wednesdays and Sundays, and that Louisa washes them—all over . . . Are you going out?

FATHER. I have to go to the school at eleven.

MOTHER. Before you go ask Alfred to come.

FATHER, *pointing to the* OFFICER. But, dear heart, he is here.

MOTHER. My sight must be going too . . . Yes, it's getting so dark. *Snuffs candle.* Alfred, come!

The FATHER *goes out through the middle of the wall, nodding goodbye. The* OFFICER *moves forward to the* MOTHER.

MOTHER. Who is that girl?

OFFICER, *whispering.* That's Agnes.

MOTHER. Oh, is it Agnes? Do you know what they are saying? That she is the daughter of the God Indra, who begged to come down to Earth so as to know what it is really like for human beings. But don't say anything.

OFFICER. She *is* a child of the Gods.

MOTHER, *raising her voice.* Alfred, my son, I shall soon be leaving you and your brothers and sisters. I want to say one thing—for you to remember all your life.

OFFICER, *sadly.* What is it, Mother?

MOTHER. Only one thing: never quarrel with God.

OFFICER. What do you mean, Mother?

MOTHER. You must not go on feeling you have been wronged by life.

OFFICER. But I've been treated so unjustly.

MOTHER. You're still harping on the time you were unjustly punished for taking that money which was afterwards found.

OFFICER. Yes. That piece of injustice gave a twist to the whole of my life.

MOTHER. I see. Well now, you just go over to that cupboard . . .

OFFICER, *ashamed.* So you know about that. The . . .

MOTHER. "The Swiss Family Robinson" which . . .

OFFICER. Don't say any more . . .

MOTHER. Which your brother was punished for . . . when it was *you* who had torn it to pieces and hidden it.

OFFICER. Think of that cupboard still being there after twenty years. We have moved so many times—and my mother died ten years ago.

MOTHER. Yes. What of it? You are always questioning everything, and so spoiling the best of life for yourself . . . Ah, here's Lina!

Enter LINA.

LINA. Thank you very much all the same, Ma'am, but I can't go to the christening.

MOTHER. Why not, child?

LINA. I've got nothing to wear.

MOTHER. You can borrow this shawl of mine.

LINA. Oh no, Ma'am, you're very kind, but that would never do.

MOTHER. I can't see why not. I shan't be going to any more parties.

OFFICER. What will Father say? After all, it's a present from him.

MOTHER. What small minds!

FATHER, *putting his head in.* Are you going to lend my present to the maid?

MOTHER. Don't talk like that! Remember I was in service once myself. Why should you hurt an innocent girl?

FATHER. Why should you hurt me, your husband?

MOTHER. Ah, this life! If you do something good, someone else is sure to think it bad; if you are kind to one person, you're sure to harm another. Ah, this life!

She snuffs the candle so that it goes out. The room grows dark and the screen is drawn forward again.

DAUGHTER. Human beings are to be pitied.

OFFICER. Do you think so?

DAUGHTER. Yes, life is hard. But love conquers everything. Come and see.

They withdraw and the background disappears. The OFFICER *vanishes and the* DAUGHTER *comes forward alone.*

The new scene shows an old derelict wall. In the middle of the wall a gate opens on an alley leading to a green plot where a giant blue monkshood is growing. To the left of the gate is the door-window of the Stage Door-

keeper's lodge. The Stage Doorkeeper is sitting with a grey shawl over her head and shoulders, crocheting a star-patterned coverlet. On the right is an announcement-board which the BILLSTICKER *is washing. Near him is a fishnet with a green handle and a green fish box. Further right the cupboard [from the previous set] has become a door with an air-hole shaped like a four-leafed clover. To the left is a small lime tree with a coal-black stem and a few pale green leaves.*

The DAUGHTER *goes up to the* DOORKEEPER.

DAUGHTER. Isn't the star coverlet finished yet?

DOORKEEPER. No, my dear. Twenty-six years is nothing for such a piece of work.

DAUGHTER. And your sweetheart never came back?

DOORKEEPER. No, but it wasn't his fault. He *had* to take himself off, poor fellow. That was thirty years ago.

DAUGHTER, *to* BILLSTICKER. She was in the ballet, wasn't she? Here—at the Opera.

BILLSTICKER. She was the prima ballerina, but when *he* went away, it seems he took her dancing with him . . . so she never got any more parts.

DAUGHTER. All complain—with their eyes, and with their voices too.

BILLSTICKER. I haven't much to complain of—not now I've got my net and a green fish box.

DAUGHTER. Does that make you happy?

BILLSTICKER. Yes, very happy. That was my dream when I was little, and now it's come true. I'm all of fifty now, you know.

DAUGHTER. Fifty years for a fishnet and a box!

BILLSTICKER. A *green* box, a *green* one . . .

DAUGHTER, *to* DOORKEEPER. Let me have that shawl now, and I'll sit here and watch the children of men. But you must stand behind and tell me about them.

The DAUGHTER *puts on the shawl and sits down by the gate.*

DOORKEEPER. This is the last day of the Opera season. They hear now if they've been engaged for the next.

DAUGHTER. And those who have not?

DOORKEEPER. Lord Jesus, what a scene! I always pull my shawl over my head.

DAUGHTER. Poor things!

DOORKEEPER. Look, here's one coming. She's not been engaged. See how she's crying!

The SINGER *rushes in from the right and goes through the gate with her handkerchief to her eyes. She pauses a moment in the alley beyond and leans her head against the wall, then goes quickly out.*

DAUGHTER. Human beings are to be pitied.

DOORKEEPER. But here comes one who seems happy enough.

The OFFICER *comes down the alley, wearing a frock-coat and top hat. He carries a bouquet of roses and looks radiantly happy.*

DOORKEEPER. He's going to marry Miss Victoria.

OFFICER, *downstage, looks up and sings.* Victoria!

DOORKEEPER. The young lady will be down in a minute.

WOMAN'S VOICE, *from above, sings.* I am here!

OFFICER, *pacing.* Well, I am waiting.

DAUGHTER. Don't you know me?

OFFICER. No, I know only one woman—Victoria! Seven years I have come here to wait for her—at noon when the sun reaches the chimneys, and in the evening as darkness falls. Look at the paving. See? Worn by the steps of the faithful lover? Hurrah! She is mine. *Sings.* Victoria! *No answer.* Well, she's dressing now. *To the* BILLSTICKER. Ah, a fishnet I see! Everyone here at the Opera is crazy about fishnets—or rather about fish. Dumb fish—because they cannot sing . . . What does a thing like that cost?

BILLSTICKER. It's rather dear.

OFFICER, *sings.* Victoria! . . . *Shakes the lime tree.* Look, it's budding again! For the eighth time. *Sings.* Victoria!

. . . Now she's doing her hair . . . *To* DAUGHTER. Madam, kindly allow me to go up and fetch my bride.

DOORKEEPER. Nobody's to go on the stage.

OFFICER. Seven years I've walked up and down here. Seven times three hundred and sixty-five I make two thousand five hundred and fifty-five. *Stops and pokes the door with the clover-shaped hole.* Then this door I've seen two thousand five hundred and fifty-five times and I still don't know where it leads to. And this clover leaf to let in the light. Who does it let the light in for? Is anyone inside? Does anybody live there?

DOORKEEPER. I don't know. I've never seen it open.

OFFICER. It looks like a larder door I saw when I was four years old, when I went out one Sunday afternoon with the maid—to see another family and other maids. But I only got as far as the kitchen, where I sat between the water barrel and the salt tub. I've seen so many kitchens in my time, and the larders are always in the passage, with round holes and a clover leaf in the door. But the Opera can't have a larder as it hasn't got a kitchen. *Sings.* Victoria! *To* DAUGHTER. Excuse me, Madam, she can't leave by any other way, can she?

DOORKEEPER. No, there is no other way.

OFFICER. Good. Then I'm bound to meet her.

Members of the Opera Company swarm out of the building, scrutinised by the OFFICER. *They go out by the gate.*

She's sure to come. *To* DAUGHTER. Madam, that blue monkshood out there—I saw it when I was a child. Is it the same one? I remember it in a rectory garden when I was seven—with two doves, blue doves, under the hood. Then a bee came and went into the hood, and I thought: "Now I've got you," so I grabbed the flower, but the bee stung through it, and I burst into tears. However, the rector's wife came and put moist earth on it—and then we had wild strawberries and milk for supper . . . I believe it's growing dark already. Where are you off to, Billsticker?

BILLSTICKER. Home to my supper.

[*Exit with fishnet and box.*]

OFFICER, *rubbing his eyes.* Supper? At this time of day? . . . *To* DAUGHTER. Excuse me, may I just step inside a moment and telephone to the Growing Castle?

DAUGHTER. What do you want to say to them?

OFFICER. I want to tell the glazier to put in the double windows. It will be winter soon and I'm so dreadfully cold.

The OFFICER *goes into the* DOORKEEPER'S *Lodge.*

DAUGHTER. Who is Miss Victoria?

DOORKEEPER. She is his love.

DAUGHTER. A true answer. What she is to us or others doesn't matter to him. Only what she is to *him,* that's what she *is.*

It grows dark suddenly.

DOORKEEPER, *lighting the lantern.* Dusk falls quickly today.

DAUGHTER. To the gods a year is as a minute.

DOORKEEPER. While to human beings a minute may be as long as a year.

The OFFICER *comes out again. He looks shabbier, and the roses are withered.*

OFFICER. Hasn't she come yet?

DOORKEEPER. No.

OFFICER. She's sure to come. She'll come. *Paces up and down.* But all the same . . . perhaps it would be wiser to cancel that luncheon . . . as it's now evening. Yes, that's what I'll do. *Goes in and telephones.*

DOORKEEPER. *To* DAUGHTER. May I have my shawl now?

DAUGHTER. No, my friend. You rest and I'll take your place, because I want to know about human beings and life—to find out if it really is as hard as they say.

DOORKEEPER. But you don't get any sleep on this job. Never any sleep, night or day.

DAUGHTER. No sleep at night?

DOORKEEPER. Well, if you can get any with the bell wire on

your arm, because the night watchmen go up on the stage and are changed every three hours . . .

DAUGHTER. That must be torture.

DOORKEEPER. So you think, but we others are glad enough to get such a job. If you knew how much I'm envied.

DAUGHTER. Envied? Does one envy the tortured?

DOORKEEPER. Yes. But I'll tell you what's worse than night-watching and drudgery and draughts and cold and damp. That's having to listen, as I do, to all their tales of woe. They all come to me. Why? Perhaps they read in my wrinkles the runes of suffering, and that makes them talk. In that shawl, my dear, thirty years of torment's hidden—my own and others.

DAUGHTER. That's why it is so heavy and stings like nettles.

DOORKEEPER. Wear it if you like. When it gets too heavy, call me and I'll come and relieve you of it.

DAUGHTER. Goodbye. What you can bear, surely I can.

DOORKEEPER. We shall see. But be kind to my young friends and put up with their complaining.

The DOORKEEPER *disappears down the alley. The stage is blacked out. When light returns, the lime tree is bare, the blue monkshood withered, and the green plot at the end of the alley has turned brown.*

The OFFICER *enters. His hair is grey and he has a grey beard. His clothes are ragged; his collar soiled and limp. He still carries the bouquet of roses, but the petals have dropped.*

OFFICER, *wandering round.* By all the signs, summer is over and autumn at hand. I can tell that by the lime tree—and the monkshood. *Pacing.* But autumn is *my* spring, for then the theatre opens again. And then she is bound to come. *To* DAUGHTER. Dear lady, may I sit on this chair for a while?

DAUGHTER. Do, my friend. I can stand.

OFFICER [*sitting*]. If only I could sleep a little it would be better.

He falls asleep for a moment, then starts up and begins

walking again. He stops by the clover-leaf door and pokes it.

OFFICER. This door—it gives me no peace. What is there behind it? Something must be. *Soft ballet music is heard from above.* Ah, the rehearsals have begun! *The lights come and go like a lighthouse beam.* What's this? *Speaking in time with the flashes.* Light and darkness; light and darkness.

DAUGHTER, *with the same timing.* Day and night; day and night. A merciful providence wants to shorten your waiting. And so the days fly, chasing the nights.

The light is now constant. The BILLSTICKER *enters with his net and his implements.*

OFFICER. Here's the Billsticker with his net. How was the fishing?

BILLSTICKER. Not too bad. The summer was hot and a bit long . . . the net was all right, but not quite what I had in mind.

OFFICER. "Not quite what I had in mind." Excellently put. Nothing ever is as one imagined it—because one's mind goes further than the act, goes beyond the object. *He walks up and down striking the bouquet against the walls until the last leaves fall.*

BILLSTICKER. Hasn't she come down yet?

OFFICER. No, not yet, but she'll come soon. Do you know what's behind that door, Billsticker?

BILLSTICKER. No, I've never seen it open.

OFFICER. I'm going to telephone to a locksmith to come and open it. *Goes into the Lodge. The* BILLSTICKER *pastes up a poster and moves away.*

DAUGHTER. What was wrong with the fishnet?

BILLSTICKER. Wrong? Well, there wasn't anything wrong exactly. But it wasn't what I'd had in mind, and so I didn't enjoy it *quite* as much . . .

DAUGHTER. How did you imagine the net?

BILLSTICKER. How? I can't quite tell you . . .

DAUGHTER. Let me tell you. In your imagination it was different—green but not *that* green.

BILLSTICKER. You understand, Madam. You understand everything. That's why they all come to you with their troubles. Now if you'd only listen to me, just this once . . .

DAUGHTER. But I will, gladly. Come in here and pour out your heart. *She goes into the Lodge. The* BILLSTICKER *stays outside and talks to her through the window.*

The stage is blacked out again, then gradually the lights go up. The lime tree is in leaf; the monkshood in bloom; the sun shines on the greenery at the end of the alley. The BILLSTICKER *is still at the window and the* DAUGHTER *can be seen inside.*

The OFFICER *enters from the Lodge. He is old and white-haired; his clothes and shoes are in rags. He carries the stems of the bouquet. He totters backwards and forwards slowly like a very old man, and reads the poster.*

A BALLET GIRL [*comes out of the Theatre*].

OFFICER. Has Miss Victoria gone?

BALLET GIRL. No, she hasn't.

OFFICER. Then I'll wait. Will she come soon?

BALLET GIRL, *gravely.* Yes, she's sure to.

OFFICER. Don't go—then you'll be able to see what's behind that door. I've sent for the locksmith.

BALLET GIRL. That will be really interesting to see this door opened. The door and the Growing Castle. Do you know the Growing Castle?

OFFICER. Do I? Wasn't I imprisoned there?

BALLET GIRL. Really, was that you? But why did they have so many horses there?

OFFICER. It was a stable castle, you see.

BALLET GIRL, *distressed.* How silly of me not to have thought of that.

[*Moves towards the Lodge. A* CHORUS GIRL *comes out of the Theatre.*]

OFFICER. Has Miss Victoria gone?

CHORUS GIRL, *gravely.* No, she hasn't gone. She never goes.

OFFICER. That's because she loves me. No, you mustn't go before the locksmith comes. He's going to open this door.

CHORUS GIRL. Oh, is the door going to be opened? Really? What fun! I just want to ask the Doorkeeper something. [*She joins the* BILLSTICKER *at the window. The* PROMPTER *comes out of the Theatre.*]

OFFICER. Has Miss Victoria gone?

PROMPTER. Not so far as I know.

OFFICER. There you are! Didn't I say she was waiting for me? No, don't go. The door's going to be opened.

PROMPTER. Which door?

OFFICER. Is there more than one door?

PROMPTER. Oh, I see—the one with the clover-leaf! Of course I'll stay. I just want to have a few words with the Doorkeeper.

[*He joins the group at the window. They all speak in turn to the* DAUGHTER.] *The* GLAZIER *comes through the gate.*

OFFICER. Are you the locksmith?

GLAZIER. No, the locksmith had company. But a glazier's just as good.

OFFICER. Yes, indeed . . . indeed. But . . . er . . . have you brought your diamond with you?

GLAZIER. Of course. A glazier without a diamond—what good would that be?

OFFICER. None. Let's get to work then. *He claps his hands. All group themselves in a circle round the door.* MALE CHORUS *in costumes of Die Meistersinger, and* GIRL DANCERS *from Aïda come out of the theatre and join them.* Locksmith—or Glazier—do your duty! *The* GLAZIER *goes towards the door holding out his diamond.* A moment such as this does not recur often in a lifetime. Therefore, my good friends, I beg you to reflect seriously upon . . .

[*During the last words the* POLICEMAN *has entered by the gate.*]

POLICEMAN. In the name of the law I forbid the opening of this door.

OFFICER. Oh God, what a fuss there is whenever one wants to do anything new and great! Well—we shall take proceedings . . . To the lawyer then, and we will see if the law holds good. To the lawyer!

Without any lowering of the curtain the scene changes to the LAWYER'S *office. The gate has now become the gate in an office railing stretching across the stage. The* DOORKEEPER'S *Lodge is a recess for the* LAWYER'S *desk, the lime tree, leafless, a coat-and-hat stand. The announcement-board is covered with proclamations and Court decrees and the clover-door is a document cupboard.*

The LAWYER *in frock coat and white tie is sitting on the left inside the railing of the gate, at this high desk covered with papers. His appearance bears witness to unspeakable suffering. His face is chalk-white, furrowed and purple-shadowed. He is hideous; his face mirrors all the crime and vice with which, through his profession, he has been involved.*

Of his two clerks one has only one arm; the other a single eye.

The people, who had gathered to witness the opening of the door, are now clients waiting to see the LAWYER, *and look as if they have always been there.*

The DAUGHTER, *wearing the shawl, and the* OFFICER *are in front. The* OFFICER *looks curiously at the cupboard door and from time to time pokes it.*

The LAWYER *goes up to the* DAUGHTER.

LAWYER. If you let me have that shawl, my dear, I'll hang it here until the stove is lighted and then I'll burn it with all its griefs and miseries.

DAUGHTER. Not yet, my friend. I must let it get quite full first, and I want above all to gather *your* sufferings up in it, the crimes you have absorbed from others, the vices, swindles, slanders, libel . . .

LAWYER. My child, your shawl would not be big enough. Look at these walls! Isn't the wall-paper stained as if by every kind of sin? Look at these documents in which I write records of evil! Look at me! . . . Nobody who comes here ever smiles. Nothing but vile looks, bared teeth, clenched fists, and all of them squirt their malice, their envy, their suspicions over me. Look, my hands are black and can never be clean! See how cracked they are and bleeding! I can never wear my clothes for more than a few days because they stink of other people's crimes. Sometimes I have the place fumigated with sulphur, but that doesn't help. I sleep in the next room and dream of nothing but crime. I have a murder case in Court now—that's bad enough—but do you know what's worst of all? Separating husbands and wives. Then earth and heaven seem to cry aloud, to cry treason against primal power, the source of good, against love! And then, do you know, after reams of paper have been filled with mutual accusations, if some kindly person takes one or other of the couple aside and asks them in a friendly sort of way the simple question—"What have you really got against your husband—or your wife?"—then he, or she, stands speechless. They don't know. Oh, once it was something to do with a salad, another time about some word. Usually it's about nothing at all. But the suffering, the agony! All this I have to bear. Look at me! Do you think, marked as I am by crime, I can ever win a woman's love? Or that anyone wants to be the friend of a man who has to enforce payment of all the debts of the town? It's misery to be human.

DAUGHTER. Human life is pitiable!

LAWYER. It is indeed. And what people live on is a mystery to me. They marry with an income of two thousand crowns when they need four. They borrow, to be sure, they all borrow, and so scrape along somehow by the skin of their teeth until they die. Then the estate is always insolvent. Who has to pay up in the end? Tell me that.

DAUGHTER. He who feeds the birds.

LAWYER. Well, if He who feeds the birds would come down to earth and see the plight of the unfortunate children of men, perhaps He would have some compassion . . .

DAUGHTER. Human life is pitiful.

LAWYER. Yes, that's the truth. *To the* OFFICER. What do you want?

OFFICER. I only want to ask if Miss Victoria has gone.

LAWYER. No, she hasn't. You can rest assured of that. Why do you keep poking my cupboard?

OFFICER. I thought the door was so very like . . .

LAWYER. Oh, no, no, no!

Church bells ring.

OFFICER. Is there a funeral in the town?

LAWYER. No, it's Graduation—the conferring of Doctors' degrees. I myself am about to receive the degree of Doctor of Law. Perhaps you would like to graduate and receive a laurel wreath?

OFFICER. Why not? It would be a little distraction.

LAWYER. Then perhaps we should proceed at once to the solemn rites. But you must go and change.

Exit OFFICER.

The stage is blacked out and changes to the interior of the Church.

The barrier now serves as the chancel rail. The announcement-board shows the numbers of the hymns. The lime-tree hatstand has become a candelabra, the Lawyer's desk is the Chancellor's lectern, and the Clover-door leads to the vestry. The Chorus from Die Meistersinger are ushers with wands. The dancers carry the laurel wreaths. The rest of the people are the congregation.

The new background shows only a gigantic organ, with a mirror over the keyboard.

Music is heard. At the sides stand the four Deans of the Faculties—Philosophy, Theology, Medicine and Law.

For a moment there is no movement, then:

The USHERS *come forward from the right.**

*This scene follows exactly the normal ceremony in a Swedish university when Doctors' degrees are conferred. As each Graduate has the wreath put on his head, a gun

The DANCERS *follow, holding laurel wreaths in their outstretched hands.*

Three GRADUATES *come in from the left, are crowned in turn by the* DANCERS *and go out to the right.*

The LAWYER *advances to receive his wreath.*

The DANCERS *turn away, refusing to crown him, and go out.*

The LAWYER, *greatly agitated, leans against a pillar.*

Everyone disappears. The LAWYER *is alone.*

The DAUGHTER *enters with a white shawl over her head and shoulders.*

DAUGHTER. Look, I have washed the shawl. But what are you doing here? Didn't you get your laurels?

LAWYER. No. I was discredited.

DAUGHTER. Why? Because you have defended the poor, said a good word for the sinner, eased the burden of the guilty, obtained reprieve for the condemned? Woe to mankind! Men are not angels, but pitiable creatures.

LAWYER. Do not judge men harshly. It is my business to plead for them.

DAUGHTER, *leaning against the organ.* Why do they strike their friends in the face?

LAWYER. They know no better.

DAUGHTER. Let us enlighten them—you and I together. Will you?

LAWYER. There can be no enlightenment for them. Oh that the gods in heaven might hear our woe!

DAUGHTER. It shall reach the throne. *Sits at the organ.* Do you know what I see in this mirror? The world as it should be. For as it is it's wrong way up.

LAWYER. How did it come to be wrong way up?

DAUGHTER. When the copy was made.

---

outside is fired. The Chancellor and the Faculties bow. Then the new doctor bows to them.

One of the Graduates should be the Officer and another the Schoolmaster of the later scene.

LAWYER. Ah! You yourself have said it—the copy! I always felt this must be a poor copy, and when I began to remember its origin nothing satisfied me. Then they said I was cynical and had a jaundiced eye, and so forth.

DAUGHTER. It is a mad world. Consider these four Faculties. Organized society subsidizes all four: Theology, the doctrine of Divinity, continually attacked and ridiculed by Philosophy claiming wisdom for itself; and Medicine always giving the lie to Philosophy and discounting Theology as one of the sciences, calling it superstition. And there they sit together on the Council, whose function is to teach young men respect for the University. Yes, it's a madhouse. And woe to him who first recovers his senses!

LAWYER. The first to discover it are the theologians. For their preliminary studies they take Philosophy, which teaches them that Theology is nonsense, and then they learn from Theology that Philosophy is nonsense. Madness.

DAUGHTER. Then there's Law, serving all but its servants.

LAWYER. Justice, to the just unjust. Right so often wrong.

DAUGHTER. Thus you have made it, O Children of Men! Child, come! You shall have a wreath from me . . . one more fitting. *She puts a crown of thorns on his head.** Now I will play to you. *She sits at the organ and plays a Kyrie, but instead of the organ, voices are heard singing. The last note of each phrase is sustained.*

CHILDREN'S VOICES. Lord! Lord!

WOMEN'S VOICES. Be merciful!

MEN'S VOICES (*Tenor*). Deliver us for Thy mercy's sake.

MEN'S VOICES (*Bass*). Save Thy children, O Lord, and be not wrathful against us.

ALL. Be merciful! Hear us! Have compassion for mortals. Are we so far from Thee? Out of the depths we call. Grace, Lord! Let not the burden be too heavy for Thy children. Hear us! Hear us!

*In Molander's production, as the Daughter put the crown of thorns on the Lawyer's head he knelt, facing the audience, his arms outstretched in the form of a crucifix.

The stage darkens as the DAUGHTER *rises and approaches the* LAWYER.

By means of lighting the organ is changed to the wall of a grotto. The sea seeps in between basalt pillars with a harmony of waves and wind.

LAWYER. Where are we?

DAUGHTER. What do you hear?

LAWYER. I hear drops falling.

DAUGHTER. Those are the tears of mankind weeping. What more do you hear?

LAWYER. A sighing . . . a moaning . . . a wailing.

DAUGHTER. The lamentation of mortals has reached so far, no further. But why this endless lamentation? Is there no joy in life?

LAWYER. Yes. The sweetest which is also the bitterest—love! Marriage and a home. The highest and the lowest.

DAUGHTER. Let me put it to the test.

LAWYER. With me?

DAUGHTER. With you. You know the rocks, the stumbling stones. Let us avoid them.

LAWYER. I am poor.

DAUGHTER. Does that matter if we love one another? And a little beauty costs nothing.

LAWYER. My antipathies may be your sympathies.

DAUGHTER. They can be balanced.

LAWYER. Supposing we tire?

DAUGHTER. Children will come, bringing ever new interests.

LAWYER. You? You will take me, poor, ugly, despised, discredited?

DAUGHTER. Yes. Let us join our destinies.

LAWYER. So be it.

The scene changes to a very simple room adjoining the LAWYER'S *office. On the right is a large curtained double bed, close to it a window with double panes; on the left a stove and kitchen utensils.*

At the back an open door leads to the office, where a number of poor people can be seen awaiting admission. KRISTIN, *the maid, is pasting strips of paper along the edges of the inner window.*

The DAUGHTER, *pale and worn, is at the stove.*

KRISTIN. I paste, I paste.

DAUGHTER. You are shutting out the air. I am suffocating.

KRISTIN. Now there's only one small crack left.

DAUGHTER. Air, air! I cannot breathe.

KRISTIN. I paste, I paste.

LAWYER, *from the office.* That's right, Kristin. Warmth is precious.

KRISTIN *pastes the last crack.*

DAUGHTER. Oh, it's as if you are glueing up my mouth!

LAWYER, *coming to the doorway with a document in his hand.* Is the child asleep?

DAUGHTER. Yes, at last.

LAWYER, *mildly.* That screaming frightens away my clients.

DAUGHTER, *gently.* What can be done about it?

LAWYER. Nothing.

DAUGHTER. We must take a bigger flat.

LAWYER. We have no money.

DAUGHTER. May I open the window, please? This bad air is choking me.

LAWYER. Then the warmth would escape, and we should freeze.

DAUGHTER. It's horrible! Can't we at least scrub the place?

LAWYER. You can't scrub—neither can I, and Kristin must go on pasting. She must paste up the whole house, every crack in floor and walls and ceiling.

[*Exit*, KRISTIN, *delighted.*]

DAUGHTER. I was prepared for poverty, not dirt.

LAWYER. Poverty is always rather dirty.

DAUGHTER. This is worse than I dreamt.

LAWYER. We haven't had the worst. There's still food in the pot.

DAUGHTER. But what food!

LAWYER. Cabbage is cheap, nourishing and good.

DAUGHTER. For those who like cabbage. To me it's repulsive.

LAWYER. Why didn't you say so?

DAUGHTER. Because I loved you. I wanted to sacrifice my taste.

LAWYER. Now I must sacrifice my taste for cabbage. Sacrifices must be mutual.

DAUGHTER. Then what shall we eat? Fish? But you hate fish.

LAWYER. And it's dear.

DAUGHTER. This is harder than I believed.

LAWYER, *gently*. You see how hard it is. And the child which should be our bond and blessing is our undoing.

DAUGHTER. Dearest! I am dying in this air, in this room with its backyard view, with babies screaming through endless sleepless hours, and those people out there wailing and quarrelling and accusing . . . Here I can only die.

LAWYER. Poor little flower, without light, without air.

DAUGHTER. And you say there are others worse off.

LAWYER. I am one of the envied of the neighbourhood.

DAUGHTER. None of it would matter, if only I could have some beauty in our home.

LAWYER. I know what you're thinking of—a plant, a heliotrope to be exact; but that costs as much as six quarts of milk or half a bushel of potatoes.

DAUGHTER. I would gladly go without food to have my flower.

LAWYER. There is one kind of beauty that costs nothing. Not to have it in his home is sheer torture for a man with any sense of beauty.

DAUGHTER. What is that?

LAWYER. If I tell you, you will lose your temper.

DAUGHTER. We agreed never to lose our tempers.

LAWYER. We agreed. Yes. All will be well, Agnes, if we can avoid those sharp hard tones. You know them—no, not yet.

DAUGHTER. We shall never hear those.

LAWYER. Never, if it depends on me.

DAUGHTER. Now tell me.

LAWYER. Well, when I come into a house, first I look to see how the curtains are hung. *Goes to the window and adjusts the curtain.* If they hang like a bit of string or rag, I soon leave. Then I glance at the chairs. If they are in their places, I stay. *Puts a chair straight against the wall.* Next I look at the candlesticks. If the candles are crooked, then the whole house is askew. *Straightens a candle on the bureau.* That you see, my dear, is the beauty which costs nothing.

DAUGHTER, *bowing her head.* Not that sharp tone, Axel!

LAWYER. It wasn't sharp.

DAUGHTER. Yes it was.

LAWYER. The devil take it!

DAUGHTER. What kind of language is that?

LAWYER. Forgive me, Agnes. But I have suffered as much from your untidiness as you do from the dirt. And I haven't dared straighten things myself, because you would have been offended and thought I was reproaching you. Oh, shall we stop this?

DAUGHTER. It is terribly hard to be married, harder than anything. I think one has to be an angel.

LAWYER. I think one has.

DAUGHTER. I am beginning to hate you after all this.

LAWYER. Alas for us then! But let us prevent hatred. I promise never to mention untidiness again, although it is torture to me.

DAUGHTER. And I will eat cabbage, although that is torment to me.

LAWYER. And so—life together is a torment. One's pleasure is the other's pain.

DAUGHTER. Human beings are pitiful.

LAWYER. You see that now?

DAUGHTER. Yes. But in God's name let us avoid the rocks, now that we know them so well.

LAWYER. Let us do that. We are tolerant, enlightened people. Of course we can make allowances and forgive.

DAUGHTER. Of course we can smile at trifles.

LAWYER. We, only we can do it. Do you know, I read in the paper this morning . . . By the way, where is the paper?

DAUGHTER, *embarrassed.* Which paper?

LAWYER, *harshly.* Do I take more than one newspaper?

DAUGHTER. Smile—and don't speak harshly! I lit the fire with your newspaper.

LAWYER, *violently.* The devil you did!

DAUGHTER. Please smile. I burnt it because it mocked what to me is holy.

LAWYER. What to me is unholy! Huh! *Striking his hands together, beside himself.* I'll smile, I'll smile till my back teeth show. I'll be tolerant and swallow my opinions and say yes to everything and cant and cringe. So you've burnt my paper, have you? *Pulls the bed curtains.* Very well. Now I'm going to tidy up until you lose your temper . . . Agnes, this is quite impossible!

DAUGHTER. Indeed it is.

LAWYER. Yet we must stay together. Not for our vows' sake, but for the child's.

DAUGHTER. That's true—for the child's sake. Yes, yes, we must go on.

LAWYER. And now I must attend to my clients. Listen to them muttering. They can't wait to tear one another to pieces, to get each other fined and imprisoned. Benighted souls!

Enter KRISTIN *with pasting materials.*

DAUGHTER. Wretched, wretched beings! And all this pasting! *She bows her head in dumb despair.*

KRISTIN. I paste, I paste!

The LAWYER *standing by the door, nervously fingers the handle.*

DAUGHTER. Oh how that handle squeaks! It is as if you were twisting my heart-strings.

LAWYER. I twist, I twist!

DAUGHTER. Don't!

LAWYER. I twist . . .

DAUGHTER. No!

LAWYER. I . . .

The OFFICER *[now middle-aged] takes hold of the handle from inside the office.*

OFFICER. May I?

LAWYER, *letting go of the handle.* Certainly. As you have got your degree.

OFFICER, *entering.* The whole of life is now mine. All paths are open to me. I have set foot on Parnassus, the laurels are won. Immortality, fame, all are mine!

LAWYER. What are you going to live on?

OFFICER. Live on?

LAWYER. You'll need a roof surely, and clothes and food?

OFFICER. Those are always to be had, as long as there's someone who cares for you.

LAWYER. Fancy that now, fancy that! Paste, Kristin, paste! Until they cannot breathe. *Goes out backwards, nodding.*

KRISTIN. I paste, I paste! Until they cannot breathe.

OFFICER. Will you come now?

DAUGHTER. Oh quickly! But where to?

OFFICER. To Fairhaven, where it is summer and the sun is shining. Youth is there, children and flowers, singing and dancing, feasting and merrymaking.

[*Exit* KRISTIN.]

DAUGHTER. I would like to go there.

OFFICER. Come!

LAWYER, *entering.* Now I shall return to my first hell. This one was the second—and worst. The sweetest hell is the worst. Look, she's left hairpins all over the floor again! *Picks one up.*

OFFICER. So he has discovered the hairpins too.

LAWYER. Too? Look at this one. There are two prongs but one pin. Two and yet one. If I straighten it out, it becomes one single piece. If I bend it, it is two, without ceasing to be one. In other words the two are one. But if I break it—like this—*breaks it in half*—then the two are two. *He throws away the pieces.*

OFFICER. So much he has seen. But before one can break it, the prongs must diverge. If they converge, it holds.

LAWYER. And if they are parallel, they never meet. Then it neither holds nor breaks.

OFFICER. The hairpin is the most perfect of all created things. A straight line which is yet two parallel lines.

LAWYER. A lock that closes when open.

OFFICER. Closes open—a plait of hair loosed while bound.

LAWYER. Like this door. When I close it, I open the way out, for you, Agnes.

Goes out, closing the door.

DAUGHTER. And now?

The scene changes. The bed with its hangings is transformed into a tent, the stove remaining. The new background shows a beautiful wooded shore, with beflagged landing stages and white boats, some with sails set. Among the trees are little Italianesque villas, pavilions, kiosks and marble statues.

In the middle distance is a strait.

The foreground presents a sharp contrast with the background. Burnt hillsides, black and white tree stumps as after a forest fire, red heather, red pigsties and outhouses. On the right is an open-air establishment for remedial exercises, where people are being treated on machines resembling instruments of torture.

On the left is part of the Quarantine Station; open sheds with furnaces, boilers and pipes.

[*The* DAUGHTER *and the* OFFICER *are standing as at the end of the previous scene.*]

The QUARANTINE MASTER, *dressed as a blackamoor, comes along the shore.*

OFFICER, *going up and shaking hands with the* QUARANTINE MASTER. What? You here, old Gasbags?*

Q. MASTER. Yes, I'm here.

OFFICER. Is this place Fairhaven?

Q. MASTER. No, that's over there. [*Points across the strait.*] This is Foulstrand.

OFFICER. Then we've come wrong.

Q. MASTER. We! Aren't you going to introduce me?

OFFICER. It wouldn't do. *Low.* That is the Daughter of Indra.

Q. MASTER. Of Indra? I thought it must be Varuna himself. Well, aren't you surprised to find me black in the face?

OFFICER. My dear fellow, I am over fifty, at which age one ceases to be surprised. I assumed at once that you were going to a fancy dress ball this afternoon.

Q. MASTER. Quite correct. I hope you'll come with me.

OFFICER. Certainly, for there doesn't seem to be any attraction in this place. What kind of people live here?

Q. MASTER. The sick live here, and the healthy over there.

OFFICER. But surely only the poor here?

Q. MASTER. No, my boy, here you have the rich. [*Indicates the gymnasium.*] Look at that man on the rack. He's eaten too much pâté-de-foie-gras with truffles, and drunk so much Burgundy that his feet are knotted.

OFFICER. Knotted?

Q. MASTER. He's got knotted feet, and that one lying on the guillotine has drunk so much brandy that his backbone's got to be mangled.

OFFICER. That's not very pleasant either.

Q. MASTER. What's more here on this side live all those who have some misery to hide. Look at this one coming now, for instance.

An elderly fop is wheeled on to the stage in a bath chair, accompanied by a gaunt and hideous coquette of sixty, dressed in the latest fashion and attended by the "Friend," a man of forty.

*Original "Ordström," meaning "Stream of Words."

OFFICER. It's the Major! Our schoolfellow.

Q. MASTER. Don Juan! You see, he's still in love with the spectre at his side. He doesn't see that she has grown old, that she is ugly, faithless, cruel.

OFFICER. There's true love for you. I never would have thought that flighty fellow had it in him to love so deeply and ardently.

Q. MASTER. That's a nice way of looking at it.

OFFICER. I've been in love myself—with Victoria. As a matter of fact I still pace up and down the alley, waiting for her.

Q. MASTER. So you're the fellow who waits in the alley?

OFFICER. I am he.

Q. MASTER. Well, have you got that door open yet?

OFFICER. No, we're still fighting the case. The Billsticker is out with his fishnet, you see, which delays the taking of evidence. Meanwhile, the Glazier has put in window-panes at the castle, which has grown half a story. It has been an unusually good year this year—warm and damp.

Q. MASTER, *pointing to the sheds.* But you've certainly had nothing like the heat of my place there.

OFFICER. What's the temperature of your furnaces then?

Q. MASTER. When we're disinfecting cholera suspects, we keep them at sixty degrees.

OFFICER. But is there cholera about again?

Q. MASTER. Didn't you know?

OFFICER. Of course I know. But I so often forget what I know.

Q. MASTER. And I so often wish I could forget—especially myself. That's why I go in for masquerades, fancy dress, theatricals.

OFFICER. Why. What's the matter with you?

Q. MASTER. If I talk, they say I'm bragging. If I hold my tongue they call me a hypocrite.

OFFICER. Is that why you blacked your face?

Q. MASTER. Yes. A shade blacker than I am.

OFFICER. Who's this coming?

Q. MASTER. Oh, he's a poet! He's going to have his mud bath.

The POET *enters, looking at the sky and carrying a pail of mud.*

OFFICER. But, good heavens, he ought to bathe in light and air!

Q. MASTER. No, he lives so much in the higher spheres that he gets homesick for the mud. It hardens his skin to wallow in the mire, just as it does with pigs. After his bath he doesn't feel the gadflies stinging.

OFFICER. What a strange world of contradictions!

POET, *ecstatically.* Out of clay the god Ptah fashioned man on a potter's wheel, a lathe, *mockingly,* or some other damned thing . . . *Ecstatically.* Out of clay the sculptor fashions his more or less immortal masterpieces, *mockingly,* which are usually only rubbish. *Ecstatically.* Out of clay are formed those objects, so domestically essential bearing the generic name of pots and pans. *Mockingly.* Not that it matters in the least to me what they're called. *Ecstatically.* Such is clay! When clay is fluid, it is called mud. *C'est mon affaire! Calls.* Lina!

Enter LINA *with a bucket.*

POET. Lina, show yourself to Miss Agnes. She knew you ten years ago when you were a young, happy, and, let me add, pretty girl. *To* DAUGHTER. Look at her now! Five children, drudgery, squalling, hunger, blows. See how beauty has perished, how joy has vanished in the fulfilment of duties which should give that inner contentment which shows in the harmonious lines of a face, in the tranquil shining of the eyes . . .

Q. MASTER, *putting a hand to the* POET'*s lips.* Shut up! Shut up!

POET. That's what they all say. But if you are silent, they tell you to talk. How inconsistent people are!

Distant dance music is heard.

DAUGHTER, *going up to* LINA. Tell me your troubles.

LINA. No, I daren't. I'd catch it all the worse if I did.

DAUGHTER. Who is so cruel?

LINA. I daren't talk about it. I'll be beaten.

POET. May be, but I shall talk about it even if the Blackamoor knocks my teeth out. I shall talk about all the injustice there is here. Agnes, Daughter of the Gods, do you hear that music up on the hill? Well, that's a dance for Lina's sister, who has come home from town—where she went astray, you understand. Now they are killing the fatted calf, while Lina, who stayed at home, has to carry the swill pail and feed the pigs.

DAUGHTER. There is rejoicing in that home because the wanderer has forsaken the path of evil, not only because she has come home. Remember that.

POET. Then give a ball and a supper every evening for this blameless servant who has never gone astray. Do that for her—they never do. On the contrary, when Lina is free, she has to go to prayer meetings where she's reprimanded for not being perfect. Is that justice?

DAUGHTER. Your questions are difficult to answer, because there are so many unknown factors.

POET. The Caliph, Harun the Just, was of the same opinion. Sitting quietly on his exalted throne he could never see how those below were faring. Presently complaints reached his lofty ear, so one fine day he stepped down in disguise and walked unobserved among the crowd to watch the workings of justice.

DAUGHTER. You do not think I am Harun the Just, do you?

OFFICER. Let's change the subject. Here are newcomers.

A white boat, shaped like a dragon, glides into the Strait. It has a light blue silken sail on a gilded yard, and a golden mast with a rose-red pennon. At the helm, with their arms round each other's waists, sit HE *and* SHE.

There you see perfect happiness, utter bliss, the ecstasy of young love.

The light grows stronger. HE *stands up in the boat and sings.*

HE. *Hail fairest bay!*
Where I passed youth's spring tide,
where I dreamed its first roses,
I come now again,
no longer alone.
Forests and havens,
heaven and sea,
greet her!
My love, my bride,
my sun, my life!

The flags on Fairhaven dip in salute. White handkerchiefs wave from villas and shores. The music of harps and violins sound over the strait.

POET. See how light streams from them! And sound rings across the water! Eros!

OFFICER. It is Victoria.

Q. MASTER. Well, if it is . . .

OFFICER. It is his Victoria. I have my own, and mine no one will ever see. Now hoist the quarantine flag while I haul in the catch.

The QUARANTINE MASTER *waves a yellow flag. The* OFFICER *pulls on a line which causes the boat to turn in towards Foulstrand.*

Hold hard there!

HE *and* SHE *become aware of the dreadful landscape and show their horror.*

Q. MASTER. Yes, yes, it's hard lines, but everyone has to land here, everyone coming from infectious areas.

POET. Think of being able to speak like that—to behave like that when you see two human beings joined in love. Do not touch them! Do not lay hands on love—that is high treason. Alas, alas! All that is most lovely will now be dragged down, down into the mud.

HE *and* SHE *come ashore, shamed and sad.*

HE. What is it? What have we done?*

*Literally "woe to us."

Q. MASTER. You don't have to do anything in order to meet with life's little discomforts.

SHE. How brief are joy and happiness!

HE. How long must we stay here?

Q. MASTER. Forty days and forty nights.

SHE. We would rather throw ourselves into the sea.

HE. Live here—among burnt hills and pigsties?

POET. Love can overcome everything, even sulphur fumes and carbolic acid.*

The QUARANTINE MASTER *goes into a shed. Blue sulphurous vapour pours out.*

Q. MASTER [*coming out*]. I'm burning the sulphur. Will you kindly step inside.

SHE. Oh, my blue dress will lose its colour!

Q. MASTER. And turn white. Your red roses will turn white too.

HE. So will your cheeks, in forty days.

SHE, *to the* OFFICER. That will please you.

OFFICER. No, it won't. True, your happiness was the source of my misery, but . . . that's no matter. [HE *and* SHE *go into the shed.*] [*To* DAUGHTER.] I've got my degree now, and a job as tutor over there. [*Indicates Fairhaven.*] Heigho! And in the fall I'll get a post in a school, teaching the boys the same lessons I learnt myself, all through my childhood, all through my youth. Teach them the same lessons I learnt all through my manhood and finally all through my old age. The same lessons! What is twice two? How many times does two go into four without remainder? Until I get a pension and have nothing to do but wait for meals and the newspapers, until in the end I'm carried out to the crematorium and burnt to ashes.

To QUARANTINE MASTER *as he comes out of the shed.*

Have you no pensioners here? To be a pensioner is the worst fate after twice two is four, going to school again

*The Poet does not speak again and is not mentioned until the end of the later quayside scene, so perhaps here he goes out.

when one's taken one's degree, asking the same questions until one dies . . .

An elderly man walks past with his hands behind his back.

Look, there goes a pensioner waiting for his life to ebb. A Captain, probably, who failed to become a Major, or a Clerk to the Court who was never promoted. Many are called, but few are chosen. He's just walking about, waiting for breakfast.

PENSIONER. No, for the paper, the morning paper!

OFFICER. And he is only fifty-four. He may go on for another twenty-five years, waiting for meals and the newspaper. Isn't that dreadful?

PENSIONER. What is not dreadful? Tell me that. Tell me that.

OFFICER. Yes. Let him tell who can.

Exit PENSIONER.

Now I shall teach boys twice two is four. How many times does two go into four without remainder? *He clutches his head in despair.*

Enter HE *and* SHE *from the shed. Her dress and roses are white, her face pale. His clothes are also bleached.*

And Victoria whom I loved, for whom I desired the greatest happiness on earth, she has her happiness now, the greatest happiness she can know, while I suffer, suffer, suffer!

SHE. Do you think I can be happy, seeing your suffering? How can you believe that? Perhaps it comforts you to know that I shall be a prisoner here for forty days and forty nights. Tell me, does it comfort you?

OFFICER. Yes and no. I cannot have pleasure while you have pain. Oh!

HE. And do you think my happiness can be built on your agony?

OFFICER. We are all to be pitied—all of us.

All lift their hands to heaven. A discordant cry of anguish breaks from their lips.

ALL. Oh!

DAUGHTER. O God, hear them! Life is evil! Mankind is to be pitied.

ALL, *as before.* Oh!

The stage is blacked out and the scene changes.
The whole landscape is in winter dress with snow on the ground and on the leafless trees. Foulstrand is in the background, in shadow.
The strait is still in the middle distance. On the near side is a landing stage with white boats and flags flying from flagstaffs. In the strait a white warship, a brig with gunports, is anchored.
The foreground presents Fairhaven, in full light.
On the right is a corner of the Assembly Rooms with open windows through which are seen couples dancing. On a box outside stand three MAIDS, *their arms round each other's waists, watching the dancing.*
On the steps is a bench on which UGLY EDITH *is sitting, bareheaded and sorrowful, with long dishevelled hair, before an open piano.*
On the left is a yellow wooden house outside which two children in summer dresses are playing ball.
The DAUGHTER *and* OFFICER *enter.*

DAUGHTER. Here is peace and happiness. Holiday time. Work over, every day a festival, everyone in holiday attire. Music and dancing even in the morning. *To the* MAIDS. Why don't you go in and dance, my dears?

SERVANTS. Us?

OFFICER. But they are servants.

DAUGHTER. True. But why is Edith sitting there instead of dancing?

EDITH *buries her face in her hands.*

OFFICER. Don't ask her! She has been sitting there for three hours without being invited to dance. *He goes into the yellow house.*

DAUGHTER. What cruel pleasure!

The MOTHER, *in a décolleté dress, comes out of the Assembly Rooms and goes up to* EDITH.

MOTHER. Why don't you go in as I told you?

EDITH. Because . . . because I can't be my own partner. I know I'm ugly and no one wants to dance with me, but I can avoid being reminded of it. *She begins to play Bach's Toccata con Fuga, No. 10.*

The waltz at the ball is heard too, first faintly, then growing louder as if in competition with the Toccata. Gradually EDITH *overcomes it and reduces it to silence. Dance couples appear in the doorway, and everyone stands reverently listening.*

A NAVAL OFFICER *seizes* ALICE, *one of the guests, by the waist.*

N. OFFICER. Come, quick! *He leads her down to the landing stage.* EDITH *breaks off, rises and watches them in despair. She remains standing as if turned to stone.*

The front wall of the yellow house vanishes. Boys are sitting on forms, among them the OFFICER *looking uncomfortable and worried. In front of them stands the* SCHOOLMASTER, *wearing spectacles and holding chalk and a cane.*

SCHOOLMASTER, *to the* OFFICER. Now, my boy, can you tell me what twice two is?

The OFFICER *remains seated, painfully searching his memory without finding an answer.*

You must stand up when you are asked a question.

OFFICER, *rising anxiously.* Twice two . . . let me see . . . That makes two twos.

S. MASTER. Aha! So you have not prepared your lesson.

OFFICER, *embarrassed.* Yes, I have, but . . . I know what it is, but I can't say it.

S. MASTER. You're quibbling. You know the answer, do you? But you can't say it. Perhaps I can assist you. *Pulls the* OFFICER's *hair.*

OFFICER. Oh, this is dreadful, really dreadful!

S. MASTER. Yes, it is dreadful that such a big boy should have no ambition.

OFFICER, *agonised.* A *big* boy. Yes, I certainly am big, much bigger than these others. I am grown up, I have left school . . . *As if waking.* I have even graduated. Why am I sitting here then? Haven't I got my degree?

S. MASTER. Certainly. But you have got to stay here and mature. Do you see? You must mature. Isn't that so?

OFFICER, *clasping his head.* Yes, that's so, one must mature . . . Twice two—is two, and this I will demonstrate by analogy, the highest form of proof. Listen! Once one is one, therefore twice two is two. For that which applies to the one must also apply to the other.

S. MASTER. The proof is perfectly in accord with the laws of logic, but the answer is wrong.

OFFICER. What is in accord with the laws of logic cannot be wrong. Let us put it to the test. One into one goes once, therefore two into two goes twice.

S. MASTER. Quite correct according to analogy. But what then is once three?

OFFICER. It is three.

S. MASTER. Consequently twice three is also three.

OFFICER, *pondering.* No, that can't be right . . . It can't be, for if so . . . *Sits down in despair.* No, I am not mature yet . . .

S. MASTER. No, you are not mature by a long way.

OFFICER. Then how long shall I have to stay here?

S. MASTER. How long? Here? You believe that time and space exist? Assuming time does exist, you ought to be able to say what time is. What is time?

OFFICER. Time . . . *Considers.* I can't say, although I know what it is. Ergo, I may know what twice two is without being able to say it. Can you yourself say what time is?

S. MASTER. Certainly I can.

ALL THE BOYS. Tell us then!

S. MASTER. Time? . . . Let me see. *Stands motionless with his finger to his nose.* While we speak, time flies. Consequently time is something which flies while I am speaking.

BOY, *rising*. You're speaking now, sir, and while you're speaking, I fly. Consequently I am time. *Flies.*

S. MASTER. That is quite correct according to the laws of logic.

OFFICER. Then the laws of logic are absurd, for Nils, though he did fly, can't be time.

S. MASTER. That is also quite correct according to the laws of logic, although it is absurd.

OFFICER. Then logic is absurd.

S. MASTER. It really looks like it. But if logic is absurd, then the whole world is absurd . . . and I'll be damned if I stay here and teach you absurdities! If anyone will stand us a drink, we'll go and bathe.

OFFICER. That's a *posterus prius*, a world back to front, for it's customary to bathe first and have one's drink afterwards. You old fossil!

S. MASTER. Don't be so conceited, Doctor.

OFFICER. Captain, if you please. I am an officer, and I don't understand why I should sit here among a lot of schoolboys and be insulted.

S. MASTER, *wagging his finger*. We must mature!

Enter QUARANTINE MASTER.

Q. MASTER. The quarantine period has begun.

OFFICER. So there you are. Fancy this fellow making me sit here on a form, when I've taken my degree.

Q. MASTER. Well, why don't you go away?

OFFICER. Go away? That's easier said than done.

S. MASTER. So I should think. Try!

OFFICER, *to* QUARANTINE MASTER. Save me! Save me from his eyes!

Q. MASTER. Come on then! Come and help us dance. We must dance before the plague breaks out. We must.

OFFICER. Will the ship sail then?

Q. MASTER. The ship will sail first. A lot of tears will be shed of course.

OFFICER. Always tears; when she comes in and when she sails. Let's go.

They go out. The SCHOOLMASTER *continues to give his lesson in mime.*

The MAIDS, *who were standing at the window of the ballroom, walk sadly down to the quay.* EDITH, *until then motionless beside the piano, follows them.*

DAUGHTER, *to* OFFICER. Isn't there one happy person in this paradise?

OFFICER. Yes, here comes a newly wed couple. Listen to them.

The NEWLY WED COUPLE *enter.*

HUSBAND, *to* WIFE. My happiness is so complete that I wish to die.

WIFE. But why to die?

HUSBAND. In the midst of happiness grows a seed of unhappiness. Happiness consumes itself like a flame. It cannot burn for ever, it must go out, and the presentiment of its end destroys it at its very peak.

WIFE. Let us die together, now at once.

HUSBAND. Die! Yes, let us die. For I fear happiness, the deceiver.

They go towards the sea and disappear.

DAUGHTER, *to the* OFFICER. Life is evil. Human beings are to be pitied!

OFFICER. Look who's coming now. This is the most envied mortal in the place. *The* BLIND MAN *is led in.* He is the owner of these hundreds of Italian villas. He owns all these bays and creeks and shores and woods, the fish in the water, the birds in the air and the game in the woods. These thousands of people are his tenants, and the sun rises over his sea and sets over his lands.

DAUGHTER. And does he complain too?

OFFICER. Yes, with good cause, as he cannot see.

Q. MASTER. He is blind.

DAUGHTER. The most envied of all!

OFFICER. Now he's going to see the ship sail with his son aboard.

BLIND MAN. I do not see, but I hear. I hear the fluke of the anchor tearing the clay bed, just as when the hook is dragged out of a fish and the heart comes up too through the gullet. My son, my only child, is going to journey to strange lands across the great sea. Only my thoughts can go with him . . . Now I hear the chain clanking . . . and there's something flapping and lashing like washing on a clothes line . . . Wet handkerchiefs perhaps . . . And I hear a sound of sighing . . . or sobbing . . . like people crying . . . Maybe the plash of small waves against the hull, or maybe the girls on the quay, the abandoned, the inconsolable. I once asked a child why the sea was salt, and the child, whose father was on a long voyage, replied at once: "The sea is salt because sailors cry so much." "But why do sailors cry so much?" "Well," he said, "because they keep going away . . . And so they're always drying their handkerchiefs up on the masts." "And why do people cry when they're sad?" I asked. "Oh," said he, "that's because the eye window must be washed sometimes, so we can see better."

*The brig has set sail and glided away. The girls on the quay alternately wave their handkerchiefs and dry their eyes. Now on the topmast is hoisted the signal "*YES,*" a red ball on a white ground.* ALICE *waves a triumphant reply.*

DAUGHTER, *to* OFFICER. What does that flag mean?

OFFICER. It means "yes." It is the lieutenant's "yes" in red, red as heart's blood, written on the blue cloth of the sky.

DAUGHTER. Then what is "no" like?

OFFICER. Blue as tainted blood in blue veins. Look how elated Alice is.

DAUGHTER. And how Edith is weeping.

BLIND MAN. Meeting and parting, parting and meeting. That's life. I met his mother, then she went away. My son was left; now he has gone.

DAUGHTER. But he will come back.

BLIND MAN. Who is speaking to me? I have heard that voice before. In my dreams, in boyhood when summer holidays began, in early married life when my child was born. Whenever life smiled, I heard that voice, like the whisper of the South wind, like the sounds of a heavenly harp, like the angels' greeting, as I imagine it, on Christmas Eve.

The LAWYER *enters, goes up to the* BLIND MAN *and whispers.*

Really?

LAWYER. Yes, it's a fact. *Goes across to the* DAUGHTER. You have seen most things now, but you have not yet experienced the worst thing of all.

DAUGHTER. What can that be?

LAWYER. Repetitions, reiterations. Going back. Doing one's lessons again . . . Come!

DAUGHTER. Where to?

LAWYER. To your duties.

DAUGHTER. What are they?

LAWYER. Everything you abominate. Everything you least want to do, and yet must. They are to abstain and renounce, to go without, to leave behind. They are everything that is disagreeable, repulsive, painful.

DAUGHTER. Are there no pleasant duties?

LAWYER. They become pleasant when they are done.

DAUGHTER. When they no longer exist. So duty is altogether unpleasant. What then can one enjoy?

LAWYER. What one enjoys is sin.

DAUGHTER. Sin?

LAWYER. Which is punished. Yes. If I enjoy myself one day, one evening, the next day I have a bad conscience and go through the torments of hell.

DAUGHTER. How strange!

LAWYER. I wake in the morning with a headache, and then the repetition begins, but it is a distorted repetition, so that everything which was charming and witty and beautiful the night before appears in memory ugly, stupid, repulsive. Pleasure stinks, and enjoyment falls to pieces. What people call success is always a step towards the next failure. The successes in my life have been my downfall. Men have an instinctive dread of another's good fortune. They feel it's unjust that fate should favour any one man, so try to restore the balance by rolling boulders across his path. To have talent is to be in danger of one's life—one may so easily starve to death. However, you must go back to your duties, or I shall take proceedings against you, and we shall go through all three Courts, first, second, third.

DAUGHTER. Go back? To the stove and the cabbage and the baby clothes?

LAWYER. Yes. And it's washing day—the big wash when all the handkerchiefs have to be done.

DAUGHTER. Oh, must I do that again?

LAWYER. The whole of life is only repetition. Look at the schoolmaster there. Yesterday he took his doctor's degree, was crowned with laurels, scaled Parnassus, was embraced by the monarch. Today he is back at school, asking what twice two is . . . and that's what he will go on doing until he dies. But come now, back to your home.

DAUGHTER. I would rather die.

LAWYER. Die? One can't do that. To begin with taking one's own life is so dishonourable that even one's corpse is dishonoured. And to add to that one is damned, for it is a mortal sin.

DAUGHTER. It is not easy to be human.

ALL. Hear, hear!

DAUGHTER. I will not go back with you to humiliation and dirt. I shall return to the place from which I came. But first the door must be opened, so that I may know the secret. I wish the door to be opened.

Enter the POET.

LAWYER. Then you must retrace your steps, go back the way you came, and put up with all the horrors of a lawsuit; the repetitions, the redraftings, the reiterations.

DAUGHTER. So be it. But first I shall seek solitude in the wilderness to find myself. We shall meet again. *To the* POET. Come with me.

A distant cry of lamentation rises.

VOICES. Oh! oh! oh!

DAUGHTER. What was that?

LAWYER. The doomed at Foulstrand.

DAUGHTER. Why do they wail so today?

LAWYER. Because here the sun is shining, here is music and dance and youth. This makes them suffer more.

DAUGHTER. We must set them free.

LAWYER. Try! Once a deliverer came, but he was hanged upon a cross.

DAUGHTER. By whom?

LAWYER. By all the righteous.

DAUGHTER. Who are they?

LAWYER. Don't you know the righteous? Well, you will.

DAUGHTER. Was it they who refused you your degree?

LAWYER. Yes.

DAUGHTER. Then I do know them.

The scene changes to a Mediterranean resort. In the background are villas, a Casino with a terrace, and a blue strip of sea. In the foreground is a white wall over which hang branches of orange trees in fruit. Below this to one side a huge heap of coal and two wheel barrows.

The DAUGHTER *and the* LAWYER *come on to the terrace.*

DAUGHTER. This is paradise.

1ST. COAL HEAVER. This is hell.

2ND. C. H. A hundred and twenty in the shade.

1ST. C. H. Shall we get into the sea?

2ND. C. H. Then the police'd come: "You mustn't bathe here!"

1ST. C. H. Can't we have a bit of fruit off that tree?

2ND. C. H. No. The police would come.

1ST. C. H. One can't work in this heat. I'm going to chuck it.

2ND. C. H. Then the police will come and take you up. *Pause.* Besides, you'll have nothing to eat.

1ST. C. H. Nothing to eat! We, who do the most work, get the least food. And the rich, who do nothing, get it all. Might one not, without taking liberties with the truth, call this unjust? What has the Daughter of the Gods up there to say about it?

DAUGHTER. I have no answer. But, tell me, what have you done to get so black and have so hard a lot?

1ST. C. H. What have we done? Got ourselves born of poor and pretty bad parents. Been sentenced a couple of times maybe.

DAUGHTER. Sentenced?

1ST. C. H. Yes. The ones that don't get caught sit up there in the Casino eating eight course dinners with wine.

DAUGHTER, *to* LAWYER. Can this be true?

LAWYER. More or less, yes.

DAUGHTER. Do you mean that everyone at some time or other deserves imprisonment?

LAWYER. Yes.

DAUGHTER. Even you?

LAWYER. Yes.

DAUGHTER. Is it true those poor men aren't allowed to bathe in that sea?

LAWYER. No, not even with their clothes on. Only those who try to drown themselves avoid paying. And they are more than likely to get beaten up at the police station.

DAUGHTER. Can't they go and bathe outside the town—in the country?

LAWYER. There is no country. It's all fenced in.

DAUGHTER. I mean where it is open and free.

LAWYER. Nothing is free. Everything is owned.

DAUGHTER. Even the sea, the vast, wide . . . ?

LAWYER. Everything. You can't go out in a boat, nor can you land, without it all being booked and paid for. It's marvellous.

DAUGHTER. This is not paradise.

LAWYER. I promise you that.

DAUGHTER. Why don't people do anything to improve conditions?

LAWYER. They certainly do. But all reformers end in prison or the madhouse.

DAUGHTER. Who puts them in prison?

LAWYER. All the righteous, all the respectable.

DAUGHTER. Who puts them in the madhouse?

LAWYER. Their own despair when they see the hopelessness of the struggle.

DAUGHTER. Has it occurred to anyone that there may be unknown reasons for this state of things?

LAWYER. Yes, the well-off always think that is so.

DAUGHTER. That there is nothing wrong with things as they are?

1ST. C. H. And yet we are the foundation of society. If there's no coal, the kitchen stove goes out and the fire on the hearth too. The machines in the factory stop working; the lights in streets and shops and homes all go out. Darkness and cold descend on you. That's why we sweat like hell carrying filthy coal. What do you give us in return?

LAWYER, *to* DAUGHTER. Help them. *Pause.* I know things can't be exactly the same for everybody, but why should there be such inequality?

The GENTLEMAN *and the* LADY *cross the terrace.*

LADY. Are you coming to play cards?

GENTLEMAN. No, I must go for a little walk to get an appetite for dinner.

Exeunt.

1ST. C. H. To *get* an appetite!

2ND. C. H. To *get* . . . !

Children enter. When they catch sight of the black workers they scream with terror [*and run off*].

1ST. C. H. They scream when they see us. They scream!

2ND. C. H. Curse it! We'd better get out the scaffolds soon and execute this rotten body.

1ST. C. H. Curse it, I say too!

LAWYER, *to* DAUGHTER. It's all wrong. It's not the people who are so bad, but . . .

DAUGHTER. But?

LAWYER. The system.

DAUGHTER, *hiding her face in her hands.* This is not paradise.

1ST. C. H. No. This is hell, pure hell.

The scene changes to [the earlier set of] Fingal's Cave. Long green billows roll gently into the cave. A red bell-buoy rocks upon the waves, but gives no sound until later. Music of the winds. Music of the waves.

The DAUGHTER *is with the* POET.

POET. Where have you brought me?

DAUGHTER. Far from the murmur and wailing of the children of men. To this grotto at the ends of the oceans to which we give the name *Indra's Ear,* for here, it is said, the King of Heaven listens to the lamentations of mortals.

POET. Why here?

DAUGHTER. Do you not see that this cave is shaped like a shell? Yes, you see it. Do you not know that your ear is shaped like a shell? You know, but you have given it no thought. *She picks up a shell.* As a child, did you never hold a shell to your ear and listen to the whisper of your heart's blood, to the humming of thoughts in your brain, to the parting of a thousand little worn-out tissues in the fabric of your body? All this you can hear in a small shell. Think then what may be heard in this great one.

POET, *listening.* I hear nothing but the sighing of the wind.

DAUGHTER. Then I will be its interpreter. Listen to the lamentation of the winds. *She speaks to soft music.*

Born under heaven's clouds,
chased were we by Indra's fires
down to the crust of earth.
The mould of acres soiled our feet,

we had to bear
the dust of roads and city smoke,
the kitchen's reek and fumes of wine.
Out to these spacious seas we blew,
to air our lungs,
to shake our wings
and bathe our feet.
Indra, Lord of Heaven,
hear us!
Listen to our sighing!
Earth is not clean,
life is not just,
men are not evil
nor are they good.
They live as best they may
from one day to another,
Sons of dust in dust they walk,
born of the dust,
dust they become.
Feet they have to trudge,
no wings.
Dust-soiled they grow.
Is the fault theirs
or Thine?

POET. So I heard once . . .

DAUGHTER. Hush! The winds are still singing.
Continues to soft music.

We, the winds, the sons of air,
bear man's lamentation.
Thou hast heard us
on autumn eves in the chimney stack,
in the stove-pipe's vent,
in the window cracks,
as the rain wept on the tiles.
Or on winter nights,
mid the pine-wood's snows,
or on the stormy ocean,
hast heard the moaning and the whine,

of rope and sail.
That is us, the winds,
the sons of air,
who from human breasts
we pierced ourselves,
these sounds of suffering learnt.
In sickroom, on the battlefield,
and most where the newborn lie,
screaming, complaining,
of the pain of being alive.
It is we, we, the winds
who whine and whistle,
woe! woe! woe!

POET. It seems to me that once before . . .

DAUGHTER. Hush! The waves are singing.
Speaks to soft music.

It is we, we the waves,
that rock the winds
to rest.
Green cradling waves,
wet are we and salt.
Like flames of fire,
wet flames we are.
Quenching, burning,
cleansing, bathing,
generating, multiplying.
We, we the waves,
that rock the winds
to rest.

False waves and faithless. Everything on earth that is not burned is drowned by those waves. Look there! *She points to the wreckage.* Look what the sea has stolen and destroyed! All that remains of those sunken ships is their figureheads . . . and the names—Justice, Friendship, Golden Peace, and Hope. That's all that's left of hope, treacherous hope. Spars, rowlocks, bailers. And see! The lifebuoy which saved itself, letting those in need perish.

POET, *searching the wreckage.* Here is the name of the ship Justice. This is the ship which sailed from Fairhaven with the Blind Man's son on board. So she sank. And Alice's sweetheart was in her too, Edith's hopeless love.

DAUGHTER. The blind man? Fairhaven? Surely that I dreamt. Alice's sweetheart, ugly Edith, Foulstrand and the quarantine, the sulphur and carbolic, graduation in the church, the lawyer's office, the alley and Victoria. The Growing Castle and the Officer . . . These things I dreamt.

POET. Of these things I once made poetry.

DAUGHTER. You know then what poetry is?

POET. I know what dreams are. What is poetry?

DAUGHTER. Not reality, but more than reality. Not dreams, but waking dreams.

POET. Yet the children of men believe that poets merely play —invent and fabricate.

DAUGHTER. It is just as well, my friend, or else the world would be laid waste from lack of endeavour. All men would lie upon their backs, gazing at the heavens; no hand would be lifted to plough or spade, or plane or axe.

POET. Do you speak thus, Daughter of Indra? You, who are half of heaven?

DAUGHTER. You are right to reproach me. I have lived too long down here, and like you have bathed in mud. My thoughts can no longer fly. Clay is on their wings and soil about their feet. And I myself—*she raises her arms*—I am sinking, sinking! Help me, Father, God of Heaven! *Silence.* No longer can I hear His answer. The ether no longer carries the sound of His lips to the shell of my ear . . . the silver thread has snapped. Alas, I am earth-bound!

POET. Do you mean then soon—to go?

DAUGHTER. As soon as I have burnt this earthly matter, for the waters of the ocean cannot cleanse me. Why do you ask?

POET. I have a prayer—a petition.

DAUGHTER. A petition?

POET. A petition from mankind to the ruler of the universe, drawn up by a dreamer.

DAUGHTER. Who is to present it?

POET. Indra's Daughter.

DAUGHTER. Can you speak the words?

POET. I can.

DAUGHTER. Speak them then.

POET. It is better that you should.

DAUGHTER. Where shall I read them?

POET. In my thoughts—or here. *He gives her a scroll.*

DAUGHTER. So be it. I will speak them. *She takes the scroll but does not read.*

> *"Why with anguish are you born?*
> *Why do you hurt your mother so,*
> *Child of man, when bringing her*
> *the joy of motherhood,*
> *joy beyond all other joys?*
> *Why wake to life,*
> *why greet the light*
> *with a cry of fury and of pain,*
> *Child of man, when to be glad*
> *should be the gift of life?*
> *Why are we born like animals?*
> *We who stem from God and man,*
> *whose souls are longing to be clothed*
> *in other than this blood and filth.*
> *Must God's own image cut its teeth?"*

Speaking her own thoughts.

Silence! No more! The work may not condemn the master.
Life's riddle still remains unsolved.

Continuing the POET*'s bitter words.*

> *"And then the journey's course begins,*
> *over thistles, thorns and stones.*
> *If it should touch a beaten track,*
> *comes at once the cry: 'Keep off!'*

Pluck a flower, straight you'll find
the bloom you picked to be another's.
If cornfields lie across your path
and you must pursue your way,
trampling on another's crops,
others then will trample yours
that your loss may equal theirs.
Every pleasure you enjoy
brings to all your fellows sorrow,
yet your sorrow gives no gladness.
So sorrow, sorrow upon sorrow
on your way—until you're dead
and then, alas, give others bread.

Her own thought.

Is it thus, O son of dust,
You seek to win the ear of God?

POET. *How may son of dust find words,*
so pure, so light, so luminous,
that they can rise up from the earth?
Child of the Gods, translate for me,
this lamentation into speech
fit for Immortal ears.

DAUGHTER. I will.

POET, *pointing.* What is floating there—a buoy?

DAUGHTER. Yes.

POET. It is like a lung with a windpipe.

DAUGHTER. It is the watchman of the sea. When danger is abroad, it sings.

POET. It seems to me that the sea is rising, and the waves beginning to . . .

DAUGHTER. You are not mistaken.

POET. Alas, what do I see? A ship—on the rocks.

DAUGHTER. What ship can it be?

POET. I believe it is the ghost-ship.

DAUGHTER. What is that?

POET. The Flying Dutchman.

DAUGHTER. He? Why is he punished so cruelly, and why does he not come ashore?

POET. Because he had seven unfaithful wives.

DAUGHTER. Shall he be punished for that?

POET. Yes. All righteous men condemned him.

DAUGHTER. Incomprehensible world! How can he be freed from this curse?

POET. Freed? One would beware of freeing him.

DAUGHTER. Why?

POET. Because . . . No, that is not the Dutchman. It is an ordinary ship in distress. Then why does the buoy not sound? Look how the sea is rising! The waves are towering, and soon we shall be imprisoned in this cave. Now the ship's bell is ringing. Soon there will be another figurehead in here. Cry out buoy! Watchman, do your duty!

The buoy sounds a four-part chord in fifths and sixths, like foghorns.

The crew is waving to us . . . but we ourselves perish.

DAUGHTER. Do you not want to be set free?

POET. Yes, yes I do! But not now . . . and not by water!

THE CREW, *singing four-part.* Christ Kyrie!

POET. They are calling and the sea is calling. But no one hears.

CREW, *singing as before.* Christ Kyrie!

DAUGHTER. Who is it coming there?

POET. Walking upon the water! Only One walks upon the water. It is not Peter, the rock, for he sank like a stone.

A white light appears over the sea.

CREW, *as before.* Christ Kyrie!

DAUGHTER. Is it He?

POET. It is He, the crucified.

DAUGHTER. Why, tell me why He was crucified.

POET. Because He wished to set men free.

DAUGHTER. Who—I have forgotten—who crucified Him?

The cave grows darker.

POET. All righteous men.

DAUGHTER. This incomprehensible world!

POET. The sea is rising. Darkness is falling on us. The storm is growing wilder.

The CREW *shriek.*

The crew are screaming with horror because they have seen their Saviour . . . and now . . . they are throwing themselves overboard in terror of the Redeemer.

The CREW *shriek again.*

Now they are screaming because they are going to die. They were born screaming and they die screaming.

The mounting waves threaten to drown them in the cave. The light begins to change.

DAUGHTER. If I were sure it was a ship . . .

POET. Indeed, I do not think it is a ship. It's a two storied house, with trees round it . . . and a telephone tower—a tower reaching to the skies. It's the modern Tower of Babel, sending up its wires to communicate with those above.

DAUGHTER. Child, man's thought needs no wires for its flight. The prayers of the devout penetrate all worlds. That is surely no Tower of Babel. If you wish to storm the heavens, storm them with your prayers.

POET. No, it's not a house . . . not a telephone tower. Do you see?

DAUGHTER. What do you see?

During the following speech, the scene changes to the alley of the Opera House.

POET. I see a snow-covered heath . . . a parade ground. The winter sun is shining behind a church on the hill, so that the tower casts its long shadow on the snow. Now a troop of soldiers comes marching over the heath. They march on the tower and up the spire . . . Now they are on the cross, and I seem to know that the first to tread on the weathercock must die . . . They are drawing near it. It's the Corporal at their head who . . . Ah! A cloud is sailing over the heath, across the sun . . . Now everything has gone. The moisture of the cloud has put out the fire of the sun. The sunlight created a shadowy image of the tower, but the shadow of the cloud smothered the image of the tower.

[*It is springtime. The tree and the monkshood are in bud. The* STAGE DOORKEEPER *sits in her old place. The* DAUGHTER *enters, followed by the* POET.]

DAUGHTER, *to* DOORKEEPER. Has the Chancellor arrived yet?

DOORKEEPER. No.

DAUGHTER. Nor the Deans?

DOORKEEPER. No.

DAUGHTER. You must send for them at once. The door is going to be opened.

DOORKEEPER. Is it so urgent?

DAUGHTER. Yes. It's thought that the answer to the riddle of the universe is locked up in there. So send for the Chancellor and the Deans of the four Faculties. *The* DOORKEEPER *blows a whistle.* And don't forget the Glazier and his diamond, or nothing can be done.

The personnel of the Opera pour from the building as in the earlier scene.

The OFFICER [*young again*], *in morning coat and top hat, comes through the gate, carrying a bouquet of roses and looking radiantly happy.*

OFFICER, *singing.* Victoria!

DOORKEEPER. The young lady will be down in a minute.

OFFICER. Good. The carriage is waiting, the table is laid, the champagne is on the ice . . . Let me embrace you, Madam. *Embraces the* DOORKEEPER. Victoria!

WOMAN'S VOICE, *from above, singing.* I am here.

OFFICER, *pacing.* Well, I am waiting.

POET. I seem to have lived through all this before.

DAUGHTER. I too.

POET. Perhaps I dreamt it.

DAUGHTER. Or made a poem of it.

POET. Or made a poem.

DAUGHTER. You know then what poetry is.

POET. I know what dreaming is.

DAUGHTER. I feel that once before, somewhere else, we said these words.

POET. Then soon you will know what reality is.

DAUGHTER. Or dreaming.

POET. Or poetry.

Enter the CHANCELLOR *and the* DEANS OF THEOLOGY, PHILOSOPHY, MEDICINE *and* LAW, [*followed by the* GLAZIER *and a group of* RIGHTEOUS PEOPLE].

CHANCELLOR. It's all a question of the door, you understand. What does the Dean of Theology think about it?

DEAN OF THEOLOGY. I don't think—I believe. Credo.

DEAN OF PHILOSOPHY. I think.

DEAN OF MEDICINE. I know.

DEAN OF LAW. I doubt—until I have heard the evidence and witnesses.

CHANCELLOR. Now they will quarrel again. Well then, first what does Theology believe?

THEOLOGY. I believe that this door ought not to be opened, as it conceals dangerous truths.

PHILOSOPHY. The truth is never dangerous.

MEDICINE. What is truth?

LAW. Whatever can be proved by two witnesses.

THEOLOGY. Anything can be proved by two false witnesses—if you're a pettifogger.

PHILOSOPHY. Truth is wisdom, and wisdom and knowledge are philosophy itself. Philosophy is the science of sciences, the knowledge of knowledge. All other sciences are its servants.

MEDICINE. The only science is natural science. Philosophy is not science. It is mere empty speculation.

THEOLOGY. Bravo!

PHILOSOPHY, *to* DEAN OF THEOLOGY. You say bravo. And what, may I ask, are you? The arch enemy of knowledge, the antithesis of science. You are ignorance and darkness.

MEDICINE. Bravo!

THEOLOGY, *to* DEAN OF MEDICINE. And you say bravo—you who can't see further than the end of your own nose in a magnifying glass. You who believe in nothing but your deceptive senses—in your eyes, for instance, which may be long-sighted, short-sighted, blind, purblind, squinting, one-eyed, colour-blind, red-blind, green-blind . . .

MEDICINE. Blockhead!

THEOLOGY. Ass!

They fight.

CHANCELLOR. Enough! Birds of a feather shouldn't peck each other's eyes out.

PHILOSOPHY. Had I to choose between these two, Theology and Medicine, I should choose—neither.

LAW. And if I had to sit in judgment over you three, I should condemn—every one of you . . . You can't agree upon a single point, and never have been able to. Let's get back to the matter in hand. What's your opinion, Chancellor, of this door and the opening of it?

CHANCELLOR. Opinion? I don't have opinions. I am merely appointed by the Government to see you don't break each other's arms and legs in the Senate in the course of educating the young. Opinions? No, I take good care not to have any. I had a few once, but they were soon exploded. Opinions always are exploded—by opponents, of course. Perhaps we had better have the door opened now, even at the risk of it concealing dangerous truths.

LAW. What is truth? What is the truth?

THEOLOGY. I am the Truth and the Life . . .

PHILOSOPHY. I am the knowledge of knowledge.

MEDICINE. I am exact knowledge . . .

LAW. I doubt.

They fight.

DAUGHTER. Shame on you, teachers of youth!

LAW. Chancellor, as delegate of the Government and head of the teaching staff, denounce this woman. She has cried "shame on you" which is contumely, and she has ironically referred to you as "teachers of youth," which is slander.

DAUGHTER. Poor youth!

LAW. She pities youth, and that's tantamount to accusing us. Chancellor, denounce her!

DAUGHTER. Yes, I accuse you—all of you—of sowing the seeds of doubt and dissension in the minds of the young.

LAW. Listen to her! She herself is raising doubts in the young as to our authority, yet she is accusing us of raising doubts. I appeal to all righteous men. Is this not a criminal offence?

ALL THE RIGHTEOUS. Yes, it is criminal.

LAW. The righteous have condemned you. Go in peace with your gains. Otherwise . . .

DAUGHTER. My gains? Otherwise what?

LAW. Otherwise you will be stoned.

POET. Or crucified.

DAUGHTER [*to the* POET]. I am going. Come with me and learn the answer to the riddle.

POET. Which riddle?

DAUGHTER. What does he mean by my "gains"?

POET. Probably nothing at all. That's what we call idle chatter. He was just chattering.

DAUGHTER. But that hurt me more than anything else.

POET. That's why he said it. Human beings are like that.

The GLAZIER *opens the door and looks inside.*

ALL THE RIGHTEOUS. Hurrah! The door is open.

The DEANS *look inside.*

CHANCELLOR. What was concealed behind that door?

GLAZIER. I can't see anything.

CHANCELLOR. He can't see anything. Well, I'm not surprised. Deans! What was concealed behind that door?

THEOLOGY. Nothing. That is the solution of the riddle of the universe. Out of nothing in the beginning God created heaven and earth.

PHILOSOPHY. Out of nothing comes nothing.

MEDICINE. Bosh! That is nothing.

LAW. I doubt everything. And there's some swindle here. I appeal to all righteous men.

DAUGHTER, *to* POET. Who are these righteous?

POET. Let him tell you who can. All the righteous are often just one person. Today they are me and mine, tomorrow you and yours. One is nominated for the post, or rather, one nominates oneself.

ALL THE RIGHTEOUS. We have been swindled.

CHANCELLOR. Who has swindled you?

ALL THE RIGHTEOUS. The Daughter!

CHANCELLOR. Will the Daughter kindly inform us what her idea was in having the door opened.

DAUGHTER. No, my friends. If I told you, you would not believe it.

MEDICINE. But there's nothing there.

DAUGHTER. What you say is correct. But you have not understood it.

MEDICINE. What she says is bosh.

ALL. Bosh!

DAUGHTER, *to* POET. They are to be pitied.

POET. Do you mean that seriously?

DAUGHTER. Very seriously.

POET. Do you think the righteous are to be pitied too?

DAUGHTER. They most of all perhaps.

POET. And the four Faculties?

DAUGHTER. They too, and not least. Four heads and four minds with a single body. Who created such a monster?

ALL. She does not answer.

CHANCELLOR. Then stone her!

DAUGHTER. This is the answer.

CHANCELLOR. Listen! She is answering.

ALL. Stone her! She is answering.

Enter LAWYER.

DAUGHTER. If she answers, or if she does not answer, stone her! *To* POET. Come, you Seer, and I will answer the riddle, but far from here, out in the wilderness, where none can hear us, none can see us. For . . .

The LAWYER *interrupts by taking hold of her arm.*

LAWYER. Have you forgotten your duties?

DAUGHTER. God knows I have not. But I have higher duties.

LAWYER. But your child?

DAUGHTER. My child? Yes?

LAWYER. Your child is calling you.

DAUGHTER. My child! Alas, I am earthbound! And this anguish in my breast, this agony, what is it?

LAWYER. Don't you know?

DAUGHTER. No.

LAWYER. It is the pangs of conscience.

DAUGHTER. The pangs of conscience?

LAWYER. Yes. They come after every neglected duty, after every pleasure, however innocent—if there is such a thing as an innocent pleasure, which is doubtful. And they also come every time one causes pain to one's neighbour.

DAUGHTER. Is there no remedy?

LAWYER. Yes, but only one. To do one's duty instantly.

DAUGHTER. You look like a devil when you say the word "duty." But when one has, as I, two duties?

LAWYER. Fulfil first one and then the other.

DAUGHTER. The higher first. Therefore, you look after my child, and I will do my duty.

LAWYER. Your child is unhappy without you. Can you let another suffer on your account?

DAUGHTER. There is conflict in my soul. It is pulled this way and that until it is torn in two.

LAWYER. These, you see, are life's little trials.

DAUGHTER. Oh, how they tear one!

POET. You would have nothing to do with me, if you knew what misery I have caused through following my vocation—yes, my vocation, which is the highest duty of all.

DAUGHTER. What do you mean?

POET. I had a father, whose hopes were centred in me, his only son. I was to have carried on his business, but I ran away from the Commercial College. Worry brought my father to his grave. My mother wanted me to be religious. I couldn't be religious. She disowned me. I had a friend who helped me when I was desperate, but that friend turned out to be a tyrant to the very people whose cause I upheld. So to save my soul I had to strike down my friend and benefactor. Since that time I have had no peace. I am considered base, contemptible, the scum of the earth. Nor do I get any comfort from my conscience when it tells me I did right, for the next moment it assures me I did wrong. That is the way of life.

DAUGHTER. Come with me, out into the wilderness.

LAWYER. Your child!

DAUGHTER, *indicating all present.* These are my children. Each one of them is good, but as soon as they are together they fight and turn into devils. Farewell!

[*Blackout. When the lights go up the scene has changed to*] *Outside the Castle.*

The set is the same as the earlier one, except that now the ground is covered with blue monkshood, aconite and other flowers. The chrysanthemum bud at the top of the tower is on the point of bursting. The Castle windows are lit with candles. [*In the foreground is a fire.*]

DAUGHTER. The hour is at hand when with the aid of fire I shall ascend again into the ether. This is what you call death and approach with so much fear.

POET. Fear of the unknown.

DAUGHTER. Which yet you know.

POET. Who knows it?

DAUGHTER. Mankind. Why do you not believe your prophets?

POET. Prophets have never been believed. Why is that? If they truly speak with the voice of God, why then do men not believe? His power to convince should be irresistible.

DAUGHTER. Have you always doubted?

POET. No, I have had faith many times, but after a while it drifted away, like a dream when one awakens.

DAUGHTER. To be mortal is not easy.

POET. You understand this now?

DAUGHTER. Yes.

POET. Tell me, did not Indra once send his son down to earth to hear man's complaint?

DAUGHTER. He did. And how was he received?

POET. How did he fulfil his mission?—to answer with a question.

DAUGHTER. To answer with another—was not the state of mankind bettered by his visit to the earth? Answer truly.

POET. Bettered? Yes, a little, a very little. Now, instead of further questions, will you tell me the answer to the riddle?

DAUGHTER. What purpose would that serve? You would not believe me.

POET. I shall believe you, for I know who you are.

DAUGHTER. Then I will tell you. In the dawn of time, before your sun gave light, Brahma, the divine primal force let himself be seduced by Maya, the World Mother, that he might propagate. This mingling of the divine element with the earthly was the Fall from heaven. This world, its life and its inhabitants are therefore only a mirage, a reflection, a dream image.

POET. My dream!

DAUGHTER. A true dream. But, in order to be freed from the earthly element, the descendants of Brahma sought renunciation and suffering. And so you have suffering as the deliverer. But this yearning for suffering comes into conflict with the longing for joy, for love. Now you understand what love is; supreme joy in the greatest suffering, the sweetest is the most bitter. Do you understand now what woman is? Woman, through whom sin and death entered into life.

POET. I understand. And the outcome?

DAUGHTER. What you yourself know. Conflict between the pain of joy and the joy of pain, between the anguish of the penitent and the pleasure of the sensual.

POET. And the conflict?

DAUGHTER. The conflict of opposites generates power, as fire and water create the force of steam.

POET. But peace? Rest?

DAUGHTER. Hush! You must ask no more, nor may I answer. The altar is decked for the sacrifice, the flowers keep vigil, the candles are lighted, the white sheet hangs in the window, the threshold is strewn with pine.*

POET. How calmly you speak! As if suffering did not exist for you.

DAUGHTER. Not exist? I suffered all your sufferings a hundred fold because my sensibilities were finer.

POET. Tell me your sorrows.

DAUGHTER. Poet, could you tell your own with utter truth? Could your words ever once convey your thoughts?

POET. You are right. No. To myself I have always seemed a deaf mute, and while the crowd was acclaiming my song, to me it seemed a jangle. And so, you see, I was always ashamed when men paid me homage.

DAUGHTER. And yet you wish me to speak? Look into my eyes.

POET. I cannot endure your gaze.

DAUGHTER. How then will you endure my words, if I speak in my own language?

POET. Even so, before you go, tell me from what you suffered most down here.

*Signs of mourning in Sweden.

DAUGHTER. From living. From feeling my vision dimmed by having eyes, my hearing dulled by having ears, and my thought, my airy, luminous thought, bound down in a labyrinth of fat. You have seen a brain. What twisting channels, what creeping ways!

POET. Yes, and that is why the minds of the righteous are twisted.

DAUGHTER. Cruel, always cruel, each one of you.

POET. How can we be otherwise?

DAUGHTER. Now first I shake the dust from my feet, the earth, the clay. *She takes off her shoes and puts them in the fire.* [*One after another the following characters come in, put their contributions on the fire, cross the stage and go out, while the* POET *and the* DAUGHTER *stand watching.*]

DOORKEEPER. Perhaps I may burn my shawl too?

OFFICER. And I my roses, of which only the thorns are left.

BILLSTICKER. The posters can go, but my fishnet never.

GLAZIER. Farewell to the diamond that opened the door.

LAWYER. The report of the proceedings in the High Court touching the Pope's beard or the diminishing water supply in the sources of the Ganges.

QUARANTINE MASTER. A small contribution in the shape of the black mask which turned me into a blackamoor against my will.

VICTORIA [SHE]. My beauty—my sorrow.

EDITH. My ugliness—my sorrow.

BLINDMAN, *putting his hand in the fire.* I give my hand which is my sight.

DON JUAN *is pushed in in the bathchair* [*accompanied by the* COQUETTE *and the* FRIEND].

DON JUAN. Make haste, make haste! Life is short.

POET. I have read that when a life is nearing its end, everything and everyone pass by in a single stream. Is this the end?

DAUGHTER. For me, yes. Farewell!

POET. Say a parting word!

DAUGHTER. No, I cannot. Do you think your language can express our thoughts?

Enter the DEAN OF THEOLOGY, *raging.*

THEOLOGY. I am disowned by God; I am persecuted by men; I am abandoned by the Government, and scorned by my colleagues. How can I have faith when no one else has faith? How can I defend a God who does not defend His own people? It's all bosh!

He throws a book on the fire and goes out. The POET *snatches the book from the flames.*

POET. Do you know what this is? A Book of Martyrs, a calendar with a martyr for each day of the year.

DAUGHTER. A martyr?

POET. Yes, one who was tortured and put to death for his faith. Tell me why. Do you believe all who are tortured suffer, all who are put to death feel pain? Surely suffering is redemption and death deliverance.

KRISTIN *enters with her paste and strips of paper.*

KRISTIN. I paste, I paste, till there is nothing left to paste.

POET. If heaven itself cracked open, you would try to paste it up. Go away!

KRISTIN. Are there no inner windows in the Castle?

POET. No, none there.

KRISTIN. I'll go then, I'll go.

Exit.

[*As the* DAUGHTER *speaks her last lines the flames rise until the Castle is on fire.*]

DAUGHTER. *The parting time has come; the end draws near.*
Farewell, you child of man, dreamer,
poet, who knows best the way to live.
Above the earth on wings you hover,
plunging at times to graze the dust,
but not to be submerged.
Now I am going, now the hour has come

to leave both friend and place,
how sharp the loss of all I loved,
how deep regret for all destroyed!
Ah, now I know the whole of living's pain!
This then it is to be a human being—
ever to miss the thing one never prized
and feel remorse for what one never did,
to yearn to go, yet long to stay.
And so the human heart is split in two,
emotions by wild horses torn—
conflict, discord and uncertainty.
Farewell! Tell all on earth I shall remember them.
Where I am going, and in your name
carry their lamentations to the throne.
Farewell!

She goes into the Castle. Music is heard. The background is lighted up by the burning Castle, and now shows a wall of human faces, questioning, mourning, despairing. While the Castle is burning, the flower-bud on the roof bursts into a giant chrysanthemum.

THE GHOST SONATA

INTRODUCTION

I have called this most famous of Strindberg's Chamber Plays, written for his own Intimate Theatre, THE GHOST SONATA, in spite of the tempting alternative SPOOK sometimes used before, because I believe "ghost" is a truer translation of the author's "spök" than "spook." The latter word has, in English, a facetious flavour—one inevitably thinks of "spooky"—which the Swedish word has not and, fantastic in part even grotesque though the play is, it is very far from being facetious.

Strindberg's original title was "Kama-Loka," reflecting the influence on him at the time of Theosophy, and the theme is merciless exposure of life's most shameful secrets. He was now writing, in 1907, at enormous speed and under great pressure. The Intimate Theatre was opening with the usual vicissitudes of small theatres and A DREAM PLAY was going into rehearsal at the Swedish Theatre. Since the end of their brief married life his domestic affairs had been all awry, and the whole situation was a strain.

Nevertheless, in THE GHOST SONATA Strindberg produced a masterpiece, once again using the dream idiom, in which everything was possible and probable, but adding to the vision of the poet the technique of the Naturalist. In THE GHOST SONATA there is no angelic child as in EASTER to bring poor mortals peace, no goddess to pity their woe. The weird mummy woman, who can stop time and undo what was done, leaves the soul only one way out of its hell—the way of retribution and death.

Strindberg's own obsession with "the labour of keeping the dirt of life at a distance" breaks the tender idyll of the Student and the Hyacinth Girl, and the huge, sinister, vampire cook is a telling piece of Symbolism. The play ends, oddly, with a view of one of Strindberg's favourite pictures: Böcklin's *Isle of the Dead.* Rereading E. M. Forster's novel *Howard's End,* I find he makes his half-German heroine say:

"My blood boils . . . when I listen to the tasteful contempt of the average islander for things Teutonic . . . 'Oh, Böcklin,' they say; 'he strains after beauty, he peoples Nature with gods too consciously.' Of course Böcklin strains, because he wants something–beauty and all the other intangible gifts that are floating about the world . . ."

The same might be said of Strindberg.

E. S.

Characters

THE OLD MAN, *Hummel, a Company Director*

THE STUDENT, *Arkenholtz*

THE MILKMAID, *an apparition*

THE CARETAKER'S WIFE

THE CARETAKER

THE LADY IN BLACK, *the daughter of the Caretaker's Wife and the Dead Man. Also referred to as the Dark Lady*

THE COLONEL

THE MUMMY, *the Colonel's wife*

THE GIRL, *the Colonel's daughter, actually the daughter of the Old Man*

THE ARISTOCRAT, *Baron Skanskorg. Engaged to the Lady in Black*

JOHANSSON, *the Old Man's servant*

BENGTSSON, *the Colonel's servant*

THE FIANCÉE, *a white-haired old woman, once betrothed to the Old Man*

THE COOK

A MAIDSERVANT

BEGGARS

SCENE ONE

Outside the house. The corner of the façade of a modern house, showing the ground floor above, and the street in front. The ground floor terminates on the right in the Round Room, above which, on the first floor, is a balcony with a flagstaff. The windows of the Round Room face the street in front of the house, and at the corner look on to the suggestion of a side-street running towards the back. At the beginning of the scene the blinds of the Round Room are down. When, later, they are raised, the white marble statue of a young woman can be seen, surrounded with palms and brightly lighted by rays of sunshine.

To the left of the Round Room is the Hyacinth Room; its window filled with pots of hyacinths, blue, white and pink. Further left, at the back, is an imposing double front door with laurels in tubs on either side of it. The doors are wide open, showing a staircase of white marble with a banister of mahogany and brass. To the left of the front door is another ground-floor window, with a window-mirror. On the balcony rail in the corner above the Round Room are a blue silk quilt and two white pillows. The windows to the left of this are hung with white sheets.†*

In the foreground, in front of the house, is a green bench; to the right a street drinking-fountain, to the left an advertisement column.

It is a bright Sunday morning, and as the curtain rises the bells of several churches, some near, some far away, are ringing.

On the staircase the LADY IN BLACK *stands motionless.*

*Set at an angle inside the window, so as to show what is going on in the street.

†Sign of mourning.

The CARETAKER'S WIFE *sweeps the doorstep, then polishes the brass on the door and waters the laurels.*

In a wheel-chair by the advertisement column sits the OLD MAN, *reading a newspaper. His hair and beard are white and he wears spectacles.*

The MILKMAID *comes round the corner on the right, carrying milk bottles in a wire basket. She is wearing a summer dress with brown shoes, black stockings and a white cap. She takes off her cap and hangs it on the fountain, wipes the perspiration from her forehead, washes her hands and arranges her hair, using the water as a mirror.*

A steamship bell is heard, and now and then the silence is broken by the deep notes of an organ in a nearby church.

After a few moments, when all is silent and the MILKMAID *has finished her toilet, the* STUDENT *enters from the left. He has had a sleepless night and is unshaven. He goes straight up to the fountain. There is a pause before he speaks.*

STUDENT. May I have the cup? *The* MILKMAID *clutches the cup to her.* Haven't you finished yet?

The MILKMAID *looks at him with horror.*

OLD MAN, *to himself.* Who's he talking to? I don't see anybody. Is he crazy?

He goes on watching them in great astonishment.

STUDENT, *to the* MILKMAID. What are you staring at? Do I look so terrible? Well, I've had no sleep, and of course you think I've been making a night of it . . . *The* MILKMAID *stays just as she is.* You think I've been drinking, eh? Do I smell of liquor? *The* MILKMAID *does not change.* I haven't shaved, I know. Give me a drink of water, girl. I've earned it. *Pause.* Oh well, I suppose I'll have to tell you. I spent the whole night dressing wounds and looking after the injured. You see, I was there when that house collapsed last night. Now you know. *The* MILKMAID *rinses the cup and gives him a drink.* Thanks. *The* MILKMAID *stands motionless. Slowly.* Will you do me a great favor?

Pause. The thing is, my eyes, as you can see, are inflamed, but my hands have been touching wounds and corpses, so it would be dangerous to put them near my eyes. Will you take my handkerchief—it's quite clean—and dip it in the fresh water and bathe my eyes? Will you do this? Will you play the good Samaritan? *The* MILKMAID *hesitates, but does as he bids.* Thank you, my dear. *He takes out his purse. She makes a gesture of refusal.* Forgive my stupidity, but I'm only half-awake. . . .

The MILKMAID *disappears.*

OLD MAN, *to the* STUDENT. Excuse me speaking to you, but I heard you say you were at the scene of the accident last night. I was just reading about it in the paper.

STUDENT. Is it in the paper already?

OLD MAN. The whole thing, including your portrait. But they regret that they have been unable to find out the name of the splendid young student. . . .

STUDENT. Really? *Glances at the paper.* Yes, that's me. Well I never!

OLD MAN. Who was it you were talking to just now?

STUDENT. Didn't you see? *Pause.*

OLD MAN. Would it be impertinent to inquire—what in fact your name is?

STUDENT. What would be the point? I don't care for publicity. If you get any praise, there's always disapproval too. The art of running people down has been developed to such a pitch. . . . Besides, I don't want any reward.

OLD MAN. You're well off, perhaps.

STUDENT. No, indeed. On the contrary, I'm very poor.

OLD MAN. Do you know, it seems to me I've heard your voice before. When I was young I had a friend who pronounced certain words just as you do. I've never met anyone else with quite that pronunciation. Only him—and you. Are you by any chance related to Mr. Arkenholtz, the merchant?

STUDENT. He was my father.

OLD MAN. Strange are the paths of fate. I saw you when you were an infant, under very painful circumstances.

STUDENT. Yes, I understand I came into the world in the middle of a bankruptcy.

OLD MAN. Just that.

STUDENT. Perhaps I might ask your name.

OLD MAN. I am Mr. Hummel.

STUDENT. Are you the? . . . I remember that . . .

OLD MAN. Have you often heard my name mentioned in your family?

STUDENT. Yes.

OLD MAN. And mentioned perhaps with a certain aversion? *The* STUDENT *is silent.* Yes, I can imagine it. You were told, I suppose, that I was the man who ruined your father? All who ruin themselves through foolish speculations consider they were ruined by those they couldn't fool. *Pause.* Now these are the facts. Your father robbed me of seventeen thousand crowns—the whole of my savings at that time.

STUDENT. It's queer that the same story can be told in two such different ways.

OLD MAN. You surely don't believe I'm telling you what isn't true?

STUDENT. What am I to believe? My father didn't lie.

OLD MAN. That is so true. A father never lies. But I too am a father, and so it follows . . .

STUDENT. What are you driving at?

OLD MAN. I saved your father from disaster, and he repaid me with all the frightful hatred that is born of an obligation to be grateful. He taught his family to speak ill of me.

STUDENT. Perhaps you made him ungrateful by poisoning your help with unnecessary humiliation.

OLD MAN. All help is humiliating, sir.

STUDENT. What do you want from me?

OLD MAN. I'm not asking for the money, but if you will render me a few small services, I shall consider myself well paid.

You see that I am a cripple. Some say it is my own fault; others lay the blame on my parents. I prefer to blame life itself, with its pitfalls. For if you escape one snare, you fall headlong into another. In any case, I am unable to climb stairs or ring doorbells, and that is why I am asking you to help me.

STUDENT. What can I do?

OLD MAN. To begin with, push my chair so that I can read those playbills. I want to see what is on tonight.

STUDENT, *pushing the chair.* Haven't you got an attendant?

OLD MAN. Yes, but he has gone on an errand. He'll be back soon. Are you a medical student?

STUDENT. No, I am studying languages, but I don't know at all what I'm going to do.

OLD MAN. Aha! Are you good at mathematics?

STUDENT. Yes, fairly.

OLD MAN. Good. Perhaps you would like a job.

STUDENT. Yes, why not?

OLD MAN. Splendid. *He studies the playbills.* They are doing *The Valkyrie* for the matinée. That means the Colonel will be there with his daughter, and as he always sits at the end of the sixth row, I'll put you next to him. Go to that telephone kiosk please and order a ticket for seat eighty-two in the sixth row.

STUDENT. Am I to go to the Opera in the middle of the day?

OLD MAN. Yes. Do as I tell you and things will go well with you. I want to see you happy, rich and honored. Your début last night as the brave rescuer will make you famous by tomorrow and then your name will be worth something.

STUDENT, *going to the telephone kiosk.* What an odd adventure!

OLD MAN. Are you a gambler?

STUDENT. Yes, unfortunately.

OLD MAN. We'll make it fortunately. Go on now, telephone. *The* STUDENT *goes. The* OLD MAN *reads his paper. The*

LADY IN BLACK *comes out on to the pavement and talks to the* CARETAKER'S WIFE. *The* OLD MAN *listens, but the audience hears nothing. The* STUDENT *returns.* Did you fix it up?

STUDENT. It's done.

OLD MAN. You see that house?

STUDENT. Yes, I've been looking at it a lot. I passed it yesterday when the sun was shining on the windowpanes, and I imagined all the beauty and elegance there must be inside. I said to my companion: "Think of living up there in the top flat, with a beautiful young wife, two pretty little children and an income of twenty thousand crowns a year."

OLD MAN. So that's what you said. That's what you said. Well, well! I too am very fond of this house.

STUDENT. Do you speculate in houses?

OLD MAN. Mm—yes. But not in the way you mean.

STUDENT. Do you know the people who live here?

OLD MAN. Every one of them. At my age one knows everybody, and their parents and grandparents too, and one's always related to them in some way or other. I am just eighty, but no one knows me—not really. I take an interest in human destiny. *The blinds of the Round Room are drawn up. The* COLONEL *is seen, wearing mufti. He looks at the thermometer outside one of the windows, then turns back into the room and stands in front of the marble statue.* Look, that's the Colonel, whom you will sit next to this afternoon.

STUDENT. Is he—the Colonel? I don't understand any of this, but it's like a fairy story.

OLD MAN. My whole life's like a book of fairy stories, sir. And although the stories are different, they are held together by one thread, and the main theme constantly recurs.

STUDENT. Who is that marble statue of?

OLD MAN. That, naturally, is his wife.

STUDENT. Was she such a wonderful person?

OLD MAN. Er . . . yes.

STUDENT. Tell me.

OLD MAN. We can't judge people, young man. If I were to tell you that she left him, that he beat her, that she returned to him and married him a second time, and that now she is sitting inside there like a mummy, worshipping her own statue—then you would think me crazy.

STUDENT. I don't understand.

OLD MAN. I didn't think you would. Well, then we have the window with the hyacinths. His daughter lives there. She has gone out for a ride, but she will be home soon.

STUDENT. And who is the dark lady talking to the caretaker?

OLD MAN. Well, that's a bit complicated, but it is connected with the dead man, up there where you see the white sheets.

STUDENT. Why, who was he?

OLD MAN. A human being like you or me, but the most conspicuous thing about him was his vanity. If you were a Sunday child, you would see him presently come out of that door to look at the Consulate flag flying at half-mast. He was, you understand, a Consul, and he reveled in coronets and lions and plumed hats and colored ribbons.

STUDENT. Sunday child, you say? I'm told I was born on a Sunday.

OLD MAN. No, were you really? I might have known it. I saw it from the color of your eyes. Then you can see what others can't. Have you noticed that?

STUDENT. I don't know what others do see, but at times. . . . Oh, but one doesn't talk of such things!

OLD MAN. I was almost sure of it. But you can talk to me, because I understand such things.

STUDENT. Yesterday, for instance . . . I was drawn to that obscure little street where later on the house collapsed. I went there and stopped in front of that building which I had never seen before. Then I noticed a crack in the wall. . . . I heard the floor boards snapping. . . . I dashed over and picked up a child that was passing under the wall. . . . The next moment the house collapsed. I was saved, but in my arms, which I thought held the child, was nothing at all.

OLD MAN. Yes, yes, just as I thought. Tell me something. Why were you gesticulating that way just now by the fountain? And why were you talking to yourself?

STUDENT. Didn't you see the milkmaid I was talking to?

OLD MAN, *in horror.* Milkmaid?

STUDENT. Surely. The girl who handed me the cup.

OLD MAN. Really? So that's what was going on. Ah well, I haven't second sight, but there are things I can do. THE FIANCÉE *is now seen to sit down by the window which has the window-mirror.* Look at that old woman in the window. Do you see her? Well, she was my fiancée once, sixty years ago. I was twenty. Don't be alarmed. She doesn't recognize me. We see one another every day, and it makes no impression on me, although once we vowed to love one another eternally. Eternally!

STUDENT. How foolish you were in those days! We never talk to our girls like that.

OLD MAN. Forgive us, young man. We didn't know any better. But can you see that that old woman was once young and beautiful?

STUDENT. It doesn't show. And yet there's some charm in her looks. I can't see her eyes.

The CARETAKER'S WIFE *comes out with a basket of chopped fir branches.**

OLD MAN. Ah, the caretaker's wife! That dark lady is her daughter by the dead man. That's why her husband was given the job of caretaker. But the dark lady has a suitor, who is an aristocrat with great expectations. He is in the process of getting a divorce—from his present wife, you understand. She's presenting him with a stone mansion in order to be rid of him. This aristocratic suitor is the son-in-law of the dead man, and you can see his bedclothes

*It was customary in Sweden to strew the ground with these for a funeral.

being aired on the balcony upstairs. It is complicated, I must say.

STUDENT. It's fearfully complicated.

OLD MAN. Yes, that it is, internally and externally, although it looks quite simple.

STUDENT. But then who was the dead man?

OLD MAN. You asked me that just now, and I answered. If you were to look round the corner, where the tradesmen's entrance is, you would see a lot of poor people whom he used to help—when it suited him.

STUDENT. He was a kind man then.

OLD MAN. Yes—sometimes.

STUDENT. Not always?

OLD MAN. No-o. That's the way of people. Now, sir, will you push my chair a little, so that it gets into the sun. I'm horribly cold. When you're never able to move about, the blood congeals. I'm going to die soon, I know that, but I have a few things to do first. Take my hand and feel how cold I am.

STUDENT, *taking it.* Yes, inconceivably. *He shrinks back, trying in vain to free his hand.*

OLD MAN. Don't leave me. I am tired now and lonely, but I haven't always been like this, you know. I have an enormously long life behind me, enormously long. I have made people unhappy and people have made me unhappy—the one cancels out the other—but before I die I want to see you happy. Our fates are entwined through your father—and other things.

STUDENT. Let go of my hand. You are taking all my strength. You are freezing me. What do you want with me?

OLD MAN, *letting go.* Be patient and you shall see and understand. Here comes the young lady.

They watch the GIRL *approaching, though the audience cannot yet see her.*

STUDENT. The Colonel's daughter?

OLD MAN. His daughter—yes. Look at her. Have you ever seen such a masterpiece?

STUDENT. She is like the marble statue in there.

OLD MAN. That's her mother, you know.

STUDENT. You are right. Never have I seen such a woman of woman born. Happy the man who may lead her to the altar and his home.

OLD MAN. You can see it. Not everyone recognizes her beauty. So, then, it is written.

The GIRL *enters, wearing an English riding habit. Without noticing anyone she walks slowly to the door, where she stops to say a few words to the* CARETAKER'S WIFE. *Then she goes into the house.*

The STUDENT *covers his eyes with his hand.*

OLD MAN. Are you weeping?

STUDENT. In the face of what's hopeless there can be nothing but despair.

OLD MAN. I can open doors and hearts, if only I find an arm to do my will. Serve me and you shall have power.

STUDENT. Is it a bargain? Am I to sell my soul?

OLD MAN. Sell nothing. Listen. All my life I have *taken.* Now I have a craving to give—give. But no one will accept. I am rich, very rich, but I have no heirs, except for a good-for-nothing who torments the life out of me. Become my son. Inherit me while I am still alive. Enjoy life so that I can watch, at least from a distance.

STUDENT. What am I to do?

OLD MAN. First go to *The Valkyrie.*

STUDENT. That's settled. What else?

OLD MAN. This evening you must be in there—in the Round Room.

STUDENT. How am I to get there?

OLD MAN. By way of *The Valkyrie.*

STUDENT. Why have you chosen me as your medium? Did you know me before?

OLD MAN. Yes, of course. I have had my eye on you for a long time. But now look up there at the balcony. The maid is hoisting the flag to half-mast for the Consul. And now she is turning the bedclothes. Do you see that blue quilt? It was made for two to sleep under, but now it covers only one. *The* GIRL, *having changed her dress, appears in the window and waters the hyacinths.* There is my little girl. Look at her, look! She is talking to the flowers. Is she not like that blue hyacinth herself? She gives them drink —nothing but pure water, and they transform the water into color and fragrance. Now here comes the Colonel with the newspaper. He is showing her the bit about the house that collapsed. Now he's pointing to your portrait. She's not indifferent. She's reading of your brave deed. . . .

I believe it's clouding over. If it turns to rain I shall be in a pretty fix, unless Johansson comes back soon. *It grows cloudy and dark. The* FIANCÉE *at the window-mirror closes her window.* Now my fiancée is closing the window. Seventy-nine years old. The window-mirror is the only mirror she uses, because in it she sees not herself, but the world outside—in two directions. But the world can see her; she hasn't thought of that. Anyhow she's a handsome old woman.

Now the DEAD MAN, *wrapped in a winding sheet, comes out of the door.*

STUDENT. Good God, what do I see?

OLD MAN. What do you see?

STUDENT. Don't *you* see? There, in the doorway, the dead man?

OLD MAN. I see nothing, but I expected this. Tell me.

STUDENT. He is coming out into the street. *Pause.* Now he is turning his head and looking up at the flag.

OLD MAN. What did I tell you? You may be sure he'll count the wreaths and read the visiting cards. Woe to him who's missing.

STUDENT. Now he's turning the corner.

OLD MAN. He's gone to count the poor at the back door. The

poor are in the nature of a decoration, you see. "Followed by the blessings of many." Well, he's not going to have my blessing. Between ourselves he was a great scoundrel.

STUDENT. But charitable.

OLD MAN. A charitable scoundrel, always thinking of his grand funeral. When he knew his end was near, he cheated the State out of fifty thousand crowns. Now his daughter has relations with another woman's husband and is wondering about the Will. Yes, the scoundrel can hear every word we're saying, and he's welcome to it. Ah, here comes Johansson! JOHANSSON *enters.* Report! JOHANSSON *speaks, but the audience does not hear.* Not at home, eh? You are an ass. And the telegram? Nothing? Go on. . . . At six this evening? That's good. Special edition, you say? With his name in full. Arkenholtz, a student, born . . . parents . . . That's splendid. . . . I think it's beginning to rain. . . . What did he say about it? So–so. He wouldn't? Well, he must. Here comes the aristocrat. Push me round the corner, Johansson, so I can hear what the poor are saying. And, Arkenholtz, you wait for me here. Understand? *To* JOHANSSON. Hurry up now, hurry up.

JOHANSSON *wheels the chair round the corner. The* STUDENT *remains watching the* GIRL, *who is now loosening the earth round the hyacinths. The* ARISTOCRAT, *wearing mourning, comes in and speaks to the* DARK LADY, *who has been walking to and fro on the pavement.*

ARISTOCRAT. But what can we do about it? We shall have to wait.

LADY. I can't wait.

ARISTOCRAT. You can't? Well then, go into the country.

LADY. I don't want to do that.

ARISTOCRAT. Come over here or they will hear what we are saying.

They move towards the advertisement column and continue their conversation inaudibly. JOHANSSON *returns.*

JOHANSSON, *to the* STUDENT. My master asks you not to forget that other thing, sir.

STUDENT, *hesitating*. Look here . . . first of all tell me . . . who is your master?

JOHANSSON. Well, he's so many things, and he has been everything.

STUDENT. Is he a wise man?

JOHANSSON. Depends what that is. He says all his life he's been looking for a Sunday child, but that may not be true.

STUDENT. What does he want? He's grasping, isn't he?

JOHANSSON. It's power he wants. The whole day long he rides round in his chariot like the god Thor himself. He looks at houses, pulls them down, opens up new streets, builds squares. . . . But he breaks into houses too, sneaks through windows, plays havoc with human destinies, kills his enemies—and never forgives. Can you imagine it, sir? This miserable cripple was once a Don Juan—although he always lost his women.

STUDENT. How do you account for that?

JOHANSSON. You see he's so cunning he makes the women leave him when he's tired of them. But what he's most like now is a horse-thief in the human market. He steals human beings in all sorts of different ways. He literally stole me out of the hands of the law. Well, as a matter of fact I'd made a slip—hm, yes—and only he knew about it. Instead of getting me put in gaol, he turned me into a slave. I slave—for my food alone, and that's none of the best.

STUDENT. Then what is it he means to do in this house?

JOHANSSON. I'm not going to talk about that. It's too complicated.

STUDENT. I think I'd better get away from it all.

The GIRL *drops a bracelet out the window.*

JOHANSSON. Look! The young lady has dropped her bracelet out of the window. *The* STUDENT *goes slowly over, picks up the bracelet and returns it to the* GIRL, *who thanks him stiffly. The* STUDENT *goes back to* JOHANSSON. So you mean to get away. That's not so easy as you think, once he's got you in his net. And he's afraid of nothing between heaven and earth—yes, of one thing he is—of one person rather. . . .

STUDENT. Don't tell me. I think perhaps I know.

JOHANSSON. How can you know?

STUDENT. I'm guessing. Is it a little milkmaid he's afraid of?

JOHANSSON. He turns his head the other way whenever he meets a milk cart. Besides, he talks in his sleep. It seems he was once in Hamburg. . . .

STUDENT. Can one trust this man?

JOHANSSON. You can trust him—to do anything.

STUDENT. What's he doing now round the corner?

JOHANSSON. Listening to the poor. Sowing a little word, loosening one stone at a time, till the house falls down—metaphorically speaking. You see I'm an educated man. I was once a book-seller. . . . Do you still mean to go away?

STUDENT. I don't like to be ungrateful. He saved my father once, and now he only asks a small service in return.

JOHANSSON. What is that?

STUDENT. I am to go to *The Valkyrie.*

JOHANSSON. That's beyond me. But he's always up to new tricks. Look at him now, talking to that policeman. He is always thick with the police. He uses them, gets them involved in his interests, holds them with false promises and expectations, while all the time he's pumping them. You'll see that before the day is over he'll be received in the Round Room.

STUDENT. What does he want there? What connection has he with the Colonel?

JOHANSSON. I think I can guess, but I'm not sure. You'll see for yourself once you're in there.

STUDENT. I shall never be in there.

JOHANSSON. That depends on yourself. Go to *The Valkyrie.*

STUDENT. Is that the way?

JOHANSSON. Yes, if he said so. Look. Look at him in his war

chariot, drawn in triumph by the beggars, who get nothing for their pains but the hint of a treat at his funeral.

The OLD MAN *appears standing up in his wheel-chair, drawn by one of the beggars and followed by the rest.*

OLD MAN. Hail the noble youth who, at the risk of his own life, saved so many others in yesterday's accident. Three cheers for Arkenholtz! *The* BEGGARS *bare their heads but do not cheer. The* GIRL *at the window waves her handkerchief. The* COLONEL *gazes from the window of the Round Room. The* OLD WOMAN *rises at her window. The* MAID *on the balcony hoists the flag to the top.* Clap your hands, citizens. True, it is Sunday, but the ass in the pit and the ear in the corn field will absolve us. And although I am not a Sunday child, I have the gift of prophecy and also that of healing. Once I brought a drowned person back to life. That was in Hamburg on a Sunday morning just like this. . . .

The MILKMAID *enters, seen only by the* STUDENT *and the* OLD MAN. *She raises her arms like one who is drowning and gazes fixedly at the* OLD MAN. *He sits down, then crumples up, stricken with horror.*

Johansson! Take me away! Quick! . . . Arkenholtz, don't forget *The Valkyrie.*

STUDENT. What is all this?

JOHANSSON. We shall see. We shall see.

SCENE TWO

Inside the Round Room. At the back is a white porcelain stove. On either side of it are a mirror, a pendulum clock and candelabra. On the right of the stove is the entrance to the hall beyond which is a glimpse of a room furnished in green and mahogany. On the left of the stove is the door to a cupboard, papered like the wall. The statue, shaded by palms has a curtain which can be drawn to conceal it.

A door on the left leads into the Hyacinth Room, where the GIRL *sits reading.*

The back of the COLONEL *can be seen, as he sits in the Green Room, writing.*

BENGTSSON, *the Colonel's servant, comes in from the hall. He is wearing livery, and is followed by* JOHANSSON, *dressed as a waiter.*

BENGTSSON. Now you'll have to serve the tea, Johansson, while I take the coats. Have you ever done it before?

JOHANSSON. It's true I push a war chariot in the daytime, as you know, but in the evenings I go as a waiter to receptions and so forth. It's always been my dream to get into this house. They're queer people here, aren't they?

BENGTSSON. Ye-es. A bit out of the ordinary anyhow.

JOHANSSON. Is it to be a musical party or what?

BENGTSSON. The usual ghost supper, as we call it. They drink tea and don't say a word—or else the Colonel does all the talking. And they crunch their biscuits, all at the same time. It sounds like rats in an attic.

JOHANSSON. Why do you call it the ghost supper?

BENGTSSON. They look like ghosts. And they've kept this up for twenty years, always the same people saying the same things or saying nothing at all for fear of being found out.

JOHANSSON. Isn't there a mistress of the house?

BENGTSSON. Oh yes, but she's crazy. She sits in a cupboard because her eyes can't bear the light. *He points to the papered door.* She sits in there.

JOHANSSON. In there?

BENGTSSON. Well, I told you they were a bit out of the ordinary.

JOHANSSON. But then—what does she look like?

BENGTSSON. Like a mummy. Do you want to have a look at her? *He opens the door.* There she is.

The figure of the COLONEL'S WIFE *is seen, white and shrivelled into a* MUMMY.

JOHANSSON. Oh my God!

MUMMY, *babbling.* Why do you open the door? Haven't I told you to keep it closed?

BENGTSSON, *in a wheedling tone.* Ta, ta, ta, ta. Be a good girl now, then you'll get something nice. Pretty Polly.

MUMMY, *parrot-like.* Pretty Polly. Are you there, Jacob? Currrrr!

BENGTSSON. She thinks she's a parrot, and maybe she's right. *To the* MUMMY. Whistle for us, Polly.

The MUMMY *whistles.*

JOHANSSON. Well, I've seen a few things in my day, but this beats everything.

BENGTSSON. You see, when a house gets old, it grows moldy, and when people stay a long time together and torment each other they go mad. The mistress of the house—shut up, Polly!—that mummy there, has been living here for forty years—same husband, same furniture, same relatives, same friends. *He closes the papered door.* And the goings-on in this house—well, they're beyond me. Look at that statue—that's her when she was young.

JOHANSSON. Good Lord! Is that the mummy?

BENGTSSON. Yes. It's enough to make you weep. And somehow, carried away by her own imagination or something, she's got to be a bit like a parrot—the way she talks and the way she can't stand cripples or sick people. She can't stand the sight of her own daughter, because she's sick.

JOHANSSON. Is the young lady sick?

BENGTSSON. Didn't you know that?

JOHANSSON. No. And the Colonel, who is he?

BENGTSSON. You'll see.

JOHANSSON, *looking at the statue.* It's horrible to think that . . . How old is she now?

BENGTSSON. Nobody knows. But it's said that when she was thirty-five she looked nineteen, and that's what she made the Colonel believe she was—here in this very house. Do you know what that black Japanese screen by the couch is for? They call it the death-screen, and when someone's going to die, they put it round—same as in a hospital.

JOHANSSON. What a horrible house! And the student was longing to get in, as if it were paradise.

BENGTSSON. What student? Oh, I know. The one who's coming here this evening. The Colonel and the young lady happened to meet him at the Opera, and both of them took a fancy to him. Hm. Now it's my turn to ask questions. Who is your master—the man in the wheelchair?

JOHANSSON. Well, he er . . . Is he coming here too?

BENGTSSON. He hasn't been invited.

JOHANSSON. He'll come uninvited—if need be.

The OLD MAN *appears in the hall on crutches, wearing a frock-coat and top-hat. He steals forward and listens.*

BENGTSSON. He's a regular old devil, isn't he?

JOHANSSON. Up to the ears.

BENGTSSON. He looks like old Nick himself.

JOHANSSON. And he must be a wizard too, for he goes through locked doors.

The OLD MAN *comes forward and takes hold of* JOHANSSON *by the ear.*

OLD MAN. Rascal—take care! *To* BENGTSSON. Tell the Colonel I am here.

BENGTSSON. But we are expecting guests.

OLD MAN. I know. But my visit is as good as expected, if not exactly looked forward to.

BENGTSSON. I see. What name shall I say? Mr. Hummel?

OLD MAN. Exactly. Yes. BENGTSSON *crosses the hall to the Green Room, the door of which he closes behind him. To* JOHANSSON. Get out! JOHANSSON *hesitates.* Get out! JOHANSSON *disappears into the hall. The* OLD MAN *inspects the room and stops in front of the statue in much astonishment.* Amelia! It is she—she!

MUMMY, *from the cupboard.* Prrr-etty Polly. *The* OLD MAN *starts.*

OLD MAN. What was that? Is there a parrot in the room? I don't see it.

MUMMY. Are you there, Jacob?

OLD MAN. The house is haunted.

MUMMY. Jacob!

OLD MAN. I'm scared. So these are the kind of secrets they guard in this house. *With his back turned to the cupboard he stands looking at a portrait.* There he is—he!

The MUMMY *comes out behind the* OLD MAN *and gives a pull at his wig.*

MUMMY. Currrrr! Is it . . . ? Currrrr!

OLD MAN, *jumping out of his skin.* God in heaven! Who is it?

MUMMY, *in a natural voice.* Is it Jacob?

OLD MAN. Yes, my name is Jacob.

MUMMY, *with emotion.* And my name is Amelia.

OLD MAN. No, no, no . . . Oh my God!

MUMMY. That's how I look. Yes. *Pointing to the statue.* And that's how I *did* look. Life opens one's eyes, does it not? I live mostly in the cupboard to avoid seeing and being seen. . . . But, Jacob, what do you want here?

OLD MAN. My child. Our child.

MUMMY. There she is.

OLD MAN. Where?

MUMMY. There—in the Hyacinth Room.

OLD MAN, *looking at the* GIRL. Yes, that is she. *Pause.* And what about her father—the Colonel, I mean—your husband?

MUMMY. Once, when I was angry with him, I told him everything.

OLD MAN. Well. . . . ?

MUMMY. He didn't believe me. He just said: "That's what all wives say when they want to murder their husbands." It was a terrible crime none the less. It has falsified his whole life—his family tree too. Sometimes I take a look in the Peerage, and then I say to myself: Here she is, going about with a false birth certificate like some servant girl, and for such things people are sent to the reformatory.

OLD MAN. Many do it. I seem to remember your own date of birth was given incorrectly.

MUMMY. My mother made me do that. I was not to blame. And in our crime, *you* played the biggest part.

OLD MAN. No. Your husband caused that crime, when he took my fiancée from me. I was born one who cannot forgive until he has punished. That was to me an imperative duty—and is so still.

MUMMY. What are you expecting to find in this house? What do you want? How did you get in? Is it to do with my daughter? If you touch her, you shall die.

OLD MAN. I mean well by her.

MUMMY. Then you must spare her father.

OLD MAN. No.

MUMMY. Then you shall die. In this room, behind that screen.

OLD MAN. That may be. But I can't let go once I've got my teeth into a thing.

MUMMY. You want to marry her to that student. Why? He is nothing and has nothing.

OLD MAN. He will be rich, through me.

MUMMY. Have you been invited here tonight?

OLD MAN. No, but I propose to get myself an invitation to this ghost supper.

MUMMY. Do you know who is coming?

OLD MAN. Not exactly.

MUMMY. The Baron. The man who lives up above—whose father-in-law was buried this afternoon.

OLD MAN. The man who is getting a divorce in order to marry the daughter of the Caretaker's wife . . . The man who used to be—your lover.

MUMMY. Another guest will be your former fiancée, who was seduced by my husband.

OLD MAN. A select gathering.

MUMMY. Oh God, if only we might die, might die!

OLD MAN. Then why have you stayed together?

MUMMY. Crime and secrets and guilt bind us together. We have broken our bonds and gone our own ways, times without number, but we are always drawn together again.

OLD MAN. I think the Colonel is coming.

MUMMY. Then I will go in to Adèle. *Pause.* Jacob, mind what you do. Spare him. *Pause. She goes into the Hyacinth Room and disappears.*

The COLONEL *enters, cold and reserved, with a letter in his hand.*

COLONEL. Be seated, please. *Slowly the* OLD MAN *sits down. Pause. The* COLONEL *stares at him.* You wrote this letter, sir?

OLD MAN. I did.

COLONEL. Your name is Hummel?

OLD MAN. It is. *Pause.*

COLONEL. As I understand, you have bought in all my unpaid promissory notes. I can only conclude that I am in your hands. What do you want?

OLD MAN. I want payment, in one way or another.

COLONEL. In what way?

OLD MAN. A very simple one. Let us not mention the money. Just bear with me in your house as a guest.

COLONEL. If so little will satisfy you . . .

OLD MAN. Thank you.

COLONEL. What else?

OLD MAN. Dismiss Bengtsson.

COLONEL. Why should I do that? My devoted servant, who has been with me a lifetime, who has the national medal for long and faithful service—why should I do that?

OLD MAN. That's how you see him—full of excellent qualities. He is not the man he appears to be.

COLONEL. Who is?

OLD MAN, *taken aback.* True. But Bengtsson must go.

COLONEL. Are you going to run my house?

OLD MAN. Yes. Since everything here belongs to me—furniture, curtains, dinner service, linen . . . and more too.

COLONEL. How do you mean—more?

OLD MAN. Everything. I own everything here. It is mine.

COLONEL. Very well, it is yours. But my family escutcheon and my good name remain my own.

OLD MAN. No, not even those. *Pause.* You are not a nobleman.

COLONEL. How dare you!

OLD MAN, *producing a document.* If you read this extract from *The Armorial Gazette,* you will see that the family whose name you are using has been extinct for a hundred years.

COLONEL. I have heard rumors to this effect, but I inherited the name from my father. *Reads.* It is true. You are right. I am not a nobleman. Then I must take off my signet ring. It is true, it belongs to you. *Gives it to him.* There you are.

OLD MAN, *pocketing the ring.* Now we will continue. You are not a Colonel either.

COLONEL. I am not . . . ?

OLD MAN. No. You once held the temporary rank of Colonel in the American Volunteer Force, but after the war in Cuba and the reorganization of the Army, all such titles were abolished.

COLONEL. Is this true?

OLD MAN, *indicating his pocket.* Do you want to read it?

COLONEL. No, that's not necessary. Who are you, and what right have you to sit there stripping me in this fashion?

OLD MAN. You will see. But as far as stripping you goes . . . do you know who you are?

COLONEL. How dare you?

OLD MAN. Take off that wig and have a look at yourself in the mirror. But take your teeth out at the same time and shave off your moustache. Let Bengtsson unlace your metal stays and perhaps a certain X.Y.Z., a lackey, will recognize himself. The fellow who was a cupboard lover in a certain kitchen . . . *The* COLONEL *reaches for the bell on the table, but* HUMMEL *checks him.* Don't touch that bell, and don't call Bengtsson. If you do, I'll have him arrested. *Pause.* And now the guests are beginning to arrive. Keep your composure and we will continue to play our old parts for a while.

COLONEL. Who are you? I recognize your voice and eyes.

OLD MAN. Don't try to find out. Keep silent and obey.

The STUDENT *enters and bows to the* COLONEL.

STUDENT. How do you do, sir.

COLONEL. Welcome to my house, young man. Your splendid behavior at that great disaster has brought your name to everybody's lips, and I count it an honor to receive you in my home.

STUDENT. My humble descent, sir . . . Your illustrious name and noble birth. . . .

COLONEL. May I introduce Mr. Arkenholtz—Mr. Hummel. If you will join the ladies in here, Mr. Arkenholtz—I must conclude my conversation with Mr. Hummel. *He shows the* STUDENT *into the Hyacinth Room, where he remains visible, talking shyly to the* GIRL. A splendid young man, musical, sings, writes poetry. If he only had blue blood in him, if he were of the same station, I don't think I should object . . .

OLD MAN. To what?

COLONEL. To my daughter . . .

OLD MAN. *Your* daughter! But apropos of that, why does she spend all her time in there?

COLONEL. She insists on being in the Hyacinth Room except when she is out-of-doors. It's a peculiarity of hers. Ah, here comes Miss Beatrice von Holsteinkrona—a charming woman, a pillar of the Church, with just enough money of her own to suit her birth and position.

OLD MAN, *to himself.* My fiancée.

The FIANCÉE *enters, looking a little crazy.*

COLONEL. Miss Holsteinkrona—Mr. Hummel. *The* FIANCÉE *curtseys and takes a seat. The* ARISTOCRAT *enters and seats himself. He wears mourning and looks mysterious.* Baron Skanskorg . . .

OLD MAN, *aside, without rising.* That's the jewel-thief, I think. *To the* COLONEL. If you bring in the Mummy, the party will be complete.

COLONEL, *at the door of the Hyacinth Room.* Polly!

MUMMY, *entering.* Currrrr . . . !

COLONEL. Are the young people to come in too?

OLD MAN. No, not the young people. They shall be spared.

They all sit silent in a circle.

COLONEL. Shall we have the tea brought in?

OLD MAN. What's the use? No one wants tea. Why should we pretend about it?

COLONEL. Then shall we talk?

OLD MAN. Talk of the weather, which we know? Inquire about each other's health, which we know just as well. I prefer silence—then one can hear thoughts and see the past. Silence cannot hide anything—but words can. I read the other day that differences of language originated among savages for the purpose of keeping one tribe's secrets hidden from another. Every language therefore is a code, and he who finds the key can understand every language in the world. But this does not prevent secrets from being exposed without a key, specially when there is a question of paternity to be proved. Proof in a Court of Law is another matter. Two false witnesses suffice to prove anything about which they are agreed, but one does not take witnesses along on the kind of explorations I have in mind. Nature herself has instilled in human beings a sense of modesty which tries to hide what should be hidden, but we slip into situations unintentionally, and by chance sometimes the deepest secret is divulged—the mask torn from the impostor, the villain exposed. . . . *Pause. All look at each other in silence.* What a silence there is now! *Long silence.* Here, for instance, in this honorable house, in this elegant home, where beauty, wealth and culture are united. . . . *Long silence.* All of us now sitting here know who we are—do we not? There's no need for me to tell you. And you know me, although you pretend ignorance. *He indicates the Hyacinth Room.* In there is my daughter. *Mine*—you know that too. She had lost the desire to live, without knowing why. The fact is she was withering away in this air charged with crime and deceit and falseness of every kind. That is why I looked for a friend for her in whose company she might enjoy the light and warmth of noble deeds. *Long silence.* That was my mission in this house: to pull up the weeds, to expose the crimes, to settle all accounts, so that those young people might start afresh in this home, which is my gift to them. *Long silence.* Now I am going to grant safe-conduct, to each of you in his and her proper time and turn. Whoever stays I shall have arrested. *Long silence.* Do you hear the clock ticking like a death-watch beetle in the wall? Do you hear what it says? "It's time, it's time, it's time." When it strikes, in a few moments, your time will be up. Then you can go, but not before. It's raising its arm against you before it strikes. Listen! It is warning you. "The clock can strike." And I can strike too. *He strikes the table with one of his crutches.* Do you hear?

Silence. The MUMMY *goes up to the clock and stops it, then speaks in a normal and serious voice.*

MUMMY. But I can stop time in its course. I can wipe out the past and undo what is done. But not with bribes, not with threats—only through suffering and repentance. *She goes up to the* OLD MAN. We are miserable human beings, that we know. We have erred and we have sinned, we like all the rest. We are not what we seem, because at bottom we are better than ourselves, since we detest our sins. But when you, Jacob Hummel, with your false name, choose to sit in judgment over us, you prove yourself worse than us miserable sinners. For you are not the one you appear to be. You are a thief of human souls. You stole me once with false promises. You murdered the Consul who was buried today; you strangled him with debts. You have stolen the student, binding him by the pretence of a claim on his father, who never owed you a farthing. *Having tried to rise and speak, the* OLD MAN *sinks back in his chair and crumples up more and more as she goes on.* But there is one dark spot in your life which I am not quite sure about, although I have my suspicions. I think Bengtsson knows. *She rings the bell on the table.*

OLD MAN. No, not Bengtsson, not him.

MUMMY. So he does know. *She rings again. The* MILKMAID *appears in the hallway door, unseen by all but the* OLD MAN, *who shrinks back in horror. The* MILKMAID *vanishes as* BENGTSSON *enters.* Do you know this man, Bengtsson?

BENGTSSON. Yes, I know him and he knows me. Life, as you are aware, has its ups and downs. I have been in his service; another time he was in mine. For two whole years he was a sponger in my kitchen. As he had to be away by three, the dinner was got ready at two, and the family had to eat the warmed-up leavings of that brute. He drank the soup stock, which the cook then filled up with water. He sat out there like a vampire, sucking the marrow out of the house, so that we became like skeletons. And he nearly got us put in prison when we called the cook a thief. Later I met this man in Hamburg under another name. He was a usurer then, a blood-sucker. But while he was there he was charged with having lured a young girl out on to the ice so as to drown her, because she had seen him commit a crime he was afraid would be discovered. . . .

The MUMMY *passes her hand over the* OLD MAN'S *face.*

MUMMY. *This* is you. Now give up the notes and the Will. JOHANSSON *appears in the hallway door and watches the scene with great interest, knowing he is now to be freed from slavery. The* OLD MAN *produces a bundle of papers and throws it on the table. The* MUMMY *goes over and strokes his back.* Parrot. Are you there, Jacob?

OLD MAN, *like a parrot.* Jacob is here. Pretty Polly. Currrrr!

MUMMY. May the clock strike?

OLD MAN, *with a clucking sound.* The clock may strike. *Imitating a cuckoo clock.* Cuckoo, cuckoo, cuckoo. . . .

The MUMMY *opens the cupboard door.*

MUMMY. Now the clock has struck. Rise, and enter the cupboard where I have spent twenty years repenting our crime. A rope is hanging there, which you can take as the one with which you strangled the Consul, and with which you meant to strangle your benefactor. . . . Go! *The* OLD MAN *goes in to the cupboard. The* MUMMY *closes the door.* Bengtsson! Put up the screen—the death-screen. BENGTSSON *places the screen in front of the door.* It is finished. God have mercy on his soul.

ALL. Amen. *Long silence.*

The GIRL *and the* STUDENT *appear in the Hyacinth Room. She has a harp, on which he plays a prelude, and then accompanies the* STUDENT'*s recitation.*

STUDENT. *I saw the sun. To me it seemed*
that I beheld the Hidden.
Men must reap what they have sown;
blest is he whose deeds are good.
Deeds which you have wrought in fury,
cannot in evil find redress.
Comfort him you have distressed
with loving-kindness—this will heal.
No fear has he who does no ill.
Sweet is innocence.

SCENE THREE

Inside the Hyacinth Room. The general effect of the room is exotic and oriental. There are hyacinths everywhere, of every color, some in pots, some with the bulbs in glass vases and the roots going down into the water.

On top of the tiled stove is a large seated Buddha, in

whose lap rests a bulb from which rises the stem of a shallot (Allium ascalonicum), bearing its globular cluster of white, starlike flowers.

On the right is an open door, leading into the Round Room, where the COLONEL *and the* MUMMY *are seated, inactive and silent. A part of the death-screen is also visible.*

On the left is a door to the pantry and kitchen.

The STUDENT *and the* GIRL (Adèle) *are beside the table; he standing, she seated with her harp.*

GIRL. Now sing to my flowers.

STUDENT. Is this the flower of your soul?

GIRL. The one and only. Do you too love the hyacinth?

STUDENT. I love it above all other flowers—its virginal shape rising straight and slender out of the bulb, resting on the water and sending its pure white roots down into the colorless fluid. I love its colors: the snow-white, pure as innocence, the yellow honey-sweet, the youthful pink, the ripe red, but best of all the blue—the dewy blue, deep-eyed and full of faith. I love them all, more than gold or pearls. I have loved them ever since I was a child, have worshipped them because they have all the fine qualities I lack. . . . And yet . . .

GIRL. Go on.

STUDENT. My love is not returned, for these beautiful blossoms hate me.

GIRL. How do you mean?

STUDENT. Their fragrance, strong and pure as the early winds of spring which have passed over melting snows, confuses my senses, deafens me, blinds me, thrusts me out of the room, bombards me with poisoned arrows that wound my heart and set my head on fire. Do you know the legend of that flower?

GIRL. Tell it to me.

STUDENT. First its meaning. The bulb is the earth, resting on the water or buried in the soil. Then the stalk rises, straight as the axis of the world, and at the top are the six-pointed star-flowers.

GIRL. Above the earth—the stars. Oh, that is wonderful! Where did you learn this? How did you find it out?

STUDENT. Let me think . . . In your eyes. And so, you see, it is an image of the Cosmos. This is why Buddha sits holding the earth-bulb, his eyes brooding as he watches it grow, outward and upward, transforming itself into a heaven. This poor earth will become a heaven. It is for this that Buddha waits.

GIRL. I see it now. Is not the snowflake six-pointed too like the hyacinth flower?

STUDENT. You are right. The snowflakes must be falling stars.

GIRL. And the snowdrop is a snow-star, grown out of snow.

STUDENT. But the largest and most beautiful of all the stars in the firmament, the golden-red Sirius, is the narcissus with its gold and red chalice and its six white rays.

GIRL. Have you seen the shallot in bloom?

STUDENT. Indeed I have. It bears its blossoms within a ball, a globe like the celestial one, strewn with white stars.

GIRL. Oh how glorious! Whose thought was that?

STUDENT. Yours.

GIRL. Yours.

STUDENT. Ours. We have given birth to it together. We are wedded.

GIRL. Not yet.

STUDENT. What's still to do?

GIRL. Waiting, ordeals, patience.

STUDENT. Very well. Put me to the test. *Pause.* Tell me. Why do your parents sit in there so silently, not saying a single word?

GIRL. Because they have nothing to say to each other, and because neither believes what the other says. This is how my father puts it: What's the point of talking, when neither of us can fool the other?

STUDENT. What a horrible thing to hear!

GIRL. Here comes the Cook. Look at her, how big and fat she is. *They watch the* COOK, *although the audience cannot yet see her.*

STUDENT. What does she want?

GIRL. To ask me about the dinner. I have to do the housekeeping as my mother's ill.

STUDENT. What have we to do with the kitchen?

GIRL. We must eat. Look at the Cook. I can't bear the sight of her.

STUDENT. Who is that ogress?

GIRL. She belongs to the Hummel family of vampires. She is eating us.

STUDENT. Why don't you dismiss her?

GIRL. She won't go. We have no control over her. We've got her for our sins. Can't you see that we are pining and wasting away?

STUDENT. Don't you get enough to eat?

GIRL. Yes, we get many dishes, but all the strength has gone. She boils the nourishment out of the meat and gives us the fibre and water, while she drinks the stock herself. And when there's a roast, she first boils out the marrow, eats the gravy and drinks the juices herself. Everything she touches loses its savor. It's as if she sucked with her eyes. We get the grounds when she has drunk the coffee. She drinks the wine and fills the bottles up with water.

STUDENT. Send her packing.

GIRL. We can't.

STUDENT. Why not?

GIRL. We don't know. She won't go. No one has any control over her. She has taken all our strength from us.

STUDENT. May I get rid of her?

GIRL. No. It must be as it is. Here she is. She will ask me what is to be for dinner. I shall tell her. She will make objections and get her own way.

STUDENT. Let her do the ordering herself then.

GIRL. She won't do that.

STUDENT. What an extraordinary house! It is bewitched.

GIRL. Yes. But now she is turning back, because she has seen you.

THE COOK, *in the doorway.* No, that wasn't the reason. *She grins, showing all her teeth.*

STUDENT. Get out!

COOK. When it suits me. *Pause.* It does suit me now. *She disappears.*

GIRL. Don't lose your temper. Practise patience. She is one of the ordeals we have to go through in this house. You see, we have a housemaid too, whom we have to clean up after.

STUDENT. I am done for. *Cor in æthere.* Music!

GIRL. Wait.

STUDENT. Music!

GIRL. Patience. This room is called the room of ordeals. It looks beautiful, but it is full of defects.

STUDENT. Really? Well, such things must be seen to. It is very beautiful, but a little cold. Why don't you have a fire?

GIRL. Because it smokes.

STUDENT. Can't you have the chimney swept?

GIRL. It doesn't help. You see that writing-desk there?

STUDENT. An unusually fine piece.

GIRL. But it wobbles. Every day I put a piece of cork under that leg, and every day the housemaid takes it away when she sweeps and I have to cut a new piece. The penholder is covered with ink every morning and so is the inkstand. I have to clean them up every morning after that woman, as sure as the sun rises. *Pause.* What's the worst job you can think of?

STUDENT. To count the washing. Ugh!

GIRL. That I have to do. Ugh!

STUDENT. What else?

GIRL. To be waked in the middle of the night and have to get up and see to the window, which the housemaid has left banging.

STUDENT. What else?

GIRL. To get up on a ladder and tie the cord on the damper* which the housemaid has torn off.

STUDENT. What else?

GIRL. To sweep after her, to dust after her, to light the fire in the stove when all she's done is throw in some wood. To see to the damper, to wipe the glasses, to lay the table over again, to open the bottles, to see that the rooms are aired, to remake my bed, to rinse the water-bottle when it's green with sediment, to buy matches and soap which are always lacking, to wipe the chimneys and trim the wicks to keep the lamps from smoking—and so that they don't go out when we have company, I have to fill them myself. . . .

STUDENT. Music!

GIRL. Wait. The labor comes first. The labor of keeping the dirt of life at a distance.

STUDENT. But you are wealthy and have two servants.

GIRL. It doesn't help. Even if we had three. Living is hard work, and sometimes I grow tired. *Pause.* Think then if there were a nursery as well.

STUDENT. The greatest of joys.

GIRL. And the costliest. Is life worth so much hardship?

STUDENT. That must depend on the reward you expect for your labors. I would not shrink from anything to win your hand.

GIRL. Don't say that. You can never have me.

STUDENT. Why not?

GIRL. You mustn't ask. *Pause.*

STUDENT. You dropped your bracelet out of the window. . . .

GIRL. Because my hand has grown so thin. *Pause.*

The COOK *appears with a Japanese bottle in her hand.*

There she is—the one who devours me and all of us.

STUDENT. What has she in her hand?

*Damper to the big stove.

GIRL. It is the bottle of coloring matter that has letters like scorpions on it. It is the soy which turns water into soup and takes the place of gravy. She makes cabbage soup with it—and mock-turtle soup too.

STUDENT, *to* COOK. Get out!

COOK. You drain us of sap, and we drain you. We take the blood and leave you the water, but colored . . . colored. I am going now, but all the same I shall stay, as long as I please.

She goes out.

STUDENT. Why did Bengtsson get a medal?

GIRL. For his great merits.

STUDENT. Has he no defects?

GIRL. Yes, great ones. But you don't get a medal for them.

They smile.

STUDENT. You have many secrets in this house.

GIRL. As in all others. Permit us to keep ours.

STUDENT. Don't you approve of candor?

GIRL. Yes—within reason.

STUDENT. Sometimes I'm seized with a raging desire to say all I think. But I know the world would go to pieces if one were completely candid. *Pause.* I went to a funeral the other day . . . in church. It was very solemn and beautiful.

GIRL. Was it Mr. Hummel's?

STUDENT. My false benefactor's—yes. At the head of the coffin stood an old friend of the deceased. He carried the mace. I was deeply impressed by the dignified manner and moving words of the clergyman. I cried. We all cried. Afterwards we went to a tavern, and there I learned that the man with the mace had been in love with the dead man's son. . . . *The* GIRL *stares at him, trying to understand.* And that the dead man had borrowed money from his son's admirer. *Pause.* Next day the clergyman was arrested for embezzling the church funds. A pretty story.

GIRL. Oh . . . ! *Pause.*

STUDENT. Do you know how I am thinking about you now?

GIRL. Don't tell me, or I shall die.

STUDENT. I must, or I shall die.

GIRL. It is in asylums that people say everything they think.

STUDENT. Exactly. My father finished up in an asylum.

GIRL. Was he ill?

STUDENT. No, he was well, but he was mad. You see, he broke out once—in these circumstances. Like all of us, he was surrounded with a circle of acquaintances; he called them friends for short. They were a lot of rotters, of course, as most people are, but he had to have some society—he couldn't get on all alone. Well, as you know, in everyday life no one tells people what he thinks of them, and he didn't either. He knew perfectly well what frauds they were—he'd sounded the depths of their deceit —but as he was a wise and well-bred man, he was always courteous to them. Then one day he gave a big party. It was in the evening and he was tired by the day's work and by the strain of holding his tongue and at the same time talking rubbish with his guests. . . . *The* GIRL *is frightened.* Well, at the dinner table he rapped for silence, raised his glass, and began to speak. Then something loosed the trigger. He made an enormous speech in which he stripped the whole company naked, one after the other, and told them of all their treachery. Then, tired out, he sat down on the table and told them all to go to hell.

GIRL. Oh!

STUDENT. I was there, and I shall never forget what happened then. Father and Mother came to blows, the guests rushed for the door . . . and my father was taken to a madhouse, where he died. *Pause.* Water that is still too long stagnates, and so it is in this house too. There is something stagnating here. And yet I thought it was paradise itself that first time I saw you coming in here. There I stood that Sunday morning, gazing in. I saw a Colonel who was no Colonel. I had a benefactor who was a thief and had to hang himself. I saw a mummy who was not a mummy and an old maid—what of the maidenhood, by the way?

Where is beauty to be found? In nature, and in my own mind, when it is in its Sunday clothes. Where are honor and faith? In fairy-tales and children's fancies. Where is anything that fulfills its promise? In my imagination. Now your flowers have poisoned me and I have given the poison back to you. I asked you to become my wife in a home full of poetry and song and music. Then the Cook came. . . . *Sursum Corda!* Try once more to strike fire and glory out of the golden harp. Try, I beg you, I implore you on my knees. *Pause.* Then I will do it myself. *He picks up the harp, but the strings give no sound.* It is dumb and deaf. To think that the most beautiful flowers are so poisonous, are the most poisonous. The curse lies over the whole of creation, over life itself. Why will you not be my bride? Because the very life-spring within you is sick . . . now I can feel that vampire in the kitchen beginning to suck me. I believe she is a Lamia, one of those that suck the blood of children. It is always in the kitchen quarters that the seed-leaves of the children are nipped, if it has not already happened in the bedroom. There are poisons that destroy the sight and poisons that open the eyes. I seem to have been born with the latter kind, for I cannot see what is ugly as beautiful, nor call evil good. I cannot. Jesus Christ descended into hell. That was His pilgrimage on earth—to this madhouse, this prison, this charnel-house, this earth. And the madmen killed Him when He wanted to set them free; but the robber they let go. The robber always gets the sympathy. Woe! Woe to us all. Saviour of the world, save us! We perish.

And now the GIRL *has drooped, and it is seen that she is dying. She rings.*

BENGTSSON *enters.*

GIRL. Bring the screen. Quick. I am dying.

BENGTSSON *comes back with the screen, opens it and arranges it in front of the* GIRL.

STUDENT. The Liberator is coming. Welcome, pale and gentle one. Sleep, you lovely, innocent, doomed creature, suffering for no fault of your own. Sleep without dreaming, and when you wake again . . . may you be greeted by a sun that does not burn, in a home without dust, by friends without stain, by a love without flaw. You wise and gentle Buddha, sitting there waiting for a Heaven to sprout from the earth, grant us patience in our ordeal and purity of will, so that this hope may not be confounded.

The strings of the harp hum softly and a white light fills the room.

I saw the sun. To me it seemed
that I beheld the Hidden.
Men must reap what they have sown,
blest is he whose deeds are good.
Deeds which you have wrought in fury,
cannot in evil find redress.
Comfort him you have distressed
with loving-kindness—this will heal.
No fear has he who does no ill.
Sweet is innocence.

A faint moaning is heard behind the screen. You poor little child, child of this world of illusion, guilt, suffering and death, this world of endless change, disappointment, and pain. May the Lord of Heaven be merciful to you upon your journey.

The room disappears. Böcklin's picture The Island of the Dead *is seen in the distance, and from the island comes music, soft, sweet, and melancholy.*

THE GREAT HIGHWAY

A Wayfaring Drama with Seven Stations

FOREWORD

The Great Highway was written in 1909, when Strindberg was sixty. It was his last play. Divorced for the third time, he was now living alone in the high Stockholm apartment he called "The Blue Tower." His health was failing and he had the urge to write, as his farewell to life, one more drama of the journey, in which he, as the Hunter, could express the unending conflict in himself between the terrible heights of heaven and the dear but dirty plains of earth. Strindberg's first pilgrimage play, *To Damascus*, written ten years before, was a trilogy, and his autobiographical novels run into many volumes; but now, with the use of poetic imagery, he condensed his soul's experience into a single composition with seven scenes. Chance helped his inspiration: a hand-painted plate for sale, brought by a child to his apartment, suggested the scenery for the Hunter's home; he heard it said that a dying man had "coughed up his heart," and the phrase became a dominant theme; the new North Road out of Stockholm, which passed his present door, so many doors in his past, and also the gate of the cemetery where he had chosen to lie, was known as "The Great Highway," and thus he named his play, adding as sub-title, thinking surely of the Cross, *A Wayfaring Drama with Seven Stations.*

Having written his earliest plays in verse and abandoned this form for terse, realistic prose, and having swung from phantasy to realism and back again, in his last play Strindberg let his inspiration dictate its own form. *The Great Highway* is full of symbolism and imagery; the higher emotional moods are expressed in unrhymed verse, containing some of Strindberg's finest poetry, while the scenes in which he satirizes society, its institutions and its successful men are written in witty colloquial dialogue.

The introduction of a Japanese character in this play reminds one that Strindberg was a considerable sinologist. As a young man, he had taught himself Chinese in order to catalogue a collection of Chinese manuscripts in the Royal Library of Stockholm, which hitherto nobody had been able to do. Doubtless he obtained some knowledge of Japanese at this time too, and all his life oriental philosophy appealed strongly to him. It is with a shock that one comes upon the name that Strindberg gave this Japanese:

> I have travelled, sinned, and suffered by
> the name "Hiroshima," after my native town.

Strindberg gave many proofs of psychic power, but surely his gift of prophecy was never so strangely manifested as in the choice of the name "Hiroshima" for the tragic Japanese figure about to commit hara-kiri.

The Great Highway was given a single performance at Strindberg's own Intimate Theatre in Stockholm in 1910, but after this, was seldom seen until it was revived with a distinguished cast at Stockholm's Royal Theatre to celebrate the centenary of Strindberg's birth in January 1949. Passages from this translation were also read at the Anglo-Swedish Society in London by Michael Redgrave to mark this anniversary. And in September 1950 the play was presented at London's Watergate Theatre. It has now also been seen in many Scandinavian and Continental cities, and Dr. Arvid Paulson's version was given at the Pasadena Playhouse in California in 1952.

I am indebted to Lady Low for her help in translating *The Great Highway*, and to Dr. Arvid Paulson for allowing me to quote from the foreword to his translation, and to print the Japanese poem, in Japanese and in English, as it appears in his version:[1]

> . . . it has been discovered that the Japanese poem quoted by Strindberg in Scene IV has been misprinted in the published editions of the play. It is by an unknown Japanese poet and is published in the famous *Kokinshu* collection. It is here reprinted as it appears in this anthology.

E. S.

[1] *The Great Highway*, translated from the Swedish by Arvid Paulson, published in *Modern Scandinavian Plays* by The American-Scandinavian Foundation—The Liveright Publishing Corporation, New York, 1954.

CHARACTERS

In order of appearance

THE HUNTER

THE HERMIT

THE TRAVELLER

MILLER ADAM

MILLER EVE

MILLER ADAM'S WIFE

THE GIRL

THE SCHOOLMASTER

THE BLACKSMITH

THE WAITRESS

THE ORGAN-GRINDER

THE PHOTOGRAPHER

EUPHROSYNE

GOTTHARD

KLARA

THE JAPANESE

MÖLLER THE MURDERER

THE CHILD

THE WOMAN

THE TEMPTER

SCENES

I. IN THE MOUNTAINS

II. AT THE WINDMILLS

III. IN ASSESDEAN

IV. THE ARCADE IN TOPHET

V. IN THE ARBOUR OUTSIDE THE CREMATORIUM

VI. AT THE LAST GATE

VII. THE DARK WOOD

During Scene VII, "The Dark Wood," Chopin's Nocturne 13, Opus 48, 1, is played softly in the distance until the end of the play.

I. IN THE MOUNTAINS

A signpost with two arms, one pointing upward, the other down.

A background of dark thunderclouds. Later the storm breaks.

THE HUNTER *enters and looks at the signpost.*

THE HUNTER. Where have I got to, and how far have I come?
Yes, there the track leads up, and there goes down.
Descent's the common way—I want to rise.
And yet the signpost has thrown out his arms,
as if in warning of the upward way.
Danger then, many dangers
on that path, so narrow and so steep.
That does not scare me—I delight in danger.
But I must pause here for a little while,
and breathe,
and think; gather up
and find myself again,
myself which they stole from me. . . .
I lived too long among humanity
and gave away my soul,
my heart, my thoughts;
the rest they took, they stole—
they fettered me with friendliness,
with gifts I did not want.
Yes, it was warm down there, passing
from home to home, with fair-spread tables,
music and flowers, glasses, light.
But it grew too warm and stifled me—

And so I cast my moorings,
threw overboard my ballast, all that weighed,
however dear—and see, I rose!
Here I can breathe, my heart's seed-leaves,
the tender lungs, can open to the air;
no dust, no smoke, no breath breathed by another
poison my blood.
White, pure snow
of sublimated vapour. Water-diamonds,
you lily flowers crystallised from frost,
you flour of heaven strained through the cloud's black sifter.
O blessed silence, draw your silken quilt
over the head of a tired traveller,
who seeks his bed while whispering this prayer!
What's to the North? A cliff of slate,
a cloud like a schoolroom blackboard, as yet
unwritten on. What a din! Now comes the Teacher
and silence falls upon the class.
Nature is silent when the Great Teacher speaks.
Look now! A lightning flash from East to West—
in flaming ink he writes his name
on blue-black cloud. I know Thee,
eternal, unseen yet seen,
thou stern Compassionate!
The mountain firs bow down,
the brooks are mute and still.
The frightened chamois falls to knee,
the vulture bends his naked head.
All nature trembles
before the mighty Lord Creator,
and I who took his name in vain,
I bow myself in shame,
meanest of all before Thy mighty throne.
Look, the cloud's burst! The curtain's pulled,
is drawn aside. What do I see?
You lovely earth! You temptress,
pulling me down again.
How you have decked yourself!
In green of hope and blue of faith
and the rose-red of love.

The pine tops painted by the setting sun,
the cypresses of tombs and night,
a marble temple set on high
to honour or to happiness,
a grotto, the grey Sybil's home,
who scares the nymphs from olive groves—

Here comes the sun. What a sparkle
of frost's rose-diamonds! The clouds are edged
with silver; the blue-black capes
are hung out in the wind to air.
But what is this? Who veils the sun
and draws a shadow on the pure white snow?
Imperial eagle, gold-breasted chrysaëtos,
knight of the air in gilded mail,
with the knight's chain around your neck—

What? Are you sinking? Do you seek the valley
when wings tire, and your rudder-tail's
no power to steer your course aloft?
Yes. That's his will. Down, down to rest
and breathe the breath of warm humanity,
and smell the fragrance of the cloverfields—
for surely there it's summer still.
There water falls down from the clouds like pearls,
here it's like brilliants, square-cut diamonds;
there the brook chirps, here it's struck dumb,
here wastes of snow, although white flowers—
down there white daisies.
Up here, down there. Hither, thither
one is driven, to equal good and equal ill.

Enter THE HERMIT.

THE HERMIT. Whither? Quo vadis, traveller?
You have come halfway and now look back.
Excelsior! That's been your motto hitherto.

THE HUNTER. It is so still.

THE HERMIT. What are you seeking here?

THE HUNTER. Myself. The self I lost down there.

THE HERMIT. What you have lost down there,
surely you cannot find again up here?

THE HUNTER. That's true. Yet were I to go down,
I'd lose still more, not find what I have lost.

THE HERMIT. You fear for your skin. . . .

THE HUNTER. Not for my skin, but for my soul. . . .

THE HERMIT. You do not love your fellow beings. . . .

THE HUNTER. Yes, all too much. Therefore I fear them too. . . .

THE HERMIT. To love is to give. Give!

THE HUNTER. But they will not receive—they only take;
nor will they take the gift without the giver too.

THE HERMIT. The shepherd gave himself for the sheep.

THE HUNTER. Dust unto dust, but the spirit belongs to God.

THE HERMIT. You fence well with your tongue, you ought to wield the pen.
In any case, half of your life has gone.
Don't force the issue—premature birth
can never bring you to full growth.
Live your life out. Return and do not fear.
The highway's dusty—brush it off.
Ditches on either side—fall in
but rise again. Where you find gates,
jump over, creep under, lift the latch.
When you meet people take them in your arms—
they will not bite, but if they bite, what harm?
If you are ducked, then shake the water off.
Scatter your coins, they'll come to you again.
Up here there is not anything to win,
for stone is stone and snow is snow—
but human nature is another thing.

THE HUNTER. I know that well. Could I but sit
among the audience and watch the play!
But I must mount the stage, take part and act,
and once I play a part, I'm lost,
forgetting who I am.

THE HERMIT. Who are you?

THE HUNTER. Well said. Now let us stop.
Truly it is too cold for me up here.

Enter THE TRAVELLER.

THE HERMIT. The air is somewhat thin, and it is lonely.
But look, here's company!

THE HUNTER. Queer fellow. Coming from above.
Looks a bit fagged. Halt, you traveller!

THE TRAVELLER. I come from the mountain tops.
I bathed in air, but could not stay in air,
so clad myself again to journey further,
with company or without—but rather with.
What is that country in the distance, Hermit?

THE HERMIT. It is called the Country of Desires.

THE TRAVELLER. Of pious desires?

THE HERMIT. Pious or pagan, whichever . . .

THE TRAVELLER. . . . whichever they may be.
Well, I'm to have company, I see.
With whom have I the honour?

THE HUNTER. I am a soldier.

During the following speech, THE HERMIT *goes out.*

THE TRAVELLER. And I a traveller.
One travels best incognito and—mark my words—
one should always make acquaintance,
but never get to know.
In fact one never can—
one only thinks one knows. And so,
in company—neither friend nor enemy—
two steps between us—not too close.
On. And down. The route is clear.
A slope up, a slope down,
an inn, a stop, a little glass—
but keeping always to the southern course.

THE HUNTER. With sun as beacon, we'll not lose our bearings.
It will not fail; that watchman never sleeps—
I think our hermit's left us.

THE TRAVELLER. Well, let him go. He has no place
down there where our way lies.
He has made his choice and bade the world farewell.

THE HUNTER. He may perhaps be right.

THE TRAVELLER. Don't look up there!
Humanity and vanity rhyme as hither, thither.
But we do not go thither—we go hither!

II. AT THE WINDMILLS

Against a background of cloudy sky stand two windmills, known as Adam and Eve.

THE TRAVELLER *and* THE HUNTER *are sitting at a table outside an inn, drinking.*

THE TRAVELLER. How still it is, here in the valley!

THE HUNTER. Too still to suit the miller,

THE TRAVELLER. sleeping no matter how much water runs,

THE HUNTER. waiting for wind and stormy weather . . .

THE TRAVELLER. which unrewarding business rouses in me a certain aversion for windmills.

THE HUNTER. Just as it did in the noble knight Don Quixote de la Mancha,

THE TRAVELLER. who did not, however, trim his sails to the wind,

THE HUNTER. but quite the reverse,

THE TRAVELLER. which is why he got into difficulties. What are we doing? Playing Beggar-my-neighbour?

THE HUNTER. Sir Incognito, why do you drink so much?

THE TRAVELLER. As I'm always lying on the operating table, I chloroform myself.

THE HUNTER. Then we'll ask no more.

THE TRAVELLER. Perhaps I said too much.

THE HUNTER. To think that I can't guess what you are.

THE TRAVELLER. Stop trying to guess. It is far pleasanter.

THE HUNTER. Certainly, yes. . . . It's been cloudy all day today.

THE TRAVELLER. Let me drink a bit more, then you'll see it's clearing up. *Drinks.* Do you know Greek? Do you understand what *oinos* means?

THE HUNTER. *Oinos* means wine.

THE TRAVELLER. Yes, it means wine. So you are educated, are you?

THE HUNTER. *Noli me tangere!* Do not touch me! I sting.

THE TRAVELLER. Have you noticed that a grape is like a bottle, and its tendrils like a corkscrew? The implication's clear.

THE HUNTER. But the juice of the grape has none of the characteristics of chloroform—

THE TRAVELLER. till the grapes have been crushed underfoot and rotted in dregs and draff,

THE HUNTER. so the spirit of wine is set free from the filthy body of matter,

THE TRAVELLER. and rises to the surface like sea-foam,

THE HUNTER. out of which Aphrodite was born,

THE TRAVELLER. naked.

THE HUNTER. Without even a vineleaf to cover herself,

THE TRAVELLER. for clothes are only a consequence of sin. Are you always as serious as this?

THE HUNTER. Are you always as frivolous as this?

THE TRAVELLER. Which of us two is the more inquisitive?

THE HUNTER. Now he is stretching out his tentacles,

THE TRAVELLER. obeying the universal law of attraction,

THE HUNTER. followed by mutual repulsion,

THE TRAVELLER. which is why it's best to keep two steps apart and march in open file,

THE HUNTER. according to the agreement made day and date as above. Full stop. Here come the actors.

MILLER ADAM *and* MILLER EVE *appear in the distance.*

THE TRAVELLER. May I borrow your pince-nez? I can't see very well.

Takes THE HUNTER'S *glasses.*

What's this on the glass? It's like hoar-frost,
or crystallised water—or salt.
A tear that has dried. Warm at the source,
very soon it cooled and became rock-salt.
The steel of the bridge has rusted.

Ah, he weeps often! But in secret.
Rivulets of tears have carved a course,
down from the eyes to the smiling mouth
to quench the smile that would kindle a laugh.
Poor human being!
Your mask is torn,
and when you show your teeth,
one cannot tell if it's to bite or smile.

THE HUNTER. The play's beginning. An idyll of the windmills.

THE TRAVELLER. A pastoral in minor-major key. We'll watch.

The MILLERS *take the stage.*

MILLER ADAM. True, neighbour, to-day we're both in the same boat, as there's no wind at all. All the same, I'm thinking of having your mill moved, as you interfere with my progress.

MILLER EVE. You mean I take the East wind from you. On the other hand, you take the West wind from me. So we're quits.

MILLER ADAM. But my mill was here first, and yours was just built out of malice. Things go badly for both of us now, so it would be better if they went well for *one* of us.

MILLER EVE. For *you,* you mean?

MILLER ADAM. For you, *you* mean?

MILLER EVE. Yes, of course.

MILLER ADAM. But when I said *one* of us, I meant the better of us, the one who has right on his side.

MILLER EVE. Which would that be?

MILLER ADAM. Is it for us to judge in the matter?

MILLER EVE. I have a better grain-bolter than you, and my Eve grinds quicker, turns more easily, and has new sails.

MILLER ADAM. But my Adam was built before your Eve, and my mill-hopper is made of boxwood—

MILLER EVE. Stop. We'll ask those gentlemen over there.

THE TRAVELLER. So now we're going to be dragged into it.

THE HUNTER. They'll grab us as witnesses, perhaps even as judges—in order, later on, to override our judgement.

Enter the WIFE OF MILLER ADAM.

WIFE. Come along now, husband, and have your dinner.

MILLER ADAM. Wait a bit.

WIFE. I can't do that.

MILLER ADAM. You should learn never to be in a hurry.

WIFE. Never?

MILLER ADAM. Never—so long as the world remains and a word holds good.

WIFE. Then the cabbage will get cold.

MILLER ADAM. Is it cabbage? Well, that's another matter. I'll come at once.

WIFE. Then the world will come to an end, and a word hold good no more.

MILLER ADAM. Did I say that? Then I take it back.

They go out.

THE TRAVELLER. He sold his birthright,

THE HUNTER. for a mess of cabbage.

THE TRAVELLER. And that's that.

THE HUNTER. But now we're to be set on by the Eve miller. Look, now he's spying on us—and hesitating. He wants something out of us—some bit of information to increase his knowledge. Look how he's examining our clothes, shoes, hair, and beards. He's a thief.

MILLER EVE. Excuse me.

THE TRAVELLER. He's trying to trick us into talking. Don't answer.

MILLER EVE. Where have you gentlemen come from?

THE TRAVELLER. That's none of your business.

MILLER EVE. Strictly speaking, no.

THE TRAVELLER. Well, we are speaking strictly, so be off with you.

MILLER EVE. I wasn't going to pinch anything.

THE TRAVELLER. That wouldn't be easy in any case.

MILLER EVE. On the contrary, I was going to give you something.

THE TRAVELLER. We don't need anything.

MILLER EVE. Huh! Well, there it is, I was going to give you gentlemen something—and ask nothing for it—a bit of information, a useful bit of information. *Pause.* They're at work blasting rock just behind here—and one, two, three, we'll get a shower of stones on our heads!

THE TRAVELLER *and* THE HUNTER *spring up.*

THE TRAVELLER. Why on earth didn't you say so at once?

MILLER EVE. You wouldn't listen. But sit down again—there's no rush. The blasters will give the alarm first.

THE TRAVELLER. Look here, is this the way to the Promised Land?

MILLER EVE. This is the straight way.

THE TRAVELLER. Will the weather hold till the afternoon?

MILLER EVE. We can expect more thunder. It's very unsettled in this district.

THE TRAVELLER. All the year round?

MILLER EVE. Always unsettled, the whole year round. Year out, year in.

THE TRAVELLER. What is the next village called?

MILLER EVE. That's none of your business. Certainly it's pleasanter to give than to take, but to be robbed isn't pleasant at all. Thief! Have you a pass?

THE TRAVELLER. What for?

MILLER EVE. There are robbers in the woods, and everyone who won't say where he comes from must be examined.

THE HUNTER. Now we are in it up to our necks.

THE TRAVELLER. And it's not exactly an idyll of the windmills we are in.

MILLER EVE. I'll go and fetch my neighbour and his men. Then we can establish alibis.

THE TRAVELLER. That's a queer idea.

MILLER EVE. Well, you see, I'm the Parish Constable, and my neighbour's the Parish Clerk. *Exit.*

THE TRAVELLER. So now Herod and Pilate have become friends.

THE HUNTER. I really started out to gain my own soul, but he who seeks to gain shall lose. Let's cast ourselves into the throng again . . .

THE TRAVELLER. at the risk of sinking,

THE HUNTER. without reaching the bottom,

THE TRAVELLER. thanks to a certain life-belt which intelligent people wear.

THE GIRL *enters.*

Here comes a woman.

THE HUNTER. As one might expect in the vicinity of Adam and Eve,

THE TRAVELLER. without, however, expecting any paradise.

THE HUNTER. Full stop. Now the scene begins.

THE TRAVELLER. I think it's advisable to take the offensive. What is your name, my pretty child?

THE GIRL. Guess!

THE TRAVELLER. Let me see. Fair, miller's daughter, not very tall, round face . . . Your name's Amelia!

THE GIRL. How did you know?

THE TRAVELLER. By your appearance.

THE GIRL. If I'd been dark and tall, with an oval face, what would I have been called then—as a blacksmith's daughter?

THE TRAVELLER. Jenny, of course.

THE GIRL. That's right.

THE TRAVELLER. Now you've had all this from me, what do I get in return?

THE GIRL. You get . . . tell me, where did you learn this gift of reading people?

THE TRAVELLER. From life, experience, certain books, an innate superior intelligence—and a good portion of acquired acuteness. Now, my dear, why won't you have the son of your neighbour miller?

THE GIRL. So you know that too.

THE TRAVELLER. But you ought to take him. Then the mill problem will be settled out of court. You will sell one of the mills and have it moved to the next parish, where it is so badly needed.

THE GIRL. How wise, how very wise you are!

THE TRAVELLER. But I see you don't want the miller's boy. You'd rather have one of the robbers from the forest, eh? The one with the black eyes and big moustaches. . . .

THE GIRL. I'm beginning to be frightened. Are you a fortune-teller?

THE TRAVELLER. As you see. But I can only tell the fortunes of young people.

THE GIRL. Why is that?

THE TRAVELLER. Because old people are so cunning.

THE GIRL, *to* THE HUNTER. Is that true?

THE TRAVELLER. Don't talk to him—he doesn't want to be involved. Talk to me. Give me something in exchange for all you have learnt in this one short moment. Otherwise you'll be in my debt, and you wouldn't like that.

THE GIRL. Very well, you shall have something, so you will go away from here rewarded, richer than you came, loaded with knowledge, for which I ask nothing.

THE TRAVELLER. That's a likely story.

THE GIRL. To begin with, I'm not called Amelia. . . .

THE TRAVELLER. But Jenny—what did I say?

THE GIRL. No, not that either. Secondly, there is no miller's son. Thirdly, the next parish already has four windmills, so the mill problem would still be unsolved. And now for one or two bits of advice into the bargain. Don't be so familiar with a strange girl—you never know to whom you are talking, however observant you think you are. And don't be disloyal to a friend when a third person comes along, or else, when you are alone again and need him, he may not be there.

THE TRAVELLER. I haven't been disloyal.

THE GIRL. Yes, just now, in order to gain my favour, you tried to make him look ridiculous. That wasn't nice. Now you are on the defensive. And if you were to ask me my name now, I wouldn't answer as you answered the miller when he was trying to save you from the robbers in the forest.

THE HUNTER, *rising*. Won't you have a seat, young lady?

THE GIRL. It's true, I am a young lady. From the manor—and not a miller's daughter. *To* THE TRAVELLER. Go to the miller and give him my compliments—then you'll get the pass. Go on. Just give him my compliments.

THE TRAVELLER. But I must know your name.

THE GIRL, *sitting down.* I don't give my name to strangers, and if you were a respectable man you wouldn't ask for it. Go along.

Exit THE TRAVELLER.

THE GIRL. You are lucky, you, who roam the world, meet people, get to know them . . .

THE HUNTER. Know them?

THE GIRL. True, one cannot know. But one grows acquainted.

THE HUNTER. Scarcely even that. But guessing riddles is a way to pass the time.

THE GIRL. Because what's said does not mean much.

THE HUNTER. Just so. It has to be translated.
For every language is a foreign one,
and foreigners we are, each to the other,
all travelling incognito.

THE GIRL. Incognito even to ourselves.
You have a grief, and yet are not in mourning.

THE HUNTER. You dress as miller-girl, yet are a lady.

THE GIRL. And your companion?

THE HUNTER. Only an acquaintance—and entirely unknown.

THE GIRL. What do you think of him?

THE HUNTER. Everything and nothing.
So far I haven't summed him up.

THE GIRL. What were you doing up there?

THE HUNTER. Breathing and forgetting.

THE GIRL. But why forget? Without memory
our life is nothing but an empty waste.

THE HUNTER. And *with* it—a cargo foundering the ship.

THE GIRL. Ships without cargo most easily capsize. . . .

THE HUNTER. Therefore one takes on ballast . . .

THE GIRL. and takes in the sails.

THE HUNTER. Like a windmill, eh?

THE GIRL. Yes, otherwise the wings would break . . .

THE HUNTER. but it turns better on the heights . . .

THE GIRL. best of all down there, out on the plains . . .

THE HUNTER. where the air is so dense . . .

THE GIRL. that you can see for miles,
can count the country churches with the naked eye.
There all the stars of night appear,

THE HUNTER. not on the horizon,

THE GIRL. but in the zenith.
The zenith is everywhere,
once the horizon has been reached.

THE HUNTER. Tell me—was I once there?

THE GIRL. You are there now—where you strove to get
this very morning. Is it not sweet
to find the new when the old is won?

THE HUNTER. And that country in the distance?

THE GIRL. Press on and you will reach it—
but if you tire, it will recede.
No mortal's reached the Pole star in the zenith;
yet still they journey and return,
and others travel the same road and are forced back.
Do as they do—but learn while on the way.

THE HUNTER. One drags and dredges, nose down in the nadir.

THE GIRL. But eyes from time to time lift to the zenith.

A horn sounds.

THE HUNTER, *alert.* Do you hear?

THE GIRL. I hear, but do not understand.

THE HUNTER. I will translate.
You hear only sound, but I hear words.

THE GIRL. What does the horn say?

THE HUNTER. "Give answer now, where are you, where?"

The horn answers: Here!

THE GIRL. It is someone calling you.

The horn is heard again.

THE HUNTER. "Come hither, come hither, come hither, hither!"

THE GIRL. I hear you are a soldier, I see it rather.
They are calling you. We part as briefly as we met.

THE HUNTER. Not quite so briefly, not so lightly. . . .
Come with me—just a little way—
to the next village.

THE GIRL. And your companion?

THE HUNTER. Such ones are found at the bar of every inn.

THE GIRL. How cruel you are!

THE HUNTER. I have been to war.
There the word's "onward," never "stop"!

THE GIRL. So I must go or else I'll stop.

THE HUNTER. If you go, you will take something with you.

THE GIRL. If I stop, you will have taken something from me.

THE HUNTER, *looking off*. Look! They are quarrelling. In a moment they'll fight.
They're fighting. And I shall be called as witness.
But you must go. You must not be involved.

THE GIRL. Are you really thinking of me?

THE HUNTER. Of you, for you,
with you and through you. And now farewell.
A flower seen through the garden fence,
for a moment delighting the traveller's eye—
fairest unpicked; its fragrance lingering
a while on the wind—and then it is gone.
And so, onward!

THE GIRL. Goodbye. And so—onward! *Exit.*

THE HUNTER. Now I am sunk. Bound, trapped,
dragged between grind-stones of the law,
wings caught in a web of emotion,
allied with a stranger and involved
in a matter which does not concern me.
Enter THE TRAVELLER.

THE TRAVELLER. Are you still here? I thought you'd gone. You must really have a faithful disposition.

THE HUNTER. Did you get into the fight?

THE TRAVELLER. I gave the miller a punch on the jaw for making a fool of me. All that stuff about blasting and robbers in the forest was a pack of lies. And now we're summoned to appear at the autumn Assizes—I as defendant, you as witness.

THE HUNTER. Did you give our names then?

THE TRAVELLER. No, I took two names at random.

THE HUNTER. What a risk! Now they can have us up for perjury as well. Going and getting oneself tangled up in this way. What did you call me then?

THE TRAVELLER. I said you travelled under the name Incognito. That satisfied the yokels.

THE HUNTER. And I am to give evidence against you?

THE TRAVELLER. Yes, in three months' time. Let's make the most of our liberty and get going. They say there's some festivity in the next village.

THE HUNTER. What sort of festivity?

THE TRAVELLER. Oh, a kind of battle of flowers—and an Asses' Gala, at which the biggest dunce in the village gets a crown of gold paper.

THE HUNTER. How very odd! What's the village called?

THE TRAVELLER. It's called Assesdean. And this one's called Liarsbourne, because only liars live here.

THE HUNTER. *Enteuthen exelaunei,*[2] and then they marched, . . .

THE TRAVELLER. *parasangas trêis,* three leagues, . . .

THE HUNTER. and so they did.

They march out together.

III. IN ASSESDEAN

Left, a smithy. Right, in a corner, a bench, on which THE HUNTER *and* THE TRAVELLER *are sitting.*

THE HUNTER. Now we have travelled quite a way together,

THE TRAVELLER. and not come any closer to each other, not even so that I have a clue as to who you are.

[2] Literally: "Thence he marched."

THE HUNTER. As I told you, I'm a soldier. I'm always fighting. Fighting to keep my personal independence . . .

THE TRAVELLER. But not always winning.

THE HUNTER. One cannot ask for that,

THE TRAVELLER. specially as lost battles are the most instructive,

THE HUNTER. for the victor,

THE TRAVELLER. but the worst of it is one never knows who's won. In the last war it was the victor who lost most.

THE HUNTER. Which war?

THE TRAVELLER. The one at the windmills.

THE HUNTER. May I borrow your penknife? I lost mine in the mountains.

THE TRAVELLER. One shouldn't be inquisitive. If you just observe this knife, it will tell you a lot. The big blade's scarcely used—so the owner's no craftsman. The little blade, on the other hand, shows traces of lead and coloured crayons. He may therefore be an artist—but perhaps only an amateur. The corkscrew's worn—that we can understand—and the bottle-opener too. But then there's also a gimlet and a saw. Yes, and a skeleton key, which is far more significant. But as it's only thrown in with the rest, taken by and large we have no information.

THE HUNTER. Well! So this is Assesdean.

Enter THE SCHOOLMASTER.

Here comes the schoolmaster. This time we'll hold our tongues so as not to be involved.

THE TRAVELLER. As if that will help.

THE SCHOOLMASTER. Abra-kadabra, abrakadabra, ab-ra-ka-da-bra! *Gazes at the strangers.* No, they did not hear. Again. Abra-ka-dabra, abra-kadabra, abra-ka-da-bra! No, they're superior beings—they have self-control. Gentlemen, he who is silent gives his consent. I've come to ask if you will receive a deputation of the leading intellectuals of the village, who will engage you in a battle of words. If I get no answer, I'll take it as affirmative. One . . . two . . . three!

THE HUNTER *and* THE TRAVELLER. No!

THE SCHOOLMASTER. Fine!

THE TRAVELLER. You're not such a fool, considering you come from Assesdean.

THE SCHOOLMASTER. I'm the only sane fellow in the place—therefore I must make myself out an imbecile, or else they'll shut me up. I had an academic education, and I've written a verse tragedy in five acts called "Potamogeton,"[3] which is so damned silly that I should have won the prize. But the village blacksmith got the better of me. He produced a memorial to the Nation's Destroyer—and so I was passed over. I am one who is always passed over. You gentlemen will think me very egotistical, talking like this about myself, but there are two reasons for it. Firstly, I have to explain myself—and secondly, you wouldn't like it if I talked about you.

THE BLACKSMITH'S *steps are heard.*

Here comes the Blacksmith. I must disguise myself, or he'll think me sane and have me shut up.

THE SCHOOLMASTER *puts on asses' ears.*

Enter THE BLACKSMITH.

THE BLACKSMITH. Abra-ka-da-bra, abra-kadabra!

THE SCHOOLMASTER. Good day, Axe-handle!

THE BLACKSMITH. Is that a hit at me?

THE SCHOOLMASTER. Life is a fight, and we're part of it.

THE BLACKSMITH. Are you referring to the emancipation question or to free trade?

THE SCHOOLMASTER. Twice two is four, and six more makes eight. Agreed?

THE BLACKSMITH. I reserve to myself all mathematics, as that is my principal subject, particularly *quatuor species*, which means the four simple rules of reckoning, fractions included, excepting, of course, simple whole fractions and decimal fractions.

THE SCHOOLMASTER. Sometimes even great Homer falls asleep.

THE BLACKSMITH. But six and four make eleven, and if one

[3] NOTE. Pondweed.

moves the decimal two points to the left, it will be straight as a nail. Isn't that so, gentlemen? Am I not right?

THE TRAVELLER. Absolutely right. Six and four make eleven, and not eight.

THE BLACKSMITH. Now we'll pass to lighter matters, or, if I may say so, subjects of conversation. Gentlemen, a subject of conversation is not blown from the nose, if I may so express myself, even if such a subject is light. A light subject of conversation, closely observed, falls into two equal parts —first comes the subject, for everything must have a subject, and then the conversation follows of its own accord. Furthermore, the subjects may be as numerous as . . . as . . . days in the year—or more still—say, as drops in the ocean—or yet more as, let me see, as sands in the desert. True, I have never been in a desert, but I can quite clearly imagine how it looks. On the other hand, I did once do a journey by steamboat. It was expensive, gentlemen—I take it you have never made such a journey—but that wasn't what I meant to say.

THE SCHOOLMASTER. The Guano Islands lie 56 degrees North, 13 degrees East by East to South.

THE BLACKSMITH. If this is a dig at me, I don't like digs.

THE SCHOOLMASTER. But that is nothing compared with Charles the Great.

THE BLACKSMITH. No. But it is harder to shoe a nag so it doesn't go lopsided.

THE SCHOOLMASTER. Hafiz also very rightly remarks in the third sura, page 78 and following: "Eat man! You never know when you'll have the chance again."

THE BLACKSMITH. I only want to explain that one says *pagīna* just as one says Carolīna, Chīna, and so forth. Or does one say *pagna?*

THE SCHOOLMASTER. Yes, yes, yes!

THE BLACKSMITH. Right's right, that's my principle. Now, Schoolmaster, do you know when Julius Caesar was born?

THE SCHOOLMASTER. The year 99 before Christ.

THE BLACKSMITH. Before Christ? That's impossible. The calendar begins at year one, and one can't count backwards, can one?

THE SCHOOLMASTER. Can't one count backwards?

THE BLACKSMITH. Take care, don't begin to argue! Take care. You've such a weak head—anything might happen. Can you tell me the difference between rye and wheat?

THE SCHOOLMASTER. Julius Caesar was born in 99 and died in 31.

THE BLACKSMITH. Look here, how can that be? Did he live backwards? The difference between rye and wheat is first of all the price of grain or the land tax, and secondly free trade—for rye is protected and wheat is free. Isn't that right?

THE SCHOOLMASTER. Yes, yes, yes!

THE BLACKSMITH. But currency, that's another matter. I deal in silver—I won't deny that. The exchange is another matter too, so are quotation rates, and agio again is something different. . . .

THE SCHOOLMASTER. What is it then?

THE BLACKSMITH. What is it? Do I have to stand here and tell you what it is? Haven't I anything else to do? Haven't I paid my taxes? Am I not married? I'm only asking. Only asking. If anyone has any objection to make, I'd like to talk to him in private—in private. Do you know what that means? Behind the stable. Don't speak. I can't stand being answered back. No one must ever answer me back. Now do you consider all these questions settled in my favour, or shall we go behind the stable? I'm a very serious man, I'm not to be trifled with. Now, gentlemen, you see what an ass you have before you. I don't mean me, but the schoolmaster, who believes a man can have been born before the calendar began. You ought to know exactly what kind of a fellow he is.

Well, he's the most miserable ignoramus that ever walked in shoes. He's so ignorant he even believes in the Guano Islands—and there's no such place. *He picks up a bottle and takes a gulp.* He doesn't know the difference between rye and wheat—and he boozes into the bargain. Perhaps you think I booze too, but I only tipple—it can't be called boozing, that's something different. Knowledge, gentlemen, is a virtue, but the schoolmaster knows absolutely nothing—and it's his place to educate children. He's a despot, a tyrant, a domineering wretch, and a bully into the bargain. Now you know what he is.

THE TRAVELLER. Stop a minute. I certainly don't intend to answer you back, because then you'd fight, and I'm not going to cross-examine you, because if I did your knowledge would show its absence. I'm not going to offer you a drink, because that's unnecessary, nor am I going to argue with you, because you wouldn't understand what I meant and you'd never admit my points. But I should like to ask you one thing.

THE BLACKSMITH. Ask, but ask nicely!

THE TRAVELLER. You consider yourself something of a character?

THE BLACKSMITH. Certainly I'm a character, a strong character at that.

THE TRAVELLER. Moreover, you deal in silver?

THE BLACKSMITH. I'm proud to say I do.

THE TRAVELLER. Don't you recognise gold as the standard in the world market?

THE BLACKSMITH. No, not gold.

THE TRAVELLER. Not in private business either?

THE BLACKSMITH. I must think a while. *Aside.* Does he mean to cheat me on the exchange? *Aloud.* I won't answer that. No one can force me to answer it. And although I'm full of sense, I can't make any sense of what you're saying.

THE TRAVELLER. Really? Were you afraid your strong character wouldn't stand the test?

THE BLACKSMITH. Are you slandering me? Don't do that, because I'm the boss here. I'm a despot.

THE TRAVELLER *laughs.*

Don't look at me, for I'm a terrible despot.

THE TRAVELLER. I wasn't looking at you. I was only laughing.

THE BLACKSMITH. Don't laugh. I have a vote in the parish as a tax-paying citizen, and that's no laughing matter. I have five children, all well educated, very gifted, specially in regard to brains. Two of them, it is true, are in America—but, well, such things do happen. And one made a false step . . . but he has paid for it, so there's nothing more to be said about that, nothing at all.

THE TRAVELLER, *aside*. He's superb.

THE HUNTER. But this must stop. I'm suffocating.

THE BLACKSMITH. I'll just go and get my manuscript; then the festivities can begin. But you gentlemen mustn't leave. I'm the Mayor and have authority. The schoolmaster is about to read from his tragedy "Potamogeton." It's not so bad for an amateur, but many hounds cause the death of the hare.

THE SCHOOLMASTER. And the lines walk by themselves like great goslings.

THE BLACKSMITH. Is that a dig at me?

THE SCHOOLMASTER. It scarcely can be, since you are full-grown.

THE BLACKSMITH. Full-fledged it's called when it's birds. Read nicely now for the gentlemen, and I'll soon be back. But don't slander me in my absence.

THE TRAVELLER. But in your presence it's impossible.

THE BLACKSMITH. That's true. Of two evils one must choose the least. So slander me in my absence and not in my presence. *Exit.*

THE TRAVELLER. What is this village—a lunatic asylum?

THE SCHOOLMASTER. Yes, they are so ill-natured they've gone mad.

THE TRAVELLER. And are you an inmate?

THE SCHOOLMASTER. I'm kept under observation because I'm suspected of being sane.

THE TRAVELLER. Come with us and we'll give them the slip.

THE SCHOOLMASTER. Then all three of us will be caught.

THE TRAVELLER. So it isn't all just folly?

THE SCHOOLMASTER. Evil is folly's mother—and its child at the same time.

THE TRAVELLER. Who is this smith?

THE SCHOOLMASTER. He is a god of filth such as Isaiah speaks of. He's composed of the hatred, jealousy, and lies of all the rest. The smith became Mayor because the baker was the most deserving man. When I had served faithfully for twenty-five years, the day was made a celebration for the blacksmith. At the last Asses' Gala the smith got the laurel wreath—because he had written the worst verses.

THE HUNTER. Better to run away than lose the battle. We can't win this, so we must run away.

THE TRAVELLER. We're in mortal danger here.

THE SCHOOLMASTER. But most dangerous of all is to run away.

THE TRAVELLER. Can't we trick them, as they're such fools?

THE SCHOOLMASTER. But like all fools, they are cunning.

THE TRAVELLER. We'll try it. *Calls.* Blacksmith!

Enter THE BLACKSMITH.

Abra-kadabra, abra-kadabra!

THE BLACKSMITH. What is it? Are you gentlemen thinking of leaving? Don't do that. On no account do that.

THE TRAVELLER. We're only going to the next village to requisition properties for the show.

THE BLACKSMITH. To do what?

THE TRAVELLER. Requisition properties.

THE BLACKSMITH. Requisition. Well, I suppose requisitions are always welcome. Are there any smithy properties at all?

THE TRAVELLER. There are shoe-nails, axle-boxes, scythes, and spades. . . .

THE BLACKSMITH. Splendid!

THE TRAVELLER. But we must have the schoolmaster to help us carry them.

THE BLACKSMITH. He's so weak and such a simpleton.

THE TRAVELLER. But the properties are only paper, so he'll be able to manage them.

THE BLACKSMITH. Very true, very true . . . but axle-boxes are heavy—they'll be too much for him.

THE TRAVELLER. Property axle-boxes are no heavier than property nails.

THE BLACKSMITH. Very true, very true. Well, go along then—but you must come back.

THE TRAVELLER. Don't you realise that if one goes, one's bound to come back.

THE BLACKSMITH. Wait a minute. What is it that goes and goes and never comes back?

THE TRAVELLER. That's the clock. But we are not clocks, so we will come back.

THE BLACKSMITH. That's logic, and I understand it. But, wait a minute. Don't your clocks come back?

THE TRAVELLER. They aren't clocks, they're watches.

THE BLACKSMITH. Ah, very true! Clocks can strike but watches are something different. And bells strike too, but they do not go.[4] Ergo . . .

THE TRAVELLER. But we're going, that's the main point.

THE BLACKSMITH. Exactly, that's the main point. And it's logical. I like logic in all walks of life, and I can only follow a strictly logical argument.

THE TRAVELLER. Then don't follow us, for we aren't a logical argument.

THE BLACKSMITH. Exactly. So I will stay here at my post and you will go. Go along.

THE TRAVELLER. Sing the praise of the ass, you great rhymesmith!

Wisest of all animals on earth,
with your long ear-trumpet
you have the finest hearing of them all.
You hear grass growing underneath the stone,
at the same moment you look both east and west,
strong character is shown in your stiff legs,
your own will is your master's law.
When you should stand, you run instead,
when whipped to run, then you stand still.

THE BLACKSMITH. That's really very well said, for the mammal in question has belonged to the world of the unappreciated,

[4] NOTE. The Swedish word *klockor* means both "clocks" and "bells." This pun cannot be exactly reproduced in English.

to the camp of the dumb, and deserves to be re-ha-bi- . . .

THE TRAVELLER. . . . litated. But did you ever hear a dumb ass?

THE BLACKSMITH. No, but I don't bother about that. I concern myself with the character, the strong character, and therefore I understand this misunderstood animal. Yes, indeed I do.

THE TRAVELLER. Do you take your stand on that?

THE BLACKSMITH. I take my stand.

THE TRAVELLER. Then we'll be off.

THE BLACKSMITH. Wait a minute. I take my stand, but I don't stand alone. I have public opinion on my side and a party. All right-thinking, enlightened, undeluded people. In short, the whole nation rallies round my banner, and from my standpoint I'll show you you are wrong. For right is right —isn't that logic?

THE SCHOOLMASTER. The highest right is the highest wrong.

THE BLACKSMITH. And the voice of the people is the voice of God. Come in, people! Rally, nation!

A few persons enter.

THE TRAVELLER. Here is the nation—but how few they are!

THE BLACKSMITH. These are few, but you don't see the massed ranks behind them.

THE TRAVELLER. No, I can't see anything like that.

THE BLACKSMITH. You can't see them for the simple reason that they are invisible. That's logical. People! These learned charlatans maintain that there's such a place as the Guano Islands. Is there such a place?

THE PEOPLE. No!

THE BLACKSMITH. Then these gentlemen are either liars or blockheads. Is there any punishment severe enough for such villains who spread lies?

THE TRAVELLER. Yes, there's one more cruel than any other, and that is exile.

THE BLACKSMITH. Not a bad idea. But we must have full evidence against them first. Here is one who asserts that Homer slept.

THE TRAVELLER. At times.

THE BLACKSMITH. At times or all the time, it comes to the same thing. That's mere sophism. Do you people believe that a poet can sleep? Have you ever heard anything so idiotic?

ONE OF THE PEOPLE. But surely he slept at night.

THE BLACKSMITH. At night? Is that an answer? Have I given permission for an answer? Come round behind the stable, and I'll give you the answer, I will.

ONE OF THE PEOPLE. Is it a matter of taking sides?

THE BLACKSMITH. Yes, people must take sides, or else they're just characterless opportunists.

THE SCHOOLMASTER, *to* THE BLACKSMITH. Aren't you going to read from your "Charles the Great" now? Then we can get away from this brawl. The visitors are in a hurry. *Aside to* THE HUNTER *and* THE TRAVELLER. His name isn't Charles the Great, but we must call him that, or else we'll be put in gaol.

THE BLACKSMITH. I heard what you said, and I saw you two sneering. He who sneers is an accomplice. Shut them up! You know what I mean—seize them! His name isn't Charles the Great, but we call him that, because he definitely was great. Give them a punch on the jaw and lock them up until they come to their senses.

THE HUNTER, THE TRAVELLER, *and* THE SCHOOLMASTER *are seized and about to be removed.*

THE HUNTER. But we have been exiled, and we must go to the town to fetch properties.

THE BLACKSMITH. That's quite right. Everything's quite right. You have leave to go, but on your word of honour to come back, and on—or rather against—your promise to be grateful, for an ungrateful person is the heaviest burden on earth. Now I have, it so happens, a wife who has a salon. Yes, it may sound ridiculous, but you see, it is a literary salon, and I shall expect you gentlemen to turn up at the first reception.

THE TRAVELLER. So we are free. But at what a price!

THE HUNTER. Can it be called freedom to be chained by one's word of honour to the forge of a literary salon?

THE BLACKSMITH. Be off with you! But the nation is to stay.

As THE HUNTER, THE TRAVELLER, *and* THE SCHOOLMASTER *go, the curtain falls.*

IV. THE ARCADE IN TOPHET[5]

In the arcade. Right, a café, then a photograph booth, then a shell shop. Left, a fruit and flower stall and a Japanese tea and perfume shop.

THE HUNTER *and* THE TRAVELLER *are sitting outside the flower stall.*

THE TRAVELLER. You're very gloomy.

THE HUNTER. I've come down too far.

THE TRAVELLER. You have been in Tophet before?

THE HUNTER. Yes. I lived here once.

THE TRAVELLER. I could see that.

THE HUNTER. We must get some chloroform. My wounds are beginning to ache.

THE TRAVELLER. *Vinum et circenses.* There'll be plenty of free shows here. This appears to be the town sewer through which everything runs. *He waves towards the café.*

A WAITRESS *brings wine.*

Won't you be recognised here?

THE HUNTER. Impossible. I've let my beard grow and cut my hair. Besides, I washed my hands this morning. In this town one is never recognised if one washes.

THE TRAVELLER. But the waitress is staring at you.

THE HUNTER. Perhaps I resemble one of her former friends.

THE TRAVELLER. Here comes a little entertainment.

Enter THE ORGAN-GRINDER *with a monkey.*

Come along, musician, and we'll redeem our heads for a good sum.

THE ORGAN-GRINDER. Heads?

[5] Hell.

THE TRAVELLER. Well, ears then. You'll get a gold coin here not to play.

THE ORGAN-GRINDER. But the monkey's the chief attraction.

THE TRAVELLER. Then we'll look at him, but without accompaniment.

THE ORGAN-GRINDER. But there's the text too.

THE TRAVELLER. Is it true that all of you in this town are descended from a monkey?

THE ORGAN-GRINDER. What a thing to ask! You'd better take care.

THE TRAVELLER. When I look at you more closely, I believe it is true. I'm sure of it, I could swear to it. May I look at the text? But this head of Zeus looks more like a ram.

THE ORGAN-GRINDER. Yes, it really does. Very well then, so it is.

THE TRAVELLER. Do you really believe that mammal in the red jacket with the gun is the father of the human race?

THE ORGAN-GRINDER. If you're a freethinker, you'd better take care. We're orthodox in this town, defenders of the faith.

THE TRAVELLER. Which faith?

THE ORGAN-GRINDER. The only true one; the doctrine of evolution.

Exit THE ORGAN-GRINDER.

THE HUNTER. Now we'll probably be charged with blasphemy. Where's the schoolmaster got to?

THE TRAVELLER. Having made use of us, he's disappeared of course.

THE HUNTER. Shall we go?

THE TRAVELLER. What's the point? It makes no difference whether we fall into the hands of these people or others.

THE HUNTER. For people lurk like robbers in the ditches ready to spring out upon each other. Look at the café window! That girl's standing there, gazing at you with eyes of entreaty, as if begging you out of kindness or pity to rescue her. She's pretty and could rouse feelings other than pity. Well, suppose you were to decide to free her from her heavy and degrading job, suppose you were to offer her a home and protection from life's worst hardships. What then? Before long she would have robbed you of your friends, separated you from your family, ruined you with your superiors and patrons. In a word, she would have devoured you,

THE TRAVELLER. and if I didn't permit that, she would sue me for cruelty,

THE HUNTER. and for having destroyed her youth. But the worst thing of all is, that you'd find yourself in a family that you don't know,

THE TRAVELLER. but can imagine . . . Yes. She's standing there drawing, sucking—creating a whirlpool. She's spinning a net that feels like warm air. . . . Wait. I'll go in and destroy it,

THE HUNTER. or be caught in it.

THE TRAVELLER *goes into the café.*

Man overboard!

Enter THE PHOTOGRAPHER *with a camera.*

THE PHOTOGRAPHER. May I take your portrait, sir?

THE HUNTER. No-o-o!

THE PHOTOGRAPHER. Please do me this favour—I'm so poor.

THE HUNTER. Very well, but you mustn't put me in the showcase or in a packet of cigarettes or on a tablet of soap. And if I come out like an Australian negro or the latest murderer, you must destroy the plate.

THE PHOTOGRAPHER. How suspicious you are, sir!

THE HUNTER. Not at all. Just a little prudent.

THE PHOTOGRAPHER *beckons to his booth.*

EUPHROSYNE *enters.*

THE PHOTOGRAPHER. Allow me to introduce my wife. She helps with the developing and printing. Come along, Euphrosyne, I have promised to take an outdoor picture of this gentleman, although I'm so busy. You talk to him, while I do the job.

EUPHROSYNE, *sitting down.* You must have been born lucky, sir, to meet such an artist as my husband. He's the cleverest one I've ever seen, and if this picture isn't good, then you can say *I* don't understand art. So you must appreciate his work and not behave as if you're doing us a favour.

THE HUNTER. Wait a minute . . .

EUPHROSYNE. No, you mustn't look so haughty. When you beg a favour of someone, you must be grateful.

THE HUNTER. Stop a moment . . .

THE PHOTOGRAPHER, *calling*. Gotthard! Come here! You've put the plate in back to front.

Enter GOTTHARD.

GOTTHARD. I didn't put the plate in.

EUPHROSYNE. Are you answering your father back? Your own father.

GOTTHARD. I don't know anything about cameras. Shells are my job. I . . .

THE PHOTOGRAPHER. Your job, yes. But do you sell any? Ask this gentleman if he wants any shells. I think he said something just now about shells.

THE HUNTER. I never mentioned shells. I only mentioned cigarettes and soap. . . .

EUPHROSYNE. Gotthard, bring some cigarettes! Didn't you hear the gentleman say he wanted some?

THE HUNTER. I wanted to avoid having my face on a cigarette packet or a soap wrapper. . . .

GOTTHARD, *sitting down*. You're difficult to deal with, I see, sir, but let's reason a little, then we'll get it straight.

EUPHROSYNE. You're right, Gotthard. When he gets to know our ways, he'll understand. Tell Klara to come out.

GOTTHARD, *calling*. Klara!

Enter KLARA, *the flower-seller*.

EUPHROSYNE. You try and sell a flower to this gentleman. He's so economical—or rather, mean—that he won't buy a single shell, although Gotthard has the most beautiful ones *I've* ever seen.

KLARA, *sitting down*. Perhaps he can be talked round, although he looks so haughty. Is he a hunter?

EUPHROSYNE. You can see he is.

KLARA. He looks cruel—like all drunkards. . . . Yes, anyone who drinks in the morning is a drunkard. He kills animals. He shouldn't do that; it's a sin.

THE HUNTER, *to* KLARA. What have you done with your husband?

KLARA *is terrified.*

It's a sin to kill people. Don't you know that?

KLARA. Is that your opinion?

THE HUNTER. Yes, that's my opinion.

KLARA. You hear, witnesses. That's his opinion.

ALL. Yes, we heard.

THE HUNTER. May I say one word? Just one?

GOTTHARD. No. Why should you?

THE HUNTER. I'm not going to say what you think, but something quite different.

EUPHROSYNE, *curious.* Say it then.

THE HUNTER. Has Möller been arrested yet?

All rise in horror.

THE TRAVELLER, *entering from the café.* What's going on now?

THE HUNTER. Has Möller been arrested yet?

All scatter but look threatening.

For the third time—has Möller been arrested yet?

All disappear.

THE TRAVELLER. What was all that about?

THE HUNTER. It's the town's secret. Everyone knows the last murder was committed by Möller, but no one dares denounce him, as there isn't sufficient evidence. As the result of the bomb I've dropped, we must take ourselves off at once. Come on!

THE TRAVELLER. I can't.

THE HUNTER. Caught?

THE TRAVELLER. In a bar. Dregs in glasses, matches and cigar ash, pawed by young men, soiled with smoke and night life —yet, in spite of all that, in spite of everything, caught.

THE HUNTER. Break loose!

THE TRAVELLER. I can't.

THE HUNTER. Let's run for it!

THE TRAVELLER. I can't.

THE HUNTER. Very well then, stay!

THE TRAVELLER. I can't. I can't do anything.

THE HUNTER. Then I must bid you farewell.

THE TRAVELLER. We shall meet again.

THE HUNTER. That's always so, when one's met once.

THE TRAVELLER. Then–goodbye.

Exit THE TRAVELLER *into the café.*

Left alone, THE HUNTER *walks a few steps in the arcade, and stops aimlessly in front of* THE PHOTOGRAPHER'S *show-case.*

THE HUNTER. This place was once my own . . .
but long ago. On rainy days
I walked beneath this roof of glass;
when murky days lay heavy on my heart,
in here the lights were always lit;
flowers and fruits rejoiced my eyes,
shells murmured fairy tales from seas.
In this case are portraits of acquaintances
and near acquaintances–
companions of my solitude.
One look, one expression was enough
for me to feel my kinship with these mortals.
There they still are. . . . Here is my oldest friend;
he must be growing grey, but his portrait,
like leaves in autumn,
has just grown yellow.
Here I see relatives, previous relatives–
a brother-in-law, brother-in-law no more–
and here–O Saviour of the world, preserve me,
for I grow faint–my child!
My child, who is no longer mine,
my child, who was, but is no longer mine.
Another's child who is yet mine . . .
And here was my café–
our table. For a long time now
all this has ceased to be,
yet it exists–in memory.
That fire which never can be quenched,
which burns, but does not warm,
which burns, but does not burn away.

The old JAPANESE *enters from the teashop. He has the appearance of a dying man.*

THE HUNTER *goes up and supports him.*

THE JAPANESE. A human being at last. Where from? Where going?

THE HUNTER. From the great highway. How can I be of service?

THE JAPANESE. Help me to die.

THE HUNTER. One can always die.

THE JAPANESE. Do not say that. I can live no longer, but I have no one to turn to for the last services, for in this Tophet there are no human beings.

THE HUNTER. What services do you mean?

THE JAPANESE. You must hold my sword, while I . . .

THE HUNTER. That I will not do. Why do you want to die?

THE JAPANESE. Because I can live no longer.

THE HUNTER. Tell me the long tale then in a few short words.

THE JAPANESE. Yes . . . yes. I left my country because I had committed an offence. I came here absolutely determined to become an honest man by strictly observing the laws of honour and conscience. I sold good wares at a reasonable price, but the inhabitants of this place only wanted bad wares at a low price. So I had but one choice, if I were not to perish. Instead of distilling the perfume of flowers, I gave them chemicals, and instead of tea leaves I gave them leaves of sloe or cherry. At first my conscience was silent–I had to live. But one day, fifteen years ago, I woke up. Then it was as if all I had been, and all I had done, was written in a book–and now the book was opened. Day and night, night and day, I read all the false entries, all the irregularities. I struggled, but in vain. Death alone can liberate me, for the evil is in my very flesh. My soul I have purified by suffering.

THE HUNTER. In what way can I help you?

THE JAPANESE. This way. I shall take a sleeping draught and become as one dead. You will have me put in a coffin, which will be carried to the crematorium.

THE HUNTER. But if you were to wake?

THE JAPANESE. That is just what I am counting on. For a moment I shall feel the purifying redeeming power of the fire. For a short while I shall suffer—then feel the bliss of deliverance.

THE HUNTER. And after that?

THE JAPANESE. After that you will gather the ashes in my most precious vase.

THE HUNTER. And put your name upon it. . . . What is your name?

THE JAPANESE. One moment. I have travelled, sinned, and suffered by the name "Hiroshima," after my native town. But in my country it is the custom, when a man dies, for him to give up his old, cursed, sullied name, and to be given a new one, which is called his Eternity Name. This name alone is put upon his tombstone with an epitaph. And then a bough of the sakaki tree is burned for him.

THE HUNTER. Have you these things ready?

THE JAPANESE. I have. Look at this.

THE HUNTER, *reading*. What does this name mean?

THE JAPANESE. *Harahara to.* It means "rustling leaf, whispering silk," but it also means "falling tears."

THE HUNTER. And the epitaph?

THE JAPANESE. *Chiru hana wo*
Nani ka uramin
Yo no naka ni
Waga mi mo tomo ni
Aran mono kawa.

THE HUNTER. And this interpreted?

THE JAPANESE. The blossoms are falling. . . .
Why should I feel aggrieved?
The gods have willed it;
And I, too, must—as the flowers—
Turn to dust some day. . . .

THE HUNTER. I will carry out your last wish. But have you no heirs?

THE JAPANESE. I had once. I had a daughter who came here three years ago, when she thought I was going to die. She came for the inheritance. But when I did not die, she grew angry, could not hide her feelings—and went away again. Since then she has been dead to me.

THE HUNTER. Where is this that we have talked of to take place?

THE JAPANESE. Outside the town—at the crematorium.

THE HUNTER. Are we to go together, or to meet there?

THE JAPANESE. We shall meet in the arbour of the inn—very shortly. I have only to bathe myself and shave.

THE HUNTER. Very well. We will meet there.

THE JAPANESE, *going towards his shop.* Here comes the murderer. Be on your guard!

THE HUNTER. Is that he?

THE JAPANESE. Be on your guard! He is the most powerful man in the town.

Exit THE JAPANESE.

Enter MÖLLER THE MURDERER. *He is stiff and pompous; his arms dangle awkwardly. He stares at* THE HUNTER.

THE MURDERER. Is it . . . ?

THE HUNTER. No, it's not.

THE MURDERER. Oh, then it is!

THE HUNTER. No, it was. The one you mean is no more.

THE MURDERER. Then you are dead?

THE HUNTER. Yes. Twelve years ago I committed hara-kiri. I executed my old self. The one you see here now, you do not know and can never know.

THE MURDERER. Yes, I remember. You were fool enough to put yourself in the pillory. On that blood-red carpet, you publicly confessed all your faults and failings. . . .

THE HUNTER. And the whole community revelled. Everyone felt themselves better people—as if they were vindicated by my social death. No one said a single word of compassion or of approval of my action.

THE MURDERER. Why should they?

THE HUNTER. However, when after ten years of suffering I had atoned and put everything right again, it occurred to me that I ought to confess your sins as well. Then the tune was changed.

THE MURDERER. Devil take you!

THE HUNTER. You who have, for example, committed murder. . . .

THE MURDERER. You can't say a thing like that . . . when you have no evidence.

THE HUNTER. I know you are the most powerful man in the community, that you bully the Grand Duke himself through the agency of a Freemason gang which . . .

THE MURDERER. What's that?

THE HUNTER. You know very well. A league which is not the holy one.

THE MURDERER. And what about you?

THE HUNTER. I've never belonged to the league, but I recognise it by certain signs. . . .

THE MURDERER. Look in the window of that paper-shop and you'll see who you are!

THE HUNTER. You mean that caricature? That's not me, that's you. That's how you look—inside. That's your creation. You're welcome to it.

THE MURDERER. You have a great talent for shaking off your vermin.

THE HUNTER. Do the same yourself in the same way—but not on to me. Execute yourself, as I did, as I had to do, when you made me into a scapegoat, on to whom you loaded all your guilt.

THE MURDERER. What are you talking about?

THE HUNTER. Take an example. Once a certain heretic wrote this piece of idiocy—that if he were standing alone on Gaurisankar, and the Flood came and drowned the whole human race, no harm would have been done at all, so long as *he* remained alive. At the next Carnival, Gaurisankar was carried in the procession, and on its summit stood not the heretic, but *I*. What have you to say about that? And on my birthday, *he* had the celebrations. When I invented the new insulators, *you* received the prize—but when you committed murder, *I* was accused. Moreover, when sugar shares went up, people blamed my insulators, although you had received the prize for the invention. To think of anything as perverse, you would have first to stand on your head and then turn yourself back to front.

THE MURDERER. Have you any evidence—that you dare call me a murderer?

THE HUNTER. Yes, I have.

THE MURDERER *appears amazed.*

But I dare not use it before a jury of your friends. They would deny the facts and have me arrested. Now tell me something. Who is that girl in there who caught my companion?

THE MURDERER. She is your daughter.

THE HUNTER *clutches his heart and his face grows white. He presses a handkerchief to his mouth. It becomes red with blood.*

THE HUNTER. That child—who has been brought up by you! . . . Now I must go to the crematorium.

He goes out.

V. IN THE ARBOUR OUTSIDE THE CREMATORIUM

Outside the Columbarium. Back, an avenue of cypresses.

A bench, a chair, a table.

Enter THE HUNTER.

THE HUNTER. What's this I see? Row upon row of urns,
but all alike?
A chemist's, a museum? No.
A columbarium, a house for doves,
but with no doves, no olive branch—
only chaff; the corn must grow elsewhere.
In the urns, ashes, so all must be alike,
as dust resembles dust.
Once human destinies, these now
bear numbers and are labelled—
"Here rests . . ." Yes, I knew you,

but you would never learn to know yourself . . .
and you, you went disguised through life,
your long and heavy life;
when I unmasked you, then you died.
Idolator! That was your name,
your character. One had to worship
your wretched wife and hateful children—
had to, or else be victimised—
each Saturday cut to pieces with a flint-knife,
or lynched, or by the Sunday press
deprived of bread and honour.

THE MURDERER, *who has been listening, enters.*

You light of Tophet's State, around your bier
you called the nation, and though dead,
counted the wreaths and threatened vengeance
on those who stayed away.

THE MURDERER. Nice things to say at a grave!

THE HUNTER. This is no grave. It's a jar with a bit of dirt in it. No, a stone. He has become slowly petrified. . . .

THE MURDERER. You mean he died of calcification—

THE HUNTER. Yes, he turned into limestone.

THE MURDERER. Tell me a little about yourself.

THE HUNTER. I did that thirteen years ago, so you're tired of the subject. But here are the ashes of one of whom I could speak well, although—or, rather, because—he was murdered by you. This victim of yours never did evil for evil's sake, only in self-defence. And when he refused to become an accomplice, he was killed and stripped of all he had.

THE JAPANESE *appears in the background.*

THE MURDERER. You go round with that rascally Japanese?

THE HUNTER. Do you mean to strike me down now, as that tycoon did?

THE MURDERER. Don't speak evil of the dead. Say "poor man."

THE HUNTER. You say that about rascals who stick their fingers in the sugar bin, but never about your victims. Now be off with you . . . quick!

THE MURDERER. I shall go when I wish.

THE HUNTER *displays his bloody handkerchief, and* THE MURDERER *turns to go.*

I can't bear the sight of blood. That's one of my peculiarities.

THE HUNTER. Since the fourth of April.

THE MURDERER *slinks out.*

To THE JAPANESE. Are you ready for your journey now?

THE JAPANESE. I am, but let us sit down here,
until the furnace has been heated up.

THE HUNTER. Gladly.

They sit.

Tell me, now life lies at your feet,
like hunted game, pursued and won,
how does the journey look?

THE JAPANESE, *after a pause.* A line with many coils,
like the image of a script
on blotting paper. Back to front—
forward and back and up and down—
but in a mirror you can read the script.

THE HUNTER. What has been hardest to bear—
of all the stones your foot has knocked against?

THE JAPANESE, *after reflection.* Once I spared an enemy,
and afterwards he stabbed me.
To have to wish a good deed never done
can be the hardest.
Another time I gave good counsel
to one oppressed. He turned my enemy,
took from me all I had,
and I was helpless in the hopeless fight,
for he—he had it written by myself
that he was the better of us two.
And yet all that is nothing,
nothing compared with life's own facts—
the humiliation of living,
a mere skeleton in a dress of flesh,
set going with tendons, strings,
by a small motor in the chest's
engine-room, run by the heat
the belly's furnace can get up.

And the soul, the spirit, sits there in the heart,
like a bird in the bosom's cage,
in a hencoop or a fish-creel.
You little bird, soon I shall open the cage,
and you can fly—to your own land,
to the glowing sunlit isles
where I was born,
but may not die.
Look! Here's my best vase, a family heritage
which now will house the mortal dust of dust,
but once held flowers,
and decked a table for a feast.
Young eyes and rosy cheeks
were mirrored in the gold-rimmed glass,
and a small hand served the children
with the treasures of the house.
Then you became a flask of tears, dear vase!
For all the good life gave us,
came later to be mourned.
I remember at the turning of the year,
the children held their festival of dolls—
with us, all dolls pass on from kin to kin.
A child!
What is so perfect in its kind
as this small being?
Not man, nor woman,
yet both and neither—
A human being in miniature.
Say, traveller—I had forgotten you
in my own sorrows—say a word
about yourself—about your fate.
How do you look on life, how did you look?
What did you find most hard, most bitter?

THE HUNTER. What I found bitterer than death,
was having to take the great joke seriously
and treat as holy what was coarse.
When I smiled at the joke, I soon must weep,
when coarseness made me coarse,
humiliation was my lot.

Then this.
I was a preacher:
in the beginning I spoke well of human nature,
brought forward all the goodness that I knew,
and set high standards up for life—
ideals, they are also called—
those bright banners on the signal posts,
calling mankind to joyfulness.
But now—how bitter! The beauty of my thoughts
and words I must take back.
Beauty does not exist in life,
cannot materialise down here.
The ideal is never found in practice.

THE JAPANESE. I know. But it's a memory,
a hope, a beacon for one's course—
and so: send up the signals!
Let the banners blow!
They're high, but so seen all the better.
They point the upward way—towards the sun.

THE HUNTER. The furnace now begins to glow . . .

THE JAPANESE. And on the cypress tops it throws
a rosy light like flush of dawn
when the sun is rising.
Welcome, day! Farewell, you night
of heavy dreams!
For the last time I strip
and go to rest, to sleep—
And when I wake—my mother will be there,
my wife, my children, and my friends.
Good night, poor human being!

The stage lights up, and the same image as in the first scene —the Country of Desires—appears in the clouds.

VI. AT THE LAST GATE

Back, two white gates opening to a low sandy beach and blue sea.

Left, a wooden house, painted red (THE HUNTER'S *home*),

in a beechwood. It has an orchard and a box hedge. Left of the house, a small table, decorated for a child's birthday party.

A shuttlecock is seen being thrown up and down beyond the hedge.

A blue-hooded baby carriage stands by the gate.

THE HUNTER *enters, lost in meditation.*

THE HUNTER. Yes. Alone. That's how it ends
if one tries to preserve one's life,
and not to barter and haggle
to get a position;
not to let oneself be stolen,
not to let oneself be cowed. . . .
When first my brain awoke,
and I grew conscious
that I was shut up in a madhouse,
a penitentiary, sanatorium,
then I wished myself out of my mind,
that no one should guess
my thoughts. . . .
"Thelō, thelō manēnai!"[6]
I desired, desired to be mad!
Then wine became my friend–
I hid, I veiled myself in drunkenness,
in the fools' garb of drunkenness forgotten,
and none guessed who I was.
Now that has changed;
the drink of oblivion has become the drink of memory.
Everything I remember, everything.
The seals are broken, the books lie open
and read themselves aloud–
and when my ears are weary, then I see.
Everything, everything I see.

Waking from his thoughts.

Where have I come to? The sea?
The beechwood and the hunter's home.
A shuttlecock rises in the air and falls,

[6] "I desire, I desire to go mad."

and here's a wicker carriage with a newborn child–
the blue hood arching like the sky
over the sleep of innocence.
Behind the shutters of that small red house
a man and woman hide their happiness–
for happiness exists, it's true,
but brief as lightning,
sunshine, or convolvulus,
one blossom and *one* day,
and then it's gone.
Smoke rises from the kitchen–
beyond's a well-stocked larder,
a little cellar underneath . . .
a verandah full of light, facing the wood . . .
I know just how it all must be–
just how it was. . . .
And here's a birthday table gaily spread
for a young child.
A little altar to all childhood,
to hope, to innocent joy built
on its own happiness,
and not on others' ruin.
And there's the beach,
with white, clean, soft, warm sand,
with shells and pebbles
and the blue water to dabble in
with naked feet. . . .
Garlands of leaves, the paths all raked–
for friends are coming to a children's party.
They have watered the flowers,
the flowers of my childhood–
blue monkshood with two doves inside,
fritillary bearing a diadem,
a sceptre, and an orb.
The passion flower of suffering
in white and amethyst with cross
and lance and nails,
sipped by the bee, which from its heart
draws honey, where we find only gall.

And here, loveliest of trees
in a child's garden,
from dark green leaves peep out in pairs
the white-heart cherries, red and white,
young children's faces, sister and brother,
playing, caressing, swinging in the wind.
Between branch and stem a warbler
has built his nest—
unseen singer, song on wings . . .
Hush! The gravel's crunched beneath small boots.
Here comes the sovereign!

THE CHILD *enters, takes* THE HUNTER'S *hand, and leads him to the baby carriage.*

THE CHILD. Walk quietly and you can look at the doll. There's the doll. That's what we call her. But you mustn't walk on the gravel, because it's been raked. Ellen raked it, for we're going to have visitors. It's my birthday today. . . . Are you sad?

THE HUNTER. What's your name, child?

THE CHILD. I'm called Mary.

THE HUNTER. Who lives in that house?

THE CHILD. Papa and Mamma.

THE HUNTER. May I look at your birthday table?

THE CHILD. But we mustn't touch anything.

THE HUNTER. No, I won't touch anything, little one.

THE CHILD. Do you know what we'll have for dinner today? We'll have asparagus and strawberries. Why are you sad? Have you lost your money? You can take a cake from the table, but you mustn't take the big one—that's for Stella. Do you know, Stella had crumbs in her bed last night, and she cried—and then there was thunder and we were frightened, so Mamma shut the damper. Yes, she'd been eating a sandwich in bed and it broke in pieces—it was that sort of crisp bread you get in the town. . . . Now shall we have a fairy story? Can you tell stories? What's your name?

THE HUNTER. My name is Cartaphilus.[7]

[7] Cartaphilus, later called Ahasuerus: The Wandering Jew.

THE CHILD. No, you're not called that.

THE HUNTER. Ahasuerus then—the one that's always wandering.

THE CHILD. Shall we talk about something else? Are your eyes hurting?

THE HUNTER. Yes, child, they hurt so much, so much.

THE CHILD. You mustn't read in bed by candlelight. That makes one's eyes hurt.

A horn sounds.

Papa's coming!

Exit THE CHILD.

THE HUNTER. My child! *My* child! She did not know me. How fortunate—how fortunate for us both!

Farewell, sweet vision.
I will not stand in the sun's path
and cast a shadow on the youngest's plot.
I know the father here—the mother too—
a lovely image, an image
wavering but lovely.
A memory perhaps, or more than that—
a hope—a summer's day out in the woods
beside the sea—a birthday table and a cradle.
A beam of sunlight from a child's eyes,
a gift from a child's hand—
and so on again and out—into the darkness.

VII. THE DARK WOOD

THE HUNTER. Alone!—I have lost my way—
In the darkness.
"And Elijah sat down under the juniper tree and he wished himself dead and said: It is enough! Take my life, O Lord!"

THE VOICE OF THE WOMAN, *in the darkness.* He who seeks to lose his life shall find it.

THE HUNTER. Who are you that speaks out of the darkness?

THE VOICE OF THE WOMAN. Is it dark?

THE HUNTER. Is it dark?

THE WOMAN *enters.*

THE WOMAN. I ask, because I cannot see. I am blind.

THE HUNTER. Have you always been blind?

THE WOMAN. No. When the tears ceased to flow, my eyes could no longer see.

THE HUNTER. It is good to be able to weep.

THE WOMAN. But I hear instead, and I know your voice. I know who you are—and I believe in you.

THE HUNTER. You must not believe in me, nor in any human being. You must believe in God.

THE WOMAN. I do that too.

THE HUNTER. But in God alone. The children of man are not to be believed in.

THE WOMAN. Weren't you once a lawyer, for the defence?

THE HUNTER. I was the defender of the only True One against the idolators. You always wanted to worship yourselves, your relatives, your friends, but you never respected simple justice.

THE WOMAN. Sometimes you abandoned the case you were fighting.

THE HUNTER. When they tricked me into pity for an unrighteous man on the pretext that he was poor, I abandoned the case of the unrighteous.

THE WOMAN. You were an evangelist once too, but you tired of that.

THE HUNTER. I did not tire, but when I found I could not live what I taught, I stopped preaching in order not to be called a hypocrite. And when I discovered that nowhere was there any putting into practice of those beautiful doctrines, I left their realisation for the land of fulfilled desires.

THE WOMAN. And now—are you dead?

THE HUNTER. Yes, socially, but not spiritually. I'm a fighter and so I live. But *I* don't exist—only what I have done. Good and evil. The evil, I confessed and suffered for—with the good, I tried to do good.

THE WOMAN. Would you still plead the human cause?

THE HUNTER. When it was right, not otherwise. Once, misled by the gratitude I owed a man, I fought a case for him, and in so doing caused great injury to an innocent person. That's how it is with even our best feelings. They beguile us into evil.

THE WOMAN. You are accusing—prosecutor!

THE HUNTER. Whom am I accusing?

THE WOMAN. The ruling powers.

THE HUNTER. Get thee behind me, Satan, before you tempt me to blasphemy.

THE WOMAN. Satan?

THE HUNTER. Yes, Satan!

THE WOMAN. No one was as black as you.

THE HUNTER. Because you blackened me, so that I should be like you. And explain this to me: when *I* confessed my sins, you felt yourselves guiltless and thanked God you were not as I—and yet you were just as bad. Once when I was a child I saw an execution. What a bunch of hypocrites the crowd was! On the way home they lamented his fate, then they went to the taverns and spoke ill of the dead man and felt better themselves. And after that, some of them went back to the gallows and took the dead man's blood—to cure epilepsy. They dipped their handkerchiefs in his blood! Look at this one! Oh, of course, you are blind. Feel it then. Your eye is in your hand. *Gives her the bloody handkerchief.*

THE WOMAN. It feels like red. And it is sticky. It smells like—butcher's meat. No, I know what it is. I had a relative who died recently. He coughed up first his lungs and finally the heart itself.

THE HUNTER. Did he cough up his heart?

THE WOMAN. Yes.

THE HUNTER, *looking at the handkerchief.* I believe it. The goat, as we know, is not a clean animal, yet on the great day of atonement he had to bear the sins of all, and thus burdened, he was driven out into the desert to be devoured by wild beasts. That was the scapegoat.

THE WOMAN. Do you mean that you have suffered for the sins of others?

THE HUNTER. For my own and others'. And so for others.

THE WOMAN. Weren't you something else, before you became a lawyer?

THE HUNTER. Yes, I was an architect. I built many houses. They weren't all good, but when I built well, they were angry with me because they were good. So they gave the work to others who did it worse. That was in the town of Tophet, where I built the theatre.

THE WOMAN. That is considered very fine.

THE HUNTER. Remember it then when I have ceased to be—and forget me.

THE WOMAN. "*I* don't exist. Only the good I did remains." Why did you have no pity for your fellows?

THE HUNTER. The question's wrongly put. Did you see any pitying me? No. Then how could I reciprocate an emotion not granted me? Besides, who was it who first preached: "Mankind is to be pitied"?

THE WOMAN *disappears.*

She's gone. They always go when one seeks to defend oneself.

THE TEMPTER *enters.*

THE TEMPTER. So now I have met you! Well, we will have a talk, but as it's rather dark here, we'll make a nice light . . . *It grows lighter* . . . so that we can see one another. It's essential to see one another if we're to talk sense. This from the Grand Duke. He admires your talents and offers you the appointment of Court Architect, with a salary of so-and-so, living quarters with fuel, etc., all found. You understand?

THE HUNTER. I don't want an appointment.

THE TEMPTER. Wait a minute! There are certain conditions. . . . Well, yes, in a word, you must conduct yourself like a human being, an ordinary human being.

THE HUNTER. I would like to hear more. It would interest me to know how an ordinary human being conducts himself.

THE TEMPTER. Don't you know that? Why do you look so distraught?

THE HUNTER. I can answer the last question in two words. I look distraught because I'm utterly confused. You see, to begin with, I was one of those people who believe what they are told—and therefore I was stuffed with lies. Everything I believed in was a pack of lies—and so my whole self is falsified. I have gone round with false opinions about people and about life; I have reckoned in false terms, passed off false coin without knowing it was false. And so I am not what I am. I can't mix with other people, can't talk, can't quote another's words of appeal to any statement, for fear it is a lie. Many times over I became an accomplice in that forge known as society, but when I grew like the rest, I went out and became a highwayman, a robber in the woods.

THE TEMPTER. All that's just twaddle. Let's get back to the Grand Duke, who is asking for your services.

THE HUNTER. He's not asking for my services, he's asking for my soul.

THE TEMPTER. He's asking you to take an interest in his great enterprise.

THE HUNTER. That I cannot do. Leave me now. I haven't long to live and I want to be alone to make up my accounts.

THE TEMPTER. Aha! If pay day is at hand,
then I will come with invoices,
with bills and summonses—

THE HUNTER. Yes, come! Come with despair,
you tempter, trying to gull me
to a coward's denial of the Good Giver.
From the height's pure air, I came down here
to walk a while yet among the sons of man
and share in their small cares.
But here there was no open road—
a ravine among thorns,
one was caught in the thicket,
leaving a shred here, a shred there.
People offered—so as to take back with interest,
gave—so as to make the gift a debt,

served—in order that they might rule,
set free—in order to confine.
I lost my companion on the way . . .
one snare was followed by another . . .
I was drawn between grindstones
and came out on the other side.
A beam of light from a child's eyes
led me here into this darkness.

THE TEMPTER *disappears.*

Now you are bringing out the bills—
What? Even he has disappeared!

So I am alone,
in night and darkness,
where the trees sleep and the grass is weeping
from the cold when the sun has set.
But some beasts wake, although not all—
the bat is weaving his cabals,
the snake coils under poison plant,
the light-shy badger makes a move
after a day of sleep.
Alone! And why?
A traveller in another's land
is always stranger and alone.
He goes through towns and villages,
stays, pays, and passes on,
until the journey's end—then he's at home.
But this is not the end . . .
I still can hear . . . a withered branch
cracks—an iron heel rings on a rock—
it is the awful blacksmith,
the idolator with his flint-knife
looking for me,
and the miller with his grindstones,
into which I was drawn
and nearly crushed.
The people in the arcade, that arcade—
a lobster pot, easy to enter
but hard to get out of.
And the murderer Möller,

with bills and summonses
and alibis and libels—
infamous man!
What do I hear now? Music!
I know your tunes—and your dear hand,
I do not want to meet you. . . .
A little way off the fire warms,
but not too near, for then it burns.
And now—a child's voice in the darkness,
you little child, last memory of light
to follow me into the dark night wood,
on the last stage to that distant land—
the land of fulfilled desires.
A vision seen from the mountain tops,
but in the valley veiled
by dust from roads and chimney smoke.
Where did you go, fair vision—
land of longing and of dreams?

If but a vision, let me see you again
in the crystal air on the snow-white height.
There with the hermit I will stay
and wait for the release.
Surely he will grant me a grave
beneath the cold white blanket,
and will write in the snow a fleeting epitaph:
Here Ishmael rests, the son of Hagar,
whose name was once called Israel,
because he fought a fight with God,
and did not cease to fight until laid low,
defeated by His almighty goodness.
O Eternal One, I'll not let go Thy hand,
Thy hard hand, till Thou bless me.

Bless me, Your creature,
who suffers, suffers from Your gift of life.
Bless me, whose deepest suffering,
deepest of human suffering, was this—
I could not be the one I longed to be.